AN INTRODUCTION TO THE LAW ON FINANCIAL INVESTMENT

Since the publication of the first edition of this book in 2005, the world of financial investment has experienced an unprecedented boom followed by a spectacular bust. Significant changes have been proposed and in some cases implemented in areas such as the structure of regulation, the organisation of markets, supervision of market participants and the protection of consumers. The second edition takes account of these developments, integrating them into an analytical framework that enables the reader to develop a critical overview of the role of general legal rules and specialised systems of regulation in financial investment. The framework focuses on the role of contract, trusts and regulation as the primary legal influences for financial investment. The first part explores the relationship between investment, law and regulation. The second part examines the nature of investments and investors, both professional and private. The third part discusses the central role of corporate finance and corporate governance in linking investors with enterprises that require external capital. The fourth part examines the nature, operation and regulation of markets and the participants that support the functioning of the market. The objective remains to provide a broadly based and critical account of the role of law in financial investment.

AN INTRODUCTION TO THE LAW ON FINANCIAL INVESTMENT

Second Edition

IAIN G MACNEIL

·H A R T·
PUBLISHING

OXFORD AND PORTLAND, OREGON
2012

Published in the United Kingdom by Hart Publishing Ltd
16C Worcester Place, Oxford, OX1 2JW
Telephone: +44 (0)1865 517530
Fax: +44 (0)1865 510710
E-mail: mail@hartpub.co.uk
Website: http://www.hartpub.co.uk

Published in North America (US and Canada) by
Hart Publishing
c/o International Specialized Book Services
920 NE 58th Avenue, Suite 300
Portland, OR 97213-3786
USA
Tel: +1 503 287 3093 or toll-free: (1) 800 944 6190
Fax: +1 503 280 8832
E-mail: orders@isbs.com
Website: http://www.isbs.com

British Library Cataloguing in Publication Data

Data Available

ISBN: 978-1-84946-050-7

Typeset by Forewords, Oxford
Printed and bound in Great Britain by
Page Bros (Norwich) Ltd, Norwich

Contents

PART 2—INVESTMENTS AND INVESTORS

PART 3—FINANCE AND GOVERNANCE

Table of Cases

Table of Legislation

European Union

Treaties

Regulations

Directives

International

United Kingdom

Statutes

FSA Handbook of Rules and Guidance

Part 1

Investment, Law and Regulation

The Nature of Investment

What is investment? The answer to that question depends on the context in which the term is being used. It is possible to identify three distinct meanings that are commonly given to the term. The first is what can be termed an economic definition of investment.

According to this view, investment means that individually, as a company or as a country we forgo the consumption of goods today in order to achieve greater consumption in the future. On this view, investment can take any form and has no particular association with the manner in which an economy is organised or the mechanisms through which investment occurs. Buying a spade with which to plant potatoes in one's garden is, from this perspective, as much 'investment' as buying a potato future in the commodities market or a share in a company that operates as a potato merchant. This approach also distinguishes investment from saving, which simply transfers consumption from one period to the next.

The economic approach to investment also distinguishes investment in real assets (such as land or machinery) from investment in financial instruments such as shares and bonds. Investment decisions relating to real assets (sometimes termed 'direct investment') are most often made within an enterprise and focus on the extent to which wealth can be created by using existing and future resources to produce goods and services now and in the future with greater value than the resources consumed. Investment decisions relating to financial instruments are generally made by investors outside these enterprises and are primarily concerned with providing finance to fund the direct investment projects of enterprises.[1] Investment in financial instruments is termed 'portfolio investment' because investors generally aim to diversify their holdings of financial instruments across a portfolio.

Portfolio investment is the main focus of this book. Its focus differs from what has become known as the law of 'finance' or 'banking', both of which are focused much more on the operation of credit markets, the techniques of debt finance and the role of banks. This book is focused more on the activities of asset managers, such as pen-

---

[1] From the perspective of the enterprise requiring finance, such decisions are referred to as financing decisions because they concern the manner in which (direct) investment decisions are financed.

sion funds, insurance funds, professional fund managers, pooled investment funds and financial advisers. Of course, a number of factors mean that there is a substantial overlap between all three areas: increasingly 'supermarket'-type financial conglomerates span all three types of activity; products in one area can increasingly be regarded as substitutes for those in another; and evolution in markets has opened up possibilities in taking and hedging risk that were not generally available in the past. Thus, the focus is not based on any clear demarcation that can be observed between the three fields; rather, it is built more around the primary legal and regulatory concerns that facilitate, shape and limit the practices associated with portfolio investment.

The second meaning of investment is what can be termed its legal definition. This focuses on investment as property and the legal rules associated with ownership of that property. The legal view of investment is intrinsically liked with the economic view because the objective of the legal rules is to create a link between the forgoing of consumption today and the delivery of greater consumption in the future. If legal rules do not provide a sufficiently strong link between the two, it is unlikely that investment (in the economic sense) will occur. In other words, legal rules must be devised so that investors have confidence in their ability to enforce their claims at some point in the future. This means that the law must make clear the nature of the claim held by the investor and make available enforcement procedures that will provide consistent enforcement of those claims over the long term.[2]

The third meaning of investment is what can be termed the process of investing. This focuses on the procedures, institutions and legal rules that are associated with investment (in the economic sense). This view encompasses matters such as the role of markets and financial institutions in channelling savings into investment as well as the regulation of markets and their participants. Investment is more likely to occur when investors believe that they are treated fairly during the process of investment. This can be understood in different ways in different contexts. For example, it can refer to the information provided by a company when it invites the public to buy its shares. Equally, it can be taken to refer to the extent to which financial markets are 'clean', meaning that they are free from manipulation and insider dealing. For private investors, it will often relate to the quality of information and advice provided at the time of making an investment decision, as well as the suitability of investments that are sold to them.

Each of these three aspects of investment is central to what follows in the book. The discussion below provides a brief overview of some of the main issues, while much of the detail is dealt with in later chapters.

---

[2] The significance of consistent enforcement over the long term becomes particularly clear in the context of equity investment, which by its nature is of an indefinite duration.

1.1 The economic nature of investment

The central feature of the economic nature of investment is the forgoing of current consumption in the expectation of achieving greater consumption in the future. A willingness to forgo current consumption in favour of investment is normally only possible when spare resources exist that are not required for current consumption. In such circumstances, surplus resources or savings will be present in the financial system and will in principle be available for investment. That is not to say that they will be automatically invested. Whether they are invested or not will depend on many different factors, two of which are particularly important. The first is the risk associated with investments and the risk preferences of the potential investors who have savings to invest. The second is the extent to which financial institutions perform the function of financial intermediation.

1.1.1 Risk

The risks associated with a particular investment can be classified as:[3]

- Uncertainty of income (sometimes referred to as project or business risk). This risk arises when an investment, such as a company share, does not have a fixed income.
- Default risk. This risk arises in respect of debt securities (which are essentially loans raised by enterprises) and is the risk that a loan will not be repaid at the due date.
- Interest rate risk. The valuation of investments is sensitive to the prevailing level of interest rates and therefore changes in interest rates cause changes in market values.[4]
- Inflation risk. This is the risk that the return on an investment that carries a fixed income (eg government securities) will be less in real terms than expected at the time of purchase as a result of higher than expected inflation.

Different investments involve different levels or risk and offer different types of return.[5] A basic distinction can be drawn between equity-based investments and fixed interest investments. The main feature of equity-based investments is that they offer no guarantee in respect of either return of capital or income. In that sense, they are risk capital. Fixed interest investments (such as bank deposits, government and corporate bonds), on the other hand, offer a guarantee in respect of both return of capital and income. In that respect,

---

[3] See J Rutterford, *Introduction to Stock Exchange Investment*, 3rd edn (Basingstoke, Macmillan, 2007).

[4] Modern portfolio theory uses a 'risk-free' rate of return to measure risk and expected return from securities. The risk-free rate of return is based on the yield available from government securities, which are regarded as a proxy for a risk-free investment. Expected returns from other securities can be compared with this risk-free rate. Changes in interest rates cause changes in the yield on government bonds and hence changes in the expected return of a particular security (eg a company share) by comparison with the risk-free rate of return.

[5] The nature of particular forms of investment is discussed in more detail in Chapter 4. See also Chapter 7.1.2 for a discussion of the characteristics of equity and debt securities.

they are safer investments than equity-based investments, but holders nevertheless face the risk of default (eg if the borrower becomes insolvent) as well as the risk of inflation.

Modern portfolio theory focuses on how to construct a portfolio of investments by reference to its degree of risk. It recognises the categories of risk mentioned above, but distinguishes between those risks that can be avoided and those that cannot.[6] Specific risk relates to particular events relevant to particular investments, such as a company losing its main customer. Those events are specific to individual companies and are not dictated by general movements in the economy as a whole. Specific risk can be reduced through diversification, which has the effect of balancing out across many investments the specific risk attached to each. In this sense, diversification reduces the overall risk of a portfolio. Market risk refers to the risks arising from general movements in the economy, for example a recession. Within a single-country portfolio this risk cannot be avoided, but for an international portfolio, diversification can reduce the risk. The availability of data on historic price movements of specific investments by comparison with the market as a whole (the beta coefficient) now enables investors to measure the relative degree of risk in their portfolios by comparison with the market as a whole.[7] That exercise enables the construction of investment portfolios in which the degree of risk is taken into consideration along with other factors that may be relevant (for example, in the case of a pension fund, the liabilities that the fund is required to pay).

The extent to which investors are willing to assume risk depends on their risk preferences. Risk preferences are measured by reference to the utility (subjective satisfaction) that an investor derives from an increase in wealth at any given level of wealth. It is generally assumed that investors are risk averse, meaning that as wealth increases they derive less utility from further increases in wealth.[8] This means that investors generally require additional expected return for taking on additional risk.[9] The specific additional return required by a particular investor in respect of a particular investment will depend on the particular utility of wealth characteristics of that investor. While that is not capable of precise expression, it underlies investment decision-making by risk-averse investors, who attempt to achieve either the highest return for a given level of risk or the lowest risk for a particular desired return.[10]

1.1.2 Financial intermediation

The second factor that determines whether funds available for investment are invested

---

[6] See generally K Pilbeam, *Finance and Financial Markets*, 3rd edn (Basingstoke, Palgrave, 2010) chs 7 and 8.

[7] See ibid, 202–03 for an explanation of beta.

[8] A risk-averse investor will always refuse a fair gamble. Assume for example that Brown is offered a 50% chance of winning £500 and a 50% chance of losing £500. If, at a given level of wealth, Brown declines the offer, she is risk averse. If she accepts she is a risk preferrer. See Rutterford, above n 3, 60 for more detail.

[9] In principle, the nature of the additional risk does not matter. Inflation and interest rate risk arising from poor macro-economic management could have a similar effect to the risk of uncertain income arising from generally poor standards of management in the corporate sector.

[10] The former would be appropriate in circumstances where the level of risk is constrained (eg trustees with limited powers of investment) and the latter to circumstances where the investments are designed to fund specified liabilities (eg in the case of a pension fund investing to meet the cost of pension payments).

is the role played by financial intermediaries. Included in this category are banks, investment management firms, insurers, unit trusts and investment trusts.[11] They act as intermediaries in the sense that they take money from their customers and in turn provide their customers with a financial instrument (such as a deposit, unit trust, life policy or share). That process has a fundamental effect on investment because it allows the intermediary to create investments with characteristics that could not be created by an investor acting alone.[12]

This transformation occurs in relation to maturity and risk. The first refers to the ability of intermediaries (such as banks) to borrow short and lend long. For example, a bank that takes short-term deposits from customers is able to lend that money on a long-term basis (eg in the form of a mortgage) because not all the depositors will want to be repaid at the same time. In this sense, financial intermediation in the form of the provision of credit helps to stabilise the cash flow of households and firms who can use credit to make long-term investment plans, such as the purchase of property, that would not be possible if credit were not available.

The second form of financial intermediation refers to the role of an intermediary in changing the risk faced by an investor. A pooled investment fund, for example, is able to transform risk because a single unit in the fund offers diversification across the entire portfolio held by the fund, whereas a single share in a company leaves the investor with a high degree of specific risk. In effect, the fund is able to offer a financial product to the investor that would not be available if the investor were to deal directly (on an individual basis) with a company. For some investors, it will be possible to replicate the diversification that can be offered by a fund, but for others (and especially the private investor) it will be more difficult to do that as well as to match the investment and administrative expertise of a fund.

Another feature of financial intermediation is that it offers a solution to the problem of asymmetric information in financial markets. This refers to circumstances in which there is an imbalance in the information available to parties who may potentially enter into a contract. Investors (particularly private investors) often face this problem as they may lack either relevant information or the ability to interpret that information. If this problem is left unresolved, it has the potential to hold back the growth of financial markets as, if investors lack the information needed to distinguish good investments from bad, they are likely to pay only average prices for all securities, with the result that high-quality issuers are likely to be deterred from raising capital.[13] Intermediaries can resolve this

---

[11] It is also possible for intermediation to occur between these financial intermediaries and investors. This occurs, for example, when a financial adviser recommends a financial product to a potential investor. See Chapter 6.1.2 for further details.

[12] The important role of intermediation in investment is evidenced by the substantial proportion of investments held through investment funds (such as unit and investment trusts and life policies). See P Myners, 'Institutional Investment in the United Kingdom: A Review' (March 2001) (Myners Report), available at http://archive.treasury.gov.uk/docs/2001/myners_report0602.html (accessed on 16 August 2011) for statistics. See also the Office for National Statistics (ONS), 'Share Ownership Survey 2008'.

[13] This is known as the problem of adverse selection. It is discussed in more detail in Chapter 2.1. See also P Spencer, *The Structure and Regulation of Financial Markets* (Oxford, Oxford University Press, 2000).

problem at relatively low cost by selecting and monitoring investments on behalf of a group of investors.

Finally, a distinction should be drawn between financial intermediation in the sense that the term is used here and 'intermediation' in the sense of an agent employed by a principal to carry out a transaction or series of transactions. An example of simple agency would be the employment of a financial adviser by an investor. The essence of financial intermediation is its capacity to change the nature of the financial product or service that is offered to the investor. Simple agency does not do that, even though it imposes an intermediary (agent) between the principal (investor) and the investee company, and brings into play obligations that arise from the law of agency and related regulatory rules. This distinction is significant because it is often the case that financial intermediation in the first sense does not represent an agency relationship in the legal sense: for example, in most instances a bank accepting a deposit from a customer or making a loan acts on an 'arm's length' basis in concluding the contract and will not be bound by the higher standards that arise from the fiduciary duties imposed on agents in the legal sense. As will be seen, the issue of identification of circumstances in which a financial intermediary acts as an agent in the legal sense when dealing with a customer, and what obligations should be attached to that role, is one of the basic problems that has been encountered in the law and regulatory rules associated with investment.

1.2 The legal nature of investment as contract and property

The fundamental challenge for the law is to devise rules that will allow investment to occur. In essence, this means devising rules that will provide legal rights to potential investors (surplus economic units) that will encourage them to become investors. The purpose of such rules is to determine the rights and obligations of an investor in relation to the entity in which the investment is made, other investors and the outside world. Without such legal rights, surplus resources or savings are unlikely to be channelled into investment because investors will be faced with legal risk as well as business risk.

Contract is the primary mechanism through which rights and obligations associated with investing are created. The essence of contract is that it creates rights and obligations only for the parties to the contract. An important example in the investment context is the 'statutory contract' that links a shareholder with a company and the other shareholders.[14] The contract comprises the articles of association and special resolutions of the company and defines, inter alia, voting rights, the right to dividends, and the distribution of power between the shareholders and the board of directors. While there is a core of mandatory rules that cannot be altered by this 'statutory contract' it is, in the UK at least, a relatively small part of company law.

---

[14] The statutory contract is recognised by s 33 of the Companies Act 2006.

It is nevertheless common for investors to be described as 'owners' of investments. From this perspective, investments are not just contracts but are also a form of property, and investors are not just party to a contract but also own a 'thing'. The implication is that investors have 'ownership' rather than just contractual rights. But how is it possible for contractual rights to become property (ie a thing that can be owned and transferred to another person)? The following sections attempt to explain this transformation, which is central to the legal meaning of investment.

1.2.1 Property—ownership and things

The two key concepts in property law are ownership and things.[15] Ownership is a set of legal rights held by an owner in respect of a thing.[16] Not all things, however, are capable of being owned.[17] Those things that are capable of being owned fall into two categories. A distinction is first made between tangible (corporeal) and intangible (incorporeal) things. A painting or a plot of land, for example, is tangible, but copyright in the painting or a right to rent from land is intangible. Tangible property is divided into real (or immoveable) property and personal (moveable) property. Real property is land and buildings, while personal property is all other types of property. In English law, tangible personal assets are referred to as 'choses in possession' or chattels and intangible personal assets are 'choses in action' or claims. In Scotland, the respective terms are 'corporeal moveables' and 'incorporeal moveables'. Investments are generally regarded by the law as falling into the category 'choses in action' ('incorporeal moveables' in Scotland or, in appropriate cases, simply debts).[18]

Also significant in the context of investment is the distinction between fungible and non-fungible property. The distinction is relevant to any situation in which there is an obligation to redeliver property, such as when a custodian[19] redelivers securities held on behalf of a client. Property is fungible if it is a commodity that has no definitive characteristics and can therefore be replaced by a similar weight, number or measure of the same commodity. Examples are money and commodities such as grain and oil. Property is not fungible if it has definitive characteristics (eg a painting, a house or a dog). Undivided securities (such as company shares of the same class) are always fungible because

---

[15] It is common to refer to the 'thing' as 'property', but that approach confuses the 'thing' with the concept of property as a set of legal rights over the 'thing'.

[16] See AM Honoré, 'Ownership' in AG Guest (ed), *Oxford Essays in Jurisprudence* (Oxford, Oxford University Press, 1961).

[17] The meaning of a 'thing' in this context is defined by DN MacCormick at para 1097 of the entry 'General Legal Concepts' in T Smith and R Black (eds), *The Laws of Scotland, Stair Memorial Encyclopedia* (Edinburgh, Butterworths, 1990) vol 11: 'Things are conceived as durable objects existing separately from and independently of persons, subject to being used, possessed, and enjoyed by persons, and thus capable of being transferred from one person to another without loss of identity.' The reference to 'durable' does not rule out a temporary existence—eg a right exercisable within a certain period of time.

[18] This categorisation is not inevitable. It is based on a distinction between a financial instrument (eg a share certificate) and the rights represented by that instrument. In the US, for example, registered securities (such as company shares) are considered to be tangible property.

[19] See Chapter 14.1.3 for an explanation of custody.

they are identical parts of a single unit (such as the capital of a company).[20] It follows that a redelivery obligation[21] in respect of such securities can be satisfied by delivery of any of the relevant class of security. In principle, this makes possible the pooling of securities of the same type held for different clients by custodians, as they are able to satisfy redelivery obligations by using any of the securities in the pool. Without that capability, custody of investments would become more complex and costly.

Ownership of a thing can take different forms. Divided ownership occurs when each person owns a thing that is legally distinct from other similar things. An example is a bearer security that promises to pay the bearer on demand. Each security is a thing in its own right, with rights and obligations that can be determined without reference to any other similar security. Undivided (or *pro indiviso*) ownership occurs when two or more people hold a thing as an undivided whole, without separate parts being attributed to each co-owner. A further distinction can be made, in the case of undivided ownership, between common property and joint property. In the case of common property (in England, tenants in common), each co-owner has a share in the *pro indiviso* whole that is separate in a legal, though not a physical, sense from shares held by other co-owners. An example is a share in a company, which is an undivided fractional part of the capital of the issuing company.[22] There are no particular parts of the share capital or assets of the company associated with a share and the issuer owes only one set of obligations to each class of shareholder. Other examples are registered debt and units in unit trusts.[23] A co-owner of any form of common property is entitled to transfer her share to another person.

Joint property (in England joint tenants) arises when there is no distinct legal title held by each of the co-owners in the *pro indiviso* whole. An example is the joint ownership of trust property by trustees (eg pension fund trustees or unit trust trustees). This type of ownership has been decribed as 'elastic'[24] as it vests in the persons who are for the time being trustees. A joint owner does not have a legally distinct share of joint property that can be transferred to another person. For example, a purported transfer of property by an individual trustee without the agreement of the others is of no effect.

1.2.2 Contractual rights as a form of property

Underlying the legal concept of property is the principle that it is capable of being owned by anyone. This implies that it is both separable and distinct from the person who owns it.[25] The logical consequence that follows the designation of a 'thing' as

---

[20] Not all securities are fungible. Some money-market instruments, for example, have distinctive serial numbers and are regarded as non-fungible.

[21] Such as occurs in a repurchase ('repo') transaction, in which a buyer of securities agrees to sell them at a future date to the original seller at an agreed price. A repo provides a means of raising short-term funds through the sale and buyback of securities.

[22] See further J Benjamin, *Interests in Securities* (Oxford, Oxford University Press, 2000) para 2.14.

[23] See Chapter 4 for the meaning of those terms and also Benjamin, above n 22, para 11.62.

[24] K Reid, 'Co-ownership' in Smith and Black (eds), above n 17, vol 18 (Property), para 35.

[25] See JA Penner, *The Idea of Property in Law* (Oxford, Oxford University Press, 1997), who explains this approach by reference to the concept of the separability of a thing from a particular person. He says (113): 'Separability is a conceptual criterion of property which defines the objects of property and gives rise to transfer-

property is that ownership should be capable of transfer.[26] Moreover, since transferability is a precondition for the existence of markets, it follows that designation of 'things' as property is the first step in the development of a legal framework for markets. Applied to financial instruments, this means that, for contractual rights (such as those arising from shares and bonds) to be capable of being transferred and traded on markets, they must first be recognised as 'property' in the legal sense.

Historically, different legal systems have varied in their recognition of contractual rights[27] as a form of (transferable) property. In Scotland, it was accepted at an early stage that such rights could in principle be transferred.[28] In England, the common law did not recognise transfers of contractual rights but they were recognised in equity and therefore capable of enforcement by the courts of equity.[29] Subsequently, statutory intervention in England expressly recognised transfer of contractual rights in specific contexts.[30] However, the potential limitations that restrictions on transferability in England (and elsewhere) posed for the development of financial markets and credit were mitigated by two important qualifications of the general policy against transferability of contractual rights. The first was the recognition that when such rights were incorporated into a negotiable instrument (such as a bill of exchange)[31] they were transferable. Moreover, not only were they transferable in the sense of transferring rights from A to B, but it was possible for C to acquire the instrument without reference to any defects in the rights held by B. In that sense, the process of 'negotiation' of a negotiable instrument differed from mere transfer and the technique was to prove a crucial development in the extension of credit and the early development of banking systems.[32] The second was the recognition that a share in a company or a partnership was property and therefore capable of transfer.[33] This recognition predated the statutory forms of companies and partnership that were

---

ability. To be conceived as an object of property a thing must first be considered as separable and distinct from any person who might hold it, and is for that reason rightly regarded as alienable.'

[26] See Penner, above n 25, 113–14.

[27] It should be emphasised that it is contractual rights and not liabilities that is being referred to here. Transfer of liabilities (ie a change in the identity of the debtor) is a different matter and generally cannot occur without the consent of the creditor because a change in the identity of the debtor fundamentally alters the contract. A change in the identity of the creditor (ie the owner of the financial instrument) does not prejudice the position of the debtor as the same obligations are owed to the new creditor.

[28] G Gretton and A Steven, *Property Trusts and Succession* (Edinburgh, Tottel, 2009) para 5.38: 'Personal rights are presumptively transferable. The consent of the debtor is not required.' See Scottish Law Commission DP No 151, 'Discussion Paper on Moveable Transactions' (June 2011) ch 4 for an outline of the current law.

[29] On the rationale for the restriction in English law on the transfer of contractual obligations see E Peel, *Treitel, The Law of Contract*, 12th edn (London, Sweet & Maxwell, 2007) 715. Scots law on the transfer of contractual rights was less restrictive than the law in England: K Reid, 'Transfer of Ownership' in Smith and Black, above n 17, vol 18 (Property), para 652.

[30] See J Dalhuisen, *Dalhuisen on Transnational and Comparative Commercial, Financial and Trade Law*, 3rd edn (Oxford, Hart Publishing, 2007) 630.

[31] Section 3 of the Bills of Exchange Act 1882 provides that: 'A bill of exchange is an unconditional order in writing, addressed by one person to another, signed by the person giving it, requiring the person to whom it is addressed to pay on demand or at a fixed or determinable future time a sum certain in money to or to the order of a specified person, or to bearer.'

[32] See generally Dalhuisen, above n 30, 759–62; E Jenks, 'The Early History of Negotiable Instruments' [1893] *Law Quarterly Review* 70; J Rogers, *The Early History of the Bills and Notes (A Study of the Origins of Anglo-American Commercial Law)* (Cambridge, Cambridge University Press, 1995).

[33] See Chapter 4.4.3 for more detail on share transfers.

introduced in 1844 and 1890 respectively, as evidenced by the existence of markets in shares from around 1600 onwards and even earlier references to transfers of partnership shares.[34] Thus, even in systems such as that in England, which did not (at least so far as the common law was concerned) facilitate the transfer of contractual rights, it remained possible for credit to be created and transferred via the negotiable instrument and for equity participations in enterprises to be transferred and traded. For the economic system as a whole, this meant that there were mechanisms that supplied basic forms of liquidity both to enterprises and to investors in those enterprises.

1.2.3 Legal title to investments

As noted earlier, property in the legal sense is a thing that has the potential to be owned by anyone. For a particular person to own a thing requires that a legal title to it becomes vested in that particular person. The process by which legal title become vested in a particular person varies as between different categories of property. In the case of registered securities (the principal example being company shares), legal title is constituted by entry of the owner's name in the relevant register. The registered owner is the legal owner and, in the case of company shares, no other interest can be recorded in the shareholders' register.[35] A distinction can be drawn between an investment and a document, certificate or other token that represents the investment. A share certificate, for example, is not itself an investment but simply evidence that the holder is a shareholder.[36] The investment is the bundle of rights held by the shareholder. The distinction between the certificate and the investment is illustrated by the approach to forged transfers. Suppose that A steals B's share certificate, forges B's signature on a transfer form, submits it to the issuer and has his name inserted on the shareholders' register. Assuming that B is able to show that A's ownership claim is false, he is entitled to have his name reinstated on the register. This remains true even if C has taken the certificate from B in good faith and for value as the certificate does not have the character of a negotiable instrument.[37]

In the case of bearer securities, a distinction between a certificate and the underlying investment cannot be drawn in the same manner. Bearer securities are regarded as tangible moveable property and can be transferred simply by delivery.[38] There is, in

---

[34] See generally WR Scott, *The Constitution and Finance of English, Scottish and Irish Joint-stock Companies to 1720* (Cambridge, Cambridge University Press, 1912) vol II; R Harris, *Industrializing English Law: Entrepreneurship and Business Organization, 1720–1844* (Cambridge, Cambridge University Press, 2000).

[35] Section 126 of the Companies Act 2006 prohibits the recording of notice of a trust on the shareholders' register of companies incorporated in England and Wales. The prohibition does not apply to companies incorporated in Scotland. The legal owner will often not be the 'ultimate' investor (the person whose money has bought the investment) as legal title to securities is nowadays often held in trust (by a trustee or custodian) for the ultimate investor. Indeed, scrutiny of the shareholders' register of many companies will in itself often reveal very little in terms of the true ownership of the company.

[36] Companies Act 2006, s 768.

[37] See further Chapter 4.4.3.

[38] Historically, this treatment evolved through a legal fiction under which the debt itself became merged with the negotiable instrument issued in respect of it, with the debt being considered to be 'locked-up' inside the investment (see Benjamin, above n 22, ch 3). In the US, but not the UK, this approach was applied to registered securities.

principle, no need for a record of ownership and any (unidentified) holder is the legal owner.[39] This gives effect to the principle that a bearer security should have a negotiable character, meaning that it is possible for a transferee to take a better title than that held by the transferor. Suppose that the same circumstances mentioned in the paragraph above occur in relation to a bearer security. While B can recover the stolen certificate while it remains in the possession of A, he cannot recover it from C if C is a bona fide purchaser for value (a 'holder in due course').

These examples illustrate the different interests that the law relating to transfer of registered and bearer securities has recognised. In the case of registered securities, priority has been given to security of title and there has been a strict application of the principle *nemo dat quod non habet* ('no one can give what he does not have'). In the case of bearer securities, priority has been given to security of transfer (to a holder in due course), reflecting the historic concern of the law merchant to facilitate the transfer of rights in the market through negotiability.[40]

Paper certificates have been replaced in many instances by an electronic record of ownership, both for registered and bearer securities. The main attraction is that it eliminates the need for transfer of paper certificates, thereby making the trading of securities less cumbersome and securities markets more efficient.[41] Dematerialisation has been adopted in many countries, including the UK. It results in an issue of securities to investors being recorded electronically by the issuer or its agent, with the investor receiving confirmation that this has occurred. Confirmation does not have the status of a document of title as it merely intimates that title is recorded in the electronic register, which is the definitive record of ownership.

Legal title to securities can be immobilised, meaning that arrangements are made for securities to be issued on the basis that there will be, in perpetuity, only one legal owner. This is a separate process from dematerialisation and its main effect is on the ownership link between an issuer and investor. It involves legal title to an entire issue of securities being taken by a central securities depositary (CSD). Investors to whom the securities are issued are recorded in the books of the CSD as holding the appropriate number of securities. However, these book entries do not give legal title to the investor as that remains with the CSD. The investor in this situation has no direct link with the issuer and his rights are derived from those held by the CSD.[42]

1.2.4 Transfer of legal title to investments

As noted earlier, the categorisation of investments represented by contractual rights as property means that they are, in principle, transferable. Put another way, the bundle of

---

[39] In practice many bearer securities are held (on behalf of the ultimate owners) by central securities depositaries (mainly for security reasons) but this does not limit their 'bearer' status.

[40] See Benjamin, above n 22, paras 3.21–3.26, on the historical significance of negotiability in England before assignment became available as a means to transfer choses in action.

[41] See further Chapter 4.4.2 and 4.4.3.

[42] Issues arising where (as is common) there is a chain of custodians linking the CSD with the ultimate investor are discussed in Chapter 14.1.3.

rights representing an investment issued to A can be transferred to B. As a general rule,[43] contractual rights are transferred by assignment.[44] That process operates on the basis that a transferee takes the same rights held by the transferor.[45] Suppose, for example, that A assigns his life assurance policy to B, who in turn assigns it to C. Assume also that the insurer is entitled to set aside (avoid) the policy on the basis of misrepresentation (eg because A lied about his health when taking out the policy). In those circumstances, the insurer has the same remedy against a subsequent holder (assignee) of the policy (B and C).[46] Assignment also requires that the debtor be notified of the assignment, thereby protecting the interest of the debtor in making payment to the correct creditor.

Assignment remains the method by which most investments other than registered or bearer securities are transferred. Thus, unregistered bonds and the rights of lenders in respect of mortgages are typically transferred by way of assignment. However, shares are transferred by a different legal process, which is referred to as novation. This is a general principle of contract law that allows a new creditor to be substituted for an existing one. The agreement of the debtor (company), existing creditor (seller) and new creditor (buyer) is necessary. The process differs from assignment in that the new creditor does not succeed to the rights of the old creditor but enters a new contractual relationship with the debtor.[47] It is possible for novation to occur in respect of company shares because of the existence of the 'statutory contract' between shareholders and the company and the shareholders *inter se*. The terms of the (new) contract (with the new member) are contained in the articles and special resloutions of the company, which together form the 'statutory contract'.[48] The agreement of the debtor (issuing company) to the process of novation is shown by it entering the name of the new shareholder (buyer) on the register and removing the name of the previous shareholder (seller).[49] Novation differs from assignment in that a transferee (buyer) is not exposed to the risk of her title being affected by defences[50] available to the issuer against the original holder. Novation also represents a technique for dealing with the potential for change in the underlying statutory contract resulting from changes to a company's constitution. Since assignment is based on the premise that the contractual rights of the creditor will be fixed at the outset and transferred without alteration, it cannot cope with changes in the terms of the contract.

---

[43] Negotiable instruments are an exception as the process of negotiation can result in a transferee having superior rights to the original creditor or a prior holder. Such instruments (and their legal infrastructure) were developed to facilitate the transfer of payment obligations as a form of trade credit.

[44] The use of assignment is linked to the categorisation of contractual rights as choses in action (in Scotland incorporeal moveable property). In the US, by way of contrast, registered securities are considered to be tangible property and can be transferred by indorsement and delivery of the relevant certificate.

[45] The principle is encapsulated by the Latin maxim *assignatus utitur jure auctoris* ('the assignee takes the rights of the assignor').

[46] The potential risks to a transferee (buyer) arising from the rule discussed above may be removed by the issuer of the relevant instrument accepting disapplication of the rule, so that a transferee takes free from any defects in the title of the original or subsequent holders.

[47] Strictly speaking, therefore, novation is not transfer but its economic effect is the same.

[48] See ss 33 and 17 of the Companies Act 2006.

[49] There may be circumstances in which the issuer can, according to its articles, refuse to register a transfer but these will be comparatively rare. See Chapter 4.4.3 for more detail.

[50] Eg if the issuer is entitled to rescind the contract or claim damages for misrepresentation. While those circumstances may be unusual, they are possible.

Novation is able to do this since each new shareholder enters into a statutory contract on the basis of the company constitution at the time when that person becomes a shareholder. Furthermore, that contract itself provides that a shareholder will be bound by subsequent changes to the constitution that are made under the relevant provisions of company law.

1.2.5 Custody of investments

It is common nowadays for investors to hold investments through intermediaries rather than directly.[51] Two explanations can be given for this trend. First, there are some investors (both professional and private) who may find it convenient to have a professional custodian hold investments on their behalf. Fund managers, for example, generally prefer to focus on portfolio management rather than be involved in the administrative arrangements associated with ownership and transfers of ownership of investments. Secondly, the introduction of dematerialised title to securities has encouraged indirect ownership because transfers of title through the system are possible only through a member.[52] If a member holds securities as custodian on behalf of investors, transfers are generally simpler and less costly.

From the legal perspective, transfer of an investment under a custody arrangement raises the question of the respective rights of the custodian (and its creditors) and the investor. Reference can usefully be made in this context to the distinction between real and personal rights in things.[53] Real rights can be exercised against the whole world, whereas personal rights can be exercised only against specific persons. The classic example of a real right is that of an owner of property against a thief. The true owner is able to vindicate his right by reclaiming stolen property because he has a real right in the property that can be exercised against everybody. The classic example of a personal right is a contractual obligation owed by a debtor to a creditor. The right is personal because it can only be exercised against the debtor. As noted earlier, investments (or in other words the legal rights that comprise the investment itself) are personal rights because they are in essence contractual rights.[54] In the case of a company, for example, the rights of an ordinary shareholder are contained in the 'statutory contract' represented by the memorandum and articles of association.[55] In the case of a lender to a company (such as a debenture holder), the rights of the holder are determined by a loan agreement (often supplemented by the taking of a security interest to guard against the possibility of default by the borrower).

It is in respect of third parties (such as custodians) who hold investments on behalf of investors that the real rights of an investor become apparent. While an investment is in essence a bundle of personal rights held by the investor, when it is 'deposited' with an

---

[51] The legal mechanism through which this occurs is normally trust. See Chapter 5.1 for more detail on the nature and operation of trusts.

[52] See Chapter 4.4.3 for more detail.

[53] In English law, the distinction is often expressed as between personal and proprietary rights.

[54] The detail of these contractual rights is discussed in Chapter 4.

[55] See above n 14.

intermediary such as a custodian the investor has real rights against the custodian. The legal nature of the investment (as a bundle of personal rights that can be exercised against the issuer) is unchanged, but there is a new legal relationship between the investor and the intermediary under which the property of the investor is deposited with the intermediary and in respect of which the investor has real rights.[56] Another way of expressing this is to say that an investor's ownership of an investment is a right that is good against the rest of the world (a real right) even though the rights represented by the investment can only be enforced against particular persons (personal rights). The position can be illustrated by reference to a simple example. A share issued by company X to Y is essentially a contractual arrangement. However, when this share is held on Y's behalf by custodian C, the law views Y as having a real right in respect of the share. The implication is that the share is not available to C's creditors should C become insolvent because the share is the property of Y and not C.[57]

This is not to say that there are not important issues that fall to be agreed by contract between an investor and an intermediary who holds securities on his behalf. Such issues include the manner in which control (voting) rights associated with an investment are to be exercised, the purposes for which the intermediary is entitled to use the investments (eg to lend to others) and the persons to whom they may be entrusted for safekeeping. These (personal) rights are, however, distinct from the real rights relating to the investment in that they are enforceable only against the custodian, whereas the real right is a right to enjoy the benefits of ownership that is good against the whole world.

1.3 The process of investment

As the focus of this book is on portfolio rather than direct investment, it is assumed that all investments are made through the financial markets. In other words, the process of investment is viewed as comprising the institutions, legal rules and procedures that together form the framework within which investments are issued, bought and sold in financial markets. An overview of that framework follows below and is developed in more detail in subsequent chapters.

---

[56] Benjamin, above n 22, para 13.10 sums up the position succinctly as follows: 'intermediation is not only compatible with property rights in relation to intangibles: it is their precondition'.

[57] The position would differ if the law recognised Y as having only a contractual (personal) right against C. This would be the case if Y deposited money with a bank. A deposit becomes the property of the bank and a depositor has only a contractual (personal) right to the return of the money. In principle, therefore, there is no 'property' which can be identified by Y as belonging to him in the event of the bank's insolvency and therefore Y will have to claim as a creditor in any insolvency procedure rather than being able to require the return of his 'property'. See generally R Cranston, *Principles of Banking Law*, 2nd edn (Oxford University Press 2002) ch 5.

1.3.1 Market structure and ownership

The structure of financial markets has been affected by a number of trends in portfolio investment in recent years. Globalisation and increasing flows of cross-border portfolio investment have been significant factors for competition among markets in respect of costs and services. Large companies no longer need to limit capital raising or the trading of their securities to their local market since exchanges and investors in other countries now stand ready to meet their needs. This trend is evident in the large numbers of foreign-listed companies which trade on the major exchanges around the world. Competition between markets has been evident in adaptations targeted at particular types of issuers: thus, it is now common for the major markets to adopt a structure in which there is a main market and a junior market which imposes less stringent listing obligations on issuers. Regulation has also been an important factor for competition and has led to the emergence of so-called 'alternative' markets which compete with public regulated markets by offering lower transactions costs to investors. Some of these alternative markets have grown to a level at which they equal or exceed the turnover of public regulated markets in some securities. The growth of trading in credit and derivative instruments has also been a significant factor in recent years and has resulted in a large volume of transactions taking place on a bilateral basis in the so-called 'over-the-counter market'. The result has been that the role of public regulated markets has declined and this has led to calls for their position to be strengthened so as to improve transparency across the financial system as a whole.[58]

Recent years have also seen significant changes in the ownership structure of financial markets. Historically, mutual ownership, in which markets were owned by the brokers and dealers trading on the market, was the standard model. Under that model, exchanges were typically run on a not-for-profit basis and performed important regulatory functions in setting and enforcing listing rules for issuers. However, that model has now been replaced in the case of all the major markets by a standard corporate model in which exchanges are listed companies owned by shareholders and operating on a for-profit basis. Taken together with the trend towards internationalisation and a greater focus on competition between exchanges as a policy objective (especially in the EU), the result has been a wave of consolidation and alliances among exchanges around the world. The move to a for-profit model has limited the regulatory role that can be entrusted to exchanges since they now operate for the benefit of their shareholders and cannot be trusted to prioritise the public interest in securing effective regulation of their own business.

1.3.2 Law and markets

From the legal perspective, contract and property law provide the basic framework within which markets operate. The role of contract law in markets of any kind is primarily to facilitate transactions and private bargaining. This can be understood in two ways. The

---

[58] See further Chapter 13.1.

first is that contract law must provide certainty that contracts will be enforced. Uncertainty surrounding the enforcement of contracts is likely to discourage investment because, even if the legal rights represented by the investment (as a form or property) are quite clear, there will be confusion over whether and on what terms any transfer is to take place. Put another way, there would be little point in the law recognising the transferability of investments if it were not able to provide certainty in respect of the enforcement of contracts under which such transfers are to take place.

Secondly, facilitation can be understood as meaning that contract law is structured so as to minimise transaction costs for the parties.[59] The most important way in which contract law pursues this objective is through the provision of standard contract terms. These mainly take the form of default rules, which are rules that apply unless disapplied or altered by the parties. Default rules are relevant both to the making of contracts that define investors' rights (such as the 'statutory contract'[60]) and to contracts under which investments are transferred.[61] The benefit of default rules is that they limit transaction costs by allowing parties to avoid drafting a new agreement every time they contract. They also provide flexibility by allowing the parties to adapt the standard terms to a form that is best suited to their own circumstances.

There are three techniques employed by the law to give effect to standard contract terms.[62] The first, and most straightforward, is for a contract to refer to a set of standard conditions that govern the contract. For example, in the case of swaps and derivatives, the model contract terms developed by the International Swaps and Derivatives Association provide standard contract terms. The second technique is that terms can be implied into contracts even when they have not been expressly agreed between the parties. The rationale for this approach is that a reasonable person in the position of the contracting parties would have agreed to the inclusion of the term. A third technique (of less relevance in modern financial markets) is that the parties will be bound by a well-established trade custom.

Property law also plays an important role in the operation of financial markets by providing a legal framework for ownership rights and the transfer of securities. Ownership rights must be clearly defined and capable of effective enforcement (both against an issuer and a custodian) so as to facilitate investment. Property law also plays an important role in facilitating transactions that transfer rights other than ownership. Rights in security, often referred to as 'collateral' in the financial markets, are an important example. Collateral is often provided in transactions to mitigate risk by making it possible for the collateral taker to sell or exercise other rights against the collateral following default

---

[59] As to the economic significance of transaction costs in determining whether and to what extent trading in legal rights (such as investments) is likely to occur, see RH Coase, 'The Problem of Social Cost' (1960) 3 *Journal of Law and Economics* 1; O Williamson, *The Economic Institutions of Capitalism* (New York, Macmillan, 1985).

[60] See above n 14.

[61] Standard contracts for the transfer of investments (eg as regards time of payment and delivery of legal title) reduce transaction costs in the process of managing investments.

[62] See generally Peel, above n 29, ch 6, and, in respect of Scotland, W McBryde, *Contract*, 3rd edn (Edinburgh, W Green, 2007) chs 7 and 9.

by the collateral giver. For this process to operate effectively, property law must define clearly the rights of the giver and taker of the collateral.

Underlying the concern with providing a legal framework for markets that combines certainty with low transaction costs is the perception that allocative efficiency will be maximised under these conditions. Allocative efficiency refers to the extent to which (scarce) resources are allocated through financial markets to those enterprises that are likely to put them to the best use. Financial markets play a role in allocating resources (in the form of finance) to enterprises in two ways. First, they act as a conduit through which enterprises can raise money directly from investors. Secondly, they provide a mechanism through which securities can be traded to those who value them most highly.[63] Both of these functions contribute most effectively to allocative efficiency when transactions costs are low because it is in those circumstances that market participants are likely to engage in transactions. As transaction costs progressively increase, it is likely that financial markets will perform their functions less effectively and allocative efficiency is likely, in aggregate, to decline. Thus, legal certainty and effective enforcement mechanisms have an important role to play both in the development of financial markets and the efficient allocation of capital.[64]

1.3.3 Regulation

Markets in which the law pursues only the objective of facilitation of private bargaining may encounter problems. If, for example, there are no controls over the terms that may be agreed between parties, those with a weak bargaining position may have little choice but to accept bad bargains. This has long been regarded as unfair (as well as inefficient, in that it is likely to discourage contracting and therefore also the process of investment), and contract law has therefore adopted a regulatory as well as a facilitative objective. That regulatory role involves the making of mandatory rules which must be observed and which cannot be excluded by agreement between the parties.[65] Such rules differ fundamentally from the main body of rules in contract law, which are default rules in the sense that they can be changed by express agreement between the parties. The most obvious examples of the regulatory role played by contract law are the relatively recent statutory controls over contract terms,[66] although there are also much older examples of

---

[63] According to the 'Coase Theorem', above n 59, all legal rights (including financial instruments) will, at least in a world with no transaction costs, be traded to those who value them most highly. The presence of transaction costs will progressively limit the extent to which this process occurs.

[64] See eg V Gessner and A Cem Budak, *Legal Certainty: Empirical Studies on Globalization of Law* (Aldershot, Ashgate, 1998).

[65] In this sense, the term 'regulation' can be applied to any circumstances in which mandatory rules limit the operation of private ordering through contract.

[66] The Unfair Contract Terms Act 1977 and the Unfair Terms in Consumer Contracts Regulations 1999. Both aim to protect consumers (broadly speaking, persons acting in a private rather than a business capacity) by prohibiting or limiting the use of contract terms that are patently unfair (eg terms that exclude liability for breach of contract).

common law controls over freedom of contract.[67] These regulatory rules are mandatory in the sense that they cannot be avoided by contracting round them.

While these aspects of the law's regulatory approach to the process of investment are important, the term 'regulation' is nowadays understood more specifically to refer to rules and procedures created by statute and administered by dedicated agencies. Some elements of regulation, in this more limited sense, have a relatively long history, but the modern form of regulation of the process of investment started in the US in the early 1930s, largely as a response to the events that culminated in the Wall Street Crash of 1929.[68] In the UK, there was less inclination to introduce statutory regulation as there was a strong tradition of self-regulation in financial markets. That tradition survived, in varying forms, until the introduction of the Financial Services and Markets Act 2000, which created a system of statutory regulation with a single regulator responsible for investment business in the UK.

The rationale for statutory regulation is that the general commercial law (primarily contract law and property law) does not provide an adequate basis for the operation of investment markets. Investment has two characteristics that differentiate it from other commercial activities, where general commercial law may be adequate.[69] The first is the presence of information asymmetry. In the absence of regulation, investors may lack the information required to make informed investment decisions. In that situation, there is information asymmetry between the investor and the entrepreneur who wants to attract investment. Such asymmetry is likely to deter investment and, if sufficiently serious, may prevent the emergence of markets for investments since investors may be unwilling to invest.

Secondly, investment often exposes investors to systemic risk. That is the risk that, even if the entity in which they invest or the entity holding their investment is sound, its solvency may be threatened by the collapse of another entity to which it is linked through the financial system. This risk arises most obviously in banking, but is also present in investment since defaults in meeting settlement obligations in investment transactions may carry implications for third parties as well as the contacting parties. For example, if A fails to pay B for shares, B may be unable to settle obligations under a separate transaction with C. Statutory regulation, such as the system established by the Financial Services and Markets Act 2000 in the UK, aims to improve the operation of financial markets by creating rules and procedures that limit the risks posed to investors by systemic risk and information asymmetry. In the wake of the financial crisis that began in 2008, regulatory systems around the world are now focusing much more closely on limiting systemic risk and developing regulatory techniques that will implement that policy.[70] The most significant development in this context has been the new capital and liquidity rules adopted

---

[67] Eg the law relating to restraint of trade. See also s 232 of the Companies Act 2006, which renders void any contract that attempts to exempt or restrict the liability of a director (to a company) for breach of duty.

[68] See JA Grudfest, 'Securities Regulation' in P Newman (ed), *The New Palgrave Dictionary of Economics and the Law* (Basingstoke, Palgrave Macmillan, 2002) 410–19.

[69] These issues are examined in more detail in Chapter 2.

[70] See generally Financial Services Authority (FSA), 'The Turner Review, A Regulatory Response to the Global Banking Crisis' (March 2009), available at http://www.fsa.gov.uk/Pages/Library/Corporate/turner/index.shtml (accessed on 16 August 2011).

by the Basel Committee on Banking Supervision in 2009, which aim to limit systemic risk by requiring a greater level of shareholder equity in banks, so as to limit the risks to customers and creditors.

1.3.4 The common law

Despite the expansion in statutory regulation of investment in recent years, the common law remains a significant influence for the process of investment. As already mentioned, contracts are central to the creation of investments as things that can be owned, but they are also important for the process of investment. In that capacity, contracts govern the relationship between investors and intermediaries who act on their behalf. Other aspects of the common law also play an important role in the process of investment and are considered below.

Trusts are a legal device that enable the legal ownership of property to be separated from the enjoyment of the benefits that flow from that property.[71] They are commonly used as the legal structure under which investments are held and managed in the UK.[72] Occupational pension funds and unit trusts are structured as trusts, thereby enabling large numbers of small investors to have an interest in a fund that is legally owned by the trustees. Custodians (sometimes referred to as nominees) hold investments on trust for their customers, thereby simplifying and centralising the administrative aspects of the ownership of investments.

Fiduciary duty arises in circumstances in which the law recognises a relationship of trust between two parties. In the investment context, important instances of fiduciary duty are the duty owed by a trustee to a beneficiary of a trust, a director to a company and an agent to a principal. Underlying the law in each instance is the objective that a fiduciary should not allow her own interest to conflict with that of the person to whom the duty is owed and should act at all times in the best interests of that person.[73]

Fiduciary duty is central to the process of investment. In the case of investment advice, for example, an independent adviser is considered the agent of the client and therefore owes a fiduciary duty to the client.[74] Trustees of a unit trust or an occupational pension scheme owe a fiduciary duty to trust beneficiaries (unit-holders or relevant employees respectively) and therefore investment (and other) decisions must be made according to the high standards the law demands from a fiduciary. In some respects, statutory regulation has replicated much of the content of fiduciary duty in regulatory rules. This is evident in rules such as suitability, which governs the standard of advice required from

---

[71] This brief introduction ignores the different doctrinal bases of trust law in Scotland and England. The English law of trusts recognises that ownership rights can be split between a legal owner (the trustee) and a beneficial owner (the beneficiary of the trust). Scots law does not recognise the possibility of ownership rights being divided in this way. In Scots law one is either a legal owner (including a common or joint owner) or not an owner.

[72] The role of trusts is discussed in more detail in Chapter 5.1.

[73] For a classic statement of the content of fiduciary duty see *Aberdeen Railway Company v Blaikie Bros* (1854) 1 MacQueen 461 (HL).

[74] See generally R Munday, *Agency Law and Principles* (Oxford, Oxford University Press, 2010) paras 8.15–8.68.

a financial adviser. However, as the courts have made clear, regulation has not super-seded the common law and, in many respects, the wide-ranging and flexible nature of fiduciary duty represents a more appropriate legal basis for governing the process of investment than regulatory rules that are often (at least for private investors) complex, counter-intuitive and inaccessible.[75]

The common law of tort (delict in Scotland) is also important in the context of invest-ment. Liability can arise in tort in circumstances in which the common law holds that one person owes a duty of care to another. For example, in the case of *Hedley Byrne v Heller* [76] it was held that a bank owed a duty of care to a third party who relied in the course of business on a reference given by the bank in respect of a customer. In the investment context, the law of tort is relevant when financial advice is given to a potential or actual customer or when information or an opinion is provided on which others rely in making investment decisions. Liability in tort is particularly important as a means of redress when there is no contractual relationship between the parties, such as when a sales representa-tive 'advises' a potential customer regarding the sale of a financial product.[77]

Common law criminal offences are now of relatively minor significance as far as the process of investment is concerned. Two related reasons can be given for this. One is that they have not proven to be an effective mechanism for punishing what may be termed 'wrongdoing' in financial transactions. Fraud is the most obvious example: it is difficult to collect adequate evidence to show intent to commit fraud and there is the added complication of ensuring that a jury is able to understand the often complicated factual circumstances associated with fraud in financial transactions. Another reason is that there has been a substantial expansion in the range of 'regulatory' criminal offences, which have been created as part of the system of financial regulation and company law. They include insider dealing, market manipulation, misleading investors and a whole array of more minor and technical offences. Moreover, there is an increasing tendency, as evidenced by the new market abuse regime,[78] for the regulatory system to ignore the criminal law altogether and to resort to sanctions imposed by the financial regulator rather than by courts.

1.3.5 Investment entities and structures

Earlier in this chapter, reference was made to the role of financial institutions in the process of financial intermediation. Nowadays, specialised investment entities and legal structures play a key role in that process. A distinction can be drawn between two types of entity or legal structure through which the process of financial intermediation takes place. The first are what may be termed fiduciary entities, which hold investments on

---

[75] See Chapter 6 for more discussion of the relative roles of the common law and regulatory rules.

[76] [1964] AC 465. It was held in this particular case that the bank had not actually breached its duty of care (because its reference included a disclaimer of liability), but the principle has nevertheless had a far-reaching impact in respect of liability for negligent financial advice.

[77] See further Chapter 6.6.2.

[78] See further Chapter 13.

trust for their clients.[79] As they act in a fiduciary capacity, they are subject to the rigorous standards required by the law from fiduciaries.[80] In this category are unit trusts, pension funds and custodians. The second category can be termed non-fiduciary entities. In the latter category are insurers and deposit-taking institutions. They have a contractual rather than a fiduciary relationship with their customer, and this has important implications for the nature of the relationship between the parties and the rights of the 'investor'. In the case of both insurance and deposits, the institution becomes the owner of the money it receives from the 'investor', who has only a contractual claim against the institution to perform the obligations contained in the relevant contract. Moreover, such an institution does not normally[81] have a fiduciary duty to the customer, with the result that the normal principles of contract law (including *caveat emptor*[82]) apply.[83]

As well as undertaking the function of financial intermediation (in the economic sense discussed in section 1.1 of this chapter), investment entities also undertake the function of repackaging investments in a form suitable for investors. For example, unit trusts, in addition to providing risk diversification, also transform the legal mechanism under which an investor owns a company share. If an investor were to own the share directly, her rights would be determined primarily by the 'statutory contract' under section 33 of the Companies Act 2006. If she owns the share indirectly through a unit trust, it is the trustees who are the legal owner (and therefore party to the 'statutory contract') and she is a beneficiary of the trust. A similar process occurs in occupational pension schemes, which operate under the legal structure of trust. In both instances, the transformation of the legal nature of the rights of the 'ultimate investor' makes possible the achievement of the economic objectives inherent in pooled investment funds (primarily risk diversification and economies of scale).

Recent years have seen a substantial increase in the use of entities that are referred to as 'special investment vehicles' (SIVs). These vehicles can take the form of companies, partnerships or trusts. What makes them 'special' is not their legal structure (although there have been some innovations in the way that the standard legal models are adapted) but the rationale for their creation. In most cases, they are used to avoid or mitigate the effects of financial regulation on the activities of a financial firm. For example, SIVs have been used frequently in the 'securitisation'[84] of mortgage portfolios to move loans off the balance sheet of banks. From the bank's perspective, there are two significant advantages of this technique. First, so long as the SIV is formally independent from the bank, there will be no need to consolidate the relevant loans in the bank's balance sheet.

---

[79] In English law, the client of such an entity can be described as the beneficial owner of the investment. In Scotland the client will either be the beneficiary of a trust or the principal in respect of an agency agreement.

[80] See further Chapter 5.5.

[81] See further Chapters 6.6 and 14.2. A fiduciary duty may arise in special circumstances.

[82] Meaning 'buyer beware'. The expression emphasises that contracts are generally made 'at arm's length', with the result that each party must look after their own interests.

[83] It is, of course, true that the principle of *caveat emptor* has been modified considerably by the regulatory obligations imposed on financial institutions (see eg the requirement of the FSA's Principles for Businesses (no 6) that 'A firm must pay due regard to the interests of its customers and treat them fairly'—see Chapter 15.2.1).

[84] Securitisation is a technique whereby debts (eg mortgages, credit-card debts) are sold by an originator to a third party, who funds the purchase through the issue to investors of bonds which are secured against the relevant debts.

Secondly, provided that there has been a true sale of the loans, which has removed the risk of default from the bank's balance sheet, the bank will benefit from a lower regulatory capital requirement as its loan book will be smaller. Thus, SIVs in principle offered the potential to banks to develop the 'originate to distribute' approach to lending in which loans were sold on to SIVs shortly after being made. The SIVs acquired the capacity to buy loan portfolios through the issue of various types of bonds to investors which were backed by the loans as collateral, with the interest payments from (mortgage) borrowers being passed on to the bond investors. This model enabled the banks to expand lending without increasing their capital to the same extent and resulted in a sharp rise in the overall leverage of the financial system in the years preceding the financial crisis.[85] It later transpired that the model was much less robust than had been claimed, especially since in many cases banks were exposed in various ways to loan defaults faced by the SIVs they had sponsored. The result has been that regulators have become more wary of this technique in the wake of the financial crisis and various techniques have been adopted that limit or require disclosure of the extent to which banks are now able to transfer loans 'off balance sheet' to SIVs.

1.3.6 Legal risk

The concept of legal risk has come to the fore in recent years. Its emergence has been driven by a number of factors. Changes in financial markets resulting from globalisation, technological change and innovation in financial instruments have meant that financial markets have become more complex, as too has the legal framework within which markets operate. Regulators around the world have become increasingly focused on risk within the financial system and categorisation of the different types of risk that are faced by markets and market participants.[86] The proliferation of sources of legal and regulatory rules is another factor that contributes to legal risk: examples are the large body of EU legislation that now interacts with national law in the EU and the prevalence of 'soft law' measures that do not have the status of formal 'hard' law but are nevertheless influential in the way that the market operates.

Moving beyond an explanation of the context in which legal risk arises to a definition of what it comprises is more problematic, since its meaning can change according to context. One succinct definition is as follows:

> As far as the financial institution is concerned, legal risk is the risk of having legal action taken, or a legal sanction enforced, against that institution, or the institution being unable to enforce a legal right, arising directly or indirectly out of the legal relationship between the institution and a contractual counterparty, a third party, or a governmental or non-governmental authority.[87]

Thus, legal risk focuses on two distinct risks.[88] One is the risk of legal action taken

---

[85] See the *Turner Review*, above n 70, chs 1.1(i) and 2.2(i).
[86] See Chapter 3.8 for a more detailed discussion of risk-based regulation.
[87] R McCormick, *Legal Risk in the Financial Markets* (Oxford, Oxford University Press, 2006) 112.
[88] This follows the approach adopted by McCormick, ibid.

by criminal prosecutors, regulators, customers or competitors seeking legal redress in relation to the conduct of the relevant financial institution. That risk encompasses matters such as market abuse sanctions that may be imposed by regulators and so-called 'mis-sellling' claims brought by customers who claim they were misled into buying financial instruments. The second focuses on the enforceability of transactions that have been entered into with counterparties. That risk encompasses matters such as the effect of legal uncertainty or a change in the law which may carry consequences for the financial institution. For example, in a series of cases dealing with swaps in the early 1990s, the House of Lords ruled that local authorities did not have the power to enter into swap agreements and as a result the contracts could not be enforced against them by banks.[89] Those cases prompted a much more intense focus on legal risk in the markets and in particular on legal uncertainty. Shortly after the decision the Bank of England established the Legal Risk Review Committee[90], which was charged with identifying and resolving areas of obscurity and uncertainty in the law with a view to limiting the effects of legal risk.

Legal risk differs from economic risk in that it is not normally sought by financial institutions or investors. In that sense, legal risk differs from economic risk since investors voluntarily undertake economic risk and their returns are linked to the degree of risk that they accept. That is not to say that legal risk is never voluntarily undertaken: in some cases, commercial considerations may lead to a decision to accept some degree of legal uncertainty in the way that a transaction is structured, especially if the risk of financial loss associated with the legal risk is small. Nor should it be assumed that all forms of legal action or sanctions that may be faced by participants in the financial markets arise from legal risk. Financial institutions face a broader set of risks, often termed 'operational', which comprise any risk that may threaten the capacity of the institution to conduct its business. This category of risk includes technical failure, natural disasters and 'rogue traders', as well as legal risk. While these operational risks may give rise to litigation or sanctions, they differ from legal risk in that the cause of the litigation or sanction is not a failure to understand and apply the law and regulatory rules to the institution's business.

---

[89] See ch 1 of McCormick, ibid, for a full discussion of these cases.
[90] The functions of that committee are now undertaken by the Financial Markets Law Committee.

Regulation of Investment—Rationale and Development

Chapter 1 drew a distinction between 'regulation' and the broader set of legal principles and rules applicable to financial investment. This chapter examines the rationale for regulation in the sphere of financial investment and its historical development. The scale and complexity of the system of regulation in the modern world is such that its existence is often taken for granted. It is true that the case for regulation is now broadly accepted, but there are at least two good reasons for exploring the rationale for regulation. The first is that such an examination is likely to provide guidance as to the objectives of a regulatory system in the sense that any system of regulation must reflect the rationale for its creation.[1] It does not, however, provide direct guidance as to the models and techniques by which those objectives are given effect, and it is for this reason that regulatory systems around the world differ despite often sharing common objectives. The second reason for exploring the rationale for regulation is that it provides a clearer picture of the costs and benefits of regulation by focusing attention on the movement from an unregulated to a regulated world. Ultimately, the value of any system of regulation must be judged by a comparison between those benefits and the costs that arise from implementing regulation.[2]

The development of regulation prior to the Financial Services and Markets Act 2000 (FSMA 2000) is also discussed in this chapter. The objective is to put the current system into historical perspective and to provide some indication of how attitudes towards financial regulation and the role of financial markets have changed over time. Finally, this

---

[1] See A Ogus, *Regulation: Legal Form and Economic Theory* (Oxford, Clarendon Press, 1994) ch 1.

[2] This is not to say that policy considerations that do not have a well-defined economic value (eg a desire to limit the extent to which individuals might experience hardship through being over-indebted) cannot form part of the assessment of whether regulation is necessary. Indeed, it might well be said that, the more fundamental the rationale for a particular form of regulation, the more difficult it is to engage in cost–benefit analysis because it is more difficult to calculate the costs and benefits relevant to broad policies (eg the reduction of financial crime) than it is in the case of regulatory techniques (eg disclosure) that have a narrower field of application.

chapter also provides an introduction to the emerging regulatory framework for financial investment at the international level and an overview of the EU system of regulation.

2.1 The need for regulation

Why do financial markets require regulation? To answer this question, we need to consider the legal framework under which markets operate without regulation. There are two aspects to consider. The first is the structure and operation of the market itself as distinct from the transactions taking place in the market. In an unregulated market, there will in principle be unrestricted and free access to the market place for buyers and sellers. In other words, there will be no requirement for licensing or authorisation as a condition for engaging in a particular activity. Nor are there likely to be 'market rules' relating to the structure and the operation of the market, such as standard rules determining when payment or delivery is due under contracts or rules governing the conduct of participants in the market[3]

The second aspect is the legal framework governing transactions in the market. The essential elements of that legal framework are property law and contract law, which together define ownership interests and their mode of transfer. In principle, a market can operate without regulation in circumstances in which the law is sufficiently developed to provide certainty in respect of ownership interests[4] and their transfer, and to punish the most obvious forms of fraudulent activity. Indeed, markets in many goods and services operate successfully on this basis without any 'regulatory' intervention.

However, an unregulated market may operate in a manner that ultimately leads to the conclusion that some form of regulation is necessary.[5] First, unrestricted access to the market may have a damaging effect if unscrupulous individuals are permitted to participate. This is a particular problem in financial markets because of the nature of the product being sold and the relationship between the product and the seller. A simple financial product such as a bank deposit account provides an example. It gives the depositor a contractual claim against the bank which can only be satisfied if the bank has sufficient funds to meet the claim. The depositor does not 'own' the deposit in the legal sense, as the money deposited in the bank is owned by the bank.[6] Instead, the depositor relies on the ongoing ability of the bank to repay deposits when they fall due. The trust placed by

---

[3] Such 'market rules' can be distinguished from contract law, although both govern the conduct of contracting parties. The former are concerned primarily with the structure and operation of the market, the latter with the rights and obligations of the contracting parties. Market rules are associated with organised markets, whereas ad hoc contracting can be governed only by contract law.

[4] It was noted in Chapter 1.2 that ownership rights in financial investments are essentially contractual rights which are considered to be 'property'.

[5] See generally Ogus, above n 1, chs 3 and 10.

[6] *Foley v Hill* (1848) 2 HL Cas 28. See generally A Hudson, *The Law of Finance* (London, Sweet & Maxwell, 2009) ch 30.

the depositor in the financial soundness of the bank is central to the transaction but, in most cases, is something that the depositor cannot independently verify. Without regulation of entry, the market is in principle open to those who would abuse this trust by running a bank in a way that threatens the interests of depositors.

The second problem, which compounds the first, is that the presence of information asymmetry is particularly severe in financial markets.[7] Two examples illustrate the problem. Consider first the position of a small group of shareholders who between them own and manage a company. They want to raise more capital through an offer of shares to the public. Clearly, their knowledge of the company and its prospects are superior to the new investors they hope to attract into the company. Applying the normal principles of contract law to the offer of new shares would result in very limited disclosure of information to the new investors because contract law generally does not require information to be volunteered to the other side. Without regulation, new investors would lack the confidence to buy the new shares. One might argue at this point that the investors could require information as a condition of investing. Well-informed investors might well do so, but others might lack the ability to define the necessary information. In any event, the lack of a minimum standard of information disclosure would have the potential to discourage investment and cause confusion among investors.

Another example is that of a private individual buying a pension. The product itself is often complex, and so too are the tax rules and the relationship between private and state pensions. In many cases, an individual will face making an important decision relating to retirement without a proper understanding of the relevant issues. This can arise simply as a result of inherent complexity in the investment even when there is adequate information available.

Unlimited access and information asymmetry may threaten both the existence and scale of the market. Unlimited access to the market poses a risk in that reputable suppliers of the same service may not be able to differentiate themselves sufficiently from disreputable suppliers and so may be unable to achieve higher prices (reflecting their financial soundness and reliability). Information asymmetry poses a problem in that investors who lack information on which to base decisions (such as the investors in the capital of the company described above) may decide not to invest or to limit their investment to less than it would have been if they had more information. It can be seen, therefore, that both suppliers and buyers of financial products may, in an unregulated market, have incentives either to withdraw from the market or to limit their involvement in it.[8]

There may also be problems in punishing fraudulent activity in an unregulated market. The criminal law of fraud is a relatively blunt instrument, which is capable of dealing with very obvious instances of fraud (eg when an instrument of transfer is forged in

---

[7] The effect of information asymmetry on the operation of markets was first elaborated by G Akerlof in 'Market for Lemons: Quantitative Uncertainty and the Market Mechanism' [1970] *Quarterly Journal of Economics* 222.

[8] This process is often referred to by economists as 'adverse selection', a concept first developed in the field of insurance to describe the process by which the presence of information asymmetry in the formation of insurance contracts is likely to lead to insurers providing cover primarily to the riskiest individuals or properties because they lack the information to evaluate risk accurately.

an attempt to gain ownership of an investment) but is less well suited to dealing with conduct that is not expressly 'criminal' but is nevertheless damaging to the operation of financial markets. For example, investors are likely to be discouraged from investing if company profits are routinely overstated in prospectuses offering shares to the public, but it is not always the case that this type of misleading behaviour would be categorised as fraud.[9]

At this point, it can be asked if unregulated markets and their legal infrastructure can evolve in a manner that resolves the problems outlined above.[10] In respect of the first issue, unrestricted access, economists have argued that there are powerful theoretical reasons for believing that self-regulation on the part of market participants will restrict market access in circumstances where the existence or scale of the market is threatened by open access.[11] The history of regulation in the London Stock Exchange (LSE) tends to support such a view. Having initially operated as a forum that was in principle open to all buyers and sellers, the LSE limited access to its members (who were required to satisfy a 'fit and proper' test) in 1801.[12] The effect was to enhance and expand the trading capacity of the market because control over entry provided a higher level of confidence among market participants that the chains of credit typically associated with transactions would be honoured. In respect of the second issue, the rules governing transactions in the market, it is more difficult to judge the extent to which evolution and adaptation could provide a solution. It is certainly true that the common law is inherently adaptable[13] but the problem is that it may not be able to evolve quickly enough to meet the needs of rapidly developing markets. Another problem is that the common law is generally based on default rather than mandatory rules, with the result that any 'investor protection' rules that arose from the common law could in principle be avoided by contract.

Financial market regulation can also be justified by reference to systemic risk. This is the risk of failure of an individual institution having a 'domino' effect, leading to the collapse of other institutions and a threat to the entire financial system. This risk is present particularly in chains of transactions that are linked by credit, where the scale of credit is large by comparison with the capital of the participants.[14] Systemic risk is

---

[9] See J Birds (ed), *Boyle & Birds' Company Law*, 8th edn (Bristol, Jordans, 2011) ch 19.34 for a discussion of common law fraud in the context of public offers of securities.

[10] See T Arthur and P Booth, *Does Britain Need a Financial Regulator? Statutory Regulation, Private Regulation and Financial Markets* (London, Institute of Economic Affairs, 2010).

[11] For theoretical analyis see P Spencer, *The Structure and Regulation of Financial Markets* (Oxford, Oxford University Press, 2000) 30–33; for an historical perspective see C Day, 'Bits and Pieces and Moral Authority: The Paradox of Success in the Unregulated 19th Century New York Capital Markets', available at http://ssrn.com/abstract=572163 (accessed on 16 August 2011).

[12] R Michie, *The LSE: a History* (Oxford, Oxford University Press, 1999) 31 observes that: 'Essentially, what the professionals wanted so as to ensure speed and trust was a market in which all present were active participants, ready to buy or sell when the opportunity arose, and each possessing a reputation for honouring their part of a bargain. In turn, those who did not fit these criteria or meet the standards set would be excluded from the market.'

[13] An example is the manner in which the general principles of contract law were adapted to suit the needs of insurance contracts in the eighteenth and nineteenth centuries through the development of the duty of disclosure, which resolved the problem of information asymmetry.

[14] See eg the account of the collapse in 1998 of Long Term Capital Management (LTCM) in S Valdez, *An Introduction to Global Financial Markets* (London, Macmillan, 2000) 343. LTCM had borrowings of 50 times its shareholders' capital.

present particularly in the banking sector, where extended chains of credit are common, but it is also present in securities markets, where firms may be linked by credit chains as a result of settlement obligations arising from buying and selling securities.[15] However, systemic risk justifies only a limited form of financial regulation in respect of the financial resources of market participants. This form of regulation is generally referred to as 'prudential' and is mainly implemented through capital adequacy rules that require sufficient regulatory capital to be available to cover the risks arising from banking and trading in financial markets. The objective of prudential regulation is to ensure that shareholders rather than customers bear the risk of loss arising from regulated activity.

Finally, regulation can be justified simply by paternalism. On this view, the state supplies regulation because it knows what is best for its citizens and acts so as to protect them. While in principle it can be used to justify extensive regulation of financial markets, paternalism is most persuasive as a basis for regulation in relation to private investors. Professional and institutional investors are better able to look after their own interests and therefore require less protection from the state.

2.2 Regulation and moral hazard

Moral hazard refers to the risk that a person's behavior may change after and as a result of entering into an agreement (explicit or implicit). The concept was originally developed in the context of insurance contracts to refer to the risk that the insured would take less care of insured property once the risk of loss or damage was covered by an insurance contract. The concept was later extended to financial regulation to explain the potential change in the behavior of financial institutions in circumstances in which there is an implicit understanding that regulators and government will step in to prevent insolvency. While regulators and government rarely provide any explicit commitment to act in that way, it is quite possible for the markets to develop an implicit understanding that they will 'bail out' failing firms, especially if there is no indication to the contrary. Such an implicit understanding is particularly strong in the case of those financial institutions which are deemed 'too big to fail', meaning that their scale is such that their failure would threaten the entire financial system.

The danger of such an implicit understanding is that it can create moral hazard by changing the behavior of financial institutions. In particular, it can encourage them to take more risks than they would if they knew that they would not be 'bailed out' by government and that shareholders would bear the full cost of failure.[16] In that sense,

---

[15] The insolvency of Lehman Brothers illustrated the extent of interconnectedness in the securities markets. Although often described as an 'investment bank', Lehman was not in legal terms a bank. It was a broker-dealer that was regulated by the SEC. See generally A Ross Sorkin, *Too Big to Fail* (Harmondsworth, Penguin, 2010).

[16] See E Greene et al, 'A Closer Look at "Too Big to Fail": National and International Approaches to Addressing the Risks of Large, Interconnected Financial Institutions' 5(2) *Capital Markets Law Journal* 117.

moral hazard has the capacity to increase risk-taking on the basis that the cost of failure can be 'externalised' to some extent through publicly funded rescue of distressed financial institutions. Following the financial crisis, one technique that has been employed to reduce moral hazard is to grant crisis management powers to the regulator, enabling it to step in to take control of a failing institution and to restructure it. Such powers have a disciplinary effect on financial institutions in that the threat of intervention and restructuring (with resultant loss of value for shareholders and bond holders) is likely to promote a more cautious attitude to risk-taking. However, it is difficult to eliminate moral hazard entirely since governments and regulators are unlikely to rule out entirely the possibility of a 'bail out' in extreme situations where the stability of the financial system as a whole may be threatened. The rescue of AIG in the US by the authorities in 2008 was just such a case. While Lehman Brothers was allowed to fail, the scale and interconnectedness of AIG was judged to be so great that there was no alternative but for the government and the regulators to coordinate a rescue plan.[17]

2.3 Regulatory models

Once the need for regulation of financial markets has been identified, the question of the form that regulation should take needs to be addressed.[18] Even a cursory examination of the manner in which financial regulation is organised in different countries around the world indicates that there are many different models. The model that operates in a particular country is closely linked with the history and development of the financial markets. In the US, for example, the regulatory framework that was put in place in the early 1930s following the Wall Street Crash of 1929 exerted a strong influence over the following decades. It reacted to the crash by limiting the creation of financial conglomerates and favouring disclosure as a regulatory technique. In the UK, the tradition of self-regulation dominated financial markets up until the 1980s and remained influential even after the introduction of a statutory system of regulation in 1986. Since financial regulation often overlaps with other legal rules and social norms, the structure that is best suited to a particular country can only be decided by reference to the local conditions. The experience of the financial crisis supports the view that no particular structure of regulation was better able to avert or deal with the crisis than the others.[19] In that sense, there is no evidence to suggest that any one structure is intrinsically better than another: much depends on the process of supervision and the quality of the regulatory personnel.

The most basic issue to be determined is whether regulation should be supplied by

---

[17] See Ross Sorkin, above n 15.

[18] See generally A Page and R Ferguson, *Investor Protection* (London, Weidenfeld & Nicolson, 1992) ch 6.

[19] Some countries were better prepared for the crisis than others as a result, inter alia, of having stronger regulatory capital rules for their banks. But that resulted more from the rules and quality of supervision rather than the structure of regulation.

government or by the market itself. The former is typically referred to as statutory regulation and the latter as self-regulation. They are not mutually exclusive. It is possible, as shown by the system of regulation created in the UK by the Financial Services Act 1986 (FSA 1986), for a hybrid to be created combining statutory regulation and self-regulation. The attraction of a statutory system is that it removes regulation from the control of market participants and provides a clear legal framework for the exercise of the regulator's powers. Self-regulation offers the potential for regulation that is more flexible and responsive to market developments, but it inevitably suffers from the risk that the system will evolve in a manner which favours the narrow interests of market participants over the broader public interest. In the main, most countries, including the UK, have now concluded that a heavy reliance on self-regulation is no longer appropriate in financial markets, but some have continued to recognise that it can be beneficial to allow for some degree of self-regulation within the system.[20]

A second issue to be considered is the manner in which the scope and operation of the system of regulation is defined. There are two possibilities. Functional regulation defines a particular type of activity (eg 'investment business') and regulates any person engaging in this type of activity. Institutional regulation focuses on particular types of institution (eg banks) and regulates whatever business is conducted by that institution. Both have strengths and weaknesses. Functional regulation takes account of the fact that particular activities are often carried on by different institutions as distinctions between different types of financial institution have become increasingly blurred. It can, however, give rise to problems of coordination when different regulators are responsible for different parts of an institution's business. Institutional regulation allows the entire business of an institution to be controlled by a single regulator, but may lead to variable regulatory treatment of institutions in respect of the same line of business if different regulators are responsible for different categories of institution.

Two other issues are linked with the choice between the institutional and functional principles of regulation. The first is the choice between a single or multiple regulators for the financial sector and the second is the issue of legal separation of different financial activities. As was the case in the UK prior to 1998, some countries adopt a system of multiple financial regulators, with responsibility typically being divided between the banking, insurance and securities sectors. This division of responsibility between regulators can be organised on either the functional (as was the case in the UK before 1998) or the institutional principle. Irrespective of the manner in which it is organised, the presence of multiple regulators is likely to raise problems, particularly in a liberal financial environment in which financial conglomerates can engage in a variety of activities. It was precisely this problem that was one of the main reasons for the UK moving to a single financial regulator in 1998. However, there is an important reason why multiple regulators survive in many other countries, which is that they are linked with legal restrictions on combining different types of financial activity within a single organisation or

---

[20] Elements of the self-regulatory approach in the UK survive in the fields of corporate governance and takeover regulation. See generally E Ferran, 'Corporate Law, Codes and Social Norms—Finding the Right Regulatory Combination and Institutional Structure' (2001) 1 *Journal of Corporate Law Studies* 381.

under common ownership. The purpose of such restrictions is to limit the accumulation of different types of risk within a single organisation. This can serve the interests of shareholders in the relevant institutions as well as the regulators, at least in circumstances in which there are real concerns over the ability to monitor and manage risk. The best known example is probably the now largely repealed Glass-Steagall Act in the US, which prohibited commercial banks from engaging in non-banking business and thereby created a 'firewall' between commercial banking on the one hand and securities and investment banking business on the other.[21] A limited form of restriction remains in the UK system, which prohibits insurers from carrying on any commercial business other than insurance business and activities directly arising from that business.[22]

The UK is now moving towards a 'twin-peaks' model of regulation.[23] The underlying premise of this model is that prudential regulation and conduct of business regulation are very different forms of regulation that are best undertaken by separate regulatory agencies.[24] According to this view, separation of the functions ensures that the objectives of each form of regulation (financial stability and investor protection) remain distinct and are not the subject of compromises within a single regulator. This means, for example, that a conduct of business regulator should not be concerned that measures to protect investors may affect the financial soundness of a financial institution as that matter is the responsibility of the prudential regulator. As part of that move in the UK, a Financial Stability Committee has already been established within the Bank of England with responsibility for financial stability. It will oversee the activities of the two new regulators, the Prudential Regulation Authority and the Financial Conduct Authority. The former will be a subsidiary of the Bank of England and will undertake firm-specific prudential supervision of banks and insurers. The latter will undertake conduct of business supervision for all authorised firms, including those operating in the wholesale markets.

2.4 Regulatory techniques

A number of different techniques are available to regulate the financial sector. Most systems, including the UK, employ all these techniques to some extent, although there are considerable differences between systems as to the importance attached to each technique and its method of implementation. A distinction should also be drawn at this

---

[21] See M Nance and B Singhof, 'Banking's Influence over Non-Bank Companies after Glass-Steagall: A German Universal Comparison' (2000) 14 *Emory International Law Review* 1305. On the role of the repeal of Glass-Steagall in the 2008 financial crisis see S Wallenstein, 'The Roots of the Financial Crisis' (2009) 4(suppl 1) *Capital Markets Law Journal* S8.

[22] Financial Services Authority (FSA) Handbook INSPRU 1.15.13R.

[23] See the HM Treasury consultation paper 'A New Approach to Financial Regulation: Building a Stronger System' (Cm 8012) and the White Paper 'A New Approach to Financial Regulation: the Blueprint for Reform' (Cm 8083).

[24] See below for a discussion of the two forms of regulation.

stage between regulation and supervision. The former refers primarily to the institutional structure of regulation and the regulatory rules; the latter focuses on the implementation of rules and the exercise of discretion by regulators.

2.4.1 Disclosure

Disclosure aims to resolve the information asymmetry which forms a substantial part of the rationale for regulation. Its function is to make information available so as to allow investors to make informed choices, with the result that the market operates more efficiently (eg in the investment context by allocating capital more efficiently to competing uses). Recognition of the role of disclosure obligations as a device to resolve information asymmetry has a long history, which predates the modern (post-1930s) phase of financial regulation. Two examples are particularly noteworthy. First, the common law, from the mid-eighteenth century onwards, began to develop an obligation of disclosure in insurance contracts as a device to resolve the information disadvantage of an insurer in respect of insured risks. Secondly, the Companies Acts, from 1844 onwards, imposed disclosure obligations on the issuer of a prospectus offering shares to the public. This occurred at a time when the Stock Exchange was a private body and there was no system of financial regulation in the modern sense. In more recent times, disclosure has been relied on heavily as a regulatory device, especially in the context of securities regulation, where mitigating information asymmetry has been viewed as the primary objective of regulation.[25]

However, the need for mandatory disclosure has at times been questioned. For example, it has been argued that the extensive disclosure obligations mandated by the Securities and Exchange Commission (in the US) ignore the capacity of markets to require the disclosure of information when it is required for efficient decision-making.[26] It has also been argued that disclosure can be of only limited value as a regulatory technique in retail financial markets since private investors lack the capacity to understand financial information and apply it to decision-making. In the wake of the financial crisis, much attention has focused on the implications of 'behavioural finance' for decision-making by investors.[27] In particular, attention has been drawn to the danger that disclosure may not lead to informed decision-making by investors when other behavioural traits are to the fore, such as overconfidence and herding. In those circumstances, reliance on disclosure as a mechanism that will lead to informed decision-making and self-correcting markets may simply be wrong.

[25] This is reflected in the approach taken by the International Organisation of Securities Commissioners (IOSCO)—see 'Objectives and Principles of Securities Regulation' at www.iosco.org (accessed on 11 November 2004). The nature and function of IOSCO is discussed in 2.5 below. See also K Lanoo, 'The Emerging Framework for Disclosure in the EU' (2003) 3 *Journal of Corporate Law Studies* 329.

[26] See H Jackson and E Pan, 'Regulatory Competition in International Securities Markets: Evidence from Europe in 1999—Part 1' (2001) 56 *Business Law* 653.

[27] See E Avgouleas, 'What Future for Disclosure as a Regulatory Technique? Lessons from Behavioural Decision Theory and the Global Financial Crisis' in I MacNeil and J O'Brien (eds), *The Future of Financial Regulation* (Oxford, Hart Publishing, 2010) ch 12.

Allied to disclosure are a number of related devices. Registration is a device for making information available to the public at large.[28] The most obvious example is the requirement imposed on companies by the Companies Act 2006 to register information with the Registrar of Companies. This is in addition to the information that has to be sent directly to shareholders. The purpose of registration is to make the information available to the public at large so that it can be used for any purpose in connection with the relevant company (eg lending, providing trade credit). Audit is intended to provide verification to investors that financial statements represent a 'true and fair' view of a company's financial position. Risk warnings are intended to encourage an evaluation of risk on the part of investors, who might not otherwise attempt to relate the characteristics of a particular investment to their own financial position. Cooling-off periods provide investors with an opportunity to reconsider a transaction and to withdraw from it. They were introduced as a response to high-pressure sales techniques and modify the general rules of contract law by allowing the investor to withdraw from a legally binding transaction.

2.4.2 Authorisation (licensing)

No modern system of financial regulation relies entirely on disclosure (and its related devices). Nowadays, authorisation (or licensing) has become a standard technique. The objective is to set conditions for entry into the various forms of activity that are within the scope of the 'regulatory perimiter'. In the UK, this has taken the form of requiring the applicant to satisfy a 'fit and proper' test as well as other specific requirements linked to the relevant activity.[29] Since authorisation typically remains a requirement to conduct the relevant business, it also provides the regulator with an ongoing form of control. The authority of the regulator ultimately rests on its ability to punish non-compliance with exclusion from the regulated activity. Regulators are typically given a wide discretion to grant authorisation.

2.4.3 Prudential regulation

Another feature of modern systems of financial regulation is prudential regulation. This focuses on controlling the solvency and liquidity of participants in financial markets. There are two objectives to this form of regulation. The first, which may be termed 'micro-prudential regulation', focuses on the solvency of individual financial firms and attempts to ensure that customers are not threatened by the risks to which financial institutions are exposed in the normal course of their business. The second, which may be termed 'macro-prudential regulation', focuses on the stability of the financial system as a whole, the risks posed to it by the collapse of a financial firm and the instability that may spread across the entire financial system in those circumstances. In the case of

---

[28] Page and Ferguson, above n 18, 50 distinguish registration in principle from certification and licensing, but note that, historically, there has been a tendency to combine registration with licensing.
[29] See further Chapter 3.4.

banks, the most obvious risk is credit risk, which is the risk that borrowers will default on loans to such an extent that the solvency of the bank is threatened. In the case of securities firms (or banks involved in securities business), the main risk is market risk, which is the risk that the value of the firm's holdings of securities will fall to such an extent as to threaten its solvency. Regulators attempt to protect customers from these risks by requiring banks and securities firms to have minimum levels of shareholders' capital (sometimes referred to as regulatory capital) and to hold a certain proportion of their assets in a liquid (readily realisable) form. This has the effect that, if the firm were to face financial difficulties, losses would be borne by shareholders before customers became affected. In this sense, prudential regulation uses regulatory capital to protect customers. Shareholders in financial institutions, on the other hand, receive no special protection from the system of prudential regulation. They are assumed to face the normal risks arising in any business, which includes insolvency.

Two other techniques can also be included within the concept of prudential regulation. The first is organisational controls, which are concerned with the legal, governance, management (including risk management) and operational structure of financial firms. The rationale for these forms of control is that they have the capacity to control risk, limit the likelihood of insolvency and thereby promote financial stability. The second is ownership controls, which require approval for shareholdings above a certain threshold (typically 10%) in financial institutions. Once again, the rationale is that this form of control promotes financial stability since the control exerted by large shareholders is a key influence in determining the strategy and risk preferences of financial firms.[30]

2.4.4 Conduct of business regulation

Conduct of business regulation is an important part of most systems of regulation. It focuses on the relationship between a financial firm and its customers, and operates through rules that control the manner in which individual financial transactions are conducted. These rules impose different types of obligations in different circumstances. Many are in effect disclosure (or related) obligations, such as the rules that require disclosure of information to a customer before a transaction is agreed. Others go beyond disclosure and limit the freedom of action of authorised persons or have important implications for the structure of the market.[31] Central to the operation of conduct of business rules is the system of customer classification used in the Financial Services Authority (FSA) rulebook.[32] The effect of this system is to provide different levels of investor protection in different circumstances. Private investors[33] are given very extensive protection by conduct of business rules, but professional investors are subject to much less regulation in their dealings with each other.

[30] See Chapter 10 for more detailed discussion of governance and risk management.
[31] The rules on 'suitability' (governing the provision of financial advice to private investors) fall into the former category, whereas the rules relating to 'polarisation' (discussed in Chapter 6) fall into the latter.
[32] See Chapters 6.3.1 and 15.1 for more detail.
[33] Referred to as 'retail clients' in the EU and UK regimes.

2.4.5 Portfolio regulation

Portfolio regulation is a technique that restricts the investments that can be made by a financial institution or a person managing investments. Historically, trustees have been subject to such restrictions in the UK under the Trustee Investment Acts, and the system of prudential supervision in respect of banks, building societies and insurers has also adopted this technique. It has also been adopted in the system of regulation for collective investment funds. The general objective has been to protect customers by requiring diversification, limiting exposure to the riskier classes of investments.

2.4.6 Intervention and crisis management powers

Powers of intervention are another regulatory technique. Historically, they were an important part of the UK system of regulation. Their purpose, broadly speaking, was to permit the regulator to intervene in the business of a regulated firm when there were grounds for concern. For the purposes of UK authorised persons, the concept of intervention was superseded under FSMA 2000 by the power of the regulator to impose requirements on permission or vary the permission of an authorised person. This was a narrower power by comparison with the power of intervention previously provided by FSA 1986 because it ruled out direct intervention by the regulator in the running of the business. The powers of intervention contained in FSMA 2000 were confined to those necessary to give effect to the relevant provisions of the EU single market directives.[34]

However, the onset of the financial crisis in 2007 resulted in a reappraisal in the UK (and elsewhere) of the value of powers of intervention. The main benefit of such powers, particularly in a crisis situation, is that the regulatory authorities can take over control of financial institutions. This provides much more flexibility in devising solutions to a crisis in that the usual legal rules that provide considerable decision-making powers to shareholders (and creditors in some circumstances) are disapplied. Thus, solutions can be adopted quickly, and shareholders and creditors can be forced to take losses that they might not voluntarily agree to. That is not to say that the regulatory authorities have a completely free hand in devising solutions, however: they will need to pay close attention to market perceptions of proposed solutions since they may have a bearing on the capacity of other financial institutions to raise capital using similar instruments to a failed institution. While there are no easy solutions to crisis situations, it is now widely recognised that effective crisis management powers allow the regulatory authorities to respond much more effectively than they could in the past. This policy was given effect in the UK by the Banking Act 2009, which introduced a 'special resolution regime' under which the regulatory authorities are able to take control of failing banks and take action to safeguard financial stability.[35] Crucially, this action allows the authorities to deal with

---

[34] See generally section 2.5 below.
[35] See Bank of England, 'The UK Special Resolution Regime for failing banks in an international context', Financial Stability Paper No 5 (July 2009); D Singh 'The UK Banking Act 2009, Pre-insolvency and Early Intervention: Policy and Practice' [2011] *Journal of Business Law* 120.

a failing bank outside the legal framework for corporate insolvency, which does not take into account public policy objectives linked with financial stability. Under the special resolution regime the authorities have a range of options, including a forced sale and a temporary transfer to public ownership, both of which may require shareholders and bondholders to accept losses.[36]

2.4.7 Deposit guarantee and compensation schemes

Finally, deposit guarantee and compensation schemes can also be considered to be a regulatory technique. Prudential supervision attempts to protect customers from insolvency, but it cannot provide a guarantee that insolvency will not occur. The purpose of deposit guarantee and compensation schemes is to provide a guarantee to investors that they will be compensated for losses resulting from the insolvency of an authorised person. A requirement that an authorised firm be a member of an approved scheme represents a technique available to a regulator to bolster the confidence of customers in the firms they use to conduct financial transactions. However, it does not remove all risk from customers, as compensation schemes may include a co-insurance provision (requiring the customer to bear a proportion of the loss) and limit the size of any financial award.[37]

2.5 Regulation in the UK prior to the Financial Services Act 1986

The perception that the pre-FSA 1986 period in the UK was dominated by self-regulation is both right and wrong. It is wrong in the sense that, historically, there have been several instances of statutory intervention in the working of the financial markets. It is right in the sense that, to a substantial extent, statutory intervention had a less significant influence on the operation of markets than self-regulatory rules.

Trading in financial securities was already well established in London when an Act was introduced to regulate trading in 1697. At this time, the market was mainly in

---

[36] Any transfer must respect the rights of shareholders and bondholders but in a failed bank those rights may be worthless: see eg the litigation that followed the nationalisation of Northern Rock in 2007, *SRM Global Master Fund LP v Treasury Commissioners* [2010] BCC 558. The relevant legislation provided for compensation for shareholders. The amount of compensation was to be determined by an independent valuer on the assumption that Northern Rock was unable to continue as a going concern and was in administration. The court held that this did not did not violate the rights of Northern Rock shareholders under the European Convention on Human Rights 1950, Protocol 1, Art 1.

[37] Compensation following insolvency of an authorised person is discussed in Chapter 6.

government securities,[38] and there was no distinction between brokers (acting as agents on behalf of their customers) and dealers acting as principals ('jobbers' or, in modern parlance, 'market-makers'). The Act required brokers and dealers to be licensed, limited the number of brokers to 100, fixed maximum commission levels and required transactions to be recorded. It was a temporary measure and lapsed when it was not renewed in 1707.

In 1801, the London Stock Exchange in its modern form came into existence. It controlled admission of members and required an annual application for readmission, thereby opening up the possibility of exclusion if a member's conduct was considered unacceptable. From 1812 onwards, all members of the LSE had to confine their business to buying and selling securities, the objective being to limit the risk arising from a member's bankruptcy.[39] At this stage, the securities market was essentially a market in government securities. However, over the course of the nineteenth century there was a transformation in the nature of the securities traded on the UK securities markets.[40] By the end of the century, corporate securities comprised a substantial part of the market. This was made possible by several key developments in corporate law during that period. One was the possibility to incorporate a company by registration, which was introduced by the Joint Stock Companies Act 1844. Before that time incorporation was not freely available.[41]

A second factor was the general availability of limited liability as a result of the Limited Liability Act 1855.[42] This had the effect of widening the pool of potential investors since individuals of modest means could now consider equity investment without the threat of bankruptcy that often accompanied failure in business as a sole trader or a partner in a partnership. A third factor, which was crucial for future developments in investor protection, was the emergence of disclosure obligations in respect of public offers of securities. At this stage, the LSE regarded itself primarily as a market for secondary trading in securities and therefore it made no attempt to regulate disclosure in relation to offers of shares to the public.[43] That was seen as a matter for the common law,

---

[38] See Michie, above n 12, 18, who describes the emergence of securities markets in theUK as follows: 'The real foundation of the securities market, that eventually led to the formation of the London Stock Exchange, took place in the year 1693 when the government, for the first time, borrowed by creating a permanent debt that was transferable. Previous to that the government's borrowing had been on a short-term basis, with the debt being either redeemed or refinanced, depending on the state of the national finances, when it became due.'

[39] The Stock Exchange was concerned that, if members were involved in other forms of trade (as they had been previously), bankruptcy could lead to trade creditors other than Stock Exchange members having claims on a member's assets. Given the extended credit and settlement chains that often existed in Stock Exchange dealings, this posed a risk for the operation of the Stock Exchange.

[40] The sheer scale of company promotions during certain periods in the nineteenth century makes the twentieth century pale by comparison. For example, Michie, above n 12, 56 refers to there being 624 joint-stock companies promoted in 1824–25. Of these, only 127 survived until the end of 1826. This was before the advent of the disclosure and registration obligations introduced by the Companies Act 1844.

[41] See, regarding the history of incorporation, P Davies, *Gower's Principles of Modern Company Law*, 6th edn (London, Sweet & Maxwell, 1997) ch 3.

[42] For an analysis of the nature and effects of limited liability see H Hansmann and R Kraakman, 'The Essential Role of Organizational Law' (2000) 110 *Yale Law Journal* 387.

[43] This is not to say that the Stock Exchange admitted the securities of any company to listing. The position was described as follows: 'the Stock Exchanges guard the public, in so far as they are able, in declining to admit to quotations the questionable enterprises of "shady" promoters, but they do not in any manner thereby indicate any opinion, personal or official, as to the value of such issues, or their real genuineness or soundness. That is entirely beyond their province, and the persons buying issues that have been "listed" should scrutinise the property

which made available a range of remedies to investors who bought securities on the basis of prospectuses that were misleading or omitted material facts.[44]

The establishment of provincial stock exchanges during the nineteenth century also had an impact on the development of regulation within the LSE. The provincial exchanges were mainly involved in trading government securities and shares in local companies. Their role in financing and trading in the shares of railway and canal companies was particularly important. They did not, in the main, compete directly with the LSE because they could not offer the liquidity or range of securities available on the LSE. There was therefore a substantial volume of business passed from brokers and jobbers in provincial exchanges to the London market, a process that was eased by the introduction of the telegraph and later telephone links. The manner in which this business was conducted had an important impact on regulation within the LSE itself. There were two main concerns. Brokers were concerned that outsiders (provincial brokers and banks) had direct access to LSE jobbers and that commissions were being forced down by competition to attract business from provincial exchanges. Jobbers were concerned that they were being bypassed as brokers made markets in securities[45] and brokers were concerned that jobbers had direct contacts with sources of business outside the Stock Exchange. This threatened the operation of the 'single capacity' market model in which jobbers were limited to acting as principals (making markets) and brokers as agents.[46] The Stock Exchange responded to both concerns by introducing rules which were to remain in place (albeit in modified form) until the 'Big Bang' in 1986.[47] In 1909, dual capacity was prohibited with the result that members could only act either as a broker or as a jobber. From the legal perspective, the requirement of single capacity introduced a strict division between the activities of agents (brokers acting for clients in accordance with fiduciary duties) and principals (jobbers acting on their own account with no duty owed to other parties). In 1912, minimum commissions were introduced, thereby limiting the possibility of competition between members based on transaction cost.

In the US, the Wall Street Crash of 1929 was an important influence in the introduction of the new statutory system of regulation established by the Securities Act 1933 and the Securities and Exchange Act 1934. In the UK, there was a more limited reaction to the crash. Attention was focused not on the activities of the Stock Exchange but on those outside the Exchange who were engaged in promoting securities to the public. One particular concern was the growth in unit trusts. They had existed for at least 50 years, having become popular in the 1870s, but had expanded considerably in the 1930s following the adoption of the more flexible legal structure (imported from the USA) which allowed continuous creation and redemption of units by the manager.

The Prevention of Fraud (Investments) Act 1939 made two significant changes to the

---

and investigate the value for themselves' (GR Gibson, *The Stock Exchanges of London, Paris and New York: A Comparison* (New York, 1889) 37, quoted in Michie, above n 12, ch 3, 96).

[44] See Birds, above n 9, ch 19.31.

[45] This issue came to the fore again during the introduction of MiFID regime in the EU: see Chapter 12.3.3.

[46] Michie, above n 12, 113 notes that this model ('single capacity') was effectively enshrined in the Stock Exchange Rules from 1847 onwards, but was not enforced.

[47] See section 2.4 below.

existing law.[48] First, it required dealers in securities either to be licensed or to be granted exempt status. Members of a recognised stock exchange were automatically granted exempt status and it was open to any dealer to apply for an individual exemption. Many of the banks (commercial and merchant), insurance companies and investment trusts gained exempt status. The result was that 'licensed dealer' status was largely confined to fringe operators who were not members of an exchange or well-established financial institutions. The second change made by the Act was the introduction of Conduct of Business Rules governing the manner in which transactions are conducted. Although, under the 1939 Act, these rules were confined to the relatively small category of 'licensed dealer', they were later to take on a much more extensive role under FSA 1986. Following some amendments made to the 1939 Act by later Companies Acts, it was re-enacted in 1958.

Although the Bank of England was nationalised in 1946 and provision was made for it to assume a statutory role in regulating the banking sector, it continued to rely on its traditional informal role in supervising banks.[49] There was no authorisation requirement and no formal rules governing the way a bank carried on its business. The Bank was reputed to rely on its power and status as the Central Bank and the disciplining effect of a 'raised eyebrow' in supervising the banking sector. This approach remained in place until 1979, when the first Banking Directive[50] required the introduction of a statutory system of banking regulation. The informal system of banking regulation that operated before 1979 facilitated the expansion of merchant banks' involvement in the securities markets. Members of the Issuing Houses Association had a long history of organising company flotations and had also developed fund management business. The post-war period brought a new development in the form of takeovers and mergers. The conduct of takeovers raised important issues for shareholders and the market, and a solution was sought through self-regulation rather than statutory control. The Notes on Takeovers and Amalgamations were introduced in 1959 and later became the Takeover Code, administered by the Takeover Panel. The Panel and the Code still survive today, though in a statutory form, sustained by a reputation for sound rule-making, rapid decision-making and effective enforcement.[51]

2.6 The Financial Services Act 1986

FSA 1986 represented the beginning of the modern era of regulation of investment business in the UK. It was introduced during a time of significant change in the financial

---

[48] See generally R Pennington, *The Law of the Investment Markets* (London, BSB Professional, 1990) paras 2.07–2.13.

[49] See E Ellinger, E Lomnicka and R Hooley, *Ellinger's Modern Banking Law*, 4th edn (Oxford, Oxford University Press, 2006) 29–32.

[50] The EU regulatory regime is discussed in more detail in Chapter 2.9 below.

[51] See Chapter 11 for more detail on the Takeover Panel and Code.

sector both within the UK and elsewhere. A number of changes had occurred before 1986 that had fundamentally altered the structure and operation of financial markets in the UK. Exchange controls were removed in 1979, encouraging the flow of investment into and out of the UK and the internationalisation of the UK financial markets. Significant changes also occurred in the London Stock Exchange. First, restrictions on outside ownership of member firms were removed as a result of a series of changes in the rules of the Exchange, thereby permitting foreign (mainly US) firms to take an ownership interest and start the process of formation of financial conglomerates. Secondly, in response to the threat of being taken before the restrictive trade practices court, the Stock Exchange abandoned its 'single capacity' rule and allowed members to act in a 'dual capacity'. The effect of this change was that members could now act at the same time as agents for clients and as principals trading in securities on their own account (ie they could become combined broker-dealers rather than having to choose between being one or the other). This change, taken together with the replacement of 'face-to-face' dealing on the floor of the Exchange with a new computerised dealing system (the Stock Exchange Automated Quotation System, or SEAQ), came to be referred to as the 'Big Bang',[52] reflecting the fundamental transformation in the operation of the Exchange that occurred on the day (27 October 1986) that these two reforms took effect.

Significant change was also evident in the retail financial market. The mortgage market expanded rapidly as the Bank of England liberalised the mortgage-lending regime. This, in turn, led to a rapid expansion in the market for endowment life assurance as a mechanism to repay mortgages. This reflected the trend established in the 1970s whereby life assurance came to be regarded as much as a form of investment as a form of financial protection against early death.

FSA 1986 made two significant changes to the existing regulatory regime. First, it created a single regulatory structure for all 'investment business'. The underlying rationale was that all those involved in this business should operate on a 'level playing field', with consequent benefits for investor protection and the promotion of competition among providers of financial services.[53] Secondly, it effectively ended the tradition of self-regulation, despite giving the appearance of continuing that type of regulation, albeit in a limited form. The Act provided for the creation of a regulator responsible for all investment business, the Securities and Investment Board (SIB), as well as self-regulatory organisations (SROs) responsible for the regulation of particular parts of the investment industry.[54] The SROs were ultimately accountable to the SIB in that they had to be 'recognised' by SIB,

---

[52] See J Littlewood, *The Stockmarket, Fifty Years of Capitalism at Work* (London, Pitman, 1998) ch 27; L Gower, '"Big Bang" and City Regulation' (1988) 51 *Modern Law Review* 1.

[53] See LCB Gower, *Review of Investor Protection*, Cmnd 9125 (London, Stationery Office Books, 1984) paras 1.11–1.20. The review was carried out for the Department of Trade and Industry by Professor Gower and became known as the 'Gower Report'. Its proposals for a fundamental change in the regulation of investment were given effect by the Financial Services Act 1986.

[54] Five SROs were recognised when the Financial Services Act 1986 took effect: the Financial Intermediaries, Managers and Brokers Regulatory Association (FIMBRA); the Investment Management Regulatory Organisation (IMRO); the Securities Association; the Association of Futures Brokers and Dealers (AFBD); and the Life Assurance and Unit Trust Regulatory Organisation (LAUTRO). The number fell to four in 1991 when the Securities and Futures Authority (SFA) was formed by a merger of the Securities Association and the AFBD, then to three in 1994 when the Personal Investment Authority (PIA) was formed by the merger of LAUTRO and FIMBRA.

a process that required them to meet certain standards laid down by the Act. There was, however, some semblance of self-regulation in that the SROs were able to make and enforce their own rulebooks largely without interference from SIB. Under this structure, recognised investment exchanges (such as the LSE) were exempt from the Act. However, as was the case with the SROs, this did not result in a system of self-regulation free from outside control as, in order to gain 'exempt' status, an exchange was required to satisfy recognition requirements laid down by the Act.

Within a relatively short period following its introduction, it became clear that the FSA 1986 system of regulation was not working as well as had been hoped.[55] The first major problem to become apparent was the system of rule-making created by the Act. Each regulator was responsible for making and enforcing rules in respect of persons they had authorised to engage in investment business. However, the rulebook of the SIB (the senior regulator) was given a special status because the rulebook of the other regulators had to provide protection at least equivalent to that afforded by the SIB rulebook.[56] This led to a tendency on the part of the other regulators to take an overly cautious and legalistic approach in writing their rulebooks, resulting in the rulebooks being complex and not be easily compared across the different investment sectors. This problem, and a number of others, was addressed by the 'new settlement', the term given to a package of amendments to FSA 1986 introduced by the Companies Act 1989. The rule-making system was amended in two ways. First, the 'equivalence' standard for SRO rule-making was changed to a test of whether there was adequate investor protection, with the result that it was no longer necessary to make direct comparisons with the SIB rulebook. Secondly, an effort was made to improve the consistency and coherence of rules across the system as a whole by introducing a tiered system of rules comprising principles, core rules and third-tier rules. The first two tiers were to be the responsibility of the SIB, with SROs assuming responsibility for the third. Principles were intended to articulate the basic values and objectives of the regulatory system, and core rules were intended to flesh out the principles in a manner that was relevant to all investment business. It was only the third-tier rules that were intended to deal with the detailed aspects of rule-making which were applicable only to individual investment sectors.

A second source of difficulty was in the effective enforcement of rules made by regulators operating under FSA 1986. This was particularly evident in the Maxwell affair,[57] in which it became clear that IMRO had failed properly to supervise authorised members who were involved in managing pension funds associated with the Maxwell group of companies. The essence of the Maxwell affair was that assets were improperly removed from those funds, with the result that pensioners suffered considerable hardship. The review of the entire system prompted by that failure[58] commented that IMRO's moni-

---

[55] See generally J Black, *Rules and Regulators* (Oxford, Clarendon Press, 1997) ch 3.

[56] FSA 1986, s 10 and sch 2, para 3.

[57] See Department of Trade and Industry (now BERR), 'Investigations under Sections 432(2) and 442 of the Companies Act 1985', available at http://pixunlimited.co.uk/Media/pdf/mirrorgroup.pdf (accessed on 12 November 2011).

[58] As well as two other regulatory failures: SIB's supervision of London FOX, a recognised investment exchange that traded futures and options on soft commodities and agricultural products; and home income

toring had been too mechanistic and insufficiently alert, its analysis of information had been too uncritical, it had failed to recognise and judge risks and its response to the crisis when it broke was inadequate.[59]

A third problem was the ability of the system to cope with new financial products. This was tested most obviously in relation to personal pensions, a new form of individual pension plan which came into existence at the same time as FSA 1986 came into effect. While there were general rules (and later core rules) governing such sales in place from the very outset of the operation of the FSA 1986 system of regulation, no detailed rules were put in place until much later. Irrespective of whether responsibility for this episode lies with the companies and advisers selling personal pensions or with the regulators, it is clear that the system failed quite comprehensively to provide adequate protection to investors.[60]

A fourth problem, brought clearly into focus by the collapse of Barings bank,[61] was that the existence of separate regulators compounded the inherent difficulty of regulating 'conglomerates' which were engaged in a number of different types of activity, such as merchant banking, commercial banking, stock-broking and investment management. It became clear from the investigation which followed the collapse of Barings that having separate regulators dealing with the banking and securities activities of such an organisation made it much more difficult to monitor the overall exposure of the group to a fall in financial markets. This incident was generally regarded as a significant factor in the decision made by the new Labour government in 1998 to strip the Bank of England of responsibility for banking supervision.[62] In that year, a single financial regulator, the FSA, was created, with the intention that it would ultimately assume responsibility for the entire financial sector, including banking and insurance.[63] That policy was later given effect by the Bank of England Act 1998 and FSMA 2000.

---

plans, which raised issues regarding the interface of regulatory responsibility as between SIB, FIMBRA and LAUTRO.

[59] See A Large, 'Financial Services Regulation: Making the Two Tier System Work' (Securities and Investment Board, May 1993).

[60] For more detail see J Black and R Nobles, 'Personal Pensions Misselling: The Causes and Lessons of Regulatory Failure' (1998) 61 *Modern Law Review* 789; G McMeel, 'The Consumer Dimension of Financial Services Law: Lessons from the Pension Mis-Selling Scandal' (1999) 3 *Company Financial and Insolvency Law Review* 29.

[61] By way of background see the report of the Board of Banking Supervision into the collapse of Barings, Session 1994–95 HC 673, discussed in C Brown, 'Report of the Board of Banking Supervision Inquiry into the Circumstances of the Collapse of Barings' (1995) 10 *Journal of International Banking Law* 446.

[62] This is made clear by the Treasury and Civil Service Committee, 6th Report 1994–95, 'The Regulation of Financial Services in the UK', vol 1, V (conclusions and recommendations). Nor had the Bank of England emerged unscathed from the aftermath of the collapse of the Bank of Credit and Commerce International (BCCI) in 1991: see The Treasury and Civil Service Committee report 'Banking Supervision and BCCI—International and National Regulation', HC 177 (1991–92).

[63] The creation of the FSA did not in itself require statutory intervention. It was achieved simply by changing the name of the SIB, which had been created as a company limited by guarantee. The name change in itself transferred no additional regulatory responsibility to the FSA.

2.7 The Financial Services and Markets Act 2000

The failings associated with the system of regulation created by FSA 1986 were widely regarded as serious, but it was less obvious that they were indicative of a systemic failure in the system of regulation. Any system of regulation can be expected to experience problems, and it is a matter of judgement as to whether such difficulties can be resolved within the system or whether the system requires replacement. Many of the changes that have been introduced by FSMA 2000 could have been introduced under FSA 1986. With the benefit of hindsight, it seems clear that much of the impetus for the introduction of the new Act was a desire to abandon a system that was associated with failure rather than to initiate 'root and branch' reform.

FSMA 2000 cannot be viewed as being a fundamental change in the system of financial regulation in the same way that FSA 1986 was. The move to a single statutory regulator for the entire financial sector, arguably the most significant of the changes made to the regulatory system, took place while FSA 1986 was still in force. Although much was made of the abandonment of self-regulation as a result of the introduction of FSMA 2000, the reality was that the Securities and Investment Board (the FSA's predecessor) had effectively operated in this way for much its existence. Moreover, at the level of the regulatory rules, much of the detail of the pre-FSMA 2000 regime was simply carried over into the new FSA Handbook.

As was the case with FSA 1986, FSMA 2000 is largely a statutory framework. It sets out some basic principles and provides various powers to the regulator. Unlike FSA 1986, the objectives of FSMA 2000 were explicitly stated by the Act.[64] The FSA was empowered to carry out the regulatory functions conferred on it by FSMA 2000. These functions included those transferred to the FSA from the Chief Registrar of Friendly Societies, the Friendly Societies Commission and the Building Societies Commission, and the regulatory functions previously carried out by the Treasury in respect of insurance. The FSA had already taken over responsibility for banking supervision from the Bank of England as a result of the Bank of England Act 1998.

The Treasury and the Bank of England did, however, retain a significant role in the system of financial regulation established by FSMA 2000. A memorandum of understanding agreed between the three organisations in 1998 set out the respective role of each, in what was commonly referred to as the 'tripartite' system of regulation, as follows:

1. The Bank of England was responsible for the overall stability of the financial system. This remit included monitoring payment systems and the broad overview of the financial system as a whole.
2. The FSA had statutory responsibility for authorisation and prudential supervision of banks, building societies, insurers and investment firms, supervision of financial markets and associated clearing and settlement systems.

---

[64] FSMA 2000, ss 3–6. See Chapter 3.2.

3. The Treasury was responsible for the overall institutional structure of regulation and the legislation which governs it. It had no operational responsibilities for the activities of the FSA or the Bank of England, but nevertheless had considerable influence on regulatory policy through the appointment, oversight and order-making powers granted by FSMA 2000.

The FSA existed prior to the Act, having been created in 1997 as result of a change in the name of the SIB. As was the case with SIB, the FSA is a private company limited by guarantee, subject to the provisions of company law. Its constitution had to comply with the provisions of schedule 1 FSMA 2000, which dealt, inter alia, with organisational structure, the maintenance of monitoring and enforcement arrangements in respect of rules imposed by or under the Act, investigation of complaints against the FSA, and the Authority's immunity from liability in respect of the exercise of its functions.

2.8 International investment

International portfolio investment has become a significant factor for financial markets.[65] It can take a variety of forms. The following are common examples:

1 Purchase, in the home state of the investor, of a security issued by a company incorporated and listed in another country.
2 Purchase, in the home state of the investor, of a security issued by a company incorporated in another country but with a foreign listing[66] in the investor's home country.
3 Purchase, outside the home state of the investor, of a security issued by a   company incorporated and listed outside the home state of the investor.
4 Purchase of an indirect form of overseas investment. This could be purchase of a depositary receipt[67] or of shares in an investment trust or units in a collective investment scheme in the investor's home country, where the underlying investments are securities issued by a company incorporated and listed in another country.

Functionally, these different techniques are equivalent in the sense that they have the capacity to expose the investor to the same investment and currency risks. However, the legal and regulatory treatment of the different techniques is quite different. The main reason is that each instance involves a different interaction between the regulatory system of the home state of the investor and that governing the issuer, the financial instrument

---

[65] See eg P Myners, 'Institutional Investment in the United Kingdom: A Review' (March 2001) (Myners Report), available at http://archive.treasury.gov.uk/docs/2001/myners_report0602.html (accessed on 16 August 2011) 27, which shows that overseas investment in UK equities rose from 7.0% in 1963 to 29.3% in 1999; for more recent data see the Office for National Statistics, 'Share Ownership Survey 2008', showing that foreign ownership of UK listed shares stood at 41.5% at the end of 2008.

[66] See Chapter 8.2.4 for an explanation of the term.

[67] See Chapter 4.9 for an explanation of the term.

and the process of investment. That interaction is now considered first in the broad international context and secondly in the context of the regional system of regulation that operates within the EU.[68]

2.8.1 International regulation?

There is no international system of regulation for portfolio investment comparable to that which exists in individual countries. This remains the case despite the substantial increase in cross-border portfolio investment and provision of financial services that has occurred in the past 30 years. Since there is no international regulatory authority that can make rules binding on individual states, attention has focused instead on the development of international institutions and the development of 'soft law' international standards that can be adopted by individual countries. It is also possible for national regulators to cooperate on an ad hoc basis or within a settled framework defined in a memorandum of understanding. However, that form of cooperation is more associated with enforcement (eg in insider dealing cases) than with policy formulation and the adoption of supervisory measures to deal with emerging risks to the global financial system.

The International Monetary Fund (IMF) was set up in 1945 as part of the Bretton Woods system of fixed exchange rates. Its main task was to oversee the international monetary and payments systems with a view to stability and the expansion of international trade. Following the collapse of the Bretton Woods system, its role is now more as 'lender of last resort' to member governments who find themselves in financial difficulty. Countries who wish to borrow or obtain standby facilities from the IMF are typically required to introduce economic and regulatory reforms so as to restore the country's economy to a healthy position. IMF involvement in these situations plays an important role in resolving economic problems since other lenders will generally only agree to debt rescheduling or additional lending once an IMF programme is in place.[69] The IMF also plays a role in surveillance of the global financial system with a view to promoting financial stability[70] and the provision of technical advice to governments.

Also of significance in the field of international financial stability is the work of the Financial Stability Board (FSB). Formed in 1999[71] by the G-7 Group, it focuses specifically on international aspects of financial market operation and in particular on systemic risk and the relationship between macro-economic regulation of the economy and micro-regulation of financial markets. Unlike the IMF, the FSB is not a separate agency with its own charter and budget: it is more of an ad hoc intergovernmental body which facilitates interaction between the respective G-7 finance ministries, central banks and regulators. The work of the FSB is carried out mainly through working groups and task forces,

---

[68] See Chapter 14.2.1 for a discussion of the principles that determine which state's courts are competent to deal with disputes (jurisdiction) and which system of law applies to contracts (the applicable law).

[69] See eg the IMF's role in the debt crises in Greece and Ireland at http://www.imf.org/external/ (accessed on 12 November 2011).

[70] See the IMF's Global Financial Stability Report at http://www.imf.org/external/pubs/ft/gfsr/2010/02/index.htm (accessed on 12 November 2011).

[71] At which time it was know as the Financial Stability Forum (FSF).

which focus on particular issues that require attention; to date, these have included highly leveraged institutions, offshore financial centres and bankers' remuneration. The FSB also performs a coordination role between different national and international regulatory authorities and promotes the implementation of international standards.[72]

'Soft law' consists of codes and standards that are adopted voluntarily by states, regulators or markets. Once implemented in national or regional legal systems (eg the EU), 'soft law' can acquire binding force. An example is the capital adequacy standards that were originally developed as 'soft law' by the Basel Committee on Banking Supervision (BCBS)[73] and have subsequently been implemented in many national legal systems.[74] In the investment field, international 'soft law' has developed through the medium of the International Organisation of Securities Commissioners (IOSCO). Formed in 1973 to promote cooperation among US securities regulators, IOSCO now has an international membership that accounts for all the major financial centres.[75] Its work includes the development of standards that can be implemented at the national level. Particularly important in this regard are IOSCO's Objectives and Principles of Securities Regulation[76] and International Disclosure Standards for Cross Border Offerings and Initial Listings by Foreign Issuers. These two documents, taken together, establish the underlying standards for securities regulation and the form and content of an internationally acceptable offering document.[77]

Another aspect of the emergence of international 'soft law' has been the movement towards harmonisation of accounting standards. There is no body with authority to set mandatory international accounting standards and therefore international investors are faced with the problem of trying to interpret accounts that have been prepared on different bases. Countries can be split into two distinct groups in terms of their approach to accounting.[78] On the one hand, there are countries where business finance is provided mainly by banks and whose approach to accounting is largely based on taxation considerations: in these countries, the preparation of accounts is geared towards the calculation of tax liabilities, and the company law often contains detailed provisions on how the accounts are to be prepared and presented. On the other hand, there are countries in which business finance is dominated by equity finance and accounting is driven more by the disclosure requirements of financial markets and professional standards than company law and tax considerations. Moreover, even within the second category, there are important distinctions between, for example, the 'detailed rule' approach of the Generally Accepted

---

[72] See eg the 12 key standards identified by the FSB as key for sound financial systems at http://www.financialstabilityboard.org/cos/key_standards.htm (accessed on 12 November 2011). The standards are those adopted by international agencies such as the IMF, BCBS and IOSCO.

[73] The Basel Committee was set up in 1974 within the Bank for International Settlements.

[74] Those standards are referred to as the Basel Accords, the third version of which was brought forward in 2010 in response to the financial crisis.

[75] See www.iosco.org for general background, documents and standards.

[76] Which are one of the 12 FSB key standards referred to in n 72 above.

[77] See D Arner, 'Globalisation of Financial Markets—An International Passport for Securities Offerings?' (London Institute of International Banking, Finance and Development Law, 2002). The UK has implemented IOSCO's International Disclosure Standards in its Listing Rules—see Chapter 8 for more details on listing and public offers.

[78] See generally Arner, ibid.

Accounting Principles (GAAP) in the US and the 'principles' approach adopted in the International Accounting Standards adopted by the International Accounting Standards Committee (IASC).

While some progress is being made, the prospects for harmonisation or convergence in international accounting standards appear more remote than in respect of securities regulation. The main body that is promoting international harmonisation is the IASC. Formed in 1973, the IASC is engaged in an effort to harmonise and improve accounting principles for the benefit of the public. Its standards are essentially recommendations in that, in themselves, they have no binding authority, although they can achieve binding authority through adoption (in whole or part) by the relevant national authorities. The EU, for example, requires all listed companies to report according to International Accounting Standards.[79] Moreover, as the IASC's standards are generally broad and allow alternative practices, it is open to question how far they can achieve the harmonisation objective, especially since that approach runs counter to the more detailed 'rules based' approach favoured by the US GAAP.

2.8.2 Regulation of international portfolio investment transactions

In the absence of any developed international system of financial regulation, it is important to determine which country's system of regulation will be applicable to a particular transaction. It is important to resolve this issue because it has the potential to affect the manner in which the transaction is carried out and the obligations owed by parties involved in its execution (including brokers, market-makers and exchanges). In the main, securities law applies to relevant transactions within a country irrespective of the company law that governs the issuer.[80] The result is that the securities law of country A will generally apply to transactions within that country even if the law applicable to the issuer of securities[81] or to the transfer of legal title[82] is that of another country. Thus, the UK market abuse regime will apply to trading on a regulated market in the UK of shares in a London-listed Chinese company, while Chinese law will govern the legal structure

---

[79] See Reg 1606/2002 [2002] OJ L243/1.

[80] See Chapter 3 for details of the jurisdictional scope of FSMA 2000.

[81] There are two approaches to this issue. The first, adopted in the UK, is that a company is governed by the company law of the country in which it is incorporated. The second is that a company is governed by the company law of the country in which its seat (*siège réel* or head office) is located. Irrespective of which approach is applied, the result is that an investor in one country buying a security issued by a company governed by the company law of another country will have his rights as a shareholder defined by the company law of that other country. In this sense, the applicable company law acts as a fixed definition of shareholders' rights irrespective of where shares are traded or held.

[82] The determination of the applicable law in respect of transfers of securities is important because different countries may have different rules regarding what constitutes a valid transfer and the respective rights of transferor and transferee. Under UK company law, the legal owner of a share is the person who is registered in the company's register of shareholders. When a UK court is faced with a question of which law applies to a transfer it will normally apply the law of the place where the shareholders' register is located, on the basis that this is where the transfer occurs. See J Fawcett and J Carruthers, *Cheshire, North & Fawcett's Private International Law*, 14th edn (Oxford, Oxford University Press, 2008) 1245–46.

and operation of the company as well as transfers of shares. It follows that, in the main,[83] the securities law of country A will not apply to securities transactions in other countries even when entered into by an investor who is a national of country A.

Unlike national systems of financial regulation, the listing rules of stock exchanges do not directly give rise to conflict of law issues.[84] Listing rules require an issuer to observe the listing rules, primarily in the form of disclosure requirements, without reference to national legal systems. In principle, company A, incorporated in the UK, and company B, incorporated in the Cayman Islands, are both bound by the listing rules in the UK in the same way if their securities are listed on the London Stock Exchange. Nor are the sanctions available to the listing authority dependent on national legal systems because the ultimate sanction (removal of listing) does not require enforcement through national courts.[85] For this reason, listing rules can be regarded as the first true form of international securities regulation because they are capable of regulating issuers of securities without reference to the jurisdiction in which the issuer of securities or the investors in those securities are based.

2.9 The European regulatory regime

The European regime for investment business reflects the broad objective of creating a single (or internal) market in services and capital within the EU. The Treaty on the Functioning of the European Union (TFEU)[86] provides:[87] 'The internal market shall comprise an area without internal frontiers in which the free movement of goods, persons, services and capital is ensured in accordance with the provisions of the Treaties.'

The main Treaty provisions that give effect to this objective in the field of investment are:

- Article 63—Free movement of capital
- Article 49—Freedom of establishment
- Article 56—Freedom to provide services

The principle of free movement of capital in Article 63 prohibits restrictions on movements

---

[83] There are some exceptions to this general principle. The most significant are the 'extraterritorial' provisions of the US securities laws. See S Choi and A Guzman, 'The Dangerous Extraterritoriality of American Securities Law' (1996) 17 *Journal of International Business Law* 207.

[84] See Chapter 7 for more detail on listing rules.

[85] In the UK, however, suspension of listing can be challenged before the Upper Tribunal: see FSMA 2000, s 77(5).

[86] The TFEU replaced the Treaty establishing the European Community when the Lisbon Treaty entered into force on 1 December 2009. For background see J Steiner and L Woods, *EU Law* (Oxford, Oxford University Press, 2009) ch 1.

[87] Art 26 TFEU.

of capital between Member States and between Member States and third countries.[88] It is therefore no longer possible for EU Member States to limit direct or portfolio investment through restrictions on capital movements. The Treaty does, however, authorise the EU, by way of exception to the general principle, to adopt restrictive measures relating to capital movements to or from third countries (outside the EU).[89]

Freedom of establishment arises from the prohibition contained in Article 49 against restrictions on nationals of a Member State establishing a business in another Member State. The prohibition applies irrespective of the form of the business as Article 49 refers expressly to the setting up of agencies, branches and subsidiaries. It includes the right to take up and pursue activities as a self-employed person and to set up and manage undertakings. 'Nationals' includes companies that are formed under the laws of a Member State and have their registered office, central administration or principal place of business within the EU. The main impact of this on financial investment is in respect of the right of providers of financial services to establish operations in EU countries other than their home country.

Freedom to provide services is in principle different from freedom of establishment in that it relates to the right to provide services on a temporary basis within another Member State (a 'host' state). This differs from operating a business from a permanent establishment in another Member State. However, freedom of services does not, in principle, allow the service provider to escape the control of the Member State in which the service is provided, as Article 50 provides that the activity can be pursued 'under the same conditions as are imposed by that state on its own nationals'. Freedom to provide services is of particular significance for the development of 'remote' services such as those delivered over the internet.

The Treaty provisions relating to establishment and services are directly effective,[90] meaning that in principle they give rise to rights that can be enforced by individuals in national courts. Why, then, have they given rise to such a complex array of secondary legislation governing EU financial markets? There are two main reasons. First, the early case law of the European Court of Justice (ECJ) dealing with these rights focused on discrimination, with the result that the emphasis was on eliminating discriminatory treatment of foreign nationals. It was only later that the ECJ began to prohibit trade barriers adopted by Member States that were equally applicable to nationals and foreign nationals, and even when this occurred there was considerable doubt over the restrictions that could be imposed by Member States on foreign nationals exercising their right of establishment or freedom to provide services.[91] This confusion was apparent in the competing claims made in the case of *Commission v Germany*[92] regarding the extent to which the German

---

[88] This Treaty provision was introduced by the Maastricht Treaty on European Union in 1993. The principle of free movement of capital between Member States had already been established by Council Directive 88/361 [1988] OJ L178/5. See generally JA Usher, *The Law of Money and Financial Services in the European Community* (Oxford, Oxford University Press, 1994) ch 2.

[89] Art 64 TFEU. Unanimity is required in the EU Council 'for measures under this paragraph which constitute a step back in Community law as regards the liberalisation of the movement of capital to or from a third country'.

[90] See generally Steiner and Woods, above n 86, ch 5.

[91] See generally ibid, ch 17.

[92] Case 205/84 [1986] ECR 3755.

Insurance Supervisory Authority could regulate the activities of foreign insurers and brokers operating in its territory.[93] Secondly, the Treaty rights, although directly effective, are subject to exceptions, some of which are contained in the Treaty and others of which have been developed by the ECJ. The result of these exceptions was that it was possible for Member States to limit the operation of the Treaty rights (and in particular freedom to provide services) on the basis that restrictions were imposed for the 'general good' of their citizens. The solution adopted by the EU was to limit the operation of this exception by creating a system of regulation that removed the need for Member States to take action to protect their citizens.

The initial approach of the EU was to focus on harmonisation of the laws of the Member States as a means of pursuing the market integration objective. It soon became clear that this approach would not work as the harmonisation proposals became bogged down by political disagreements. In the mid-1980s, the approach was changed so as to focus on the principle of mutual recognition of laws of different Member States combined with minimum harmonisation. The objective of mutual recognition was to recognise the laws of each Member State as being equivalent to each other, with the result that it would no longer be necessary, in principle, to apply the laws and regulatory rules of state A to the supply of services in that state by a supplier based in state B. For example, mutual recognition would allow a bank based in the UK to engage in banking business in Germany without having to go through an authorisation process in Germany. The objective of minimum harmonisation was to create the conditions under which the assumption of equivalence between the laws of a home and a host state was factually correct. If it were not, it would not be possible for mutual recognition to work because there would remain differences between the laws of Member States that would eventually make the system unworkable.

The principles of minimum harmonisation and mutual recognition led directly to the development of the two key principles adopted in the EU financial market directives: the 'single licence' and 'home country control'. The former provides that an authorisation granted in the home state provides a basis for engaging in relevant business in a host state through a branch or through the provision of services. It does not extend to conducting business through a subsidiary, which is a legal person formed under the laws of the host state and is therefore governed by the laws of the host state. Home country control is a technique for allocating regulatory responsibility between home and host states. As implemented by the EU directives, it results in a home state taking primary responsibility for all business undertaken under an authorisation that it has granted. The main exception to this principle was that a host state could apply its conduct of business rules to transactions occurring within that state.[94] There also remained in place, however, a residual exception based on the concept of the 'general good', which permitted Member States to limit the operation of the principle of freedom of services (and by implication

---

[93] See further I MacNeil, 'Does the EC Have a Single Market in Insurance?' (1995) 10 *Butterworths Journal of International Banking and Financial Law* 122.

[94] That exception has now been largely removed as a result of the adoption of the provisions of MiFID: see section 2.9.1 below.

the 'single licence' and 'home country control') on the basis that such restrictions were necessary for the protection of investors in that country.

The introduction of the euro as a common currency removed currency risk and enhanced price transparency within the eurozone. Its effect was felt both in financial markets and in their regulation. In the markets, the single currency encouraged a shift to asset allocation at the European rather than the country level and, assisted by technological advances, encouraged the emergence of competitors to the long-established stock exchanges.[95] The European Commission responded to these changes and attempted to shape their future development by adopting the Financial Services Action Plan (FSAP),[96] an ambitious programme of legislative proposals comprising 42 separate measures. A parallel development in the sphere of legislative process was the adoption of the 'Lamfalussy' model in 2001, which aimed to accelerate the adoption of European legislative measures and to break the process down into several levels that would allow political and strategic issues to be separated from technical rules.[97] The FSAP emphasised two aspects of the integration process: first, the construction of deep and liquid capital markets that would serve issuers and investors better; and secondly, the removal of barriers to cross-border financial services so as to expand consumer choice while maintaining consumer confidence with a high level of consumer protection. However, as well as promoting market integration, the FSAP adopted a much clearer policy of explicit regulation, which was evidenced by a move away from the mutual recognition/minimum harmonisation model that had previously been relied on. The FSAP programme made use of the 'maximum harmonisation' technique, which requires Member States to adopt European legislative measures as they stand, with no changes.[98] That marked a move towards a model in which European regulation plays the leading role and national regulation a secondary role. It also marked a rejection of the possible benefits of 'regulatory competition', which has been argued to bring benefits in the form of experimentation between different forms of regulation, resulting in the survival of the best models and the elimination of the weakest.[99] That did not imply any change in the respective roles of the European and national authorities in the process of supervision (the application of regulatory rules to markets and their participants): it remained the case that the European authorities had no active role in supervision. However, as discussed below, developments in the European regulatory structure in the post-crisis phase are likely to result in the European authorities playing a greater role in the process of supervision.

---

[95] See further Chapter 12.3.

[96] Commission Communication on Implementing the Framework for Financial Markets: Action Plan, COM(1999) 232.

[97] See N Moloney, *EC Securities Regulation*, 2nd edn (Oxford, Oxford University Press, 2008) 1016 for more detail.

[98] Maximum harmonisation can be equated with unification of laws since it represents both a minimum and a maximum standard for Member States to observe.

[99] The theory and benefits of regulatory competition remain contentious: see Moloney, above n 97, 27–31 for an overview of the debate.

2.9.1 The European regime for investment

The core of the European regulatory regime for investment is contained in the Markets in Financial Instruments Directive[100] (MiFID) and its implementing measures;[101] in the text below (and subsequent chapters), they are referred to collectively as the 'MiFID regime'. There are several key definitions which determine the scope of the regime.[102] The first is 'investment firm', which means any legal person whose business is the provision of investment services to third parties and/or the performance of one or more investment services or activities on a professional basis. Investment services and activities are defined in the Directive as well as ancillary services. The latter cannot be the sole activity of an investment firm since MiFID does not permit authorisation to be granted for ancillary services alone. The definition of financial instruments has been extended from that adopted under the Investment Services Directive (ISD)[103] to include credit derivatives, financial contracts for differences, exotic derivatives and commodity derivatives. By delimiting its scope in these terms, the MiFID regime adopts a functional regulatory model, meaning that it applies to any person that carries out the relevant activity. Thus, banks or other financial institutions, which often have large investment divisions, are subject to the MiFID regime when they engage in business falling within its scope. This approach is intended to ensure that there is a 'level playing field' between different types of entity who are engaged in the same activity.

The MiFID regime further develops the market access and integration policy that was pursued through the ISD. Facilitating market access through the MiFID regime promotes the objective of capital market integration within the EC. This policy recognises the increasing role that market-based financing (both equity and debt) is playing in the financing of European enterprises, which, outside the UK, have tended historically to rely more heavily on bank loans. MiFID continues the 'single licence' and 'home country control' approach that was adopted by the ISD but limits the role of the host state by allocating responsibility for conduct of business regulation to the home Member State.[104] That alters the approach under the ISD according to which the host state was responsible for conduct of business regulation. Moreover, since there is extensive harmonisation of conduct of business rules under the MiFID regime, there is much less scope to restrict the provision of services by investment firms authorised in other Member States than was the case under the ISD since it is much more difficult to establish that additional restrictions based on the 'general good' are required for customers in a particular location.

In pursuit of the market integration objective, the MiFID regime facilitates access on the part of investment firms in country A to regulated markets in country B. It does this by requiring country B to ensure that investment firms authorised in country A can

---

[100] Directive 2004/39/EC [2004] OJ L145/1.

[101] The MiFID regime was implemented through the 'Lamfalussy' legislative process. Two implementing measures were adopted at 'level 2' of that process: Commission Directive 2006/73/EC [2006] OJ L241/26 and Commission Regulation (EC) No 1287/2006 [2006] OJ L241/1.

[102] Art 4 of MiFID. The definitions in the Directive are paraphrased in the text.

[103] Directive 93/22/EC [1993] OJ L141/27.

[104] Art 31. An exception applies in the case of business conducted through a branch: in that case responsibility for conduct of business regulation lies with the Member State in which the branch is located (Art 32(7)).

become members of or have access to the regulated markets in country B.[105] That in itself does not provide a right of remote access to a regulated market in country B for an investment firm in country A. However, where the regulated market in country B operates without a requirement for a physical presence, there is a right to have remote membership or access.[106] Provision is also made for this process to work in reverse so as to facilitate access by a regulated market in country A to investment firms in country B. In circumstances in which a regulated market in country A has no requirement for a physical presence on the part of investment firms, that regulated market has the right to provide 'appropriate facilities' in country B so as to enable investment firms to exercise their right of remote membership or access.[107]

The MiFID regime also gives effect to a policy of opening up competition between different transaction venues so as to lower transaction costs for investors. It does this primarily by giving a more prominent role to alternative markets on the basis that they provide valuable competition to regulated markets and can contribute to market efficiency, provided adequate transparency rules are in place to enable investors to observe activity across the market as a whole.[108] In the past, the focus on 'regulated markets' in the ISD adopted what has been referred to as the 'public utility' approach to market regulation.[109] This evolved during the era when national stock exchanges often enjoyed a monopoly (legal or de facto) over securities trading and the main regulatory concern was to control the modus operandi of the exchange so as to limit anti-competitive behaviour.[110] Associated with this was the desire on the part of some Member States to protect their financial market from competition from more developed markets following liberalisation and also from 'alternative markets'.[111] The 'concentration' provision in the ISD reflected these concerns. It gave Member States the option of requiring that transactions in securities be carried out on a regulated market when certain conditions were met. In effect, it gave Member States the option of prohibiting the execution of transactions on 'alternative' markets (although not on regulated markets in another Member State). The rationale for the provision was that there were benefits for investors in having transactions centralised in a large and liquid market. By repealing the concentration provision, MiFID opened up the potential for the development of alternatives to regulated markets as locations for the execution of transaction. As discussed in more detail in Chapter 12, that was a key development in the recent reconfiguration of market structure.

Significantly, the MiFID regime's objectives go beyond market integration. The rationale for the regime remains ostensibly linked to market integration; thus, recital two of MiFID states that 'it is necessary to provide for the degree of harmonisation needed

---

[105] Art 32 of MiFID.

[106] Art 33 of MiFID.

[107] Art 42(6) of MiFID. See also Art 46 regarding the provision of clearing and settlement facilities in country B for the settlement of trades conducted in a market in country A.

[108] See Chapter 12 for more details on the structure and regulation of trading markets.

[109] See G Ferrarini, 'The European Regulation of Stock Exchanges: New Perspectives' (1999) 36 *Common Market Law Review* 569.

[110] See eg J Littlewood, above n 52, 317–18 regarding concerns over anti-competitive practices in the London Stock Exchange in the early 1980s.

[111] See Chapter 10 for a discussion of alternative markets.

to offer investors a high level of protection and to allow investment firms to provide services . . . on the basis of home country supervision'. However, it seems clear from the scope and detail of the MiFID regime, as well as its use of the maximum harmonisation technique[112], that the objective has moved much more towards the creation of a European system of regulation rather than the more limited focus on market integration that was evident under the ISD. This is evident in particular with regard to conduct of business regulation. The MiFID regime governs conflicts of interest; provision of information to clients; 'suitability' requirements; execution of client orders; and the obligations of investment firms who appoint 'tied agents'.[113] The broadening of the scope of the regime by comparison with the ISD, along with the use of maximum harmonisation, has the effect of displacing national regulation to a considerable extent with rules derived from the MiFID regime. Enforcement under the MiFID regime is still a matter for the national authorities, leaving open the possibility that market integration will be limited by differences in the intensity of supervision and enforcement among Member States. However, two features of MiFID attempt to limit the extent to which that risk will materialise: one is the requirement that all national authorities have a common set of enforcement and investigatory powers; the other is that national authorities are subject to a strict duty of cooperation with each other so as to improve the capacity of the system to deal effectively with regulatory infringements in the case of cross-border operations.

Central to the European regulatory regime for investment is the requirement that investment firms satisfy regulatory capital requirements. As in the case of the banking regime, the purpose of these requirements is to protect the customers of investment firms from the risk of the insolvency of the firm and to promote financial stability by ensuring that firms can meet their obligations to their counterparties. In the case of investment firms that engage in trading for their own account (in the form of market-making or proprietary trading), the main risk for the firm and its customers is market risk; that is, the risk that the value of the investments held by the firm will fall and cause insolvency. To protect against such risk, investment firms (including banks engaged in investment activity falling within the MiFID regime) are required to hold regulatory capital to cover market risk. They are also required to hold capital to cover two other risks. The first is counterparty risk, which is the risk that a counterparty to a transaction will not be able to settle on the due date. The second is operational risk, which is the risk arising from failure of internal systems, disruption to payment and settlement systems, or external shocks such as natural disasters. While the calculation of the amount of regulatory capital required is complex, the principle is quite simple: regulatory capital should be set at a level that allows the firm to absorb the expected losses[114] arising from market risk, counterparty risk and operational risk. The relevant requirements are set

---

[112] Use of the techniques is evident in the implementing measures rather than in MiFID itself.

[113] These issues are considered in more detail in Chapters 5, 6 and 15.

[114] This concept is problematic since it opens up a host of related questions, such as: the range of expected losses that should be covered (eg how far should the 'tail' of the statistical distribution of expected losses be covered?); the techniques by which losses are estimated (eg 'mark to market' accounting); and the respective role of regulators and investment firms in the process (eg how far should regulators rely on internal models?).

out in the Capital Requirements Directive,[115] which is considered in more detail in the following section.

In the case of investment firms that do not deal in or hold investments for their own account (eg asset managers), market risk does not threaten their solvency in the same way because losses are absorbed by their customers, whose funds they manage. Those firms are therefore subject to less onerous regulatory capital requirements. However, such firms are subject to the MiFID rules requiring segregation of client assets to ensure that legal ownership rests with the client in the event of the firm's insolvency and thus ensure that the firm's creditors do not have access to those assets to satisfy their claims against the firm. They are also subject to capital requirements linked to their overhead costs, which is designed to ensure business continuity in the event that revenue (which is often linked to fund value) falls as a result of a decline in asset prices.

2.9.2 The European regime for banking

The European regime for banking is of considerable relevance to investment for several reasons. One is that the major 'broker-dealers' who trade in investments for their own account are part of banking conglomerates. Another is that banks often have substantial asset management divisions and in that capacity act as fund managers/institutional investors. Finally, banks play an important role as distributors of retail financial products and providers of financial advice. These investment activities, which bring banks within the scope of the MiFID regime, can be contrasted with the deposit-taking and lending business of banks. Banking business poses different risks to those that arise in investment business. For banking business, credit risk and liquidity risk are the two main concerns. Credit risk focuses on the possibility of borrowers defaulting on loans. Liquidity risk arises from the maturity transformation function of banks: because they fund long-term lending with short-term deposits, banks face the risk of being unable to repay deposits as they fall due. Regulatory capital requirements for banks require capital to be held against credit risk so as to provide a buffer that can absorb loan defaults without posing a risk to depositors and other creditors. When account is taken of the types of capital that can count as regulatory capital (mainly equity), it can be seen that it is mainly shareholders in banks who bear the risk of failure.[116] Liquidity requirements also play a role in promoting financial stability by ensuring that banks have access to sufficient liquid funds to pay their debts as they fall due. As illustrated by the collapse of Northern Rock in the UK in 2007,

---

[115] Although it is generally referred to as a single measure, the CRD in fact comprises two directives: the Banking Directive (2006/48/EC [2006] OJ L177/1) and the Capital Adequacy Directive (2006/49/EC [2006] OJ L177/201). The CRD (as amended) is implemented in the UK by the Capital Requirements Regulations 2006, SI 2006/3221 and FSA regulatory rules.

[116] That is not to say that holders of other instruments that can count as regulatory capital should not bear losses. However, government bailouts during the crisis have mainly imposed losses on shareholders and have generally been protective of bondholders in failed banks. That treatment poses 'moral hazard' risks in relation to the valuation of bank debt and the conduct of bondholders.

liquidity problems can be a catalyst for a bank run and ultimate collapse even when the underlying balance sheet of a bank is sound.[117]

The European regime for banking is closely linked to the Basel Accords developed by the Basel Committee.[118] The Capital Requirements Directive[119] implemented the 2004 Basel II Accord in the EU. Basel II was intended to make the regulatory capital regime for banks more risk sensitive and less costly than the first Basel Accord. It introduced a more sophisticated approach to the risk weighting of assets (loans) for the purposes of setting regulatory capital requirements. Credit ratings were used to assign risk weightings to assets, with the result that considerable reliance was placed on those ratings in setting regulatory capital. Moreover, banks themselves became much more directly involved in setting their own capital requirements as a result of Basel II's introduction of the 'Internal Ratings Basis', which permitted banks to develop models that measured risk and allocated appropriate levels of capital against that risk. From that perspective, Basel II was clearly deregulatory in its overall effect, and in hindsight has been viewed as taking that agenda too far, thereby contributing to the financial crisis.[120]

As well as setting minimum capital requirements (Pillar I), Basel II was structured around two other pillars that were intended to work alongside Pillar I so as to promote financial stability. Under Pillar II (supervisory review) it was envisaged that banking supervisors would determine if the minimum capital requirements set by Pillar 1 were adequate in individual cases. In hindsight, it seems clear that this power was all too often overlooked or sidelined by the (apparent) explanatory power of banks' own models in measuring risk and setting appropriate levels of capital. Pillar III (market discipline) was intended to strengthen the regulatory regime by requiring banks to disclose information relating to their financial position and quality of their assets. While in principle that approach had the potential to encourage market counterparties to exert market discipline to force weaker banks to strengthen their capital and liquidity, it seems clear in hindsight that the deregulatory force of Basel II was simply too strong to permit market discipline to play a significant role. Moreover, since booming asset prices created an illusion of strong capital positions for the banks in the pre-crisis phase (at least by comparison with the Basel II minimum standards), there was no clear or imminent danger on which market discipline could focus and take action.

The Capital Requirements Directive[121] imposes a uniform set of regulatory capital requirements on banks and investment firms in respect of their 'trading book', which comprises all positions in financial instruments and commodities that are held 'with trading intent'. This applies most obviously to the 'market-making' positions of brokers-dealers and proprietary trading positions, but not to investments that are held on behalf

---

[117] See FSA, 'The Supervision of Northern Rock: a Lessons Learned Review' (March 2008) B7 (available at http://www.fsa.gov.uk/pubs/other/nr_report.pdf).

[118] See generally S Gleeson, *International Regulation of Banking, Basel II: Capital and Risk Requirements* (Oxford, Oxford University Press, 2010).

[119] Above n 115.

[120] See eg the critique of the Basel II regime in 'The Report of the High-Level Group on Financial Supervision in the EU' (February 2009) (the de Larosière Report), available at http://ec.europa.eu/internal_market/finances/docs/de_larosiere_report_en.pdf (accessed on 16 August 2011).

[121] The requirements are contained in the Capital Adequacy Directive.

of clients. The Directive adopts standard models for measuring position and counterparty risk, but also permits the use of value at risk models so long as they are approved by the relevant (national) regulatory authority. There is also a specific regulatory capital charge to cover operational risk arising from failure in internal systems, external shock and legal risk.

The Basel III Accord[122], adopted by the BCBS is September 2010, requires considerably higher levels of regulatory capital. Basel I had established a minimum capital requirement of 8% capital to risk adjusted assets. Within that overall ratio, a core tier 1 ratio of 2% was set by reference to fully paid-up share capital and retained earnings only.[123] Under Basel III the core tier 1 ratio is more than doubled, to 4.5%. This is supplemented by an additional conservation buffer of 2.5%, which takes the core tier 1 ratio to 7%. Systemically important institutions will be subject to a 9% minimum core tier 1 ratio and regulators will retain discretion (which they already had under Pillar 2 of Basel II) to impose higher standards in individual cases. These changes are in principle applicable to investment firms and banks with a 'trading book' of investments. Thus, the higher levels of capital apply across the board to all the (risk-adjusted) assets held by the relevant firm. However, as far as the trading book alone is concerned, the 2009 Basel reforms to the Basel II market risk framework represent the most significant change. Addressing their implementation in the UK, the FSA said that 'On average, these changes will increase the capital held against trading activities in large banks to more than three times current levels'.[124]

However, while the regulatory requirements are substantially higher, market discipline had already provided an impetus for the strengthening of capital (primarily by banks in Europe and the US) and therefore the incremental effect will not be so great.[125] Moreover, as the Basel III standards will be implemented over an extended period (until 2019), there is time for national regulatory regimes and banks to adjust and possibly also for the rigour of the regime to be diluted through adjustment and during the course of implementation. At the European level, Basel III will be implemented through changes to the Capital Requirements Directive and therefore much of the reform will be common to all Member States. That process will not in itself disrupt the long-standing arrangement in the European system under which supervision and enforcement are the responsibility of the national authorities and that poses risks to the extent to which a common version of Basel III will be implemented in Europe.[126]

---

[122] See http://www.bis.org/bcbs/basel3.htm.

[123] Thus core tier 1 capital excludes other forms of capital that may count for regulatory capital purposes (such as subordinated debt). The rationale is that share capital is the best form of protection for bank customers since shareholders have no protection against losses suffered by a bank. The core tier 1 ratio is therefore the strictest and most robust measure of the capital strength of a bank.

[124] FSA DP 10/4, 'The prudential regime for trading activities, a fundamental review' (August 2010).

[125] It does, of course, remain open to national regulators to impose stricter requirements, as Switzerland has already done in the form of the so-called 'Swiss finish', under which regulatory capital is around twice the Basel III minimum requirement.

[126] Proposals for a 'maximum harmonisation' implementation of Basel III in the EU would go some way to mitigating that risk, but at the cost of removing flexibility from national supervisors. That approach has attracted criticism in the UK.

2.9.3 The European regime for insurance

Whilst insurance in its basic form represents protection against risk, there are many insurance products that have an investment dimension. The overlap with investment is evident in the substantial share of insurance products in the retail financial market. Moreover, particularly prior to the financial crisis, the insurance sector played a significant role in underwriting credit risk through credit default swaps (CDSs),[127] which had the effect of transferring credit risk from the banking sector to the insurance sector.

Before considering the approach to insurance regulation in the EU, it is important to draw attention to the very different risk profile of insurers by comparison with banks.[128] At the most basic level, there are two important differences between the business models of banks and insurers. First, banks rely on leverage to expand their lending activities beyond the level that can be sustained by their deposit base. Insurers cannot use leverage in that manner because their business is self-funded by premiums and leverage cannot in itself represent a technique to expand the business. Secondly, as insurers do not engage in maturity transformation in the way that banks do, they do not face the same liquidity problems that arise from mismatch in the maturity of assets and liabilities. Moreover, there are also other considerations that lead to the conclusion that the systemic risk associated with insurers is much less than in the case of banks. One is the nature of their investment management activities, which are quite small by comparison with bank assets and the overall size of capital markets, and do not have the capacity to transmit material losses to other financial institutions.[129] Another is that, even if heavy losses are sustained through risks underwritten by insurers, the timing of claims payments means that the liquidity risk is not as great as in the case of bank runs. Thus, the nature of the insurance business suggests that regulatory intervention should focus more on policyholder protection through ensuring the solvency of individual firms rather than focusing on systemic stability, which has become the dominant theme in banking regulation since the financial crisis.

Within the EU, a fundamental restructuring of insurance regulation will result from the implementation of the Solvency II Directive.[130] In recognition of the limited systemic risk posed by insurers, the Directive provides that:

> The main objective of insurance and reinsurance regulation and supervision is the adequate

---

[127] See Chapter 4.3.5 for an explanation of CDSs. While often referred to as a form of insurance, CDSs differ from insurance in that there is no pooling of risk (as in the case of insurance) and no requirement of insurable interest, with the result that losses on CDSs may exceed the value of the financial instruments (typically bonds) that they reference. The larges losses sustained by AIG in CDSs during the financial crisis were not in its core insurance operations.

[128] See generally 'Systemic Risk in Insurance, An Analysis of Insurance and Financial Stability', Special Report of the Geneva Association Systemic Risk Working Group (March 2010).

[129] Unlike banks, insurers' links to non-insurance financial institutions are primarily as owners or creditors, whereas banks are often both creditors and debtors to each other. The nature of the interconnectedness therefore differs and there is less risk of transmission of losses from the insurance sector to other financial institutions.

[130] Directive 2009/138/EC [2009] OJ L335/1. The Directive is generally a maximum harmonisation measure. Its provisions must be implemented by Member States by 1 November 2012. It applies also to reinsurance activities.

protection of policy holders and beneficiaries. The term beneficiary is intended to cover any natural or legal person who is entitled to a right under an insurance contract. Financial stability and fair and stable markets are other objectives of insurance and reinsurance regulation and supervision which should also be taken into account but should not undermine the main objective.[131]

As regards its 'single market' dimension, the Directive follows the approach outlined above with respect to investment firms and banks. The most significant change relates to capital requirements that are imposed on insurers. The basic objective remains to ensure that adequate resources are available to meet policyholders claims, but Solvency II adopts a prospective and risk-based approach to this issue.[132] The directive's requirements start with governance[133] and risk management,[134] then move to the details of calculation of claims provisions and capital. All insurers are required to have in place an 'own risk solvency assessment', which is the principal means by which the Directive draws together risk management, governance, controls and capital into a single picture which is the responsibility of senior management and must be used in decision-making.

The central requirement related to capital is that insurers hold own funds[135] covering the Solvency Capital Requirement.[136] This requirement is not a minimum requirement[137] but a threshold for supervisory intervention, as failure to meet the requirement triggers the obligation to submit a recovery plan for approval by the supervisory authority and empowers the authority to take necessary measures to ensure compliance with the requirement.[138] The Solvency Capital Requirement can be calculated either according to a standard method set by the Solvency II Directive or on the basis of an internal model that has been approved by the competent authority. Whichever method is adopted, the Solvency Capital Requirement must take into account the following risk modules: non-life underwriting risk, life underwriting risk, health underwriting risk, market risk and counterparty default risk.[139]

The objective of policyholder protection is also evident in the provisions relating to the investment of insurers' assets, which are principally reserves for the payment of policyholders' claims. The high-level requirement that investments should be in accordance with the 'prudent person' principle follows a long-standing approach, as do the more detailed rules relating to diversification and liquidity. However, Member States are not permitted

---

[131] Recital 16 to the Directive.

[132] See Art 29(1).

[133] See Art 41(1), requiring 'an effective system of governance which provides for the sound and prudent management of the business'.

[134] See Art 41(1), requiring an effective and continuous risk management process that is integrated into the decision-making process.

[135] Own funds are defined by Arts 87–98. Basic own funds are defined as the excess of assets over liabilities (valued in accordance with the Directive) and subordinated liabilities (those that are paid after all other creditors). As is the case for banks, own funds are divided into three tiers according to the extent that they are available to absorb losses.

[136] Art 100.

[137] A separate minimum requirement is set by Arts 128 and 129.

[138] See Art 138.

[139] The Directive requires that a 'value-at-risk' measure of basic own funds, with a 99.5% confidence level, over a 1 year period, be used to calculate the capital requirement.

to require insurers to invest in particular categories of asset, nor to subject investment decisions to any kind of prior approval. The crisis management powers provided by the Solvency II Directive to the supervisory authorities are extensive, empowering them to take 'all measures necessary to safeguard the interests of policyholders' in situations where insurers fail to comply with the Directive's capital requirements.[140] Finally, the Directive provides that, in a winding-up of an insurer, policyholders' claims take precedence over all other claims (with limited exceptions).[141]

2.9.4 The de Larosière Report and changes to the European structure of regulation

In the wake of the financial crisis, the European Commission appointed a high-level group led by Jacques de Larosière to advise on the future of European financial regulation and supervision. The report which followed (the de Larosière Report[142]) highlighted a number of lessons that were learnt from the crisis and made recommendations for reform. The report drew attention to specific defects in the European system that exacerbated the crisis: failure to challenge supervisory practices on a cross-border basis; lack of frankness and cooperation between supervisors; lack of consistent supervisory powers across Member States; and no means for supervisors to take common decisions. The Report made a number of recommendations to remedy these defects and, in common with developments elsewhere, to shift the regulatory focus more towards macro-prudential regulation.

The European Commission responded to the de Larosière report by proposing the creation of a European Systemic Risk Board (ESRB) and a European System of Financial Supervisors (ESFS).[143] This proposal was duly approved in late 2010.[144] The ESRB is primarily a forum for coordination and discussion among the heads of the central banks of the Member States, the European Central Bank and the ESFS. Although it lacks formal regulatory powers, the ESRB is expected to play a significant role in the monitoring of systemic risk and in the development of macro-prudential regulation. In that capacity, it will collaborate with the IMF and the FSB in developing an early warning system to draw attention to risks to financial stability at the international level.

The ESFS is of more direct relevance to investment firms. It comprises three new European supervisory authorities (ESAs): the European Banking Authority (based in London), the European Securities and Markets Authority (based in Paris) and the European Insurance and Occupational Pensions Authority (based in Frankfurt). The market-sector responsibilities of the new ESAs correspond with those of their predecessor committees (banking; securities; and insurance and occupational pensions) at level 3 of the

---

[140] See Art 141.
[141] Art 275.
[142] The de Larosière Report, above n 120.
[143] See Communication from the Commission, 'European Financial Supervision', COM(2009) 252 final.
[144] In respect of the ESRB see Regulation 1092/2010 [2010] OJ L331/1 and Regulation 1096/2010 [2010] OJ L331/162; and in respect of the ESFS, Regulation 1095/2010 [2010] OJ L331/84 (ESMA), Regulation 1094/2010 [2010] OJ L331/48 (EIOPA) and Regulation 1093/2010 [2010] OJ L331/12 (EBA).

'Lamfalussy' legislative process. However, there are important changes in their powers and objectives. The new ESAs are legal persons with expanded powers encompassing rule-making, acting in emergency situations, settling disputes, and issuing instructions to national supervisors and financial institutions.[145] These changes are likely to result in a fundamental recalibration of the operation of financial regulation at the European level and of the relationship between the European authorities (including the Commission) and the national authorities.[146]

The new structure for rule-making in the ESFS is likely to have two effects. First, it is likely to lead to greater harmonisation in rulebooks across Member States as the new ESAs begin to exercise their powers to develop common technical standards and implementing measures. While the Commission will still be responsible for overseeing the process, its stated intention is to rely, as a rule, on the standards submitted to it by the new ESAs. The scope of harmonisation is potentially broad, since each of the new ESAs is empowered to act not only in respect of relevant directives applicable to each sector but also in respect of matters relating to corporate governance, auditing and financial reporting, provided such actions are necessary to ensure the effective and consistent application of those acts. Adaptation of technical standards at the national level is effectively ruled out since they will be adopted in the form of regulations and decisions which are directly applicable in Member States without the need for implementing measures. Moreover, the new structure adopts a 'comply or explain' model in respect of guidelines and recommendations made by the new ESAs, which (unlike technical standards adopted as regulations or decisions) are not legally binding; thus, national authorities and financial market participants may be required both to notify their non-compliance and state their reasons.

Secondly, it is likely that greater convergence will also be evident in the process of supervision. The impetus for this is likely to come from two sources. One is the role of the new ESAs in resolving disagreements between national authorities in cross-border situations and across market sectors. In the absence of agreement under the conciliation procedure, the matter can be settled by the relevant ESA. The other is the broader power to require national supervisors to act (or to refrain from acting) and, as a last resort in cases of non-compliance, to issue an individual decision directly to a financial institution requiring the necessary action to comply with its obligations under EU law. While the failure to put in place an enforcement mechanism for these decisions at the outset may cast some doubt over how far the balance of power will in fact be tilted away from national authorities to the new ESAs, there can be little doubt that at least a foundation has been laid for the emergence of a European system of supervision.

While the new system envisages a 'swift and concerted response' at the European level to crisis situations, the tools available to deal with a crisis are essentially the same as those applicable in other circumstances. Once an emergency situation has been determined by the Council of the EU, it is possible for the ESAs to adopt a faster decision-making

---

[145] Supervision will remain in the hands of the national authorities other than in the case of credit rating agencies (see Chapter 14.1.7) and trade repositories (under the proposed European Markets Infrastructure Regulation).

[146] The so-called 'Omnibus Directive', Directive 2010/78/EU [2010] OJ L331/120, makes changes to the major EU financial sector directives so as to accommodate the expanded role of the new ESAs.

process requiring national supervisors or financial institutions to act. However, the substance of the decision is determined by the same body of law (including technical standards) that applies outside an emergency situation. In that sense, the ESAs do not have the special powers that are typically available to national authorities to deal with crisis situations. It is envisaged that the ESAs will contribute to and participate actively in the development and coordination of effective resolution and recovery plans, but that is largely a supporting role by comparison with the leading role of the national authorities. That impression is supported by the requirement that no decision on emergency action (or on the settlement of disputes between national supervisors) shall impinge on the fiscal responsibilities of Member States.

The role of the new ESAs in relation to financial innovation and consumer protection reflects the more sceptical attitude towards financial innovation that has become apparent in the wake of the financial crisis. Thus, the new ESAs are required to establish committees on financial innovation bringing together national authorities with a view to achieving a coordinated approach to the regulatory and supervisory treatment of new or innovative financial activities and providing advice to the new ESAs. Moreover, the power temporarily to prohibit or restrict certain financial activities that threaten the orderly functioning and integrity of financial markets opens up the possibility of a much more centralised form of control over financial innovation than has been practised in the past. While the temporary and exceptional nature of the power means that it will not be used routinely, it does provide a reserve power that is of considerable value in setting the relationship between the new ESAs and the markets. As in other areas, such as crisis resolution, the availability of powers often has the capacity to alter the dynamics of regulatory relationships such that the exercise of formal powers may not be necessary.

The Regulatory System in the UK

This chapter examines the regulatory system currently in place in the UK. It provides an overview of the structure and objectives of regulation, the role of the regulator and the techniques that are employed in regulating firms and individuals who engage in investment business.

3.1 Background: the financial crisis and regulatory reform

3.1.1 Responding to the financial crisis

In the UK, as elsewhere, the onset of the financial crisis exposed deficiencies in financial regulation and led to calls for regulatory reform. The Treasury Select Committee[1] led the way, with its hearings into the collapse of Northern Rock exposing serious deficiencies in supervision and risk management.[2] In October 2008, the Chancellor of the Exchequer asked Lord Turner, the newly appointed chairman of the Financial Services Authority (FSA), to review the causes of the crisis and to make recommendations on the changes in regulation and supervisory approach needed to create a more robust banking system for the future. The Turner Review,[3] published in March 2009, made a number of

---

[1] The Treasury Select Committee is a parliamentary (House of Commons) committee that scrutinises the activity of the regulatory authorities in the UK.

[2] See House of Commons Treasury Committee, 'The Run on the Rock', HC 56-1 (Fifth Report of Session 2007–08).

[3] FSA, 'The Turner Review, A Regulatory Response to the Global Banking Crisis' (March 2009), available at http://www.fsa.gov.uk/Pages/Library/Corporate/turner/index.shtml. See also the FSA publication that accompanied the Turner Review: 'A Regulatory Response to the Global Banking Crisis', FSA Discussion Paper 09/2 (March 2009), available at http://www.fsa.gov.uk/pubs/discussion/dp09_02.pdf. For a more detailed discussion of both see I MacNeil, 'The Trajectory of Regulatory Reform in the UK in the Wake of the Financial Crisis' (2010) 11(4) *European Business Organization Law Review* 483.

recommendations to create a stable and effective banking system. In particular, it focused on the need for an increase in the quantity and quality of overall capital in the global banking system so as to allow banks to absorb losses without threatening financial stability or requiring governments to intervene through so-called 'bailouts'. It also recommended that liquidity regulation and supervision should be recognised as of equal importance to capital regulation, reflecting the experience during the crisis in which many solvent banks experienced problems in disposing of illiquid assets to meet their obligations. Turner also recommended that much more emphasis be placed on macro-prudential analysis and supervision, focusing on stability of the financial system as a whole rather than just the solvency of individual financial institutions. Finally, while Turner identified deficiencies in the FSA's supervisory approach, he favoured retention of the FSA as an integrated regulator, although he did recommend that the supervisory approach should be changed to a more intrusive approach with a greater emphasis on risk-taking by large complex banks.

Even before the Turner Review was published, legislation had been passed to deal with three aspects of the regulatory system that had been exposed as deficient following the collapse of Northern Rock in the autumn of 2007. The first was an increase in the level of deposits covered by the Deposit Guarantee Scheme.[4] This was intended to limit the possibility of a 'run' on a bank similar to that experienced by Northern Rock once rumours of its financial problems began to circulate. The second was the introduction of a statutory financial stability objective for the Bank of England by the Banking Act 2009. That objective requires the Bank to 'contribute to protecting and enhancing the stability of the financial systems of the UK'.[5] The third was the introduction of a 'special resolution regime' under the Banking Act 2009, enabling the tripartite authorities[6] to intervene in failing banks. The significance of that regime is that the authorities are freed from the constraints that would otherwise be imposed by the law of corporate insolvency. In particular, it permits earlier intervention and the imposition on shareholders and creditors of a range of solutions devised by the authorities, such as the sale of the institution to a third party.

3.1.2 The Financial Services Act 2010

Following publication of the Turner Review, the Treasury published a consultation paper entitled 'Reforming Financial Markets' in July 2009.[7] It made a number of legislative proposals which were ultimately enacted in the Financial Services Act 2010 (FSA 2010). While that Act made no changes to the institutional structure of regulation, it did introduce some changes in response to the financial crisis and the Turner Review. These are set out below.

---

[4] The increase (effective from 1 October 2007) resulted in deposits up to £35,000 being fully covered by the Financial Services Compensation Scheme established under FSMA 2000. Prior to that, the maximum payable in respect of a protected deposit was £31,700, comprising 100% of the first £2,000 and 90% of the next £33,000. For the current deposit protection arrangements see Chapter 6.7.

[5] See s 2A of the Bank of England Act 1998, inserted by s 238 of the Banking Act 2009.

[6] The Treasury, the Bank of England and the FSA.

[7] Cm 7667.

Financial stability

FSA 2010 provides that financial stability should be one of the regulatory objectives of the FSA, replacing 'public awareness'. The Act adopts a rather circular definition of the meaning of 'financial stability',[8] with the result that the real meaning is something that awaits clarification, most likely through its practical implementation by the regulatory authorities.

Remuneration of executives of authorised firms

FSA 2010 empowers the Treasury to make regulations about the preparation, approval and disclosure of executives' remuneration reports in relation to authorised firms. These provisions reflect political pressure in the wake of the financial crisis to constrain remuneration and risk-taking, and to make executives more accountable to shareholders. The Act also empowers the FSA to require authorised firms to have a remuneration policy that is consistent with the effective management of risk.[9]

Short-selling rules

FSA 2010 provides express powers to the FSA to make rules either prohibiting or requiring disclosure of short-selling. There were no express powers under the Financial Services and Markets Act 2000 (FSMA 2000), and therefore the temporary rules made by the FSA in 2008 were based on the premise that short-selling or failure to disclose short-selling constituted market abuse.[10] The express powers provided by FSA 2010 strengthen the legal basis for short-selling rules and remove the need for them to be justified by reference to market abuse considerations alone.

FSA disciplinary powers

FSA 2010 extended the FSA's disciplinary powers in several significant ways. These powers are considered in subsection 3.10.2 below.

Consumer redress schemes

The new provisions in FSA 2010 relating to consumer redress schemes enhance the powers of the FSA to require authorised firms to conduct a review of past business and pay compensation to consumers. While the old provision of FSMA 2000 (section 404) required Treasury and parliamentary authority for such action, the new provisions[11]

---

[8] New s 3A of FSMA 2000 (inserted by s 1(3) FSA 2010) provides that: 'The financial stability objective is: contributing to the protection and enhancement of the stability of the UK financial system.'

[9] See further Chapter 10.2.4.

[10] See Chapter 13.5 for a discussion of short-selling and market abuse.

[11] FSMA 2000, ss 404, 404A–404G.

enable the FSA to make rules establishing such a scheme in appropriate cases and to require compensation to be paid.

Power to require information

FSA 2010 provides for an expansion in the information-gathering powers of the FSA contained in FSMA 2000. Previously, the FSA's powers could be exercised only within the regulatory perimeter, even though this extends to collection of information on unregulated activity that is undertaken by a regulated entity and on exposure to unregulated counterparties of regulated entities. The expanded power[12] will enable the FSA to collect information that is relevant to the stability of the financial system directly from owners or managers of investment funds or persons connected to them and service providers to authorised firms.[13] While the effective exercise of this power may in some cases be limited by the territorial limits of the FSA's jurisdiction (eg in respect of 'offshore' funds managed from the UK), its overall effect is likely to be beneficial in facilitating the development of a more complete picture of the nature and scale of risk accumulation and transfer, especially in the less transparent areas of the market.[14]

3.1.3 Reform proposals

In February 2011 the government's reform proposals were fleshed out in more detail when the Treasury published its consultation paper 'A New Approach to Financial Regulation: Building a Stronger System' (hereinafter Treasury Cm 8012).[15] That was followed in June 2011 by a further consultation document and white paper including draft legislation.[16] The proposals will result in significant changes to the institutional structure, regulatory objectives and style of regulation. Each of these issues is discussed in more detail below.

The original plan was for the new regulatory framework to be in place by the end of 2012[17], but that target was dropped[18] in Cm 8083 in favour of the more open-ended

---

[12] FSA 2010, s 18.

[13] Moreover, the Treasury is empowered to prescribe further categories of person in respect of whom the FSA's extended information-gathering power may be exercised.

[14] While the transaction reporting regime established by Art 25 of MiFID provides regulators with transaction details from the over-the-counter (OTC) market in respect of trading in financial instruments admitted to trading on regulated markets, there remains a substantial volume of OTC trade that is not in such instruments (eg credit default swaps). See further Chapter 13.1.

[15] Cm 8012, available at http://www.official-documents.gov.uk/document/cm80/8012/8012.pdf (accessed on 16 August 2011).

[16] HM Treasury, *White Paper: A New Approach to Financial Regulation: The Blueprint for Reform*, Cm 8083 (London, HM Treasury, 2011).

[17] Treasury Cm 8012, above n 15, stated (at para 8.2) that: 'The Government is committed to putting the new regulatory architecture in place by the end of 2012. The Government believes that this remains an appropriate and achievable target.'

[18] The Treasury Select Committee had expressed concern over the potential effect of too short and rigid a timetable on the quality of legislation: see House of Commons Treasury Committee, 'Financial Regulation: A Preliminary Consideration of the Government's Proposals', HC 430-1 (Seventh Report of Session 2010/11) vol 1, ch 2.

formulation that 'the Government remains committed to implementing these reforms as quickly as possible, recognising the need to minimise regulatory uncertainty for firms'.

Also relevant in this context is the review of structure and competition in banking undertaken by the Independent Banking Commission. The Commission published an interim report in April 2011[19] and its final report in September 2011. As was generally expected, the Commission recommended that the structure of UK banking be altered by introducing a 'ring-fence' between retail activities and other banking activities. Four principles underlie the reforms proposed by the Commission. First, structural separation of retail and other activities should make it easier and less costly to resolve ring-fenced banks that get into trouble. Secondly, structural separation should help insulate retail banking from external financial shocks, including by distancing them from the global interconnectedness of the financial sector. Thirdly, according to the Commission, structural separation would help sustain the UK's position as a pre-eminent international financial centre while UK banking is made more resilient. Finally, separation, accompanied by appropriate transparency, should facilitate the operation of market discipline and regulatory supervision. The Treasury has already indicated that it will accept and implement the proposals made by the Commission, although the commitment to introduce legislation by 2015 and implement any measures by 2019 does not create the impression of any urgency.

3.2 Regulatory objectives

The regulatory objectives of the system of regulation established by FSMA 2000 are set out in sections 3–6 of the Act.[20] They provide a form of high-level control and accountability over the actions of the FSA since the Act requires the Authority to discharge its general functions[21] in a way that is compatible with the regulatory objectives.[22]

Market confidence

The market confidence objective is maintaining confidence in the financial system. The financial system includes financial markets and exchanges, regulated activities, and other activities connected with financial markets and exchanges. This objective therefore

---

[19] Independent Banking Commission, 'Interim Report, Consultation on Reform Options'; and 'Final Report', available at http://bankingcommission.independent.gov.uk/ (accessed on 20 November 2011). See also GA Walker, 'Structural Regulation and Financial Reform: the Independent Commission on Banking' (2011) 5(6) *Law and Financial Markets Review* 418.

[20] This was an innovation when the Act was passed as FSA 1986 had not referred to regulatory objectives.

[21] The general functions of the Authority are stated by s 2(4) of FSMA 2000 to be: (i) rule-making; (ii) issuing codes; (iii) giving general guidance; and (iv) determining the general principles and policy for the performance of its particular functions.

[22] FSMA 2000, s 2.

extends beyond activities which are regulated activities under the Act. Market confidence does not imply a policy of preventing all failures, but involves minimising the impact of failures and providing mechanisms to protect consumers.[23]

Financial stability

The financial stability objective of the FSA is: contributing to the protection and enhancement of the stability of the UK financial system. In considering that objective, the Authority must have regard to—

1. the economic and fiscal consequences for the UK of instability of the UK financial system;
2. the effects (if any) on the growth of the economy of the UK of anything done for the purpose of meeting that objective; and
3. the impact (if any) on the stability of the UK financial system of events or circumstances outside the UK (as well as in the UK).

The Authority must, in consultation with the Treasury, determine and review its strategy in relation to the financial stability objective.

The protection of consumers

The consumer protection objective is securing the appropriate degree of protection for consumers. In considering what is appropriate, the FSA must have regard to risk, expertise, the need for information and advice, and the general principle that consumers should take responsibility for their decisions. 'Consumer' is defined broadly, and includes (i) companies and persons entering into transactions in a business capacity; and (ii) persons who derive rights from persons who are 'consumers'.[24]

The reduction of financial crime

The reduction of financial crime objective is reducing the extent to which it is possible for a business carried on (i) by a regulated person or (ii) in contravention of the general prohibition against carrying on regulated activity without authorisation, to be used for a purpose in connection with financial crime. Financial crime includes any offence involving fraud or dishonesty; misconduct in, or misuse of information relating to, a financial market; and handling the proceeds of crime. The offence includes an act or omission that would be an offence if it took place in the UK. The Act itself establishes offences falling within the scope of this objective, such as making misleading statements and engaging in market manipulation.[25]

---

[23] See FSA 'Reasonable Expectations: Regulation in a Non-Zero Failure World' (2003).
[24] FSMA 2000, ss 425A and 425B. The Office of Fair Trading (OFT) retains responsibility for licensing and supervision under the Consumer Credit Act 1974.
[25] FSMA 2000, s 397.

The Act also refers to principles of good regulation to which the FSA must have regard in carrying out its duties.[26] They are:

(a) the need to use its resources in the most efficient and economic way;
(b) the responsibilities of those who manage the affairs of authorised persons;
(c) the principle that a burden or restriction which is imposed on a person, or on the carrying on of an activity, should be proportionate to the benefits, considered in general terms, which are expected to result from the imposition of that burden or restriction;
(d) the desirability of facilitating innovation in connection with regulated activities;[27]
(e) the international character of financial services and markets and the desirability of maintaining the competitive position of the UK;
(f) the need to minimise the adverse effects on competition that may arise from anything done in the discharge of those functions;
(g) the desirability of facilitating competition between those who are subject to any form of regulation by the Authority; and
(h) the desirability of enhancing the understanding and knowledge of members of the public of financial matters (including the UK financial system).

The experience of the financial crisis has caused some re-evaluation of these principles. Thus Treasury Cm 8012 indicated that principles (d), (f), (g) and (h) are likely to be removed when the new regulatory framework is put in place. Part of the reason for this is a policy decision that each of the new regulatory authorities should have a single regulatory objective that should not be complicated by potentially conflicting objectives. In the case of (d), it is clear that there is a more cautious approach to the benefits of financial innovation as a result of the key role of innovative products in the financial crisis. In the case of (f), it is argued that the competition objective will be subsumed into the objectives and operation of the Prudential Regulation Authority and the Financial Conduct Authority:[28] in the former case, the financial stability objective will strengthen the competitiveness of the UK system, whereas in the latter case, the clean, fair and efficient markets objective will have the same effect. In the case of (f), the creation of the Consumer Financial Education Body (CFEB) by the Financial Services Act 2010[29] gives effect to that regulatory objective in a specific manner by requiring the FSA to establish a body to enhance the understanding and knowledge of the public of financial matters and the ability of members of the public to manage their own affairs.

---

[26] FSMA 2000, s 2(3).

[27] For a general discussion of innovation in financial services see S Lumpkin, 'Consumer Protection and Financial Innovation: A Few Basic Propositions' (2010) 2010(1) *Financial Market Trends* 117; E Engelen, I Erturk, J Froud, A Leaver and K Williams, 'Reconceptualizing Financial Regulation: Frame, Conjuncture and Bricolage' (2010) 39(1) *Economy and Society* 33.

[28] See section 3.3 below for more detail about these new regulatory bodies.

[29] See s 2(5), inserting a new s 6A into FSMA 2000.

3.3 The institutional structure of regulation

Prior to the May 2010 general election, the Conservative Party had made clear that it intended to disband the FSA and place the Bank of England at the centre of a reformed regulatory system. The proposed new system follows the 'twin peaks' model that has already been adopted in some other countries, with prudential regulation and conduct of business regulation to be undertaken by separate regulatory bodies.[30] Underlying that approach is the proposition that the two forms of regulation are very different in nature and are therefore best undertaken by separate agencies. Prudential regulation focuses on capital, liquidity and balance sheets, while conduct of business regulation focuses on a firm's business process and its relationships with customers. Another relevant factor is that there may be conflicts between the objectives and outcomes of each type of regulation, so separate agencies avoid the likelihood that an integrated regulator may not enforce regulation if it threatens solvency. Thus, for example, if action proposed by a conduct of business regulator weakens the financial position of an authorised firm, an integrated regulator may be less willing to take the necessary action because it is concerned about financial stability whereas an independent conduct of business regulator is not directly concerned with that issue. That argument for a 'twin peaks' approach is, however, only as good as the independence of the relevant regulators, and in any system it is quite likely that there will be external and political pressures to act or not to act in specific situations.

While similar to a number of other systems,[31] the proposed UK model does have distinctive characteristics, in particular the positioning of the central bank (the Bank of England) at the centre of the regulatory system, with the result that it has responsibility both for monetary policy and financial stability. The proposed new structure responds to perceived deficiencies in the old system, in which the FSA operated as an integrated regulator within a 'tripartite' system, in which the Bank of England was responsible (under the triparite memorandum of understanding (MOU), though not the legislative framework) for financial stability and the Treasury for policy. In particular, the Treasury highlighted the following problems resulting from the tripartite structure:

- the Bank of England, while having statutory responsibility for financial stability,[32] has only limited tools to deliver it;
- the FSA, by contrast, has regulatory tools for delivering financial stability, but with such a wide mandate prior to the crisis—including consumer protection, public awareness, market confidence and the reduction of financial crime—was not sufficiently focused on stability issues; and
- perhaps most significantly, the linkage between firm-level and systemic stability issues

---

[30] The EU regulatory framework does not require this type of institutional structure but does require a clear division between prudential and conduct of business regulation for the purposes of the 'passporting' regime and the allocation of responsibilities to home and host states: see Chapter 2.9.

[31] Such as Australia, Hong Kong and the Netherlands.

[32] Under the Banking Act 2009. That responsibility was not formally recognised by FSMA 2000.

has fallen between the institutional cracks, with no one body having the remit to tackle this fundamentally important issue. This has created a significant area of regulatory 'underlap' within the UK's framework.[33]

Another aspect of the UK reform is a policy of separating macro-prudential regulation (to be located in the Bank of England) from micro-prudential regulation (to be located in the Prudential Regulation Authority (PRA)). Thus the Bank of England will have responsibility for financial stability (to be given effect through macro-prudential regulation) and for operating the special resolution regime for failing banks introduced by the Banking Act 2009, as well as the traditional role of any central bank as the 'lender of last resort' to banks who can no longer raise funds in the markets. The Treasury consultation paper argues that:

> By locating these distinct but complementary functions within the Bank of England group, the Government will ensure that systemic and firm-specific regulation are coordinated, and that the market knowledge and economic expertise of the central bank is fully brought to bear on financial stability.[34]

The Treasury consultation paper also indicates that the Treasury is likely to take a more active stance in determining the style of regulation that it is adopted within the new structure. While the FSA had a relatively free hand in developing its style[35]—most obviously characterised by 'light touch' and 'principles-based' regulation—the initial indications are that the new legislative framework and Treasury guidance will play a greater role in the new structure. This is evident in the extensive discussion of the regulatory style and approach that should be adopted by the PRA and Financial Conduct Authority (FCA) in the Treasury consultation Cm 8012.

It remains to be seen how far the reform of the institutional structure will lead to better regulation and supervision. Some commentators have argued that there is little or no evidence that some institutional structures are better able to avert or mitigate crises than others:[36] on that view, there is little point in principle in reforming the institutional structure in response to the crisis. Focusing more specifically on the UK, it has been argued the FSA's performance before and during the crisis does not justify its break-up.[37] While it does seem clear that regulatory reform could have focused only on the regulatory rules and style of supervision without disturbing the institutional structure, perhaps the crucial issue is whether the reform to the institutional structure will strengthen the capacity of regulators to act at the appropriate time to constrain risk-taking and protect financial stability. Only time will tell if that is the case.

---

[33] Cm 8012, above n 15, 4.

[34] Ibid, 5.

[35] FSMA 2000, s 2(4)(d) expressly provides for the Authority to develop the general principles and policy for the performance of its particular functions.

[36] See eg J Cooper, 'The Regulatory Cycle: From Boom to Bust' in I MacNeil and J O'Brien (eds), *The Future of Financial Regulation* (Oxford, Hart Publishing, 2010) ch 28.

[37] E Ferran, 'The Break-Up of the Financial Services Authority', available at http://ssrn.com/abstract=1690523 (21 August 2011).

3.3.1 The Financial Policy Committee

The Financial Policy Committee (FPC), which was established on an interim basis in February 2011 as a committee of the Court of Directors of the Bank of England, will sit at the top of the UK's new regulatory structure.[38] It will undertake the macro-prudential function that will be formalised in statute in due course and will contribute to the Bank's financial stability objective by identifying, monitoring and taking action to remove or reduce systemic risks with a view to protecting and enhancing the resilience of the UK financial system. That function will encompass research and analysis, the provision of advice to the Treasury and coordination with the 'twin peaks' regulators who will carry out supervision of financial firms. The FPC's function will also involve using the 'levers' which are at its disposal to achieve its objectives. They include:

- public pronouncements and warnings;
- influencing macro-prudential policy in Europe and internationally;
- making recommendations to bodies other than the PRA and FCA;
- powers over the PRA and FCA: to make recommendations (backed up by a 'comply or explain' mechanism) and to direct the regulators where explicitly provided for by macro-prudential tools designed in secondary legislation.

The FPC will eventually supersede the Financial Stability Committee established under the Banking Act 2009 once the new statutory framework is in place. The new FPC has a broader remit and more extensive powers within the regulatory system than the committee it will replace, which was focused only on the Bank of England's financial stability objectives and powers. That change reflects the new regulatory structure that is being put in place by the Conservative government, under which the Bank of England is at the centre of, and to a large extent controls, the system of financial regulation.[39]

3.3.2 The Prudential Regulation Authority

The PRA will be established as a subsidiary of the Bank of England and will undertake prudential regulation and supervision of deposit-taking institutions, insurers (including the Lloyd's of London insurance market) and systemically significant investment firms. The identification of systemically significant investment firms will be based on their capacity to pose risks to financial stability as a result of the nature and scale of their activities. Only firms which have permission to deal in investments as a principal will fall into this category, and within that only the larger firms will be regarded as systemically significant. Thus, large 'broker-dealers' or investment banks (irrespective of whether they

---

[38] These comments on the role of the FPC are based on Treasury Cm 8012, above n 15.

[39] The Labour government had proposed to legislate to replace the Standing Committee of the tripartite Authorities with a Council for Financial Stability: see HM Treasury Cm 7667, supra n 7, 138. The conservative opposition (now in government) opposed the creation of the Council on the basis that it did not address fundamental defects in the current institutional structure: see Hansard (House of Lords, Report and Third Reading), 8 April 2010, col 1663.

take deposits) will fall within the scope of regulation of the PRA. The strategic objective of the PRA (in common with the FPC) will be the promotion of financial stability, while its operational objective will be promoting the safety and soundness of PRA authorised firms in a way that does not rule out the possibility of firm failure.[40] As regards style of regulation, the PRA will continue with and extend the 'principles-based' approach developed by the FSA, focusing on compliance with the spirit as well as the letter of the rules. It will also develop a 'Proactive Intervention Framework', which is intended to support the capacity of regulators to act at the appropriate time. In the words of the Treasury Cm 8012:

> The framework will have two clear purposes: firstly, to create presumptions that regulatory actions will be taken at certain points with a view to increasing probability of recovery, and secondly to initiate coordination measures between the authorities so that the failure and/or resolution can be more effectively controlled with minimum systemic disruption. The introduction of this framework will ensure that the judgement-led approach will be applied proactively where a supervisor has concerns and that action is taken.[41]

3.3.3 The Financial Conduct Authority

The FCA will undertake conduct of business regulation for all authorised firms. These firms will therefore be 'dual regulated' by both the PRA and the FPC. Importantly, however, it will also undertake prudential regulation and supervision for investment firms that are deemed not to be systemically significant (and therefore excluded from the PRA's remit). Thus, measured by number of firms, the FCA will undertake prudential regulation and supervision of more firms than the PRA, although, measured by scale and complexity, the activity of the PRA will be greater. The UK Listing Authority (UKLA) will also form part of the FCA's remit, as will conduct issues in the 'wholesale' markets such as the operation of the 'market abuse' regime. The FCA's strategic objective will be to protect and enhance confidence in the UK financial system, while its operational objectives will be: to facilitate efficiency and choice in the market for financial services; to secure an appropriate degree of protection for consumers; and to protect and enhance the integrity of the UK financial system. Given the FCA's strategic and operational objectives, its prudential regulation will focus less on acting to avoid the failure of firms and more on preventing consumer detriment. In the event of failure, the FCA's main objective will be to ensure that customers are not disadvantaged and that risks to confidence in the UK's financial system are minimised.

The control of style of regulation by the government via the Treasury is evident to an even greater extent than in the case of the PRA. Thus Cm 8012 sets out in extensive detail how the FCA will be expected to engage in regulation and supervision. In particular, it requires the FCA to focus on consumer detriment through a more interventionist approach

---

[40] See further The Bank of England, Prudential Regulation Authority, 'Our Approach to Banking Supervision' (May 2011) and 'Our Approach to Insurance Supervision' (June 2011).

[41] Treasury Cm 8012, above n 15, 51.

than had been practised by the FSA in the past and to intervene at an earlier stage in the lifecycle of financial products where consumer detriment is likely rather than waiting for the harm to occur.

3.3.4 Hierarchy and collaboration in the new institutional structure

The introduction of a 'twin peaks' system, combined with the enhancement of the role of the Bank of England in financial stability and the 'resolution regime' for failing banks, represents a significant change from the FSMA 2000 structure, under which the FSA acts as a integrated regulator for all matters in respect of all authorised firms. In particular, the new structure raises issues regarding the hierarchy of the regulatory authorities and the extent to which they will collaborate. The issue is of considerable practical importance, since the theoretical division between 'prudential' and 'conduct of business' on which the 'twin peaks' model is based cannot be applied quite so easily in practice. In some areas, such as decisions on granting or limiting authorisation and the operation of the 'approved persons' regime, it may not be entirely clear whether the matter falls within 'prudential' or 'conduct of business' regulation, and it may indeed be better to assume that it falls within both.

So far as hierarchy is concerned, the proposed solution reflects greater political control (through the Treasury) and the central role of financial stability as a regulatory objective within the new system. Thus, the Treasury will be able to provide 'guidance' to the FPC, which in turn will be able to issue directions and recommendations to the PRA in respect of macro-prudential tools.[42] The FPC will also be able to require information from the PRA, though it will not have any powers over individual firms. The PRA will in turn have a power of veto over actions proposed by the FCA which are likely to lead to the disorderly failure of a firm or wider financial instability. The PRA and FCA will also be subject to a statutory duty to coordinate activity with each other, and that will be supported by cross-membership of boards and a statutory obligation to prepare a MOU that deals with specific regulatory processes for which cooperation is essential.

---

[42] Relevant tools are counter-cyclical buffers; variable risk weights; leverage limits; liquidity tools; collateral requirements: see Treasury Cm 8012, ibid, 25.

3.3.5 Accountability of the regulators

While the FSA was established with the intention of creating an independent regulator, FSMA 2000 provides for a degree of accountability to government ministers, Parliament and stakeholders.[43] The most significant form of ministerial control is the power of the Treasury to appoint and remove the chairman and members of the governing body of the FSA. This gives the Treasury a significant role in influencing the manner in which the FSA approaches its regulatory remit. It is possible for the Treasury to require the FSA to alter its rules, but only when they have a significantly adverse affect on competition[44] or in order to comply with the UK's EU or international obligations.[45] It is also possible for the Treasury to commission value-for-money audits and to arrange independent inquiries into regulatory matters of serious concern.[46]

Some measure of parliamentary scrutiny of the FSA is made possible by the requirement that its annual report be laid before Parliament.[47] The FSA is also in principle subject to Select Committee scrutiny, though serious doubts have been expressed over the effectiveness of such oversight.[48]

The main mechanism for securing accountability to stakeholders has been the requirement that the FSA establish Consumer and Practitioner Panels.[49] The FSA must consider representations made by either Panel and, if it disagrees with it, must give the Panel a statement in writing of its reasons for disagreeing.

The need for greater accountability on the part of the regulatory authorities has been one of the main concerns in the development of the new regulatory structure in the UK. The June 2011 White Paper[50] proposed many changes to the governance of the regulators and to their accountability. Of particular note are the following proposals:

- The Financial Policy Committee will be required to publish a record of each meeting within 6 weeks.
- The PRA (and FCA) will be under a duty to make a report where there may have been regulatory failure, and that the trigger will be set out in legislation.
- The National Audit Office (NAO) will be able to initiate value for money (VFM) studies of the PRA.[51]

---

[43] See generally A Page, 'Regulating the Regulator—A Lawyer's Perspective' in E Ferran and C Goodhart (eds), *Regulating Financial Services and Markets in the 21st Century* (Oxford, Hart Publishing, 2001).

[44] FSMA 2000, s 163.

[45] FSMA 2000, s 410.

[46] See ss 12 and 14 FSMA 2000 respectively. See eg the Penrose Report (2003) into the collapse of Equitable Life at http://www.thecashquestion.com/penrose/intro.pdf. (21 August 2011). In 2010 the new coalition government decided to award compensation to the policyholders of Equitable Life as a result of maladministration in the regulation of Equitable Life: see http://www.hm-treasury.gov.uk/fin_equitable_life.htm (accessed on 8 August 2011).

[47] FSMA 2000 sch 1 para 10(3).

[48] See Page, above n 43, 134.

[49] FSMA 2000, s 8.

[50] Above n 16.

[51] Section 6 of the National Audit Act 1983 provides that the NAO can undertake a VFM study of any body whose accounts are required to be examined and certified by, or are open to the inspection of, the Comptroller

• The draft legislation provides for audit of the FCA by the NAO (which will enable the NAO to launch VFM investigations into the FCA).[52]

3.4 Authorisation

FSMA 2000 adopts the basic rule, on which most systems of financial regulation are based, that authorisation is required to engage in regulated activities.[53] Authorisation is achieved, in most cases, by applying to the FSA for permission to engage in the relevant activity.[54] An applicant must meet the 'threshold conditions' contained in the Act before permission will be granted.[55] These conditions cover several matters and in particular leave considerable discretion to the FSA in deciding whether three requirements are met. The first is whether the applicant (and the group of which it is a member) has adequate financial resources in relation to the regulated activities it seeks to carry on. The second is the nature of the risks that are undertaken and how they are managed. The third is whether the applicant is a fit and proper person (natural or legal) having regard to all the circumstances. These tests formed part of the authorisation procedure under the Financial Services Act 1986 (FSA 1986). Special provisions apply to firms from other EU Member States who wish to become authorised by exercising rights under the EU financial market directives or the TFEU.[56] Such firms are able to exercise 'passport' rights so as to be recognised as authorised persons in the UK. There are also a number of important exemptions from the requirement for authorisation. These issues are discussed below.

3.4.1 Permission

Permission is normally granted only for specified activities and may be subject to requirements imposed by the Authority.[57] That in itself constitutes authorisation for the purposes of the Act, with the result that any form of permission means that the criminal offence of engaging in unauthorised activity cannot be committed. However, engaging in activity in respect of which a person does not have permission is a regulatory contravention which will result in disciplinary action being taken by the FSA. It is not,

---

and Auditor General. As to the role of the Comptroller and Auditor General see the History of the National Audit Office at http://www.nao.org.uk/about_us/history_of_the_nao.aspx (accessed on 8 August 2011).

[52] See Cm 8083, above n 16.

[53] This is the 'general prohibition' contained in s 19 FSMA 2000.

[54] Under the 'twin peaks' model dual regulated firms will require authorisation from both the PRA and the FCA.

[55] See s 41 of and sch 6 to FSMA 2000.

[56] See Chapter 2.9 for an overview of the EU regime.

[57] See generally pt IV of FSMA 2000. A requirement to 'ring-fence' the 'retail' activities of banks so as to protect them from the risks inherent in investment banking could be implemented in part through this regulatory technique.

however, a criminal offence, and the contravention has no effect on the validity of a contract. The scope of permission can be varied at the request of an authorised person subject to meeting the 'threshold conditions' in relation to all permitted activities. The Authority is empowered to vary or revoke permission in three circumstances: first, when an authorised person fails to satisfy the 'threshold conditions'; secondly, when an authorised person fails, within 12 months, to carry on a regulated activity for which he has permission; and thirdly, when it is desirable to meet any of its regulatory objectives.

3.4.2 EEA (European Economic Area) and Treaty Firms

It is also possible for authorisation to be achieved by an EEA firm exercising its rights under the various EU directives which give effect to the TFEU's principles of freedom of establishment and freedom to provide services.[58] This is referred to in FSMA 2000 as the exercise of 'passport rights' by EEA firms. The EU directives relating to banking, insurance and investment are based on two principles. The first is a 'single licence' under which a firm authorised in an EEA state is entitled to provide services or establish a branch (but not a subsidiary) in other EEA states. The second is 'home country control', under which a firm is supervised by its home state in respect of all its business conducted under the single licence.

Subject to satisfying certain conditions associated with the exercise of these rights (mainly the giving of notice to its home state regulator), an EEA firm qualifies for authorisation in the UK.[59] It is also possible for an EEA firm to gain authorisation for an activity in respect of which there is no EEA right to carry on the activity in the manner proposed by the applicant. For this to occur, the firm must have authorisation in its home state, and the laws of the home state must provide equivalent protection or conform with a relevant provision of EU law.[60] This possibility is referred to by FSMA 2000 as the exercise of 'treaty rights' and is designed to ensure that the UK conforms with EU law relating to freedom to provide services.[61]

3.4.3 Exemptions

A number of exemptions from the general prohibition against engaging in regulated activity without an authorisation are provided by FSMA 2000. Section 285 establishes the general framework under which investment exchanges and clearing houses[62] are regulated. It provides that investment exchanges and clearing houses which have been 'recognised' by the FSA are exempt from the general prohibition in section 19 of the Act. There are two important aspects of exempt status. First, the exemption is not a

---

[58] See Chapter 2.9.

[59] FSMA 2000, s 31(1)(b) and sch 3.

[60] FSMA 2000, s 31(1)(c) and sch 4.

[61] The TFEU Treaty rules relating to freedom of services are broader than the regime established by the financial market directives, hence the need for this rule.

[62] See Chapter 12 for more detail regarding the nature and operation of exchanges and clearing houses.

true exemption from the regulatory framework of FSMA 2000 because exchanges and clearing houses can only become recognised if they meet certain criteria.[63] Secondly, the scope of the exemption is limited. For a recognised investment exchange (RIE), it relates to activities carried on as part of the business of an exchange or in connection with the provision of clearing services. For a recognised clearing house (RCH), it relates to activities connected with the provision of clearing services by the clearing house. There is no exempt person status in respect of other activities undertaken by RIEs or RCHs. Any application for permission in respect of such other activities is to be treated as an application relating only to that other activity.

Appointed representatives are also exempt from the requirement for authorisation. They are persons (human or legal) who act on behalf of an authorised person in carrying on a regulated activity. They cannot themselves be authorised persons. The exemption applies only if:[64]

- the appointed representative is a party to a contract with an authorised person, referred to as the principal, which permits the appointed representative to carry on regulated activities and complies with such requirements as may be prescribed; and
- the principal has accepted responsibility in writing for the conduct of those regulated activities.

The consequence of accepting responsibility for the actions of an appointed representative is that the principal bears responsibility for them in any disciplinary action taken by the FSA or civil action taken by a customer. There is, however, a limitation of the principal's liability in respect of criminal offences in that the knowledge and intentions of the appointed representative are not attributed to the principal unless in all the circumstances it is reasonable for them to be attributed to him. The type of activity carried on by appointed representatives and some aspects of the relationship between the principal and appointed representative are controlled by regulations made by the Treasury.[65]

Although appointed representatives do not require authorisation, they require approval under the 'approved persons' regime if they undertake 'controlled functions' in respect of the principal's business.[66]

Members of designated professions are also exempt from the general prohibition against engaging in regulated activity without authorisation. This is mainly an issue for firms of accountants, solicitors and actuaries who, in the normal course of their business, may find themselves engaging in regulated activities (eg an accountant engaging in tax-planning advice on pensions or a solicitor arranging for the investment of a trust fund). The main problem faced by the regulatory system is differentiating between cases in which such activity can safely be left outside the regulatory perimeter (leaving it to be controlled by the relevant professional body) and cases in which the scale of the

---

[63] See Chapter 12 for more detail.

[64] FSMA 2000, s 39.

[65] The Financial Services and Markets Act 2000 (Appointed Representatives) Regulations 2001, SI 2001/1217 (as amended). See Chapter 6.1.2 for more details.

[66] See below section 3.8.4.

regulated activity justifies treating members of professions on an equal footing with other authorised persons.

The central provision of FSMA 2000 is that a professional firm or person can only be exempt if the carrying on of regulated activity is incidental to the provision of professional services.[67] Whether or not regulated activity is incidental to a profession is determined by the 'Professions Order',[68] which distinguishes between completely non-exempt activities and non-exempt activities that are subject to conditions. If the 'incidental business' requirement is breached, there is no exemption available, and the firm or person can be considered to be undertaking unauthorised activity. However, the likelihood of that occurring is reduced by the requirement that designated professional bodies should make rules that give effect to the 'incidental business' requirement. Moreover, the firm or person must not receive from any other person any pecuniary reward (such as commission) for which he does not account to his client. This is not a prohibition on charging clients for services comprising regulated activities. The intention is that there should be no payment made to the member of the profession that is hidden from the client.

The Treasury is authorised to designate professional bodies for the purposes of this exemption. To qualify for designation, a professional body must show that it has rules which satisfy the conditions mentioned above. It must also demonstrate the legal basis for its regulatory function in respect of the profession. Following designation, responsibility for oversight of professional bodies lies with the FSA. It is required to keep itself informed of the manner in which professional bodies exercise their supervisory function and the way in which members of the profession carry on their activities. The FSA also has residual powers to 'knock out' the exemption for the professional body in whole or in part or to 'knock out' a particular firm if it is not a fit and proper person to carry on the relevant regulated activity subject to an exemption.[69]

3.4.4 Jurisdiction

The 'general prohibition' contained in section 19 FSMA 2000 applies to the carrying on of regulated activity in the UK. Section 418 identifies five cases in which a person carrying on a regulated activity, who would not otherwise be regarded as carrying it on in the UK, will be regarded as doing so. They relate to cases in which persons based in the UK (according to various criteria) carry on regulated activities overseas (whether in the EU under Treaty or Directive rights or elsewhere in the world). The general principle is that such persons are treated as carrying on regulated activity in the UK and therefore subject to FSMA 2000 system of regulation. The objective is 'anti-avoidance' and it is consistent with the general 'home country control' principle that is now well established in the EU and gaining increasing acceptance across the world.

---

[67] FSMA 2000, s 327(4). See also Art 2(1)(c) of MiFID.
[68] The FSMA 2000 (Professions) (Non-exempt activities) Order 2001, SI 2001/1227.
[69] See respectively ss 328 and 329 FSMA 2000.

3.4.5 Unauthorised activity

Engaging in regulated activities without authorisation is a criminal offence.[70] It is not, however, a criminal offence for an authorised person to engage in activities for which no permission has been granted by the FSA, but this may give rise to disciplinary action. An agreement made by a person acting in contravention of the general prohibition (ie an unauthorised person) cannot be enforced against the other party.[71] The latter is entitled to recover any money or property transferred and compensation for any loss sustained as a result of having parted with it. However, provision is made for a court to allow an agreement made by an authorised person to be enforced against the customer if it is just and equitable to allow the agreement to be enforced.[72] The court must consider whether the authorised person reasonably believed he was not contravening the general prohibition.[73]

3.5 Regulated activities

The definition of regulated activities is central to the system of regulation because it defines the sphere of activity in respect of which authorisation is required (the 'regulatory perimeter'). Section 22(1) FSMA 2000 provides as follows:

> An activity is a regulated activity for the purposes of this Act if it is an activity of a specified kind which is carried on by way of business and—
>
> (a) relates to an investment of a specified kind;
> (b) in the case of an activity of a kind which is also specified for the purposes of this paragraph, is carried on in relation to property of any kind.

This rather opaque formulation creates two routes through which activity may be regulated. The first is that it is a specified activity relating to an investment of a specified kind.[74] The second is that it is a specified activity carried on in respect of any property. The purpose of paragraph (b) of section 22(1) is to bring within the scope of regulation activities that would not otherwise be regulated. For example, property (land and buildings) is not a specified investment, but paragraph (b) allows direct property investment to be brought within FSMA 2000 in certain circumstances. This has occurred in respect of

---

[70] FSMA 2000, s 19.

[71] FSMA 2000, s 26. In effect, a party entering an agreement with an unauthorised person is given the option of enforcing the agreement. That section does not apply to unauthorised deposit-taking, in respect of which there is a special provision in s 29.

[72] FSMA 2000, s 28.

[73] For an example of such an agreement being enforced see *Helden v Strathmore Ltd* [2010] EWHC 2012 (Ch).

[74] Para (a) of s 22(1) (quoted above).

direct property investment undertaken by collective investment schemes and stakeholder pension schemes.[75]

The Treasury is authorised to make an order defining what is meant by a specified activity or specified investment, and has made the Financial Services Services and Markets Act 2000 (Regulated Activities) Order 2001[76] (RAO). The RAO provides a more detailed definition of specified activities and investments than the Act itself. Before turning to the detail of the RAO, it should be noted that, to fall within the scope of FSMA 2000, the relevant activity must satisfy three requirements. First, the activity must be carried on by way of business. Whether an activity is carried on in this manner is determined by an order (the 'Business Order'[77]) made by the Treasury.[78] Persons (natural or legal) acting solely for their own account do not fall within the scope of the Act. Secondly, the activity must relate to a specified investment or be carried on in relation to property of any kind. Investments are defined in schedule 2 to the Act and in the RAO, and are discussed in more detail in Chapter 4. Finally, the activity must be of a kind specified by schedule 2 FSMA or the RAO. The activities specified by the RAO are set out below.[79]

Accepting deposits

This activity has been the traditional foundation on which banking regulation has been based in the UK. It reflects the emphasis in banking regulation on the protection of depositors. Certain types of deposit made other than in the context of banking business (eg a deposit that is a pre-payment for goods) are excluded from the RAO. Deposits will not be considered to be accepted by way of business if a person does not hold himself out as accepting deposits on a day-to-day basis and any deposits which he accepts are accepted only on particular occasions. However, the point at which this threshold will be crossed is not entirely clear, and over-reliance on the exemption opens up the real possibility of engaging in unauthorised activity.[80]

Issuing electronic money

The RAO has recently been amended to include the issuing of electronic money. 'Electronic money' means electronically (including magnetically) stored monetary value as represented by a claim on the electronic money issuer which—

---

[75] Arts 51 and 52 respectively of the RAO.

[76] SI 2001/544.

[77] See FSMA 2000 (Carrying on Regulated Activities by Way of Business) Order 2001 (SI 2001/1177) for more detail.

[78] See *Helden v Strathmore Ltd* [2010] EWHC 2012 (Ch) para 85 for a discussion of the 'by way of business' test in s 22 FSMA 2000 and the 'business of engaging in that activity' test in Art 3A of the Business Order.

[79] This section is intended to provide an overview of the RAO. As each regulated activity is subject to detailed conditions and exceptions, reference must be made to the RAO to decide whether a particular activity falls within its scope.

[80] See *FSA v Anderson* [2010] EWHC 599 (Ch) for an instance in which the exemption was held not to apply as a result of the regular taking of substantial deposits with a view to making money on the interest rate 'spread' as between the rate paid to depositors and the rate achieved on the invested fund.

1. is issued on receipt of funds for the purpose of making payment transactions; and
2. is accepted by a person other than the electronic money issuer.[81]

The EU Directive on Electronic Money requires that issuers be authorised by the relevant authority in their home state and that a register of issuers be maintained by that authority. The primary requirements of the Directive and the Regulations in respect of the issuance and redemption of electronic money are that:

An electronic money issuer must—

(a) on receipt of funds, issue without delay electronic money at par value; and
(b) at the request of the electronic money holder, redeem—
   (i) at any time; and
   (ii) at par value,

the monetary value of the electronic money held.[82]

Insurance

Effecting or carrying out a contract of insurance as a principal is a regulated activity. While there is no general definition of a contract of insurance in FSMA 2000, the RAO does refer to contracts that cover 'miscellaneous financial loss'.[83] While the FSA has issued guidance[84] on the identification of insurance contracts for the purposes of FSMA 2000, it does not provide clarity with regard to the issue of whether credit default swaps (CDSs) fall within the definition.[85] The RAO excludes from its scope the activities of EEA insurers carried out under freedom of services and in relation to co-insurance, in respect of which there are EU directives in force. Annuity contracts (such as personal pensions or 'insured' group pensions) are included within the definition of insurance, as is 'breakdown' insurance provided by motoring organisations.

Dealing in investments as a principal

This category applies most obviously to market-makers[86] and 'proprietary trading' activities within investment banks, whose business consists principally of buying and

---

[81] The Electronic Money Regulations 2011, SI 2011/99, Art 2. The Regulations implement EU Directive 2009/110 on the taking up, pursuit and prudential supervision of the business of electronic money institutions with effect from 30 April 2011. As it represents 'stored value', electronic money is not consumer credit within the meaning of the Consumer Credit Act 1974.

[82] SI 2011/99, Art 39.

[83] SI 2001/544, sch 1, pt 1, para 16. It was held in *Re Digital Satellite Warranty Cover Ltd* [2011] EWHC 122 (Ch) that this covered extended warranty insurance, even though the obligation was to repair or replace rather than pay money. It followed that the sale of such warranties without authorisation from the FSA was a breach of s 19 FSMA 2000.

[84] See FSA Handbook, PERG 6.

[85] See further L Gullifer and J Payne, *Corporate Finance Law* (Oxford, Hart Publishing, 2011) ch 5.3.3, referring to a leading legal opinion that has been widely relied on to support the view that CDSs are not insurance. The issue carries significant implications for the regulatory position of participants in the CDS Market.

[86] On the role of market-makers, see Chapter 14.1.2.

selling investments as a principal with a view to making a profit. The RAO makes clear that this category of specified activity applies only to persons engaged in dealing as a business and not persons who deal in investments in the course of carrying on a separate business (eg fund management).[87]

Dealing in investments as agent

Buying, selling, subscribing for or underwriting securities or relevant investments (such as options) as an agent is a specified activity. There are exclusions from this type of activity. An important one relates to transactions arranged by an agent who is not an authorised person where the client enters the transaction on advice given by an authorised person. Another exclusion is acting as an agent in respect of 'hedging' risks (such as fluctuations in currencies or commodity prices) arising in a business that is not engaged in 'regulated activity' (eg oil companies).

Arranging deals in investments

Making arrangements for another person (whether as principal or agent) to buy, sell, subscribe for or underwrite particular investments[88] is a specified kind of activity. This category is intended to deal with persons involved in making arrangements for other persons in circumstances in which they are not the agent of that person. An example would be a person operating, on an independent basis, a system that enables investors to buy and sell securities from each other (a 'multilateral trading facility'[89]). Included in this category are arrangements made for another person to enter into a regulated mortgage contract. However, mere 'introductions' to an authorised or exempt person with a view to the provision of independent advice or the independent exercise of discretion (eg as an asset manager) are excluded.[90]

Managing investments

Managing investments belonging to another person, in circumstances involving the exercise of discretion, is generally a specified kind of activity.[91]

Managing the investments of an occupational pension scheme (defined in the RAO as a scheme limited to providing benefits to a defined category of employees) is, subject to exceptions, a specified activity. Authorisation is not required if a trustee[92] does not hold himself out as providing an investment management service or if the trustee is not acting in a business capacity. A trustee does not act in a business capacity when:

---

[87] The RAO also makes clear that companies who (i) issue their own shares or (ii) purchase their own shares to be held in 'treasury' under s 724 of the Companies Act 2006 do not engage in regulated activity.

[88] See Art 25 of the RAO.

[89] See Chapter 12.3.2.

[90] Art 38 of the RAO, but note that the exclusion does not apply to insurance contracts.

[91] Art 37 of the RAO.

[92] A trustee is responsible for the investment of trust funds and an occupational pension fund is a trust fund. See generally Chapter 5.1.

- routine investment decisions are delegated to an authorised person with relevant permission, an exempt person or an overseas person;
- the trustee is a beneficiary of the scheme (eg an employee); or
- the trustee has no part in routine investment decisions.[93]

The activity of managing investments is not carried on by a person acting under a power of attorney if all routine investment decisions are taken by an authorised person with permission to carry on this activity.

Assisting in the administration and performance of a contract of insurance

This specified activity is in principle wide ranging, but is subject to several exclusions which narrow its scope considerably. [94] The following do not fall within this specified activity:

1. expert appraisal;
2. loss adjusting on behalf of a relevant insurer;[95] or
3. managing claims on behalf of a relevant insurer, and that activity is carried on in the course of carrying on any profession or business.

Safeguarding and administering investments

This is a regulated activity if the assets include any investment which is a security or contractually based investment or may do so.[96] It is immaterial that the title to assets is held in uncertificated form.[97] An authorised person with permission to engage in this activity is a 'qualifying custodian'. Arranging for another person to safeguard or administer investments is a regulated activity, but mere introduction of a customer to a qualifying custodian is not.

Sending dematerialised instructions

This category is intended to bring within the scope of FSMA 2000 persons involved in sending instructions relating to the transfer of legal title to securities that are held in dematerialised form (ie ownership is recorded in a computer system rather than on a paper certificate).[98] The activity relates to instructions sent within a relevant system in respect of which an Operator is approved under the Uncertificated Securities Regulations 2001. There are exemptions from the scope of this activity, notably in respect of participating issuers (who are not normally engaged in regulated activity).

---

[93] Art 66(3) of the RAO and Art 4 of the Business Order (SI 2001/1177).
[94] Arts 39A and 39B of the RAO.
[95] Meaning an insurer that is authorised to carry on insurance business under FSMA 2000.
[96] Art 40 of the RAO.
[97] See Chapter 4.12 as to the meaning of uncertificated securities.
[98] Art 45 of the RAO. See Chapter 4.4.2 regarding dematerialisation.

Collective investment schemes [99]

The following are specified activities:

1. establishing, operating or winding up a collective investment scheme;
2. acting as trustee of an authorised unit trust scheme;
3. acting as the depositary or sole director of an open-ended investment company (OEIC).

These activities are also specified for the purposes of section 22(1)(b) FSMA 2000, with the result that they are regulated activities when carried on in respect of property of any kind (eg investing scheme assets in land and buildings, which are not specified investments).[100]

Stakeholder and personal pension schemes

Establishing, operating or winding up a stakeholder or personal pension scheme[101] is a specified kind of activity and is also specified for the purposes of section 22(1)(b) FSMA 2000.[102] Operating an occupational pension scheme is not a specified activity under the RAO, but, as noted above, managing the investments of such a scheme may be one.

Advising on investments

This is generally a specified activity. Included within the scope of the activity is advice given to a person in his capacity as agent for an investor or potential investor. Also included is advice given on insurance contracts (both life assurance and general insurance); this extension of the scope of the activity of 'advising' became effective on 14 January 2005, and a new section of the FSA Handbook entitled 'Insurance: Conduct of Business Sourcebook (ICOB)' was created for this purpose. ICOB also implemented two European Community measures that have significant implications for general insurance broking: the Insurance Mediation Directive[103] and the Distance Marketing Directive.[104] Advising on mortgages is covered by a specific regulated activity (below). Generic investment advice in newspapers and other publications is excluded if it does not advise on particular investments or lead or enable persons to deal in securities. Providing basic advice to a retail consumer on a stakeholder product is a distinct form of specified activity.[105]

Activities linked with Lloyd's of London

Underwriting contracts of insurance as a principal in the Lloyd's insurance market is

---

[99] The structure, operation and regulation of collective investment schemes is discussed in Chapter 4.10.
[100] Art 4(2) of the RAO.
[101] See Chapter 4.12 for the meaning of these terms.
[102] See the comment on collective investment schemes in the text above.
[103] Directive 2002/92/EC [2003] OJ L9/3.
[104] Directive 2002/65/EC [2002] OJ L 271/16.
[105] Art 52B of the RAO.

covered by the specified activity of insurance (above) in the RAO. Other activities which are specified are:[106]

- advising a person to become, or continue or cease to be, a member of a particular Lloyd's syndicate;[107]
- managing the underwriting capacity of a Lloyd's syndicate as a managing agent;
- the arranging of deals in contracts of insurance written at Lloyd's by the Society of Lloyd's (ie the activity of a Lloyd's broker).

Funeral plan contracts

Entering as provider into a funeral plan contract is a specified activity, subject to exclusions.[108] The purpose of a funeral plan contract is to meet the costs of the funeral of the customer.

Regulated mortgage contracts

Mortgages often represent a major, and often the largest, long-term financial committment of households. Despite this, mortgages were not included in the definition of investments under FSA 1986, with the result that neither mortgage lending nor advising on mortgages fell within the scope of regulated activities under that Act. The regulatory gap was eventually filled in 1997 by a self-regulatory 'Mortgage Code', which was overseen by a body called the Mortgage Code Compliance Board. However, it soon became clear that some form of statutory regulation would be introduced. The Treasury's initial proposal was to bring mortgage lending within the scope of regulated activities, and appropriate provisions were included in the RAO. They did not, however, come into effect as originally planned in September 2003. Instead, regulation of mortgage lending was introduced at the same time as regulation of mortgage advice on 31 October 2004. From that date, a number of activities that are undertaken in respect of 'regulated mortgage contracts' are specified activities,[109] and a new part of the FSA Handbook, the Mortgage Conduct of Business Rules (MCOB), took effect.

To qualify as a 'regulated mortgage contract', the following conditions must be met:[110]

1. the borrower must be an individual or trustee;
2. the contract must be entered into after mortgage regulation comes into force (31 October 2004);
3. the lender must take a first charge over UK property;
4. the property must be at least 40% occupied by the borrower or his immediate family.

---

[106] Arts 56–58 of the RAO.

[107] Generic advice on whether to become a member of Lloyd's is not included in this activity.

[108] Art 60 of the RAO.

[109] See FSMA 2000 (Regulated Activities) (Amendment) (No 1) Order 2003, SI 2003/1475.

[110] See Art 61 of the RAO. Loans that do not fall within this definition (eg a mortgage which is a second charge) may be subject to regulation under the Consumer Credit Act 1974. Responsibility for licensing under that Act lies with the OFT.

The following are specified activities in respect of such contracts:

- entering into or administering;[111]
- arranging;[112]
- advising.[113]

Appointed representatives (also known as 'tied agents') do not have the option of becoming authorised for the purposes of mortgage advice, as the FSMA does not permit the same person to be both exempt from authorisation[114] in respect of some activities and authorised for others. Professional firms that carry on regulated activity that is incidental to their profession can engage in a similar fashion in arranging and advising on mortgages. This activity does not include recommending particular products to clients, for which authorisation is necessary. With the introduction of mortgage regulation, the scope of the financial promotion regime[115] has been extended to include promotion relating to arranging and advising in respect of regulated mortgage contracts.

Regulated agreements relating to land and homes

The RAO specifies as regulated activities the entering into and administering of three types of agreement that have become quite common in recent years as techniques to release equity tied up in a home so as to fund retirement or care home expenses. The three types of agreement are as follows:

1. Home reversion plans. Under this type of agreement a provider agrees to buy an interest in land or a home. The seller remains entitled to live in the property, but that right terminates on the occurrence of specified events, such as admittance to a care home.
2. Home purchase plans. This type of agreement is similar to 1 above except that the seller does not lose the right to occupy the home. In this case, the purchase price effectively acts as a form of income for the seller over the specified period, but leaves the seller with no asset at the end of the period.
3. Sale and rent back agreements. Under this form of agreement the seller transfers ownership to the provider, but then has the right to remain in the home as tenant rather than owner.

Agreeing to carry on activities

Agreeing to carry on most of the activities referred to above is a specified activity.[116] This brings within the scope of FSMA 2000 persons who have not yet commenced the relevant

---

[111] Art 61 of the RAO.
[112] Art 25A of the RAO.
[113] Art 53A of the RAO.
[114] Under s 39 FSMA 2000, appointed representatives are exempt from authorisation.
[115] See section 3.6 below.
[116] Exceptions are accepting deposits, effecting and carrying out contracts of insurance or carrying on any of the collective investment scheme activities or activities in relation to stakeholder pension schemes.

activity but have agreed to do so. It has implications for persons who plan to provide services in respect of which they do not currently have permission.

Dormant account funds

The Dormant Bank and Building Societies Accounts Act 2008 put into place a legislative framework that allows dormant accounts (ie those that have been inactive for 15 years and therefore appear to have no claimant) to be used for social and environmental purposes. As part of that framework, the Act enables the creation of so-called 'reclaim funds' to whom dormant accounts can be paid. Two activities associated with such reclaim funds are specified activities: the meeting of repayment claims to (dormant) account holders or their successors;[117] and the management of dormant account funds (including the investment of such funds) by a reclaim fund.

Exclusions applying to several specified kinds of activity

This part of the RAO excludes certain types of activity from its scope. These are:

1. some of the activities of trustees and personal representatives;
2. activities carried on in the course of a profession or non-investment business which are a necessary part of that business and are not remunerated separately;
3. the provision of information on an incidental basis about an insurance contract;
4. activities carried on in connection with the sale of goods or the supply of services;
5. transactions between members of corporate groups and joint enterprises;
6. activities carried on in connection with the sale of a body corporate;
7. activities carried on in connection with employee share schemes; and
8. various activities carried on by an overseas person.

The general policy of these exclusions is to ensure that the scope of regulated activities does not require businesses and professional firms whose main activity is not financial services to be authorised under FSMA 2000.

3.6 The financial promotion regime

The financial promotion regime had no direct counterpart under FSA 1986. It has two main purposes. First, it prohibits financial promotion on the part of unauthorised persons. Authorised persons are permitted to engage in financial promotion and when they do so are regulated by FSA rules.[118] Secondly, it unites in a single regime a variety of regulatory

---

[117] In which case the designation of the account as 'dormant' is effectively lifted.

[118] These rules form part of the Conduct of Business Sourcebook (COBS, part 4) rather than being part of the financial promotion regime itself.

controls relating to financial promotion that had in the past existed under FSA 1986, the Banking Act 1987 and the Insurance Companies Act 1982. These controls related to the advertising, marketing and sales techniques used to promote the financial products falling within each of the three regulatory regimes (above) that predated FSMA 2000. Of particular significance in the context of investment were the controls over advertising (section 57 FSA 1986 and rules made under it), unsolicited calls (section 57 FSA 1986 and relevant rules), promotion of unregulated collective investment schemes (section 76 FSA 1986) and promotion of certain long-term insurance contracts (section 130 FSA 1986). By consolidating these controls, the Financial Promotion Regime provides a single point of reference for determining whether a person can engage in financial promotion.

Financial promotion is not the same as regulated activity. While the distinction introduces considerable complexity into the regulatory system, it has been justified on the basis that the FSA should be able to take action when an unauthorised person attempts to induce a potential customer into a transaction without waiting until regulated activity has commenced. Under FSA 1986, 'investment business' included 'offering' to engage in such business, with the result that promotion fell within that Act's definition of regulated activity.[119] That is no longer the case, as under FSMA 2000 an unauthorised person contravenes the general prohibition only at the stage of agreeing to carry on a regulated activity and not before.[120] It has also been justified on the basis that the territorial scope of the financial promotion regime should be broader than that of 'regulated activities' so as to limit promotions aimed at the UK from overseas persons falling outside the scope of the RAO.

Section 21 of the FSMA forms the basis of the financial promotion regime. It provides:

(1) A person ('A') must not, in the course of business, communicate an invitation or inducement to engage in investment activity.
(2) But subsection (1) does not apply if—
  (a) A is an authorised person; or
  (b) the content of the communication is approved for the purposes of this section by an authorised person.
(3) In the case of a communication originating outside the United Kingdom, subsection (1) applies only if the communication is capable of having an effect in the United Kingdom.

A number of points can be made. First, 'in the course of business' appears to mean in the course of any business and not just regulated activity. 'Communicate' appears to include not just the source of the communication but also persons involved in its delivery (in whatever format) to the potential customer. The FSA, in its Financial Promotion Guidance,[121] takes the view that a person communicates where he is responsible for giving or transmitting material to a third party. Thus publishers and broadcasters who publish advertisements fall within the regime while printers, postal services, advertising

---

[119] See FSA 1986 (repealed), sch 1, 2.
[120] See Art 64 of the RAO. The reference to 'agreeing' indicates that there must be a legally binding contract for the carrying on of a regulated activity.
[121] See FSA Handbook, PERG 8.

agencies and courier services would either not be considered to be communicating or could take advantage of the 'mere conduit' exemption.[122]

'Engaging in investment activity' is defined by section 21(8) as:

(a) entering or offering to enter into an agreement the making or performance of which by either party constitutes a controlled activity; or
(b) exercising any rights conferred by a controlled investment to acquire, dispose of, underwrite or convert a controlled investment.

'Controlled activities' and 'controlled investments' are defined (at some length) in an Order made by the Treasury under section 21 FSMA 2000.[123] Although these categories overlap to a significant extent with 'specified activities' and 'specified investments' under the RAO, there are important differences. In general, the exclusions set out in the RAO do not apply, so that. while a person may not require authorisation because he is not carrying on a regulated activity by way of business, he may find that his communications are subject to the financial promotion prohibition.

The restriction on financial promotion does not apply to a communication if the content of the communication is approved for the purposes of section 21 by an authorised person. The approval process is controlled by Conduct of Business Rules made by the FSA.[124] As far as territorial application is concerned the prohibition applies to communications originating outside the UK that are capable of having an effect within the UK but does not generally apply to communications made to persons receiving it outside the UK or which is directed only at persons outside the UK.[125] The restriction does not prevent the provision of information to a customer at the customer's initiative nor communications that enable such a customer to acquire a controlled investment or to be supplied with a controlled service.[126]

3.7 Rule-making

3.7.1 Powers

The nature of FSMA 2000 is that it is an enabling statute. It contains only a basic framework for the system of financial regulation, leaving much of the detail to rules made by the regulator and the style of supervision adopted by the regulator. The rule-making powers of the FSA are therefore central to the whole system.

The FSA has both general and specific rule-making powers. The general rule-making

---

[122] Art 18 of the Financial Promotion Order (below).
[123] The FSMA 2000 (Financial Promotion) Order 2005 SI 2005/1529, replacing SI 2001/1335.
[124] See FSA Handbook, COBS 4.10.
[125] Art 12 of the Financial Promotion Order.
[126] Art 13 of the Financial Promotion Order.

power authorises it to make rules that apply to authorised persons with respect to them carrying on any activities (whether or not regulated activities) as appear necessary or expedient for the purpose of meeting any of its regulatory obligations.[127] Statutory recognition that rules may apply in different ways to different persons or activities allows the Authority to continue the practice of distinguishing between different types of customer and investor in its rulebook.[128] There are also specific rule-making powers.[129] Also relevant here are the FSMA provisions relating to the manner in which the FSA carries out its functions. One of the FSA's general functions under the Act is making rules, and the Act requires that, in discharging its general functions, the Authority must have regard to, inter alia, the principle that the costs of regulation should be proportionate to the benefits.[130]

The rule-making procedure under FSMA 2000 is more formal and detailed than that under FSA 1986.[131] The FSA must publish a draft of proposed rules for public consultation and must take account of any representations when making the rules. Such representations are likely to be made by the Consumer and Practitioner Panels which the Authority is required to establish and maintain.[132] The consultation draft must be accompanied by an explanation of the purpose of the proposed rules. The FSA must also, in most circumstances, publish a cost–benefit analysis with a draft of the rules. If the rules differ significantly from the consultation draft, the FSA is required to publish details of the difference and another cost–benefit analysis.

3.7.2 The FSA Handbook

The FSA has used these powers to make its rulebook, the Handbook of Rules and Guidance.[133] The Handbook is divided into several blocks, which are in turn divided into topics. There are seven main blocks as follows:

1 High-level standards. This contains, inter alia, statements of principle applicable to businesses and approved persons.
2 Prudential standards. This block contains standards for regulatory capital and liquidity for banks, insurers and investment firms.
3 Business standards. This block contains the Conduct of Business (COBS) and Market Conduct sourcebooks.

---

[127] FSMA 2000, s 138 (as amended by s 3(4) FSA 2010). FSA 2010 extended the FSA's general rule making power to include any regulatory objective: it had previously been limited to rules that were necessary or expedient to protect consumers (which included professional investors as well as retail investors).

[128] See s 156(1) FSMA 2000.

[129] See ss 144–47 FSMA 2000, which empower the Authority to make price stabilising rules, financial promotion rules, money laundering rules and control of information rules.

[130] FSMA 2000, s 2(3)(c). The costs of regulation are borne initially by authorised persons and ultimately by investors (assuming that such costs are passed down the chain of transactions to final investors).

[131] See s 155 FSMA 2000.

[132] See ss 8–10 FSMA 2000.

[133] The handbook is available online at www.fsa.gov.uk (accessed on 22 August 2011). See the Reader's Guide to the Handbook for details regarding structure and content.

4 Regulatory processes. Included in this block are the Authorisation, Supervision (SUP) and Enforcement manuals.
5 Redress. This contains the complaints and compensation sourcebooks.
6 Specialist sourcebooks, including those applicable to collective investment schemes, recognised exchanges and the Lloyd's insurance market.
7 Listing, prospectus and disclosure. This block contains the UKLA Listing Rules, the rules for public offers and prospectuses, and the disclosure obligations of issuers whose securities are listed.

The status of each provision in the Handbook is indicated by a letter attached to it as follows:

R indicates rules, which can be general rules made under section 138 FSMA 2000 or rules made under other specific powers provided by the Act. Included in this category are the FSA's Principles for Businesses. Most of the rules in the Handbook create binding obligations on firms. If a firm contravenes such a rule, it may be subject to enforcement action and, in certain circumstances, to an action for damages.
D indicates directions and requirements given under various powers conferred by the Act. They are binding upon the persons or categories of person to whom they are addressed.
P indicates Statements of Principle for Approved Persons made under section 64 of the Act. The Statements of Principle are binding on approved persons.
C indicates 'safe harbours' (conclusive descriptions of compliant behaviour in respect of the market abuse regime) specified under section 119(2) of the Act.
E indicates evidential provisions, specified in section 149 FSMA, which are discussed below.
G indicates guidance given by the Authority under section 157 FSMA (discussed below).

It follows from this structure that the FSA Handbook comprises diverse provisions that have different effects. Some have no binding effect (guidance). Others are binding but are expressed with differing levels of detail (principles and rules). Some are binding but only for the purposes of disciplinary action by the FSA, and are not actionable in law (principles).[134] Others serve the purpose of more clearly delimiting the scope and application of related rules (safe harbours and evidential provisions). Evidential provisions are intended to make clear when compliance with or contravention of one rule (A) will result in compliance with or contravention of another rule (B). An evidential provision must either provide that contravention of rule A tends to establish contravention of rule B or that compliance with rule A tends to establish compliance with rule B. Their effect is to move the burden of proving compliance with rule B on to a firm when it is in contravention of rule A and of proving contravention of rule B on to the FSA when a firm is in compliance with rule A. In that sense, they create rebuttable presumptions of compliance with or contravention of the binding rules to which they refer. 'Safe harbours' differ from evidential provisions in two important ways. First, they relate only to the

---

[134] See section 3.7.3 for more detail.

market abuse regime. Secondly, behaviour in conformity with a safe harbour is, by virtue of section 122 FSMA 2000, conclusively not market abuse. In this sense, safe harbours provide guarantees in respect of behaviour while evidential provisions do not.

Guidance can consist only of information and advice, and therefore cannot impose obligations.[135] It can take the form of general guidance given to the public, regulated persons or a class of regulated persons, or, alternatively, specific guidance given to an individual or firm.[136] Compliance with guidance provides no immunity from regulatory action taken by the FSA in respect of a contravention of the Act or rules made under it, but the FSA has made clear that action will not normally be taken against a firm or individual in respect of behaviour in line with general or specific guidance.[137]

Finally, the FSA may also, in some circumstances, give directions. For example, when it decides to modify or waive the application of a particular rule, the FSA gives a direction to that effect. There are normally particular conditions attached to the making of directions.

3.7.3 Principles versus rules

A contrast is often made between regulatory systems as regards the extent to which they are based on principles and rules respectively.[138] According to this approach, principles are broadly based standards that encourage compliance with their spirit as well as their letter. Their broad formulation permits the regulator considerable discretion in interpreting and applying the principles but, viewed from the perspective of the regulated community, they create some uncertainty as to the precise nature of the regulatory obligations. By way of contrast, a system that focuses more on rules formulates regulatory obligations more precisely and concentrates on compliance with the letter of the rules; this provides greater certainty to the regulated community but opens up more scope for 'creative compliance',[139] which respects the letter of the rule but not the spirit. While it is often claimed that systems are either 'principles based' or 'rules based', it is probably more accurate to say that all system use both principles and rules to varying degrees, and that the differences relate to the extent to which each is employed.[140]

The FSA has been a strong proponent of the principles-based approach, primarily on the basis that it represents a better way to structure regulatory obligations than a more

---

[135] See ss 157 and 158 FSMA 2000.

[136] The FSA can make a reasonable charge for guidance given to a person on request.

[137] See FSA Policy Statement, 'The FSA's Approach to Giving Guidance and Waivers to Firms' (September 1999).

[138] See generally J Black, M Hopper and C Band, 'Making a Success of Principles-based Regulation' (2007) 1(3) *Law and Financial Markets Review* 191.

[139] See generally D Mc Barnet and C Whelan, *Creative Accounting and the Cross-eyed Javelin Thrower* (Chichester, John Wiley, 1999).

[140] See CL Ford, 'New Governance, Compliance and Principles-Based Securities Regulation', available at http://ssrn.com/abstract=970130. A cursory glance at the sheer scale of the FSA Handbook of Rules and Guidance (see www.fsa.gov.uk) serves to illustrate the point.

rules-based approach. Prior to the global financial crisis, the FSA's case for principles-based regulation was that:[141]

1. detailed prescriptive standards have not in the past prevented misconduct;
2. the current volume and complexity of FSA standards acts as both a barrier to entry and a barrier to compliance;
3. prescriptive rules divert attention towards compliance with the letter rather than the spirit of the standard;
4. many issues are not dealt with adequately by prescriptive standards, or can be dealt with in that way only at the cost of making the system overly complex;
5. prescriptive standards are costly for FSA and consumer resources.

While the FSA's principles-based approach was widely viewed as successful in the pre-crisis era, the onset of the global financial crisis, and in particular the severity with which it affected UK financial institutions and the broader economy, caused some re-evaluation. It was clear, ever since the FSA Chief Executive remarked that 'A principles-based approach does not work with individuals who have no principles',[142] that some change was likely in the FSA's approach. While there is little evidence to date of any substantial change in the formal position of principles within the FSA rulebook, both the FSA's re-denomination of principles-based regulation as 'outcomes-focused regulation' and the change in basic regulatory philosophy and style outlined below[143] suggest that there may well be significant changes 'in action'.

On the other hand, a recent test case[144] brought by the British Bankers Association (BBA) challenging the manner in which the FSA treated principles as imposing obligations on authorised firms provides important legal authority for the FSA's principles-based approach. The dispute in this case focused on whether it was lawful for the FSA to rely on principles to impose obligations on firms requiring them to compensate customers for their breach. The context of the dispute was that the FSA had responded to widespread concern about consumer detriment resulting from mis-selling of payment protection insurance (PPI) in connection with consumer loans by amending the FSA Handbook provisions on handling PPI sales complaints and issuing an Open Letter identifying common failings. The BBA challenged the lawfulness of the FSA Policy Statement that set out these changes by arguing that:

• the FSA could not rely on principles to create obligations for firms since they are not actionable in law; and
• that, since the FSA had made specific (conduct of business) rules on PPI sales, it was unlawful for the FSA to provide in its Policy Statement that a customer might

---

[141] See A Whittaker, FSA Director General Counsel, 'Professional and Financial Regulation—Conflict or Convergence?', speech delivered at the Fountain Court Chambers Conference, 31 January 2006, available at http://www.fsa.gov.uk/pages/Library/Communication/Speeches/2006/0131_aw.shtml4.

[142] H Sants, 'Delivering Intensive Supervision and Credible Deterrence', speech delivered at the Reuters Newsmaker Event, 12 March 2009, available at www.fsa.gov.uk/pages/Library/Communication/Speeches/2009/0312_hs.shtml.

[143] See below section 3.8.3.

[144] *R (ex parte British Bankers Association) v FSA* [2011] EWHC 999 (Admin).

be entitled to redress by reference to principles which conflicted with or augmented those specific rules.

The High Court rejected both of these arguments and, in so doing, provided an important endorsement of the lawfulness of the FSA's policy of principles-based regulation. The court's reasoning provides a succinct overview of the legal context and the manner in which principles-based regulation operates:

> The Principles are the overarching framework for regulation, for good reason. The FSA has clearly not promulgated, and has chosen not to promulgate, a detailed all-embracing comprehensive code of regulations to be interpreted as covering all possible circumstances. The industry had not wanted such a code either. Such a code could be circumvented unfairly, or contain provisions which were not apt for the many and varied sales circumstances which could arise. The overarching framework would always be in place to be the fundamental provision which would always govern the actions of firms, as well as to cover all those circumstances not provided for or adequately provided for by specific rules.[145]

Thus, the FSA has a solid legal basis for continuing to rely on principles as a source of obligations. However, that in itself does not resolve the issue of whether the principles-based approach represents the best way for the FSA to pursue its regulatory objectives. Indeed, to the extent that the PPI test case can be viewed as a case study of the failure of principles-based regulation (prior to FSA intervention) to secure appropriate outcomes for consumers in situations where there are gaps in the detailed rules, it might well be argued that it does not support a principles-based approach to regulation. However, that is probably an overly pessimistic reading of the case, and a more balanced view would be that the case demonstrates the capacity of principles-based regulation to signal to authorised firms how to deal with (inevitable) gaps in detailed rules by reference to high-level principles.

3.8 Risk-based regulation

3.8.1 Risk-control strategies[146]

While the descriptor 'risk-based regulation' is of relatively recent origin, the technique itself is not. The concept of controlling excessive or abusive instances of activity that is prima facie socially beneficial has a long history both within discrete regulatory regimes and in the general law. Regulatory regimes generally adopt three high-level strategies

---

[145] Ibid at para 161 (Ousely J).

[146] This section is drawn substantially from I MacNeil, 'Risk Control Strategies: An Assessment in the Context of the Credit Crisis' MacNeil and O'Brien, above n 36, ch 9.

for controlling risk-taking:[147] prohibition, limitation or remedy (see Table 1). Whilst, in principle, each represents a different approach, there is some overlap, and regulatory regimes typically combine the three approaches. The three generic approaches remain the same irrespective of the institutional arrangements for regulation within any system, although there may well be issues as to how well each strategy can operate when responsibility is split across different regulatory authorities.

Table 1 Generic Risk Control Strategies

	Prevent	**Limit**	**Remedy**
Substance	Prohibition	Risk threshold	Liability standard
Process			
Ex ante	Licensing	Supervision	Deterrence
Ex post	Enforcement:exclusion/ containment/penalty	Negotiated correction/ penalty	Enforcement: restitution/ compensation/penalty

The prohibition strategy is used for three main purposes: (i) to control entry[148] into regulated activity; (ii) to constrain the activities of authorised firms; and (iii) to prohibit conduct within the system that directly threatens the objectives of the regulatory system. Examples of the first within the UK regulatory system are the criminal offence of engaging in regulated activity without authorisation and the prohibition on 'controlled activities' being performed by anyone other than an 'approved person'.[149] An example of the second is the constraint imposed on authorised firms by the concept of 'permitted activities', which represent the subset of regulated activity in which an authorised firm is permitted to engage. An example of the third is the 'market abuse' regime.[150] The attraction of the prohibition strategy is that it draws a clear dividing line between what is and what is not permitted. It does, however, have several disadvantages. First, at least in it simplest form, it is a crude mechanism that lacks flexibility. Moreover, in its more sophisticated forms (eg the market abuse regime) it risks losing legal certainty since the prohibition becomes so nuanced that it can be difficult to understand and apply. Secondly, the prohibition strategy limits the potential role of the regulator as a supervisor as opposed to an enforcer of regulatory rules. The extent to which that occurs will depend on how the prohibition is framed. Thus, for example, a 'fit and proper' test for entry into regulated activity by firms and individuals can in itself open up a broad role for a regulator even within a system that emphasises prohibition. Thirdly, the prohibition strategy is open in some cases to avoidance through regulatory arbitrage. That will be the case particularly when activities can be transferred to jurisdictions in which the activity is not prohibited

---

[147] Risk-taking behaviour is a subset of the entire set of risks that a regulatory system confronts. It is most obviously linked with credit risk, market risk and systemic risk.

[148] And in some cases exit: see the rules on de-listing of SEC-registered companies, which constrain the ability of companies to de-list in the US.

[149] Respectively, FSMA 2000 s 19 and s 59.

[150] FSMA pt XVIII, implementing the EC Directive on Market Abuse (Directive 2003/6 [2003] OJ L96/16).

or can be functionally replicated through alternative techniques (eg 'off-balance sheet' financing or derivatives).

The limitation strategy is more sophisticated in the sense that it permits activity subject to the observance of risk thresholds that cannot be exceeded. Such risk thresholds can be either quantitative (eg regulatory capital requirements by reference to tiers of capital) or qualitative (eg the requirement to have 'adequate financial resources'). From the perspective of process, the limitation strategy focuses on supervision, undertaken through provision of information and direct contact between regulators and the firm. As the experience of the credit crisis has shown, breach of risk thresholds tends to be dealt with as a matter of negotiated correction rather than formal enforcement. This reflects both the priority given to supervision over enforcement within the limitation model and the practical constraints imposed on the possibility of formal enforcement where regulators have failed to use their full range of powers prior to the emergence of a crisis. In such a situation, regulators cannot credibly claim that there has been non-compliance when the exercise of discretionary powers would have averted (or at least mitigated) the crisis.[151] The limitation strategy is particularly appropriate in situations where alignment of the interests of regulated firms and their customers creates an incentive to observe the regulatory thresholds without resort to enforcement.[152] It also offers the potential to respond more quickly through supervision than through formal enforcement. The drawback of the limitation strategy is that it depends heavily on the capacity of the regulator to engage in effective supervision and, as recent events demonstrate, that may not always be a realistic expectation.

The remedial strategy attracts less attention as a regulatory technique probably for two reasons. One is that regulation is often equated with a model in which the regulator has an active supervisory role, whereas the remedial strategy does not envisage such an active role for the regulator but relies instead on the deterrent effect of the liability standard. The limitation strategy typically gives a significant role to the courts in enforcing the liability standard, although it is also possible for this process to take place within the regulatory system.[153] By setting a standard that may trigger liability (to investors, customers), a liability standard has the capacity to control risk-taking *ex ante*, at least to the extent that risk-taking can be causally linked with harm.[154] A second reason for its lower profile is that the remedial strategy bridges the divide between the general law and discrete regulatory systems (in the pure sense as something distinct from law), and can therefore be characterised as much as a general legal strategy as a regulatory strategy associated with

---

[151] This was the position in respect of regulatory capital since the FSA was already empowered to require levels of capital above the minimum requirement prior to the financial crisis.

[152] That has been the case with regard to the recent strengthening of the regulatory capital of banks, but only as a result of the onset of the financial crisis. It is clear that banks (and their counterparties in the wholesale markets as well as regulators) were prepared to tolerate much lower levels of regulatory capital during the boom years.

[153] For example, FSMA 2000 authorises the FSA on its own initiative to make restitution and compensation orders in connection with regulatory contraventions (see s 384). While there is little formal use of this power, it does provide a 'stick' to back up negotiated settlement in individual or industry-wide cases (eg pensions mis-selling).

[154] It is for this reason that a liability standard is of little use in controlling systemic risk, whereas it does have a major role to play in regulating individual transactions.

risk-based regulation. However, it remains the case that the remedial strategy plays an important role in many systems of financial regulation. Prime examples in the UK are the liability associated with false or misleading statements in prospectuses and disclosures to the market and actions in damages or for restitution for regulatory contraventions. In the US, securities class actions stand out as the most distinctive example of the remedial approach. The strategy in principle encompasses both public and private enforcement, albeit that the relative role of each will depend on a range of factors.[155] The objective of enforcement under the remedial model is to secure compensation (or restitution) in respect of loss caused by breach of the liability standard. That objective also represents a restriction on the potential use of the strategy since there are instances in which the avoidance of the materialisation of risk is such a priority within the system that it is inappropriate to deploy a regulatory strategy that focuses on resolution *ex post*.[156]

Regulatory systems can and do adopt different combinations of the three generic strategies outlined above. It is the mix that largely defines the individual character of any regulatory system, and this is likely to be driven by a range of different factors. The legislative framework has a direct effect on the mix to the extent that it adopts clear choices as between the three strategies. As far as the UK system is concerned, the legislative framework does adopt the prohibition and remedial strategies to a significant extent, but does not emphasise the limitation strategy. That does not mean, however, that the limitation strategy is excluded. On the contrary, the wide discretion enjoyed by the regulator in the UK in defining its approach to regulation opens up the possibility of adopting the limitation technique across the board. That is precisely what has occurred through the adoption of risk-based regulation. Linked with this is the fact that the UK legislative framework does not deal with the issue of the risk preference that should be favoured by the regulatory system and it has therefore fallen to the FSA to delimit tolerable risk. In so doing, the FSA has implicitly prioritised the limitation strategy, albeit that there are important elements of the prohibition and remedial strategy within the system. The limitation strategy offers a more active role and greater flexibility to a regulator than do the other two options. and in that sense is hardly a surprising choice within a system that leaves the determination of basic regulatory policy to the regulator.

Another factor that should influence the mix but does not always clearly do so is how the system of financial regulation meshes with the general legal system, and in particular the extent to which corporate and fiduciary law as well as governance codes provide a normative substratum on which the system of financial regulation is built. That issue is relevant not only for the determination of whether regulatory intervention should occur, but also for the manner in which it should occur. In this context, attention should be paid to the regulatory strategies adopted in regimes that operate in parallel with FSMA 2000.[157] They are significant since, to the extent that they pursue similar objectives to the

---

[155] They include the powers of the regulator and the incentives for private lawsuits in the legal system generally and in the system of financial regulation.

[156] That argument applies both to the risk of insolvency of individual firms and systemic risk, although it is possible for *ex post* mechanisms such as deposit protection to prevent the materialisation of (insolvency and liquidity) risk.

[157] Such as corporate governance: see Chapters 9 and 10.

FSMA, different regulatory strategies are liable to lead to confusion and lack of coherence. The principles/rules debate is also relevant in this context since principles-based regulation maps very directly on to the limitation strategy, with its focus on flexibility and supervisory engagement.

3.8.2 Risk assessment and monitoring

The FSA now operates what it refers to as a 'risk-based' system of regulation. The risks to which this refers are those that pose a risk to the achievement of the statutory objectives set by FSMA 2000.[158] This is a fundamentally different perspective of risk from that of an authorised firm that is managing risk within its business, albeit that the risks faced by firms must inevitably form the focus of the FSA's general functions. Essentially the risk with which the FSA is concerned is the risk of regulatory failure, meaning failure to achieve the statutory objectives set by FSMA 2000.[159]

In identifying and assessing risks, the FSA focuses on their impact (the scale of the effect on the statutory objectives if the issue or event crystallises) and their probability (the likelihood of the particular issue or event crystallising). Firms that are assessed by the FSA as being 'low impact' (in the sense of posing little risk to the achievement of the statutory objectives) do not have an individual risk assessment or mitigation programme. They are monitored through the more traditional approach of scrutinising returns made by firms and conducting sample exercises to monitor compliance standards.

For those firms subject to individual risk assessment, the FSA identifies the following types of risk:

1. Firm-specific risk. This is the risk that arises from the structure and method of operation of a particular business. It can be broken down into two components:
   (a) Business risk. This is the risk that arises from the nature of the business. For example, in banking there is a risk of customers defaulting on loans, and in general insurance there is the risk posed by the multiple occurrence of insured risks (eg as a result of an earthquake).
   (b) Control risk. This risk arises from the way in which a business is organised and operates. It includes issues such as the management structure, internal controls and the way in which the business sells financial products to or advises customers.
2. Environmental risk. This category describes risks that are external to the firm but which directly or indirectly affect firm specific risk. It comprises the following types of risk:
   (a) Political/legal. This would include threats to a firm's business posed by changes in legislation.
   (b) Socio-demographic. An example would be the long-term effect on an annuity provider of increasing life expectancy.

---

[158] See above section 3.2.
[159] See generally FSA, 'The FSA's Risk Assessment Framework' (2006).

(c) Technological. An example is the threat posed to recognised investment exchanges by developments in computerised dealing systems.[160]

(d) Economic. Changes in interest rates may, for example, increase loan defaults for banks.

(e) Competition. Some firms may face pressure from new competition (domestic or international).

(f) Market structure. This may be affected by changing customer preferences (eg a preference for renting over home ownership) or regulatory developments.

The next step is to link these risks to the statutory objectives. This is achieved through an assessment of how these risks affect one or more of seven regulatory risks, which are termed 'risk to objectives' (RTO) groups. In essence, the RTOs provide a technique for mapping business and control risks on to the statutory objectives. The RTOs are as follows:

- Financial failure. This is the risk posed to market confidence and consumer protection from the failure of a firm.
- Misconduct and/or mismanagement. An example is the risk to consumer protection and market confidence arising from 'mis-selling'.[161]
- Consumer understanding. This is the risk posed to the consumer protection and public awareness objectives by lack of understanding on the part of consumers of products bought from firms.
- Incidence of fraud or dishonesty. This poses a threat to the financial crime, consumer protection and market confidence objectives.
- Incidence of market abuse. This also poses a threat to the financial crime, consumer protection and market confidence objectives.
- Incidence of money laundering. This poses risks for the financial crime objective.
- Market quality. This is the risk posed to market confidence and consumer protection arising from possible deterioration in the functioning of a market.

In respect of each firm, the business and control risks are scored against the RTO groups. This process provides an overall probability score in respect of each statutory objective that falls into one of the following catgeories: high, medium high, medium low or low. The next step is for the FSA to develop a risk mitigation programme (RMP) by reference to the score of a particular firm.[162] In so doing, the FSA takes account of the principles of good regulation by aiming to ensure that the intensity of the RMP is proportionate to the risk posed by the firm. The RMP is then communicated to the firm together with an indication of the regulatory period, which is the period between formal risk assessments. The period varies between 12 and 36 months, according to the risk profile of firms, and, when longer than 12 months, an interim risk assessment will be undertaken which may result in changes to the RMP.

---

[160] See Chapter 12 for further discussion.
[161] See Chapter 6 for a discussion of 'mis-selling'.
[162] See Appendix 2 to the FSA's Risk Assessment Framework, above n 159, for an example of an RMP.

3.8.3 'Light-touch' regulation

Although the FSA never explicitly endorsed the 'light-touch' descriptor[163] with which it became associated, there can be little doubt that it was in the ascendancy prior to the financial crisis and represented a de facto limitation on the very broad powers and extensive discretion that were given to the FSA by FSMA 2000. The approach was described by the FSA itself in the following terms:

> The historical philosophy was that supervision was focused on ensuring that the appropriate systems and controls were in place and then relied on management to make the right judgment. Regulatory intervention would thus only occur to force changes in systems and controls or to sanction transgressions which were based on historical facts. It was not seen as a function of the regulator to question the overall business strategy of the institution or more generally the possibility of risk crystallising in the future.[164]

In the wake of the crisis, changes to the model of supervision were implemented through the 'Supervisory Enhancement Programme', which focused attention on 'high-impact firms' (HIFs, firms whose failure has the potential to have systemic implications). It was based on the premise that 'The new model of supervision is designed to deliver a more intrusive and direct regulatory style than the FSA has previously adopted and requires a "braver" approach to decision-making by supervisors'.[165] Among the changes it introduced were:

- A compulsory and irreducible programme of regular meetings with the senior management, control functions and non-executive directors of firms subject to our 'close and continuous' regime (that is, HIFs). This is to establish and communicate to the firm the minimum level of interaction the FSA expects, and will now include:
  - an annual meeting with the firm's senior management to focus specifically on the business and strategic plans for the firm;
  - an annual meeting with the external auditors; and
  - specific items of management information to support these meetings (such as annual strategy documents, operating plans, particular Board reports and the Management Letter provided from the external auditors).
- A regulatory period between formal ARROW[166] assessments of maximum two years for each HIF. During this period, we are now holding more formal internal 'checkpoints' on a six-monthly basis to provide more FSA senior management input and oversight of the supervisory approach for the firm.
- Increased scrutiny of candidates for Significant Influence Functions (SIFs), particularly the Chair, CEO, Finance Director and Non-executive Directors of HIFs. This scrutiny includes interviewing SIF candidates where appropriate and a greater focus on their personal accountability in post.

---

[163] See the Turner Review, above n 3, 86, which refers to it as 'somewhat of a caricature, and a term which the FSA never itself used'.

[164] FSA Regulatory Response, above n 3, para 11.14.

[165] Ibid, para 11.15.

[166] See below section 3.9.2.

- A new group of supervision advisory specialists who will conduct a regular quality review of the supervisory process for all HIFs. It will also provide support to the supervisory teams.[167]

3.9 Risk control and supervision under FSMA 2000

3.9.1 Risk as a Determinant of Regulatory Response

Risk identification and assessment, driven by the statutory objectives, lies at the heart of the regulatory system in the UK because it is what determines the regulatory response. In principle, the regulatory response encompasses the entire range of powers that are made available to the FSA by the legislative framework. The appropriate regulatory response will depend on a range of factors. If there are no regulatory rules in place, the risk must justify regulatory intervention and the FSA follows economic orthodoxy in maintaining that intervention is only justified when there is market failure. Moreover, even when there is some evidence of market failure, regulatory intervention will only be justified when other mechanisms (eg contracts[168]) cannot mitigate the risk effectively. If there are already regulatory rules in place, risk identification and assessment across the market may result in changes to the rules or a decision that the matter can be adequately dealt with through supervisory engagement. In that sense, the determination of the regulatory response at the market level is linked with the model of supervision for individual firms since the latter can be adjusted by the FSA for different levels of risk tolerance. As risk tolerance levels rise for individual firms, it can be expected that the capacity of the system to generate rules or rule changes will decline and vice versa. There may also be a form of reflexive relationship here since it may also be expected that a greater tolerance of risk across the system will feed back into greater tolerance of risk at the firm level.

3.9.2 Risk as a Determinant of Supervisory Intensity at the Firm Level

The 'ARROW' risk model used by the FSA to model the risk of individual firms focuses on the impact of the occurrence of a risk event and the probability of the event.[169] The risk profile of a firm is a combination of these two characteristics and results in a firm being categorised as falling into one of four risk categories: low, medium low, medium

---

[167] Extracted from FSA, 'Supervisory Enhancement Programme: Closing Summary' (February 2009).

[168] Contracts can only operate in this way when there is access to adequate information and regulation will often be framed (in the form of disclosure obligations) to allow it to occur.

[169] For more detail see the FSA's Risk Assessment Framework, above n 159, chs 3 and 4. Under the new regulatory structure, a 'proactive intervention framework' will be developed and implemented: see The Bank of England, Prudential Regulation Authority, 'Our Approach to Banking Supervision' (May 2011).

high and high. In the case of low-impact firms, the FSA undertakes supervision primarily through remote monitoring of the firm and thematic assessment. For other firms, the FSA undertakes individual assessments that vary in their intensity according to the risk profile of the firm and result in RMP being agreed with the FSA. The FSA monitors the RMP and follows up the actions within it to ensure that its objectives are achieved. In the periods between these formal assessments the FSA undertakes 'baseline monitoring' for all firms and 'close and continuous monitoring' for firms that are designated 'high-impact'.

These two processes are intended to identify emerging risks promptly, verify the reliance placed on senior management and the control systems of a firm, and keep up to date with organisational and personnel changes in complex firms.[170] In cases where the FSA encounters an uncooperative or obstructive attitude from authorised firms or has reason to doubt assurances given by the senior management, it has powers to require an independent investigation or a skilled person report.[171] Crucially, the ARROW risk model can be adjusted to reflect changes in the risk tolerance of the FSA. In the FSA's own words:[172] 'We have constructed the ARROW II risk model to be very flexible. The model contains parameters that can be set by our senior management to reflect their risk appetite.'

This approach provides a mechanism through which changes in the FSA's risk tolerance have a direct effect on the RMP of individual authorised firms and on the process of supervisory engagement.

The regulatory rules that form the basis for risk-based supervision are discussed below. As shown in Table 2, they are based primarily on the limitation and risk threshold strategies identified in Table 1 (above).

3.9.3 Risk Control through Capital Adequacy and Liquidity Rules

The principle of controlling risk-taking in banks by reference to the capital of the bank has a long history, at least in its most basic form. Risk-weighting of assets was introduced by the first Basel Accord, while the second Basel Accord refined the system and emphasised the role of supervisory engagement and market discipline in ensuring capital adequacy for individual institutions. In the EU, the Basel Accords were implemented by a series of directives which have overlaid a market integration framework objective on the Basel rules and applied them to investment firms which face market risk as a result of trading in financial instruments. Both the Basel and EU systems have focused on the solvency of individual institutions, with much less attention being paid to systemic risk or liquidity, both of which have featured prominently in the credit crisis.

---

[170] It seems clear that the model may not always work as it should and the FSA itself has admitted as much in the context of its supervision of Northern Rock: see FSA, 'The supervision of Northern Rock: A Lessons Learned Review' (March 2008).

[171] See FSMA 2000, ss 166, 167 and 168 and FSA Handbook, SUP 5.3. The effect of these provisions is to remove barriers to the availability of information, but the timing of the provision of the information and its interpretation may nevertheless remain problematic.

[172] The FSA's Risk Assessment Framework, above n 159, 15.

Table 2 Risk Control under FSMA 2000

Risk	Strategy	Substance
Failure to meet regulatory capital requirements (solvency and liquidity)	Risk threshold	FSA Principle 4, FSA GENPRU
Internal systems and control (firms)	Risk threshold	FSA Handbook, SYSC
Competence and integrity (individuals)	Prohibition Risk threshold	FSA Handbook, APER

In the UK context, the minimum levels of regulatory capital set by the Basel Accords and the EU directives are of limited practical relevance for two reasons. First, market counterparties may demand higher levels of capital as a condition for access to certain forms of money-market finance and higher levels of capital will, *ceteris paribus*, generate a higher credit rating for a bank's own debt, thereby lowering its funding cost. Secondly, the FSA is empowered to set individual capital adequacy standards for banks in the form of individual capital guidance (ICG), which then represents 'a regulatory intervention point' for the purposes of supervision.[173] However, following the principles-based approach that prevails in the UK, responsibility for ensuring adequate regulatory capital and liquidity rests with the management of an authorised firm. This is made clear by the FSA Handbook: 'A firm must at all times maintain overall financial resources, including capital resources and liquidity resources, which are adequate, both as to amount and quality, to ensure that there is no significant risk that its liabilities cannot be met as they fall due.'[174] Moreover, the FSA makes clear in its risk assessment of individual firms that: 'The FSA's issuance of the ICG should not be seen as an alternative to the responsibility of a firm's management to monitor and assess the level of capital appropriate to its needs.'[175]

Thus, in theory the regulator is in a powerful position as regards capital adequacy in that it can both adjust the required level of regulatory capital and, if that goes wrong, can ultimately hold the senior management to account for getting it wrong. That seems too good to be true, and in reality it is. The problem for the regulator is twofold. First, if it fails to set the ICG at a sufficient level, it is difficult to hold the senior management to account (even if possible in a technical legal sense) when the regulator has failed to identify and/or act on the problem. Secondly, even if the regulator acts against the senior management, there may be little to gain since some form of systemic risk may already have been activated. Of course, to the extent that action against the senior management in those circumstances would promote deterrence and individual responsibility, there would be some benefit for the system a whole.

---

[173] Ibid, 39.
[174] FSA Handbook, GENPRU 1.2.26R.
[175] The FSA's Risk Assessment Framework, above n 159, 38.

3.9.4 Risk Control through the 'Senior Management, Systems and Controls' (SYSC) and 'Approved Persons' (APER) Components of the FSA Handbook

In tandem with the regulatory capital regime, the UK regulatory system attempts to control risk-taking through two distinct but related components of the rulebook. One (SYSC) focuses on organisational structure, governance and risk management, while the other (APER) is more clearly focused on the competence and integrity of individuals who carry out a range of functions referred to as 'controlled functions'.[176] The FSA may designate a function as a controlled function if one of the following conditions is met:[177]

(a) the function is likely to enable the person responsible for its performance to exercise a significant influence on the conduct of the authorised person's affairs, so far as it relates to the regulated activity; or

(b) the function will involve the person performing it in dealing with customers of the authorised person in a manner substantially connected with the carrying on of the regulated activity; or

(c) the function will involve the person performing it in dealing with the property of customers of the authorised person in a manner substantially connected with the carrying on of the regulated activity.

Significantly, the scope of APER is much wider than SYSC since APER operates without reference to the seniority of the relevant individual.[178]

The objective of the SYSC component of the FSA Handbook of Rules and Guidance is expressed by Principle 3 of the Principles for Business:[179] 'A firm must take reasonable care to organise and control its affairs responsibly and effectively, with adequate risk management systems.' In more detailed terms, the FSA Handbook describes the purposes of SYSC as being:[180]

(1) to encourage firms' directors and senior managers to take appropriate practical responsibility for their firms' arrangements on matters likely to be of interest to the FSA because they impinge on the FSA's functions under the Act;

(2) to increase certainty by amplifying Principle 3, under which a firm must take reasonable care to organise and control its affairs responsibly and effectively, with adequate risk management systems;

(3) to encourage firms to vest responsibility for effective and responsible organisation in specific directors and senior managers; and

---

[176] One of the innovations of FSMA 2000 was to introduce an 'approved person' regime ('APER' in the FSA Handbook) under which persons performing 'controlled functions' require the approval of the FSA. Approval is subject to the FSA being satisfied that the relevant person is 'fit and proper' to perform the relevant controlled function. Controlled functions are defined in general terms by s 59(4)–(9) and more specifically by the FSA Handbook: see FSA Handbook, SUP 10.

[177] Section 59(5)–(7) FSMA 2000.

[178] It should be noted that the scope of APER is limited by the fact that the regime does not apply to firms who carry on regulated business in the UK under an 'EEA' or 'Treaty firm' authorisation. This respects the 'single licence' and 'home country control' principles of the EU regime.

[179] These are high-level principles that bind authorised firms.

[180] See FSA Handbook, SYSC 1.2.

(4) to create a common platform of organisational and systems and controls requirements for firms subject to the CRD[181] and/or MiFID.[182]

The third of the purposes listed above represents the first step in a move towards individual responsibility because it requires the implementation of management systems that provide a basis for identification of individual responsibility. The second step is the link between SYSC and the mechanisms that are available for taking enforcement action against individuals. Persons to whom SYSC functions are allocated are automatically included within the APER regime because such functions are designated as 'controlled'. This has the effect that the sanctions[183] available for breach of APER are available in respect of persons performing or failing to perform SYSC functions. Moreover, it has been noted that close linkage in rule formulation between the SYSC and APER ensures that failings in relation to SYSC can be positively identified as contraventions of the APER regime, thereby opening up the possibility of action against an individual.[184] Furthermore, accessory liability, in circumstances in which an approved person is 'knowingly concerned' in a contravention for which a firm bears primary responsibility represents another route for enforcement action against individuals.[185]

3.9.5 The Role of Regulatory Discretion in Risk Control

Regulatory discretion is a key feature of risk-based regulation in the UK. It is evident both at the level of design of the regulatory system and at the level of the regulator's relationship with authorised firms. At the level of design, the legislative framework leaves considerable freedom to the FSA to select the appropriate regulatory technique (eg disclosure, conduct of business regulation), to determine the structure of its rulebook (eg as between principles and rules) and to allocate responsibility for regulatory compliance (as between authorised firms and individuals). This remains true even when account is taken of the substantial extent to which the UK regulatory system is based on standards and regulatory rules emanating from international sources (such as the Basel Committee) and the EU. At the level of the regulator's relationship with individual firms, discretion is evident in: the manner in which the regulator can issue individual capital and liquidity guidance to a firm that exceeds the levels set by the FSA Handbook; the ability to review and update a firm's RMP as a result of specific events that affect a firm; and the ability

---

[181] The EC Capital Requirements Directive: Directive 2006/49 [2006] OJ L177/201.

[182] The EC Markets in Financial Instruments Directive: Directive 2004/39 [2004] OJ L145/1.

[183] The relevant sanctions provided by FSMA 2000 are: withdrawal of 'approved person' status (s 63); a financial penalty (s 66); or a public statement of misconduct (s 66). A prohibition order (under s 56) preventing an individual from engaging in specified regulated activities is a broader sanction that is not limited to the approved persons regime and is regarded by the FSA as a more serious penalty than withdrawal of approval.

[184] See J Gray and J Hamilton, *Implementing Financial Regulation: Theory and Practice* (Wiley, 2006), 75.

[185] See FSMA 2000, s 66; see also the enforcement action against Deutsche Bank/David Maslen discussed in I MacNeil 'The Evolution of Regulatory Enforcement Action in the UK Capital Markets: A Case of "Less is More"' (2007) 2 *Capital Markets Law Journal* 345.

to adjust the permitted activities of an authorised firm when this is desirable to meet the Authority's regulatory objectives.[186]

3.10 Compliance and Enforcement

All authorised firms are required to establish procedures and working practices that will ensure the firm is in compliance with FSMA 2000 and rules made under it. Principle 3 of the FSA's Principles for Business provides that 'A firm must take reasonable care to organise and control its affairs responsibly and effectively, with adequate risk management systems'.

Contravention of the Act or a rule is likely to result in a range of measures being taken against the relevant firm and, in some cases, against individuals within the firm. These measures include disciplinary action taken by the FSA, a criminal prosecution or a private action in damages brought by a client for breach of statutory duty. However, FSMA 2000 does not require that the Authority take enforcement action, and therefore both the occasions on which enforcement occurs and the form that it takes are matters that have been left to the FSA to determine as a matter of policy.

3.10.1 The role of enforcement in the regulatory system[187]

According to the 'responsive regulation' model, enforcement represents only the final option that is available to secure compliance with regulatory obligations.[188] Other options that are available include persuasion and more intensive supervisory engagement. Applied to the financial sector, this model corresponds quite closely to the approach that has been adopted by the FSA, according to which, at least in the pre-crisis era, it was not an enforcement-led regulator. From an international perspective, it is well known that the FSA is much less active than its US counterpart—the Securities and Exchange Commission (SEC)—in taking enforcement action: even adjusting for different levels of market capitalisation, the number of enforcement cases initiated by the SEC and the financial penalties imposed are much greater.[189] One interpretation of the low incidence of enforcement in the UK is that the FSA does not give it sufficient prominence. One influential commentator has argued that the greater intensity of enforcement action in the US contributes towards a lower cost of capital, as evidenced by the enduring valuation

---

[186] FSMA 2000 s 45.

[187] This section draws substantially on MacNeil, above n 185.

[188] See generally I Ayres and J Braithwaite, *Transcending the Deregulation Debate* (Oxford, Oxford University Press, 1992).

[189] For the relevant statistics see JC Coffee Jr, 'Law and the Market: The Impact of Enforcement', 35–37, available at http://ssrn.com/abstract=967482.

premium[190] that can be observed for foreign companies (including those from the UK) that cross-list in the US by comparison with their peers who do not cross-list.[191] The argument in essence is that cross-listed firms gain a valuation premium by 'bonding' to the system of regulation in the US, which is superior to other systems largely because of its strong focus on enforcement action. According to this approach, the most obvious disparity in enforcement activity between the FSA and SEC lies in the area of insider dealing restrictions, which can be viewed as a possible explanation for the (sustained) valuation premium recorded for companies that cross-list in the US.

If a strong emphasis on enforcement is indeed capable of generating such a beneficial outcome, a strong case would have to be made for its rejection in the UK context. In response, the FSA would no doubt counter that formal enforcement action is only one of the regulatory tools available to the FSA to deal with contraventions.[192] Alternatives, which focus more on an *ex ante* rather than an *ex post* approach to dealing with contraventions, include supervisory action, theme work[193] and the policy consultation process. That debate is a particularly difficult one to resolve because it is not easy to estimate the impact that either the level of enforcement or its mix (as between different techniques) has on compliance.[194] While it is clear, for example, that the FSA devotes proportionately much less resource to enforcement than does the SEC, it is not entirely clear what may safely be concluded from such an observation. It would be rash to conclude, for example, that the low level of enforcement in the UK results in a lower level of compliance. That would imply that the other regulatory activities in which the FSA engages have a lower compliance value than enforcement action, yet there is no clear evidence of that being the case. Equally, it would be wrong to conclude that a higher level of enforcement activity in the US implies a higher level of compliance: it may simply be the result of a higher ratio of enforcement action to contraventions.

In the wake of the financial crisis, however, the FSA has shifted its policy to concentrate on what it terms 'credible deterrence', which focuses more on the capacity of enforcement against particular firms and individuals to encourage better compliance across the system as a whole. Recent high-profile investigations into insider-dealing rings said to be operating among market professionals[195] has provided plenty of high-profile evidence of the new approach, but it remains to be seen how far it will be carried into other areas, especially since the FSA has in the past emphasised that supervisory engagement was often a superior alternative to formal enforcement.

---

[190] As measured by Tobin's *q*, calculated for this purpose as: (book value of total assets – book value of equity + market value of equity)/(book value of total assets).

[191] See Coffee, above n 189. See Chapter 8.2.4 regarding cross-listing.

[192] See FSA Handbook, Enforcement Guide, para 3.2.

[193] This refers to investigation and supervisory engagement on specific issues across a range of firms.

[194] See generally HE Jackson and MJ Roe, 'Public Enforcement of Securities Laws: Preliminary Evidence', available at http://ssrn.com/abstract=1000086.

[195] See eg 'Seven Charged Over Insider Trading Ring', *Financial Times*, 31 March 2010.

3.10.2 Disciplinary measures and sanctions

The FSA has a range of disciplinary measures at its disposal.

Public censure

The most straightforward sanction is public censure,[196] which simply involves publication of the fact of a contravention of the Act or rules made under it by an authorised person. The FSA is not required to establish a contravention of the Act or its rules according to any objective standard before issuing a public censure.[197] This sanction relies on the deterrent effect that adverse publicity can have on reputation in the financial market.

Financial penalty

Another option is to impose a financial penalty. This was a power that the FSA lacked under the FSA 1986 regulatory system: only the self-regulatory organisations (SROs) were empowered to impose financial penalties, and that was a matter of contractual agreement between the SROs and authorised persons rather than a statutory power. There is, in principle, no limit to the amount of the penalty, but the FSA is required to publish guidance on its policy regarding penalties and the amount of penalties.[198] No firm, except a sole trader, may pay a financial penalty imposed by the FSA on a present or former employee, director or partner of the firm or of an affiliated company.[199] A penalty may be imposed at the same time that authorisation is withdrawn.[200]

Variation or cancellation of permission

Although not categorised by FSMA 2000 as disciplinary measures, there are several other options that might be considered by the FSA in response to a contravention. One is a variation in the regulated activities included in an authorised person's 'permission'.[201] In the past, this was limited to circumstances in which an authorised firm no longer met the 'threshold conditions' for authorisation, but that restriction was removed by FSA 2010 so as to enable the Authority to vary permission to meet any of its regulatory objectives. At the same time, the Authority was authorised to suspend permission or to impose restrictions or limitations that it considers appropriate.[202]

A second, and more drastic, response would be complete cancellation of permission to engage in any regulated activity. That, in itself, does not result in withdrawal of authori-

---

[196] See s 205 FSMA 2000.

[197] See FSA Handbook, DEPP 6.4.2G regarding factors relevant to the issue of a public censure.

[198] See ss 206 and 210 FSMA 2000. The guidance is published at DEPP 6.

[199] FSA Handbook, GEN 6.1.4A R. For background see FSA, 'Decision Procedure and Penalties manual and Enforcement Guide Review', Policy Statement 11/3 (February 2011).

[200] See s 10 FSA 2010, amending s 206 FSMA 2000. Cancellation of permission had already been permitted at the same time as the imposition of a financial penalty.

[201] This is possible at the FSA's initiative under s 45 FSMA 2000.

[202] See new s 206A FSMA 2000, inserted by s 9 FSA 2010.

sation because a separate direction from the FSA is required for that to occur.[203] The purpose of this procedure is to ensure that, when an authorised person is no longer able to engage in regulated activity as a result of cancellation of permission, it remains subject to the jurisdiction of the FSA because it is still an authorised person.

Prohibition orders

The FSA may prohibit an individual (ie a human person) from performing any regulated activities carried on by an authorised person if it considers that the individual is not a fit and proper person to carry on that function.[204] The prohibition may apply to any or all regulated activity, and may prohibit employment by a particular firm or type of firm. An order may also prohibit an individual from performing functions in relation to the regulated activity of an exempt person (such as an appointed representative or a recognised investment exchange or clearing house) and persons covered by an exemption under part XX (provision of financial services by members of the professions). In most cases the FSA will consider whether the particular unfitness can be adequately dealt with by withdrawing approval[205] or other disciplinary sanctions, for example public censure or financial penalties, or by issuing a private warning.[206] The FSA will consider making a prohibition order only in the most serious cases of lack of fitness and propriety. In the case of an individual who is not an approved person, a prohibition order may be the only enforcement option. The FSA will also take into account other enforcement action against the individual by the FSA, other agencies or professional bodies.

It is an offence for an individual to perform or agree to perform a function in breach of a prohibition order.[207] The offence is one of strict liability (not requiring *mens rea*), but it is a defence for the accused to show that he took all reasonable precautions and exercised all due diligence to avoid committing the offence. The FSA may, on the application of the individual named in a prohibition order, vary or revoke it.

An authorised (or exempt) person is required to take reasonable care to ensure that no function of his, in relation to the carrying on of a regulated activity, is performed by a person who is prohibited from performing that function by a prohibition order. Such orders are recorded in the register maintained by the FSA.[208] Reasonable care would appear to require that an authorised person search the register before engaging any employee. Any breach of this duty of care is actionable at the suit of a private person who suffers loss as a result of the contravention.[209]

---

[203] FSMA 2000, s 33.
[204] FSMA 2000, s 56.
[205] This refers to approval under the APER regime to perform 'controlled functions'.
[206] FSA Handbook, Enforcement Guide (EG) 9 sets out the FSA's policy on making prohibition orders. The Authority considers that a prohibition order is a more serious penalty than the withdrawal of approval (in relation to an approved person) because a prohibition order will usually be much wider in scope.
[207] FSMA 2000, s 56(4).
[208] As required by s 347 FSMA 2000.
[209] FSMA 2000, s 71(1).

Approved persons

The FSA is empowered to take disciplinary action against approved persons if two conditions are met.[210] The first is that the person is guilty of misconduct. This will occur if an approved person has failed to comply with the FSA's Principles for Approved Persons or has been knowingly concerned in a contravention on the part of an authorised person. The second is that it is appropriate in all the circumstances to take action against the approved person. In this regard, statements made by the Authority shed some light on what will be considered appropriate circumstances:[211] 'For example, action will be unlikely where an individual's behaviour was in compliance with the rules imposed on his firm in respect of his controlled function' and

> The FSA does not consider that it would be appropriate to discipline senior managers, approved for the purpose of [s 59 FSMA 2000], simply because a breach of the regulatory requirements has occurred in an area for which they are responsible. There will only be a breach of a Statement of Principle where there is personal culpability.[212]

The Authority must bring disciplinary proceedings against an approved person within 3 years[213] of becoming aware of the misconduct. It is also possible that the Authority might simply give a private warning rather than take formal action.[214] The FSA is also empowered to take action against persons registered with SROs under arrangements that predated the 'approved persons regime', in respect of contraventions occurring before FSMA 2000 took effect.[215] The Authority will generally be able to take action against such persons in respect of contraventions that relate to activities which, if performed after the commencement of FSMA 2000, would be considered 'controlled activities'. The sanctions available to the FSA if misconduct on the part of an approved person is established are a financial penalty or public censure.

As a separate matter, the Authority is now also empowered to impose a financial penalty on an individual who performs a 'controlled function' without approval if the individual could be reasonably expected to have known that to be the case.[216]

3.10.3 Disciplinary procedure

The disciplinary procedure provisions of FSMA 2000 attracted considerable attention during the committee stages in Parliament as debate focused on their compatibility with

---

[210] FSMA 2000, s 66.

[211] FSA Consultation Paper 26, 'The Regulation of Approved Persons' (1999) paras 98 and 115 respectively.

[212] See FSA Handbook, APER 3.2.1E for factors relevant in determining if approved persons are in compliance with the Principles.

[213] Extended to three from two by s 12 FSA 2010, amending s 66(4) of FSMA 2000. That change is linked with the increased focus on individual responsibility in the reforms introduced by FSA 2010.

[214] See FSA Handbook, EG 7.10–19.

[215] See FSMA 2000 (Transitional Provisions and Savings) (Civil Remedies, Discipline, Criminal Offences) (No 2) Order 2001, SI 2001/3083, Art 9.

[216] FSMA 2000, s 63A, inserted by s 11 FSA 2010.

the Human Rights Act 1998.[217] The main issue was the compatibility of the procedures with article 6 of the European Convention on Human Rights (ECHR), which provides for the right to a fair trial. Potential contraventions were identified by reference to the following:[218]

1. the extent to which the disciplinary procedure and the role of the FSA provided for a fair trial;
2. the absence of legal assistance to secure representation for persons appearing before the Financial Services Tribunal;[219]
3. the standard of proof to be required in hearings before the Financial Services Tribunal;
4. the use of compelled evidence in disciplinary proceedings; and
5. the absence of legal certainty in the definition of market abuse.

The disciplinary framework ultimately adopted by the Act took account of these concerns. The relevant powers of the FSA are spread across various provisions of the Act and in the relevant part of the FSA Handbook (designated DEPP). The key points are as follows:

1. The first stage in the disciplinary process is the issue of a 'warning notice' to a firm or individual. This gives reasons for the proposed action and allows a period of time during which representations may be made to the FSA.
2. The Regulatory Decisions Committee (RDC) is responsible for reaching decisions on disciplinary matters raised in a warning notice. The members of this Committee are independent of the FSA.[220] When making decisions, the RDC meets in private and is required to adopt procedures that will result in the case before it being dealt with fairly.
3. Following intimation of the RDC's conclusions to the FSA, either a decision notice or discontinuance notice will be issued to the firm or person concerned.[221] A decision notice must set out the action that the FSA proposes to take and, if relevant, draw attention to any right of appeal to the Upper Tribunal and any right of access to material relevant to the decision. If there is no referral to the Upper Tribunal, a final notice will be issued before the relevant action is taken. If there is a referral to the Upper Tribunal (or a subsequent appeal to the court), the Authority must give the relevant person a final notice before taking action in accordance with the direction of the Upper Tribunal or court.

---

[217] The Act gives effect in the UK to the European Convention on Human Rights. See the First (H of L 50 I–II; H of C HC328 I–II) and Second (H of L 66; H of C HC465) Reports of the Joint Parliamentary Committee on Financial Services and Markets. Para 147 of the First Report notes: 'According to the Progress Report [on the Bill] "The main focus of comment on the draft Bill has been on the disciplinary process. There has been a perception that the FSA internal procedures may lack fairness and transparency, or be unduly costly and burdensome, and that the FSA will be able to act as prosecutor judge and jury."'

[218] See Annexes C and D to the Joint Committee First Report on the draft Bill, ibid.

[219] This was replaced by the Upper Tribunal with effect from April 2010.

[220] This gives effect to the requirement of s 395 FSMA 2000 that such decisions must be made by persons independent of those who investigated the matter.

[221] FSA 2010 amended s 391 FSMA 2000 so as to permit the FSA to publicise a decision notice.

4. The Upper Tribunal has a wide-ranging jurisdiction over many of the FSA's decisions, including those of a disciplinary nature.[222] It is not an 'appeals' tribunal in the strict sense as it determines matters *de novo* and is able to consider fresh evidence that was not available to the RDC. The Tribunal must determine what (if any) is the appropriate action for the FSA to take. Decisions of the Tribunal can no longer be appealed to the courts on a point of law.[223]

5. The Act makes provision for persons to whom notices are issued to have access to material that the Authority relied on in making the decision regarding issue of the notice.[224] The objective is to give effect to the right to a fair trial (Article 6 ECHR), which includes the right to have knowledge of and comment on evidence relied on in the proceedings.

6. In respect only of market abuse cases that are referred to the Upper Tribunal, there is a legal assistance (or 'legal aid') scheme.[225]

3.10.4 Consumer redress schemes

In cases of widespread regulatory failure, the FSA is authorised to establish a consumer redress scheme.[226] The purpose of such a scheme is to require relevant firms to investigate potential regulatory contraventions and to provide redress to consumers[227] where loss or damage has been caused to them. While the provision in its original form required the Treasury's approval for a scheme to be established, the amendments introduced by FSA 2010 authorise the FSA to establish a scheme on its own initiative.[228] It was argued by the British Bankers Association in a test case relating to payment protection insurance[229] that, since section 404 FSMA 2000 prescribed a specific statutory procedure for dealing with widespread cases of regulatory failure by firms, it 'occupied the field' and precluded the use of other regulatory powers from achieving similar objectives. That argument was rejected by the High Court and therefore leaves open the possibility for the FSA to deal with widespread regulatory failure through other powers, such as rule-making, guidance and open letters.

---

[222] The tribunal hears appeals against FSA decision notices concerning authorisation and permission, market abuse, disciplinary matters and official listing.

[223] FSMA 2000, s 137 (which permitted appeals on a point of law) was repealed by the Transfer of Tribunal Functions Order 2010, SI 2010/22, sch 2, para 46 with effect from 6 April 2010.

[224] FSMA 2000, s 394.

[225] This reflected advice given to the government during the passage of the bill through Parliament that the market abuse regime could be considered 'criminal' rather than 'civil' for the purposes of human rights law. Categorisation as 'criminal' would increase the likelihood of triggering the requirement of Art 6(3)(c) ECHR that legal assistance be provided 'when the interests of justice so require'.

[226] FSMA 2000, s 404.

[227] Consumers includes for this purpose business and professional customers: s 404E FSMA 2000. It also includes customers who have not complained to the relevant firm: see FSA, 'The Assessment and Redress of Payment Protection Insurance Complaints', Policy Statement 10/12 (August 2010).

[228] The amended version of s 404 FSMA 2000 applies to regulatory failures that occurred before that provision took effect (on October 12, 2010).

[229] *R (British Bankers Association) v FSA* [2011] EWHC 999 (Admin). See section 3.6 for more details about the case.

3.10.5 Prosecution of criminal offences

There are a number of criminal offences created by FSMA 2000. They include:

- breach of the general prohibition against carrying on regulated activity without authorisation;[230]
- the making of false claims to being an authorised or exempt person;[231]
- the use of misleading statements and practices to induce another person to enter into an investment agreement;[232]
- engaging in market manipulation;[233] and
- misleading the Authority.[234]

In England and Wales, prosecutions in respect of offences under FSMA 2000 may be instituted by the FSA, by the Secretary of State (Department of Business, Innovation and Skills[235]) or by or with the consent of the Director of Public Prosecutions. The FSA is also empowered to bring prosecutions under other statutes.[236] In exercising its powers, the FSA must comply with any conditions or restrictions imposed by the Treasury. In Scotland, prosecutions for offences under FSMA 2000 remain the responsibility of the Crown Office.[237]

A contravention that is a criminal offence may or may not be pursued through the criminal courts. A decision on whether to prosecute or take disciplinary action will depend on a range of factors, including:

1. whether, in the FSA's opinion, the taking of civil or regulatory action might unfairly prejudice the prosecution, or proposed prosecution, of criminal offences;
2. whether, in the FSA's opinion, the taking of civil or regulatory action might unfairly prejudice the defendants in the criminal proceedings in the conduct of their defence; and
3. whether it is appropriate to take civil or regulatory action, having regard to the scope of the criminal proceedings and the powers available to the criminal courts.[238]

The FSA has made clear that prosecution will not normally be pursued alongside disciplinary measures.

FSMA 2000 also provides for personal criminal liability on the part of certain indi-

---

[230] FSMA 2000, s 23.

[231] FSMA 2000, s 24.

[232] FSMA 2000, s 397.

[233] FSMA 2000, s 397(3).

[234] FSMA 2000, s 398.

[235] Formerly known as BERR (Department for Business, Enterprise and Regulatory Reform) and the Department of Trade and Industry (DTI).

[236] It was held in *R v Rollins* [2010] UKSC 39 that the Authority had the power of a private individual to bring any prosecution which fell within its memorandum and articles of association and was not precluded by the terms of the relevant statute. Sections 401 and 402 did not define exhaustively the FSA's prosecutorial powers, and accordingly the FSA had power to prosecute money laundering offences under ss 327 and 328 of the Proceeds of Crime Act 2002.

[237] The same applies to those offences which fall within the remit of the SFO in England.

[238] See FSA Handbook, EG 12.

viduals in circumstances in which an offence is committed by an organisation with the consent or connivance of, or as a result of the negligence of, that individual. The provision[239] applies to officers of a company,[240] partners in a partnership, and officers or members of the governing body of an unincorporated association. The Treasury has power to extend this section to bodies established outside the UK.

Under the Criminal Justice Act 1987, the Director of the Serious Fraud Office (SFO) may investigate any suspected offence which appears on reasonable grounds to involve serious or complex fraud and may also conduct, or take over the conduct of, the prosecution of any such offence. The SFO may investigate in conjunction with any other person with whom the Director thinks it is proper to do so; this includes a police force, the FSA or any other regulator.

3.10.6 Civil action for damages

A contravention of FSMA 2000 or a regulatory rule made under the Act[241] opens up the possibility of an action in damages at the suit of a private person.[242] A private person includes any individual, unless he suffers the loss in the course of carrying on any regulated activity, and any person who is not an individual (eg a company), unless he suffers the loss in question in the course of carrying on a business of any kind.[243] Non-private persons can take action in three circumstances only:

1. where the rule that has been contravened prohibits an authorised person from seeking to make provision excluding or restricting any duty or liability;
2. where the rule that has been contravened concerns the misuse of unpublished information for the purposes of effecting transactions (ie criminal or regulatory forms of insider dealing and market abuse[244]); or
3. where the action can only be brought in a fiduciary capacity by a non-private person on behalf of the private person.[245]

The basis of an action under section 150 is that the contravention represents a breach of statutory duty which has caused loss to the investor. As it is of most direct relevance to private investors, the requirements for a successful action are discussed in Chapter 6.[246] The equivalent provision in FSA 1986 was little used, and this has remained so under FSMA 2000, largely as a result of the possibility of cases being referred to the Financial Ombudsman Service or through bulk settlements negotiated by the FSA on behalf of private investors.

---

[239] FSMA 2000, s 400.
[240] The term includes controllers (large shareholders) who are individuals, and members of a Limited Liability Partnership (see SI 2001/1090).
[241] Not all rules are actionable: see Chapter 6.5.
[242] FSMA 2000, s 150.
[243] FSMA 2000 (Rights of Action) Regulations 2001, SI 2001/2256, Art 3.
[244] See Chapter 13.2.
[245] SI 2001/2256, Art 6.
[246] See Chapter 6.5.

Part 2

Investments and Investors

4

Investments—Nature and Typology

This chapter explains the legal nature and characteristics of different types of investment, focusing in particular on those that fall within the scope of the Financial Services and Markets Act 2000 (FSMA 2000). It assumes that the reader is familiar with the concepts discussed in the first three chapters.

In Chapter 1 it was noted that investments are personal rights over incorporeal moveable property (intangibles). The nature of these rights is the subject of this chapter. For some investments, such as company shares, investors' rights are largely determined in the market (through contract), with little regulatory control. In the case of other forms of investment (eg some forms of investment fund) there is much less scope for private bargaining, as the investor's rights are largely determined by regulation. As will be seen, regulation can control both the (contractual) relationship between an issuer and investor and the legal structure of an investment entity.

It was also noted in Chapter 1 that legal title to investments can be constituted in different ways. The main distinction is between registered and unregistered securities. The implications of this distinction for the mode of transfer of investments and the rights acquired by a transferee are considered in this chapter.

In Chapter 3, the scope of the regulatory system established by FSMA 2000 was discussed. Central to the scope of that system is the concept of a 'specified investment' because any 'specified activity' carried on by way of business in respect of a 'specified investment' or specified property of any kind is a regulated activity falling within the Act.[1] The Regulated Activities Order (RAO) defines both specified activities and specified investments. The scope of the former was outlined in Chapter 3, while the scope and nature of the latter is explained in this chapter. The treatment of the different forms of investment follows the sequence of the RAO for ease of reference. In addition to the specific forms of 'investment' that are 'specified' by the RAO, there is also a catch-all provision which brings into the definition of specified investments any right to or interest in a specified investment.[2] This means that rights or interests derived from 'indirect'

---

[1] See s 22 FSMA 2000.
[2] Art 89 of the RAO.

forms of investment (such as a trust) in which the legal owner is not the beneficial owner do not fall outside the scope of regulation.

There is no discussion in this chapter of 'product wrappers' into which investments may be organised. They include Individual Savings Accounts (ISAs), Personal Equity Plans and Investment Trust Savings Plans. These wrappers are not in themselves investments or property (in the legal sense);[3] they are essentially contractual arrangements for the administration of investments, designed mainly to take advantage of various tax incentives. They do not alter the legal nature and structure of the underlying investments that are included in the product wrapper.

4.1 Deposits

A deposit is an arrangement under which the depositor transfers ownership of the deposit to the deposit-taker (normally a bank or building society), who is free to use the deposit in the course of its business, which will normally mean that the deposit becomes part of the institution's funds available for lending to borrowers. As ownership of the deposit is transferred to the deposit taker, a depositor has no real (proprietary) right in respect of the deposit;[4] the depositor has only a contractual claim for the repayment of the deposit on the agreed terms (eg as to interest and time). A depositor therefore ranks only as an ordinary creditor on the insolvency of a bank, and for that reason special measures have put in place to guarantee the repayment of deposits.[5] It is normal for deposit agreements to provide for repayment on demand or subject to a period of notice being given by the depositor.

Deposits are specified investments for the purposes of FSMA 2000 and the business of deposit-taking falls within FSMA 2000 because deposit-taking is a specified activity (under the RAO).[6] While this represents an expansion of the scope of the FSMA 2000 regulatory system by comparison with that created by the Financial Services Act 1986 (FSA 1986) (which did not cover the business of deposit-taking), it is in reality just a transfer to FSMA 2000 of the system of banking regulation previously contained in the Banking Act 1987.

---

[3] They cannot be considered property as they are personal to the account holder. No one person's tax exemption or incentive may be transferred to another. They therefore fail to meet the basic criterion of property that it should be capable of being owned by anyone. See generally J Gray, 'Personal Finance and Corporate Governance: The Missing Link: Product Regulation and Policy Conflicts' (2004) 4 *Journal of Corporate Law Studies* 187, 208–10.

[4] *Foley v Hill* (1848) 2 HL Cas 28.

[5] See Chapter 6.7.

[6] See Arts 5 and 74 of the RAO (SI 2001/544). Note that mortgage lending is not included within the definition of the regulated activity of deposit-taking, although it is often funded by deposits; see Chapter 3.5 regarding the regulation of mortgage lending.

4.2 Electronic money

The RAO designates electronic money as a 'specified investment' and defines it as follows:[7]

> 'electronic money' means electronically (including magnetically) stored monetary value as represented by a claim on the electronic money issuer which—
> (a) is issued on receipt of funds for the purpose of making payment transactions;
> (b) is accepted by a person other than the electronic money issuer; and
> (c) is not excluded by article 3 of the electronic money regulations.[8]

4.3 Rights under a contract of insurance

Rights under a contact of insurance are specified investments.[9] A distinction can be drawn between investment-related life assurance, which is often used as a form of saving and investment, and general (or non-life) insurance, which is a pure risk transfer mechanism that protects the insured from the financial consequences of risks covered by the insurance policy.

4.3.1 Investment-related life assurance

In its early forms, life assurance provided financial protection only against premature death. It still performs this function, but has also taken on the characteristics of an investment. This has happened for a number of reasons. One is that the traditional manner in which life assurance was organised was similar in character to investment funds and therefore life offices had the organisational and contractual mechanisms in place to enable them to change their focus from protection to investment. Another reason is that life assurance made investment accessible to lower income groups who lacked the wealth to invest directly in company shares or indirectly in unit trusts. This was particularly so in the case of 'industrial' life assurance, which developed as a system of regular collection of relatively small premiums from policyholders' homes. Another influence was the use of life assurance as a mechanism to repay a mortgage from the proceeds of a life policy. This greatly expanded the market for investment-related life assurance in the 1980s, but

---

[7] Art 3.
[8] SI 2011/99. That article excludes forms of electronic money that are valid only within a limited network.
[9] FSMA 2000, s 22(2) and sch 2, para 20; RAO Art 75.

that process went into reverse in the 1990s as interest rates fell and regulators became concerned that such products had been sold in inappropriate circumstances.

4.3.2 The with-profits system

Although its use has declined in recent years, the 'with-profits' mechanism has been the traditional method by which life assurance companies have allocated the investment returns (both income and capital gains) arising from the fund representing premiums paid by 'with-profits' policyholders (the 'with-profits' fund). The mechanism works by allocating bonuses to individual policies. In order for bonuses to be allocated, the value of the life office's assets must exceed the present value of its future liabilities, which are mainly sums accrued by policyholders as policy benefits. In this situation the life office has an actuarial surplus, which is in principle available for distribution to policyholders in the form of bonuses.[10]

The normal practice has been for life offices to declare two types of bonus: annual (or reversionary) and final (or terminal). Annual bonuses are contractually guaranteed additions to the policy which become payable when the policy matures and are normally made at a conservative level as the life offices must include them in the calculation of liabilities. Terminal bonuses are allocated and paid when a policy matures, and are intended to increase the value of the policy to a level which reflects the actual investment return achieved by the with-profits fund rather than the generally lower return assumed in calculating annual bonuses.

The overall objective of bonus allocation in respect of with-profits policies is that the value of the benefits should equate to the policyholder's notional 'asset-share' in the with-profit fund, that is, the notional part of the total fund that has been created over time by the investment of the premiums paid by an individual policyholder. The attraction of the system is that it provides a mechanism that allows the policyholder to participate in the growth of the with-profits fund while at the same time having some protection against sharp fluctuations in the value of investments (through contractually guaranteed annual bonuses). This is generally referred to as 'smoothing' of investment returns. From the perspective of the life office, the with-profits mechanism provides very broad powers for distributing actuarial surplus among policyholders in a manner that is equitable to different generations of policyholders who have participated in the fund through periods in which different investment returns have been achieved. It is also attractive to the life office in that no specific investment return is normally guaranteed to the policyholder when the policy is issued, the understanding being that the policyholder accepts, through the bonus allocation process, whatever investment return is achieved by the with-profits fund.

It has always been accepted that annual and final bonus rates could change from year to year and could be set at different levels for different generations of policyholders.

---

[10] The articles of association govern the distribution of surplus. In a shareholder-owned company they normally provide for the surplus to be split 90:10 between policyholders and shareholders, whereas in a mutual company they normally provide for the entire surplus to be distributed to policyholders.

Prior to the *Equitable Life* case,[11] however, it remained unclear whether the discretion enjoyed by a life office in respect of the bonus allocation process could be employed so as to eliminate or reduce contractual obligations to policyholders. Following that case, the first in which the operation of the with-profits system had been subjected to judicial scrutiny, it seems clear that in most instances life companies will not be able to act in that manner. While the facts of that case are not universally applicable, it is indicative of judicial resistance to the use of discretionary powers to override contractual rights.[12]

4.3.3 Unit-linked contracts

Unit-linked contracts were developed to provide a more transparent form of investment than was provided by the 'with-profits' system. Although the life fund in which premiums are invested may invest in a similar fashion to a with-profits fund, the manner in which the policyholder participates in the fund differs. A unit-linked policyholder is allocated units in the fund, which are priced on a daily basis by reference to the underlying investments.[13] In contrast to a 'with-profits' contract, the value of the policy is evident on a continuous basis. Charges levied from the policyholder are also explicit (usually expressed as a percentage of the value of units) rather than being hidden (and encompassed in the bonus calculation) in the case of with-profits contracts. In addition to its investment value, a unit-linked contract normally carries a minimum guaranteed payment on death.

4.3.4 Regulatory considerations

All contracts of life assurance are specified investments for the purposes of FSMA 2000.[14] Insurers therefore require authorisation and permission from the Financial Services Authority (FSA), and are subject to prudential supervision so as to safeguard the interests of policyholders. However, the FSA does not (and cannot) regulate the terms of life assurance contracts.

Considerable regulatory attention has been focused in recent years on the operation of the 'with-profits' system. The following issues in particular have given rise to concern:

1 the manner in which life offices exercise their discretion, particularly as regards the allocation of bonuses to policies;

---

[11] *Equitable Life v Hyman* [2000] 2 All ER 331, [2002] 1 AC 408 (HL). See I MacNeil, 'When is a Guarantee Not a Guarantee?' [2000] *Company Financial and Insolvency Law Review* 154 and 'Contract, Discretion and the With-Profits Mechanism' [2000] *Company Financial and Insolvency Law Review* 354.

[12] The House of Lords implied into the society's articles of association (under which the directors were empowered to declare bonuses) a prohibition on linking bonuses to the manner in which policyholders chose to exercise contractual rights under their policies. See the MacNeil articles, ibid.

[13] This distinguishes a unit-linked policy from a 'unitised with-profits' policy, which, although it allocates units to the policyholder, preserves the life office's discretion in allocating units and hence 'smoothing' of investment returns. See FSA, 'A Description and Classification of With-Profits Policies' (October 2000) for more detail.

[14] FSMA 2000, s 22(2) and sch 2, para 20; RAO Art 75.

2 the manner in which the 'inherited estate' accumulated by many life offices should be used; and

3 the feasibility of making the with profits system simpler and more transparent for policyholders.

All three issues are relevant to the nature of a with-profits policy as an investment and are therefore discussed below.

Discretion is an inherent feature of with-profits policies because they are based on the principle that a policyholder will share in the (smoothed) investment returns of the with-profits fund. Its presence, however, poses risks for policyholders in that, during the term of their policy, they may encounter instances of the exercise of discretion that are unexpected or perhaps even unfair. Unfairness in this sense could mean different treatment for different generations of policyholders or the favouring of the interests of shareholders over policyholders. Legal controls over the exercise of discretion comprise primarily the FSA's Principles for Businesses[15] and the regulations applicable to all contract terms.[16] The FSA's concern arises from the wide nature of the discretion typically given to insurers by 'with-profits' policies, which could potentially be considered unfair under the Unfair Terms in Consumer Contract Regulations 1999.[17] Disclosure of the principles and practices applicable to the exercise of discretion is the solution favoured by the FSA to make with-profit contracts compliant with these legal and regulatory obligations. The objective is to improve policyholders' understanding of the role of discretion and the manner in which it is likely to be exercised.

The 'inherited estate' (sometimes referred to as 'orphan assets') refers to the assets that have been accumulated over time by a with-profits fund that are not required to meet policyholders' reasonable expectations.[18] The latter expression refers to how a policyholder could reasonably expect a life office to use its discretion, particularly as regards bonus policy. An 'inherited estate' arises as a result of the discretion given to a life office in distributing investment returns in a with-profits fund to policyholders. In some instances, life offices have exercised that discretion with caution and have accumulated assets over and above those required to satisfy policyholders' reasonable expectations.

Two issues give rise to regulatory concern. The first is the attribution of ownership of the inherited estate as between shareholders and policyholders. This has been largely settled by the 1995 Ministerial Statement, which has the effect in most cases of attributing it 90:10 between policyholders and shareholders.[19] The second is the reattribution of an

---

[15] Principle 6, which states that 'A firm must pay due regard to the interests of its customers and treat them fairly'.

[16] In particular, the Unfair Terms in Consumer Contract Regulations 1999, SI 1999/2083.

[17] See FSA, 'Discretion and Fairness in With-Profits Policies', With-Profits Review Issues Paper 4 (2002) paras 22–26.

[18] Policyholders' reasonable expectations are referred to in the Ministerial Statement on 'Orphan Estates' issued by the Department of Trade and Industry on 24 February 1995 and the term has since been regularly used by the FSA. Although widely used in the actuarial profession, it does not have a technical legal meaning and is not referred to by FSMA 2000.

[19] See above n 17. This follows the same ratio normally applied to the distribution of actuarial surplus. The logic is that the inherited estate could potentially form part of surplus. In mutual companies, the inherited estate belongs to the policyholders (there are no shareholders).

inherited estate to shareholders, that is, the buy-out by shareholders of policyholders' interests in the inherited estate. There are two main regulatory concerns that arise in respect of both attribution and reattribution exercises.[20] The first is that they are commercial negotiations between shareholders and current policyholders in which policyholders have no explicit and distinct negotiator to act on their behalf. The second is that both attribution and reattribution are complex exercises that are difficult for policyholders to understand.[21] Since 2007, reattribution has been subject to detailed FSA regulation, including the appointment of a policyholder advocate who is free from conflicts of interest,[22] and a requirement to secure the consent of the firm and policyholders to the process.

The feasibility of making the with-profits system simpler and more transparent for policyholders came to the fore largely as a result of the recommendations of the Sandler Report.[23] It found that the opaque nature of with-profits policies inhibited effective competition and created inherent conflicts of interest in shareholder-owned companies, particularly over the selection of investment opportunities.[24] The Sandler Report made extensive recommendations for improving the with-profits system. Two points in particular are worthy of note. First, it proposed restructuring with-profits funds so as to separate the interests of shareholders and policyholders and limit the potential for conflicts of interest. Secondly, it proposed a clearer definition of policyholders' rights and improved disclosure to policyholders.

The FSA responded to these concerns in three ways. First, it established a framework under which firms must disclose the manner in which their with-profits business is being run. This requires firms carrying on a with-profits business to establish and maintain Principles and Practices of Financial Management (PPFM).[25] The Principles are enduring statements describing the standards the firms adopt in managing with-profits business and the business model used by the firm in meeting its duties to policyholders and in responding to longer-term changes in the business and economic environment. The Practices must describe the manner in which the with-profits fund is managed and contain

---

[20] See FSA, 'Process for Dealing with Attribution of Inherited Estates', With-Profits Review Issues Paper 1 (October 2001) para 23; FSA, 'Treating With Profits Policyholders Fairly', Consultation Paper 207 (December 2003).

[21] See FSA Consultation Paper 207, ibid, 28 for an overview of the legal framework relevant to 'reattribution'.

[22] See FSA Handbook, COBS 20.2.42R–20.2.60R.

[23] 'Medium & Long Term Retail Savings in the UK—A Review' (HM Treasury, 2002), available at www.hm-treasury.gov.uk (accessed on 11 November 2004). The government commissioned this review in June 2001 to 'identify the competitive forces and incentives that drive the industries concerned, in particular their approaches to investment, and, where necessary, to suggest policy responses to ensure that consumers are well served'. It was prompted by P Myners, 'Institutional Investment in the United Kingdom: A Review' (March 2001) (Myners Report), available at http://archive.treasury.gov.uk/docs/2001/myners_report0602.html (accessed on 16 August 2011), which was concerned that investment decision-making was suboptimal as a result of the structure and operation of the retail investment market. Its focus on industry efficiency, value for money and effectiveness of investment decision-making distinguishes it from the FSA's review of with-profits business, which, as a result of the FSA's statutory objectives, focused more on consumer protection and consumer understanding.

[24] Sandler Report, ibid, paras 60–61.

[25] The requirement is contained in the FSA Handbook, COBS 20.3.1R. For background see FSA, 'With Profits Governance, the Role of Actuaries in Life Insurers and Certification of Insurance Returns', Consultation Paper 167 (January 2003).

sufficient detail to enable a knowledgeable observer to understand the material risks and rewards arising from maintaining a with-profits policy with the firm. The PPFM must also cover the firm's management of any inherited estate and the uses to which the firm may put that inherited estate. Firms are required to report to policyholders each year stating whether they have complied with the obligations relating to PPFM.[26]

Secondly, for firms writing with-profits business, the (single) role of appointed actuary was abolished and replaced by two roles: that of 'with-profits actuary' and the 'actuarial function'.[27] These two roles can be performed by a single person acting in a different capacity and are 'controlled functions' for the purposes of the approved persons regime. That change was based primarily on the premise that the appointed actuary represented the interests of both the policyholders and the firm, and that this inevitably involved a conflict of interest. The identification of two separate roles (albeit performed by the same person) is intended to separate the interests of the firm from those of the with-profits policyholders, and in particular to ensure that firms comply with their obligation to treat customers fairly when exercising their discretion in the operation of with-profits business.

The third strand of the FSA's response was to create new sections of the Conduct of Business (COBS) Sourcebook dealing specifically with treating with-profits policyholders fairly and the attribution of inherited estates.[28] These provisions are regarded by the FSA as a codification of good practice rather than new rules that are being imposed on insurers.

4.3.5 Rights under a contract of general insurance

Rights under a contract of general insurance are not normally considered to be investments according to the normal meaning of that term, reflecting the fact that the premium paid for cover is a price paid for the transfer of risk rather than a sum paid over that will be returned at some point in the future. However, since general insurance represents an important technique for financial planning and protection against risk, it is entirely appropriate that it should be treated similarly to investments in the conventional sense for the purposes of regulation. The designation of general insurance as an investment for the purposes of FSMA 2000 gives effect to that policy and integrates activities relating to general insurance into the regulatory framework.

It is not clearly settled whether credit default swaps (CDSs)[29] are contracts of insurance. There is considerable support for the view that they are not,[30] but FSA guidance[31] on the matter does not resolve the issue conclusively. The significance of the issue lies

---

[26] FSA Handbook, COBS 20.4.7R. There must be some independent judgment in the assessment of compliance with PPFM (COBS 20.3.2G). One way of providing such independent judgement is through the creation of a with-profits committee with external members to advise on the interests of policyholders (see FSA Consultation Paper 167, ibid, part 5 'Governance Arrangements for With-Profits Business').

[27] See FSA Handbook, SUP 4.3.13R.

[28] See COBS 20.2.

[29] A CDS is a contract under which a protection buyer pays a protection seller to provide cover in respect of the risk of default by a borrower. The CDS buyer need not be a lender to the borrower.

[30] See L Gullifer and J Payne, *Corporate Finance Law* (Oxford, Hart Publishing, 2011) at Chapter 5.3.3.

[31] FSA Handbook, PERG 6.

in two matters. The first is the regulatory treatment of participants in the CDS market. Insurers are limited to insurance business,[32] and therefore banks would not be able to conduct CDS business through a banking entity if CDSs were considered to be insurance contracts. The second is whether buyers of CDSs owe a duty of disclosure to the seller similar that that which is owed in the context of insurance contracts. The scale and significance of the CDS market suggest that a resolution of these issues is a matter of some urgency, but it is unlikely that the UK would be able to move alone as the CDS market operates on a global basis.

4.3.6 Transfer of rights

Rights under a life assurance contract are a form of incorporeal moveable property (in England, choses in action) and are in principle capable of being assigned to a third party. It is possible for a policy to prohibit assignment, but that is unusual as many policies are taken out on the basis that the right to payment will be assigned, for example in connection with the repayment of a mortgage.[33] Assignment is only effective if written notice[34] is given to the insurer, but there is no requirement to obtain the insurer's consent. An assignee takes the policy subject to equities (in Scotland, subject to the principle *assignatus utitur jure auctoris*), meaning that any defence that is available to the insurer against the original policyholder is also available against an assignee.[35]

Rights under a contract of general insurance can be transferred only with the consent of the insurer as the contract is one in which the identity of the creditor (the insured) is crucial to the obligations that are undertaken by the debtor (the insurer).[36] Thus, for example, in the case of motor insurance, the age and driving record of the insured are important factors for the decision to insure and the setting of the policy terms. In practice, since an insurer would not normally agree to the transfer of a policy, rights under a general insurance policy cannot be transferred. However, there is no restriction on the transfer through assignment of the benefits of an insurance policy, whether before or after the occurrence of an insured event. In this case, the risk faced by the insurer remains the same and the policy benefits (ie a sum of money) are a distinct form of 'property' from the rights under the policy. It follows that the benefits of a policy can be transferred through assignment without the consent of the insurer so long as notice of the assignment is given to the insurer.

---

[32] FSA Handbook, INSPRU 1.5.13R.

[33] In this case the life assured remains the same, but the policy is transferred in security to the mortgagee, who is entitled to the proceeds to the extent necessary to repay the loan advanced to the mortgagor. Another reason for assignment is that there is now a market in 'secondhand' with-profits life policies, which may offer a policyholder a higher price than the surrender value offered by the life office.

[34] This is a requirement of the Policies of Assurance Act 1867, which governs assignment of life polices in England and Scotland. It is also a requirement of the Law of Property Act 1925, which provides an alternative basis for assignment in English law.

[35] See generally J Birds, *Modern Insurance Law*, 7th edn (London, Sweet & Maxwell, 2001) ch 9.

[36] The restrictions are linked to the operation of the principle of *delectus personae* in contract and its implications for assignment. The theoretical and historical background is discussed in R Anderson, *Assignation* (Edinburgh, Edinburgh Legal Education Trust, 2008) 27–34.

4.4 Company shares

Company shares are specified investments for the purposes of FSMA 2000.[37] This section considers their nature, legal title and transfer. It assumes that the reader is familiar with the more general analysis of these issues presented in Chapter 1.

4.4.1 Nature of company shares

It was noted in Chapter 1 that a share is a form of intangible personal property (in Scotland, incorporeal moveable property).[38] That observation, however, leaves unresolved the more fundamental issue of what the property actually comprises.[39] So too does the statutory definition of a share as '[a] share in the share capital of a company'.[40] However, related statutory provisions make clear the nature of a share. Membership of a company is dependent on owning a share[41] and members are parties to the statutory contract[42] between each member and the company and between the members *inter se*. The statutory view is therefore essentially of a share as a contractual relationship.

Judicial definitions of a share support that view. In *Borland's Trustee v Steel Bros & Co Ltd* it was said that:[43]

> A share is the interest of a shareholder in the company measured by a sum of money, for the purpose of liability in the first place, and of interest in the second, but also consisting of a series of mutual covenants entered into by all the shareholders *inter se* in accordance with s 16 of the Companies Act 1862 [now section 33 of the Companies Act 2006]. The contract contained in the articles of association is one of the original incidents of the share. A share is not a sum of money settled in the way suggested, but is an interest measured by a sum of money and made up of various rights contained in the contract, including the right to a sum of money of more or less amount.

A similar approach was adopted in *Commissioners of Inland Revenue v Crossman*.[44] In that case, the interest of a shareholder was defined as being 'composed of rights and obligations which are defined by the Companies Act and by the memorandum and articles of association of the company'. Even those definitions that focus on the property rather than contractual characteristic of shares recognise that the property is essentially a set of

---

[37] See para 11 of sch 2 to FSMA 2000 and Art 21 of the RAO.

[38] Companies Act 2006, s 541.

[39] See, for an historical analysis of this issue, R Pennington, 'Can Shares in Companies be Defined?' (1989) 10 *Company Lawyer* 140.

[40] Companies Act 2006, s 540(1).

[41] Companies Act 2006, s 112. This is the case for a company with a share capital—see also s 113.

[42] See s 33(1) Companies Act 2006.

[43] [1901] 1 Ch 279, 288, per Farwell J.

[44] [1937] AC 26, 66 per Lord Russell of Killowen.

contractual rights.[45] In this respect, the position of a shareholder is different from a trust beneficiary, who (at least in English law) has an equitable interest in the assets comprising the trust fund.

Shareholders' rights are defined by company law and by a company's articles of association and special resolutions, which together form a company's constitution.[46] Company law recognises that the constitution forms the basis of a 'statutory contract' between shareholders and the company and among the shareholders *inter se*.[47] This means that members can require the company to observe the constitution and can enforce the constitution against each other (eg in respect of provisions relating to the sale of shares or the issue of new shares). While the precise legal boundaries of the enforceability of the 'statutory contract' remain unclear—the Companies Act 2006 did not clarify the uncertainty arising from the common law—there have been relatively few problems in practice. In any case, shareholders who have concerns about enforceability of provisions in the constitution can often protect themselves through a shareholders' agreement.[48]

Companies can have different classes of shares with different rights.[49] Ordinary shares are by far the most common category, and if there is only one class of share they are assumed to be ordinary. In respect of ordinary shares, the articles of association of companies normally provide that each share carries one vote.[50] That remains the default rule in the Companies Act 2006.[51] While this is assumed to be standard practice nowadays, there have been variants, particularly in continental Europe, where in the past voting rules were derived from the principle that each member rather than each share carried a vote.[52] It is possible for the articles to provide that a certain class of share has no voting rights, but this is less common nowadays, particularly in the case of public listed companies, in respect of which institutional investors have an established policy opposing the creation of non-voting shares.[53] Enhanced voting rights attaching to particular shares are also possible, for example allowing a particular shareholder to veto certain decisions or actions of the company. Shareholders' agreements, although not part of the articles of association of a company, may attach special conditions to voting rights in certain circumstances. These agreements may be enforced by shareholders against each other through remedies such as

---

[45] See R Pennington, *Pennington's Company Law*, 8th edn (London, Butterworths, 2001) 6 for a definition of a share as a species of intangible movable property which comprises a collection of rights and obligations relating to an interest in a company of an economic and proprietary character.

[46] Companies Act Act 2006, s 17.

[47] Companies Act 2006, s 33.

[48] While common in private companies, shareholders agreements are not common in public companies because they are not normally public documents and bind only the shareholders who enter the agreement.

[49] See also Chapter 7.1.

[50] See Art 54 of Table A (Regulations for Management of a Company Limited by Shares) in the Companies (Tables A to F) Regulations 1985, SI 1985/805. These articles (subject to amendment) continue to govern companies formed prior to the entry into force of the relevant provisions of the Companies Act 2006 (on 1 October 2009).

[51] Companies Act 2006, s 284.

[52] See CA Dunlavy, 'Corporate Governance in Late 19th Century Europe and the US, The Case of Shareholder Voting Rights' in KJ Hopt, H Kanda, MJ Roe, E Wymeersch and S Prigge (eds), *Comparative Corporate Governance—The State of the Art and Emerging Research* (Oxford, Oxford University Press, 1998).

[53] Regarding shareholder voting see generally Chapter 9.6.1.

injunctions[54] (preventing breach) or damages (providing compensation for breach). Individual numbering of shares was common in the past, but has now died out.[55] Therefore, within a particular class, shares are a fungible form of property, meaning that any one is the equivalent of another.

Ordinary shareholders have no legal right to payment of a dividend. Companies are free to retain profits or distribute them to shareholders as they see fit, and the balance between retention and distribution will vary over time and across different industry sectors. Ordinary shareholders ultimately control this issue through voting on dividend resolutions at the annual general meeting.[56]

Taken together, the right to dividends (at the company's discretion) and the right to vote are the essence of what is 'owned' by an ordinary shareholder. This becomes clearer if the focus of the enquiry into the nature of ownership moves from the assets of the company to its earnings and dividends. The company itself, as an independent legal person, owns the assets, but shareholders are entitled to dividends, which are paid from profits. That entitlement is realised through the power of shareholders to vote on a resolution for the payment of dividends.[57] When shares are issued or transferred, it is essentially these rights that are allocated to the owner, hence the assumption in finance theory that the value of a share is the present value of the future stream of dividend income.[58] Viewed in this light, shareholders are holders of legal title to a stream of income in the form of dividends. A share price (or in the aggregate, the market capitalisation of a company) is simply an estimate of the present value of that right and has no necessary link with the value of the company's assets or the share capital recorded in the company's accounts.

Preference shares, as the name suggests, provide investors with preferred rights in respect of any or all of voting, dividends and rights on liquidation of the company. Preference shares normally carry a fixed right to dividend expressed as a percentage of their par value. The dividend is often stated to be cumulative, and will be assumed to be so unless the articles provide otherwise. This means that if the company fails to pay the dividend in one year, the preference shareholders are entitled to payment in the following year(s) before any distribution of profit can be made to the ordinary shareholders.

If a company becomes insolvent, ordinary shareholders are in a weak position. Preferred creditors, ordinary trade creditors and preference shareholders rank ahead of them in terms of claims on the remaining assets of the company. As liquidation is most often the result of insolvency, ordinary shareholders often face the prospect of being paid little or nothing in a liquidation. This is the price to be paid for their equity interest in the company: they are better rewarded than other stakeholders if the company does well and they suffer more if the company fails. Preference shareholders are in a better position than

---

[54] In Scotland, interdict.

[55] The authority to dispense with individual numbering of shares is provided, subject to certain conditions, by s 543(2) of the Companies Act 2006. In particular, the shares must be fully paid and rank *pari passu* (equally) for all purposes with all shares of the same class for the time being issued and fully paid up. That option was first introduced by the Companies Act 1929. Prior to that it was common for shares to be re-designated following issue as 'stock', to which the numbering requirement did not apply, thereby facilitating transfer.

[56] See generally Chapter 7.4.3 re dividend distributions.

[57] Company law controls the circumstances in which a dividend can be paid. See Chapter 7 for more detail.

[58] See K Pilbeam, *Finance and Financial Markets*, 3rd edn (Basingstoke, Palgrave, 2010) ch 9.

ordinary shareholders, but may also face the prospect of losing much of their investment on insolvency.

4.4.2 Legal title

A shareholder is the registered owner of shares in a company. Every company is required to keep a register of its members, and this register is prima facie evidence of the legal title of the shareholder to the relevant shares.[59] The register is not conclusive evidence of membership of the company because (i) section 112 of the Companies Act 2006 also requires agreement for a person to become a member; (ii) it may be that the requirements of the company's articles of association have not been met (eg as a result of pre-emption rights in a private company[60]); or (iii) in the case of dematerialised shares settled through CREST, there may be a discrepancy between the issuer company's register and the Operator register of members.[61] In the case of listed companies, whose shares must be freely transferable, the Operator register will in practice be conclusive in almost every case.

In the past, a share certificate provided evidence of ownership of shares. While it is still possible for this to occur, dematerialisation of share certificates has resulted in relatively few investors holding paper certificates. When they do, the Companies Act 2006 provides that the certificate is prima facie evidence of the legal title of the shareholder to the shares.[62] It is not conclusive evidence, as that issue turns ultimately on who is entitled to have their name entered in the share register. A bona fide purchaser of shares is entitled to rely on a certificate as evidence of the legal title of the seller. If the seller does not in fact have title to sell, the buyer cannot be registered as a member but is entitled to damages from the company at the market price of the shares.[63]

Dematerialisation of share certificates was made possible by section 207 of the Companies Act 1989, which permits the Treasury to make Regulations 'for enabling title to securities to be evidenced and transferred without a written instrument'. The relevant regulations are the Uncertificated Securities Regulations 2001,[64] which set out the principles for dematerialised transfers and establish the CREST computer system through which transfers are made. CREST is not a compulsory system, as the consent of CRESTCo (the operator), the issuer and the shareholder are required for transfers to be made through

---

[59] See ss 113 and 127 Companies Act 2006.

[60] See section 4.4.3 below.

[61] In these circumstances Art 24 of the Uncertificated Securities Regulations 2001 states that entry of a person's name in the issuer register shall not be treated as showing that person to be a member unless: (i) that register shows him as holding shares in certificated form; (ii) the Operator register shows him as holding shares in uncertificated form; or (iii) he is deemed to be a member of the company by Art 32(6)(b) of the Uncertificated Securities Regulations 2001. See below for an explanation of transfer procedures.

[62] Companies Act 2006, s 768. In Scotland, a share certificate is sufficient evidence of legal title unless the contrary is shown.

[63] *Re Bahia and San Francisco Rlwy Co* (1868) 3 QB 584, 594. The company's liability is based on the principle of estoppel: it cannot deny the title of the seller because the certificate issued by the company causes the buyer to believe that the seller had a valid title.

[64] SI 2001/3755. These regulations superseded the 1995 Regulations of the same name (SI 1995/3272).

the system. In particular, a shareholder can choose to retain shares in certificated form, although this will generally lead to higher transaction costs. A small shareholder will generally have little option but to hold the shares in a nominee account run by the purchasing broker.[65] That affects the relationship with the issuer, as the nominee is recorded as the shareholder in the relevant registers and the investor therefore ceases to have a direct relationship with the issuer.

4.4.3 Transfer

Before considering the law relating to how shares are transferred, it is necessary to consider possible limitations on transferability. In principle, a shareholder has a right to transfer shares and, unless expressly authorised by the articles of association, the directors of a company have no power to refuse to register a transfer.[66] In the case of public listed companies, no restriction is possible because it is a condition for listing that the shares be freely transferable. In the case of non-listed public companies or private companies, it is possible for the articles of association to limit transfer.[67] This occurs most often in the case of private companies, whose articles frequently provide that a member may not sell shares without first offering them to existing members at a price determined by an independent valuation (a pre-emption provision).[68] Transfers which do not comply with such a provision in the articles can be set aside so that a transferor is required to make a pre-emptive offer in accordance with the articles.[69]

An agreement to transfer shares, whether made within or outside a regulated market, has no immediate effect on the ownership of the shares. It is necessary for the name of the buyer to be inserted in the company's share register for legal ownership of shares to be transferred. This normally occurs some time after the making of the agreement to transfer ('dealing'). A company can only register a transfer if:

1. A proper instrument of transfer has been delivered to it. The Stock Transfer Act 1963 provides a standard form of stock transfer for registered shares[70] but does not prevent the use of other forms of instrument.

---

[65] The alternatives of becoming a sponsored or full member of CREST are generally not realistic options for small investors.

[66] *Re Smith & Fawcett Ltd* [1942] Ch 304.

[67] The standard articles of a private company authorise the directors to refuse to register a transfer (Art 26(5)) without giving any reason, although this power must be exercised in the best interests of the company: *Re Smith & Fawcett*, ibid. The standard articles of a public company permit the directors to refuse to register a transfer only in limited circumstances (Art 63(5)).

[68] This right of pre-emption, which is contractual in nature, should be distinguished from the statutory rights of pre-emption provided by ss 560–77 of the Companies Act 2006, which do not limit the transfer rights of shareholders (see Chapter 7.3.2). There cannot be restrictions on transfers of shares in public listed companies as the Listing Rules require such shares to be freely transferable.

[69] See J Birds (ed), *Boyle & Birds' Company Law*, 8th edn (Bristol, Jordans, 2011) ch 9.2.2.

[70] The standard form can also be used for gilts and units in unit trusts—see s 1(4).

2. The transfer is made in accordance with the regulations made under section 207 of the Companies Act 1989.[71]

The legal process by which a transferee becomes a member of a company is novation. This is a general principle of contract law that allows a new creditor to be substituted for the existing creditor. The agreement of the debtor (company), existing creditor (seller) and new creditor (buyer) is necessary for novation to take place. The process differs from assignment[72] in that the new creditor does not succeed to the rights of the old creditor but enters a new contractual relationship with the debtor.[73] The terms of the (new) contract are contained in the constitution of the company, which forms the basis of the 'statutory contract'. The agreement of the debtor (issuing company) to the process of novation is shown by it entering the name of the new shareholder (buyer) on the register and removing the name of the previous shareholder (seller).[74]

Transfer of shares held in dematerialised form is effected by an instruction to the company (or the registrar acting for it) to make a change in its share register. In principle, only the operator of the transfer system (CRESTCo) can give such an instruction, although there are some exceptional circumstances (such as a court order) in which instructions from other parties are binding. The company is generally obliged to register a transfer instruction given by the operator and must confirm to the operator that the transfer has occurred. The Regulations contain provisions[75] governing liability for fraudulent or unauthorised instructions, but they do not cover such acts emanating from a computer that is part of the system. This reflects the general approach of the Regulations, which is to require that system participants should be able to rely on properly authenticated dematerialised instructions sent by other system participants.[76] The potential risk faced by investors arising from fraudulent or unauthorised instructions emanating from within the system are dealt with by the inclusion of sending dematerialised instructions on behalf of others within the categories of regulated activities for the purposes of FSMA 2000.[77] This means that persons sending such instructions fall within the rule-making and disciplinary powers of the FSA and could potentially face restitutionary claims as well as financial penalties.[78]

Shares in companies (including public companies) that are not listed or admitted to trading on a regulated market are not held in dematerialised form. Transfers of such shares take place outside regulated markets and do not fall within the standard clearing

---

[71] This is a reference to the Uncertificated Securities Regulations 2001 (SI 2001/3755), which enable transfer through CREST.

[72] Assignment cannot form the legal basis for share transfer since only rights can be transferred through that process whereas novation enables all shareholder rights as well as obligations that bind the company to pass to a new shareholder.

[73] Strictly speaking, therefore, novation is not transfer. Novation does not bind a new shareholder to a shareholders' agreement, which is an agreement made by the shareholders outside the articles.

[74] There may be circumstances in which the issuer can, according to its articles, refuse to register a transfer, but these will be comparatively rare.

[75] Art 36.

[76] Art 35.

[77] See Art 45 of the RAO.

[78] See Chapter 3 regarding the powers of the FSA.

and settlement procedures that apply to listed securities. The transfer procedure for unlisted securities involves the seller providing a completed transfer form and certificate to the buyer in return for the price. The buyer then sends these documents to the company secretary, who, assuming everything is in order, will enter the buyer on the shareholders' register (in place of the seller) and issue a new certificate to the buyer.[79]

4.4.4 Special types of share (investment trust)

Investment trusts are not trusts; they are public limited companies whose business is the management of a portfolio of investments. To become an investment trust, a company normally passes through two regulatory hurdles. First, it becomes an investment company for the purposes of section 833 of the Companies Act 2006. This provides that the company should have given notice to the Registrar of Companies of its intention to carry on business as an investment company and that it complies with the requirements of section 833(2), which imposes restrictions on the manner in which the company operates.[80] The benefit of 'investment company' status is that the company becomes subject to the favourable rules on dividend distributions contained in section 832 of the Companies Act 2006.[81] An investment company must then comply with section 1159 of the Corporation Tax Act 2010 (CTA 2010)[82] in order to qualify as an investment trust. It must also comply with the requirement of S1158 CTA 2010 that it should not be a 'close company' for tax purposes. It is possible, although unusual, to gain 'investment trust' status without being an investment company under section 833 Companies Act 2006. The main benefit of investment trust status is that the fund itself (but not shareholders)

---

[79] For more detail see Birds, above n 69, ch 9.3.2. In the case of transfer of voting control to a new shareholder in a private company, it is standard practice for a share purchase agreement to be concluded between the buyer and the seller setting out detailed terms governing the sale.

[80] The requirements are: (i) that the business of the company consists of investing its funds mainly in securities, with the aim of spreading investment risk and giving members of the company the benefit of the results of the management of its funds; (ii) that none of the company's holdings in companies (other than those which are for the time being investment companies) represents more than 15% by value of the investing company's investments; (iii) that, subject to subs 2A, distribution of the company's capital profits is prohibited by it memorandum or articles of association; and (iv) that the company has not retained, other than in compliance with this part, in respect of any accounting reference period, more than 15% of the income it derives from securities.

[81] See further J Birds et al (eds), *Annotated Companies Legislation* (Oxford, Oxford University Press, 2010) 932.

[82] Section 1159 CTA 2010 requires each of the following conditions to be met: *Condition A*: The company must be UK resident throughout the accounting period; *Condition B*: The shares making up the company's ordinary share capital (or if they are of more than one class, those of each class) must be included in the official UK list throughout the accounting period; *Condition C*: The company's income of the accounting period must be derived wholly or mainly from shares or securities; *Condition D*: The company must not retain in respect of the accounting period an amount which is greater than 15% of the income it derives from shares or securities (but see s 1161); *Condition E*: The company must not at any time in the accounting period have a holding in a company that represents more than 15% by value of the investing company's investments (but see s 1162); *Condition F*: The company's memorandum or articles of association must prohibit the distribution as dividend of surpluses arising from the realisation of investments.

is exempt from capital gains tax.[83] Shareholders pay capital gains tax in the normal way on gains in the value of their investment trust shares.[84]

The portfolio of an investment trust is created initially by raising capital through issuing shares in the company to investors. As the capital and number of shares is fixed, an investment trust is a 'closed-end' fund. It is possible for the capital to be varied in accordance with the normal procedure applicable to companies generally,[85] but that procedure does not lend itself to a process of continuous issue and redemption of shares such as occurs in the case of units in unit trusts and shares in open-ended investment companies (OEICs). Thus, while investment trusts are functionally similar to other investment funds in that they offer a diversified form of pooled investment, the mechanism through which an investor participates (ie the share) is indistinguishable from that which is used in ordinary trading companies.

The reference to 'trust' survives from the late nineteenth century, when investment companies were commonly established by a 'deed of settlement', which was a form of trust.[86] Investment trusts are listed in the UK and admitted to trading on the London Stock Exchange. Their internal organisation and the rights of their shareholders are, like any other listed company, controlled by three main legal sources: company law; their articles of association; and the Listing Rules. A company that is an investment trust is (like any other company) a separate legal person and owns the investments that comprise the fund. Shareholders have no direct claim to the underlying investments.

Investment trusts are sometimes described as 'unregulated'. This is true in the sense that they are not 'collective investment schemes' for the purposes of FSMA 2000 and therefore do not fall under the regulations applicable to such schemes. They are, however, subject to the UKLA Listing Rules, which apply to all listed companies. One of the requirements for 'investment trust' status under CTA 2010 is that the entire ordinary share capital of the company must be listed. The Listing Rules contains special provisions for closed-end investment funds with a premium listing, dealing with matters such as: the restriction of the business to investment; the requirement for a board that is independent from the investment manager; and disclosure of the investment policy.[87]

Investment managers who manage the assets of investment trusts must be authorised under FSMA 2000 and private customers who are advised on investment trusts are protected by the FSA's Conduct of Business Rules.[88]

Purchase and sale of shares in an investment trust differs from unit trusts and OEICs in two significant ways. First, in the case of unit trusts and OEICs, the issue/redemption process is managed internally (by the manager or ACD respectively), whereas the sale or purchase of shares in an investment trust occurs in the (public) secondary market for shares. Secondly, the price at which units/shares in unit trusts and OEICs are issued and

---

[83] Taxation of Chargeable Gains Act 1992, s 100. The same principle applies to an authorised unit trust.

[84] The same is true for unit-holders in an authorised unit trust.

[85] See Chapter 7.

[86] See KF Sin, *The Legal Nature of the Unit Trust* (Oxford, Oxford University Press, 1997) 13–19; and *Gower's Principles of Modern Company Law*, 4th edn (London, Sweet & Maxwell, 1979) 266–72.

[87] See FSA Handbook, LR 15.2.

[88] See Chapter 6 for more detail.

redeemed is related to the net asset value of the fund and is regulated by the FSA. In the case of investment trust shares, there is no necessary link between the price at which the shares are transferred between investors and the net asset value of the fund. The price of an investment trust share is determined in the open market, just like any other share. Hence, investment trust shares can and often do trade at either a discount or premium to their net asset value.[89]

A split capital investment trust is an investment trust with a fixed life span.[90] Unlike a conventional investment trust, which has no fixed life, a split capital trust is wound up on a predetermined date. 'Split capital' refers to the existence of different classes of share with different rights. The objective of a split capital structure is to target different types of investor, some of whom require income and others of whom are more concerned with long-term capital appreciation. Split capital trusts, especially those with more complex structures, involve structural gearing because the return on any one class of share is determined not only by the entitlement of that class but also by that of others. This can be distinguished from financial gearing that arises when an investment trust borrows money to increase the size of the fund available for investment.

The early forms of split capital trust issued income and capital shares. The former were entitled to the entire income from the fund while the latter were entitled to the capital. Over time, more complex structures were introduced. They often included:[91]

- Zero dividend preference shares. These are preference shares that have no entitlement to income. They have a predetermined capital return that is not guaranteed and is dependent on sufficient assets being available at winding-up.
- Income shares. These shares vary in their entitlement as to capital and income.
- Ordinary income shares. These shares offer potential for a rising income. They have no predetermined capital value, but on winding-up are entitled to all surplus assets after prior ranking charges (which usually include zero dividend preference shares).
- Capital shares. These shares are entitled to all surplus assets after prior ranking charges. The prior ranking charges may include some or all of the share classes above.

The split capital investment trust sector expanded rapidly during the 1990s,[92] driven largely by the rising equity market. However, the collapse in the equity market from 1999 onwards resulted in fundamental problems in the sector being exposed. The two main problems were high levels of borrowing (gearing) and investment in other split investment trusts (cross-holdings). These two characteristics meant that many trusts faced severe financial difficulties as a result of the fall in the equity market. Illustrative figures produced by the FSA show the effect of the fall in the market over the period March 1999 to March 2002. While the FTSE 100 Index fell by 16.2% over that period, a typical

---

[89] While this explains how discounts/premiums can arise, it does not adequately explain why they do. That remains something of a mystery in the sense that the general principles of finance would predict that a basket of shares should have the same value as the aggregate of its components.

[90] See generally FSA, 'Split Capital Closed End Funds', Discussion Paper 10 (December 2001).

[91] This is an overview of typical share classes. Each split capital trust has a unique pattern of entitlement and order of priority on winding-up.

[92] FSA Policy Statement, 'Split Capital Investment Trusts' (May 2002) notes that 55 were launched between 1990 and 1999 and 34 between 1999 and 2001.

split capital investment trust with no cross holdings fell by 39.1% and one with cross-holding representing between 41 and 70% of its portfolio fell by 98%.[93] Many investors suffered heavy losses, exacerbated by the fact that the insolvency of an investment trust is not an event in respect of which a claim can be made under the Financial Services Compensation Scheme.[94]

Following its investigation of the split capital debacle, the FSA introduced changes to the listing rules applicable to investment trusts and to the conduct of business rules applicable to transactions in the securities issued by them.[95] Two changes are particularly significant:

- Cross-holdings. There is a new listing rule (in the form of a condition for admission to listing and a continuing obligation) that limits to 10% in aggregate the value of the gross assets that may be invested in other listed investment companies. The rule does not apply if the relevant investment company has a stated investment policy to invest no more than 15% of their gross assets in other listed investment companies.
- The Board of Directors. The split capital debacle showed that the requirement of the listing rules that the board must be able to demonstrate that it will act independently of any investment manager was often not borne out in practice. The result was that the role of the board of directors in promoting the interests of shareholders and monitoring the performance of the manager was often compromised. To remedy this, the listing rules have been altered so as to cast a wider net over persons who will not be considered to be independent of the manager.[96]

4.4.5 Special types of share (ETF)

Exchange traded funds are open-ended funds that are structured as listed companies. They are relatively new to the UK, having been launched in April 2000, but are well established in other countries such as the US and Canada. The ETF sector in the UK is composed entirely of index-tracking funds and is able to avoid stamp duty (normally 0.5% of the purchase cost of securities) by being based in Dublin (where, confusingly from the UK perspective, they are classified as mutual funds). They are therefore capable of offering exposure to a diversified portfolio at lower cost than other forms of pooled investment fund.

In financial terms, the process of issue/redemption of ETF shares is in principle similar to that for OEICs and unit trusts in that there is a direct link between the price and the net asset value of the fund. ETFs are not, however, 'collective investment schemes' for the

---

[93] Ibid, 6.

[94] See Chapter 6.5. Other potential remedies for private investors, such as a complaint to the Financial Ombudsman or an action for damages arising from breach of a regulatory rule, are considered in Chapter 6.

[95] The changes were contained in the Investment Entities (Listing Rules and Conduct of Business) Instrument 2003, made under a variety of powers contained in FSMA 2000. On the background and rationale for the changes see FSA, 'Investment Companies (including Investment Trusts) Proposed Changes to the Listing Rules and Conduct of Business Rules', Consultation Paper 164 (January 2003).

[96] See FSA Handbook, LR 15.2.12A R. These rules are in addition to the requirements of the UK Code of Corporate Governance that are applicable to investment trusts. See Chapter 10.

purposes of FSMA 2000, with the result that their regulatory position is more similar to investment trusts. As entities, ETFs are regulated primarily by the listing rules (in respect of admission to listing, financial reporting and continuing obligations), while transactions in ETF shares are regulated by the COB Sourcebook.

4.5 Debt instruments

This category of specified investment[97] refers to loans that are raised by organisations other than the government or public sector bodies. Companies frequently raise loans to finance their business in addition to share capital.[98] Such loans can take the following forms:

- Debentures. This term has no technical legal meaning, but is used in the UK to refer to long-term secured loans.
- Loan stock. This refers to long-term unsecured loans.
- Bonds. This is a generic term referring to any form of long-term loan.
- Commercial paper. This refers to short-term loans of up to one year.

An investor holding any of these instruments is in a better position than a shareholder (ordinary or preference) in the event of liquidation because his claim to the assets of the company ranks ahead of shareholders. This results from the nature of the relationship between the holder of loan capital and the issuer, which is that of debtor (issuer)/creditor (holder). An investor who makes a loan to a company is a creditor in respect of the loan, whereas a shareholder is not a creditor of the company for his share capital although he has a contractual and statutory right to share in surplus assets (after payment of creditors) on a winding-up.

4.5.1 Definition and categorisation

The term 'debenture' is not in itself a legal term of art and its broad scope is reflected by the most widely quoted judicial definition:[99]

> In my opinion a debenture means a document which either creates a debt or acknowledges it, and any document which fulfils either of these conditions is a 'debenture'. I cannot find any precise legal definition of the term, it is not either in law or commerce a strictly technical term, or what is called a term of art.

It is clear from this definition that the legal term 'debenture' can be applied to any form of

---

[97] See Art 77 of the RAO.
[98] See generally Chapter 7.
[99] *Levy v Abercorris Slate and Slab Co* (1887) 37 Ch D 260, 264 per Chitty J.

loan made to a company irrespective of the terminology applied to the loan by commercial practice. Debentures can take a variety of forms. They can have a redemption date that is fixed or dependent on a future contingency or they can be perpetual (irredeemable).[100] Interest payable on the loan can be fixed or variable ('floating') by reference to a specified benchmark such as LIBOR.[101] They can be secured on the company's assets or unsecured.[102] They can be listed and traded on a stock exchange or unlisted.[103] They may or may not carry the right to vote at company meetings. Some debentures carry special privileges in addition to the right to interest.[104]

Debentures can be in the form of a loan made by a single lender or (as is more often the case) can comprise a fund lent by a group of lenders ('debenture stock'). In the latter case, it is common for trustees to be appointed to represent the collective interest of lenders in dealing with the company.[105] In principle, the duties of trustees include taking charge of documents of title to property on which the debt is secured, safeguarding the interests of debenture stockholders (eg in relation to compliance with the company's obligations under the loan agreement) and enforcing the security.[106] There are, however, no specific provisions in company law relating to the duties of trustees for debenture holders, with the result that the general law relating to trustees is applicable. Company law does, however, make any exclusion of the liability of trustees for debenture holders void.[107]

Debentures can be issued in registered or bearer form. Unlike the position in relation to shares, there is no legal obligation to maintain a register of debenture holders.[108] There are, however, two reasons for companies to do so. First, it will normally be required by a trust deed creating debenture stock in registered form. Secondly, a company is required to open and maintain such a register as a condition for dematerialisation and settlement by electronic transfer within the CREST settlement system.[109] As discussed below, the function of the register of debenture holders differs from the register of members.

When debentures are issued in bearer form, the company has no ownership record or manner of identifying the holder. Such debentures may or may not be negotiable instruments; they are, though, if they are promissory notes within the meaning of the Bills of

---

[100] Companies Act 1985, s 193. As Pennington, above n 45, 564 observes, the term 'irredeemable' is not entirely accurate as perpetual debentures can be redeemed by the holder on the default of the borrower.

[101] The London Interbank Offered Rate, which is the rate at which banks can borrow in the wholesale money market.

[102] Commercial practice in the UK generally refers to secured loans as 'debentures' and unsecured loans as either 'loan stock' or 'loan notes', depending on the duration of the loan. See Chapter 7 for an overview of security interests granted by companies.

[103] Listed loan instruments are often referred to as corporate bonds and are generally unsecured. The terms of such loans are linked to the credit rating of an issuer issued by credit rating agencies: see Chapter 14.1.7.

[104] Eg those relating to sporting venues, such as Wimbledon and Murrayfield.

[105] See J Benjamin, *Interests in Securities* (Oxford, Oxford University Press, 2000) 13.

[106] Pennington, above n 45, 577 notes that in practice trustees rarely fulfil the second and third functions.

[107] Companies Act 1985, s 192(1).

[108] However, s 741 of the Companies Act 2006 introduced a requirement to register an issue of debentures with the Registrar of Companies. That is in addition to the requirement to register a charge that secures the issue (see Chapter 7.4.5). However, registration of an issue of debentures is not linked with ownership (as it is in the case of shares).

[109] Uncertificated Securities Regulations (SI 2001/3755), Arts 18(2), 19(2) and 19(3).

Exchange Act 1882.[110] A single debenture or series of debentures could fall within this definition, but debenture stock issued in bearer form cannot fall within the definition as the promise to pay the debt is made to the trustees rather than directly to holders (bearers) of the debentures. Whether or not a debenture issued in bearer form is a negotiable instrument has implications for the rights of a transferee (see below).

Some bonds are convertible into ordinary shares on the basis of a formula that typically allows x bonds to be converted into y shares. This provides investors with a security that has both debt and equity characteristics. The fixed interest rate attached to a bond provides a guaranteed return and the option to convert allows the holder to benefit from a rise in the value of the ordinary shares into which conversion is possible. A variant of the convertible bond is a bond with warrants attached, entitling the holder to subscribe for a fixed number of ordinary shares at an agreed price at some point in the future. Some issues allow for such warrants to become detached from the securities and to be sold or transferred independently.

Holders of convertible bonds are not protected by law from the negative impact of changes in the share capital of the issuer. For example, suppose that five bonds can be converted into three ordinary shares after 5 years. Assume the company increases its share capital by 25% through a (one-for-four) rights issue in the third year. As a result of this issue the three-for-five conversion option is less valuable because the three represents a smaller proportion of the issuer's ordinary shares. A contract term will not be implied into a convertible or warrant issue that adjusts the conversion or subscription formula to reflect the change in the issuer's share capital.[111] However, it is possible for the terms of issue to provide this protection to the bondholders.

Eurobonds are a form of corporate bond that have particular characteristics. They are bearer bonds issued in a currency other than that of the domicile of the issuer (eg bonds issued in US dollars by a UK company). They are generally unsecured. A trustee is appointed to safeguard the interests of bondholders. The 'Euro' designation reflects the historic origin of the market, which developed as a means to invest large bank deposits that were built up in European financial centres as a result of the oil price boom in the 1970s and the introduction by the US of withholding taxes on foreign bank deposits. These deposits were available to lend to companies who were willing to borrow in a foreign currency. The market in Eurobonds is not limited to European issuers, lenders or currencies.[112]

The Eurobond market is an 'over-the-counter' market, meaning that it has no central location or organisation and each transaction is conducted on an ad hoc basis. The 'market' itself is not regulated under FSMA 2000 but the market participants are, as they are normally dealing in investments in the course of a business. Transfer of Eurobonds (as with other forms of bearer bond) was in the past effected simply by delivery of the

---

[110] Section 83 provides that: 'A promissory note is an unconditional promise in writing made by one person to another signed by the maker, engaging to pay, on demand or at a fixed or determinable future time, a sum certain in money, to, or to the order of, a specified person or to bearer.' The most common example is a bank note.

[111] *Forsayth Oil and Gas NL v Livia Pty Ltd* [1985] BCLC 378.

[112] Many Eurobond issues are raised simply because the cost of borrowing is lowest in that currency and are later swapped into the currency in which the issuer really wants to have the money.

instrument to the transferee. Following dematerialisation of Eurobond issues, the standard practice now is for a global bond to be issued to a depositary institution,[113] which records the acquisition of a given number of bonds by an investor in its register. Below this level, there may also be a custodian who 'holds' the bonds on behalf of an investor.[114]

'Junk bonds' is a generic term for bonds that are below 'investment grade'. This is determined by the rating attached to a bond by rating agencies.[115] A rating below 'BBB' generally results in a bond not being eligible for inclusion in investment portfolios of institutional investors. To attract investors and offset the risk of default, such bonds have to offer interest rates considerably higher than those of investment grade bonds.

4.5.2 Transfers

A debt in any of the forms discussed above is, from the perspective of property law, a legal chose in action (in Scotland incorporeal moveable property) and can therefore in principle be transferred by assignment. Even if a company maintains a register of debenture holders in respect of an issue of debentures, it does not have the status of the register of members. Entry in the register of members is necessary to become a member (shareholder), but it is possible to be a debenture holder without being entered in a register of debenture holders (eg if a company does not have such a register). In other words, ownership of debentures is not based on registration, whereas ownership of ordinary shares is. The result is that the legal process for the transfer of debentures is assignment (in Scotland assignation), which is the standard legal process for the transfer of debt.

The provisions of the Companies Act 1985 and the Uncertificated Securities Regulations 2001 relating to transfers of shares (above) apply equally to debentures in registered form, assuming that the debentures take the form of debenture stock and not a single mortgage or charge over the company's property. However, as registered debentures are transferred by assignment (assignation), the assignee (buyer) in principle takes subject to any defects in the title of the assignor (seller). The law is based on the principle that an assignee of a debt (as opposed to a negotiable instrument) cannot acquire a better title than the assignor.[116] A defect could exist, for example, if the issue of the debenture was induced by misrepresentation and the contract is therefore voidable.[117]

Debentures issued in bearer form are transferred simply by delivery. The rights of a

---

[113] See Chapter 14.1.4 regarding the nature of securities depositaries. The depositary institutions are normally Cedel or Euroclear, based in Luxembourg and Brussels respectively.

[114] See Chapter 14.1.3 regarding custody of securities.

[115] Rating agencies are private sector bodies that grade bonds. The three most prominent agencies are Moody's Investors Services Inc, Standard & Poor's Ratings Services and Fitch Investors Service Inc, all based in the USA. For a general discussion of the role of rating agencies in financial markets see S Schwarcz, 'Private Ordering of Public Markets: The Rating Agency Paradox' 2002(1) *University of Illinios Law Review* 1. See also Chapter 14.1.7.

[116] The Latin maxim 'assignatus utitur jure auctoris' encapsulates the principle.

[117] See eg *Stoddart v Union Trust Ltd* [1912] 1 KB 181.

transferee depend on whether the debenture is or is not a negotiable instrument,[118] which is a form of debt that occupies a privileged position for the purposes of transfer. If it is, a holder in due course[119] takes free from any defect in the title of a transferor. If it is not (as is generally the case for debenture stock) a transferee takes subject to any defects in title of a transferor. It is, however, possible (and common) for debentures to be issued by a company on the basis that a holder takes the debenture free from any claim of the company against an original or intermediate holder. This frees a holder from the potential risk arising from the common law rule that an assignee takes only the rights of an assignor. Unaltered, that rule would have the effect that any claim of the company against an original holder would be passed down the chain of assignees (debenture holders).

4.6 Alternative finance investment bonds

These bonds are specified investments under the RAO. Although the term is not used, the reference is to so-called 'sukuk' instruments, which are 'Shari'ah-compliant' financial instruments that perform an equivalent function to loans or bonds in the western financial system.[120] The key differentiating feature of these instruments is that they do not pay interest in the conventional sense, but are structured so as to pay a return linked to the assets which the bond has funded. In that sense, they can be regarded as a form of asset-based and profit-sharing financial instrument. Recognition of these instruments as recognised investments, along with special provisions of tax law applicable to them, is intended to meet several policy objectives. The first is that all individuals, irrespective of belief, should have access to competitively priced financial products. The second is a policy objective of ensuring that London is at the forefront of developments in the 'Shari'ah-compliant' international financial market. The third objective is to bring these instruments within the conventional regulatory regime so as to ensure that providers of different types of product are subject to equivalent forms of regulation. This carries implications much more for regulatory capital and conduct of business than for product design, which is largely within the control of any product provider subject to the constraints imposed by the general law.

---

[118] That issue is dependent on the debenture falling within the definition of a promissory note in s 83 of the Bills of Exchange Act 1882. The provisions of that Act relating to bills of exchange (such as their negotiable character) apply equally to promissory notes (see s 89(1)). A debenture in bearer form would, in principle, fall within this definition, but see n 119 below.

[119] See s 29 of the Bills of Exchange Act 1882. An essential element of the definition is that a holder in due course takes a bill in good faith without notice of any defect in the title of the person from whom he took it. See the Financial Markets Law Committee, 'Property Interests in Investment Securities' (July 2004) para 6.8, available at http://www.justice.gov.uk/lawcommission/docs/fmlc_report.pdf (15 Aug 2011), suggesting that investors in bonds, legal title to which is held by an intermediary (eg custodian), are not holders in due course.

[120] See generally A Al Elsheikh and J Tanega, 'Sukuk Structure and its Regulatory Environment in the Kingdom of Saudi Arabia' (2011) 5(3) *Law and Financial Markets Review* 183.

4.7 Government and public securities

Government (sometimes referred to as 'Treasury') and public securities are loans raised by the government and public authorities. They are specified investments for the purposes of FSMA 2000.[121] The term 'gilt-edged stock' (or 'gilts') is used in respect of government borrowing because of the security attaching to the loan as a result of the government's promise to repay the loan. Loans are raised for different periods at different interest rates, and are categorised as being short (up to 5 years), medium (up to 10 years) or long (over 10 years) dated. The interest rate is fixed. The par value, at which the loan will be redeemed, is normally £1. However, gilts need not be issued at par, and the prices at which they trade will reflect movements in interest rates since their issue.[122]

Gilts are registered securities[123] and are therefore transferred by the legal process of novation.[124] Legal title is now generally held in dematerialised form[125] and transfers normally take place through CREST.[126] It does, however, remain possible for transfers of certificated securities to be effected outside the CREST system by means of a stock transfer.[127]

4.8 Instruments giving entitlement to investments

Warrants are the main form of investment in this category.[128] A warrant is a contractual entitlement to acquire securities at an agreed price at a future date. Warrants are generally issued by companies in conjunction with new securities with the objective of attracting investors who will be able either to exercise the warrants (thereby acquiring additional shares in the company) or sell the warrants in the market. They are specified investments for the purpose of FSMA 2000.[129] From a financial perspective, they can be regarded either as a discount applied to the price of the issue of securities with which they are

---

[121] See Art 78 of the Regulated Activities Order (SI 2001/544). Instruments issued by the National Savings Bank are excluded from the definition of specified investments.

[122] Regarding the structure and movements in interest rates see K Pilbeam, *Finance and Financial Markets* (3rd edn, Basingstoke, Palgrave, 2010) ch 4.

[123] The register is held either by CREST (for dematerialised issues) or by the Bank of England (for certificated stock).

[124] See section 4.4.3 for an explanation of novation.

[125] Legal title is recorded and transferred electronically rather than by the use of paper records.

[126] See section 4.4.2.

[127] See s 1 of the Stock Transfer Act 1963 and Regulation 15(1) of the Government Stock Regulations 2004, SI 2004/1611.

[128] Subscription shares are functionally equivalent to warrants. They provide rights to subscribe for shares but are not in themselves shares.

[129] See Art 80 of the RAO.

associated or as a form of dilution of future earnings (as exercise of the warrants will increase the number of shares in issue and thereby reduce the earnings per share). From either perspective, it is clear that an issue of warrants represents a cost to the company as it dilutes the capital raised from the relevant issue of securities.

Warrants can generally be traded in the secondary market and transfer occurs in accordance with the principles outlined above in respect of debt securities. This remains so even if the warrants relate to registered securities such as ordinary shares, because a warrant itself is not a registered security and is therefore transferred through the process of assignment.

Covered warrants are a relatively new development. A covered warrant is issued by a financial institution and gives the holder the right, but not the obligation, to buy or sell an underlying asset at a specified price, on or before a predetermined date. It resembles an option in the sense that there is no obligation to buy or sell and the maximum loss that can be suffered by an investor is the premium paid for the warrant. The term 'covered' denotes the fact that when issuers sell a warrant to an investor, they will 'cover' (hedge) their exposure by buying the underlying securities in the market. In the UK, covered warrants are available on a wide range of UK and international blue chip and midcap shares and indices. Covered warrants have on average a life of 6–12 months, although some have a lifespan of up to 5 years.

4.9 Certificates representing certain securities

Depositary receipts (DRs) are the main example of this specified investment.[130] They facilitate indirect investment in foreign securities and serve the needs of investors in a variety of circumstances.[131] Examples are where there is a restriction on foreign ownership of investment or where dealing in such investments is administratively complex and costly.[132] DRs are in essence receipts issued by a legal owner of securities to investors specifying that the depositary holds the securities as trustee for the depositary receipt holders.[133] The process can be undertaken either with ('sponsored') or without ('unsponsored') the cooperation of the issuer of the underlying shares. In the former case, it is common for a specific issue of shares to be made to the depositary, whereas in the latter case the shares have to be bought by the depositary in the market.

The terms under which a depositary holds the underlying shares for the DR holders

---

[130] Ibid.

[131] Although they share the characteristic of indirect investment with collective investment funds, they are not categorised as such under FSMA 2000.

[132] For details of the American Depositary Receipt programmes of FTSE 100 companies, see RC Nolan, 'Indirect Investors: A Greater Say in the Company?' (2003) 1 *Journal of Corporate Law Studies* 73.

[133] The term 'depositary receipt' and references to a 'depositary' in this context should be distinguished from the use of the term 'depositary' in the context of the immobilisation of securities. Securities in respect of which depositary receipts are issued may or may not be immobilised.

will be set out in a deposit agreement. This will cover matters such as voting rights in respect of the underlying shares, the payment of dividends and the procedure for transfer of the DRs. In common with many other instances of investment, the rights held by the DR holder are interests in securities derived from the depositary and not direct legal ownership of the underlying securities. Transfers of DRs are arranged through movements between accounts held by investors (or their custodians) with the depositary, who is always the legal owner of the security (assuming immobilisation of legal title).

4.10 Units in a collective investment scheme

4.10.1 Nature and typology of investment funds

Investment funds can be defined as arrangements under which individuals contribute to a common fund managed on their behalf by a professional investment manager. They are attractive to both institutional and private investors for a number of reasons. They offer a degree of diversification that would often be difficult to replicate through direct investments, such as when an investor wants exposure to an overseas market. They also offer economies of scale in respect of dealing, custody and transfer as the fund benefits from operating on a larger scale than its contributors. Finally, a fund may be able to offer improved market access for investors by having access to some investments that are offered only to institutional investors.[134]

The most basic distinction is between open- and closed-end funds. Closed-end funds take the form of investment companies, which are public companies whose business is the investing of its funds in securities.[135] The capital of such a company can only be increased or reduced by following the normal rules of company law that apply in this situation. Investment trusts are the main example of closed-end funds. In most respects, they are similar to any other listed company. The main difference is that they do not engage directly in trade. Rather, their assets are investments, and their business is to manage these investments on behalf of their shareholders. The main disadvantage of closed-end funds is that they cannot vary their capital on an ongoing basis.[136] This means that investors in such funds can only buy or sell a participation in the fund (in the form of shares) in the market, in the same way as they would in respect of any other listed

---

[134] This includes in some circumstances depositary receipts and new issues offered only to a limited circle of institutional investors.

[135] Companies Act 1985, s 266.

[136] As limited companies, they are subject to the normal company law rules on changes to capital. These rules were developed to protect creditors and limit the extent to which a company can make changes to its capital.

(trading) company. Moreover, there is often a disparity between the price of the shares in investment trusts and the value of the underlying portfolio of investments.[137]

Open-end funds differ in that they have a variable capital structure. This means that they can adjust their capital according to the demand for investment in the fund. They do this by creating and redeeming participations in the fund on a continuous basis. New units are created when a new investor wants to participate in the fund and existing units are cancelled when an investor wants to withdraw. This process is managed internally by the operator of the fund on a continuous basis, with the result that an investor always has liquidity in relation to his holding. Moreover, as a result of the relevant regulatory rules, the pricing of units on issue or redemption is directly related to the value of the underlying portfolio. This means that, by comparison with closed-end funds, the investor avoids the risk of the value of his (indirect) investment deviating from the underlying investments to which it is linked.

Open-end funds exist in two main forms. Unit trusts, as the name suggests, are organised on the basis of a trust deed. As they are not companies, they were able to avoid the historic prohibition on companies having a variable capital structure. They have a relatively long history, dating back to the late 1800s.[138] Investment funds that are organised as companies with variable capital (referred to as 'mutual funds' in the US) are a relatively recent innovation in the UK, made possible by a relaxation of the historic prohibition against such companies. Such open-ended investment companies (OEICs) have now become the preferred method of organising investment funds as they are more familiar to investors in jurisdictions in which the unit trust is not recognised.

A distinction can also be drawn between regulated and unregulated investment funds. Regulated schemes are referred to as 'collective investment schemes' or 'authorised schemes' by FSMA 2000.[139] A collective investment scheme is defined by FSMA 2000 as follows:[140]

> any arrangements with respect to property of any description, including money, the purpose or effect of which is to enable persons taking part in the arrangements (whether by becoming owners of the property or any part of it or otherwise) to participate in or receive profits or income arising from the acquisition, holding, management or disposal of the property or sums paid out of such profits or income.

The main examples of collective investment schemes are unit trusts and investment companies with variable capital (ICVCs).[141] Investment trusts do not fall within the scope of collective investment schemes as the term excludes funds organised as companies

---

[137] This is commonly referred to by saying that investment trusts trade at a discount to their underlying net asset value. It is not clear why this should be so. The discount has varied considerably over time and some trusts have even traded at a premium.

[138] See *Gower's Principles of Modern Company Law*, above n 86, 266–72 for an historical account of the unit trust.

[139] See ss 235–37 FSMA 2000 and FSMA 2000 (Collective Investment Schemes) Order 2001, SI 2001/1062.

[140] FSMA 2000, s 235. The definition does not require that the contributors be the legal owners of the assets in the fund.

[141] While the term OEIC is used generically to refer to any open-ended investment company, ICVC refers to a UK-authorised OEIC. FSMA 2000, sch 5.1(3) provides that an authorised open-ended investment company is an authorised person.

other then OEICs.[142] The benefit of being constituted as an authorised scheme is that an investment fund can then be promoted to the public. Unauthorised investment funds can be established, but they suffer from the drawback that they cannot be promoted to the public under the regulations applicable to collective investment schemes.

Collective investment schemes that qualify as UCITS schemes can be marketed throughout the EU on the basis of an authorisation granted by the home state. The UCITS Directive,[143] adopted by the EC in 1985, was the first example of the operation of the system of 'single licence' and 'home country control' that has since been extended to the remainder of the financial sector.[144] The UCITS Directive was quite restrictive as to the type of investment that could be held by a qualifying fund, but a later directive extended the range of permissible investments.[145]

Two common types of unauthorised investment fund are hedge funds and venture capital funds formed as general partnerships. The term 'hedge fund', while widely used, has no precise meaning but is generally taken to refer to funds with a number of distinct characteristics.[146] Usually, hedge funds:

- are organised as private investment partnerships or offshore investment corporations;
- use a wide variety of trading strategies involving position-taking in a range of markets;
- employ an assortment of trading techniques and instruments, often including short-selling, derivatives and leverage;
- pay performance fees to their managers; and
- have an investor base comprising wealthy individuals and institutions and a relatively high minimum investment limit (set at US$100,000 or higher for most funds).

Hedge funds can be marketed in the UK to professional clients and eligible counterparties.[147] At present, they cannot generally be freely offered to private customers in the UK as they are classified as unregulated collective investment schemes. However, the FSA Handbook does permit marketing to private customers in certain circumstances, such as when a firm takes reasonable steps to ensure that the fund is suitable.[148]

Venture capital (or 'private equity') funds are created for the purpose of investing on a pooled basis in relatively new business ventures. They typically invest at various stages in the development of new ventures with a view to selling that investment at a later date (either to another venture capitalist or through a public offering when the company is 'floated' on the stockmarket). Such funds are normally constituted as limited partnerships under the Limited Partnership Act 1907 and generally comprise a general partner (the

---

[142] See SI 2001/1062, Art 21.

[143] Directive 85/611/EEC on the co-ordination of laws, regulations and administrative provisions relating to undertakings for collective investment in transferable securities (UCITS) [1985] OJ L375/3 (as amended).

[144] See Chapter 2.9 regarding the EU system of regulation.

[145] See Directive 2001/108/EC [2002] OJ L41/35, commonly referred to as the 'Product Directive'. It was implemented in the UK by changes to the FSA Handbook of Rules and Guidance.

[146] See FSA, 'Hedge Funds and the FSA', Discussion Paper (DP) 16 (2002) for a more detailed explanation of the operation of hedge funds. The FSA did canvass a relaxation of the rule relating to the marketing of hedge funds in the UK (see DP 16), but concluded that it was not appropriate on the basis that the current regime provides the right balance of consumer protection and access.

[147] COBS 4.12.1R. See Chapter 15.1 for an explanation of customer classification under FSMA 2000.

[148] Ibid.

venture capitalist) and a number of limited partners. The general partner bears unlimited liability, whereas the liability of the limited partners is limited to their capital contribution to the partnership. The partnership normally has a fixed duration and will often make provision for the proceeds of disposals of investments to be distributed before the end of that period. The distribution of profits is a matter for agreement between the partners, but the higher risk assumed by the general partner is normally associated with a right to a higher proportion of profits than the limited partners.

4.10.2 Unit trusts

Unit trusts can be traced back to the second half of the nineteenth century, but their modern form originated in the US in the 1930s.[149] Unlike some of the older forms of unit trust, such as the fixed trust based on a fixed portfolio with a fixed duration, the modern form of unit trust offers unit-holders transferability and liquidity. The manager and trustee are required to issue and redeem units on a continuous basis, so that the unit-holder always has a two-way market available in the units. The issue and redemption process is undertaken by reference to the value of the underlying investments, with the result that, from an investment perspective, the unit-holder is in the same position as if he were the direct owner of the underlying investments, which he is not.

Under the unit-trust form of organisation, the ownership interest of a contributor is in the units that are allocated to him by the operator. The contributor has no legal ownership in respect of the assets (investments) held within the fund.[150] The legal owner of the investments is the trustee, who holds the investments on behalf of the contributors (beneficiaries). The investor's stake can be expressed as an entitlement to a proportionate share of the profits (capital gains as well as income) in any period of account.

A fundamental characteristic of the unit trust is that unit-holders are able to realise their investment at a price related to the net asset value of the fund.[151] While the net asset value of the fund is subject to changes in the value of the underlying portfolio, there is no market pricing of the units held by a unit-holder. Pricing of units in a unit trust is undertaken internally by the manager of the trust, subject to regulatory rules set by the FSA. This distinguishes the unit trust from an investment trust, in which a shareholder does not have this guarantee and will often find that the investment can be sold only at a discount to the underlying value of the portfolio. In the case of the unit trust, the pricing

---

[149] Regarding the history of unit trusts see Sin, above n 86, ch 1, 7–44.

[150] In England, a contributor is the beneficial owner of the underlying assets. The legal position of a holder of units in a unit trust in England can be described as that of a person with an indirect and unallocated interest in a changeable pool of securities that is owned beneficially by all unit-holders. In Scotland, a contributor does not have ownership of the underlying assets because trust law in Scotland does not recognise division of ownership. A contributor in Scotland is a beneficiary of the trust.

[151] This is a requirement for all collective investment schemes under the UCITS Directive (85/611/EEC). FSMA 2000, s 243(10) provides that: 'The participants must be entitled to have their units redeemed in accordance with the scheme at a price related to the net asset value of the property to which the units relate and determined in accordance with the scheme.'

mechanism is located within the manager of the fund and is regulated by the COLL component of the FSA Handbook.

Historically, UK unit trusts used a 'dual-pricing' system, which involves the manager making an 'offer price' at which a customer can buy and a (lower) 'bid price' at which customers can sell. The bid/offer 'spread' includes dealing costs, fiscal duties and other front-end charges associated with the fund. More recently, the 'single-pricing' system, which is generally used in continental Europe, has become common in the UK.[152] This involves the manager quoting a single price to buyers and sellers of units, with front-end management charges being shown separately. From the investor's perspective, neither system is inherently superior. The regulatory approach to any pricing system must be based on three objectives: transparency; fairness as between incoming, outgoing and continuing investors; and competitiveness.[153]

4.10.3 Investment companies with variable capital

ICVCs are UK-authorised OEICs.[154] As is the case with a unit trust, there is no requirement for an OEIC to become authorised, but an unauthorised scheme cannot be promoted to the general public.[155] OEICs were not, historically, used as a form of collective investment in the UK. The catalyst for change was the introduction of the UCITS Directive[156] in 1985, which made possible the cross-border marketing of funds within the EU. A problem for UK funds was that the trust form of organisation was not used or well understood in continental Europe and therefore the ICVC structure was a more appropriate structure for funds that wanted to qualify as UCITS funds. The UK introduced Regulations permitting the formation of OEICS in 1996 and these have now been replaced by the 2001 Regulations.[157] These regulations are concerned mainly with the organisational structure of ICVCs, while the FSA Handbook (COLL) controls other matters such as investment powers, dealing and pricing of shares. Although a form of limited liability company, ICVCs are not subject to the Companies Act 1985.[158] They are constituted by an instrument of incorporation, which must comply with the OEIC Regulations.[159]

Under the company form of organisation represented by an ICVC, the ownership rights of an investor are similar to those of a shareholder in a limited company incor-

---

[152] For background see FSA, 'Single Pricing of Collective Investment Schemes: A Review', DP 8 (October 2001).

[153] Ibid, para 7.2.

[154] See s 236 FSMA for the statutory definition, which requires that an investor be able to realise his investment on a basis that reflects the value of the underlying investments. This rules out the possibility of shares in OEICs being issued or redeemed at a discount to the underlying net asset value.

[155] FSMA 2000, s 238.

[156] Directive 85/611/EC [1985] OJ L375/1.

[157] The Open-Ended Investment Companies Regulations 2001, SI 2001/1228.

[158] CA 2006 s 1(1) provides that it applies only to companies formed and registered under the Act. Many of the core provisions of CA 2006 are, however, replicated in the OEIC regulations.

[159] See Art 14 (conditions for authorisation) and sch 2 (instrument of incorporation).

porated under the Companies Act 2006.[160] The main difference is that, in common with a unit-holder in a unit trust, a shareholder in an ICVC is entitled to redeem his shares on an ongoing basis by reference to the net asset value of the underlying portfolio.[161] The redemption process is managed internally by the ICVC, rather than occurring in the market (as is the case for shares held in an investment trust).

4.11 Options, futures and contracts for differences

4.11.1 Nature and typology of derivatives

Financial derivatives are instruments whose value is derived from other (underlying) investments.[162] The essence of a derivative is that it can have no independent existence because it is based on and its value is quantified by reference to the underlying investment. The general policy of FSMA 2000 is to classify derivatives entered into for investment purposes as specified investments but to exclude derivatives entered into for commercial purposes (eg an industrial firm hedging against fluctuations in commodity prices).

Historically, futures contracts were the first form of derivative and were developed in relation to commodities rather than investments.[163] Futures are commitments to buy or sell a given quantity of an underlying product in the future at an agreed price. For example, a grain merchant might want to avoid the risk of fluctuations in the price of grain by fixing in advance the price at which he will buy from farmers. The contract cannot be abandoned and the potential gain or loss for each party is unlimited because it is dependent on the movement in the price of the underlying product. Futures contracts can be settled physically (eg by delivery of a commodity at the agreed price) or through payment by reference to the respective gains and losses on the contract at maturity. The gains and losses on futures contracts are symmetrical in that any deviation in the future spot price of a commodity or financial instrument from the contract price will generate a profit for one party that is the same as the loss for the other.[164] A market in these contracts developed so as to allow merchants to adjust their requirements for commodities on an ongoing basis. This allowed one merchant to transfer the contract to another, while at the same time preserving the fundamental characteristics of the contract—that it cannot be abandoned before expiry and that gain or loss is in principle unlimited. The use of futures

---

[160] For a complete definition of a shareholder's rights in a particular ICVC, it is necessary to examine the instrument of incorporation. This will be the case in particular when there are different classes of share. The OEIC Regulations (Regulation 45) permit different classes of share.

[161] See Art 15 of the OEIC Regulations 2001 (requirements for authorisation).

[162] See generally A Hudson, *The Law on Financial Derivatives*, 3rd edn (London, Sweet & Maxwell, 2002).

[163] See generally E Swann, *The Regulation of Derivatives* (London, Cavendish, 1995). The terms 'future' and 'forward' are often used interchangeably. Hudson, ibid, 41 reserves the term 'future' for derivatives traded on an exchange, while others (OTC derivatives) are termed 'forwards'.

[164] See Pilbeam, above n 122, ch 14.10.

in the context of modern financial markets can be envisaged by substituting financial securities and market indices for grain in this example.[165]

Contracts for difference share the same basic characteristics as futures in that the gains and losses are symmetrical and in principle unlimited. They are agreements whereby the difference in the price of an index, currency, commodity or share at the end of the contract from the reference price at the beginning is paid by one party to the other: if the difference is positive, the seller pays the buyer; if the difference is negative, the buyer pays the seller. So-called 'spread betting' is a form of contract for difference and is a specified investment if it relates to securities. Derivative instruments for the transfer of credit risk are included in the definition of contracts for difference. Thus CDSs are included but not if they are contracts of insurance, which are excluded. As already mentioned,[166] that issue remains unresolved and creates some uncertainty for the operation of what has become a very large market.

Options differ from futures in that the buyer has an option rather than an obligation to buy (call) or sell (put) the underlying investment. The price paid for an option is in the form of a premium paid by the buyer to the writer of the option. The maximum loss that can be suffered by the buyer of an option is the premium paid to the writer.[167] If the price of the underlying investment moves so as to make exercise of the option economically unattractive,[168] the buyer can simply abandon the option. In the case of a simple share option, the buyer pays a premium to the writer of the option for the right to buy or sell shares at an agreed price during a certain period of time. In most cases, the contract is settled (performed) by cash transfers between the option holder and the writer by reference to the value of the option at the time of exercise rather than by transfers of the underlying investment. For example, the exercise of an option to buy 1,000 shares in company X on 4 July at 100p when the price is 150p is normally settled by payment of £500 to the holder, rather than the writer delivering 1,000 shares to the holder for purchase at 100p.

In principle, all derivatives contracts are structured from combinations of features derived from the basic options and futures contracts just described. Basic forms of options and futures, as well as more exotic derivatives based on them, are now available in respect of many underlying investments, commodities and market indices. They are attractive to companies and investors for a variety of reasons. For companies raising finance, derivatives offer the opportunity of repackaging obligations so as to gain access to funding on more attractive terms. Swaps are a good example.[169] They became popular in the era of exchange controls because they allowed corporate borrowers to evade exchange controls and raise finance in more attractive jurisdictions. The essence of swaps is that the manner in which companies want to borrow money is not always the manner

---

[165] Note that futures undertaken for commercial rather than investment purposes are not specified investments (Art 84 of the RAO). Thus, the grain merchant would not normally fall with the FSMA regulatory perimeter.

[166] See section 4.3.5.

[167] Therefore, unlike futures, the profit/loss profile of an option contract is not symmetrical as between the writer and the holder of the option. (See Pilbeam, above n 122, ch 14.11 for a worked example of the different profit/loss profiles that result from hedging currency risk through futures and options respectively.)

[168] In market parlance, an 'out-of-the-money' option.

[169] See the definition of an interest rate swap given by Woolf LJ in *Hazell v Hammersmith & Fulham LBC* [1991] 1 All ER 545, 550.

that is most economically efficient for them. Some may be able to raise a fixed-rate loan on better terms than a floating rate loan or may be better able to borrow in euros than in sterling. The swaps market allows a company to exchange cash flows with another borrower (or a bank) so as to achieve a lower cost of funding. For example, A plc borrows £20m from B bank at a floating rate of 'LIBOR + 100 basis points'.[170] It then agrees with C bank that the latter will pay this interest to B in return for A paying a fixed rate of 6% to C. A has now fixed its borrowing cost and will make a profit if 'LIBOR + 100 basis points' exceeds 6% (ie if the floating rate it would have had to pay before arranging the swap exceeds the fixed rate it now has to pay).[171] The rationale for C's involvement in the transaction is that it believes that the interest rate represented by 'LIBOR + 100 basis points' will remain less than 6%, the margin between the two being C's profit.

From the perspective of investors, derivatives are attractive as a means of speculation and for managing risk. Derivatives are a geared form of investment in the sense that movements in the underlying investment cause a proportionately greater movement in the value of the derivative. It is therefore possible to use derivatives to speculate on relatively small movements in the price of underlying investments. The role of derivatives in managing or reducing risk within a portfolio is less well appreciated, but derivatives can be used for a variety of purposes in this context. They can reduce or increase the overall risk profile, introduce diversification by sector, currency or country, or replicate transactions in assets in which it is difficult to deal. For example, a portfolio manager in the US could gain exposure to the UK equity market by buying FTSE 100 options rather than by buying the underlying investments, or could use a currency derivative to hedge the risk of a fall in the value of sterling if investments are already held in the UK.

4.11.2 OTC and exchange-traded derivatives

Derivative contracts can be arranged on an ad hoc basis between two parties or they can be bought in a standardised form on exchanges. The former are referred to as over-the-counter and the latter as exchange-traded. The term 'over-the-counter' (OTC) is slightly misleading because it gives the impression that there is some form of market infrastructure. In reality, there is none, as such contracts are arranged on an ad hoc basis between parties, one of which is normally a bank acting as a principal. There is, however, considerable standardisation in the terms of OTC derivative contracts as most are formulated by reference to the standard terms set by the International Swaps and Derivatives Association.[172] It is common for collateral (typically in the form of a security interest or trust) to be given by one or both sides to an OTC derivative transaction. This offers some protection against the default of the other side to the transaction.[173]

---

[170] Each whole number of an interest rate is broken down into 100 basis points for the purposes of financial market transactions.

[171] This example is adapted from Hudson, above n 162, 46.

[172] See www.isda.org (accessed on 14 November 2011).

[173] As is the case with any security interest, the basic objective is to provide a real right in respect of property should a counterparty fail to perform the obligations contained in the derivative contract. The practice of each

The OTC market is one in which mainly large companies and banks are involved. It has grown rapidly in the last 20 years and is now considerably larger than the exchange-traded market.[174] The attraction for companies is that OTC derivatives offer a mechanism to restructure obligations in a manner which better suits a company than the form in which the obligation currently exists. The OTC market is not an organised market and is therefore not regulated in the same manner as organised markets such as the London Stock Exchange.[175] The absence of any market infrastructure, organisation or rules means that the OTC market cannot be regulated in this way.

However, for the purposes of FSMA 2000, OTC derivative contracts may be 'specified investments',[176] with the result that persons engaging in specified activities[177] fall within the scope of FSA regulation. Banks involved in the OTC derivatives market are already subject to prudential supervision and capital adequacy requirements in respect of their mainstream banking business. Non-bank counterparties to OTC derivative contracts do not normally fall within the FSMA 2000 regulatory perimeter. Their involvement in the market is in principle unregulated, but is subject to disclosure obligations set by company law, listing rules and accounting standards.[178]

Exchange-traded derivatives are a more recent development. They offer standard contracts to investors over a wide range of commodities, investments and market indices. Contracts relating to investments are generally settled by payment of money rather than by delivery of the underlying investment. The comments made above in relation to OTC derivatives falling within the definition of 'specified investments' for the purposes of FSMA 2000 apply equally to exchange-traded derivatives. Trading is subject to the rules set by the relevant exchange. These rules normally provide for the payment of margin on futures contracts, which is intended to ensure that each party meets their obligations under the contract.[179] This means that, when the holder sells a derivative through the exchange, profits/losses arising from that instrument have already been settled between the holder and issuer through the margining process. The comments made above in relation to regulation of participants in the OTC derivatives market are equally applicable to

party taking collateral allows derivatives to be treated by each as secured, with the result that less regulatory capital is required for banks to engage in such activity.

[174] See the Turner Review, ch 1.

[175] See Chapter 12 for a description of the regulation of recognised investment exchanges in the UK.

[176] See Arts 83, 84 and 85 of the Regulated Activities Order (SI 2001/544, discussed in Chapter 3.4). They include within their ambit futures, options and contracts for differences. As noted earlier, all derivatives can, in principle, be regarded as combinations of options and futures, with the result that even exotic derivatives can be considered to fall within the RAO. Futures contracts made for commercial rather than investment purposes (eg an oil company using futures to hedge the price of oil) are excluded from the RAO.

[177] Specified activities falling within the scope of FSMA 2000 are discussed in Chapter 3.

[178] That issue came to the fore following the collapse of ENRON, which had engaged in extensive derivatives trading disclosed in only a limited form to investors. See WC Powers et al, 'Report of Investigation by the Special Investigative Committee of the Board of Directors of Enron Corp 2003', available at http://i.cnn.net/cnn/2002/LAW/02/02/enron.report/powers.report.pdf (accessed on 16 August 2011).

[179] 'Initial margin' is normally set by the exchange at the level of the expected maximum daily movement in the relevant instrument. Once it has been paid, 'variation margin' becomes payable by one party to the other based on the daily profits/losses arising from the instrument. This is sometimes referred to as the process of 'marking-to-market'.

participants in the exchange-traded market. The exchanges on which trading occurs can choose to become 'recognised' for the purposes of FSMA 2000.[180]

Exchange-traded derivatives are normally 'cleared' by a clearing house prior to settlement.[181] The benefit of this procedure is that the clearing house acts as a central counterparty, thereby guaranteeing the performance of obligations of its clearing members. As part of this function, the clearing house is responsible for the collection of margin, which acts as a form of performance bond, providing assets to the clearing house in the event of default. Some, but not all, OTC contracts are cleared through a clearing house.

4.12 Rights under a pension scheme

A pension can be defined in simple terms as an arrangement through which a person makes provision for an income in retirement. In the UK, there are two main ways in which such arrangements can be structured in the private sector.[182] The first is possible when contributions are paid into a scheme run by an employer (an occupational pension scheme). Such schemes can be structured so that employees receive a pension that is related to their salary at retirement.[183] From the employee's perspective, this offers certainty and predictability of retirement income, but from the employer's perspective it results in some uncertainty and risk as regards costs. This arises mainly from the possibility that growth in the accumulated fund of pension contributions will not match liabilities (present and future pension payments), which rise in line with the growth in earnings, leaving the employer with the obligation to make good any shortfall. The 'final-salary' structure (under which an employee's pension represented a proportion of salary at retirement) was popular for many years, but its use has declined in recent years as a result of employers' concerns over risk and cost.

The second type of structure is based on the principle that an individual pays contributions into a plan managed by an organisation independent from his employer (eg an insurer) and then uses the proceeds of that plan to purchase an annuity, which is a contract under which an insurer agrees to pay an income for life in return for a capital sum. The second system is referred to as a 'money-purchase' system as the fund available to buy an annuity at retirement is dependent mainly on the market value of the fund at retirement. It results in some uncertainty for employees as regards their retirement income but can be

---

[180] See Chapter 12 for an explanation of the process of 'recognition'.

[181] See Chapter 12.5 regarding the clearing process.

[182] The state provides a basic pension on a universal basis, but the payments have over time been eroded by inflation and are widely regarded as inadequate to support a decent standard of living. The state scheme is unfunded, meaning that payments are made from current taxation rather than an accumulated fund. Increasing longevity and a resulting increase in the proportion of the population represented by pensioners poses a problem for both state and private sector schemes.

[183] For discussion of the legal structure of OPS, see section 4.15.2.

more attractive for employers as they are able to fix and predict their costs more easily than in the case of final salary schemes.

Occupational pensions are organised by employers on behalf of employees and are open only to employees. In general, there is no obligation imposed on an employer to provide an occupational pension scheme for employees. When they are provided, they can be organised either as final-salary or money-purchase schemes.[184] Rights in such schemes are not investments for the purposes of FSMA 2000. This may appear anomalous in view of the fact that, for many people, pensions represent their largest investment (in the economic sense of the word), but the legal categorisation of such rights can be justified on two grounds. First, occupational pension schemes are subject to a special regulatory regime. The legal regime applicable to occupational pension schemes is that of trust and the regulatory regime is that created by the Pensions Act 1995.[185] Secondly, although not stated explicitly in the Act, the FSMA regulatory regime is focused on transferable investments and occupational pensions do not fall into that category. While rights arising from an occupational pension scheme can be considered 'property' in the legal sense,[186] assignment is prohibited by statute[187] and therefore the 'investment' represented by those rights is not transferable.

Alternatives to occupational pension schemes have existed for a long time in the form of self-employed pensions and the State Earnings Related Pension Scheme. However, the market for such alternatives expanded rapidly as a result of legislation introduced in the late 1980s that created 'personal pensions'. The policy underlying their introduction was that of promoting greater personal responsibility for retirement planning so as to reduce the role of the state in funding retirement income. The new personal pensions were categorised as investments for the purposes of FSA 1986.[188] That approach was continued under FSMA 2000,[189] with the result that providers of such pensions are subject to authorisation and conduct of business rules.[190]

For regulatory purposes, a personal pension scheme is defined as a scheme of investment that provides benefits on retirement, on reaching a certain age or on termination of employment.[191] It is a money-purchase contract, which means that it provides a mechanism through which a person can accumulate a fund with which to purchase an annuity.[192] The annuity can be purchased either from the provider of the personal pension or from

---

[184] Recent years have seen a significant decline in the number of final salary schemes and growth in money purchase schemes.

[185] The 1995 Act was a response to R Goode, *Pension Law Reform: The Report of the Pension Law Reform Review Committee* (London, HMSO, 1993), which was prompted mainly by the Maxwell pensions scandal, which involved the removal of assets from the Mirror Group pension fund.

[186] See *Re Landau* [1988] Ch 223.

[187] Pensions Act 1995, s 91.

[188] They were considered to be long-term insurance contracts under FSA 1986 (repealed), sch 1, para 10. For a discussion of the insurance characteristic of a personal pension, see J McMeel, 'The Consumer Dimension of Financial Services Law: Lessons from the Pension Mis-Selling Scandal' [1999] *Company Financial and Insolvency Law Review* 29, 31.

[189] See RAO Arts 75, 3 and sch 1, pt 2. 'Group' personal pensions, which are an alternative to occupational pension schemes, are also specified investments.

[190] Insurers, who are the main providers of personal pensions, are also subject to prudential supervision.

[191] FSA Handbook, Glossary.

[192] Use of the fund for other purposes is constrained by tax law.

another provider of annuities. Alternative methods of accumulating a fund can be considered, but the attraction of a personal pension is that it offers considerable tax advantages in comparison to other forms of investment (eg unit trusts) that might be used for the same purpose.

Rights under personal pension schemes are property in the legal sense and can, in principle, be transferred by way of assignment.[193] However, assignment is prohibited as a condition of approval of a personal pension scheme for tax relief.[194] This means that, for practical purposes, rights under personal pension schemes are not transferable. This distinguishes them from rights under a life assurance policy, which are generally transferable, and limits their use as collateral in connection with mortgages and other forms of lending.[195]

The Welfare Reform and Pensions Act 1999 introduced a new form of low-cost pension, the 'stakeholder pension', aimed primarily at those who do not have access to an occupational pension scheme. Underlying this development was a recognition that state pension provision (whether in the basic or earnings-related form) could not provide a financially secure basis for retirement and that the take-up of a private sector 'second pension' should therefore be encouraged. Stakeholder schemes are organised as trusts, are open to employees of different employers and are required to meet a number of conditions set by the Act. Among the conditions are that the scheme must be structured on a money-purchase basis [196] and that annual charges are limited to 1% of the value of the fund per annum. Employers are required to provide employees with access to a stakeholder pension scheme unless they are exempt.[197]

4.13 Lloyd's syndicate capacity and syndicate membership

The RAO designates the following as specified investments:

1. The underwriting capacity of a Lloyd's syndicate.
2. A person's membership (or prospective membership) of a Lloyd's syndicate.[198]

While this definition does not add much to the specified activity of 'Activities linked with Lloyd's of London',[199] it does have the effect of limiting those activities to the investments

---

[193] Applying the reasoning of *Re Landau*, above n 186, by way of analogy to personal pensions. The effect of that decision (holding that rights under a personal pension policy formed part of a bankrupt's estate) has been reversed by s 11 of the Welfare Reform and Pensions Act 1999.

[194] Income and Corporation Taxes Act 1988 ss 620, 634 and 635.

[195] For example, while a lender can require assignment of a life policy as security against repayment of a loan, it is not possible to assign rights under a personal pension policy as security for repayment of a loan.

[196] Welfare Reform and Pensions Act 1999, s 1(4).

[197] An employer is exempt if it has fewer than five employees or offers an occupational pension scheme to employees within one year of their starting work.

[198] Art 86 of the RAO.

[199] Arts 56–58 of the RAO: see Chapter 3.

specified above. Activities linked with Lloyd's that do not relate to the investments above are not within the regulatory perimeter.

4.14 Miscellaneous 'retail' investment products[200]

- Funeral plan contracts: rights under a funeral plan contract are a specified investment under FSMA 2000.[201]
- Regulated mortgage contracts: rights under a regulated mortgage contract are a specified investment under FSMA 2000.[202]
- Regulated home reversion plans: rights under a regulated home reversion plan are a specified investment under FSMA 2000.[203]
- Regulated home purchase plans: rights under a regulated home purchase plan are a specified investment under FSMA 2000.[204]
- Regulated sale and rent-back agreements: rights under a regulated sale and rent-back agreement are a specified investment under FSMA 2000.[205]

4.15 Investments outside the FSMA 'specified investment' regime

4.15.1 Direct property investment

A distinction can be drawn between direct property investment and investment in financial instruments (portfolio investment). The former is investment in real (tangible) things, such as land and buildings, art or wine. The latter form of investment represents a more complex relationship between persons and property. An investor in a financial instrument cannot identify physical property over which she holds legal rights (eg a company shareholder has no direct ownership in respect of assets owned by the company). Thus, although the holder of a financial instrument is commonly termed its owner, the nature of ownership differs fundamentally from direct investment in property. A direct property investor has real rights that can be exercised against tangible property (eg taking

---

[200] For more detail on each of these investments see the matching regulated activities at Chapter 3.5.
[201] Art 87 of the RAO.
[202] Art 88 of the RAO.
[203] Art 88A of the RAO.
[204] Art 88B of the RAO.
[205] Art 88C of the RAO.

possession), whereas a portfolio investor has personal (contractual) rights that cannot normally be exercised in that way.[206]

Direct property investment is familiar to most people in the form of home ownership. It is also undertaken by companies who buy premises and by fund managers who buy property as part of their portfolios. While direct investment in property gives an investor a real right in the property, this is not to say that the investor has exclusive rights in the property because more than one real right can exist in respect of the same property.[207] Common examples of the coexistence of real rights are when security interests are granted over property (eg a mortgage) or the grant of the real right of possession through a lease. The coexistence of such real rights can have important implications for the direct investor, such as restricting the ability to sell or take possession of the property.

Direct property investment is not a specified investment for the purposes of FSMA 2000. It follows that regulated activities that are defined by reference to specified investments (eg dealing, managing, advising) do not, when carried out in respect of direct property investment, fall within the scope of FSMA 2000. However, there are two ways in which direct property investment may fall within the scope of regulation. The first is when an activity is 'specified' by the RAO by reference to property of any kind. This is the case for the following activities:

- the activities mentioned in Chapter 3.5 in respect of collective investment schemes;
- the activities mentioned in Chapter 3.5 in respect of dormant account funds.

The second way in which direct property investment may fall within the scope of FSMA regulation is in respect of activities relating to the financing of that investment. The most common form of finance is secured lending, commonly referred to as a mortgage.[208] As from 31 October 2004, entering into (ie lending), administering, arranging or advising on regulated mortgage contracts became regulated activities.[209] That definition includes within its scope most forms of residential mortgage activity, but not activities related to commercial mortgage lending.

4.15.2 Rights under an Occupational Pension Scheme

Occupational pension schemes are in essence a trust in which the settlor (trustee) is the employer and the beneficiaries the employees.[210] Trustees (often directors of the employer) are responsible for the operation of the trust and beneficiaries' interests are protected in

---

[206] See Chapter 1 for a discussion of real and personal rights. It was noted in Chapter 1 that the holder of a financial instrument may have real (proprietary) rights against persons who hold the instrument on his behalf. Such rights do not, however, transform the nature of the financial instrument. They relate to the manner in which rights are held rather than their nature.

[207] See Chapter 1 for a discussion of property rights in the context of investment.

[208] Although the term 'mortgage' is now commonly used throughout the UK, it has no technical meaning in Scotland, where a security interest over land granted by a borrower to a lender is termed a 'standard security'.

[209] See Chapter 3.5 for an explanation of regulated activity.

[210] This is the conventional view. Hudson, above n 162, 148 takes the view that the employees should also be considered settlors when they provide capital for the trust fund through contributions.

the normal manner by the application of the law of trusts. The Occupational Pensions Regulatory Authority was created by the Pensions Act 1995 and has an oversight role in respect of occupational pensions. It reports on an annual basis to the Secretary of State and has powers to remove trustees, prohibit persons from acting as trustees of a particular scheme and suspend persons from acting as trustees of a scheme.[211]

---

[211] See ss 3 and 4 of the Pensions Act 1995.

Institutional Investment

While the nature of investments has changed over time, there has probably been an even more significant change in the nature of investors. Private individuals were the dominant type of investor in the nineteenth century, although insurance companies had begun to build up substantial holdings of government bonds in the early part of the century and had accumulated significant equity investments by its end.[1] The post-Second World War period witnessed a transformation in the ownership distribution of financial securities as institutional ownership of investments grew to become much more significant than individual ownership. Several factors lay behind this trend. One was the growth of collective investment schemes and in particular the flexible form of unit trust imported from the US in the 1930s. This provided risk diversification for private investors and also lower transaction costs by comparison with individual ownership of securities. Another was the development of insurance as an investment through products such as with-profits endowments and later unit-linked life assurance. The growth in pension provision was another factor, resulting in pension funds reaching a position where they matched the importance of insurance companies as institutional investors.

Institutional investment operates under a variety of legal structures, each with their own special characteristics. Trust law is relevant because two of the most important forms of institutional investment (pensions and unit trusts) are structured as trusts.[2] Corporate law is relevant for those investment funds that take the form of a registered company. The partnership structure has become increasingly popular as investors have been attracted by the relative privacy that it offers in comparison to the corporate form. Contractual structures differ from the three forms just mentioned in that they provide the contributor/investor with only a contractual claim against the relevant financial institution. This means that, in the event of insolvency, there is no 'property' that is owned by the investor and repayment depends on the assets that are available for payment of creditors.[3]

---

[1] R Michie, *The London Stock Exchange: A History* (Oxford, Oxford University Press, 1999) 73 observes that the assets of British life assurance companies rose almost fivefold between 1870 and 1930, while their holdings of stocks and shares rose tenfold.

[2] Trusts are also an important legal structure for private investors. The general principles of trust law were developed in the context of family trusts. The use of trusts as a legal structure for institutional investment was a later development.

[3] Deposit guarantee and compensation arrangements are also relevant in these circumstances: see Chapter 6.7.

Irrespective of the legal form in which institutional investment is structured, it is common for the process of investment to be delegated through an investment management contract to a professional fund management firm. In principle, a distinction can be made within the process of investment between investment strategy (or asset allocation) and selection of individual investments.[4] Investment strategy involves making decisions as to what type of assets to hold. It involves choices between different types of investment (eg equities v fixed interest securities), different currencies in which investments are denominated and different types of business risk (eg across different business sectors). In principle, it is a separate process from the selection of individual investments within the parameters set by the investment strategy. Investment management contracts may in principle cover both strategy and selection, although it is now more common for the two aspects to be dealt with separately.

Regulation also plays an increasingly important role in institutional investment, especially since the scope of the EU regime has been extended by the MiFID regime[5] to apply organisational and conduct of business requirements to investment firms. These requirements have been superimposed on the pre-existing Financial Services and Markets Act 2000 (FSMA 2000) regulatory obligations, such as those relating to authorisation, senior management arrangements systems and controls, and the approved persons regime.[6]

5.1 The trust structure

Several forms of institutional investment are conducted under the legal structure of trust. Pension funds and unit trusts each represent a form of trust with a specific purpose and a specific regulatory regime that is not applicable to other trusts, such as family or charitable trusts. However, subject to the provisions of their special regulatory regime, unit trusts and pension trusts remain subject to the basic principles of the general law of trusts.[7] They are, however, expressly excluded from the scope of most of the provisions of the Trustee Act 2000, which is discussed below.[8] They are also excluded from the provisions of the Trusts (Sc) Act 1921 relating to the investment powers of trustees.[9]

The general law of trusts (ie excluding the special regulatory regime for unit trusts and pensions) developed originally from equitable and common-law principles, but over time was also influenced by a number of statutory provisions. There are important differences

---

[4] See generally P Myners, 'Institutional Investment in the United Kingdom: A Review' (March 2001) (Myners Report), available at http://archive.treasury.gov.uk/docs/2001/myners_report0602.html (accessed on 16 August 2011) ch 3, 'Investment Decision-Making by Trustees'.

[5] See Chapter 2.9.1 for the meaning of this term.

[6] See Chapter 3 for an explanation of these terms.

[7] *Cowan v Scargill* [1984] 2 All ER 750, 763 per Sir Robert Megarry VC. See generally G Moffat, 'Pension Funds: A Fragmentation of Trust Law' (1993) 56 *Modern Law Review* 471.

[8] See ss 36 and 37 of the Trustee Act 2000. That Act applies to England and Wales only.

[9] Section 4(1B) (as amended).

in the nature and statutory regulation of trusts between Scotland and England. In English law, trusts can be characterised as a mechanism that divides ownership between the legal rights of a trustee and the equitable (or beneficial) rights of the beneficiary.[10] The nature of a trust in England has been described as follows:

> The essence of a trust is the imposition of an equitable obligation on a person who is the legal owner of property (a trustee) which requires that person to act in good conscience when dealing with that property in favour of any person (the beneficiary) who has a beneficial interest recognised by equity in the property. The trustee is said to 'hold the property on trust' for the beneficiary. There are four significant elements to the trust: that it is equitable, that it provides the beneficiary with rights in property, that it also imposes obligations on the trustee, and that those obligations are fiduciary in nature.[11]

Whereas in England ownership is split and the beneficiary of a trust enjoys equitable (or beneficial) ownership of the trust property, in Scotland the rights of a beneficiary have been characterised as being personal (*in personam*), meaning that they are more analogous to contractual rights than they are to property rights. The legal nature of a trust in Scotland has been explained by the Scottish Law Commission in the following terms:

> In Scots law the essential element of a trust is the concept of fiduciary ownership. Fiduciary ownership arises when the owner of property is under a duty to use it for the benefit of another and not for himself . . . At every stage of the administration of the trust, the trustee must always put the beneficiaries' interests before his own. This is the concept of fiduciary ownership. The beneficiary has a corresponding right to compel the trustee to administer the trust funds in accordance with the provisions of the declaration of trust. This is a personal right. It is axiomatic that in Scots law the beneficiaries do not have a real right or a quasi-real right in the trust property. They have no proprietary interest in the trust fund.[12]

However, while the doctrinal foundations of trusts as a legal device differ between Scotland and England, there are three issues central to the role of trusts in institutional investment in regard to which their approach is very similar. The first is the role of trusts in segregating assets: once assets are transferred to a trustee they are no longer available to the creditors of the truster who transfers the property or of the trustee who takes legal title to the property. This function of trusts is crucial to the protection of client assets and money that are held by a trustee or the trustee's agent. The second issue is the default investment powers of trustees (applicable unless varied by a trust deed), which are now very similar in the two countries. The third issue is the duty of skill and care that applies to the performance of the investment function of trustees, which is also very similar in the two countries. Thus, despite quite different starting points in terms of the basic nature of a trust, in the context of institutional investment the legal framework is similar as regards its central provisions, even if some of the detail differs.

Trustees have to consider the implications of FSMA 2000 for their activities. In principle, they could be regarded as falling within a number of regulated activities, such

---

[10] The possibility of division of ownership in this way is rejected in many civil law jurisdictions, but is generally followed in other common law jurisdictions around the world.

[11] G Thomas and A Hudson, *The Law of Trusts*, 2nd edn (Oxford, Oxford University Press, 2009) para 1.01.

[12] Scottish Law Commission, 'The Nature and Constitution of Trusts', Discussion Paper No 133 (2006).

as dealing in investments as principal (as they are the legal owners of the investments held in trust), arranging deals in investments, managing investments, and safeguarding and administering investments. However, as the scope of FSMA 2000 extends only to regulated activity carried on by way of business, the Regulated Activities Order (RAO)[13] makes it clear that trustees who do not carry on these activities by way of business do not require authorisation, provided that they are not paid for these activities in addition to any payments received as trustee.[14] It follows that trustees who provide and charge for services such as fund management or dealing cannot be exempt from authorisation whereas trustees who act only as trustees are exempt even if they do from time to time engage in activity falling within the scope of FSMA 2000.

Professional trustees who are authorised under FSMA 2000 also need to consider the implications of regulatory rules made under the Act. This issue arises when services additional to trusteeship are provided to the trust. In these circumstances, an authorised firm will be required to categorise the trust as a customer, thereby triggering the application of the relevant Conduct of Business Rules (COBs).[15] This relationship between authorised firm and customer provides an additional layer of protection to the beneficiaries, but is probably best viewed as providing little in the way of substantive protection for the beneficiaries that is not already provided by the fiduciary duty owed by the trustee. In the case of professional trustees who are exempt from authorisation as members of a recognised professional body,[16] the Financial Services Authority (FSA)'s COBs are not applicable, but there are usually professional rules relating to such services.

The starting point for determining the investment powers of trustees is the trust deed. The statutory provisions relating to investment powers[17] are default provisions, meaning that they take effect subject to any contrary provision in the trust deed (eg restricting or expanding the statutory investment powers) or relevant legislation. Most trust deeds make express provision regarding the investment powers of trustees, with the result that the statutory default provisions apply to a relatively small number of trusts, such as those that arise on intestacy. Nevertheless, as these statutory powers form the backdrop against which express powers evolved, it is worthwhile considering them.

5.1.1 Trustees' powers of investment

Restrictions on the powers of investment of trustees that previously applied under the Trustee Investment Act 1961 (TIA 1961) have been removed in both England and Scotland. The new default powers of investment for trustees provide them with much broader powers.[18] The rationale for this relaxation is mainly the change in perception

---

[13] The RAO (SI 2001/544) defines the scope of FSMA 2000 system of regulation by reference to 'specified activities' and 'specified investments'. See generally Chapter 3.

[14] Art 66 of the RAO.

[15] See Chapter 15.1 regarding customer classification.

[16] See Chapter 3.3.3 for an explanation of the authorisation regime applicable to the professions.

[17] Those contained in the Trustee Act 2000 and (in Scotland) in the Trusts (Sc) Act 1921 (as amended by the Charities and Trustee Investment (Scotland), Act 2005, asp 10 (Scottish Act)).

[18] See the Trustee Act 2000, s 3 for England and the Trusts (Sc) Act 1921, s 4 (as amended).

of investment risk that has resulted from the application of modern portfolio theory. Historically, the common law and the Trustee Act 1925 had taken a cautious approach to the investment powers of trustees by defining a range of 'authorised investments', which excluded equity investments. Underlying this approach was a perception that the interests of beneficiaries were best served by requiring trustees to invest in fixed interest securities and by prohibiting speculation in equities.

Two main factors contributed to a change in approach, leading to the authorisation of equity investment by TIA 1961. One was the realisation that beneficiaries holding fixed interest securities were under threat from inflation and that they could be protected from this risk by holding equities. Another factor was the realisation that a diversified equity portfolio considerably reduced the risk associated with holding individual shares.[19] The upshot was that TIA 1961 authorised equity investment for the first time, but did so in a manner that initially restricted it to 50% of the fund, a limit that was later increased to 75%.[20] Following the repeal of TIA 1961 in both England and Scotland, this limit on equity investment is no longer applicable.

The central provision of the Trustee Act 2000 is that a trustee can make any kind of investment that he could make if he were absolutely entitled to the assets of the trust.[21] This is referred to as 'the general power of investment'. It can be expanded or restricted by specific provisions in the trust deed. Similar provision is made in the relevant Scottish legislation.[22]

In exercising any investment power, a trustee must have regard to the standard investment criteria contained in the Act. These are:

- the suitability to the trust of investment of the same kind as any particular investment proposed to be made or retained and of that particular investment as an investment of that kind; and
- the need for diversification of the trust, so far as is appropriate to the circumstances of the trust.[23]

The requirement for suitability follows an approach that is now well established in the regulatory sphere and attempts to ensure that trustees give careful consideration to the type of fund and the degree of risk that is appropriate in the circumstances. The scope for diversification (as a technique for limiting risk) will depend on the scale and objectives of the trust, and may be limited by the express objectives of the trust (for example, a trust with an express objective of investing in 'green' companies will not be able to diversify to the same extent as a trust with a broader investment objective).

Before exercising any investment power a trustee must normally take professional advice, other than when the trustee concludes that, under all the circumstances, it is unnecessary or inappropriate to do so. These provisions apply to trusts irrespective of

---

[19] See Chapter 1.1 regarding risk and diversification.

[20] The Trustee Investments (Division of Trust Fund) Order 1996, SI 1996/845, made under s 13 of TIA 1961.

[21] Section 3. A similar provision is contained in s 34(1) of the Pensions Act 1995.

[22] The Trusts (Sc) Act 1921, s 4(1)(ea) (as amended) now permits trustees 'To make any kind of investment of the trust estate (including an investment in heritable property)'.

[23] Trustee Act 2000, s 4(2) and Trusts (Sc) Act 1921, s 4A(1).

whether they were created before or after commencement of the relevant legislation extending trustees' powers in England or Scotland. The effect is to apply the new powers to all trusts except those containing express restrictions or those excluded from the relevant provision (eg pension trusts and unit trusts).

5.1.2 Express investment clauses

Most trust deeds provide trustees with express investment powers that are wider than the default statutory powers discussed above. The main issue that arises in these circumstances is to determine the meaning and scope of the relevant clause(s) in the trust deed. An important issue is the meaning of 'investment' for the purposes of such clauses, especially when the trust deed does not specify the type of investment that it permitted. Where it does specify an investment, there can be no question of the power being interpreted so as to exclude that type of investment. Where it does not, it has been observed that the term 'invest' implies an income yield, thus ruling out non-income-producing property (eg derivatives, zero dividend preference shares).[24]

In the nineteenth century the Chancery Court in England adopted a restrictive approach by developing the concept of 'authorised investments', to which trustees were restricted.[25] In 1882, for example, a clause authorising trustees to invest 'on such securities as they might think fit' was taken merely to give discretion to select from such authorised investments.[26] However, a more liberal approach was developed in the twentieth century as the courts gave effect to clauses which clearly intended that trustees should enjoy investment powers extending beyond authorised investments. For example, in *Re Wragg* investment in land was approved under a clause which did not expressly authorise investment in land but clearly intended the trustees to have absolute discretion.[27] Moreover, although the general rule is that express provisions in trust deeds that expand trustees' powers of investment beyond those authorised by law will be strictly construed, it has been recognised that this does not require a court to take an unduly restrictive approach to particular investment clauses.[28]

There may be circumstances in which both express investment powers and the statutory powers apply to a trust. This could arise, for example, where a trustee is expressly

---

[24] See *Re Power* [1947] Ch 572, holding that an express power in a will trust to invest in any manner that the trustee thought fit as if he were the beneficial owner did not authorise the purchase of a house for the testator's widow to live in. The rationale was that such a purchase was for some other purpose than the receipt of income. The decision was criticised by the Law Commissions, 'Trustees' Powers and Duties', Law Commissions' Report No 260/Scottish Law Commission Report No 172 (1999), 134 on the basis that a beneficiary's possession or occupation is equivalent to receipt of rental income.

[25] This approach was later adopted in the statutory provisions relating to trustees' investment powers, such as TIA 1961.

[26] See *Re Braithwaite* (1852) 21 Ch 121.

[27] [1919] 2 Ch 58. The clause permitted investments of whatever nature and wheresoever as his trustees should in their absolute and uncontrolled discretion think fit to the intent that they should have the same full and unrestricted powers of investing as if they were absolutely entitled to the trust money beneficially.

[28] Re Peczenik's Settlement, *Cole and Another v Ingram and Others* [1964] 2 All ER 339. The recent expansion of trustees' powers of investment clearly limits the necessity to resort to the principles established in this case.

authorised to invest a specific proportion of the fund in specific assets, such as shares in a single private company. In that situation, the balance of the fund would be subject to the default statutory powers of investment (above), which would, subject to the nature of the trust, require diversification across a broader range of investments.

5.1.3 Delegation of investment powers

Trustees must determine whether and to what extent they can delegate their powers. This is normally dealt with by the express terms of the trust deed. If it is not, there is a power to delegate investment management functions.[29] In England, this power is subject to the requirement that the trustees prepare a policy statement relating to the exercise of those powers and that the agent agrees to comply with this statement.[30] When delegation occurs under this power it may relate to any or all of the trustees' investment powers, and the 'duty of care' required by section 1 of the Act applies to the selection of the agent. The terms on which a trustee in England may delegate investment management functions are also controlled. Unless it is reasonably necessary for them to do so,[31] there cannot be terms (i) permitting the agent to appoint a substitute, (ii) restricting the liability of the agent or (iii) permitting the agent to act in circumstances capable of giving rise to a conflict of interest.[32]

The liability of trustees for the acts of an agent is governed in England by the Trustee Act 2000 and in Scotland by the common law.[33] A distinction can be made between the selection and supervision of an agent. In England, the statutory 'general duty of care' of a trustee[34] applies to selection of an agent by a trustee. In Scotland, the common law imposes a similar requirement.[35] As regards supervision of the agent, the Trustee Act 2000 in England discharges the trustee from liability other than in cases where loss arises from a failure to comply with the statutory duty of care imposed by the Act. This provision does not apply to Scotland, where supervision of agents is subject to the same common law duty of care as applies to selection of agents.[36] Thus, in both England and Scotland a trustee can be liable for careless selection of an agent (eg an investment manager) and/or careless supervision.[37]

---

[29] Trustee Act 2000, s 11 and Trusts (Sc) Act 1921, s 4C.

[30] Trustee Act 2000, s 15.

[31] The Law Commissions, above n 24, 32 noted that it would often be necessary for this to occur when investment management is delegated to a discretionary fund manager as the standard terms of business of fund managers commonly permit further delegation.

[32] Trustee Act 2000, s 14.

[33] In each case, the rules differ to those found in the context of delegation by an agent who is not a trustee, where the agent assumes full responsibility for the actions of the subcontractor. See R Munday, *Agency Law and Principles* (Oxford, Oxford University Press, 2010) para 8.57; in respect of Scotland see W McBryde, *Contract*, 3rd edn (Edinburgh, Thomson W Green, 2007) 319.

[34] See below section 5.1.4.

[35] *Carruthers v Carruthers* (1896) 23 R (HL) 55.

[36] See *Carruthers*, ibid.

[37] Despite the practice of extensive delegation by trustees of large funds (eg to investment consultants who then recommend investment managers for different parts of the fund), it seems unlikely that the duties of trustees with respect to selection and review of investment managers can be entirely delegated to agents as

5.1.4 Investment strategy and selection

When there has been no delegation of the investment management function, the trustees must take account of the relevant law relating to the manner in which they should determine investment strategy and make individual investment decisions. Depending on the terms of the trust,[38] the relevant law can be the common law or the statutory powers of investment contained in the Trustee Act 2000 in England or the Trusts Act 1921 in Scotland. Where there has been delegation of the investment management function to an external fund manager, the principles set out below represent the default rules that govern the actions of the fund manager. However, those default rules may be adjusted by the contract between the trustees and the fund manager.[39]

Both the strategy and selection aspects of the process of investment may be limited by the trustees' powers of investment, but even within relatively narrow powers it is possible for the distinction to remain meaningful, as the trustees may choose to ignore a permitted category of investment. It is likely in most circumstances that both strategy and selection will have a material influence on the performance of the fund.[40] The legal principles encompass both aspects of investment management, although the focus has been much more on selection than on strategy. The central legal principle is the duty of care and skill owed by trustees to beneficiaries in exercising their investment powers.[41] The standard of care required to discharge that duty is that of the 'ordinary prudent man of business'. It has been described as follows:[42]

> Business men of ordinary prudence may, and frequently do, select investments which are more or less of a speculative character; but it is the duty of a trustee to confine himself to the class of investments which are permitted by the trust, and likewise to avoid all investments of that class which are attended with hazard.

In *Bartlett v Barclays Bank Trust Co Ltd*[43] it was held that a corporate professional trustee owed a higher standard of care to beneficiaries than did other (ie individual non-corporate) trustees. Such trustees are required to show the skill and experience that they profess to

---

that would result in a form of 'inactive' trustee with no real function. See, by way of analogy, the decision in *Re Barings Plc* (No 5) [2001] 1 BCLC 523 (CA) regarding the limitations on delegation of the functions of a company director.

[38] See above regarding express and default (statutory) powers of investment.

[39] See further section 5.6.

[40] See R Sandler, 'Medium and Long-Term Retail Savings in the UK' (HM Treasury, 2002), available at www.hm-treasury.gov.uk (accessed on 11 November 2004) 127.

[41] That duty arises in tort/delict from the assumption of responsibility for the property or affairs of others: Millet LJ in *Bristol and West Building Society v Mothew* [1998] Ch 1, 16. There is no separate 'fiduciary' duty of care: ibid. For an analysis of Scots law along similar lines see G Gretton and A Steven, *Property Trusts and Succession* (London, Tottel Publishing, 2008) ch 23.28.

[42] *Learoyd v Whiteley* (1887) 12 App Cas 727, 733 per Lord Watson. In that case a mortgage on a freehold brickfield, which was prima facie within the investment powers of the trustees, was held to be a breach of trust on the basis that the particular property was a wasting asset and therefore hazardous. A similar approach was adopted in Scotland in the case of *Raes v Meek* (1889) 16 R (HL) 31. See J Chalmers, *Trusts, Cases and Materials* (Edinburgh, W Green, 2002) 173 for a comparative analysis of the English and Scots law formulations of the standard of care required on the part of trustees.

[43] [1980] 1 All ER 139.

have as professional trust managers. Precisely how this differs from the standard of the 'ordinary prudent man of business' is not entirely clear, nor is it obvious why trustees who are paid professionals (eg a solicitor) are excluded from the ambit of the enhanced duty that applies to trust corporations.[44] The Trustee Act 2000 has modified that principle as far as English law is concerned. It requires trustees acting under its powers to exercise such care and skill as is reasonable in the circumstances, having regard in particular:

1. to any special knowledge or experience that he has or holds himself out as having; and
2. if he acts as a trustee in the course of a business or profession, to any special knowledge or experience that it is reasonable to expect of a person acting in the course of that kind of business or profession.[45]

This clearly brings paid professionals (as well as trust corporations) within the scope of the section one duty of care as regards the exercise of powers under the Trustee Act 2000. Moreover, since the Act makes clear that such powers include "any other power of investment, however conferred", the section one duty of care is not limited to the default statutory powers of trustees in England. In Scotland, the duty of care and skill remains part of the common law.[46] There remains some doubt over whether remunerated trustees in Scotland are subject to a higher standard of diligence and knowledge, although trustees subject to professional standards (such as lawyers and accountants) will be judged according to the (enhanced) standard of diligence and knowledge required by those standards.[47]

An element of the basic duty of care owed by any trustee to beneficiaries is to take advice in appropriate circumstances.[48] This duty arises under both the common law and statute. The common law requires a trustee to take advice on matters that the trustee does not understand, to consider the advice and act on it in accordance with the standard of the 'ordinary prudent man of business'.[49] This involves the exercise of judgement. A trustee (or an agent exercising the powers of a trustee) cannot hide behind advice as a means of avoiding consideration of whether a particular course of action is in the best interests of the beneficiaries. In England, the Trustee Act 2000 follows this approach, requiring trustees to take advice except where they conclude that in all the circumstances it is not necessary.[50]

When exercising any power of investment, trustees are required to have regard to the 'standard investment criteria' established by the Trustee Act 2000 and the Trusts (Sc)

---

[44] The Law Commissions, above n 24, regarded the higher standard as being applicable to 'remunerated and professional' trustees (see para 2.15).

[45] Section 1.

[46] For articulation of the common law duty in Scotland see *Clarke v Clarke's Trustees* 1925 SC 693, holding trustees liable for failing to exercise the required standard of care in the retention of shares in a company which became insolvent.

[47] On this point see the Law Commissions, above n 24, 26; Chalmers, above n 42, para 9.08.

[48] The Law Commissions, above n 24, 23 noted that 'appropriate circumstances' would depend upon a number of variables, including the size, nature and purpose of the particular trust, the composition of its investment portfolio and the skills and experience of the trustees. The report also notes that modern trust deeds do not generally oblige a trustee to take advice before exercising an express power of investment, however wide (24).

[49] *Cowan v Scargill* [1984] 2 All ER 750, 752 per Megarry V-C.

[50] Section 5.

Act 1921.[51] They are that the investments should be suitable for the trust and should be diversified. The suitability obligation requires trustees to consider characteristics of investments such as risk, duration and liquidity, by reference to the trust purposes. A trustee will be liable for breach of duty in the event that unsuitable investments are selected and cause loss to the trust.

The purpose of diversification is to reduce the overall risk associated with the fund.[52] Risk can be categorised for investment purposes as being either market risk or specific risk. Market risk describes the risk arising from movements in the general level of the market in a particular class of investment. Specific risk describes the risk arising from a particular investment, such as the risk of insolvency making a share worthless. While market risk cannot generally be avoided,[53] specific risk can be reduced through diversification, which, by spreading risk across a number of holdings, limits the effect of specific risk on the fund as a whole.

Diversification gives rise to a further problem. It is the issue of the liability of trustees who have diversified the fund but have fallen short of the growth that could have been achieved had the fund been invested in different proportions in the relevant asset classes. In other words, are trustees liable for a shortfall in relative performance against comparable funds[54] and, if so, for what are they liable? The matter was considered in *Nestlé v National Westminster Bank plc*.[55] The plaintiff alleged that a combination of failure on the part of the trustees to understand their investment powers and to review the performance of the fund led to the beneficiary suffering a loss in excess of the value of the fund. The plaintiff was unable to prove the loss and therefore the case failed. The legal reasoning in that case suggests that it will be very difficult to attach liability to a trustee in circumstances in which relative performance falls short of comparable funds in the absence of some other failing, such as failing to take advice or to conduct periodic reviews. The following extracts from the judgments in that case contribute to this conclusion:

> Of course it is not a breach of trust to invest a trust fund in such a manner that its real value is not maintained. At times that will be impossible, at others it will require extraordinary skill or luck.[56]
>
> The trustees' performance must not be judged with hindsight: after the event even a fool is wise, as a poet said 3000 years ago.[57]

---

[51] Sections 4(2) and s 4A respectively.

[52] See Chapter 1 regarding risk.

[53] Although there are many instruments through which it can now be hedged.

[54] This issue becomes particularly relevant when a fund manager has a mandate to manage on the basis of a 'peer group total fund benchmark'. In this situation the manager is responsible for both strategy and selection, and his performance is measured against what is believed to be a relevant peer group (normally other funds managed under a similar mandate). See generally the Myners Report, above n 4, ch 2, 'Pension Funds: the Context for Investment Decision-Making'.

[55] The first instance decision was handed down in June 1988 but only belatedly reported in (1996) 10 *Trust Law International* 112. The Court of Appeal decision is reported at [1993] 1 WLR 1260.

[56] Staughton LJ at 1275 (CA).

[57] Staughton LJ at 1276 (CA).

> The starting point must, in my judgment, be that as the plaintiff is claiming compensation, the onus remains on her to prove that she has suffered loss because from 1922 to 1960 the equities in the annuity fund were not diversified.[58]

Another important issue for trustees is the extent to which they can take account of considerations other than financial return when exercising their investment powers. This issue arises mainly when ethical or political considerations influence investment decisions. In *Cowan v Scargill*[59] the issue was whether the trustees of a pension scheme for mineworkers could exercise their power of investment so as to prohibit future investment overseas, require the sale of existing overseas investment and prohibit investment in energies in direct competition with coal. The court held that the trustees could not act in that way as it was inconsistent with their fiduciary duty to act in the best interests of the beneficiaries, which was normally their best financial interest. It was recognised that there could be cases[60] where other considerations could coincide with the best financial interest of the beneficiaries, but they could not take priority to that interest. A similar approach was adopted in *Martin v City of Edinburgh District Council*,[61] a case involving sale by trustees of shares with a South African interest following the adoption of an anti-apartheid policy by Edinburgh District Council. It was held that the members of the council as trustees had not applied their minds separately and specifically to the question whether the changes in investments would be in the best interests of the beneficiaries of the trusts. In *Harries v The Church Commissioners for England* [62] the court was required to review the investment policy of trustees (the commissioners) in respect of South Africa as well as the compatibility of that policy with basic Christian values. It was held that the trustees were entitled to follow an ethical policy that precluded investment in South African companies or other companies with more than a small part of their business in South Africa. It was stressed, however, that financial return must be the main criterion for trustee investments and that 'the circumstances in which trustees are bound or entitled to make a financially disadvantageous investment decision for ethical reasons are extremely limited'.[63] It is, of course, a different matter when trustees are specifically authorised to take account of non-financial considerations, as occurs when trust funds are established on an 'ethical' basis.[64]

5.1.5 Trustees' powers to employ nominees and custodians

The position in England prior to the Trustee Act 2000 was that, in the absence of an

---

[58] Dillon LJ at 1269 (CA).

[59] [1984] 2 All ER 750.

[60] The court referred to the US case of *Withers v Teachers' Retirement System of the City of New York* 447 F Supp 1248 (1978), where a pension fund bought bonds issued by the City of New York as part of a strategy of ensuring continuation of the City's contributions to the (unfunded) pension scheme.

[61] 1988 SLT 329.

[62] [1992] 1 WLR 1241.

[63] Ibid, 1250.

[64] See generally L Kurtz, 'Socially Responsible Investment and Shareholder Activism' in A Crane et al (eds), *The Oxford Handbook of Corporate Social Responsibility* (Oxford, Oxford University Press, 2009) ch 10.

express power in the trust instrument or an express statutory exception, trustees could neither vest trust property in nominees[65] nor place trust documents in the custody of a custodian—to do so would result in a breach of trust.[66] Two statutory exceptions were relevant:

1. Section 21 of the Trustee Act 1925 empowers trustees to deposit any documents held by them relating to the trust, or to the trust property, with any banker or banking company, or any other company whose business includes the undertaking of the safe custody of documents.
2. Under section 7(1) of the same Act, trustees have a statutory duty to deposit bearer securities with a banker or banking company for the purposes of safe custody and the collection of income. There is no similar statutory duty in respect of any other form of trust property.

The Law Commissions regarded these rules as being unduly restrictive for trustees. In particular, they did not allow for legal title to assets to be vested in a nominee unless there was an express power to do so. The default rule was that legal title had to be held in joint names so that the consent of all trustees was required for transfer. This posed particular problems following the dematerialisation of title to securities traded through the CREST system (as well as similar overseas systems) because that system was designed on the basis that nominees would normally hold legal title on behalf of investors.[67]

The result was that the Law Commissions recommended that the law be changed. In so doing, they recognised that the use of nominees and custodians posed risks in respect of fraud and loss of shareholders' rights. The fraud risk arises from the loss of (legal) ownership and control of trust assets on the part of trustees while the loss of shareholders' rights arises from the principle that rights (eg to vote at company meetings or receive dividends) follow legal ownership.[68] The Trustee Act 2000 introduced default powers enabling trustees to appoint nominees and custodians.[69] Unlike the position in respect of delegation of investment powers to fund managers, there is no requirement that the nominee or custodian be authorised to conduct investment business under FSMA 2000. The rationale for this is that the FSMA system of regulation does not extend to all cases in which it would be appropriate for trustees to employ nominees and custodians.[70]

The Law Commissions' recommendation was implemented in Scotland several years later, thereby aligning the law in the two countries.[71]

---

[65] Nominees are trustees whose only function is to hold legal title to assets.

[66] See Law Commission Report No 260, above n 24, 160, citing *Browne v Butter* (1857) 24 Beav 159, 161, 162; 53 ER 317, 318, per Romilly MR. The rationale underlying the law is that trustees are bound to preserve the trust fund under their own control.

[67] On dematerialisation and the CREST system, see Chapter 4.2.

[68] Under s 112 of the Companies Act 2006 it is the registered holder of a share who is prima facie entitled to exercise the rights of a member (shareholder) of the company. Regarding the rights of investors when shares are registered in the name of a nominee see R Nolan, 'Indirect Investors: A Greater Say in the Company' (2003) 3 *Journal of Corporate Law Studies* 73.

[69] Sections 16 and 17.

[70] An example would be a nominee who holds land, which does not fall within the scope of FSMA 2000.

[71] Trusts (Sc) Act 1921, s 4B (as amended).

5.1.6 Breach of trust and exclusion of trustees' liability

Breach of duty on the part of trustees in principle gives rise to legal liability to the beneficiaries of the trust. However, a distinction is drawn between two types of breach of duty. The first, which is of most direct relevance in the context of investment management, is breach of the duty of care and skill in respect of the investment functions of the trustees.[72] Such claims would typically relate to the selection or retention of investments that were permissible under the terms of the trust but not suitable for the trust by reference to their risk profile. These claims are based on breach of a duty that arises in tort/delict and damages for loss are limited to what a reasonable person could have foreseen in the circumstances.[73]

The second type of breach of duty is breach of the terms of the trust[74] or of the fiduciary duties that are owed by trustees to beneficiaries. Examples of this type of breach are the investment of trust assets in a category of investment that is not permitted by the trust or the taking of a secret profit by the trustee. This type of breach gives rise to the following remedies: restoration of trust property that has been removed in breach of duty; accounting for profits resulting from the breach of trust; and compensation for loss caused to the trust.[75] In assessing compensation for breach of trust, it is necessary to show that the breach caused a loss to the trust. Once that is shown, damages are not limited by foreseeability of loss and extend to all losses necessary to restore the trust to the position it would have been in had there been no breach.[76] The date for assessing compensation is the date of the court judgment, which means that events or market movements subsequent to a breach of trust may result in there being no claim for loss against the trustees.[77] Moreover, losses for which trustees are liable cannot be offset against profits that have been achieved elsewhere in the fund.[78] Thus, the law isolates and quantifies each breach of trust and does not excuse it even if the performance of the trustees has in other respects been exemplary.

However, it may be that the trust deed exempts the trustees from liability in defined circumstances. The common law in both Scotland and England allows a trust deed to do this. The authorities were reviewed in England in the case of *Armitage v Nurse*,[79] in which a widely drawn clause exempted the trustees from liability other than in cases involving 'actual fraud'. It was argued that such a clause could not be given effect because it was contrary to public policy to allow such a wide exemption in the context

---

[72] In Scotland, this is termed '*intra vires* breach of duty'.

[73] These claims should be distinguished from contractual claims made by trustees against investment managers to whom they delegate the investment management function: see section 5.6 in that regard. The significance of the characterisation of the claims as contractual or based on tort/delict lies primarily in the measure of damages which can be recovered for loss: contractual damages are based on losses arising naturally from the breach or within the knowledge of the party in breach. See further L Van Setten, *The Law of Institutional Investment Management* (Oxford, Oxford University Press, 2009) 3.6.

[74] In Scotland, this is termed '*ultra vires* breach of trust'.

[75] *Target Holdings v Redferns* [1996] 1 AC 421.

[76] Ibid, 434.

[77] Ibid, 437.

[78] *Clarke v Clarke's Trustes* 1925 SC 693.

[79] [1998] Ch 241.

of a relationship of trust. This argument was rejected in favour of an approach analogous to that in contract, with the result that any exemption clause other than in respect of fraud is acceptable and the role of the court is essentially to determine the meaning of the exemption. The position was explained as follows:[80] 'In my judgment clause 15 exempts the trustee from liability for loss or damage to the trust property no matter how indolent, imprudent, lacking in diligence, negligent or wilful he may have been, so long as he has not acted dishonestly.'

It was also noted in this case that the Scottish authorities supported a similar conclusion in respect of the scope and validity of exemption clauses under Scots law.[81] It is also possible in the case of Scottish trusts for a court to relieve trustees from liability for breach of trust if they have acted honestly and reasonably.[82]

The Trustee Act 2000 does not alter the position in respect of exclusion of trustees' liability as the duty of care created by the Act is not a mandatory rule. The possibility of exclusion of the duty in whole or part is referred to expressly in the Act.[83] The position differs in respect of trustees of occupational pension schemes,[84] trustees of issues of debentures[85] and trustees of unit trusts,[86] all of whom are subject to statutory limitations in respect of the validity of exclusion clauses.

Responding to concern over the widespread use of exemption clauses in trust deeds, the (English) Law Commission commented in 2002 that:

> It is now relatively common to find express provisions in modern trust instruments inserted to protect trustees from their liabilities in respect of acts or omissions that would normally be regarded as breaches of trust. As the powers of trustees have increased as a result both of express provisions in trust instruments and by legislation, so has the breadth of trustee exemption clauses. When coupled with the less restrictive approach recently adopted by the courts to the construction of exemption clauses, it can be strongly argued that the protection offered to beneficiaries, one of the prime concerns of trust law, is weaker than in the past.[87]

The Law Commission proposed changes to the law according to which:

- All trustees should be given power to make payments out of the trust fund to purchase indemnity insurance to cover their liability for breach of trust.[88]

---

[80] Millet J at 251.

[81] Reference was made to *Knox v Mackinnon* (1888) 13 AC 753 and *Raes v Meek* (1889) 16 R (HL) 33. The Scottish Law Commission, however, are of the view that it is not possible under Scots law to exclude the liability of trustees in respect of gross negligence (*culpa lata*): see para 3.16 of the Scottish Law Commission, 'Breach of Trust', Discussion Paper No 123 (2003).

[82] Trusts (Sc) Act 1921, s 32. A similar provision is contained in s 61 of the Trustee Act 1925 (England).

[83] See s 1 and sch 1, para 7.

[84] See s 33 of the Pensions Act 1995.

[85] Companies Act 2006, ss 750 and 751. See Chapter 4 for an explanation of debentures.

[86] FSMA 2000, s 253.

[87] Law Commission, 'Trustee Exemption Clauses', Consultation Paper No 171 (2002). For parallel proposals applicable to Scotland see Scottish Law Commission, above n 81.

[88] While the default statutory powers to insure trust property do not extend to insuring trustees' liability, it is possible for this power to be granted by the trust deed and such cover is available in the insurance market. By way of contrast, company directors are expressly authorised to take out insurance to cover liability for negligence, default, breach of duty or breach of trust: see Companies Act 2006, s 233.

- Professional trustees should not be able to rely on clauses which exclude their liability for breach of trust arising from negligence.
- Insofar as professional trustees may not exclude liability for breach of trust, they should not be permitted to claim indemnity from the trust fund.
- In determining whether professional trustees have been negligent, the court should have power to disapply duty exclusion clauses or extended powers clauses where reliance on such clauses would be inconsistent with the overall purposes of the trust and it would be unreasonable in the circumstances for the trustee to be exempted from liability.[89]

Legislation would be required to give effect to these changes, but none has yet been brought forward.

5.2 Special forms of trust

5.2.1 Occupational pension schemes

Occupational pension schemes (OPSs) are normally organised as trusts. The trust fund comprises the contributions made by the employer and employees and the trustees act on behalf of the beneficiaries, who are the employees covered by the scheme. OPSs are governed by both the general law of trusts[90] and various statutory provisions, the most comprehensive being the Pensions Act 1995, which establishes a regulatory framework for the operation of occupational pension schemes.[91] The Act was introduced following recommendations made by the Pensions Law Reform Committee,[92] which was set up following the Maxwell pension funds scandal in the early 1990s. Smaller pension funds are organised either as an insured scheme or as pooled funds. The former is in effect simply an insurance policy, with the result that beneficial ownership of the assets rests with the insurer and the insured has a contractual claim similar to other insurance policies (ie they form part of the overall life fund). The funds from such schemes are treated similarly to those from other policies. Pooled funds differ only in that the funds from a number of pension schemes are aggregated into a single fund that is distinct from the general life fund. Ownership and control of the investments comprising this fund also lie with the insurer. The only asset held by the trustees of insured or pooled pension funds is the insurance policy (ie a contractual rather than a proprietary claim).

The main function of trustees is to invest (or, as is more often the case, enter into

---

[89] Ibid.

[90] See *Cowan v Scargill* [1984] 2 All ER 750, 763.

[91] Occupational pension schemes are not 'specified investments' for the purposes of FSMA 2000 but managing the investments of an OPS is a 'specified activity': see generally Chapter 3.4.

[92] See *Pension Law Reform* (The Goode Report) Cm 2342, 1993.

arrangements for the investment of) the contributions of the employer and employees so as to provide a fund that can pay pensions to employees on retirement.[93] Unless the scheme provides otherwise, decisions of the trustees of an occupational pension scheme may be taken by agreement of the majority of trustees. The investment powers of trustees are determined in the first instance by the trust deed that creates the scheme. If no provision is made in the trust deed, the default provision in the Pensions Act 1995 applies, with the result that the trustees are free to make investments as if they themselves were the beneficial owners of the assets.[94] It is possible for the trustees to delegate their investment powers internally to a subcommittee of two or more trustees, although the trustees collectively remain responsible for the acts of the subcommittee.[95]

The larger pension schemes are directly invested, meaning that the scheme controls its own investments. Such schemes can use an 'in-house' investment manager or, as is more common, an external manager.[96] Irrespective of how the investment is organised, the employees covered by the scheme remain the beneficial owners of the investments. However, voting and information rights associated with shares are likely to be held by other parties. While, under trust law, the exercise of voting rights is a matter for the trustees, it is likely that these rights will be delegated to an external fund manager when the investment management function is delegated by the trustees. It is also possible that the registered owner of the shares will be a nominee (eg a custodian) who has voting rights under company law.[97] However, as a nominee holds the shares as trustee, trust law (and usually also a contract between the pension fund trustees and the custodian) requires that he follow the voting instructions of the trustee or investment manager. The beneficial interest of the trustees in shares cannot be recorded on the shareholders' register of an English company and they have no direct right against the company.[98]

The discretion given to trustees (or fund managers when delegation has occurred) in making investments means that, in principle, any form of investment (in the broad sense of the word, not its narrower regulatory sense of specified investments under FSMA 2000) is eligible for inclusion in the fund. There are, however, a number of safeguards. When choosing investments, the trustees or fund manager must have regard to the need for diversification and the suitability of investments.[99] They also need to comply with regulations made under the Pensions Act 1995.[100] In particular:

---

[93] See Chapter 3 as regards the authorisation requirements for trustees.

[94] Pensions Act 1995, s 34(1).

[95] Pensions Act 1995, s 34(5).

[96] Delegation of the investment powers of pension fund trustees is permitted by s 34(2) of the Pensions Act 1995, including delegation to a fund manager operating outside the UK as regards overseas investment business. See the Myners Report, above n 4, for a description of the differing types of mandate typically given to external fund managers.

[97] Companies Act 2006, s 284(1).

[98] See s 126 Companies Act 2006. The prohibition does not apply to Scotland and it is common for the existence of a trust to be recorded in the shareholders' register of Scottish companies.

[99] Pensions Act 1995, s 36.

[100] The Occupational Pensions Schemes (Investment) Regulations 2005, SI 2005/3378 (OPS Regulations), made under s 36 of the Pensions Act 1995.

1. The assets must be invested—
   (a) in the best interests of members and beneficiaries; and
   (b) in the case of a potential conflict of interest, in the sole interest of members and beneficiaries.
2. The powers of investment, or the discretion, must be exercised in a manner calculated to ensure the security, quality, liquidity and profitability of the portfolio as a whole.
3. Assets held to cover the scheme's technical provisions must also be invested in a manner appropriate to the nature and duration of the expected future retirement benefits payable under the scheme.
4. The assets of the scheme must consist predominantly of investments admitted to trading on regulated markets.
5. Investment in assets which are not admitted to trading on such markets must in any event be kept to a prudent level.
6. The assets of the scheme must be properly diversified in such a way as to avoid excessive reliance on any particular asset, issuer or group of undertakings, and so as to avoid accumulations of risk in the portfolio as a whole. Investments in assets issued by the same issuer or by issuers belonging to the same group must not expose the scheme to excessive risk concentration.
7. Investment in derivative instruments may be made only insofar as they—
   (a) contribute to a reduction of risks; or
   (b) facilitate efficient portfolio management (including the reduction of cost or the generation of additional capital or income with an acceptable level of risk), and any such investment must be made and managed so as to avoid excessive risk exposure to a single counterparty and to other derivative operations.[101]

Trustees who have retained responsibility for selecting investments are required to take proper advice before making investment decisions, other than in respect of 'narrow-range investments not requiring advice' under the Trustee Investment Act 1961.[102] This means that, in the case of advice that is a regulated activity under FSMA 2000, trustees should be advised by an authorised person, and in other cases (eg direct property investment) they should be advised by a person believed by the trustees to have appropriate expertise. The trustees or fund manager must exercise their powers of investment in accordance with the statement of investment principles (SIP), which the trustees are required to prepare and maintain. The SIP must include:[103]

1. the policy regarding diversification and suitability of investments as required by section 36 of the Pensions Act 1995;
2. the principles for the investment of the fund, including types of investment risk and expected return; and
3. the trustees' policy on socially responsible investment and their policy on voting their shares.

---

[101] Art 4 of the OPS Regulations.
[102] Pensions Act 1995, s 36(3).
[103] Pensions Act 1995, s 35(2) and Art 2 of the OPS Regulations.

There are also safeguards relating to employer-related assets and the extent to which non-financial considerations can be taken into account by trustees. Investment in employer-related assets gives rise to concern because of the potential risk posed by failure of the employer's business. A substantial investment in the employer's business might result in employees losing their jobs and a substantial part of their pension entitlement simultaneously. Reflecting this concern, the general rule is that occupational pension schemes cannot invest more than 5% of their assets in employer-related investments.[104] Additionally, the investment must be in line with the SIP and be capable of justification in financial terms by comparison with other similar investments.

Pension fund trustees are unlikely to incur personal liability if they follow the procedures outlined above. If the trustees retain the power to select investments, they are required to take advice, and any negligent advice will give rise to legal liability on the part of the adviser.[105] If the trustees have delegated responsibility for making investments to a fund manager, they are not liable for the acts or defaults of the fund manager in the exercise of discretion where the trustees have taken all such steps as are reasonable to satisfy themselves that the fund manager has appropriate knowledge and experience for managing the investments of the scheme and that he is carrying out his work competently and in compliance with the provisions of the Pensions Act 1995 regarding the selection of investments.[106] It is not, however, possible for a trustee (where there has been no delegation), or an investment manager to whom the investment function has been delegated, to exclude liability for breach of an obligation under any rule of law to take care or exercise skill in the performance of any investment functions.[107] There are also regulatory sanctions available to the Occupational Pensions Regulatory Authority to fine or disqualify trustees who do not comply with the provisions of the Child Support, Pensions and Social Security Act 2000 or regulations made under it.[108]

5.2.2 Unit trusts

The legal structure of a unit trust combines elements of contract and trust. The parties involved are the manager (also known as the operator), the trustee and the unit-holder. The trust is executed by the manager and trustee, neither of whom can be considered to be in the position of a settlor of a private trust, because the trust makes no provision in respect of their property. Another problematic issue in analysing the unit trust according to standard trust law principles is whether the manager is or is not to be considered a trustee. Arguments have been made for and against considering the manager to be a trustee.[109] The significance of the issue lies in the potential liability of the manager arising

---

[104] Pensions Act 1995, s 40(1) and Art 12 of the OPS Regulations.

[105] Under the general principles of the law of negligence. See G McCormack, 'Liability of Trustees for Negligent Investment Decisions' (1997) 13 *Professional Negligence* 45.

[106] Pensions Act 1995, s 34(4).

[107] Pensions Act 1995, s 33.

[108] Pensions Act 1995, ss 3 and 10.

[109] KF Sin, *The Legal Nature of the Unit Trust* (Oxford, Oxford University Press, 1997) argues against the manager being considered a trustee on the basis that the trust fund is owned by the trustee and that there can be

from breach of the investment powers contained in the trust deed. If the manager is a trustee, there is potentially increased liability arising from the high standard of conduct expected by the law from a trustee and a wider range of remedies available to the unit-holders.[110]

The trust deed provides for the safekeeping and investment of sums paid by unit-holders, who are the beneficiaries of the trust.[111] The trust is, in effect, the contractually agreed mechanism under which the manager and trustee deal with the unit-holder's money. The manager and trustee of a unit trust must each be an incorporated body, be independent of each other, be authorised under FSMA 2000 and have permission to act as manager or trustee respectively.[112] It is not possible for the manager or trustee to exclude liability for any failure to exercise due care and diligence in the discharge of their functions in respect of a unit trust scheme.[113]

5.3 The corporate structure

A substantial proportion of institutional investment is structured in the corporate form, with a company buying investments with funds contributed by the shareholders in the company (the underlying investors). The main examples are investment trusts and investment companies with variable capital (ICVCs).[114] The latter have grown in popularity to overtake unit trusts largely as a result of the movement towards a single market in pooled investment funds in the EU. That process has benefited the ICVC at the expense of the unit trust mainly because the ICVC was a more common structure in most EU countries, whereas the unit trust was a structure that was largely confined to the UK. The legal structure of an ICVC makes provision for the management of investments, which is the responsibility of the authorised corporate director, with the result that there is no need for a separate investment management agreement with an external manager. In the case of an investment trust, it is common for an external manager to be appointed by the board to act on behalf of the company.

Responsibility for the operation of an ICVC is split between an authorised corporate director (ACD), other directors (if there are any) and the depositary. The ACD must be

---

no trust (on the part of the manager) without property. A Hudson, *Law of Investment Entities* (London, Sweet & Maxwell, 2000) 207 argues that the manager is a trustee on the basis that the trust deed expressly allocates investment powers to the manager and therefore the manager is functionally in the position of a trustee. On this view, the trustee function in a unit trust is split between the manager and trustee.

[110] For example, if the manager is a considered a trustee, it could be required to make good any deficiency in the trust fund arising from a breach of investment powers and duties. While contractual remedies are also available to unit-holders against the manager, it is more difficult to judge whether, in financial terms, they would be functionally equivalent to remedies for breach of trust.

[111] For discussion of the rights of the beneficiaries and the nature of their investment see Chapter 4.10.

[112] See ss 237 and 243 FSMA 2000 and FSA Handbook, AUTH, Annex 2G T7.

[113] FSMA 2000, s 253.

[114] See generally Chapter 4.4.4 and 4.10.

a body corporate that is authorised for the purposes of FSMA 2000 and has permission to act as a director of an ICVC. It is the ACD that has effective power of management of the ICVC,[115] although where there are other directors they have a role in monitoring the performance by the ACD of its allocated functions. The depositary is responsible for custody of the assets of the ICVC (which are owned by the company) and also has a duty to ensure that the scheme is managed in accordance with the CIS Sourcebook.[116] The directors (including the ACD) and the depositary can retain the services of others (eg a professional custodian) to assist with their duties.

5.4 The partnership structure

Another possible structure for institutional investment is partnership, whether in the standard form, as a limited partnership (LP) or possibly even a limited liability partnership (LLP). Of the three forms, the LP is by far the most popular as a structure for investment management. There are two major attractions of the LP. The first is limited liability for investors, meaning that they can restrict their exposure to their capital contribution.[117] This characteristic has typically been employed so that the investors become limited partners in the LP, with the fund manager being the general partner, who is required to have unlimited liability.[118] As only the general partner is allowed to manage the business of the partnership, the LP structure is well suited to the creation of a fund in which investment management is delegated to the general partner while the other partners do no more than contribute capital. The second attractive characteristic is a substantial degree of privacy. While an LP must be registered with the Registrar of Companies, the information disclosed at that stage is minimal and there are no ongoing disclosure requirements.[119] Thus, by comparison with an LLP or a company, the LP affords a considerable degree of privacy to the contracting parties. Another consideration, relevant in the case of family run businesses, is that an LP can be used as an alternative to a trust for the purposes of succession and tax planning.

The LP is the most common legal structure for private equity funds in the UK. It provides a legal structure that distinguishes the role of the private equity firm (or the fund manager, as it is sometimes called) from the investors in the fund. All limited partnerships

---

[115] See FSA Handbook, CIS 7.3.1R (Functions of the ACD). In this sense, the role of the ACD is similar to that of a manager of a unit trust.

[116] Hudson, above n 109, 219 argues that a depositary might be considered a fiduciary in respect of the fund. Even if that were the case, it is not clear that it would result in a material expansion in a depositary's potential liability under contract, tort and regulatory rules.

[117] By way of contrast, partners in a standard partnership have unlimited liability. In Scotland, another consideration is that a partnership is a separate legal person, which can own property and contract in its own right.

[118] All LPs must have at least one general partner with unlimited liability: s 4(2) of the Limited Partnerships Act 1907 (LPA 1907).

[119] See s 8 LPA 1907 for initial disclosure requirements.

must have at least one general partner with unlimited liability, and the limited partners are not permitted to participate in the management of the firm.[120] In the context of private equity, the role of general partner is taken by a limited company and the role of limited partners by the investors. The limited company general partner is normally a subsidiary[121] of the private equity firm that is appointed to manage the investments of the fund. The management agreement is entered into between the fund (as a limited partnership) and the private equity firm, with the result that there is no direct contractual relationship between the individual investors in the fund and the private equity firm. The rights of investors in the fund depend on the partnership agreement and, where the agreement contains no relevant items, the default rules of partnership law.[122]

Unlike companies (which normally have an unlimited duration), private equity funds are established with a limited duration, typically 10 years. The size of a fund is a function both of the projected investor interest and the possibility that the private equity firm may place a limit on the size of the fund. As investors are required to remain committed for the lifetime of the fund or until all the investments have been successfully divested, their investment in the fund is by its nature illiquid. A secondary market in private equity fund participations has developed, but it provides only very limited liquidity because a potential buyer will require a substantial period of time to investigate and value the participation being offered. It is common for some equity finance to be provided also by the executives of the private equity firm. This is normally structured so that their investment is made through an entity which, just like the other investors in the fund, has limited partner status.

5.5 The contractual structure

The main example of the use of a contractual structure for institutional investment is investment-related life assurance. While insurers are often structured as companies, their relationship with customers who pay premiums into a life fund is contractual. This means that the rights of the policyholder are determined solely by the contract of insurance, and the policyholder has no proprietary rights comparable to those of a contributor to a pension fund or a shareholder in an investment company. While this implies that policyholders are in a weaker position than indirect investors in other forms of institutional investment, regulation of the solvency of insurers as well as the availability of compensation on

---

[120] Section 6(1) of the Limited Partnerships Act 1907 prohibits limited partners from taking part in the management of the firm. If they do take part, they assume liability for debts of the firm incurred during that period of time.
[121] The definition of 'parent and subsidiary undertakings' in s 1162 of the Companies Act 2006 recognises that a partnership can be the parent undertaking of a limited company if it satisfies the 'control' requirements set by s 1162.
[122] This is LPA 1907 or the Partnership Act 1890 (where the 1907 Act does not have specific provisions covering the matter).

insolvency limits the risks to a considerable degree. Insurance contracts are not subject to the Unfair Contract Terms Act 1977 but may be subject to the Unfair Terms in Consumer Contracts Regulations1999.[123] Insurers are also subject to Principle 6 of the FSA's Principles for Businesses, which requires that an authorised person treat customers fairly. This is particularly important in contracts (such as with-profits insurance) in which considerable discretion is given to the insurer as to the allocation of profits between different generations of policyholders.[124]

5.6 Investment management contracts

It is possible for an investment fund organised under any of the structures discussed above to manage its own investments. However, as 'in-house' management of a diversified portfolio requires substantial investment in personnel and support systems, it is more common for investment management (and in some cases investment strategy) to be delegated to professional fund managers through an investment management contract. It is normal practice in the investment management business for such contracts to be termed a 'mandate', although in strictly legal terms the contract is not one of mandate.[125] Subject to the general law of contract, restrictions arising under trust law and obligations arising from the FSA's regulatory rules, the parties to such an agreement are free to agree whatever terms they wish. The general law of contract contains some restrictions on freedom of contract (eg contracts to commit a crime are unenforceable), but none are directly relevant to investment management agreements. Neither the Unfair Contract Terms Act 1977 nor the Unfair Terms in Consumer Contracts Regulations 1999, which apply mainly to contracts between a business and a private individual, regulate the terms of such contracts.

Over time, the standard terms of these contracts have changed.[126] In the 1980s, most funds were managed on a 'balanced' basis. This type of contract involved a single fund manager being given responsibility for the entire portfolio of a pension fund, including both asset allocation and stock selection. Contracts would specify an objective of outperforming, or being in the top quartile of, a peer group of funds ('peer group benchmarking') and provision would be made for performance to be evaluated by independent consultants. By the mid-1990s, balanced mandates were seen to have produced disappointing results,

---

[123] The manner in which the regulations apply to insurance is complex: they do not apply to the main terms of the contract (often referred to as the core terms) or to the price (premium), but may apply to the remainder of the contract. See N Legh-Jones (ed), *MacGillivray on Insurance Law* (London, Sweet & Maxwell, 2003) para 10.18.

[124] See Chapter 4.3.2 for a discussion of this issue.

[125] Mandate in its true legal sense is a form of gratuitous representation which differs from agency in that the mandatory becomes bound to contracts entered into on behalf of the mandator (unlike agency in which the principal becomes bound by contracts entered into by an agent).

[126] See the Myners Report, above n 4, 75.

and the focus shifted to employing specialist managers for asset allocation and different asset classes. More recently, the focus (especially in the case of pension funds) has shifted to 'liability driven investment'. This approach aims to match investment returns with the liabilities that they are required to fund and to manage portfolio risk within that context.

An investment management agreement is a contract for the provision of services.[127] A typical agreement will include terms:

- providing for the appointment of the manager to manage a certain portfolio of investments for a specified period of time;
- obliging the investor to pay a fee and providing for the method of calculation of that fee;
- setting out the specified risk and return objectives;
- requiring the manager to use professional judgement, knowledge and skill, as the investor's agent, to attain the investment objectives subject to the relevant investment constraints ('the investment duty');
- an 'entire agreement' clause, limiting the contract terms to those expressly set out in the agreement;
- 'jurisdiction' and 'applicable law' clauses, which determine in which country's courts and according to which system of law disputes are to be settled.

It follows from the nature of the agreement as one for the provision of services that the manager aims to deliver a certain return but does not guarantee that return. The discretion enjoyed by the manager will be subject to any constraints that are applicable to the relevant fund, by reference, for example, to the geographical area for investment, the size of company, constituents of a particular index or the exclusion of certain industry sectors (eg in an 'ethical' fund). Regulatory controls applicable to the fund represent another form of constraint.[128] There may also be more detailed specification of the style of investment in the agreement through prescriptive risk parameters such as 'value-at-risk', which attempts to quantify risk by reference to the historic volatility of financial instruments. In tandem with the investment discretion, the agreement will also provide the manager with authority as agent to bind the investor to transactions with or through third parties.[129] The precise scope of the authority requires careful matching with the investment discretion to enable the manager to enter into the full range of transactions (eg futures, options) that may be required to achieve the investment objective, although it may be possible for necessary powers that are not expressly stated in the agreement to be implied by reference to the intentions of the parties or standard market practice. Consideration also has to be given as to whether fund investments may the subject of

---

[127] For a more detailed discussion see generally Van Setten, above n 73.

[128] Regulatory constraints are discussed in more detail in sections 5.8 and 5.9.

[129] See eg the Investment Management Association (IMA) Model Terms of Business with Brokers, available at http://www.investmentfunds.org.uk/assets/files/industry-guidance/20090702-modeltermsofbusiness.pdf (accessed on 15 November 2011).

stock-lending[130] or collateral agreements entered into by the fund manger in connection with transactions in derivatives.

It is the conduct of the manager by reference to the investment objectives and constraints that must form the basis for any claim that the manager is in breach of the investment duty. The actual results delivered by the manager (whether above or below the objectives set by the agreement) are not of direct relevance for the purposes of this evaluation. The standard of skill and care required from the manager is determined primarily by the law of agency, as the manager is designated by the agreement as the investor's agent. The standard is very similar to that mentioned above in the context of professional trustees or those acting under powers granted by the Trustee Act 2000.[131] Every professional agent acting for reward is required to exercise such skill, care and diligence as is usual or necessary in, or for the ordinary or proper conduct of, the profession.[132] It is this standard that must be applied to the exercise of investment discretion by the manager to determine if the manager has discharged the investment duty. In making that assessment, proof of common practice among peers will be relevant, as may be any relevant professional codes of conduct and regulatory rules.[133] Thus, as illustrated by the extreme example of *Nestle v National Westminster Bank plc*,[134] it is possible for the manager's performance to fall far short of benchmarks that fall within the investment objectives and constraints of the agreement/trust without being in breach of duty.

An 'entire agreement' clause is a defensive mechanism that protects the manager from claims made by the investor in connection with false representations that are made by the manager during pre-contractual negotiations. Such representations may relate to matters such as the past performance of the manager, business processes, investment selection methods or expectations of future performance. The risks faced by a manager are twofold. First, a court may consider that a representation has become a term of the contract or that it has created a separate 'collateral' contract. While primacy is given to the written document and the barriers to introducing extrinsic evidence of additional express terms to a contract are relatively high, the risk is still real. Secondly, a court could consider that the manager had made an actionable misrepresentation relating to facts that the investor relied on in entering into the agreement. In both cases, the outcome would be that the manager would face a claim for compensatory damages for any loss caused to the investor. A basic form of 'entire agreement' clause limits this risk by limiting the contract

---

[130] Stock-lending is a form of loan of securities. The lender is usually an institutional investor and the borrower a market-maker or proprietary trader with a short position who borrows to meet settlement obligations. The fee paid by the borrower boosts the investment performance of the fund. See further Chapter 13.5; see also the IMA, 'Survey of Fund Managers' Engagement with Companies for the Two Years Ended 30 June 2008', 25–27, available at http://www.investmentfunds.org.uk/research/ima-annual-industry-survey/ams (accessed on 15 November 2011) for more details on the practice of stock-lending.

[131] See above section 5.1.4.

[132] *Bowstead & Reynolds on Agency*, 18th edn (London, Sweet & Maxwell, 2006) 6-015–6-018.

[133] See *Gorham v BT plc* [2001] WLR 2129 and *Seymour v Caroline Ockwell & Co (a firm)* [2005] EWHC 1137 (QB) for judicial endorsement of regulatory rules as a relevant consideration for establishing the scope and content of common law duties.

[134] Above n 55.

terms to those expressly set out in the contract.[135] A more sophisticated version of the clause would also exclude liability for misrepresentation, although that option presents some difficulties in satisfying the requirements of the general law of contract relating to exclusion clauses.

An investment management contract may also carry implications for the manner in which ownership rights, and particularly the right to vote, are exercised. In many instances, legal title to investments such as shares is held by an investment manager rather than by the investment fund. This results in the investment manager having the right to vote on resolutions at a company meeting. It is possible, however, for voting rights to be passed down to an indirect investor by contractual agreement.[136] This can take the form of an agreement between the investment manager and the indirect investor (the fund) that the former will appoint the latter as proxy in respect of the shares, with discretion as to how the votes attached to the shares should be cast.[137]

5.7 Institutional investment organisations

There are a number of organisations through which institutional shareholders coordinate their activity and promote their interests as shareholders. The members of the Institutional Shareholders' Committee are particularly influential. These are as follows:

The Association of British Insurers (ABI)

The ABI is a trade body which represents the interests of its members, who are engaged in all forms of insurance business. As insurance, and in particular life assurance, involves holding and investing substantial funds accumulated from premiums (as well as shareholders' capital), insurers occupy an important position as investors in bonds and equities.

The National Association of Pension Funds (NAPF)

The NAPF is the principal UK body representing the interests of the employer-sponsored pensions movement. Among its members are both large and small companies, local authority and public sector bodies. NAPF members also include the leading businesses

---

[135] This includes terms that can be implied from the intentions of the parties as evidenced by the contact. However, implied terms based on 'trade custom' or 'business usage' are excluded by an 'entire agreement' clause.

[136] See Nolan, above n 68.

[137] As a registered shareholder always has a right to appoint a proxy under s 324 of the Companies Act 2006, such an agreement provides an ongoing mechanism for votes to be passed down to the ultimate investor. The position becomes more complicated when there is a chain of indirect ownership, but the same mechanism can be employed within the extended chain.

providing professional services to pension funds, such as consultancy, actuarial, legal, trustee, administration, IT and investment services.

The Investment Management Association (IMA)

The IMA represents the UK unit trust and investment management industry. It acts as a trade body to promote its members' interests to government and regulators, and to promote the general principle of investing through collective funds to the general public. The IMA was formed on 1 February 2002, when the Association of Unit Trusts and Investment Funds and the Fund Managers Association merged to establish a new association. It publishes an annual Asset Management Survey that covers recent trends in the industry and regulatory developments.

The Association of Investment Trust Companies (AITC)

The AITC is the non-profit-making trade body of the investment trust industry and was formed in 1932. It represents investment trust companies and their shareholders, but also works closely with the management groups that administer the companies. The individual trusts provide funding for AITC, and its activities are focused on providing value to them and their shareholders (eg by promoting the benefits of investment trusts to the public). An example of the work of the Institutional Shareholders' Committee is the Statement of Principles dealing with the responsibilities of institutional shareholders and agents, which was superseded in 2010 by the Stewardship Code.[138] The Principles (and now the Code) provide a framework within which institutional shareholders will carry out their responsibilities within investee companies to ensure that institutional investors act in the best interests of ultimate investors (whose money they manage) in the manner in which they deal with investee companies. The Stewardship Code plays an important role in articulating the fiduciary duties of institutional investors and their agents. That function is important because few disputes between institutional investors ever reach the courts.

The ABI and NAPF are particularly active in producing specific guidance for members on issues relating to institutional investment. They have, for example, formulated guidelines on share options and executive remuneration, shareholders' pre-emption rights and voting policy.[139] The dominant role of institutions in the ownership of investments in the UK means that these self-regulatory measures have *de facto* a similar status to formal legal measures.

British Private Equity &Venture Capital Association (BVCA)

The BVCA is the industry body and public policy advocate for the private equity and venture capital industry in the UK. It has been particularly prominent in addressing public concern over the manner in which private equity firms run portfolio companies and the

---

[138] See Chapter 9.4.2.
[139] See Chapter 9.4.

secrecy that surrounds the operation of the funds.[140] Guidelines published by the BVCA in November 2007 provide for enhanced disclosure by some portfolio companies and private equity firms, and will operate on a 'comply or explain' basis, leaving open the possibility of conformity through explanation (for example, where compliance might risk competitive disadvantage). The enhanced disclosure regime provides for more disclosure than is required for other private companies under company law. The BVCA is responsible for monitoring compliance and for review of the guidelines.

Alternative Investment Management Association (AIMA)

The AIMA is the trade association for hedge funds and associated support services. As well as acting as an advocate for the industry in the development of the regulatory regime, AIMA has also been active in developing best practice standards for hedge funds.

5.8 The EU regulatory framework

The EU 'MiFID regime'[141] applies to 'investment firms'. This category includes investment firms who directly manage investments on behalf of their clients 'in house' and fund managers who act on behalf of an institutional investor operating under any of the legal structures discussed above. The MiFID regime excludes from its scope: insurers; collective investment undertakings (UCITS), and their depositaries and managers; and pension funds.[142] As the excluded entities account for the majority of funds under management in the UK, it might be argued that the 'footprint' of the MifID regime in the sphere of institutional investment is quite limited. While that conclusion may be valid when the MiFID regime is viewed in isolation, there are two other relevant considerations: first, the inclusion of fund managers effectively brings within the MiFID regime any form of institutional investment that operates through an external fund manager; and secondly, insurers and UCITS are subject to separate EU regulatory regimes that pursue very similar objectives to MiFID but take into account the special characteristics of those forms of investment.

The requirements of the MiFID regime can be broadly separated into three categories: organisational; conduct of business; and capital adequacy. As regulatory rules, they do not carry direct implications for investment management contracts, although courts may well

---

[140] See generally I MacNeil, 'Private Equity: The UK Regulatory Response' (2007) 3(1) *Capital Markets Law Journal* 18.

[141] See Chapter 2.9.1 for the meaning of this term.

[142] Credit institutions (such as banks) are not exempt from the MiFID regime, but are exempt from the requirement to gain separate authorisation for investment business.

refer to regulatory rules when interpreting those contracts.[143] Each of the three categories is discussed below.

The organisational requirements can be characterised as operational requirements or compliance requirements.[144] The operational requirements focus on:

- ensuring continuity and regularity in the performance of investment services and activities through requirements related to systems and controls;
- ensuring compliance with applicable regulatory rules through recordkeeping requirements that allow the firm's regulator to monitor compliance;
- establishment of a transparent organisational structure that allocates functions and responsibilities in a clear manner to individuals with the requisite skills, knowledge and expertise to discharge those responsibilities.

The compliance requirements focus on:

- ensuring that a firm has adequate compliance procedures by reference to the nature and range of the business, and that adequate procedures are put in place to minimise the risk of the firm failing to deal with its regulatory obligations;
- establishing procedures to identify conflicts of interest between the firm and its clients or between one client and another, and ensuring that a policy[145] is in place to prevent such conflicts prejudicing the interests of clients.

The conduct of business requirements of MiFID fall into two categories: one covers requirements relating to dealings *with* clients; the other, requirements relating to dealing *for* clients. Two issues within the first category are of particular significance:

- Client classification. Under the MiFID regime, all client relationships must fall under the category of 'professional' or 'retail'. Prior to the provision of any investment service, the firm must notify the client of the appropriate designation.[146] That designation carries important consequences for the regulatory rules that apply to the client relationship, as MiFID adopts a policy of applying a more protective regulatory regime to 'retail' clients. Importantly, however, MiFID also recognises that a professional client may, for certain purposes, be treated as an 'eligible counterparty', with the result that relevant MiFID rules are disapplied. Thus, in the case of transactions with an 'eligible counterparty', the assumption is made that each party is a well-informed professional who is capable of looking after their own interests and that the transaction is concluded on an 'arm's length' basis.
- Suitability and 'know your customer'. In the case of portfolio management:

> the firm shall obtain the necessary information regarding the client's or potential client's knowledge and experience in the investment field relevant to the specific type of product

---

[143] For cross-references to cases see Van Setten, above n 73.

[144] Van Setten, ibid, 37.

[145] It must be a written policy specifying procedures to be followed and measures to be adopted to manage identified conflicts of interest.

[146] MiFID generally permits firms authorised under FSMA 2000 to be professional clients as well as pension funds, national and regional governments, and companies meeting certain financial thresholds.

or service, his financial situation and his investment objectives so as to enable the firm to recommend to the client or potential client the investment services and financial instruments that are suitable for him.[147]

While an investment firm is entitled to assume that a professional client has the requisite knowledge and experience in this context, it is not clear that it is entitled to assume that the client is able to bear financially any related investment risks consistent with its investment objectives.[148]

The MiFID conduct of business rules relating to dealing for clients can be characterised broadly as a regulatory articulation of the common law duties owed by an agent to a client. They focus on the following issues:

- Inducements. The policy underlying these rules is that the nature of payments paid or received by a firm in connection with the provision of investment services should not compromise the duty of the firm to act in the best interests of the client. The rules require that payments made and received in connection with the service be disclosed to the client in a manner that is comprehensive, accurate and understandable.
- 'Best execution'. This requirement focuses on achieving the best possible results for clients in the way that transactions in financial instruments are carried out. The obligation is to take 'all reasonable steps', taking into account the various characteristics of the order, such as price, speed, size and settlement. While it applies most obviously to brokers who act as agents for clients in concluding transactions, it also applies to portfolio managers who place orders with such brokers. However, in that case, the manager is entitled to rely on confirmation by the relevant brokerage firm that it is subject to and complies with the MiFID requirements. This provides an indirect form of compliance by the portfolio manager and reduces duplication of regulatory obligations.
- Client order handling. The MiFID rules on client orders recognise that the location, timing and sequence of order execution in financial markets carry significant implications for the terms that can be achieved by an investment firm when it deals on behalf of a client. Firms are required to have an order execution policy and to take all reasonable steps to obtain the best possible results for their clients, taking into account price, costs, speed, likelihood of execution and settlement, size, nature or any other consideration relevant to the execution of the order.

The regulatory capital requirements for investment firms operate in tandem with those applicable to banks and aim to apply equivalent standards to firms that undertake the same risks irrespective of the nature of the firm. The EU Capital Adequacy Directive (CAD)[149] sets out the regulatory capital requirements for firms engaging in investment activity such as portfolio management, brokerage and market-making, whereas the EU Banking Directive[150] deals with firms engaged in deposit-taking and lending. Insurance

---

[147] Art 19(4) MiFID. See also Art 35 of the MiFID Implementing Directive 2006/73 [2006] OJ L241/26.
[148] See Van Setten, above n 73, 53 for further discussion of this issue.
[149] Directive 2006/49 [2006] OJ L177/201. See also Chapter 2.9.1.
[150] Directive 2006/48/EC [2006] OJ L177/1.

companies fall outside the banking and MiFID regimes as their regulatory capital is governed by a separate EU directive.[151]

In the case of portfolio management, the risks that are undertaken by the firm are relatively low by comparison with the credit risks faced by commercial banks and the market risk that is faced by investment banks that engage in market-making and proprietary trading. The lower risk profile of asset managers reflects the fact that their clients bear the risk of the fall in the value of their investment portfolio (market risk) and they do not normally undertake significant credit risk by lending money to clients. Thus, the regulatory capital requirements for fund managers are relatively low by comparison with banks and other investment firms as a result of their lower risk profile.[152] There are two main requirements for fund managers, one of which relates to initial capital and distinguishes between firms that provide only advice and those that hold client money and/or securities and provide a full portfolio management service.[153] The former are subject to lower requirements reflecting the lower risk posed to clients as a result of their limited services. The other requirement relates to operational risk, which focuses on the ability of the firm to continue to operate its business on stable basis. This imposes an additional requirement for a fund management firm to have capital equivalent to 25% of the previous year's fixed overheads.[154]

The UCITS regime provides a distinct regulatory framework for collective investment schemes.[155] It applies the 'single licence' and 'home country control' principles to UCITS, thereby enabling authorised UCITS schemes to be marketed across the EU. The UCITS regime is unusual in the EU context as it relies primarily on regulation of the product (the units in the fund acquired by an investor) as a technique to protect the mainly retail investors in such funds. The investment objectives of UCITS funds have been widened considerably over time, by extending the range of assets in which they can invest. Controls over the managers of such funds, which were originally regulated quite lightly, were strengthened in 2001, when the EU passport was extended to managers (having been originally limited to UCITS schemes). The prudential controls over managers of UCITS run broadly in parallel with those applicable to managers under MiFID (above), albeit that broader discretion is given to the home state to set the relevant rules than in the case of the MiFID regime, which is more prescriptive.

The EU Alternative Investment Fund Managers Directive (AIFMD)[156] also has impor-

---

[151] See Chapter 2.9.3.

[152] The risk profile of a fund management firm should not be confused with its investment strategy in managing client portfolios. A high-risk investment strategy implies a high degree of risk for the client but does not in itself imply that the firm faces a higher risk of insolvency.

[153] See Arts 5(1) and 5(3) of the CAD. A full portfolio management service will require authorisation for portfolio management and arranging deals in addition to the provision of advice.

[154] Art 21 of the CAD.

[155] The regime comprises the UCITS Directive 85/611 EC [1985] OJ L375/3 as amended by the 'UCITS III' revisions in the Product Directive 2011/108 EC [2002] OJ L41/35 and the Management Company and Prospectus Directive 2001/107/EC [2002] OJ L41/20. See generally N Moloney, *EC Securities Regulation*, 2nd edn (Oxford, Oxford University Press 2008) ch 3.

[156] Directive 2011/61 [2011] OJ L174/1. See generally, D Awrey, 'The Limits of EU Hedge Fund Regulation' (2011) 5(2) *Law and Financial Markets Review* 119.

tant regulatory implications for fund managers who fall within its scope.[157] The Directive applies in particular to the managers of hedge funds, private equity funds and real estate funds.[158] While such managers already fell within the scope of MiFID (because they offer portfolio management services on a professional basis), the funds themselves fell outside the scope of EU regulation.[159] Moreover, since many alternative funds are based outside the EU and are therefore beyond the jurisdiction of its laws and regulations, the EU chose an indirect approach to regulation in the form of an enhanced regulatory regime for managers of AIFs. Many of the basic elements of that regime are not materially different from the requirements imposed by MiFID: the references to risk management, conflicts of interest and capital requirements follow the general approach of MiFID, although the level 2 implementing measures may in due course specify more detailed requirements that differentiate the AIFMD regime more clearly from the MiFID regime.[160] There are, however, three distinctive requirements:

- Third-party valuation and safekeeping requirements. The AIFMD requires that an AIFM appoint an independent third party to value both the portfolio assets of the AIFs it manages and their issued securities. This reflects the potential problems that arise in the valuation of illiquid assets, which tend to be more important for alternative funds than their conventional counterparts. It also requires that a depositary be appointed to receive and hold subscriptions from investors and for the purposes of safekeeping portfolio assets.
- Disclosure requirements. The AIFMD lays down a series of initial, periodic and event-driven disclosure requirements designed to enhance the transparency of AIF activities to investors and regulators. This includes a requirement to make audited accounts available to investors on an annual basis and to report to investors and regulators periodically regarding investment in illiquid securities and management of risk.
- Leverage requirements. Responding to the perception that leverage employed by hedge funds may have exacerbated the financial crisis by contributing to market instability, the AIFMD empowers the EU Commission to set leverage requirements for AIFMs where it deems them necessary to ensure the stability and integrity of the financial system. It requires that AIFM employing leverage on a systematic basis above a defined threshold disclose aggregate leverage in all forms, and the main sources of leverage both to investors and to the home authority of the AIFM.

---

[157] The Directive does not seek to regulate the funds, which are often based in 'offshore' jurisdictions.

[158] See Chapter 4.10 regarding the nature of hedge funds and section 5.4 regarding the nature of private equity funds.

[159] In particular, the UCITS regime does not apply to such funds.

[160] There is also considerable overlap with the best practice standards developed by the hedge funds trade association, the Alternative Investment Management Association (AIMA).

5.9 The FSMA 2000 regulatory framework

Reference was made at the beginning of this chapter to the role of the FSMA 2000 system of regulation in controlling risks to which contributors to funds managed by institutional investors (and their agents) are exposed. Those risks are primarily management risk (arising from incompetent or fraudulent management) and investment risk (the assumption of risk beyond that which is appropriate for a particular fund).[161] The role of FSMA 2000 in controlling exposure to such risk is apparent both at the point of entry into regulated activity (authorisation and permission) and during the conduct of the activity.

Once authorised, all forms of institutional investment become subject to those parts of the FSA Handbook that in principle extend to all forms of regulated activity. Of particular importance are the Handbook components relating to regulatory capital requirements,[162] the senior management arrangements, systems and controls,[163] the approved persons regime[164] and the market abuse regime.[165] The MiFID regulatory regime (above) is another significant factor for institutional investment, although implementation through 'intelligent copy out' rather than 'gold-plating'[166] means that the FSA Handbook mostly replicates the provisions that are to be found within that regime.

The provisions of the FSA Handbook relating to the treatment of client money and client assets held by investment firms are unusual in the regulatory context in that they carry direct implications for the property rights of clients. In the case of client money, FSMA 2000 enables the FSA to specify that it is held on trust.[167] The Client Assets (CASS) section of the FSA Handbook gives effect to this provision by specifying that firms receive and hold client money subject to a statutory trust.[168] The result is that, in the event of the firm's insolvency, client money is kept separate from the assets of the firm that are available to its creditors to meet its debts. There is no parallel statutory power enabling the FSA to specify that other assets (mainly financial instruments) held by investment firms on behalf of clients be held on trust. However, the regulatory obligations imposed on firms lead to the same result in practice. Firms are required to hold client assets in a way that safeguards the clients' ownership rights, especially on insolvency.[169] This is achieved mainly through organisational requirements (eg in respect of separate

---

[161] This follows the classification adopted by O Loistl and R Petrag in *Asset Management Standards* (Basingstoke, Palgrave MacMillan, 2003).

[162] These requirements differ between different types of firm, although they are all risk based and aim for equivalence is setting capital requirements by reference to risk: see FSA Handbook GENPRU, BIPRU and IPRU-INV.

[163] See Chapter 3.

[164] See Chapter 3.

[165] See Chapter 13.

[166] 'Gold-plating' is prohibited by Art 4 of the MiFID Implementing Directive. See Chapter 2.9 for the meaning of this term.

[167] FSMA 2000, s 139.

[168] FSA Handbook, CASS 7.7.2R.

[169] FSA Handbook, CASS 6.2.1R.

identification of firm and client assets) and the recording of legal title in a manner that ring-fences the relevant assets on insolvency. The normal procedure for recording legal title is that it is taken in the name of a custodian who must be authorised under FSMA 2000,[170] and the result is that a trust is created in which the custodian acts as trustee and the client is the beneficiary.[171]

In addition to those generally applicable parts of the FSA Handbook just mentioned, there are also parts that apply only to particular types of institutional investor. For example, in the case of life assurance, the FSA's solvency rules have the effect of limiting the manner in which the life fund can be invested, but these rules are not applicable to investment funds, which have their own rules. Thus, the regulatory position in respect of institutional investors is complex and is best approached from the perspective of the specific activity concerned.

5.9.1 Insurance companies

The funds available for investment by insurance companies are derived from three main sources. First, life funds, which comprise the premiums paid by policyholders and are available to meet claims on life policies. These funds can be organised on the with-profits or unit-linked basis.[172] Secondly, claims reserves relating to non-life policies. These are funds derived from premiums paid under non-life policies that have been allocated to the payment of claims. Thirdly, in the case of shareholder-owned companies, shareholders' capital and reserves are available for investment. Mutual companies do not have shareholders and hence no shareholders' capital is available for investment, but there will normally be accumulated reserves. The policyholders of insurance companies (whether life or non-life) have no direct ownership interest in the investment funds of the insurer. This is true of insurers organised both as shareholder-owned companies and as mutual organisations.[173] The claims of policyholders are entirely contractual.[174] Policyholders who are members (ie shareholders in registered companies or members of mutual organisations) have no ownership rights in investment funds because the assets held in the fund are owned by the insurer, which is a separate legal person.

Insurers are not subject to direct controls over their investments, but there are indirect controls arising from the FSA's prudential supervision sourcebook for insurers. FSMA 2000 imposes solvency requirements on insurers in the following terms: 'A firm must at all times maintain overall financial resources, including capital resources and liquidity

---

[170] See Chapter 14.1.3 regarding custodians.

[171] The trust may be subject to sub-trusts as a result of ownership of securities being recorded successively in the books of intermediaries operating at different levels in the financial markets. The position of the client as the ultimate beneficiary remains unaltered.

[172] See Chapter 4.10 for an explanation of these terms.

[173] See Chapter 7, n 10 regarding the nature of mutual organisations.

[174] See Chapter 4.3 and 5.5 for more detail.

resources, which are adequate, both as to amount and quality, to ensure that there is no significant risk that its liabilities cannot be met as they fall due.'[175]

While the calculation of risk plays an important role in the regulation of solvency, so too does the determination of what counts as regulatory capital. From the investment management perspective, a significant factor for insurers is whether regulatory capital is invested in 'admissible assets', meaning assets which can be counted as regulatory capital for the purpose of solvency calculations.[176] If assets are inadmissible for these purposes, it will be more difficult for an insurer to cover its liabilities and comply with the general solvency rule above. Regulatory capital requirements therefore represent a substantial constraint for the investment of insurance funds and distinguish them from other investment funds that are not subject to those requirements.

5.9.2 Pension funds

Occupational pension schemes do not fall within the scope of the MiFID regime or FSMA 2000. However, since investment management is normally delegated to an external fund manager, the process of investment of the assets of such a scheme is brought within the scope of the regulatory regime through regulation of the fund manager. In particular, the fund manager will be subject to the relevant requirements of the MiFID regime and FSMA 2000.

5.9.3 Investment companies

The investment powers of an investment company (including an investment trust[177]) are determined by its articles of association and will reflect the purpose for which it was established. Unlike the position in respect of authorised unit trusts and ICVCs, the FSA has no regulatory remit in respect of investment trusts and there is therefore no regulatory control of their investment powers.[178] Responsibility for investment of the company's assets may be retained 'in house' or delegated to a fund management firm under an investment management agreement. Whichever option is selected, it will be necessary for the manager to secure authorisation in respect of those regulated activities that form a normal part of the duties of a fund manager.

---

[175] FSA Handbook, GENPRU 1.2.36R. This rule is an articulation of Principle 4 of the FSA's General Principles for Business (see Chapter 15.2.1).

[176] See GENPRU 2 Annex 7 for a list of admissible assets. Note that land and buildings are not admissible.

[177] See Chapter 4 for the distinction between an investment company and investment trust.

[178] While shares in investment trusts are a form of 'specified investment', they are not 'units in a collective investment scheme' and therefore not subject to the special regulatory regime that applies to those schemes. However, listed shares in investment trusts are governed by the FSA Listing Regime in the same way as any other listed company: see generally Chapter 8.

5.9.4 Fund managers

Fund managers may operate on an independent basis or as part of a larger financial conglomerate (such as a 'universal bank'). They will normally require authorisation for the following forms of regulated activity: managing investments, arranging deals in investments and advising on investments.[179] As investment firms, they fall within the scope of the MiFID regime[180] (above) as well as the CAD for the purposes of regulatory capital. The FSMA 2000 regime implements both the MiFID and CAD requirements, and categorises firms according to the type of investment activity that they undertake.[181] Fund managers who deal with professional clients (such as pension funds or large undertakings, partnerships and trusts) are subject to less intense conduct of business regulation by MiFID than those who deal directly with retail clients (eg through collective investment funds). As regards financial resources, fund managers fall within the regime established by CAD.[182] Fund managers are in many cases able to take advantage of the limited exemption from the CAD regime offered to 'limited activity' firms who do not deal as a principal for their own account. The benefit of that exemption is that the firm is not required to apply the regulatory capital charge required by CAD against operational risk.[183] That results in a considerable saving, and represents a proportionate and risk-based approach to the limited systemic risk that is posed by fund management activities.

The Myners Report[184] identified the potential for two practices in investment management to give rise to conflicts of interest and to distort the market for dealing services and investment research. They are 'bundled brokerage' and 'soft commission'. The former is an arrangement in which a broker provides a client (eg a fund manager) with a combination of trade execution services and other services, such as investment research, paid for through the commission payable to brokers for executing orders on behalf of clients. The components of the bundle are not usually offered or priced as separate services. There is an expectation, but no obligation, that the fund manager will deal through the broker. Under a 'soft commission' arrangement, the fund manager receives goods and services (usually from third parties) which are paid for by the broker. There is an explicit prior agreement that links the value of the 'softed' goods and services to a specified volume of commission from dealing orders.

Following the Myners Report, the FSA reviewed the manner in which the regulatory regime dealt with these issues. Its report[185] identified a number of regulatory concerns:

1. The contractual basis under which UK fund managers typically operate permits dealing costs to be incurred (at the discretion of the manager) over and above the fee agreed

---

[179] See Chapter 3.5.

[180] Fund managers acting for institutional investors are unlikely to be exempt under Art 3 MiFID, which applies mainly to small investment firms operating in the retail market.

[181] See FSA Handbook, PERG 13 Guidance on the scope of MiFID and the recast CAD.

[182] See generally Chapter 15.4. Fund managers cannot be CAD exempt firms under Art 3(1)(b)(iii) CAD.

[183] See further Chapter 15.4.3.

[184] Above n 4.

[185] See FSA, 'Bundled Brokerage and Soft Commission Arrangements', Consultation Paper 176 (April 2003).

for investment management. The resulting costs are often opaque and accountability to customers (typically pension funds and collective investment funds) is poor.

2. Bundled brokerage and soft-commission arrangements distort fund managers' decisions on the routing of business because additional services provided by brokers may be a more significant factor than execution quality.

3. Competition between fund managers focuses on the management fee, not on dealing costs. Moreover, there is only very limited disclosure of the effect of transaction costs on fund performance (the main criterion against which fund managers are judged).

The FSA proposed two regulatory measures to resolve these problems. The first was that the nature of goods and services that can be bought from a broker with commission payments should be limited to trade execution (dealing) and investment research.[186] The rationale was that the fund manager should be incurring the cost of other services directly rather than including them in transaction costs to be paid by the customer. The second proposal was that, where a fund manager buys any services additional to trade execution with his customer's commission, he should determine the cost of those services and rebate an equivalent amount to his customer's funds. This was envisaged as providing fund managers with an additional incentive to control the purchase of additional services.

However, the FSA eventually decided to pursue only the first option.[187] It is given effect in the FSA Handbook by the following rule:

(1) An investment manager must not accept goods or services in addition to the execution of its customer orders if it:
    (a) executes its customer orders through a broker or another person;
    (b) passes on the broker's or other person's charges to its customers; and
    (c) is offered goods or services in return for the charges referred to in (b).
(2) This prohibition does not apply if the investment manager has reasonable grounds to be satisfied that the goods or services received in return for the charges:
    (a)
        (i)   are related to the execution of trades on behalf of the investment manager's customers; or
        (ii) comprise the provision of research; and
    (b) will reasonably assist the investment manager in the provision of its services to its customers on whose behalf the orders are being executed and do not, and are not likely to, impair compliance with the duty of the investment manager to act in the best interests of its customers.[188]

The effect of the exception in part 2(b) of the rule is to leave considerable discretion in

---

[186] This would exclude services such as market information provided by third parties (eg the Reuters news agency), custody services, computer hardware, telephone lines and payment of fees for seminars and publications.

[187] See FSA, 'Bundled Brokerage and Soft Commission Arrangements', Policy Statement 04/13 (May 2004). The abandonment of the second option reflected a number of considerations including: (i) the concern expressed by fund managers regarding the practical aspects of calculating rebates across a varied customer base; (ii) a desire not to stifle market developments in view of changing attitudes among industry participants to their traditional business models and (iii) industry-led developments that are likely to result in greater disclosure by fund managers to customers as to how costs incurred by the manager are broken down.

[188] COBS 11.6.3R.

the hands of the investment manager as to what exactly comprises research and whether the goods or services provided assist in the provision of services to customers. It leaves unresolved the concern expressed by the FSA that ancillary costs incurred by investment managers are hidden in transaction costs charged directly to clients rather than being included in fund management fees (which are the main focus of attention in competition between investment managers).

Fund managers who fall within the scope of the AIFMD will also need to comply with the additional requirements imposed by that measure.[189]

5.9.5 Managers of collective investment schemes

These schemes comprise mainly unit trusts and ICVCs.[190] The investment powers of the manager are determined by both the instrument constituting the scheme and the regulatory rules contained in the FSA Handbook.[191] The regulatory rules take priority over the instrument constituting the scheme and must be complied with to gain authorisation.[192] The general approach of the regulatory rules is to protect consumers by setting minimum standards for the type of investments that can be held and the spreading of risk.

The FSA Handbook requires a number of basic principles to be observed by all author-ised unit trusts and ICVC managers when exercising their powers of investment. They include:

- a requirement that the assets provide a prudent spread of risk, taking account of the objectives of the fund;
- detailed rules limiting the concentration of risk by reference to particular financial instruments and issuers of those instruments;
- restrictions on investment in derivatives by reference to value, counterparties and the process for valuation of the relevant positions; and
- a prohibition on holding funds in cash, other than in schemes designed for that purpose or to meet operating requirements.[193]

There is a general power to borrow up to 10% of the value of the fund. This allows the fund manager to use 'gearing' as a technique to improve returns in rising markets, but also involves greater exposure to loss in falling markets (hence the relatively low limit on borrowing). Lending money and assets from the funds is prohibited because it would expose investors to credit risk (which does not fall within the objectives of the fund), but stock-lending[194] is permitted as the risks arising in such transactions are normally offset to a large extent by the provision of collateral held on behalf of the lender (the

---

[189] See above section 5.5.

[190] Both types of scheme can qualify as UCITS under the EU regulatory regime and thereby market their units in other EU Member States.

[191] See FSA Handbook, COLL (Collective Investment Schemes).

[192] The instrument constituting the scheme can however impose more restrictive rules for the operation of the scheme (eg in respect of investment powers).

[193] See FSA Handbook, COLL 5.2 for the detailed formulation of all these rules.

[194] See n 130 above.

investment fund). Voting rights attached to the property of a scheme must be exercised or not exercised as directed by the manager, reflecting the fact that voting rights are central to the management of the investments that are selected by the manager.[195]

Collective investment schemes are also subject to prudential standards, which mainly take the form of what are termed 'financial resources rules'. The objective of these rules is to set minimum capital and other risk management standards, thereby mitigating the possibility that firms will be unable to meet their liabilities and commitments to investors and counterparties. This is achieved by requiring the firm to have financial resources (mainly capital and reserves) sufficient to cover the higher of (i) a percentage of assets under management and (ii) a fraction of annual fixed expenditure.[196] Thus, assets under management and fixed expenditure are employed as proxies for the scale of the business to determine the level of capital required to cover operational risk under the assumption that market risk is already effectively controlled by the provisions mentioned above.

The regulatory rules require a scheme to publish a prospectus that contains details regarding the operation of the scheme. The prospectus represents a contract between the unit-holders and the manager.[197] The authorised fund manager is subject to a general duty to disclose in scheme particulars information required by the COLL Sourcebook, as well as any other material information.[198] That information covers matters such as the investment objectives of the fund, borrowing policy, arrangements for distribution of income, the remuneration of the fund manager, and arrangements for the sale and redemption of units. The prospectus must be available to any person free of charge on request. Changes to the scheme must be incorporated into an updated version of the prospectus and significant changes (such as fundamental changes in the nature and risk profile of the scheme or changes in the rights of investors) must be approved by a resolution adopted in a general meeting of the investors.

---

[195] FSA Handbook, COLL 6.6.3R. See Chapter 9.4.1 regarding voting rights generally.

[196] See FSA Handbook, UPRU 2.1 (Prudential Sourcebook for UCITS Firms).

[197] See Sin, above n 109, 81, citing the Australian case *Graham Australia Pty Ltd v Corporate West Management Pty Ltd* (1990) 1 ACSR 682, 687.

[198] FSA Handbook, COLL 4.2.5R (Contents of Prospectus).

Private Investors and the Retail Financial Market

This chapter considers the way in which the Financial Services and Markets Act 2000 (FSMA 2000) system of regulation and the common law deal with private investors. The 'retail' investment market is the market for investment products and services that are sold to private individuals. While almost all investments are available to private individuals, there are some, such as life assurance savings schemes, personal pensions and collective investment schemes, that have been designed specifically for the private rather than the professional or institutional investor. Moreover, while investment services such as portfolio management are available to both institutional and private investors, the nature of the services and their regulatory treatment differ. It is therefore useful to distinguish the 'retail' investment market from the 'wholesale' investment market in which professionals and institutions are active. The distinction is based on the participants in each market and their different regulatory treatment.

6.1 Market structure and regulatory framework

The structure of the retail investment market and the products and services available to private investors reflect a number of influences. First, there is considerable diversity among private investors in terms of the type of investment they want and the degree of risk they are prepared to assume. There is also considerable diversity in terms of how much money private investors are able to invest. The market therefore encompasses a spectrum ranging from risk-averse investors with very little money available for investment to wealthy individuals with a substantial appetite for risk. The products and services offered in the retail market reflect this diversity. Secondly, the structure of the retail market reflects the constraints imposed by the regulatory system on the manner in which investments can be sold to private investors. In particular, the rules relating to the status of different types of seller and the provision of financial advice have had a major influence on the structure of the market. Thirdly, long-standing resistance on the part of private investors to pay for financial advice in respect of most financial products has influenced the development of remuneration patterns, which have been a major concern of the regulatory system since the introduction of the Financial Services Act 1986 (FSA 1986).[1]

In common with the investment market generally, the basic regulatory structure of the retail market is built around the authorisation and financial promotion regime. The authorisation regime creates a perimeter within which, broadly speaking, all providers of investments and advisers on investments are regulated by the Financial Services Authority (FSA).[2] The financial promotion regime controls the promotion of investments by unauthorised persons and the manner in which promotion is undertaken by authorised persons. Broadly speaking, it prohibits unauthorised persons approaching customers with a view to entering into an agreement to buy an investment or to provide investment services.[3] However, the main distinguishing feature of the retail market is that conduct of business regulation is employed much more extensively than in the wholesale markets as a tool to promote investor protection. This policy reflects the imbalance in knowledge and understanding of financial instruments in the retail market between customers and firms who provide financial products and financial advice.

Implementation of the MiFID regime[4] has been a significant factor in the development of the regulatory regime for the retail market in recent years. Two aspects of the regime are of particular significance. The first is that it harmonises some organisational and conduct of business rules across the EU. The former relate to the management structure and business processes of a firm whereas the latter relate to the manner in which a firm does business with its customers. While FSMA 2000 rules on these issues that were in place before the MiFID regime pursued the same high-level objective of investor protection, considerable adjustment was required to give effect to the detailed rules of the MiFID regime. The second relevant consideration, which is linked with the first, is that the MiFID regime does not generally permit 'gold-plating'.[5] Thus, it is not normally possible for Member States to retain or introduce regulatory rules that differ from those set out in the MiFID regime other than in exceptional cases that require notification to the European Commission.[6] The result is that much of the FSA's conduct of business rulebook is a direct copy from the MiFID regime.

Central to the regulatory regime for the retail market is the definition of a 'packaged product' and a 'retail client' as the regulatory regime for the retail market is largely con-

[1] See FSA, 'Price of Retail Investing in the UK', Occasional Paper 6 (2000).

[2] See Chapter 3 for a more detailed discussion of the scope of the regulatory regime and the requirement for authorisation.

[3] See Chapter 3 for a more detailed analysis.

[4] See Chapter 2.9.1 for the meaning of this term.

[5] See Art 4 of the MiFID Implementing Directive.

[6] The UK made use of this procedure for certain elements of its regulatory regime for 'packaged products' when MiFID was introduced and intends to do so again in relation to its changes to adviser status and adviser charging which will take effect at the end of 2012: see FSA, 'Distribution of retail investments: Delivering the RDR', Consultation Paper (CP) 09/18 (June 2009).

cerned with sales of 'packaged products' to 'retail clients'.[7] The concept of a packaged product is that it is a product that has been assembled from underlying financial instruments in a manner that makes it suitable for the retail market.[8] The regulatory definition of a packaged product is:[9]

1. a life policy;
2. a unit in a regulated collective investment scheme;
3. an interest in an investment trust savings scheme;
4. a stakeholder pension scheme; or
5. a personal pension scheme;

whether or not (in the case of 1–3) held within an Individual Savings Account (ISA).[10]

The definition of a retail client is also of central significance because some of the FSA's conduct of business rules are limited in their operation to retail clients. This issue is discussed in more detail in 6.2 below.

There are a number of different ways in which investments are sold in the retail market. This is a function not just of long-established market practices, but also of regulatory rules. In particular, the polarisation regime introduced under the FSA 1986 had a fundamental impact on the structure of the retail market by creating a strict regulatory division between different types of person selling and advising on investments. While that regime was brought to an end in 2005, regulatory requirements relating to the status of firms selling and advising on investments in the retail financial market remain a major factor in determining the structure of the market. The different marketing and sales models and their respective regulatory regimes are discussed below.

6.1.1 Execution-only business

Execution-only business refers to transactions executed by a firm upon the specific instructions of a client where the firm does not give advice on investments relating to the merits of the transaction.[11] A common example is 'execution-only' dealing services provided by 'discount' stockbrokers. It is also sometimes referred to as 'non-advised business' so as to distinguish it from 'advised' transactions in which additional conduct of business rules apply to the adviser.[12] However, the fact that only limited advice on

---

[7] The 'retail' market is not itself a formal regulatory concept, although the term is commonly used in the market and in regulatory circles.

[8] As noted in Chapter 1, the creation of a packaged product generally involves transformation of the maturity and risk characteristics of the underlying financial instruments. A unit trust, for example, offers a degree of diversification in equity investment that would not normally be available to a private investor of modest means.

[9] See the glossary to the FSA Handbook of Rules and Guidance. See Chapter 4 for a discussion of the nature of the underlying investments to which the definition refers.

[10] Personal Equity Plans and Individual Savings Accounts offer tax advantages to investors who hold qualifying investments in designated accounts.

[11] This follows the definition given in the glossary to the FSA Handbook of Rules and Guidance which adds 'and in relation to which the rules on assessment of appropriateness (COBS 10) do not apply'. See also Art 18 MiFID.

[12] See FSA CP 09/18, above n 6, for use of this terminology.

investments is given to a private client in respect of a particular transaction is not enough to make it execution only.[13] The consequence of business being transacted on this basis is that (i) the rules on adviser status and charging do not apply and (ii) the conduct of business rules relating to 'appropriateness' (see section 6.3.5 below) do not apply and the client is therefore required to take full personal responsibility for the selection of investments.[14]

'Direct offers' differ from execution-only business in that they are offers made to the public (often with conditions attached) that can result in a binding contract being made if an offeree accepts the offer and meets the conditions.[15] Since the circumstances of the potential buyer are not known to the seller, there is no opportunity for the seller to assess the suitability of the product for the buyer or to engage in the giving of advice (irrespective of how limited or conflicted it might be). In these circumstances there are two main regulatory controls: the first is the financial promotion regime,[16] which requires that the offer be made or approved by an authorised person; the second is the requirement of the FSA conduct of business rules that relevant information about the firm and the investment be made available to offerees.

6.1.2 Intermediaries and financial advice

Intermediaries have always been important in the retail financial market because many private investors lack the information, expertise or judgment required to make fully informed investment decisions. Intermediaries can potentially solve these problems by providing advice about financial products and how they can meet the needs of the customer. The nature of intermediaries and the type of service that they can and do offer varies considerably. Some are very small local firms while others are large national or international networks that may form part of larger financial conglomerates. The nature of the services offered carries implications for the regulated activities for which an adviser requires permission under the Financial Services and Markets Act 2000 (FSMA 2000). In most cases it is likely that an adviser will require permission for the following activities: advising on investments, arranging deals in investments, and arranging for another person to safeguard and administer investments.[17]

---

[13] See *Loosemore v Financial Concepts* [2001] 1 Lloyd's Rep PN 235.

[14] See *Wilson v MF Global UK Ltd* [2011] EWHC 138 for an unsuccessful attempt by a client who had selected 'execution only' status to recover trading losses from his broker. The court stressed that the broker and client were not in an advisory relationship and that the conduct of business rules applicable to such a relationship could not be taken into consideration.

[15] A common example is a direct offer of life assurance made in a newspaper or magazine, usually subject to satisfying some basic conditions as regards health. Direct offers cannot include listed securities, which are subject to restrictions regarding public offers: see Chapter 8.

[16] See Chapter 3.6.

[17] See Chapter 3.5 for more detail.

Adviser status

Prior to FSA 1986, the provision of investment advice was not regulated in terms of the status of the adviser or the substance of the advice. It was therefore primarily controlled by the common law of agency. Under the common law, it is possible for an agent to offer a limited range of services to a principal because the nature of the service to be provided is a matter for private agreement. Before FSA 1986 took effect, it was common for agents to offer advice to private investors based on a limited product range. The rationale for this practice was that it was often considered uneconomic for agents to act for a large number of product providers and that most customers' needs could be met from the products provided by a limited range of companies.

The position changed with the introduction of FSA 1986. The so-called 'polarisation' rule made by the Securities and Investment Board required anyone selling packaged products to be either a company representative or an independent financial adviser. The former was restricted to selling products of his marketing group[18] and the latter was required to advise the customer by reference to the entire market for the relevant product. The result was that the market for financial advice became polarised between these two extremes. The rule was intended to address two perceived deficiencies of the existing legal regime for financial advice. The first was information asymmetry as between an adviser and a private customer regarding the nature of the advice being given. The polarisation rule was intended to remove any doubts as to the nature of the advice by indicating the status of the adviser clearly to the customer.[19] It was also intended to deal with conflicts of interest in the advisory process, such as agents who were ostensibly independent favouring the products of a particular company so as to earn higher remuneration.[20]

Despite the Office of Fair Trading (OFT) concluding that it had anti-competitive effects,[21] the polarisation rule was carried over to the regulatory regime established under FSMA 2000. However, its value for private investors was increasingly questioned both within the FSA and externally.[22] The potential benefits of reforming or ending polarisation were primarily that consumers are likely to be offered a wider range of advice options, greater variety and higher quality of financial products, and that there was likely to be a greater degree of competition between direct-selling providers.[23] In recognition of these benefits, the FSA concluded that the polarisation rule (as well as some related rules) should be repealed. It was brought to an end in 2005 and replaced by a new regime for

---

[18] A marketing group (as defined by the FSA Handbook Glossary) is a group of persons or firms who are allied together (either formally or informally) for purposes of marketing packaged products of the marketing group.

[19] Note that the rule applied only when advice was given, with the result that products outside that of the marketing group could be sold on an 'execution-only' basis.

[20] See FSA, 'Reforming Polarisation: Making the Market Work for Consumers', CP 121 (2002) ch 2.

[21] See *The Rules on the Polarisation of Investment Advice* (August 1999) available from www.oft.gov.uk/News/Publications (accessed on 11 November 2004).

[22] The FSA commissioned several reports by external consultants on the operation and effects of the polarisation regime. See FSA CP 121, above n 20, for details. As noted in CP 121, 27, no other country uses the concept of polarisation.

[23] For a discussion of the background to these conclusions see generally FSA CP 121, above n 20; FSA, 'Reforming Polarisation: Removing the Barriers to Choice', CP 166 (January 2003).

advisers that provided more choice to advisers regarding their regulatory status.[24] The new regime allows advisers to choose between offering three types of advice: entire market, limited range and single provider. The introduction of 'limited range' advice opened up the possibility of firms occupying a mid-point between the two polarised options under the old regime by offering advice relating to a limited range of investments. A central focus of the new regime is the 'Initial Disclosure Document', which makes clear the nature of the advice being offered (from the three options just mentioned), and a 'Keyfacts' document, which sets out details of the services offered and their likely cost (on a comparative basis against market averages). It is also a requirement for independent advisers to offer a fee-based payment option to clients as an alternative to commission payment by a product provider.[25]

However, not long after the abolition of polarisation the FSA began a fundamental review of the distribution of retail products, the Retail Distribution Review (RDR).[26] The RDR focused on some fundamental problems in the retail markets. The FSA expressed its concerns as follows:

- Many retail investment products have complex charging structures and it is often not clear how benefits accrue to consumers.
- Consequently, many consumers rely heavily on advisers through whom retail investment products are sold. Product providers often remunerate advisers, and there can be a misalignment of advisers' interests with those of consumers.
- The costs of poor quality advice may not be fully faced (or perceived to be faced) by advisers as unsuitable sales may be identified only years after the sale, if at all.[27]

Following consultation on these issues, the FSA eventually decided to make changes to its rules on adviser status in 2009. Under rules which will take effect at the end of 2012, advisers will have to choose between offering 'independent' or 'restricted' advice. In order to offer independent advice, an adviser must be able to advise on all retail investment products that are capable of meeting the investment needs and objectives of a retail client.[28] A form of 'simplified advice' that could be provided by advisers operating under either independent or restricted status is under development, but will not be adopted as a separate regime.[29] A 'basic advice' regime for charge-capped 'stakeholder' products will remain in place and will be subject to the new status rule, with the result that advisers providing basic advice will have to disclose that they are providing restricted advice.

---

[24] See FSA, 'Reforming Polarisation: A Menu for Being Open with Consumers', CP 04/3 (2004) for details of the regulatory rules that replaced polarisation.

[25] COBS 6.2.15.

[26] See FSA, 'A Review of Retail Distribution', Discussion Paper (DP) 07/1 (June 2007).

[27] Ibid, 2 and 3.

[28] The scope of the products to which the independence requirements applies has been widened from 'packaged products' to a new category of 'retail investment product', which includes unregulated collective investment schemes, all investments in investment trusts (not just those in investment trust savings schemes), structured investment products and other investments which offer exposure to underlying financial assets, but in a packaged form that modifies that exposure compared with a direct holding in the financial asset.

[29] See FSA CP 09/18, above n 6, ch 3 for more detail.

The implementation of the MiFID regime in the UK also had an impact on the regulatory status of advisers. Article 3 of MiFID permits investment firms to be exempt from the MiFID regime if (i) they do not hold client funds and (ii) their services are limited to the transmission of orders to authorised firms and the provision of related advice. The UK has taken advantage of this option, with the result that small firms of financial advisers can be exempt from the MiFID element of the regulatory system while remaining subject to the FSMA 2000 system.[30] This carries important implications for the intensity of the conduct of business rules to which they are subject and the relevant financial resources rules. The result is that regulatory costs are minimised for these firms in recognition of the lower risk that their limited activities pose to their customers. However, a potential drawback for these 'Article 3' firms is that they do not benefit from the MiFID provisions relating to 'passporting' activities into other Member States.

Adviser charging

As a matter of market practice, intermediaries selling packaged products are normally remunerated by the product provider rather than by the customer. This remains the case even when a product is sold to a customer by a person considered by the law to be the agent of the customer (eg an independent financial adviser). Remuneration generally takes the form of a commission based on the sum to be invested. This practice carries with it considerable risks to the interests of the customer. It can quite easily lead to a situation in which an intermediary's advice is focused more on earning commission than taking care of the best interests of the customer. This will be the case in particular if the customer is not aware of the scale of the intermediary's remuneration and the potential impact it is likely to have on investment returns.

Prior to the entry into force of FSA 1986, the remuneration of agents was controlled by the common law. While it focuses primarily on the more usual situation in which an agent is remunerated by the principal, it does not forbid the agent being remunerated by a third party (such as a product provider). Moreover, even if it were not expressly agreed between a customer and an agent that the agent would be remunerated by the product provider, it would be possible to imply such a term into an agency agreement as a result of the widespread practice of commission payments in the retail financial market.[31] The common law allows the principal to require the agent to disclose any payments from a third party; but there is no obligation imposed on an agent to volunteer this information. In the absence of customer understanding of the law and financial market practices, it was inevitable that commission payments would remain largely undisclosed.

The confusion and lack of transparency resulting from the common-law approach to commission payments resulted in the introduction of conduct of business rules under the FSA 1986 regime that required the disclosure of commission paid to intermediaries. These rules were carried over into the FSMA 2000 system of regulation and are discussed

---

[30] See further N Moloney, *How to Protect Investors* (Cambridge, Cambridge University Press, 2010) 24.

[31] It could be considered to be part of the usual or customary authority of such an agent. See generally R Munday, *Agency Law and Principles* (Oxford, Oxford University Press, 2010) paras 3.24–3.27.

in more detail in 6.3.3 below. However, following the completion of the Retail Distribution Review in 2009, the FSA decided to make a fundamental change to the regulatory regime for adviser charging. The policy change is encapsulated by the following extract from the FSA consultation paper:

> At present, firms that give advice on investments face the prospect of earning different amounts of money depending on which particular firm they recommend a product from and which type of product they recommend. This creates a potential conflict of interest that can be damaging to consumers and undermine trust in the investment industry.
>
> We propose that adviser firms should only be paid for the advice and related services that they provide through 'adviser charges'. By this, we mean that adviser firms should be paid by charges that are set out up-front and agreed with their clients, rather than by commissions set by product providers to secure distribution of their products (including so-called 'soft' commissions, paid in non-monetary forms).[32]

Following this change, which takes effect (along with the changes to adviser status mentioned above) at the end of 2012, it will no longer be possible for advisers to be remunerated in the form of commission payments. The new rules apply only to situations where a firm makes a personal recommendation to a retail client and do not apply to business transacted with professional clients or eligible counterparties (nor to 'execution-only' business). Once the new rules are in place, advisers will have to set their own charging structures, which cannot compromise their obligations to act in the best interests of their clients under the FSA's regulatory rules and the common law.

Appointed representatives

'Appointed representatives' (also known as 'tied agents') were a creation of the FSA 1986 regulatory system that has been carried over to the FSMA 2000 system.[33] They are persons (often legal persons, such as companies) who enter into agreements with an authorised person to act (eg by advising or selling) on behalf of that authorised person (the principal). In respect of designated investment business[34] with retail clients, an appointed representative is permitted to have only one principal, but in respect of other business (eg non-investment insurance) there is no restriction.[35] The limitation to one principal in the former case is based on making clear the status of the appointed representative, whereas the freedom granted in the latter case reflects a judgement that this is necessary to prevent disruption to existing distribution systems and business models.[36]

---

[32] FSA CP 09/18, above n 6, paras 4.1. and 4.4.

[33] See FSMA 2000, s 39 and FSMA 2000 (Appointed Representatives) Regulations 2001, SI 2001/1217.

[34] See below n 75.

[35] FSA Handbook, SUP 12.5.6A R. Note that there are other categories covered by the prohibition, such as regulated mortgage business. Note also Art 3 SI 2001/1217, requiring contracts between a principal and the appointed representative to permit the principal to restrict the business of the appointed representative in this manner.

[36] See FSA Policy Statement (PS), 'Appointed Representatives—Extending the Current Regime' (September 2003).

Appointed representatives differ from a firm's employed sales force because their business is separate from that of the principal (they are engaged under a contract for services rather than an employment contract). However, they are similar to the employed sales force in that the principal is required to accept responsibility for the actions of the appointed representative.[37] An appointed representative is exempt from FSMA 2000, meaning that it does not have to seek authorisation and is not directly subject to the FSA rulebook.[38] However, many rules do apply to appointed representatives, and the principal takes responsibility for compliance.

Financial resources rules

Intermediaries operating in the retail financial market are subject to financial resources (also known as 'capital adequacy') rules, which operate in principle in a manner similar to those in the 'wholesale' market.[39] The financial resources that a firm is required to maintain depend on the business conducted by the firm, the objective being to require firms to have resources commensurate with the risks posed to clients and the extent (if any) to which the firm may pose systemic risk as a result of failure to fulfil its obligations to clients and counterparties. Intermediaries in the retail market are likely to benefit from some form of exemption from the CAD[40] regime that applies to investment firms as defined by MiFID. Exemption from the CAD regime may result from:

- the firm benefiting from the exemption provided by MiFID for firms with restricted activities;[41]
- the limited exemption in CAD provided for firms that are not authorised to deal on their own account, offer portfolio management services or investment advice;[42] or
- the exemption in CAD relating to capital held against operational risk.[43]

Those intermediaries that fall within the first exemption are subject to the regulatory capital requirements set out in the IPRU (INV) component of the FSA Handbook. The minimum requirement is £10,000, and is conditional on appropriate professional

---

[37] Under s 39 FSMA 2000. This provision creates a statutory form of vicarious liability on the part of the principal in respect of the actions of the appointed representative 'for which he has accepted responsibility'. As to the meaning of this statutory provision see *Emmanuel v DBS Management plc* [1999] OJ Lloyd's Rep PN 593, where it was observed that a principal is not responsible for the theft of money by its appointed representative if the latter is acting in a different capacity.

[38] Exempt status also means that an appointed representative cannot be authorised under FSMA 2000 as it is not possible to be exempt and authorised at the same time in respect of the same activities. See generally FSA Handbook, PERG 5.13.

[39] See Chapter 15.4.

[40] The Capital Adequacy Directive, 2006/49/EC [2006] OJ L177/201.

[41] Art 3(1) of MiFID exempts firms that: are not allowed to hold clients' funds or securities and which for that reason are not allowed at any time to place themselves in debit with their clients; are not allowed to provide any investment service except the reception and transmission of orders in transferable securities and units in collective investment undertakings and the provision of investment advice in relation to such financial instruments; and, in the course of providing that service, are allowed to transmit orders only to authorised investment firms or banks. Such a firm is 'an exempt CAD firm' for the purposes of the FSA Handbook.

[42] See Chapter 15.4.2. This exemption relates only to the level of initial capital required for authorisation.

[43] See Chapter 15.4.3.

indemnity insurance being in place.[44] If advice is offered on mortgage and general insurance products, further capital requirements are imposed by reference to the annual income of the business.[45] In the case of firms that are not CAD exempt firms, their position will depend on whether they can benefit from the second or third exemptions. The third is likely to be most significant as it offers a considerable saving on an ongoing basis by comparison with the capital charge that would otherwise be required by CAD against operational risk.[46]

Advice by members of the professions

Advice on investments provided by members of the professions is also an important part of the retail market. Members of a designated profession can provide such advice without authorisation provided it represents 'incidental business'.[47] The relevant professional bodies regulate their own members in respect of this activity. If the activity does not fall within the 'incidental business' category but is carried on as a separate activity in its own right, the member (or firm) will require authorisation and will be regulated in the normal manner by the FSA. It is possible for members of the professions to carry on regulated activities as an appointed representative as that activity is itself exempt under the regime applicable to appointed representatives (above).[48]

6.1.3 Vertically integrated firms

Vertical integration occurs when a product provider and an adviser operate within the same firm or within the same marketing group. In the context of a single integrated firm, it sometimes referred to as 'direct selling', meaning that the sales force of the provider advise the customer regarding the sale; in a marketing group context, it is often referred to as 'bancassurance', meaning that the products of an insurer within the group are distributed through its bank branch network.[49] In the first case there is little risk of product bias, since, under both the existing regulatory regime and its pending replacement,

---

[44] FSA Factsheet, 'Financial Resources for Investment Firms' (2009).

[45] Ibid.

[46] See further Chapter 15.4.3.

[47] See Chapter 3 for more detail on the authorisation regime for members of the professions.

[48] However, that is not to say that the rules of the relevant professional body permit members to act in that way. On the basis that appointed representatives can act for only one principal in respect of designated investment business, the status of appointed representative is arguably inconsistent with the independent role of members of the professions.

[49] See the Sandler Report, 'Medium and Long-Term Retail Savings in the UK' (HM Treasury, 2002), available at www.hm-treasury.gov.uk (accessed on 11 November 2004) ch 4 for an analysis of distribution methods in the retail market. Sandler notes that the numbers of sales representatives employed by life offices fell from 190,000 in 1991 to 20,000 in 2001. The decline was attributed to a failure to appeal to high-income customers, high staff turnover and high compliance costs. Over the same period, the share of the life assurance market taken by independent financial advisers (IFAs) rose sharply, reaching 55% (by value of sales) in 2000. For more recent data on market structure and shares see Treasury Select Committee, 'Retail Distribution Review, 15th Report of Session 2010–12, Volume II Additional Written Evidence', 181, showing that IFAs market share had risen further to 65%.

the nature of the restricted advice will be clear to the customer. Nevertheless, an adviser in those circumstances makes a recommendation to the customer and that is the rationale for the application of conduct of business rules to the sale. The advisory nature of the relationship is made clear by the obligation of the adviser not to recommend a product if a suitable product is not available from the product range of the relevant firm.[50] In the second case there is a risk of conflict of interest distorting the investments that the adviser recommends to its customer and also a risk that the respective charges of the product provider and of the adviser may not be clear.[51] While the first risk has for a long time been the focus of conduct of business rules such as 'suitability', the latter was not addressed directly until the FSA brought forward its RDR reforms in 2009. Under those reforms, integrated firms will be required to separate provider charges and adviser charges.[52] The rationale is that this will provide a level playing field between vertically integrated firms and other adviser firms by making clear that adviser charges are payable in addition to product charges irrespective of the distribution method that is used.

6.1.4 Platforms

Platforms are described by the FSA in the following terms:

> Platforms are online services, used by intermediaries (and sometimes consumers directly) to view and administer their investment portfolios. As well as providing facilities for investments to be bought and sold platforms are often used to aggregate, and arrange custody for, customers' assets.[53]

The term covers so-called 'fund supermarkets' and 'wraps'. The former typically provides access to third party funds without any explicit charge made to the customer or her adviser. Remuneration for that form of platform operator is typically through rebates received from product providers (the operators of the third party funds). The latter type of platform is broader in terms of the range of assets that are covered (eg life assurance investment products and individual pensions), the availability of tax wrappers (such as ISAs) and explicit charging to customers whose investment are managed through the platform. In recent years such platforms have grown to represent a substantial part of the retail investment market.[54]

From the regulatory perspective a platform is a service provided by the operator. Providing access to a platform is not in itself a regulated activity under FSMA 2000 but,

---

[50] Put another way, the regulatory rules disapply the common law principle of *caveat emptor* and require the seller to consider the suitability of the investment for the buyer.

[51] While the nature of these conflicts suggest that an alternative approach to regulation would be to prohibit vertical integration of product providers and independent advisers, that approach has not been adopted in the UK, mainly due to fears that it would lead to a reduction in the availability of independent advice.

[52] See FSA PS 10/6, 'Distribution of Retail Investments: Delivering the RDR—Feedback to CP 09/18 and Final Rules' (2009) paras 4.32–4.34.

[53] See FSA, 'Platforms: The Role of Wraps and Fund Supermarkets', DP 07/2 (June 2007).

[54] FSA DP 10/2, 'Summary of Feedback to the Turner Review Conference Discussion Paper (DP 09/4)' (2009), refers to platforms holding around £110bn of assets and accounting for around half of new sales of retail investment funds (para 2.1).

depending on the type of service offered, it is likely that a platform operator will require authorisation in respect of the following regulated activities:

- dealing in investments as agent;
- arranging deals in investments;
- safeguarding and administering assets; and
- sending dematerialised instructions.

Financial advisers who use platforms need to ensure that the manner in which they use platforms matches the regulatory activities covered by their permission from the FSA. Thus, it may well be necessary to hold permission for regulated activities other than advising, especially if customers agree that the adviser can act on a discretionary basis in buying and selling investments on their behalf. However, there is no dedicated regulatory regime for platforms and therefore, as with other technological developments in financial markets, it is a case of fitting an innovative distribution and administration technique into existing regulatory principles. The FSA's Principles for Business provide a high-level starting point for such an exercise, and the FSA has commented on the application of those principles to platforms as follows:

- Principle 3 (Management and control): 'A firm must take reasonable care to organise and control its affairs responsibly and effectively, with adequate risk management systems.' This will be of particular relevance to intermediaries adopting platforms as part of wider changes to the services they provide.
- Principle 6 (Customers' interests): 'A firm must pay due regard to the interests of its customers and treat them fairly.' This is of wide-ranging relevance to both platform providers and users.
- Principle 7 (Communications with clients): 'A firm must pay due regard to the information needs of its clients, and communicate information to them in a way which is clear, fair and not misleading.' This is relevant, for example, to platform providers producing information for intermediaries and consumers.
- Principle 8 (Conflicts of interest): 'A firm must manage conflicts of interest fairly, both between itself and its customers and between a customer and another client.' This may be relevant to intermediaries when choosing platforms.
- Principle 9 (Customers: relationships of trust): 'A firm must take reasonable care to ensure the suitability of its advice and discretionary decisions for any customer who is entitled to rely upon its judgement.' This will be relevant to intermediaries assessing the appropriateness of using a platform for a customer.

Advisers who use platforms must have regard to the regulatory framework mentioned above concerning their status and remuneration, since their use of a platform must be in compliance with those rules. This is particularly the case in circumstances where an advisory firm has an ownership interest in a platform, since that relationship clearly poses a risk of the rules on status and remuneration being compromised to the detriment of the client.

6.2 Product regulation

Regulation of financial products does not, in the main, form part of the regulatory approach adopted under FSMA 2000, which favours regulation of the process of investment and in particular the process whereby advice (in whatever form) is provided to a client.[55] However, a limited form of product regulation has been developed in recent years as a means of creating simpler and less costly financial products for the retail sector that are likely to appeal in particular to those on lower incomes.[56] Two techniques have been adopted. The first is the concept of 'CAT-marked' products and the second is the so-called 'stakeholder' suite of products.

'CAT' standards, short for 'comparability, access and terms', are voluntary benchmarks of quality and charges for retail financial products.[57] They were first introduced with ISAs in April 1999 and then extended to residential mortgages. The FSA largely replaced CAT standards for mortgages with relevant rules in 2004, when mortgage lending and advising became regulated activities.[58] The objective of CAT standards is to help consumers identify suitable products and to permit lighter regulation of the sales process (and thereby lower charges) in appropriate cases. There is no requirement for any product to become CAT marked, the objective being that consumer demand would lead providers to offer CAT-marked products. However, this initiative did not meet with a very enthusiastic response, with the result that the market for these products remains small.

The concept of a 'stakeholder suite' of simplified financial products was first put forward in the Sandler Report,[59] which concluded that low- to middle-income consumers were being driven out of the market because the heavy costs of compliance were making it uneconomic for providers and intermediaries to sell products to them. The report proposed that a simplified suite of products should be developed in which risk and charges would be controlled.[60] This was seen as a means of limiting the need for regulation of the sales process, thereby cutting compliance costs and ultimately charges to the consumer. The report proposed that there should be three products in the suite (a mutual fund[61] or unit-linked life fund, a with-profits fund and a pension) and that the annual charge should

---

[55] Quite apart from its likely effect on innovation and competitiveness (see HM Treasury, 'Standards for Retail Financial Products' (2001) 23–24, available at http://archive.treasury.gov.uk/pdf/2001/cat_standards_3001.pdf (accessed on 15 November 2011)), product regulation would put the UK in breach of its obligations under EU law, which permits cross-border market access based on the single licence and home country control.

[56] Interestingly, this initiative was developed by the Treasury, not the FSA. It was not based on any of the statutory powers given to the Treasury by FSMA 2000 but on the policy that the government should act as an 'intelligent sponsor' of the financial services industry: see HM Treasury, 'Proposed Product Specifications for Sandler 'Stakeholder' Products' (February 2003).

[57] See generally HM Treasury, 'Standards for Retail Financial Products' (2001), above n 55.

[58] See Chapter 3.5.

[59] 'Medium and Long-Term Retail Savings in the UK' (HM Treasury, 2002), available at www.hm-treasury.gov.uk (accessed on 11 November 2004).

[60] Paragraph 10.14 of the report states 'Product regulation provides an embedded means of protection that does not rely on advice and so minimises the fixed cost element of interacting with customers'.

[61] This is the generic term used in the US to describe pooled investment funds (see Chapter 4.9).

be limited to 1%. The product suite has now been expanded and the annual charge for the investment and pension products capped at 1.5% for the first year and 1% thereafter.[62] The new products became available in April 2005 and are sold through a 'basic advice' process that has been developed by the FSA. That process is described by the FSA in the following terms:

> With Basic Advice, the consumer is asked some pre-scripted questions about their income, savings and other circumstances to identify the consumer's financial priorities and suitability for a stakeholder product, but a full assessment of their needs is not conducted nor is advice offered on whether another stakeholder product may be more suitable.[63]

To the extent that both developments offered the possibility of improving access to financial products with modest charges, they can hardly be criticised. The potential problem, however, is that they add to rather than remove the complexity associated with buying financial products, as consumers have the choice not only of the type of financial product they want but also the type of regulatory regime under which the product is sold (CAT, stakeholder or mainstream FSA regulation). Thus, it is difficult to avoid the conclusion that CAT and stakeholder products are 'bolt-on' solutions that do not address the fundamental problems of cost and complexity[64] in the regulation of sales of financial products.

In the wake of the financial crisis, a more interventionist policy has been evident with regard to product regulation. Underlying that policy is the premise that financial innovation may pose risks to financial stability and investor protection by introducing forms of risk into the financial system that are not well understood. While EU law effectively rules out any form of prior approval for financial products, it has been proposed that the new conduct of business regulator in the UK should adopt a more interventionist stance.[65] Additional powers that have been put forward by the FSA for consultation include the power to ban products, mandating or banning product features or exclusions, controls over pricing (including capping) and additional capital requirements for products that pose particular risks to consumers.[66]

---

[62] See HM Treasury press release of 17 June 2004. The increase in the permissible charge reflected industry concerns that a 1% cap would not generate a return sufficient to attract providers into this market as well as an independent study of the effects of different price caps.

[63] FSA CP 09/18, above n 6, para 3.9. See COBS 9.6 for the rules governing the basic advice sales process.

[64] See J Gray, 'Personal Finance and Corporate Governance: The Missing Link: Product Regulation and Policy Conflicts' (2004) 4 *Journal of Corporate Law Studies* 187, stating at 215 that CAT standards 're-design and re-price the product'.

[65] See HM Treasury, *White Paper: A New Approach to Financial Regulation: The Blueprint for Reform*, Cm 8083 (London, HM Treasury, 2011) 30.

[66] FSA, 'Product Intervention', DP 11/1 (2011), ch 5.

6.3 Conduct of business rules

The principle that the regulatory system ought to treat investors acting in a private capacity differently from those acting in a professional capacity was recognised in FSA 1986, and this approach has been continued under FSMA 2000. Section 156(1) of FSMA 2000 provides that: 'Rules made by the Authority may make different provision for different cases and may, in particular, make different provision in respect of different descriptions of authorised person, activity or investment.'

This provision forms the basis of the system of customer classification created by the FSMA regulatory system, which distinguishes between retail clients, professional clients and eligible counterparties.[67] A retail client is a client who is not a professional client or an eligible counterparty.[68] The term applies most obviously to individuals acting in a private capacity, but also includes small businesses (who fall below certain financial thresholds[69]) who are not FSA-authorised firms. The general approach of the conduct of business rules is that retail clients require more protection than do professional clients or eligible counterparties. The rationale is that retail clients suffer most from the information asymmetry problem that forms the basis for regulation.[70] They have problems acquiring information, processing it and using it to make appropriate decisions.

The policy of protecting the retail client is given effect largely through conduct of business rules that regulate the manner in which transactions are conducted. These rules distinguish between different types of customer through a process of rules being 'switched on' or 'switched off' in respect of different categories of customer. In the case of eligible counterparties, for example, most of the conduct of business rules do not apply.[71] However, since the implementation of the MiFID regime, conduct of business obligations owed to professional clients have expanded, although in many instances the nature of business transacted with professional clients limits the application of the relevant rules. This is particularly the case for 'non-advised' and 'principal-to-principal' transactions, which are common in the professional market.[72]

The scope of conduct of business regulation is narrower than the scope of the regulatory regime as a whole since the relevant part of the FSA Handbook (Conduct of Business, COBS) applies only to designated investment business.[73] As a result of mortgage lending

---

[67] COBS 3.3, implementing Art 4(1)(12) MiFID. Note that the term 'client' includes persons to whom a firm provides, intends to provide or has provided a service in the course of carrying on a regulated activity (COBS 3.2.1R). Prior to the implementation of the MiFID regime, the FSA Handbook used the terms 'private customers', 'intermediate customers' and 'market counterparties'.

[68] For definitions of these terms see Chapter 15.1.

[69] See COBS 3.5.2R.

[70] See Chapter 2 regarding information asymmetry.

[71] See Chapter 15 for more detail.

[72] See Chapters 14 and 15 for more discussion of professional and wholesale markets.

[73] The COBS sourcebook applies in general only to 'Designated Investment Business' (see the glossary to the FSA Handbook). This category of business relates to a subset of 'specified activities' (see Chapter 3). The definition serves the purpose of distinguishing 'mainstream' investment business from the other activities

and advising and general insurance broking becoming regulated activities[74] after the entry into force of FSMA 2000, two new conduct of business sourcebooks took effect: the Mortgage Conduct of Business Sourcebook (MCOB), effective from 31 October 2004; and the Insurance Conduct of Business Sourcebook (ICOB), effective from 14 January 2005. Extensive changes to COBS were also made necessary by two European measures: first, the EC Distance Marketing Directive,[75] which provides rights to consumers of financial services that are already available to consumers of other products under the EC Distance Selling Directive;[76] and secondly, the MiFID regime, which has resulted in harmonisation of a number of conduct of business rules and the reframing of the FSA rules to fall into line with its requirements. The MiFID regime has also complicated the conduct of business rulebook as it is necessary to make provision both for MiFID firms and non-MiFID firms (such as 'Article 3' firms, which are exempt from MiFID, and firms from outside the EU).

The discussion of conduct of business rules below follows the sequence of rules in the FSA Handboook and focuses on issues that are of particular significance for retail clients. It is based on the broader set of conduct of business rules that applies to MiFID firms. Those aspects of the conduct of business regime that are of more direct relevance to market professionals (primarily dealing and managing; and investment research) are discussed in Chapter 15.

6.3.1 Accepting clients

A firm is required to notify its clients of the category into which they fall. The purpose of classification is to achieve appropriate application of the conduct of business rules, bearing in mind that the rules apply in different ways to different customers. A client who would otherwise be classified as a retail client can be classified as a professional client if he has sufficient experience and understanding. The result is that he loses some of the safeguards provided by the regulatory system, and therefore the client's informed consent is necessary for this to occur. Similarly, a client who would otherwise be a professional client can be classified as an eligible counterparty if certain conditions are met (mainly relating to the size of the organisation). It is also possible for clients to be recategorised so as to increase their protection (eg by moving from the professional to the retail category). It is the responsibility of a professional client or eligible counterparty

(such as deposit-taking) that are included within the scope of regulation of FSMA 2000. It corresponds to what was termed 'investment business' under FSA 1986: see FSA, 'The Conduct of Business Sourcebook', CP 45a (February 2000). See COBS 1.1 for the precise scope of the regime.

[74] See Chapter 3.5 for more detail.

[75] Directive 2002/65/EC [2002] OJ L271/16, implemented in respect of FSA regulated activities by the Distance Marketing Directive Instrument 2004 (FSA 2004/39) with effect from 9 October 2004 (and 31 October 2004 and 14 January 2005 for MCOB and ICOB respectively). See FSA, 'Implementation of the Distance Marketing Directive's Proposed Rules and Guidance', CP 196 (2003) and FSA, 'Implementation of the Distance Marketing Directive', Policy Statement 04/11 (2004).

[76] Directive 97/7/EC [1997] OJ L144/19.

to ask for a higher level of protection when it deems it is unable to properly assess or manage the risks involved.

Accepting a retail client triggers a requirement for the firm to enter into a client agreement setting out the essential rights and obligations of the client and the firm. Moreover, before the retail client becomes bound to the agreement or services are provided, the client must be provided with the terms of the agreement and information about the firm and its services, including information on communications, conflicts of interest and authorised status.[77]

6.3.2 Fair clear and not misleading communications

The relevant conduct of business rules are derived from Principle 7 of the FSA's Principles for Businesses, which provides: 'A firm must pay due regard to the information needs of its clients and communicate information to them in a way which is clear fair and not misleading.'

The more detailed application of that principle for retail clients is contained in COBS 4.5.2R:

A firm must ensure that information [provided to the client]:
(1) includes the name of the firm;
(2) is accurate and in particular does not emphasise any potential benefits of relevant business or a relevant investment without also giving a fair and prominent indication of any relevant risks;
(3) is sufficient for, and presented in a way that is likely to be understood by, the average member of the group to whom it is directed, or by whom it is likely to be received; and
(4) does not disguise, diminish or obscure important items, statements or warnings.

There is some overlap here with the common law relating to misrepresentation. The result is that liability may arise from the same set of circumstances under both heads.[78] From the perspective of the retail client, however, the attraction of a case based on a regulatory rule breach is that it may be pursued at no cost through the FSA or the Financial Ombudsman.[79] The courts have taken the view that the experience of customers is relevant in determining whether the rule has been breached. In *Maple Leaf Macro Volatility Master Fund v Rouvroy and Trylinski*[80] the court took the view that there was no breach of this rule,[81] relying in particular on the experience of the defendants and the severe time constraints under which the firm they instructed was asked to act. Tellingly, it concluded that, even if the firm was in breach of that rule, there was no causal link to the loss suffered by the defendants as the evidence pointed to the likelihood that they would have acted as they did even if the firm had made clear to them that they were entering a legally binding agreement.

---

[77] See COBS 8.1.
[78] See *Black Horse Ltd v Speak* [2010] EWHC 1866 (QB).
[79] See sections 6.5 and 6.6 below for further discussion of remedies available to retail clients.
[80] [2009] EWHC 257 (Comm).
[81] As formulated in COB 2.1.3 prior to the post-MiFID restructuring of the FSA Handbook.

6.3.3 Disclosure about services, fees and commission

The relevant conduct of business rules are framed by reference to firms that make personal recommendations, deal as agents for or make arrangements for retails clients in relation to packaged products.[82] The disclosure is made through a document, the services and costs disclosure document, which must be made available to the client in good time, which means before a personal recommendation is made to the client or the client becomes bound to any agreement.[83] The disclosure document enables a firm to comply with a range of disclosure obligations imposed by the conduct of business rules and in particular it clarifies:

• The nature of the products offered by the firm. This is linked with the status of the adviser as discussed above.
• The services that the firm will offer, indicating whether or not it will provide advice. This carries implications in particular for the operation of the suitability and appropriateness rules below.
• The method of payment for the services provided by the firm. There is currently no restriction on the form that payment can take.[84] If commission is to be paid by a product provider, then typical commission levels must be disclosed; before the investment is completed, the actual commission level that will be received must also be disclosed.[85] A fee payment option must be offered by a firm that is an independent adviser[86] and the rates must be set out clearly. A combination of commission and fee payment is possible. With effect from 2013, changes to the FSA Handbook will mean that it is no longer possible for advisers to receive payment in the form of commission.[87]

6.3.4 Suitability

The suitability rule is expressed at a general level by Principle 9 of the Principles for Business as follows: 'A firm must take reasonable care to ensure the suitability of its advice and discretionary decisions for any customer who is entitled to rely upon its judgment.'

It is expressed in more detail by COBS 9.2R as follows:

(1) A firm must take reasonable steps to ensure that a personal recommendation, or a decision to trade, is suitable for its client.
(2) When making the personal recommendation or managing his investments, the firm must obtain the necessary information regarding the client's:

---

[82] See text at n 9 above for the definition of a packaged product.
[83] COBS 6.3.3G.
[84] COBS 2.3.1R. This rule permits charging in the form of fees, commission or non-monetary benefits so long as they do not impair compliance with the firm's duty to act in the best interests of clients.
[85] COBS 6, Annex 1 G, note 21.
[86] COBS 6.2.15R.
[87] See section 6.1.2, Adviser charging, above.

(a) knowledge and experience in the investment field relevant to the specific type of designated investment or service;
(b) financial situation; and
(c) investment objectives;

so as to enable the firm to make the recommendation, or take the decision, which is suitable for him.[88]

The delimitation of the scope of the rule by reference to a personal recommendation has the effect that it applies to advisers who offers such recommendations irrespective of their regulatory status in the sense discussed above. It applies also to 'advised' sales made directly by product providers through their own sales force. Moreover, since a personal recommendation can be made without an agency relationship existing between the seller/adviser and the customer, the regulatory rule cannot be co-extensive with any common law suitability obligation imposed on an agent.[89]

The formulation of the suitability requirement is linked to the old FSA 'know your customer' rule[90] in that the information obtained through the 'fact-find' undertaken when accepting a customer is relevant when considering what constitutes a suitable recommendation. The rule refers to 'reasonable steps', with the result that the liability of the firm is based on fault and is not a strict liability. The reference to reasonable steps presumably includes those arising directly or indirectly from regulatory requirements. It is not entirely clear, however, whether—and, if so, to what extent—a firm is expected to go beyond express regulatory requirements in taking reasonable steps. What is clear, however, is that it is not enough for the firm as an organisation to have taken reasonable steps, for example by giving adequate training to staff. That approach was rejected in *Black Horse Ltd v Speak*,[91] where it was held that the adequacy of reasonable steps would be judged by reference to the actions of the individual who acted on behalf of the firm in dealing with the customer.

6.3.5 Appropriateness (for non-advised services)

The rules relating to appropriateness apply to the provision of investment services other than making a personal recommendation and managing investments on a discretionary basis. In the case of retail clients, the breadth of the suitability rule (above) taken together with the exclusion of 'execution-only' business means that the scope of the rule is quite narrow.[92] Moreover, the scope of the rule has the effect that it cannot apply to transactions that fall within the suitability rule (above).[93] The rule requires that:

---

[88] COBS 9.2.1R, implementing Art 19(4) of MiFID, Art 12(2) of the Insurance Mediation Directive.
[89] See section 6.6 below for discussion of the common law.
[90] See the first edition of this book at 178.
[91] [2010] EWHC 1866 (QB).
[92] Most sales of packaged products in the retail market are subject to the suitability rule. It is only in the case of sales of complex products to retail clients that appropriateness will normally apply, as in that case the exclusion of 'execution-only' business does not apply. See Art 19(6) MiFID.
[93] See COBS 10.6.1G, making clear that appropriateness does not apply if the transaction is subject to the suitability rule.

(1) When providing a service to which this chapter applies, a firm must ask the client to provide information regarding his knowledge and experience in the investment field relevant to the specific type of product or service offered or demanded so as to enable the firm to assess whether the service or product envisaged is appropriate for the client.

(2) When assessing appropriateness, a firm:
  (a) must determine whether the client has the necessary experience and knowledge in order to understand the risks involved in relation to the product or service offered or demanded;
  (b) may assume that a professional client has the necessary experience and knowledge in order to understand the risks involved in relation to those particular investment services or transactions, or types of transaction or product, for which the client is classified as a professional client.[94]

If the firm concludes, after assessing appropriateness, that the client does not have the necessary experience and knowledge, it is obliged to warn the client, but the firm is still able to complete a transaction should the client decide to proceed after receiving the warning.[95]

6.3.6 Producing and providing product information to clients

While the suitability and appropriateness rules outlined above provide some protection to retail clients, considerable reliance is nevertheless placed on disclosure of information so as to enable the client to make an investment decision based on their own personal circumstances. Disclosure performs two functions in this context: first, it allows a customer who is considering purchasing a packaged product to identify the main features of the product so as to determine if that type of product meets his needs; and secondly, it allows a customer to make a comparison between different providers of the same product, all of which may meet his basic needs but with differences in design, risk and charges. The foundation of the disclosure regime in relation to packaged products[96] is that firms must prepare a 'Key Features Document' and a 'Key Features Illustration' for each packaged product that it produces in good time before these documents have to be provided to clients.[97] The former focuses on the aims and risks of the product whereas the latter focuses on projected performance and the effect of charges under standardised assumptions. The key features document must be provided to the client in good time before the relevant business is undertaken. An overlapping obligation is imposed on firms to provide clients with a general description of the risks posed by designated investments, taking into account the client's categorisation as a retail or professional client.[98]

---

[94] COBS 10.2.1R, implementing Art 19(5) MiFID and Art 36 of the MiFID Implementing Directive.

[95] See COBS 10.3. Note that the firm is not obliged to communicate its own assessment of the risk (COBS 10.2.8).

[96] While personal recommendations of investments in listed equities and bonds are excluded from this regime, those investments are subject to their own disclosure regime (see Chapter 8) and retail investors benefit from the influence of professional investors in setting prices for those investments in public markets. Packaged products are not traded on public markets and therefore retail investors do not benefit from that influence.

[97] COBS 14.2.1R. The restriction of the rule to 'packaged products' means in effect that it is not relevant for professional clients.

[98] COBS 14.3. This must include risk, volatility, costs and margin requirements.

The need for retail clients in particular to understand the risk that they are running in making an investment is central to the system of regulation because no amount of information can compensate for a failure to appreciate this aspect of an investment. Failure to understand risk lies at the root of many disputes and reflects the fact that there are many aspects of risk that can go unrecognised or be misunderstood. The following are typical examples:

1. Failure to distinguish the market risk from the specific risk attaching to a particular investment (eg even 'blue chip' investments will tend to decline in value when economic fundamentals deteriorate).[99]
2. Failure to understand risks in the underlying business of the entity in which the investment is made (eg political and environmental risks in mineral extraction companies).
3. Failure to understand risks arising from the complexity of the investment (eg derivatives or split capital investment trusts).
4. Failure to understand risks arising from the different underlying bases of competing investments (eg in relation to pension opt-outs, the difference between 'defined benefits' and 'money purchase' schemes).

These examples illustrate the potential problems that arise from reliance on disclosure as a regulatory technique to protect retail investors as there always remains the risk that they cannot properly use the disclosed information to make informed investment decisions in the way that professional investors are assumed to do.[100]

6.3.7 Cancellation rights

The purpose of cancellation rights is to give a customer the opportunity to reconsider an investment. Cancellation rights arise after a contract has been concluded and permit the customer to cancel the contract within a defined period. They modify the common law of contract, which would otherwise permit the customer's offer (to enter into an investment agreement on the terms proposed by the product provider) to be accepted at any time before it is withdrawn and would not allow the customer to cancel the contract except on grounds applicable to contracts generally (eg misrepresentation, undue influence).

The rules relating to cancellation rights are complex.[101] The first issue that must be determined is whether the particular investment agreement carries with it a right to cancel.[102] The second issue that must be determined is the period of reflection available to the customer, which varies between 14 and 30 calendar days.

Customers must be given notice of the right to cancel when it is available.[103] They can exercise the right to cancel by serving notice upon the firm. A notice is valid when it is served on the firm, its appointed representative or an agent with appropriate authority.

---

[99] See Chapter 1 for a discussion of risk.
[100] For further discussion of the role of disclosure in retail markets see Moloney, above n 30, ch 5.
[101] The rules are contained in COB 6.7.
[102] See the table at COBS 15.2.1R.
[103] See COB 15.5.52R.

The customer is not required to state any reason for cancellation. In most cases, exercise of the right of cancellation has the effect that the customer withdraws from the entire agreement. The process is in effect rescission of the contract as the conduct of business rules make clear that *restitutio in integrum*[104] must follow exercise of the right. This means that the firm must return any sums paid in connection with the agreement and the customer must return any property transferred to him under the agreement (eg units in a unit trust) and any money paid by the firm. Special provisions apply in circumstances in which the market falls during the cancellation period: their effect is that the customer bears the loss.[105]

6.3.8 Client assets and client money

The client asset and client money rules in the FSA Handbook (CASS) are generally applicable rules which apply to all clients of a firm. They are discussed in Chapter 15.[106]

6.4 Complaints and redress

This part considers the options available to a private investor when there has been a contravention of any applicable regulatory rules. A major achievement of the regulatory system has been to improve the scope for redress on the part of the private investor, at low cost and without having to resort to litigation.

6.4.1 Complaints

The most obvious starting point for a dissatisfied private customer is to complain to the authorised firm with which he has dealt. Resolution of any dispute at this stage will result in the costs associated with a reference to the Financial Services Ombudsman, a complaint to the FSA or a lawsuit being avoided. In recognition of this and of the FSA's statutory objective to promote consumer protection,[107] the FSA Handbook requires firms[108] to have in place effective written procedures for dealing with complaints from

---

[104] This is a general principle of contract law that requires the parties to be returned to their pre-contractual position if rescission occurs.

[105] See COBS 15.4.3R for the rule described as 'shortfall'.

[106] See Chapter 15.2.4.

[107] See FSA, 'Consumer Complaints Part III', CP 4 (1997).

[108] Recognised investment exchanges and clearing houses, while 'exempt' from FSMA 2000, are required by the recognition requirements to have effective arrangements for the investigation and resolution of complaints: see FSMA 2000 (Recognition Requirements for Investment Exchanges and Clearing Houses) Regulations 2001, SI 2001/995, sch 1, paras 9 and 23. As an authorised firm is responsible for the actions of its authorised representatives, it is the appropriate person to handle complaints.

eligible customers and to publish summary details of their complaints procedure and refer eligible customers to those details. Customers fall within this category if they are eligible to refer a complaint to the Financial Ombudsman Service (FOS).[109]

Once a complaint has been received by a firm, it must:

(1) investigate the complaint competently, diligently and impartially;
(2) assess fairly, consistently and promptly:
   (a) the subject matter of the complaint;
   (b) whether the complaint should be upheld;
   (c) what remedial action or redress (or both) may be appropriate;
   (d) if appropriate, whether it has reasonable grounds to be satisfied that another respondent may be solely or jointly responsible for the matter alleged in the complaint;
   taking into account all relevant factors;
(3) offer redress or remedial action when it decides this is appropriate;
(4) explain to the complainant promptly and, in a way that is fair, clear and not misleading, its assessment of the complaint, its decision on it, and any offer of remedial action or redress; and
(5) comply promptly with any offer of remedial action or redress accepted by the complainant.[110]

The FSA Handbook sets a time limit of 8 weeks for a final response to complaints.[111] The final response must inform the complainant of the right to refer the matter to the FOS within 6 months and enclose a copy of the FOS explanatory leaflet. Firms are required to keep records of complaints in different categories and to report to the FSA twice a year on this.

6.4.2 The Financial Services Ombudsman

Before FSMA 2000 came into effect, there were eight different Ombudsman schemes in place. Some operated on a voluntary basis (eg the Insurance and Banking Ombudsmen), while the jurisdiction of others was based on a statute (the Building Societies Ombudsman) or a regulatory requirement (the Personal Investment Authority Ombudsman). The FOS replaces all of these with a single scheme. It is operated by a company established by the FSA, Financial Ombudsman Service Ltd.[112] This company is required to have operational independence[113] from the FSA, but the FSA nevertheless exerts a strong influence over the working of the FOS through the appointment of the chairman and members of the board, approval of the FOS annual budget and the making of rules governing the compulsory jurisdiction of the FOS.[114] The costs of the FOS are borne by authorised firms.

---

[109] FSA Handbook, DISP 1.1.3R (DISP is the Dispute Resolution part of the FSA Handbook).
[110] DISP 1.4.1R.
[111] DISP 1.6.2R.
[112] See www.financialombudsman.org.uk (accessed on 11 November 2011).
[113] FSMA 2000, s 225(4) and sch 17, para 3(4).
[114] See E Ferran, 'Dispute Resolution Mechanisms in the UK Financial Sector', available at SSRN: http://ssrn.com/abstract=298176 (accessed on 22 August 2011), who comments at 15: 'The powerful controls enjoyed by the FSA make it possible to question whether the FOS can actually achieve operational independence.'

Jurisdiction

The jurisdiction of the FOS, split between compulsory and voluntary categories, reflects the varied background from which it evolved. Compulsory refers to the obligation imposed on a regulated firm to submit to the procedure and comply with the decision of the Ombudsman; no such obligation is imposed on the complainant. As the name implies, there is no obligation imposed on regulated firms to submit to the voluntary jurisdiction of the FOS.

The FSA Handbook limits both the type of complaint that can be referred to the FOS and the type of customer who is entitled to refer. The types of complaint that can be made generally cover the entire range of relationships between firms and customers that may arise from regulated activity.[115] Some types of complaint arise from an indirect rather than a direct relationship between the complainant and the firm.[116] A person referring a complaint must also be an eligible complainant. Authorised firms cannot be eligible complainants in respect of activities which they are authorised to carry on. The following are eligible to complain:

1. a consumer;[117]
2. a micro-enterprise:[118]
    (a) in relation to a complaint relating wholly or partly to payment services, either at the time of the conclusion of the payment services contract or at the time the complainant refers the complaint to the firm; or
    (b) otherwise, at the time the complainant refers the complaint to the firm;
3. a charity which has an annual income of less than £1 million at the time the complainant refers the complaint to the firm; or
4. a trustee of a trust which has a net asset value of less than £1 million at the time the complainant refers the complaint to the firm.

A potential customer falling into one of the above categories is also an eligible complainant. This allows the FOS to consider issues arising from the act or omission of a firm in circumstances in which no transaction has been concluded (eg loss suffered as a result of a failure to act according to the FSA's rules). Complaints must refer to a matter that an authorised firm has failed to resolve satisfactorily within 8 weeks of the date of receipt (the time limit for making a final response to complaints).

---

[115] See generally DISP 2.7.6R.

[116] Examples are: the complainant is a beneficiary under a trust or estate of which the firm is trustee or personal representative; the complainant is a person for whose benefit a contract of insurance was taken out or was intended to be taken out; and the complainant is a person on whom the legal right to benefit from a claim under a contract of insurance has been devolved by contract, statute or subrogation.

[117] For these purposes a 'consumer' means any natural person acting for purposes outside his trade, business or profession. Professional clients are no longer automatically excluded.

[118] This is defined as an enterprise which: (i) employs fewer than 10 persons; and (ii) has a turnover or annual balance sheet that does not exceed €2 million. In this definition, 'enterprise' means any person engaged in an economic activity, irrespective of legal form, and includes, in particular, self-employed persons and family businesses engaged in craft or other activities, and partnerships or associations regularly engaged in an economic activity.

All authorised firms are subject to the compulsory jurisdiction of the FOS. It covers the following types of activity:

1. regulated activities;
2. payment services;[119]
3. consumer credit activities,[120] including lending money and operating credit cards;
4. lending money secured by a charge on land (ie mortgage lending); and
5. the provision of ancillary banking services;

or activities ancillary to them (for example, advice provided by a firm in connection with these activities). Activity is understood to include a failure to act and encompasses activity for which a firm is responsible, such as the activity of an appointed representative. Complaints relating to 'non-mainstream regulated activity' undertaken by a professional firm that can be handled by a designated professional body are excluded from the FOS.[121]

The FOS voluntary jurisdiction is a service open to unauthorised firms and authorised firms in respect of complaints not covered by the compulsory jurisdiction. There is no requirement to join, but if a firm does join it becomes bound by the standard terms governing the voluntary jurisdiction.[122] The rules for determining eligible complainants are the same as for the compulsory jurisdiction (above). However, the type of complaint that can be considered is different. In particular, a complaint can only be made under the voluntary jurisdiction if it is not covered by the compulsory jurisdiction.

The territorial scope of the FOS compulsory jurisdiction covers complaints about the activities of firms carried on from an establishment in the UK. It therefore covers firms operating from a permanent place of business, including EEA firms and Treaty firms but excluding business conducted on a services basis.[123] Complaints about business conducted by branches of UK-authorised firms outside the UK are excluded from the compulsory jurisdiction. Firms subscribing to the voluntary jurisdiction are covered in respect of business conducted from an establishment in the UK and EEA, but business conducted on a services basis falls within the voluntary jurisdiction of the FOS only if certain conditions are met.[124]

The adjudication process

The Ombudsman is entitled to deal with complaints on the basis of written submissions made by the parties, but also has the option of inviting the parties to attend a hearing. The parties are entitled to request a hearing, but ultimately this is a matter for the Ombudsman,

---

[119] The definition is complex and follows the approach in the Payment Services Regulations 2009 (SI 2009/209).

[120] Activities falling within the scope of the Consumer Credit Act 1974.

[121] See Chapter 3 for an account of the regulatory regime for professional firms. The exclusion is achieved by excluding professional firms from the definition of a 'respondent' (in DISP) against whom a complaint may be made.

[122] See DISP 4.

[123] See Chapter 2 for the meaning of these terms.

[124] See DISP 2.6.4R. Among the conditions is the requirement that the relevant contract is governed by the laws of one of the jurisdictions in the UK.

who is required to have regard to the provisions of the European Convention on Human Rights.[125] Parties must, however, be informed of their right to make representations before the Ombudsman makes a determination. A complaint can be dismissed without consideration of its merits for a number of reasons. They include the following:

1. the complainant has not suffered loss;
2. the firm has already made an offer of compensation which is fair and reasonable;
3. the matter has been previously considered or excluded under the FOS or a previous scheme;
4. the subject matter of the compliant has been the subject of court proceedings where there has been a decision on the merits;
5. the complaint is the subject of current court proceedings unless proceedings are stayed or sisted so that the matter may be considered by the FOS; and
6. the complaint relates to investment performance.[126]

Determination of complaints

Complaints are determined according to what is fair and reasonable in all the circumstances of the case.[127] In considering what is fair and reasonable, the Ombudsman will take into account the relevant law, regulations, regulators' rules and guidance and standards,[128] relevant codes of practice[129] and, where appropriate, what he considers to have been good industry practice at the time. When a complaint has been determined,[130] the Ombudsman must give both the complainant and the firm a written statement of the determination, stating reasons for it. The statement will invite the complainant to notify the Ombudsman

---

[125] This is relevant to the manner in which the hearing is held.

[126] See DISP 3.3.4R for more detail.

[127] In the case of the compulsory jurisdiction, s 228(2) FSMA 2000 provides a statutory basis for this approach. In the case of the voluntary jurisdiction, FSA Handbook, DISP 3.6.1R provides a contractual basis for the Ombudsman to determine a complaint in this manner. For further discussion of the meaning of 'fair and reasonable' and its implications for legal certainty see I MacNeil, 'Consumer Dispute Resolution in the UK Financial Sector: The Experience of the Financial Ombudsman Service' (2007) 1(6) *Law and Financial Markets Review* 515.

[128] It was held in *R (ex parte British Bankers Association) v FSA* [2011] EWHC 999 (Admin) that the Ombudsman is entitled to take into account FSA rules even if they are not actionable under s 150 FSMA 2000 (breach of statutory duty). In that case, this approach permitted the Ombudsman to take into account a Policy Statement issued by the FSA in connection with the application of its Principles for Business to claims made by customers in connection with the mis-selling of payment protection insurance (PPI).

[129] See, in this regard, *Norwich and Peterborough Building Society v The Financial Services Ombudsman Service* [2002] EWHC 2379. This was a judicial review of an award made by the FOS in respect of a complaint relating to 'downgrading' (the practice of offering new customers better terms than existing customers). In making its award, the FOS (in accordance with the Building Societies Act 1986, sch 12, pt II, para 4c) had regard to the Banking Code. It also based its decision on a standard, developed in previous decisions, which it called 'relative onerousness', which involved comparing the terms of accounts with their relative interest rates. The court held that while interpretation of the Banking Code was ultimately a matter for the court, the FOS's power to decide what was fair was not limited to compliance with legal obligations. The approach based on 'relative onerousness' was therefore upheld. For a discussion of the case see R Nobles, 'Rules, Principles and Ombudsmen: Norwich and Peterborough Building Society v The Financial Services Ombudsman Service' (2003) 66 *Modern Law Review* 781.

[130] A provisional decision, which gives both parties an opportunity to comment, is issued before the final decision.

in writing before the date specified in the statement whether he accepts or rejects the determination. If the complainant accepts the determination within the time limit set by the Ombudsman, it is final and binding on both the complainant and the firm. If not, the firm is not bound by the determination and both sides are free to pursue legal remedies in court.

If a complaint is determined in favour of the complainant, the determination may include:

- a money award subject to a maximum of £100,000;[131]
- a direction that the firm take such steps in relation to the complainant as the Ombudsman considers just and appropriate; or
- both of these.

In the case of a money award, the Ombudsman may decide to award compensation for the following kinds of loss or damage (in addition to or instead of compensation for financial loss):

- pain and suffering;
- damage to reputation; or
- distress or inconvenience.

The limit on the maximum money award has no bearing on any direction that the Ombudsman may make as part of a determination. The result is that the complainant can receive benefits in excess of the monetary limit in circumstances in which a direction has a financial benefit for the complainant (eg a direction that a person be readmitted to a pension fund). Where the Ombudsman finds in a complainant's favour, he may also award an amount which covers some or all of the costs which were reasonably incurred by the complainant in respect of the complaint. A money award under the compulsory jurisdiction is enforceable through the courts in the same way as money awards made by the lower courts.[132]

No appeal to the courts is possible from a determination made by the Ombudsman. The rationale for excluding a right of appeal from FSMA 2000 was that it would be inconsistent with the objective of resolving disputes quickly and with minimum formality.[133] In principle, judicial review is available, but this provides only a limited basis on which to mount a challenge. Nor is it possible to recover losses above the limit for FOS awards through subsequent court action following acceptance of an FOS award.[134]

---

[131] This will rise to £150,000 in respect of complaints referred to the FOS on or after 1 January 2012. See DISP 3.7.4R and FSA, Consumer Complaints: The Ombudsman Award Limit and Changes to Complaints-Handling Rules', CP 11/10 (2011).

[132] FSMA 2000, sch 17, para 16.

[133] See FSA, 'FSMA 2 Year Review: Financial Ombudsman Service', CP 04/12 (2004) 27. The possibility of establishing a right of appeal (which would require amendment of s 228(5) FSMA 2000) was canvassed by the FSA in that paper, which noted that there was considerable support among authorised persons for a right of appeal but that consumer groups were generally content with the existing arrangements.

[134] *Andrews vs SBJ Benefit Consultants* [2010] EWHC 2875 (Ch).

'Wider implications cases'

The boundary between the regulatory role of the FSA and the role of the FOS in adjudication of individual cases has been a live issue for some time. Concern was expressed by some authorised persons that the involvement of the FOS in 'wider implication cases' had resulted in the FOS setting standards rather than resolving individual disputes.[135] The argument is that the FOS may make a decision in an individual case that has wide implications for firms and consumers because it concerns issues that arise in a large number of similar cases and is likely to be followed in those cases. In response, the FSA and FOS have agreed a memorandum of understanding governing 'wider implication cases', which is intended to ensure that both the FOS and FSA can carry out their respective functions. In the case of the FSA, the relevant action may involve disciplinary proceedings, issuing or amending rules or guidance and taking action to secure redress for consumers.[136]

6.4.3 Redress required or initiated by the FSA

A complaint from a private customer may lead the FSA to take disciplinary proceedings against a firm or individual. If the FSA imposes a sanction for a contravention of the Act or rules made under it, this may carry no direct benefit for the complainant. This will be the case if the sanction is a fine (payable to the FSA) or a public censure. However, it is also open to the FSA to order restitution in cases:

1. where a person has accrued profits as a result of a contravention of a relevant requirement or a person has suffered loss as a result of the contravention; or
2. in market abuse cases when a contravention has resulted in the making of a profit for the person concerned in it or a loss for another person.[137]

The amount of the restitution is the amount of the profit gained or the loss suffered from the contravention. FSA action is not intended to duplicate the functions of the FOS, but there may be cases, such as where many persons have suffered loss, in which it is deemed appropriate. The FSA has set out its policy in the following terms:

---

[135] Examples of such cases are mis-selling of 'endowment' life assurance policies and PPI.

[136] The process was implemented in connection with the sale of Lehman-backed structured investment products following the collapse of Lehman Bros in 2008. Structured products typically offer a return linked to a particular index over a fixed period of time, with either full or partial protection of the initial investment provided through a guarantee. The FSA found that over 5,000 UK retail investors had invested a total of £107m in structured investment products where the capital protection at maturity was provided solely by firms within the Lehman Group. Three firms who had packaged and marketed Lehman-backed structured products went into administration and investors who bought through them became entitled to compensation from the Financial Services Compensation Scheme. This resulted in the implementation of the 'wider implications process'. As part of that process adjudication of complaints pending with the FOS was suspended and the FSA undertook a thematic review of advice given to customers to invest in structured investment products. The outcome was clarification issued by the FSA as to the standards it expects in relation to such advice, provision of guidance to investors on bringing a complaint to the FOS and the referral of several cases to the FSA enforcement division for further action.

[137] FSMA 2000, s 384. Restitution can be ordered in favour of any person, not just private customers. It can be exercised against any person, whether authorised or not. There was no parallel power under FSA 1986, with the result that the FSA (and previous regulators) had to apply to court for restitution orders.

When deciding whether to exercise these powers, the FSA will consider whether this would be the best use of the FSA's limited resources taking into account, for example, the likely amount of any recovery and the costs of achieving and distributing any sums. It will also consider, before exercising its powers: other ways that persons might obtain redress, and whether it would be more efficient or cost-effective for them to use these means instead; and any proposals by the person concerned to offer redress to any consumers or other persons who have suffered loss, and the adequacy of those proposals. The FSA expects, therefore, to exercise its formal restitution powers on rare occasions only.[138]

In the case of widespread regulatory failure that has resulted in consumer detriment, it is open to the FSA to require firms to establish and operate a consumer redress scheme.[139] For these purposes, consumers are not limited to retail customers, although the requirement that the relevant consumers have a legal cause of action may limit the use of a scheme in other cases.[140] It is the responsibility of the relevant firm to:

- investigate whether it has complied with the relevant regulatory rules;
- determine if a breach has caused loss to consumers;
- determine an appropriate form of redress; and
- make redress to the customer.[141]

However, even with this substantial delegation of the operation of a scheme to the relevant firms, the FSA remains in control through its monitoring of the process and its power to alter the rules of the scheme, should that become necessary.

Another possibility, which is relevant when an authorised person is experiencing financial difficulty, is for the FSA to initiate or intervene in insolvency procedures. The relevant powers[142] enable the FSA to take action to safeguard the interests of consumers of financial services. When insolvency is looming or has already occurred, consumers of financial services may face considerable difficulty in taking independent action to safeguard their interests: the possibility of FSA action therefore promotes market confidence and discourages financial crime.

It is also open to the FSA to act in its capacity as a 'qualifying body' under the Unfair Terms in Consumer Contracts Regulations 1999.[143] The objective of the regulations is

---

[138] FSA Handbook, Enforcement Guide (EG), 11.1.

[139] FSMA 2000, s 404. The section was amended by the Financial Services Act 2010 so as to allow the FSA to take action under its own initiative rather than with the approval of and under terms set by the Treasury. For the background to the introduction of s 404 into FSMA 2000 and its links with the uncertain legal basis of the review of pensions mis-selling which began (under the FSA 1986 regime) in the 1990s, see J Gray, 'The Legislative Basis of Systemic Review and Compensation for the Mis-selling of Retail Financial Services and Products' (2004) 25(3) *Statute Law Review* 196.

[140] For example, as only 'private investors' can take action under s 150 FSMA 2000 in respect of a breach of conduct of business rules, professional investors have no legal cause of action in respect of such a breach.

[141] Redress is required under s 404 FSMA 2000 even if a defence of limitation would otherwise be available to the firm.

[142] See pt XXIV of FSMA 2000 as amended by the Enterprise Act 2002. These powers are distinct from the 'special resolution regime' contained in the Banking Act 2009, in which the Bank of England plays the leading role: see Chapter 2.2.6.

[143] SI 1999/2083. The FSA has agreed with the OFT that the FSA will take lead responsibility for contracts in the areas of investments, pensions, life and general insurances, mortgages and banking. Contracts covered by the Consumer Credit Act 1974 remain the responsibility of the OFT. See the Memorandum of Understanding

to prevent the use of unfair terms in contracts concluded between a business and a consumer. In its capacity as a qualifying body, the FSA is able to consider the fairness of contact terms on its own initiative or following the making of a complaint by a consumer. The FSA's policy is to talk constructively with firms to deal with unfair terms,[144] but if that fails it is able to apply for an injunction to prevent the use of the term.[145] The Regulations do not authorise the FSA to make a financial award or otherwise compensate consumers, but it remains open in principle for a consumer to refer the case to the FOS or for the FSA to require restitution if the use of an unfair contract term also amounts to a breach of FSA rules.

Also relevant in this context are the Consumer Protection from Unfair Trading Regulations 2008.[146] While the FSA is not under an express statutory duty to enforce these regulations, it has an interest in compliance to the extent that unfair practices as defined by the Regulations[147] may take place in carrying on regulated activity. In recognition of this interest, these regulations are covered by the memorandum of understanding between the FSA and the OFT regarding their respective roles in consumer protection.[148]

6.5 Statutory claims

6.5.1 Breach of statutory duty

The availability of the FOS removes much of the need for litigation on the part of private investors. However, there may be circumstances in which litigation is deemed appropriate, such as where the loss suffered by an investor exceeds the limit set by the FOS or where it is likely that a court would take a view more favourable to the complainant in relation to the common law duties of an authorised person than would the FOS Ombudsman (eg because the relevant law is in a state of flux or development).

The first option that should be considered is an action for breach of statutory duty. Several different sections provide for this action to be available to an investor, the most wide-ranging being section 150 FSMA 2000.[149] This provides that a contravention by an

---

between the OFT and the FSA (2009), available at http://www.oft.gov.uk/shared_oft/general_policy/674008/MOU.pdf.

[144] See FSA, 'The FSA's Approach to the Use of its Powers under the Unfair Terms in Consumer Contracts Regulations', CP 148 (1999) para 4.11.

[145] An injunction as to future use does not affect the validity of unfair terms in existing contracts. Only a court could apply the provision (Art 8 SI 1999/2083) that provides for an unfair term to have no binding effect on a consumer.

[146] SI 2008/1277, implementing EC Directive 2005/29 on unfair business-to-consumer commercial practices in the internal market [2005] OJ L149/22.

[147] See Art 3 of and sch 1 to the regulations for practices that are considered unfair.

[148] See above n 144.

[149] The others are ss 20(3), 85(4) and 202(2).

authorised person of a rule[150] is actionable at the suit of a private person[151] who suffers loss as a result of the contravention, subject to the defences and other incidents applying to actions for breach of statutory duty.[152] The availability (or otherwise) of a section 150 action does not alter the function of rules in any other way: thus the fact that a breach of a rule is not actionable carries no consequences for obligations owed to customers under the relevant rules.[153] Section 150 also provides that rules may prescribe circumstances in which this remedy is available to a non-private person.[154]

The section 150 (and its predecessor, section 62 of FSA 1986) remedy has not been popular with investors for two main reasons. First, its restriction to private persons means that it is generally not available to those institutional investors who might be more inclined to pursue litigation. Secondly, the plaintiff in a section 150 case is required to show not only a breach of the relevant rule but also a causal link between the breach and the loss.[155]

The availability of the section 150 remedy does not exclude the possibility of legal action based on the common law. The most obvious options are the law relating to agency, negligence, fiduciary duty and contract. While much of the substance of the common-law rules in these fields are reflected in regulatory rules, they are not co-extensive, a point made clear by the Court of Appeal in *Gorham v British Telecommunications*.[156] The approach taken in that case suggests that it may be better in some circumstances to ground a case on basic common-law principles, such as negligence, rather than attempting to establish a rule breach and its causal link with loss under section 150 FSMA 2000.

It is also possible for the FSA to take legal action on behalf of investors. The purpose of such action is to require persons who have contravened rules or been knowingly concerned[157] in such a contravention to make restitution.[158] The FSA will normally consider

---

[150] Listing rules, financial resources rules and short-selling rules are not rules for the purposes of this section: see s 150(4). Principles set out in the PRIN section of the FSA Handbook are also excluded: s 150(4) and PRIN 3.4.4R.

[151] Private person is defined by Art 3 of FSMA 2000 (Rights of Action) Regulations 2001, SI 2001/2256. See *Titan Steel Wheels Ltd v The Royal Bank of Scotland Plc* [2010] EWHC 211 (Comm) for an unsuccessful attempt by a commercial company to bring itself within the definition of a private person (with the aim of pursuing a claim for losses on structured products which speculated on currency movements). Note that the regulatory definitions of 'retail client' and 'private person' are not co-extensive.

[152] This includes contributory negligence as a partial defence. See *Spreadex Ltd v Sanjit Sekhon* [2008] EWHC 1136 (Ch), where a customer was found to be 85% responsible for losses sustained on spread bets.

[153] *R (ex parte British Bankers Association) v FSA* [2011] EWHC 999 (Admin), per Ousley J at para 71: 'The statutory provision being construed is s 150. S150(1) deals with contraventions of rules by making them actionable as breaches of statutory duty. "Actionable" means giving rise to a cause of action in a court of law. S150(2) removes that actionability. S150(2) does nothing else. "Actionable" in s 150(1) simply does not mean "capable of giving rise to obligations or compensation". So s 150 does not apply to the Principles. It does not alter their function in any other way. It leaves intact any other function or effect which a non-actionable rule might have. The clear words of the section are wholly inapt to prevent rules which are not actionable giving rise to obligations as between firms and customers.'

[154] It is available to institutional investors in respect of contraventions of rules that relate to dealing on the basis of unpublished price-sensitive information: see SI 2001/2256, Art 6.

[155] As to the difficulties involved in so doing, see I MacNeil, 'FSA 1986: Does s 62 Provide an Effective Remedy for Breaches of Conduct of Business Rules?' (1994) 15 *Company Lawyer* 172.

[156] [2001] 1 WLR 2129.

[157] See *SIB v Pantell SA (No 2)* [1993] 1 All ER 134.

[158] FSMA 2000, s 382.

using its administrative powers[159] to require restitution before applying to the court for a restitution order. The court can order these persons to pay to the FSA such a sum as appears just, having regard to the profits appearing to have accrued to them or the loss suffered by others as a result of the contravention. Any amount paid to the authority in pursuance of such a restitution order must be paid by it to such a qualifying person or distributed by it among such qualifying persons as the court may direct.

6.5.2 Statutory control of unfair contract terms

Unfair contract terms are controlled by the Unfair Contract Terms Act 1977 and the Unfair Terms in Consumer Contracts Regulations 1999.[160] However, the availability of adjudication through the FOS and the capacity for decisions made by the FOS to take account of matters other than the law mean that litigation based on unfair terms legislation is not common. A rare example arose in the case of *Maple Leaf Macro Volatility Master Fund v Rouvroy and Trylinski*,[161] which concerned a dispute that arose from a funding arrangement entered into between a hedge fund (Maple Leaf) and the two defendants with the objective of securing control of Belvedere, a French company in which they were respectively CEO and deputy CEO as well as substantial shareholders. The funding arrangement was negotiated in the form of a 'termsheet', and Maple Leaf claimed that the defendants were in breach of the agreement and liable in damages. The defendants denied that the termsheet represented a legally enforceable agreement and that, even if it did, it was unfair under the Unfair Terms in Consumer Contracts Regulations 1999. To the extent that the 1999 Regulations could be applied to the funding arrangement (and they could not apply to the price/remuneration aspects), the court followed *Bryen & Langley v Boston*,[162] holding that, as long as the relevant terms were not imposed on the 'consumer' in contravention of the requirements of good faith, there could be no issue of unfairness. The court found no indication of breach of the requirement of good faith (fair dealing) in this case.

6.6 Private law claims

When FSA 1986 came into effect, the role of the common law in developing investor protection standards became marginalised.[163] From that time onwards, the main

---

[159] See section 6.4.3 above.

[160] SI 1999/2083. Section 3 of the Misrepresentation Act 1967 controls contractual exclusions of liability for misrepresentation but is unlikely to be relevant in the retail financial market.

[161] [2009] EWHC 257 (Comm).

[162] [2005] EWCA 973.

[163] Of course, to the extent that the introduction of statutory regulation reflected the perceived failure of the common law to apply effective controls to investment, it can be argued that the common law had in the past

developments, in terms of both setting standards and enforcement, occurred within the regulatory system, which focused more on *ex ante* prevention rather than *ex post* redress. However, there are now indications that the common law may have a more active role to play. As discussed below, the courts have begun to apply common law agency and tort principles in situations where regulatory rules apply.

6.6.1 Agency

The agency relationship

As noted earlier, private customers often buy investments through agents rather than directly from the representatives of product providers. They do so primarily to take advantage of the knowledge and experience of the agent in dealing with the type of transaction they propose to enter. While, prior to FSA 1986, the term 'agent' was capable of being understood in different ways, there were only two types of agent that were recognised by FSMA 2000 under the polarisation system.[164] Following the demise of the polarisation rule in 2005, the FSA rules regarding adviser status recognise three categories of agent by reference to the type of advice that they offer: entire market, limited range and single provider. The FSA Handbook sets out conduct of business requirements for the provision of all these types of advice but does not make clear how these rules interact with the common law of agency.

Approaching this issue from the basic principles of the law of agency, it would seem that it is only in the case of the first two types of advice (above) that an agent can be considered to be the agent of the customer. An adviser who sells only the products of a single provider is subject to FSA conduct of business rules but cannot be taken to be an agent in the legal sense of a person who acts on behalf of the customer and is therefore subject to a fiduciary duty to act in the best interests of the customer. It follows that an agent providing advice relating to a single provider is the agent of the provider.[165] Thus, the common-law duties owed by such an 'agent' are to the provider and not to the customer, even if advice is provided to the customer.[166]

If an agency relationship exists, several issues require consideration. The following are of particular importance:

---

contributed little to investor protection. See generally A Page and R Ferguson, *Investor Protection* (London, Weidenfeld & Nicolson, 1992) ch 2.

[164] Under that system an independent intermediary (or a member of a 'recognised' profession) was the agent of the client. A company representative was the agent of the company for which it acts (as was an appointed representative). There could be no confusion between these two categories because the polarisation regime required that any person selling investments must choose between being one or the other and must identify themselves as falling into one category or the other. The result was that, for the purposes of applying the common-law rules of agency, the polarisation rule effectively removed any doubt regarding the issue of whom an agent represents.

[165] Such an agent bears some similarity to an 'appointed representative' under s 39 FSMA 2000, except that the latter is exempt from authorisation whereas the former is not.

[166] In support of this view see *Barnes v Black Horse Ltd* [2011] EWHC 1416 (QB). In that case the court refused to find that a lender who sold payment protection insurance (PPI) in tandem with a personal loan owed a fiduciary duty to the customer. It was said that 'mere giving of advice does not of itself import a fiduciary relationship' (para 17).

- the extent of the authority of an agent and the related issue of when an agent can bind the principal to a contract;
- the liability of the agent for breach of fiduciary duty; and
- the liability of the agent for breach of the duty of care.

The first two issues are examined below, while breach of a duty of care is examined under the heading of tort claims below.

The authority of an agent

It is a basic principle of agency law that a principal is only bound by acts of the agent that are within the authority of the agent. Provided that an agent acts within his authority, he can bind his principal to a contract with a third party. Similarly, a principal can be liable in tort (delict) for acts done or omitted by an agent acting within his authority. A significant difference between the regulatory system and the common-law rules of agency is that the latter do not use the regulatory concept of a 'retail client'. In principle, agency law applies in the same manner to all customers. However, agency law responds to the context in which it operates and is therefore able to take account of the needs of private investors. A clear example is the case of *Martin v Britannia Life Ltd*, discussed below.

The authority of an agent can be express, implied or ostensible. Express authority arises where the principal expressly authorises the agent to undertake a particular task (eg an instruction given by a client to a stockbroker to sell 1,000 shares in company A at a minimum price of 150p during the next week). Implied authority arises where no express authority has been given but it can be implied from the contract terms and the context in which the contract was concluded that the parties intended that the agent should have that authority. Ostensible (or apparent) authority arises where the principal[167] has represented to a third party (by word or action) that the agent has the necessary authority for a particular transaction.

These principles were considered in the context of the regulatory regime established by FSA 1986 in the case of *Martin v Britannia Life Ltd*.[168] The case concerned financial advice given by an appointed representative of the defendant company. As is the case under FSMA 2000, a principal was required under FSA 1986 to assume responsibility for anything said or done or omitted by an appointed representative in carrying out the investment business for which the principal has accepted responsibility.[169] At issue in this case was the extent of the authority of the appointed representative in acting on behalf of Britannia Life Ltd. The issue was of significance because the advice given to the plaintiff had included advice relating to a remortgage provided by another company, which was not classified as an 'investment' under FSA 1986 and therefore did not fall within the scope of the Act or its regulatory rules. It was contended by the defendant that

---

[167] It is clear from The Ocean Frost case (*Armagas Ltd v Mundogas* [1986] AC 717) that the representation must be made by the principal. Ostensible authority cannot be created by a false representation as to authority made by an agent to a third party.

[168] [2000] OJ Lloyd's Rep PN 412.

[169] FSA 1986 (repealed), s 44 and FSMA 2000, s 39.

the authority of the appointed representative could not extend beyond 'investment' advice as defined by FSA 1986 and that its responsibility was similarly limited.

The court rejected this contention and chose to define the actual authority of the appointed representative very broadly. The rationale for this approach was stated as follows:[170]

> In my judgement, advice as to the 'merits' of buying or surrendering an 'investment' cannot sensibly be treated as confined to a consideration of the advantages or disadvantages of a particular 'investment' as a product, without reference to the wider financial context in which the advice is tendered.

This was despite a limitation in the contract between the appointed representative and Britannia Life Ltd, which provided that the former was engaged solely to advise, market and sell the products of the latter. The reasoning of the court was that the statutory agency created by section 44(6) FSA 1986 overrode the express contractual limitation and had to be understood as referring to the broad concept of 'investment advice' indicated above. It followed that the appointed representative had actual authority to advise on the remortgage. Moreover, even if there were no actual authority, there was ostensible authority arising from the description of the appointed representative as a 'financial adviser' on the business card supplied to him by the defendant. The court's view was that this description represented that the appointed representative had authority to engage in transactions ancillary to or associated with insurance.

Applying the rationale of this case to FSMA 2000 points to the following conclusions. First, contractual limitations on the authority of an appointed representative are unlikely to have much effect in protecting a principal. They are likely to be overriden by a broad view of the statutory agency created by section 39 FSMA 2000 (the successor to section 44 FSA 1986). Secondly, appointed representatives who engage in activities outside the 'permission' of their principal are still likely to be considered as acting within their actual authority, at least as far as associated transactions are concerned. Thirdly, even when authorised representatives engage in unregulated activity, they can in principle be considered to be acting within their authority, at least as far as associated transactions are concerned.

Breach of fiduciary duty

An agent owes a fiduciary duty to act in the best interests of the principal.[171] The essence of fiduciary duty has been described in the following terms: 'The distinguishing obligation of a fiduciary is the obligation of loyalty. The principal is entitled to the single-minded loyalty of his fiduciary.'[172]

In cases where financial products are sold without advice being given, there is no fiduciary duty. Such transactions can be described as 'arm's length', and typically arise when a firm sell its own products directly to customers or provides services on an 'execu-

---

[170] [2000] OJ Lloyd's Rep PN 412, J Parker J at 431.
[171] *Boardman v Phipps* [1967] 2 AC 46.
[172] Millet J in *Bristol & West Building Society v Mothew* [1998] Ch 1, 18.

tion only' basis. In the normal course of events there is no fiduciary relationship between a banker and a customer, but there can be if the bank offers advice relating to financial products. However, the mere giving of advice does not in itself give rise to a fiduciary relationship.[173] Fiduciary relationships arise either in the context of recognised relationships[174] or on an ad hoc basis, as a result of a relationship of trust and reliance between two parties.

While much of the content of the common-law duty has been subsumed within the FSA conduct of business rules, the scope of the two regimes is not coterminous.[175] Thus, breach of fiduciary duty remains a potential basis for action by a private investor. However, since many cases are based on allegations of negligence in the provision of advice and there is no separate 'fiduciary' duty of care,[176] it is more likely that claims based on negligence will be pursued by investors. A rare example of a claim of breach of fiduciary duty being upheld in connection with a transaction with a retail client was in the case of *Lloyd's Bank v Bundy*.[177] In that case, the defendant, an existing customer of the bank, guaranteed the overdraft of his son's business and provided a charge over his house as security to the bank. When his son's business failed and the bank called in the guarantee and sought an order to sell the house, the defendant argued that the bank owed him a fiduciary duty and was in breach of it by not advising him to take independent advice on the transaction. The Court of Appeal held that, although the transaction did not fall within the established categories of fiduciary relationship, an ad hoc fiduciary relationship existed as a result of the reliance placed by the defendant on the advice given by the bank.

6.6.2 Liability in tort/negligence

Liability in negligence is based on the existence of a duty of care in the law of tort (delict in Scotland). To establish liability, it is first necessary to show that a duty of care exists. A duty of care is an implied term of an agency contract[178] and therefore it follows that agents, other than those that act for a single company,[179] owe a common-law duty of care to the customer. Once it is clear that a duty of care exists, it is then necessary to show that a breach of the duty caused loss to the person to whom the duty is owed. There are no special rules of tort relating to 'retail clients' but, as in the case of agency,

---

[173] *Barnes v Black Horse Ltd* [2011] EWHC 1416, para 16.

[174] The established categories are: trustee/beneficiary; solicitor/client; agent/principal; director/company; and partner/partner. The relationship of banker and client gives rise to a duty of confidentiality in respect of the customer's financial affairs but that does not in itself make it a fiduciary relationship.

[175] This follows from the fact that the existence of a fiduciary duty and duties owed under the COBS do not necessarily arise in the same circumstances.

[176] The duty of care owed by an agent arises from tort and there is no separate fiduciary duty of care: see Millet, LJ in *Bristol and West Building Society v Mothew* [1998] Ch 1, 16.

[177] [1975] 1 QB 326.

[178] *Bowstead & Reynolds on Agency*, 8th edn (London, Sweet & Maxwell, 2006) 6-015–6-018.

[179] See *Barnes v Black Horse Ltd* [2011] EWHC 1418 (QB), paras 32–35 for support for this view. Reference to 'advice' provided by an agent who distributes the products of only one company is indeed a misnomer since the agent does not 'advise' the client in the normal sense. Such an agent acts on behalf of the provider she represents not the customer who buys the product.

the common-law rules respond to context and are capable of accommodating the special needs of private investors. This is made clear by the decision in *Gorham v British Telecommunications plc*.[180]

This case involved financial advice given by a company representative of the Standard Life Assurance Company in 1991 in connection with the pension arrangements of an employee of British Telecom plc. Following that advice, the plaintiff took out a personal pension plan. He was under the misapprehension that he was a member of his employer's pension scheme because he had not returned an opt-out form after joining the company. When he realised that he could not have both a personal pension and be a member of his employer's scheme he contacted Standard Life, who informed him that he would be better off in the employer's scheme. As a result, he stopped contributing to the personal pension, assuming that he was a member of the employer's scheme. He died shortly thereafter. Had he joined the employer's pension scheme following the advice from Standard Life his family would have been eligible for a lump sum payment but not other pension rights which were payable only after two years' membership. Standard Life admitted that they owed Mr Gorham a duty of care and that their representative had been negligent in failing to advise him about the differences between an occupational scheme and a personal pension, and in selling him the personal pension without being satisfied that he had made an informed choice between the two, but they denied owing the plaintiffs (his wife and children) any duty of care.

The Court of Appeal held that Standard Life owed the plaintiffs a duty of care. The rationale for the existence of this duty was articulated by Pill LJ in the following terms:[181]

> The advice in this case was given in the context in which the interests of the dependants were fundamental to the transaction, to the knowledge of the insurance company representative giving advice as well as to his customer, and a duty of care was owed additionally to the intended beneficiaries.

The implication of this principle is that there may be a duty of care in other contexts in which these circumstances exist. Nor is this process limited by FSMA 2000 and its regulatory rules. The relationship between the system of regulation and the common-law principles of tort was explained as follows:[182]

> Had Parliament not intervened, remedies for the abuses which existed in this field would almost certainly have been developed by the courts. The courts now do so in the context, and with the benefit of, rules and codes of practice laid down by those concerned with the maintenance of proper standards. The courts can be expected to attach considerable weight to the content of codes drafted in these circumstances but they are not excluded from making their own assessment of a situation.

The implication is that tort liability exists independently of the regulatory system even if 'considerable weight' is given to it in determining the existence of a duty of care. Nor does articulation of elements of the common-law duty of care in regulatory rules

---

[180] [2000] 1 WLR 2129.
[181] At 2142.
[182] At 2141.

necessarily exhaust the scope of the common-law duty as the two spheres are not necessarily co-extensive.[183]

Once the existence of a duty of care has been confirmed, it is necessary to establish the standard of care associated with that duty. This addresses the issue of the standard of conduct necessary to discharge the duty of care. Failure to discharge the duty will result in a finding of negligence and liability in damages to the person who has suffered loss. In *Gorham v BT*, it was said that the standard of care expected from Standard Life was a duty to the dependants not to give negligent advice to the customer that adversely affected their interests as he (the customer) intended them to be. It was also said that[184] 'The restrictions imposed by statute on what products the adviser can recommend do not have the effect of relieving him of the duty not to recommend his principal's products unless they are suitable'.

This reference to a suitability requirement was to one imposed by the common law and not by the regulatory system. The implication is that there is both a regulatory and a common-law suitability requirement and that they are not necessarily co-extensive.[185]

6.6.3 Contractual claims

Breach of contract may overlap with claims under the law of agency, tort and fiduciary duty above, especially since the scope of liability under each of these headings may be adjusted by contract. This section considers only those breaches of contract that do not overlap and may therefore be considered to be examples of breach of contract in the simple sense.

Common law claims against financial advisers tend to fall within the categories mentioned above. This is mainly because contracts do not generally define precisely the nature or standard of the advice that is to be given and therefore disputes generally have to be resolved by reference to the default rules of the law of agency, tort and fiduciary duty.

Claims against product providers in respect of breach of contract are possible but are rare as a result of the tendency for the terms of financial products not to guarantee any particular results in respect of financial performance. Moreover, adherence to codes of conduct relevant to the particular activity does not in itself result in the code being incorporated into the contract.[186]

Apart from breach of contract, common law claims may also arise in respect of the negotiation phase of the contract. The most common example is misrepresentation which,

---

[183] See Ousley J in *R (ex parte BBA) v FSA* [2011] EWHC 999 at para 182. It follows that a common law claim may succeed even where a claim based on breach of statutory duty has failed.

[184] Schiemann J at 2144.

[185] On suitability obligations generally see L Lowenfels and A Bromberg, 'Suitability in Securities Transactions' (1999) 54 *Business Law* 1577.

[186] See eg *Barnes v Black Horse Ltd* [2011] EWHC 1416, where it was held that adherence to the Code of the General Insurance Standards Council (now superseded by the Insurance Conduct of Business component of the FSA Handbook, ICOB) did not in itself make that code part of a contract through which a customer purchased payment protection insurance (PPI).

if established, may allow the customer to rescind the contract or to claim damages for loss suffered as a result of the misrepresentation.[187]

6.7 The Financial Services Compensation Scheme

The purpose of compensation schemes is to provide some reassurance to investors that their investment or other assets will be secure in the event that an authorised firm becomes insolvent. The rationale for establishing such schemes and their role in a regulatory system was explained by the FSA in the following terms:

> The justification for establishing compensation schemes is that individual investors, depositors and policyholders are not generally in a position to make an informed assessment of the risk that the firm to which his or her funds are entrusted may fail. As well as providing protection in the last resort for consumers, the existence of compensation schemes also helps to reduce the systemic risk that a single failure of a financial firm may trigger a wider loss of confidence in the rest of the financial sector concerned (eg through a run on deposit-taking institutions).[188]

A new system of compensation following the failure of a regulated firm was established under FSMA 2000. It rationalised the previous arrangements for compensating customers of failed firms and implements the provisions of the two relevant European directives, the Deposit Guarantee Directive[189] and the Investor Compensation Directive.[190] Before the new system took effect, there were different arrangements in place for banking (The Deposit Protection Scheme) insurance (The Policyholders' Protection Scheme and The Friendly Societies Protection Scheme) and investment (The Investors' Compensation Scheme). Each of these schemes had different rules for eligible claimants, the maximum amount payable and the claims procedure. The new scheme replaced these schemes and is run by a new body established for that purpose, the Financial Services Compensation Scheme Ltd,[191] which is operationally independent from the FSA but accountable to it.[192] The scheme is funded through levies paid by authorised firms.[193]

A claimant must meet several criteria to make a claim against the Financial Services Compensation Scheme (FSCS). A claimant must:

- be an eligible complainant;
- have a protected claim; and

---

[187] For more detail about this type of claim see Chapter 14.2.2.

[188] FSA, 'Consumer Compensation', CP 5 (1997) para 11.

[189] Directive 94/19/EC [1994] OJ L135/5, as amended by Directive 2009/14 [2009] OJ L68/3.

[190] Directive 97/9/EC [1997] OJ L84/22.

[191] See www.fscs.org.uk (accessed on 11 November 2011).

[192] See ss 212 and 218 FSMA 2000.

[193] See s 214 FSMA 2000. For a discussion of the way in which costs are allocated between firms (and a failed attempt to challenge a levy imposed by the FSA through judicial review) see *R (on the application of ABS Financial Planning Ltd) v Financial Services Compensation Scheme Ltd* [2011] EWHC 18 (Admin).

- be claiming against a relevant person.

Further,

- the relevant person must be in default.

Each of these aspects is now considered.

Eligible complainants are defined as any person who does not fall within a long list of excluded persons.[194] The effect of the exclusions is generally to limit access to the FSCS on the part of persons other than private individuals and small businesses.[195] A protected claim can be:

- a claim for a protected deposit;
- a claim under a protected contract of insurance;
- a claim in connection with protected investment business;
- a claim in connection with protected home finance mediation; or
- a claim in connection with protected non-investment insurance mediation.

The definitions of each category are complex, largely as a result of their giving effect to the principle that 'passporting firms' (whether incoming or outgoing) are not required to join the compensation scheme of the host state in which they engage in 'passported' activities.[196] In European law, the compensation schemes that Member States must maintain for the protection of depositors and investors in securities markets operate on a home country basis.[197] This means that 'passporting firms' operating in the UK are not required to join the FSCS, although they have the option to do so.[198] If such firms undertake regulated activities in the UK not covered by their EU passport they are required to join the FSCS. The definition of protected contracts of insurance includes contracts that, under the EU choice of law rules for insurance,[199] are governed by UK law, irrespective of whether they are underwritten by a firm exercising passport rights. This avoids the potential problems that would arise if contracts subject to UK insurance law were to become subject to the compensation scheme of a Member State whose insurance law differs materially from the UK.

---

[194] See COMP 4.2.1R and 4.2.2R.

[195] A small business for this purpose is a partnership, body corporate, unincorporated association or mutual association with an annual turnover of less than £1 million (or its equivalent in any other currency at the relevant time).

[196] See Chapter 2.5.2 for an explanation of the concept of 'passporting'.

[197] This approach caused considerable problems for UK depositors following the collapse of Icelandic banks operating in the UK under their EEA passport. For more detail see FSA, 'The Turner Review, A Regulatory Response to the Global Banking Crisis' (March 2009), available at http://www.fsa.gov.uk/Pages/Library/Corporate/turner/index.shtml) 37 and http://www.hm-treasury.gov.uk/fin_stability_icelandic_banks.htm (18 August 2011).

[198] Provision is made for passporting firms to 'top-up' the cover provided by their home state if it falls short of the levels provided by the scheme in the host state. As the relevant EU directives are based on minimum standards, levels of compensation vary between different Member States.

[199] See generally I MacNeil, 'UK Report' in M Frigessi di Rattalma and F Seatzu (eds), *The Implementation Provisions of the EC Choice of Law Rules for Insurance Contracts. A Commentary* (The Hague, Kluwer Law International, 2003).

Relevant persons against whom claims can be made are participant firms[200] and appointed representatives of such firms. Such relevant persons are considered to be in default whenever the FSA determines that this is the case or (if earlier) a judicial authority has made a ruling that has the effect of suspending the ability of eligible claimants to bring claims against the participant firm (eg the making of an administration order). The FSA can make such a determination when a relevant person (natural or legal) is subject to specified insolvency proceedings.

The FSCS may make an offer of compensation conditional on the assignment of rights to it by a claimant so as to enable it to pursue claims against failed firms. The result will be that any sum payable in relation to the rights so assigned will be payable to the FSCS and not the claimant. This is subject to the proviso that any recovery that exceeds the compensation payable to the claimant must be returned to the claimant and that the FSCS must endeavour to ensure that a claimant must not suffer disadvantage resulting from prompt acceptance of the FSCS offer of compensation.[201]

Prior to the changes that were prompted by the financial crisis, the amount of compensation payable by the FSCS reflected the principle that claimants should not have their claims met in their entirety. The rationale for requiring claimants to bear part of the loss lay in the concept of moral hazard, which predicts that the behaviour of parties may change after the making of a contract or the provision of a guarantee (eg by not taking precautions they would otherwise take). The FSA explained its approach as follows:[202]

> It would be possible to structure compensation arrangements as a complete safety net for all consumers. Such a provision would be more in the nature of an indemnity for consumers, providing total protection for anything that goes wrong. It could undermine the encouragement which we would otherwise wish to give to individuals to enter into transactions in financial services only after proper consideration, to the best of their ability, of the balance of risk and reward.

However, the financial crisis highlighted the key role of deposit protection in maintaining financial stability and preventing a 'run' on banks that were perceived to be in financial difficulty. This led to a change in approach whereby 100% of deposits are covered by the new rules. In the case of other categories of claim, the full amount is not always covered.[203]

The maximum payable in respect of a protected deposit is £85,000.[204] A distinction is drawn in the case of general insurance between compulsory insurance and other categories: in the former case, 100% of the claim is covered and the amount is unlimited, whereas in the latter case, only 90% of the claim is covered (with no limit). Claims relating to protected non-investment insurance mediation follow the same pattern. In

---

[200] Excluded from the definition are, inter alia, EEA banks and investment firms 'passporting' into the UK, authorised professional firms that are subject to the rules of the Law Society (England and Wales) or the Law Society of Scotland, and investment companies with variable capital. See COMP 6.2.1R.

[201] See the example at COMP 7.2.6G.

[202] FSA CP 5, above n 188, 6.

[203] See the table at COMP 10.2.3R for more detail.

[204] This represents the sterling equivalent of the minimum coverage level of 100,000 euros set by Art 7 of the Deposit Guarantee Directive 94/19/EC [1994] OJ L135/5 (as amended).

the case of life assurance, 90% of the claim is covered with no limit. Claims relating to protected investment business are fully covered up to a limit of £50,000, as are claims relating to protected home finance mediation.

These limits apply to the aggregate amount of claims in respect of each category of protected claim that an eligible claimant has against the relevant person.[205] Payment of compensation must normally be made to a claimant as soon as is reasonably possible after the claim has been verified and calculated, and in any event within 20 working days for a protected deposit and 3 months in other cases, unless an extension is granted by the FSA.[206] Provision is also made for accelerated payment of deposits (only) by the FSCS without an application being made by depositors.[207] The objective is to permit the FSCS to support rapid restructuring or sale by the authorities of banks that are in difficulty.[208]

There are no statutory or FSA Handbook provisions dealing with appeal against decisions made by the FSCS. It seems clear, however, that such decisions can, in principle, be the subject of judicial review.[209]

---

[205] COMP 10.2.2G. In this context a person is a natural or legal person. Thus, the corporate structure under which a group operates carries direct implications for compensation as subsidiaries which are legal persons (eg companies) are a relevant person for these purposes, whereas a 'brand' through which a firm markets services may not always operate through a separate subsidiary and will not therefore be a relevant person.

[206] COMP 9.2.1R. The deadline for payment of claims relating to protected deposits was shortened in response to the financial crisis with the objective of limiting the possibility of a 'run' on a bank perceived to be in difficulty by depositors whose deposits would be fully covered but nevertheless wished to avoid delay in the payment of their claim. This approach recognises that a 'run' on a bank can result from liquidity as well as solvency concerns.

[207] COMP 15.1.

[208] See Chapter 3.1.1 regarding the resolution powers that are available to the authorities to deal with troubled financial institutions.

[209] See *R v Investors Compensation Scheme Ltd, ex Bowden* [1996] AC 261. Although this case was an unsuccessful attempt to challenge the discretion given to the operator of the compensation scheme established under s 54 of the Financial Services Act 1986, it did establish that compensation decisions are open to judicial review.

Part 3

Finance and Governance

7

Corporate Finance— General Principles

Financing refers to the way in which enterprises fund the projects that form their business. Corporate finance, the focus of this chapter, is concerned with the legal rights of the providers of finance to companies and the operation of the markets through which companies can gain access to finance. Finance is linked with investment because enterprises often rely on funds raised through the process of investment for their establishment and expansion. Put another way, financing is the process that leads to the creation of the set of legal rights (comprising an investment) issued to investors in an enterprise. Three dimensions of those rights are of particular significance: their duration; whether the return to be paid to the investor is fixed or at the discretion of the company; and whether the investor has any role in the governance structure of the company. Equity investors are willing in principle to make an investment of unlimited duration with no fixed return, but typically have control rights in the form of votes at the general meeting of shareholders. By way of contrast, investors in debt instruments have a preference for certainty of return and priority in repayment over voting rights. In each instance the nature of the investment reflects both the financing requirement that it is intended to meet and the willingness of investors to meet that need. Thus, for example, equity finance may be the only option available to a start-up business which faces an uncertain future, whereas a mature and stable business represents a more attractive proposition for debt finance.

The law of corporate finance is relevant to investors in three ways. First, it establishes a framework within which the rights of contributors of the original or new finance to a company are defined. Secondly, it defines the role of existing shareholders in the raising of new finance. Thirdly, it governs the process by which new finance can be raised and the relationship of a company and its investors with public markets on which financial instruments issued by a company may be traded. The first two matters have traditionally been dealt with by company law, while the third has become increasingly separated from company law as capital market regulation (in the form of the Financial Services and Markets Act 2000 (FSMA 2000) and the Financial Services Authority (FSA) rulebook) has become an increasingly important area in its own right.

7.1 Sources of finance and capital structure

7.1.1 Internal and external finance

A business can finance investment in productive activity either from funds generated by the business itself (internally) or from external sources such as banks and investors. Internal funds are principally profits that are retained within a company (as reserves) rather than distributed to shareholders. The extent to which internal funds can finance investment varies greatly and depends, inter alia, on the nature of the business, its cash flow pattern, the extent to which it is capital-intensive and the dividend policy pursued by the company. External funds include the proceeds of issues of shares and debt instruments as well as bank loans. In aggregate, internal finance is a more important source of funds for investment for UK companies than external finance.[1] This means that companies typically finance their investment in productive capacity from internal resources rather than from external finance.

The balance between internal and external finance is ultimately controlled by shareholders in a company. There are two ways in which this occurs. First, shareholders set the dividend policy. This is crucial because the dividend policy determines the balance between the proportion of profits that are distributed as dividends to shareholders and the proportion that is retained within the company. Retained profits are generally the most significant source of internal finance available to a company. Secondly, shareholders' approval is normally required for a substantial issue of new shares. There is generally greater freedom given to companies to raise debt finance and shareholder approval is not normally required. However, it is common for a company's constitution to limit borrowing and there are self-regulatory restraints imposed by institutional investors in the case of listed companies.

7.1.2 Equity and debt finance

When a company's investment plans require external finance, a choice has to be made between equity and debt financing. Equity financing refers to financing through the issue of share capital, the most common form being ordinary share capital. It has the benefit of making finance available to the company on the basis that returns paid to the shareholders (in the form of dividends) are discretionary. Reliance on equity funding, however, carries the disadvantage that equity finance may not be available (whether from existing or new shareholders) on a scale that is capable of financing the growth of a company.

---

[1] See Office for National Statistics (ONS) *Financial Statistics* No 591 (July 2011), ch 6: data on the issue of financial instruments by companies. Recent years have seen a greater reliance on debt than equity finance. For earlier data see H Davies, 'Industrial Investment—Can the Market Respond?'(1996) 36 *Bank of England Quarterly Bulletin* 216.

Debt financing refers to financing through loans under which a company enters into a debtor/creditor relationship with a lender. Some of the characteristics of debt financing are variable, such as the duration of the loan, whether or not it is secured on the company's property and the obligations undertaken by the company in the loan agreement concluded with the lender. All forms of debt finance, however, share some common features. First, unlike equity, debt finance provides a contractually guaranteed return to the lender in the form of interest, which may be at a fixed or a floating rate (eg by reference to a benchmark). Secondly, lenders are entitled to repayment on a predetermined date (maturity of the loan). Equity investors (shareholders) have no such right as they provide in effect a perpetual form of financing to the company, although they can transfer their investment by selling their shares to another investor. Thirdly, lenders assume less risk than shareholders as, in the event of the company's insolvency, they take priority over shareholders in claiming the remaining assets of the company. Linked with their lower level of risk is the absence of profit-sharing on the part of lenders. They are entitled only to contractual interest and repayment, and have no claim to share in either the profits of the company or any rise in value in the company's assets.

Some forms of finance are described as hybrid in that they combine both equity and debt characteristics. These include preference shares, convertible bonds and bonds with warrants attached.[2] The attraction of these instruments for investors is that they offer the security and fixed income of debt instruments combined with some of the profit-sharing features of equity investment.

Another factor to be considered is control. From the perspective of the existing shareholders, a new issue of equity capital to outsiders dilutes their influence (through voting) whereas loan capital has the potential to provide additional capital without any loss of control. However, while it is unusual for control rights in the form of votes to be allocated to anyone other than company members (shareholders), lenders often require a company to accept loan covenants which limit the freedom of action of the company (and therefore also the control rights of the members) during the term of a loan.[3]

Debt financing introduces gearing (or leverage) into the financial returns of shareholders, with the result that changes in the financial performance of the company have a greater effect on shareholders than if the company is financed entirely by equity capital. This is because debt financing carries a fixed cost whereas dividends paid to shareholders are discretionary and are paid only after interest on the debt capital has been paid. Another relevant factor is that interest on debt is generally tax deductible, whereas dividends paid on shares are not. Gearing increases risk, delivering benefits when times are good and, at least at high levels, posing the threat of substantial losses or insolvency when times are bad.[4]

---

[2] See Chapter 4 for an explanation of the legal nature of these instruments
[3] Loan covenants are discussed below at section 7.3.
[4] For a worked example of the effect of gearing on profits and company value see R Pike and B Neale, *Corporate Finance and Investment, Decisions and Strategies*, 5th edn (London, FT Prentice Hall, 2006) ch 18.4.

7.1.3 Capital Structure

The choice between equity and debt finance is influenced by a number of factors. Cost of capital, control rights and gearing are particularly important. In the case of debt finance, the cost of capital is the interest payable (and, in the case of convertibles or attached warrants, the earnings dilution[5] resulting from the exercise of the relevant rights). In the case of an equity issue, the cost is the dividend payable on the shares (the dividend yield). The higher the price at which shares can be issued, the lower the cost of the equity capital. Taxation also plays a role in comparing the cost of equity and debt because interest on loans is paid from pre-tax profits whereas dividends are paid from profits after tax. Another element of cost, in the case of debt, is the credit rating[6] of the borrower, which is itself influenced by the existing level of debt and the company's historic record of servicing its debt. Risk is another important factor in judging the appropriate balance between debt and equity, and attitudes towards risk may vary considerably between different companies and their shareholders.

The extent to which the choice between debt and equity affects the cost of capital or the value of a company remains a matter of some controversy. According to a seminal paper by Modigliani and Miller,[7] the choice does not matter because the cost of capital is a constant regardless of the debt ratio. Thus, any attempt to improve financial returns to shareholders through leverage will lead to a corresponding increase in the cost of equity because the equity is more risky (and vice versa). However, that prediction is based on certain assumptions that do not hold good in the real world, such as the absence of taxes, perfect capital markets in which all investors have access to equal information, and the absence of insolvency and transaction costs. Once those assumptions are relaxed, it seems clear that there may well be scope to adjust the capital structure so as to reduce the overall cost of capital.

Several explanations have been offered as to how companies make (or should make) adjustments to capital structure to lower their aggregate cost of capital.[8] One is the 'trade-off theory', which predicts that firms will borrow up to the point at which the marginal value of the tax shields on additional debt is just offset by the increase in the present value of possible costs of financial distress. However, that approach does not fit well with the observation that many profitable and tax-paying firms have very low levels of debt. Another approach is the 'pecking-order' theory, which focuses on the information advantage of corporate managers in issuing and pricing equity. That advantage exposes equity investors to the risk of errors in valuing the firm that may result from that information advantage, whereas in the case of debt that risk does not arise. Thus, the pecking-order theory predicts that equity issues will be spurned by investors if debt is available on fair terms, and in equilibrium only debt will be issued. The theory does have some empirical

---

[5] Earnings dilution arises as a result of aggregate earnings being divided among a larger number of shares in issue following exercise of the relevant rights.

[6] See Chapter 14.1.7 re credit rating agencies.

[7] F Modigliani and MH Miller, 'The Cost of Capital, Corporate Finance and the Theory of Investment' (1958) 48(3) *American Economic Review* 261.

[8] SC Myers, 'Capital Structure' (2001) 15(2) *Journal of Economic Perspectives* 81.

support, in that the majority of external financing is in the form of debt rather than equity.[9] The 'free cash flow' theory provides another perspective. It focuses on the disciplinary effect of a high debt ratio in constraining the freedom of managers in wasteful investment of the free cash flow since it forces them to concentrate their efforts on servicing a high level of debt. It presumes that managers are self-interested and that limiting their discretion will result in a clearer focus on maximising value for shareholders.

7.1.4 Legal structure and financing

There exists a close relationship between the legal structure of a business and its financial structure because the legal structure governs the type of financing that is available to a business.[10] For this reason, legal structure is central to the initial establishment of a business and to its subsequent development.

The most basic distinction in terms of legal structure is between incorporated and unincorporated businesses. The main example in the former category is a company formed by registration under the Companies Act 2006. Unincorporated businesses are either sole traders or partnerships. Neither of these forms of unincorporated business organisation was developed for the purpose of facilitating investment by outsiders who are not involved in running the business, although it is possible for a partnership to be structured in a way that achieves this purpose.[11] It follows that, from the perspective of portfolio investment, unincorporated businesses do not generally provide investment opportunities.

A further distinction can be drawn between businesses that have a financing structure involving share (equity) capital and those that do not. The main example in the former category is companies limited by shares. The extent to which such companies are able to attract investment depends to some extent on whether they are private or public companies, an issue considered further below. Companies that do not have a share capital include companies limited by guarantee, in which the members agree to contribute a certain sum in the event of insolvency and their liability is limited to that amount. Included in this category are some 'mutual' companies.[12]

The legal distinction between public and private companies is important in considering the extent to which there can be 'investment' in a company. Only public companies are permitted to offer their shares to the general public and to have their shares traded on a regulated market. Therefore, companies that want access to institutional investment and

---

[9] See sources cited in n 1 above.

[10] It is possible also to regard the relationship as working in the opposite direction. From that perspective, the law facilitates different forms of financing by creating financial instruments that meet different financing needs.

[11] Limited partnerships, formed under the Limited Partnership Act 1907, are commonly used as a legal structure for venture capital funds. See Chapter 5.4.

[12] The concept of 'mutuality' is not an essentially legal one: the law does not and probably could not provide a definition of a mutual organisation that is capable of encompassing the wide range of organisations which operate on the basis of mutual principles. There are, however, two features which are common to mutual organisations: first, the members are both the customers and providers of capital for the organisation; and secondly, the organisation is run on the basis that all members have equal voting rights irrespective of their capital investment.

liquid markets for their securities must be public companies. Such companies must be designated as such by their certificate of incorporation, have a minimum alloted share capital of £50,000 (of which at least £12,500 must be paid up) and must include 'plc' in their name.[13] Any other company is a private company.[14] The vast majority of companies are private companies, and almost all companies start out as such. Conversion to public company status is possible at a later date. Only a relatively small proportion of public companies have a stockmarket listing.[15]

7.2 Equity finance: overview

At the time of its formation (through incorporation), a new limited company is required to have a share capital. It may or may not require further share capital during its lifetime. Whether it does so will depend on a number of factors, including its cash flow, profitability, dividend policy and ability to borrow money. All these factors influence the extent to which a company can remain self-financing.

A decision to issue new shares is likely to be made at one of the following stages in the life of a company:

1. when it is still a private company;
2. when it has become a public company but before its shares are listed;
3. at the time of listing; or
4. subsequent to listing.

Other than at stage 1, the issue of new shares is likely to involve a public offer. This process will trigger the application of the legal provisions relevant to public offers and possibly also listing. These issues are considered in Chapter 8. In the current chapter, the focus is on the relevant provisions of company law that must logically be considered before any decision regarding a public offer or listing can be made. A number of issues are relevant. First, what is the relevance of the company's capital structure to its ability to issue new shares? Secondly, who can authorise the issue of new shares, and in what circumstances? Thirdly, to whom can new shares be issued? Fourthly, what controls are

---

[13] See ss 4(2), 58, 761 and 763 of the Companies Act 2006.

[14] In the past, private companies were required to impose restrictions on the transfer of their shares. Although that is no longer a statutory requirement, it is common for the articles of private companies to restrict transfer. The result is to create a closed shareholding structure that is similar to a partnership. In contrast, listed company shares must be freely transferable.

[15] As at 31 March 2011 there were over 2.4m private companies and 7,900 public companies registered in Great Britain (see Companies House Statistical Tables on Companies Registration Activities 2010/11). The number of public companies fell from the 12,400 registered as at March 2000 (see the first edition of this book at 211). As of June 2011, there were 1002 companies listed on the Main Market of the London Stock Exchange and 1,151 companies listed on AIM (see London Stock Exchange Main Market Statistics June 2011).

imposed over the price at which new shares can be issued? Each of these issues is now considered.

7.2.1 Capital structure and share issues

The Companies Act no longer requires a company to state its authorised share capital in its memorandum of association.[16] The result is that there is no legal or theoretical limit as to the share capital that can be issued by a company. That matter is effectively left to private bargaining between the company and investors. The statement of capital and shareholdings that must be delivered to the Registrar of Companies on formation[17] specifies the nominal (or par) value of each share. This is simply the result of dividing the total share capital on formation by the number of shares, and serves the purpose of apportioning a fixed participation in the entire share capital to each share.[18]

Shares may be issued on a fully paid, partly paid or nil paid basis. This means that, in each case, an investor pays the full price, a proportion of the price or nothing when shares are issued. In the case of a public company, at least 25% of the nominal value, plus the whole of any premium, must be paid when shares are allotted.[19] When an issue is made other than on a fully paid basis,[20] shareholders are liable to pay the balance. The payment dates may be set by the articles or left to the discretion of the directors. The paid-up share capital of a company refers to that part of the issued capital that has been paid up and the called-up share capital refers to the paid-up capital plus the amounts due in respect of calls (for payment) made on shares that are not fully paid.[21] Allotted share capital refers to shares that have been allotted by the company to a subscriber who has not yet been entered on the register of shareholders. Other than at the time of allotment of new shares, the allotted share capital should equal the issued share capital.

[16] The requirement previously contained in the Companies Act 1985, s 2(5)(a) was not carried forward to the Companies Act 2006. However, the concept of authorised share capital remains relevant in the case of companies formed under earlier Acts. A provision relating to authorised share capital in its memorandum will continue to have effect (as part of the articles) and may be revoked or amended by the company by ordinary resolution: Companies Act 2006 (Commencement No 8, Transitional Provisions and Savings) Order 2008, SI 2008/2860, sch 2, para 42.

[17] See Companies Act 2006, ss 9 and 10.

[18] It is now generally agreed that there is no need for par values in respect of shares and some countries operate without them. There is, however, a need for some alternative mechanism to determine the extent of the (typically limited) liability of members in a company if par values are abolished. See R Pennington, *Pennington's Company Law*, 8th edn (London, Butterworths, 2001) 161 regarding the history of par values. See also the Company Law Review Group's comments at para 7.3 of their Final Report (DTI, 2001).

[19] Companies Act 2006, ss 761 and 763.

[20] This is not normally possible in the case of private companies: see Art 21(1) of the model articles for private companies limited by shares (SI 2008/3229).

[21] For public companies the main relevance of called-up share capital is in determining if a distribution (eg a dividend) can be paid to members. See section 7.4 below.

7.3 Equity finance: issuing shares

7.3.1 New share issues

The provisions of the Companies Act 2006 relating to share issues restate the prohibition, derived from the Second EC Directive on Company Law,[22] against directors exercising any power of the company to allot shares or to grant rights to subscribe for, or to convert any security into, shares in the company, except in accordance with section 550 (private company with a single class of shares) or section 551 (authorisation by the company). In line with the Company Law Review Group's view[23] that the prohibition did not meet the needs of most private companies, section 550 removes private companies from the prohibition where the private company will have only one class of share following the allotment. Section 550 is formulated as a default rule as it is possible for the articles to prohibit or limit the power of the directors in this context.[24]

In the case of public companies or private companies with more than one class of shares, section 551 authorises directors to issue shares (or grant rights to subscribe for shares or to convert any security into shares) if they have been given prior authorisation for the proposed allotment by ordinary resolution or by the articles of association. An ordinary resolution suffices to give authority to the directors even when it has the effect of altering the company's articles (which normally requires a special resolution). The authorisation can be general or limited to a specific issue of shares, and the choice between the two carries implications for the power of the directors to make share issues other than on a pre-emptive basis. Neither the model articles[25] for public companies nor the model articles for private companies limited by shares give directors such authority.[26]

The authority must state the maximum number of shares (or shares that may be allotted under rights granted by the company) that may be allotted under it, and specify its duration, which must be no more than 5 years. In the case of listed companies, institutional investors are expected to follow the Statement of Principles adopted by the Pre-Emption Group, which represents the interests of institutional investors. The Statement of Principles indicates that the number of shares which the directors should be authorised to issue should be the lesser of (i) the unissued ordinary share capital and (ii) a sum equal to one-third[27] of the issued ordinary share capital. The circular issued in connection with a resolution under this section must, in the case of a listed company, include, inter alia,

---

[22] Directive 77/91/EEC [1977] OJ L26/1.

[23] Final Report, above n 18, para 4.5.

[24] The section applies to companies formed before 1 October 2009 only if the members have resolved that the directors should have the power under it, although such resolution can be an ordinary resolution even if it alters the company's articles: Companies Act 2006 (Commencement No 8, Transitional Provisions and Savings) Order 2008, SI 2008/2860, sch 2, para 43.

[25] See SI 2008/3229.

[26] See Art 43 of the former and Art 22 of the latter.

[27] Two-thirds in the case of fully pre-emptive rights issues. This guidance relates to the number of shares that directors are authorised to issue. Whether shareholders will approve a non pre-emptive issue is a separate matter.

a statement by the directors as to whether they have any present intention of exercising the authority and, if so, for what purpose.[28]

7.3.2 Pre-emption rights

New issues of shares are controlled by the principle of pre-emption in company law. The objectives of a pre-emption rule are to protect the existing shareholders against two risks that arise from the process of issuing new shares. The first is the risk that the proportion of voting shares held by an existing shareholder may be diluted by an issue of new shares. This can be illustrated by reference to a simple example. Assume that company A has an issued share capital of 1000 ordinary shares. If the company proposes to increase its equity capital by 30%, it can in theory do this by offering the new shares either to existing shareholders or to third parties outside the company. If the shares are offered to and taken up by the existing shareholders, then the result is that the proportionate shareholding and voting power of each shareholder remains the same. Alternatively, if the shares are issued to outsiders in their entirety, the proportionate shareholding and voting power of existing shareholders will be diluted: in this situation, a 15% shareholder would see their shareholding fall to 11.5%. A range of intermediate solutions would also be possible in a situation in which the new shares were taken up by different combinations of existing shareholders and outsiders. It is also possible for dilution to occur in a similar manner when shares are offered only to a select group of shareholders, with the result that the remaining shareholders suffer dilution.[29] Protecting shareholders against the risk of dilution in their voting power assumes, of course, that they have an interest in exercising their votes—an assumption that is not always supported by empirical evidence.[30]

The second risk against which a pre-emption rule seeks to protect shareholders is that of reduction in the value of their shares resulting from a share issue made to outsiders at a price below the prevailing market price. The example already given can also be used to illustrate this point. Assume that Company A makes an issue of 300 new shares to outsiders at a price of 150p at a time when the market price of the shares is 200p. In this situation, the new shareholders will have paid less than the market value of the shares and the share price will fall, causing a loss to the existing shareholders.[31]

---

[28] See FSA Listing Rule LR 13.8.1R.

[29] See Law Commission, 'Shareholders' Remedies' Consultation Paper No 142 (1996) paras 9.36–9.38, which discusses this issue from the perspective of s 459 'prejudicial conduct' actions relating to breach of pre-emption rights.

[30] See Chapter 9.4.

[31] The fall in the share price will reflect the fact that, ceteris paribus, the number of shares in issue will have increased to a greater extent than the company's capital and dividend-paying capability. The ABI/NAPF Joint Position Paper (1996) (see www.abi.org.uk (19 Nov 2004)) states, 'any discount [in the price of a new issue relative to existing shares] represents a transfer of wealth from, and therefore a cost to, existing shareholders'. In contrast, a new issue made to existing shareholders at less than the prevailing market price (the typical rights issue in the UK equity market) has no significant effect on an existing shareholder's financial position. The ABI/NAPF Paper goes on to say, 'It makes no difference to an existing shareholder whether new shares issued by way of rights are issued at a deep discount to the market price, at a modest discount or at the market price itself'.

The absence of a common law rule of pre-emption in the UK meant that shareholders were not regarded as having the right to control the entry of new members into a company in the way that partners can control entry into a partnership.[32] The adoption of the Second Directive on Company Law[33] in 1976 resulted in pre-emption becoming a statutory right, and is now contained in sections 560–77 of the Companies Act 2006. The right of pre-emption under these provisions arises only when a company is proposing to make an allotment of 'equity securities'.[34]

The right of pre-emption is granted only to holders of ordinary shares[35] and is excluded when a company makes a share issue for a cash consideration.[36] It may also be restricted where a company's memorandum or articles contain a provision requiring that an issue of shares of a particular class[37] be offered first on a pre-emptive basis to the holders of that particular class of share.[38] In this situation, the pre-emptive rights of the holders of other classes of shares (to which the general right of pre-emption relates) apply only to those shares which are not taken up by the holders of the relevant class to whom the offer was required to be made.

The effect of the rule requiring that any offer of equity securities be on a pre-emptive basis is that a company is not able to offer such securities to any other person unless an offer on the same or more favourable terms has been made to holders of ordinary shares.[39] In that sense, the pre-emption rule allows a shareholder to maintain his proportionate shareholding in the company when an allotment of new shares is made. If that were not the case, a shareholder would face the prospect of dilution of the relative voting power of his shareholding following the allotment of new shares. He might also face the possibility of dilution in the value of his shares if the allotment were made at less than market value. A company is prohibited from allotting securities in respect of which a pre-emptive offer to shareholders is required unless the period during which the offer may be accepted has

---

[32] Gower comments that it was odd for company law to have developed in this way, given the willingness of the legislature and the courts to adopt partnership principles in other situations (LCB Gower, 'Some Contrasts between British and American Corporation Law' (1956) 69(8) *Harvard Law Review* 1369, 1380). The common law in the US did contain a principle of pre-emption, but this was removed by individual state corporation laws: see I MacNeil, 'Shareholders' Pre-Emption Rights' [2002] *Journal of Business Law* 78.

[33] Directive 77/91/EEC [1977] OJ L26/1.

[34] This term is defined in s 560(2) as (i) ordinary shares; or (ii) rights to subscribe for, or convert shares into, ordinary shares. Ordinary shares means shares other than those that as respects dividends and capital carry a right to participate only up to a specified amount in a distribution. An issue of preference shares will normally fall outside the definition of 'equity securities'. An issue either of warrants or convertible loan stock that can be converted into ordinary shares will generally fall within the definition of an allotment of 'equity securities'.

[35] Companies Act 2006, s 561(1)(a). Note that while an issue of convertible securities can trigger the operation of pre-emption rights, it is only the holders of ordinary shares than benefit from the right.

[36] Companies Act 2006, s 565, replicating Art 17(1) of the Second EC Company Law Directive, above n 33. This means that 'vendor consideration' issues, which are issues in respect of which the consideration for the share issue is either property or share capital (of another company), do not fall within the scope of statutory pre-emption rights.

[37] For this purpose, a class of shares is defined as shares to which the same rights are attached as to voting and as to participation, both as respects dividends and as respects capital, in a distribution.

[38] Companies Act 2006, s 568.

[39] For example, in the case of a company with a share capital of 100 ordinary shares that proposes to allot 20 new shares, it will be obliged to offer 5 of those new shares to a holder of 25 shares. The rule also has the effect that an offer of 'equity securities' to the holders of a particular class of share must be made to all ordinary shareholders unless the exception in s 568 applies.

expired or the company has received notice of the acceptance or refusal of every offer so made. Irrespective of this element of the prohibition, it is in any case only when the outcome of all pre-emptive offers are known that the company would be in a position to determine the scale of an offer that might be made to other persons.

The articles of a private company may exclude pre-emption rights.[40] In the case of a public company, where the directors have a general authority to allot shares (under section 551), pre-emption rights can be excluded or modified by the articles of association[41] or by a special resolution.[42] If the directors are authorised only in relation to a particular allotment, a special resolution is required to disapply pre-emption rights. Although the listing rules do not restrict disapplication of statutory pre-emption rights, self-regulation on the part of institutional investors does. Guidelines drawn up by the Stock Exchange Pre-Emption Group[43] in 1987[44] limit the size of share issues not involving pre-emption rights that will be approved by Association of British Insurers (ABI)/National Association of Pension Funds (NAPF) members when voting on a disapplication resolution and control the price at which such an issue can be made. Such resolutions for an annual disapplication of pre-emptive rights will be approved by ABI/NAPF members provided they do not exceed 5% of the issued ordinary share capital shown in the latest published annual accounts. A cumulative limit is also applied to restrict issues made over a 3 year period by a company using its disapplication entitlement to 7.5% of issued ordinary share capital shown by the latest published annual accounts. As regards the price of an issue to non-shareholders, the Pre-Emption Guidelines provide that any discount should not exceed 5%, and the Stock Exchange monitors this guideline both before and after an issue is made.[45]

A shareholder's financial position will not normally be affected by a decision to take up or decline a share issue made in accordance with pre-emption rights (ie a rights issue). This is because it is normally possible to sell in the market the right to buy the new shares at a discount. The principle of pre-emption does not restrict the sale of these rights by a shareholder. The price at which the rights trade in the market will reflect the size of the discount to the prevailing market price at which the rights issue is made. Therefore, a shareholder will be in the same financial position irrespective of whether the rights are sold or exercised.[46]

---

[40] Companies Act 2006, s 567. The Second Company Law Directive, above n 33, does not apply to private companies and therefore the application of pre-emption to private companies remains a matter for the Member States of the EU.

[41] The model articles for neither private nor public companies disapply pre-emption rights.

[42] This requires a 75% majority of members who vote on the resolution. Section 571 also provides that such a special resolution cannot be proposed unless it is recommended by the directors and there has been circulated, with the notice of the meeting at which the resolution is proposed, a written statement by the directors setting out the reasons for the recommendation, the amount to be paid in respect of equity securities allotted and the directors' justification of that amount.

[43] The group comprises representatives of institutional investors, investment banks and listed companies.

[44] For the current version see Pre-Emption Group, 'Disapplying Pre-emption Rights, a Statement of Principles' (July 2008), available at http://www.pre-emptiongroup.org.uk/documents/pdf/Statement%20of%20Principles%20July%202008.pdf.

[45] The Pre-Emption Guidelines require companies to complete a form showing the projected discount at which the new shares will be issued and the actual discount at which the shares are issued. The actual discount will reflect market conditions at the time that the pricing decision is made.

[46] See the example in section 7.2.4 below.

If shares are issued in contravention of a shareholder's pre-emptive rights, there are two remedies available to the shareholder. First, the company and every officer of it who has knowingly authorised or permitted the contravention are jointly and severally liable to compensate any person to whom an offer should have been made.[47] This requires the shareholder to show that a loss has resulted from the contravention. In the case of a rights issue from which the shareholder was excluded, this would be the value of the nil paid rights.[48] Secondly, the shareholder could apply to the court to have the company's share register rectified. Failure to observe pre-emption rights does not automatically invalidate an issue, but the court can exercise its power to rectify the share register in such circumstances.[49]

7.3.3 Pricing of new shares

The minimum price at which a company can issue shares is the nominal (or par) value of the shares. If shares are issued at a discount to their nominal value, the allottee and any subsequent holder (other than a good faith purchaser for value[50]) is liable to pay the company the amount of the discount in cash.[51] In setting the price for a pre-emptive issue of shares (a 'rights issue'), directors must consider the potential dilution in the value of the shareholding of shareholders unable to take up the offer (at least where that is known or foreseeable). An issue at par in circumstances where a higher price could have been obtained is a breach of fiduciary duty and may be 'unfairly prejudicial' for the purposes of section 994 of the Companies Act 2006.[52]

The actual price at which a company can issue shares is the price at which investors (and in particular the existing shareholders) are prepared to subscribe to a new issue, and that may be a determining factor in deciding whether or not to make an issue. Any difference between the nominal price and the issue price is referred to as a premium, and is treated in much the same way as capital. It is available to finance the company's activity, but is not generally available to distribute to shareholders as dividend.[53]

---

[47] Companies Act 2006, s 572.

[48] See the example in section 7.3.3 below.

[49] Companies Act 2006, s 125. See *Re Thundercrest Ltd* [1995] BCLC 117 for an example of the exercise of this power in the context of a private company.

[50] This refers to a person who is a purchaser for value without actual notice of the issue at a discount at the time of the purchase or who derived title directly or indirectly from such a purchaser: see Companies Act 2006, s 588(2).

[51] Companies Act 2006, s 580(2). The statutory provisions give effect to a long-established common law principle which aimed to ensure that companies did not overstate their capital by issuing shares at a discount to their nominal value. The rationale for the principle was to protect creditors who relied on the stated capital being available to pay their debts: see *Ooregum Gold Mining Co of India Ltd v Roper* [1892] AC 25.

[52] *Re Sunrise Radio Ltd (Kohli v Lit)* [2009] EWHC 2893 (Ch). In that case, the court held that, where it was foreseen that a minority shareholder would not or might not have the money or inclination to subscribe to a rights issue, the directors should consider the price that could and should be paid by shareholders willing to subscribe. Failure to do so, such as by issuing new shares at par, would represent a breach of fiduciary duty and would be unfairly prejudicial to the minority (since their shareholding would be diluted by an under-priced issue of shares).

[53] The legal framework governing the distribution of dividends is considered at section 7.5 (below).

Just as there is no direct relationship between the nominal value of shares and their issue price, there is no direct relationship between the nominal value of shares and the price at which they trade in the secondary market. A company has no involvement in the trading of its shares between investors and is not directly affected by that process because, irrespective of who owns the shares, its share capital remains the same.[54] The value of assets that represent the share capital (such as land, buildings, and plant and machinery) will fluctuate in value according to market movements and the fortunes of the company, and will have a direct effect on the market value of a company's shares. However, that process has no effect on the share capital or nominal value of shares, both of which remain fixed unless altered in accordance with the procedure set by company law.

A rights issue is a share issue in which shareholders have a legal right to participate.[55] The size of the issue is measured by reference to the existing issued share capital. For example, in a one-for-three rights issue, the issued share capital is being increased by 33% and shareholders have a right to buy one new share for every three that they already own. It is normal for a rights issue to be made at a discount to the prevailing market price and sometimes at a 'deep discount'. The only limit on the size of the discount is that shares cannot be issued below their par (nominal) value. While directors who allot shares to outsiders at a discount to market value may be guilty of a breach of duty and liable to pay the premium that could have been obtained as damages,[56] there is no restriction on offering shares at a discount to market value to shareholders.[57] As discussed below, this reflects the fact that any discount in the price at which shares are offered to shareholders (in a rights issue) does not prejudice their financial position.

In principle, the size of the discount is neutral for the financial position of an individual shareholder, irrespective of whether she takes up the offer or sells her entitlement to the offer in the market (in the form of nil paid rights). However, as the size of the discount acts as a measure of shareholders' demand for the company's shares and the attractiveness of the project that the issue is to fund, deep-discount issues are regarded by many companies and investors as less attractive than those priced close to the prevailing market price.[58]

The effect of a (discounted) rights issue on the position of a shareholder can be analysed by calculating the 'theoretical ex-rights price' price of the shares. This is an estimate of the price at which the share should trade in the market after the rights issue. It is only an estimate as it ignores factors such as the expected return earned by the company on the funds raised by the issue, which in reality will have an important influence on the market's response to a rights issue.

---

[54] A company is indirectly affected in that a new issue of shares will be made by reference to the price at which the company's shares trade in the market.

[55] The right is that of pre-emption, considered at Chapter 7.3.2.

[56] *Lowry v Consolidated African Selection Trust Ltd* [1940] AC 648 at 679 per Lord Wright. For an analysis of this and other cases dealing with the price at which new shares are issued see MacNeil, above n 32.

[57] *Mutual Life Insurance Co of New York v Rank Organisation Ltd* [1985] BCLC 11.

[58] Companies also face the problem that they may not be able to maintain the same level of dividend on the increased share capital. However, as it is normal for earnings and dividends to be adjusted (downwards) for a rights issue, this is essentially a problem of investor expectations rather than an inherent defect in the deep-discount financing technique.

Assume that company A's shares trade at 150p. It announces a one-for-five rights issue at 100p. The position of a shareholder with 20 shares who takes up the offer is as follows:

20 'old' shares @ 150p	£30.00
4 'new' shares @ 100p	£ 4.00
24 shares in total	£34.00
Each share is worth	142p

In this example, the theoretical ex-rights price is 142p, and this is the price at which the shares could be expected to trade in the market after the rights issue. The value of the 'rights' is the difference between the theoretical ex-rights and the subscription price payable to the company, in this case $142 - 100 = 42$p. A shareholder can sell the rights in the market as nil paid rights at this price, giving the buyer the rights to buy the shares at 100p. If the shareholder in this example were to do this as opposed to taking up the offer, her position would be:

20 shares @ 142p	£28.40
sale of nil paid rights over 4 'new' shares	£ 1.68
Combined total	£30.08

This can be compared with the position after taking up the rights, which is that the shareholder has a shareholding of 24 shares worth £34.08 but has paid £4 for the new shares. Adjusting for the £4 paid for the new shares, the position is the same irrespective of whether the shareholder takes up the rights offer or not. This remains true irrespective of the fraction of the share capital represented by the rights issue or the size of the discount.

An open offer is similar to a rights issue in that it is an offer of new securities to existing investors in those securities in proportion to their existing holdings, but is not made by means of a renounceable letter of allotment.[59] This form of offer means that existing shareholders who do not take up the offer will suffer dilution without compensation, whereas in a rights offer they will be compensated by sale of their nil paid rights. An open offer may also operate on the basis of a shorter timetable than a rights issue,[60] which can help to minimise costs associated with the issue, such as underwriting costs.[61]

A capitalisation issue of shares (also referred to as a bonus or scrip issue), unlike a rights issue, does not involve the raising of new capital by a company. It is a mechanism by which a company can use retained profits[62] to pay up unissued shares in the company which are then issued to existing shareholders pro rata to their existing shareholding.[63]

---

[59] *Listing Rules*, LR App 1.1: Relevant definitions.

[60] See LR 9.5.7R requiring the timetable for an open offer to be approved by the recognised investment exchange on which the shares are traded. There is no comparable requirement under the Companies Act 2006 to the 14 day open period for rights offers.

[61] The matter of underwriting charges in the UK capital markets has been a controversial area and the subject of a reference to the Competition Commission. On this, see Bank of England, 'Guide to Share Issuing Good Practice for Listed Companies' (October 1999).

[62] It is also possible for such an issue to be funded by a transfer from the share premium account (Companies Act 2006, s 610(3)) or the capital redemption reserve (Companies Act 2006, s 733(5)).

[63] This definition is contained in s 853(3) Companies Act 2006.

The result is that the number of shares in issue is increased but shareholders' funds (net assets) remain the same. The market price is likely to fall to reflect the new issue[64] and so a shareholder's financial position will remain the same. Companies make such issues for a variety of reasons, one being that it is sometimes believed that the liquidity of shares (and hence their value) may benefit from a lower price per share.

7.3.4 Underwriting and bookbuilding

A contract of underwriting[65] is an agreement that, if the whole or a certain proportion of an issue of securities is not applied for by the public, the underwriters will themselves apply or find persons to apply for the balance or a certain proportion of the balance of the issue. The underwriters receive a commission whether they are called upon to take up any securities or not. There is no legal or regulatory requirement for an issuer to enter into an underwriting agreement and it is therefore a matter of commercial judgement as to whether it is necessary. The advantage from an issuer's perspective is that the success of the issue is guaranteed but the disadvantage is the cost (over and above the other costs of an issue).[66] Two issues are particularly relevant for the underwriting decision. The first, which is relevant in the case of a rights issue, is the scale of the discount to the prevailing market price at which new shares are offered. Where the discount is large (a deep-discount issue), existing shareholders have a substantial incentive to take up the issue to avoid dilution in their shareholding, thus limiting the need for underwriting. The second, applicable to any issue, is the level of anticipated demand for the new issue. The increasing use of the 'bookbuilding' technique for new issues makes it possible to predict demand more accurately at different price levels. The process involves the publication of a prospectus[67] in which an indicative price range is set along with the conditions for determination of the final price. Investors make binding bids for shares at specific price levels and, following the determination of the final price, are allocated shares by the bookrunner (typically an investment bank). Bookbuilding thus tends to maximise the price for the issuer, though it raises potential regulatory problems as to the manner in which the bookrunner makes allocations, especially when duties are owed to both the issuer and its own investment clients.

---

[64] For example, a bonus issue of 1 new share for every 5 held will result in a 20% fall in the share price but as a shareholder will have 20% more shares the overall impact is neutral.

[65] The meaning of 'underwriting' was declared by the Court of Appeal after hearing evidence in *Re Licensed Victuallers' Mutual Trading Association* (1889) 42 ChD 1. A modern judicial analysis of underwriting structures is provided by Hobhouse LJ in *County Ltd v Girozentrale Securities* [1996] 1 BCLC 653, 670. See also *Eagle Trust plc v SBC Securities Ltd* [1995] BCC 231 (role and duties of underwriter).

[66] The maximum amount of commission that can be paid to underwriters from the proceeds of an issue of shares is regulated by ss 552 and 553 of the Companies Act 2006.

[67] See generally Chapter 8.3.2.

7.4 Equity finance: maintenance of capital

Although it now forms the basis for several of the provisions of the Companies Act 2006, the doctrine of maintenance of capital was first developed by the courts.[68] The underlying rationale for the principle is that creditors are entitled to rely on capital paid into a company remaining in the company to meet its debts. While it is recognised that capital may be lost in the course of a company's trading, it should not in principle be capable of removal by the shareholders. In that sense, the capital is 'locked in' to the company. Moreover, since creditors will be paid on insolvency before the shareholders, the capital acts as a form of buffer that protects the creditors.

The premise underlying the principle of maintenance of capital—that creditors do in fact rely on the legal concept of capital in extending credit to a company—has increasingly been questioned.[69] It has been argued that the concept of legal capital may provide creditors with a very poor measure of the creditworthiness of a company because the legal capital may bear little relationship to the current financial position of the company. One reason is that legal capital is a historic record of capital (based on the nominal value of shares) and does not focus on the current assets and liabilities of the company. Another argument is that creditors are able to devise more sophisticated mechanisms to protect their interests and therefore a crude measure such as legal capital is a weak foundation on which to build other legal rules. Despite these doubts, the concept of legal capital and the principle of maintenance of capital still survive largely intact in the EU regime[70] and the Companies Act 2006. Some inroads have been made by the introduction of a solvency-based test for reduction of capital (in the case of private companies) and share buy-backs, but that falls short of the acceptance of general principle that solvency certification should replace the principle of maintenance of capital in regulating the return of capital to shareholders.

The various statutory options that are made available for companies to return capital to shareholders do mean, however, that in its modern form the principle of maintenance of capital is very different in its effect to the old common law principle. The Companies Act 2006 provides several ways in which capital can be returned to shareholders. The techniques are to some extent functionally equivalent from an economic perspective in that they all have the effect of returning money to shareholders. However, there are important differences between them as regards the procedure for approval and the extent to which dissenting shareholders can be compelled to participate

---

[68] See in particular *Trevor v Whitworth* (1887) 12 App Cas 409, HL.

[69] See L Gullifer and J Payne, *Corporate Finance Law, Principles and Policy* (Oxford, Hart Publishing, 2011) 4.2 and 4.5 for a review of the debate.

[70] Principally the Second Directive on Company Law, above n 33.

7.4.1 Reduction in Capital

There are various reasons why a company may consider reducing its capital. One is that the level of capital may exceed what is required to finance the business. If that is the case, it is likely that the return on capital will be low and shareholders may be able to earn a better return by investing the capital elsewhere. Another is that the stated level of capital may no longer be matched by assets. That situation would be likely where the capital has been eroded over time by losses and is overstated by reference to the assets of the company. In that situation, a reduction in capital would bring the capital into line with the assets without making any payment to the shareholders.

The Companies Act 2006 permits a company to reduce its capital in any way, but refers specifically to three techniques:

1. extinguish or reduce the liability on any of its shares in respect of share capital not paid up;
2. either with or without extinguishing liability on any of its shares, cancel any paid up share capital that is lost or unrepresented by available assets; and
3. either with or without extinguishing liability on any of its shares, pay off any paid up share capital that is in excess of the company's wants.[71]

A reduction in capital must first be approved by a special resolution of the shareholders. That has the effect of binding all shareholders, including those who oppose the reduction in capital. It must then be approved by the court under a procedure that is intended to protect the rights of creditors. The court can confirm a reduction of capital on such terms as it thinks fit. In the case of a private company (only), a reduction of capital is also possible under the solvency statement procedure. In this case, there is no requirement for the court procedure, but directors must provide a solvency statement confirming that the company is able to pay its debts at the date of the statement and is likely to remain able to do so during the year immediately following that date.[72] The statement must be made by all the directors, with the result that any disagreement would have to be resolved by resignation or removal before the statement is made.

Failure to follow the statutory requirements for reduction of capital would mean that, under the common law, the reduction is void,[73] that responsible directors are in breach of their duties owed to the company[74] and that the recipient shareholders may be held liable to repay any capital that has been distributed to them.[75] Moreover, in the case of a private company, directors who make a false solvency statement are guilty of a criminal offence punishable by up to 2 years' imprisonment.[76]

---

[71] Companies Act 2006, s 641.
[72] Companies Act 20006, s 643.
[73] *MacPherson v European Strategic Bureau Ltd* [2000] 2 BCLC 683, CA.
[74] *Aveling Barford Ltd v Perion Ltd* [1989] BCLC 626.
[75] *Re Halt Garage* (1964) Ltd [1982] 3 All ER 1016.
[76] Companies Act 2006, s 643(4)–(5).

7.4.2 Share buy-backs (and redemption)

A share buy-back is an arrangement whereby a company buys shares from its shareholders. The purpose of a share buy-back is generally to boost those financial ratios (such as earnings and assets) that are commonly measured on a per share basis. Those ratios will be boosted because there will be a lower number of shares as the divisor of total earnings or assets. Put another way, a share buy-back should in principle boost the share price because the number of shares with a right to participate in the profits of the company will be reduced. The same principle can be applied if shares are bought back from the proceeds of a loan raised for that purpose. The effect is to replace equity with debt and, if the financing cost (interest) of the debt is lower than the cost of paying dividends on the equity, earnings per share will improve. The same analysis can be applied to redeemable shares, which, unlike ordinary shares, are issued on the basis that they will be bought back at some point in the future.

Historically, the law has viewed share buy-backs with suspicion.[77] The common law prohibited a company purchasing its own shares on the basis that it represented a mechanism by which a company could return capital to its members.[78] The common law rule is restated in the Companies Act 2006.[79] Contravention of the prohibition makes the company liable to a fine and the officers of the company liable to a fine or imprisonment, or both. A purported acquisition of shares contrary to the prohibition is void.

The prohibition is, however, disapplied in respect of a purchase or redemption of shares made in compliance with the provisions of the Act.[80] As a result of its potential to damage the interests of creditors, the process is strictly controlled but is nevertheless commonly used by listed companies. The relevant provisions of company law vary according to whether the purchase is a 'market purchase' or an 'off-market purchase'. The latter is a purchase other than on a recognised investment exchange (RIE) or on an RIE in circumstances in which the shares are not subject to a marketing arrangement on that RIE.[81] A marketing arrangement exists if shares are listed or the RIE provides ongoing facilities for dealing in the shares (such as on the Alternative Investment Market). 'Market purchases' are those made on an RIE other than off-market purchases. The stricter regulation of 'off-market' purchases reflects the fact that such purchases are not subject to a valuation determined (by market forces) in a regulated market, in which it is expected that the price formation process (in respect of the shares being purchased or redeemed) will be fair and efficient.

---

[77] It was only in 1981 that the law was amended to permit share buy-backs.

[78] *Trevor v Whitworth* (1887) 12 AC 409.

[79] Companies Act 2006, s 658.

[80] See Companies Act 2006, ss 684 and 690. A company must be authorised by its articles of association to purchase or redeem its own shares. The model articles made under the Companies Act 2006 do not provide such authorisation, with the result that a change to the articles may be necessary to permit the issue and redemption of redeemable share or the purchase of ordinary shares.

[81] See Chapter 12 for a discussion of recognised investment exchanges.

In the case of a 'market purchase',[82] the purchase must be authorised by an ordinary resolution of the company.[83] The authorisation must state the maximum number of shares that may be purchased, together with the maximum and minimum price to be paid.[84] The resolution must state the duration of the authority, which must not exceed 5 years.[85] It is common for such resolutions to provide authority for only 12 months until the next annual general meeting, when a similar resolution will be adopted so as to provide a continuing mandate to repurchase shares.[86] In the case of 'off-market' purchases, authority (for a maximum of 5 years) can be given only by special resolution and the terms of the purchase contract must be approved in advance by the shareholders.[87]

It is also possible for a company to buy its own shares through a contingent purchase contract. This is a contract under which the company may, subject to conditions, become entitled or obliged to purchase shares in itself but there is no immediate obligation.[88] A typical example would be a 'put' contract, under which the company would become obliged to buy shares from a shareholder at an agreed price. Such a contract must be approved by a special resolution and is subject to the same rules as an 'off-market' purchase. Shares that are to be repurchased must be fully paid and the payment to shareholders must be in the form of cash paid at the time of purchase.[89] A repurchase cannot be made if it would result in only redeemable shares being held by members,[90] the rationale being that a company would then face the eventual prospect of having no members (when the redeemable shares were redeemed). Contracts entered into contrary to the statutory provisions outlined above are void as a contract to perform an illegal act.[91]

For a public company, the main source of finance for share buy-backs is distributable profits.[92] It is also possible for the proceeds of a fresh issue of shares to be used to finance a repurchase, though there are restrictions associated with the use of such funds.[93] Private companies benefit from a less restrictive regime governing the sources from which repurchases may be financed. In particular, provision is made for repurchases to be made, in some circumstances and subject to safeguards, from capital.[94] Shares that have been purchased by a company must be cancelled, with the result that the issued

---

[82] In the case of a market purchase, the requirements set by the Listing Rules must be followed by companies with a premium listing: see LR 12. The Disclosure and Transparency Rules may also be relevant: see DTR 5.

[83] Companies Act 2006, s 701. In practice, many companies adopt a special resolution, as recommended by the ABI: see ABI 'Own Share Purchase', available at http://www.ivis.co.uk/PDF/3.2_Own_Share_Purchase.pdf.

[84] The prices may be expressed as a formula so long as it is not reliant on any person's discretion or opinion.

[85] The period was increased from 18 months as a result of the implementation of Directive 2006/68 [2006] OJ L264/32, which introduced limited reform of the capital maintenance regime.

[86] This is the procedure recommended by the ABI.

[87] Companies Act 2006, s 694. The time limit of 5 years applies only to public companies. It was increased from 18 months as a result of the implementation of Directive 2006/68 [2006] OJ L264/32, which introduced limited reform of the capital maintenance regime.

[88] Companies Act 2006, s 694(3).

[89] Companies Act 2006, s 691.

[90] Companies Act 2006, s 690(2).

[91] *Re RW Peak (Kings Lynn) Ltd* [1998] 1 BCLC 193, holding that the statutory requirements cannot be set aside by unanimous consent of the shareholders.

[92] For a definition of distributable profits see Chapter 7.4.3.

[93] See Companies Act 1985, s 692(3).

[94] See ss 709–23 Companies Act 2006.

share capital is reduced by the nominal value of the repurchased shares.[95] In the case of a repurchase funded from distributable profits, this would result in a reduction in the issued share capital of the company and pose a potential risk to creditors.[96] To protect against this risk, a company must, following a purchase funded from distributable profits, transfer to its capital redemption reserve an amount equivalent to the fall in its issued share capital (equivalent to the nominal value of the shares repurchased). The capital redemption reserve is treated as paid-up share capital, except that it can be used to fund an issue of fully paid bonus shares to members of the company.

In addition to the requirements imposed by company law, listed companies must also comply with the requirements of the Listing Rules.[97] Companies are required to notify the market of a decision to seek shareholder approval for purchases (other than a renewal of authority) and of actual purchases when they occur. The content of circulars seeking shareholder approval is controlled by the Listing Rules, and in some circumstances (such as a purchase from a related party) prior approval of circulars is required. The price of dealings is also controlled. For purchases of less than 15% of any class of shares, a ceiling is set at 5% above the average of the market value of the shares for the 5 days preceding the purchase. For purchases of more than 15%, a tender offer (open to all shareholders) must be made at a stated maximum or fixed price.

Redeemable shares differ from ordinary shares in that they are issued with the intention that they will be redeemed (purchased) by the company at some point in the future. Any company whose articles permit it can issue redeemable shares, but a company cannot only have members holding only redeemable shares. The terms and manner of redemption are a matter to be determined by a company's articles or by a resolution of the company.[98] Authority for redemption is provided on a continuing basis by the articles as opposed to the more limited authorisation provided by a shareholders' resolution for the purchase of non-redeemable shares. When redemption of shares is financed from distributable profits, the same potential problem arises as in the case of purchases (above), and the same solution is adopted by requiring a transfer to be made to the capital redemption reserve equivalent to the nominal value of the shares to be redeemed.[99] Only fully paid shares can be redeemed.[100]

---

[95] It is also now possible for shares to be held in 'treasury' by the company. This provides a mechanism through which a company can manage its equity financing requirements.

[96] A repurchase funded from a new issue of shares does not pose this risk as the new issue will result in the issued capital remaining at the level it stood prior to repurchase and cancellation.

[97] See generally LR 12. These requirements apply to repurchases of any security, not just shares.

[98] Companies Act 2006, s 685. The articles may authorise the directors to set the terms before issue of the shares.

[99] Companies Act 2006, s 733. This has the effect of maintaining the issued capital at the same level after the redemption has occurred and gives effect to the company law principle of maintenance of capital.

[100] Companies Act 2006, s 691.

7.4.3 Distributions to shareholders

Dividends are central to equity investment, yet shareholders have no legal right to be paid a dividend. The apparent conundrum implicit in this statement is explained by the very nature of equity investment. It is a form of risk-taking under which an investor agrees to provide capital in return for a residual[101] claim to all the profits and surplus assets of a company. Dividends are essentially a mechanism through which investors are able to share in profits during the time that a company is a going concern.

The payment of dividends is encompassed by the principle of maintenance of capital. The objective is to ensure that dividends are not paid from capital, as that would represent a form of return of capital to the shareholders. A dividend can only be paid if 'distributable profits' are available for this purpose. They are defined as a company's 'accumulated, realised profits, so far as not previously utilised by distribution or capitalisation, less its accumulated, realised losses, so far as not previously written off in a reduction or reorganisation of capital duly made'.[102]

Realised capital gains are included within this definition, but not unrealised gains, which are treated as undistributable reserves. The availability of distributable profits is determined by reference to a company's relevant accounts, which may be either the last audited annual accounts or interim accounts.[103]

Public companies are subject to a further constraint in paying dividends: a dividend can only be paid if (i) at that time the amount of the company's net assets is not less than the aggregate of its called-up share capital and undistributable reserves; and (ii) if, and to the extent that, the distribution does not reduce the amount of those assets to less than that aggregate.[104] The purpose of this provision is to ensure that share capital and undistributable reserves (which are regarded as equivalent to capital) are represented by assets. This can never be guaranteed, as assets are always open to erosion from trading losses, but at least it prevents such an outcome being the result of the payment of dividends to the shareholders.

The Companies Act specifically provides that a payment of dividend in circumstances where there are no distributable profits (an unlawful distribution) must be repaid by the recipient.[105] However, that provision is made subject to the requirement that the recipient must know or have reasonable grounds for knowing that the distribution is unlawful. If that requirement is not satisfied, the statutory liability to repay the dividend does not apply.[106] However, the statutory liability is without prejudice to any other obligation to repay. This might arise, for example, if the recipient was considered to be a constructive trustee of the payment. For this to occur, it must be shown that the payment was made

---

[101] The residual nature of the claim is reflected in the priority given to creditors' claims in the event of insolvency.

[102] Companies Act 2006, s 830(2).

[103] Companies Act 2006, s 836.

[104] Companies Act 2006, s 831.

[105] Companies Act 2006, s 847.

[106] As occurred, for example, in *Precision Dippings Ltd v Precision Dippings Marketing Ltd* [1986] Ch 447.

by the directors in breach of their fiduciary duty and that the recipient was aware of the factual circumstances, though not necessarily the illegality of the payment.[107]

The procedure for declaring dividends is not mandated by the Companies Act and is therefore determined by a company's articles. They normally provide that decisions on dividend payments should be made by ordinary resolution of the company in general meting and that no payment greater than that recommended by the directors may be paid.[108] Provision is also made for the directors to declare an interim dividend without the approval of shareholders.[109]

Dividends can be paid in the form of assets, in cash or in the form of scrip dividends. Most dividends are paid in the form of cash. Under the common law, dividend payments were calculated by reference to the nominal value of shares,[110] but it is now common for the articles to provide that payments be calculated by reference to the amounts paid up on shares.[111] The purpose of such a provision is to link the amount paid by way of dividend to the capital contributed to the company by a member (shareholder) rather than to the number of shares held.

Some companies are authorised by their articles to pay 'scrip dividends'. This allows shareholders to elect to receive new shares as an alternative to the payment of a cash dividend. The attraction for companies is that scrip dividends retain cash within the company that would otherwise have been paid out in the form of dividends. In this sense, scrip dividends are the economic equivalent of reinvestment in the company, as shareholders are in effect reinvesting their dividend in the company. For shareholders, the main attraction is that they can increase their holding in the company without incurring transaction costs.

Transfers of shares raise the issue of the person to whom dividends should be paid. The common law rule is that the dividend is paid to the registered owner at the date of declaration of the dividend.[112] Companies and stock exchanges have overcome the potential uncertainty resulting from the application of this rule by adopting a device that makes clear who is entitled to a dividend. Shares are quoted either cum (with) or ex (without) dividend on either side of a date (the record date) fixed by the company (as authorised by its articles) for payment of dividends to shareholders. The matter really only assumes significance around the time of the record date, as for the remainder of the year shares are traded cum dividend. The process of going 'ex-dividend' is in principle associated

---

[107] See *Re Cleveland Trust plc* [1991] BCLC 424. It is possible for illegal dividend payments to be traced in the hands of shareholders and payments to be recovered from directors.

[108] See Art 70 of the Model Articles for PLCs (SI 2008/3229). It is very unusual for the directors' recommendation regarding dividend payment to be rejected by the shareholders.

[109] Ibid, Art 70(6).

[110] *Oakbank Oil Company Ltd v Crum* (1882) 8 App Cas 65 (HL).

[111] See Art 70(3) of the Model Articles for PLCs. Art 21(1) of the Model Articles for Private Companies Limited by Shares provides that all shares in a private company must be fully paid and therefore Art 30(4) of the Model Articles for Private Companies Limited by Shares simplifies matters by providing that dividends are to be distributed according to the number of shares held, subject to the ordinary resolution to declare, or the directors' decision to pay, a dividend specifying otherwise or the terms on which the shares are issued providing otherwise.

[112] *Re Wakley, Wakley v Vachell* [1920] 2 Ch 205.

with a fall in the value of the shares equal to the dividend payment, as a buyer will not have the right to that payment.[113]

7.5 Debt finance

Companies can raise debt finance either through issuing financial instruments such as debentures or bonds to investors or through various forms of bank loan. The focus here is on the former category, which can be considered as a form of financial investment since it is undertaken typically through the issue of transferable financial instruments that may be traded on organised markets. Whichever option is chosen, the basic relationship of creditor and debtor is the same, and so too are the main legal techniques that are used to protect the lender.

7.5.1 Borrowing powers and procedures

Companies generally have greater freedom to issue loans than share capital. A company formed to carry on a trade or business has an implied power to borrow and give security for loans made to it, but it is normal for express powers to be included in a company's constitution. In the absence of any restriction in its constitution,[114] the amount of money a company can borrow is unlimited. The directors' authority to issue loan capital is also in principle unlimited unless limitations are imposed by the constitution.[115] Existing lenders to a company have no statutory protection against further borrowing by a company comparable to the pre-emption rights enjoyed by shareholders, but they can protect themselves through contractual provisions and security interests.

In the UK, the term 'debenture' is associated with secured long-term loans, although that usage runs counter to the legal meaning of the term and to its meaning in the US.[116] Unsecured long-term loans are typically referred to as loan stock, while short- or medium-term unsecured loans are often termed 'loan notes'. Short- and medium-term loans of up to 7 years' duration, which comprise mainly fixed-term bank loans and overdrafts, are generally excluded from the term 'loan capital'.[117] Such loans include money-market instruments, which are short-term debt instruments (with less than a year's maturity)

---

[113] Expectations relating to the next dividend payment will, in principle, be reflected in the share price over the period that the shares are traded cum dividend before the next dividend payment.

[114] There are none in the model articles for PLCs or private companies.

[115] See Pennington, above n 18, 234 for historic restrictions requiring shareholders' approval for loans above a certain threshold. In the case of listed companies, the ABI generally expects borrowing to be limited to twice capital and reserves and such a limitation can be included in the articles of association.

[116] See Chapter 4.5 for an explanation of the legal nature of debentures.

[117] Short-term loans of up to one year's duration are generally referred to as commercial paper.

used by treasury departments to manage the short-term financing needs of companies. Eurobonds are a special type of loan issued by companies.[118]

Debentures and loans are frequently issued in the form of 'stock'. Old forms of debenture were issued to a single lender, but over time the process of issuing debentures adapted to the need to raise loan capital from large numbers of investors. The modern procedure is for the loan to be made to trustees, who are the creditors of the company for the whole amount of the loan plus interest. This offers the benefit that the company does not have to deal directly with large numbers of small creditors. The individual subscribers are issued with 'debenture stock', which evidences their share in the loan but does not make them creditors of the company. The debenture stockholders' rights are primarily against the trustees who act on their behalf. The trust deed normally provides that the debenture stockholders rank *pari passu* (equally) as regards their rights, thereby avoiding the possibility that any one holder can gain a preference or priority over the others.

Like shares, instruments representing loan capital have a nominal value, which is the sum repayable to the lender on maturity. Unlike shares, they can be and are issued at a discount to their nominal value. This has the effect that the amount of the discount repayable at maturity is capital rather than income, which may give rise to tax benefits. It also allows the contractual rate of interest for loan capital (the 'coupon' in market parlance) to be set well in advance of the issue date, as the issue price can be fixed closer to the issue date so as to make the redemption yield[119] on the issue attractive in relation to comparable securities.

Redemption of debentures can occur in a variety of ways, according to the loan agreement. It is unusual for repayment of the entire loan to be made at a fixed date. More commonly, repayment is made by instalments over a period of between 2 and 5 years before the final date for repayment. The loan agreement can provide for repayments to be distributed pro rata across all holders, or alternatively it can provide for lots to be drawn to determine which debentures shall be repaid from each instalment. It is possible for a premium to be payable by the company on redemption of debentures. This can be provided for by the loan agreement (eg if the company wants to pay the loan before maturity) or can be agreed at the time of repayment.

7.5.2 Loan agreements

In principle, loans to companies can be made on any terms.[120] The terms of a loan agreement, including the rate of interest, will reflect the creditworthiness of the borrowing company. In the case of loan capital that is to be listed and offered to the public, it is common for the borrower to arrange for a credit rating to be attached to the loan by

---

[118] See Chapter 4.5.

[119] The redemption yield is the return earned by holding a fixed-interest security to maturity. It may vary over the term of a fixed interest security according to prevailing interest rates. See J Rutterford, *An Introduction to Stock Exchange Investment*, 3rd edn (Basingstoke, Palgrave MAcmillan, 2007) 87.

[120] Controls over interest rates do not apply (as they potentially do to consumer credit under s 140A of the Consumer Credit Act 1974), nor do the controls over contract terms contained in the Unfair Contract Terms Act 1977 or the Unfair Terms in Consumer Contracts Regulations 1999, SI 1999/2083.

a credit rating agency.[121] The purpose of a credit rating is to provide an independent assessment of the ability of a borrower to meet its loan obligations. In general terms, the better the credit rating, the better the terms on which a company can borrow.

Lenders generally adopt three techniques to protect against the risks inherent in lending to companies. First, loan agreements generally guarantee the accuracy of the information on which a lender has made a lending decision. This is achieved through conditions precedent and representations and warranties in loan agreements. Secondly, covenants in loan agreements protect lenders against the risk of a debtor acting in a manner that prejudices the interests of the lender after the loan has been advanced. Thirdly, lenders often take a security interest so as to ensure that, in the event of a borrower defaulting, assets will be available from which the debt can be repaid. Each technique is now considered in turn.

7.5.3 Conditions precedent; representations and warranties

The purpose of conditions precedent is to ensure that the lender is only required to advance the money to the borrower if the conditions are met. If the conditions are not met the loan agreement remains valid, but the obligation to advance money cannot be enforced until there is compliance with the conditions precedent.[122] The conditions typically relate to the legal capacity of the borrower to enter into the agreement and the delivery to the lender of satisfactory security documents.

The purpose of representations and warranties in a loan agreement is to guarantee the accuracy of the information on which a lending decision is based. Factors relevant to that decision include the financial position of a company; the authority given to directors to enter into loan agreements; litigation pending against the company; pre-existing loans and security interests; and compliance with relevant laws and regulations. A loan agreement will normally specify that an incorrect representation or warranty is an act of default, giving the lender the right to call for repayment of the loan. This avoids the technical arguments which would otherwise arise as a result of the different implications in contract law arising from a breach of a warranty and a misrepresentation.[123]

7.5.4 Covenants

Covenants in loan agreements vary according to the bargaining position of the lender and the nature of the loan.[124] They are intended to ensure that a borrower remains able to fulfil its loan obligations, which are the repayment of both interest and capital. The most

---

[121] See Chapter 10.

[122] See Gullifer and Payne, above n 69, 167.

[123] These terms have a specific meaning in the law of contract in England: see E Peel, *Treitel, The Law of Contract*, 12th edn (London, Sweet & Maxwell, 2007) 362 and 879–83. While they may be used in loan agreements subject to Scots law, they do not have the same default meaning in that context: see W McBryde, *Contract*, 3rd edn (Edinburgh, W Green, 2007) ch 20.

[124] See P Wood, 'Bondholders and Banks—Why the Difference in Protections?' (2011) 6(2) *Capital Markets Law Journal* 188, who concludes that bondholders benefit from bank monitoring of covenants as bonds issued in the capital markets do not generally contain the covenants that are typically found in bank loans. For typical

common forms of covenant are those relating to the financial position of the company. They can include minimum requirements as to a company's level of working capital and net assets or prohibitions on dividend distributions above a certain level or substantial asset disposals. They can also include reporting covenants, which require the debtor to provide the lender with ongoing financial information, in addition to that which is publicly available.[125] It is also possible to prevent or restrict the creation of new security interests during the term of a loan, through the insertion of a 'negative pledge' clause. Breach of a covenant is normally an act of default under the loan agreement, giving the lender the right to terminate the loan agreement and demand repayment of the loan. However, there is no automatic termination, leaving the lender with the option of adopting a policy of forbearance in the hope that the financial position of the borrower may improve such that repayment in the agreed manner can be resumed later.

7.5.5 Security Interests

There are several reasons for taking security in connection with the making of loans.[126] One is that legal regimes governing insolvency generally permit various forms of security interest to be given priority in the distribution of assets that are available on insolvency.[127] Another is that a security interest may permit the lender to take over the project against which the loan has been made.[128] Thirdly, in international transactions, it may be difficult to enforce contractual rights against a borrower, in which case rights against specific assets may encourage compliance or facilitate enforcement. Fourthly, in the financial markets security may be taken not just for the purposes of providing protection against default by the borrower but also so as to provide liquidity to the lender, through the right to use the secured assets to secure the lender's obligations to third parties.[129] Finally, the capital requirements imposed on banks[130] are lower in the case of secured loans than unsecured loans, with the result that there is an economic benefit in taking security where possible.

bond covenants see The Bond Covenant Group (ABI/BVI/IMA/NAPF) 'Model Covenants in Sterling and Euro Bond Issues', available at http://www.ivis.co.uk/Model_Covenants_In_Stg_and_Euro_bond_Issues.aspx.

[125] In that situation, it is possible for a lender of loan capital to be better informed than a shareholder. However, in the case of listed loan capital, lenders need to exercise caution in the use of inside information. See Chapter 13 for a discussion of legal controls over the use of such information.

[126] See generally C Bamford, *Principles of International Financial Law* (Oxford, Oxford University Press, 2011) ch 10.

[127] That remains the case even in systems that claim to prioritise the *pari passu* principle in their insolvency regime: see generally R Goode, *Principles of Corporate Insolvency Law* (London, Sweet & Maxwell, 2005) 3-01.

[128] This consideration is applicable more to project finance than to the typical issue of debentures or bonds to investors, where that solution is not usually appropriate.

[129] As noted by Bamford, above n 126, recognition of that possibility in Regulation 16 of the Financial Collateral (No 2) Regulations, SI 2003/3226 was not a novel departure in English law. The same could equally be said of Scots law.

[130] See Chapter 2.9.2.

The floating charge is the most common technique used by lenders to take security from companies.[131] It offers the benefit that it can cover any or all of the company's property and the company can continue to deal (buy and sell) in the property subject to the charge. Under a fixed charge[132] relating to specific property, by way of contrast, it is not possible for the company to sell the relevant property. The 'floating' characteristic reflects the fact that, prior to enforcement, property subject to the charge is constantly changing.

The Companies Act requires details of floating charges to be made available to the Registrar of Companies within 21 days of their creation, for the purposes of registration.[133] The purpose of registration is to publicise the existence of the security interest, as it may affect the likelihood of other creditors (in particular, ordinary trade creditors) recovering their debts in the event of the company's insolvency.[134] Information held by the Registrar of Companies is available to the general public.[135] Details of the charge must also be entered in the register of charges maintained by the company at its registered office.[136] If a floating charge is not registered within the statutory period, the holder loses her priority as against other secured creditors.[137] The precise meaning of that expression remains a matter of some doubt as the statute makes clear that the charge is not void, but does not make clear what the loss of priority means in all circumstances.[138]

When certain events occur, the floating charge is said to 'crystallise' or 'attach' to the relevant property. When the charge relates (as is commonly the case) to 'all the property and undertaking of the company', all the assets owned[139] by the company at that point in time become subject to the charge and cannot be sold. The effect of attachment is that the floating charge becomes a fixed charge, an event which has important consequences for the priority of the holder as against other creditors of the company.

The events that can result in attachment of a floating charge differ between England and Scotland, and represent different approaches to the manner in which creditors are

---

[131] The floating charge was recognised under the common law in England but was not recognised in Scotland until 1961. It is a statutory exception to the general rule in Scotland that transfer of possession to the creditor is necessary to create a valid security interest over property.

[132] Eg a legal mortgage in England or a standard security in Scotland.

[133] Companies Act 2006, s 860(1) for England and s 878(1) for Scotland. The requirement applies to other charges but does not cover quasi-security interests such as retention of title clauses in contracts of sale.

[134] However, the 21 day period for registration creates an 'invisibility' problem for creditors if registration is delayed within that period.

[135] There is a Registrar of Companies for companies incorporated in England in Cardiff and for companies incorporated in Scotland in Edinburgh.

[136] This register can be inspected freely by members and creditors and by the public on payment of a small charge.

[137] Companies Act 2006, s 874 for England, s 889 for Scotland. The substance of the provisions is the same but the separate system of property law and security interests in Scotland led to separate provisions in the Companies Act 1985, which have been carried forward. Measures to reform the law in Scotland are contained in pt 2 of the Bankruptcy and Diligence (Sc) Act 2007 but have not yet been brought into effect. Reform of the law in England has been considered, but no action has yet been taken: see generally the Law Commission, 'Company Security Interests', Law Com No 296, Cm 6654 (2005).

[138] See Gullifer and Payne, above n 69, ch 6.3.3.2; G Gretton, 'Registration of Company Charges' (2002) 6 *Edinburgh Law Review* 146.

[139] Assets held by a company as trustee or as agent are not owned by the company and do not become subject to the charge. As regards the status of property in respect of which a contract of sale has been agreed but no transfer has taken place, see *Sharp v Thomson* 1997 SLT 636.

treated on the insolvency of a company. In England, it is possible for the instrument creating a floating charge to specify which events will give rise to crystallisation, without any action being necessary on the part of the creditor ('automatic crystallisation').[140] In the absence of express provision, the instrument will be assumed to create implied terms providing for crystallisation in three circumstances. These are the appointment of a receiver by the holder of the floating charge, the commencement of the winding up of the company and the cessation of its business.

In Scotland, a more restrictive approach is adopted. A floating charge only attaches to the relevant property when a company goes into liquidation or on the appointment of a receiver.[141] It is not possible to have an 'automatic crystallisation' provision (as occurs in England). This restriction reflects concern over the potential prejudice that could be created for other creditors as a result of the occurrence of 'automatic crystallisation' events of which they are not aware. Liquidation and receivership, by way of contrast, are events that attract publicity and are therefore likely to put creditors on notice that they face problems in recovering debts from the relevant company.

Following the changes introduced by the Enterprise Act 2002, it is now more common for an administrator rather than a receiver to be appointed to a company that is in financial distress. The role of an administrator is essentially to ensure the continued survival of the company as a going concern.[142] If that is not possible, administration will normally be followed by liquidation. In those circumstances, the floating charge holder is entitled to repayment only after payment of, inter alia, holders of fixed charges[143] that rank ahead of the floating charge and preferential creditors. Fixed charges that have been created in accordance with relevant legal requirements[144] before a floating charge becomes a fixed charge (on attachment) take priority over the floating charge.[145]

The statutory priority in which a company's debts are to be repaid in receivership or liquidation can be varied by contract through the process of 'subordination'.[146] Secured debt can be subordinated by the making of a ranking agreement among the relevant creditors under which the holder of the secured debt accepts a lower priority than would otherwise be the case. Unsecured debt can be similarly subordinated if the relevant creditor simply agrees to accept that her claim ranks behind those of other creditors.[147]

---

[140] See *Re Brightlife Ltd* [1987] Ch 200 and *Re Permanent Houses (Holdings) Ltd* (1989) 5 BCC 151.

[141] Companies Act 1985, s 463(1) and Insolvency Act 1986 s 53(7).

[142] The appointment of an administrator does not in itself cause attachment of a floating charge.

[143] Such as a legal mortgage in England or standard security in Scotland. The position in Scotland will change following implementation of the 2007 Act: see s 40.

[144] Eg as to registration.

[145] The priority given to holders of fixed charges created before the floating charge crystallises (or attaches) means that it is important for lenders taking security in this form to ensure that there are no pre-existing fixed charges and that none is created while the charge remains 'floating'. This can be achieved through the use of a 'negative pledge' clause.

[146] This is not an attempt to place a debt outside the liquidation procedure, in which the *pari passu* principle applies, meaning that creditors are in principle treated equally unless they hold preferential rights. It should be distinguished from attempts to contract out of the (mandatory) scheme for distribution of debts on insolvency provided by the Insolvency Act 1986, which is prohibited by the common law rule principle of anti-deprivation: see further Gullifer and Payne, above n 69, 99.

[147] As there can be no question of the rights of other creditors being prejudiced in these circumstances, their consent is not required.

The purpose of subordination is generally to allow a company to borrow in a manner that does not threaten the interests of existing creditors. The subordination agreement can be enforced either by the company[148] against the relevant debenture holders or by a creditor[149] who is intended to benefit from the subordination.

---

[148] *Beswick v Beswick* [1968] AC 58.

[149] In England, under the Contracts (Rights of Third Parties) Act 1999, s 1(1)–(3); in Scotland, under the common law based on the *ius quaesitum tertio* (the right of a third party).

8

Corporate Finance— Listing and Public Offers

This chapter focuses on the regulatory regime that applies when a company wishes to raise capital through a public offer of its shares[1] or to have its shares traded on a public market. A public offer of shares is a form of external capital raising in the sense that the term was used in Chapter 7. Such an offer can be of new shares that are to be issued by the company or of shares that are already in issue, or a combination of both. In the case of new shares, the company will have identified the need for new capital and will set out its plans for use of the new capital in its offer document. In the case of an offer of shares already in issue, existing shareholders sell to new investors. The two forms of offer can be combined and both are said to take place in the 'primary market', which is distinguished from the 'secondary market', in which trading of shares occurs following their issue or sale. Companies coming to the public market for the first time to make an offer and have their shares traded on the market are described as making an 'initial public offer' (IPO). The process is also sometimes referred to as 'flotation' or 'going public'. These are forms of market rather than legal terminology and, as discussed below, the legal regime is based on concepts that overlap with but are not co-extensive with them.

There are a range of different reasons for IPOs. One is that the company may have exhausted the financing options that are available to it. This may be because the activity is too risky for debt finance or the scale of the financing necessitates access to a broad pool of investors. An IPO opens up the possibility of bringing in new investors, especially since the liquidity[2] of a company's shares will be greatly improved following an IPO. While shares that are not traded on a public market can be bought and sold privately, they lack the liquidity that arises from being continuously traded on an organised market. This feature is said to give rise to a 'liquidity premium' that investors are willing to pay for the benefit of liquidity.[3]

---

[1] The chapter also deals with other securities (eg bonds and derivatives), but the discussion focuses in particular on shares.

[2] Liquidity refers to the ease with which a financial instrument can be converted into cash.

[3] The rationale for the premium is that investors face less risk if they can liquidate their investment quickly. However, the recent credit crisis provides a salutary lesson as to how liquidity can quickly evaporate in crisis situations, even in asset classes not directly associated with the crisis.

Another reason for IPOs is what may be termed 'exit'. In the case of shares that are already in issue, a public offer provides an opportunity for existing shareholders (e.g the founder shareholders) to sell part of their shareholding. In that sense, a public offer provides an 'exit' for those shareholders, although it is normal for the founders to remain with the company in a significant management role so as to provide continuity. However, in its public-listed form, it is unlikely that founder-shareholders will be able to exert the same influence as when the company was in its formative stage, since both the regulatory regime and the presence of institutional investors are likely to cause significant changes in the relationship between the founder-shareholders and the company. In the case of venture capital and private equity firms,[4] 'exit' has become a standard part of their business model, meaning that they invest with the aim of realising their investment subsequently through an IPO.

The pattern of IPOs can be linked also with other influences. One is the prevailing political view of the role of state ownership in the economy. Thus, there have been periods during which privatisation has formed an important factor in the pattern of IPOs. Another, which is particularly noticeable in the context of IPOs undertaken by foreign companies, is regulation. While the relationship between regulation and the attractiveness of particular markets for IPOs is complex, changes in IPO numbers have been associated with changes in regulation.[5]

Finally, although the focus of this chapter is on companies 'going public', it should be noted that there has also been considerable traffic in the opposite direction in recent years as investors have concluded that companies can be run more effectively as private companies. This trend has been associated in particular with private equity 'buyouts', through which public-listed companies have been acquired through takeover and then converted to private companies. Among the reasons given for such buyouts has been that the regulatory regime for public listed companies has become unduly onerous, forcing boards of directors to focus as much on disclosure and public scrutiny as on strategic management.

8.1 Regulatory background

8.1.1 Listing and Public Offers

Listing is a regulatory process which makes the securities of a public company eligible for trading in a regulated market.[6] A public offer of securities is an invitation to the

---

[4] For an explanation of this term, see Chapter 5.4.

[5] For example, there was a marked decline in foreign company IPOs in the US following the introduction of the Sarbanes-Oxley Act in 2002.

[6] See Chapter 12.1 for the meaning of a regulated market.

general public to buy securities.[7] A public offer can be made in respect of listed or unlisted securities, and in practice it is common for a public offer to be made of securities that are to be listed. The focus of the law relating to public offers runs parallel to that relating to listing in that it aims to ensure that adequate disclosure is made in respect of the securities offered for sale. However, as a public offer will not always involve securities that are to be traded on an organised market, the law relating to public offers is more directly concerned with the fairness of the particular sale transaction involved in the public offer, whereas the law relating to listing has a broader focus on the fairness of the operation of the market as a whole.

Public offers of securities can take different legal forms. An offer for subscription invites the public to subscribe for shares that have not yet been issued. It therefore involves the raising of new capital by the company. An offer for sale is an offer made by shareholders to sell shares already in issue to the public: it does not in itself involve the raising of new capital. An investment bank can make this type of offer as an agent for the shareholders or as a principal, following acquisition of the shares by the bank. In the latter case, the bank will expect to sell the shares to the public at a profit. A public offer can be a combination of an offer for subscription and an offer for sale. A placing is another form of public offering in the sense that new shareholders are introduced to the company. It involves an offer being made to a limited number of professional investors and is thereby exempt from the requirement for the publication of a prospectus. A rights issue involves a company making an offer to existing investors pro rata to their existing shareholding.[8] An open offer is similar to a rights issue in that it is an offer of new securities to existing investors in those securities in proportion to their existing holdings but is not made by means of a renounceable letter of allotment.[9]

Other than when an investment bank acts as principal, the company (in the case of an offer for subscription) and selling shareholders (in the case of an offer for sale) face the risk that the offer may not be taken up. This may present serious problems, such as creating uncertainty over the funds available to the company for its future development. A solution is available in the form of underwriting. This involves an underwriter (or more likely a group of underwriters and sub-underwriters) agreeing to take up the offer to the extent that it is not taken up by public subscription. In return, the underwriters are paid a fee expressed as a percentage of the value of the issue.[10]

8.1.2 Regulatory objectives

There are three broad approaches to the regulation of listing. 'Merit-based' regulation involves a regulator reviewing the merits of securities in respect of which an application

---

[7] This is an explanatory definition. The legal definition (below) is more complex.

[8] See Chapter 7.3.2.

[9] See Chapter 7.3.3.

[10] For judicial comment on the nature of underwriting see *County Ltd v Girozentrale Securities* [1996] 1 BCLC 653, 670–73. For discussion of the role and duties of underwriters see *Eagle Trust plc v SBC Securities Ltd* [1995] BCC 231. See further Chapter 7.3.4.

for listing has been made.[11] The objective is to restrict listing to securities that are regarded, on objective criteria, as sound investments. 'Mandatory disclosure' is an alternative approach which assumes that investors can be left to make their own decisions so long as full disclosure is made by issuers.[12] In the UK, the latter approach has generally prevailed, although there have always been conditions for listing, which have had the effect of excluding some types of company from listing. Nevertheless, the broad powers[13] given to the Financial Services Authority (FSA) to determine which securities should be admitted to listing have not been viewed as a mandate for the introduction of 'merit-based' regulation. The main concern of the law and regulatory rules relating to listing in the UK is to ensure that, following listing of a company's securities, there will be a proper market, meaning one in which investors are able, at any point in time, to make fully informed investment decisions (eg to buy, sell or hold). Finally, although not generally favoured, it would in principle be possible to leave disclosure to be determined by market forces. This could result in either disclosure requirements being set on an individual basis or (more likely) some form of self-regulation being agreed between issuers and (professional) investors.[14]

8.1.3 The EU dimension and regulatory evolution

A feature of the regulatory regime for both listing and public offers is that they incorporate measures designed to facilitate the operation of the single market in the EU. As has been the case elsewhere in the financial sector, the EU's approach has been based mainly on the principles of minimum harmonisation and mutual recognition.[15] The rationale for this approach is that the creation of a core of common minimum standards across the EU enables (and obliges) Member States to recognise and give effect to regulatory approvals granted by other Member States. The intention is to make it easier for issuers to access the capital markets in other Member States, thereby increasing their potential sources of capital and possibly also lowering their cost of capital.

This minimum harmonisation approach has been followed in the Consolidated Admissions and Reporting Directive (CARD),[16] which sets the conditions that must be met for companies that are admitted to 'official listing'. That term is not itself defined in the

---

[11] Merit-based regulation was adopted by most states of the USA prior to the introduction of the federal securities laws in the 1930s. It was referred to as 'blue sky' law because it was claimed that many securities salesmen were so dishonest that they would sell 'buildings in the blue sky' to investors. For background and history see P Mahoney, 'The Origins of the Blue Sky Laws: A Test of Competing Hypotheses', available at SSRN: http://ssrn.com/abstract=296344 (accessed on 20 August 2011).

[12] It is linked with the efficient market hypothesis, which, in its semi-strong form, predicts that the prices of securities will reflect all publicly available information (ie there will be no pricing anomalies in respect of that information). For a discussion of the role of disclosure in modern securities markets see S Schwarcz, 'Rethinking the Disclosure Paradigm in a World of Complexity' (2004) 1 *University of Illinois Law Review* 1.

[13] FSMA 2000, s 74(2) provides that 'The competent authority may admit to the official list such securities and other things as it considers appropriate'.

[14] See generally J Coffee, 'Market Failure and the Economic Case for a Mandatory Disclosure System' (1984) 70 *Virginia Law Review* 717.

[15] See generally Chapter 2.9.

[16] Directive 2001/34/EC [2001] OJ L184/1.

Directive and therefore the delimitation of 'official listing' falls to the competent authorities of the Member States so long as admission meets the requirements of the Directive. Following the minimum harmonisation approach, the CARD leaves open the possibility of Member States imposing more stringent requirements.[17] Thus, it is envisaged that the conditions for admission to 'official listing' will not be uniform across Member States and that even within Member States there will be the possibility to 'segment' the official list so as to create listing categories that may be attractive to different types of issuer. As discussed below, this option has been used in the UK to create different listing segments.

Following the adoption of the Financial Services Action Plan (FSAP) by the European Commission in 1999, there was a move away from reliance on minimum harmonisation and mutual recognition as regulatory techniques. This was evident in particular in the adoption of 'maximum harmonisation' in the Prospectus Directive[18] (PD). The main reason for this change was that the old approach had achieved only very limited progress in overcoming national barriers to cross-border listing and public offers. Maximum harmonisation, meaning in effect standardisation within the EU within the relevant field, held out the possibility of removing such barriers and simplifying the process of cross-border listing and capital raising.

Another development associated with the FSAP initiative was the decline in the significance of the concept of official listing as the cornerstone of the regulatory system. Two key developments lay behind this change. The first was a move away from the old regulatory model under which national exchanges had a virtual monopoly over listing and trading in securities. Associated with that process were changes in the structure of many stock exchanges, which converted from member-controlled mutual organisations to shareholder-owned and for-profit entities.[19] Since it seemed inappropriate to entrust regulatory functions (with an inherent public interest dimension) to the stock exchanges (in their new form), a distinction was drawn between admission to listing (overseen by a competent regulatory authority) and admission to trading on a 'regulated market' (overseen by the market). The second was the emergence of alternative trading systems which competed with but were not regulated as stock exchanges.[20] By referencing regulatory obligations to the new concept of 'regulated markets', the EU regulatory system created a structure under which alternative trading systems could compete directly with the older established stock exchanges. The objective of increasing competition was implicit in this approach, since new exchanges were given the choice between becoming regulated markets, with the same status as the older established stock exchanges, or, alternatively, operating without that designation but with a less onerous regulatory regime. In the post-FSAP framework for listing and public offers, regulatory obligations are referenced to official listing only in connection with admission criteria (set out in CARD). The other FSAP directives (the Prospectus, Transparency Obligations and Market Abuse Directives)

---

[17] Such requirements must apply generally to all issuers or for individual classes of issuer.

[18] Directive 2003/71/EC [2003] OJ L345/64.

[19] See generally A Fleckner, 'Stock Exchanges at the Crossroads' (2006) 74 *Fordham Law Review* 2541, available at SSRN: http://ssrn.com/abstract=836464 (accessed on 20 August 2011).

[20] See further Chapter 12.3.

are applicable across all regulated markets, irrespective of whether or not the relevant securities are admitted to official listing.

The PD provides for 'passporting' of a prospectus following its approval by the home Member State.[21] This means that the passport remains valid for a 12 month period after its publication for offers to the public or admission to trading on a regulated market anywhere in the EU. Validity is made conditional on the publication of a supplement should new factors or information emerge that affect the assessment of the securities. Reflecting the barriers that had in the past been placed in the way of 'passporting' by Member States, the PD limits the role of a host Member State in the process. It expressly provides that 'Competent authorities of host Member States shall not undertake any approval or administrative procedures relating to prospectuses'.[22] The host Member State is entitled to receive notification from the competent authority in the home Member State that the prospectus has been duly approved, but that does not form a basis for intervention unless there are matters that require the publication of a supplementary prospectus. In the past, a host Member State could insist on the translation of the entire prospectus into their local language, but that right has been curtailed by the option given to issuers to publish the prospectus in a 'language customary in the field of international finance'. The PD also provides for the possibility of securities that are already admitted to trading on one regulated market to be admitted to another, provided that the issuer is in compliance with the listing obligations of the relevant market.[23] This is achieved by exempting such an admission to trading from the usual requirement for the publication of a prospectus at that time.[24]

While these provisions had the potential to facilitate cross-border listing and public issues in the EU, the reality is that they have been used very little. There are several reasons for this. One is that the necessity for cross-border listing has declined as investors have been prepared to trade on exchanges in other countries and links between markets have improved (eg through remote access and clearing arrangements). This has removed the need to list in other countries to gain access to local investors. Another has been the use of 'exempt' public offers by issuers. This offers the possibility of raising capital without the need to produce an approved prospectus and carries benefits in terms of the speed with which an issuer can access the market. A variant of the exempt offer is an 'international-style offering', which takes the form of a regulated public offer in one state (typically one such as the UK, with a well-developed capital market) and 'exempt' offers in other Member States. The exemption is based on one or more of those provided by the PD, such as the exemption relating to qualified investors.[25] Such an offer is capable of being taken up by the public at large in the first state and by qualified investors in other

---

[21] The home Member State is normally the state where the issuer has its registered office (Art 2(1)(m) of the PD).

[22] Art 17(1).

[23] This possibility was originally provided for in respect of 'listing particulars' by the CARD (Art 23(4)).

[24] See Art 4(1)(h) of the PD for the exemption.

[25] See section 8.3.2 below.

Member States. It thereby provides a mechanism through which a large pool of capital can be tapped through a prospectus that is regulated by only one country.[26]

The Transparency Obligations Directive (TD)[27] and the Market Abuse Directive (MAD),[28] while not directly concerned with the process of listing or the making of public offers, are of considerable significance for both purposes. The former is concerned primarily with the obligations of listed entities, and both amends and augments the regime for disclosure established in the CARD (above).[29] It has been implemented in the UK primarily by changes made to the FSA Handbook.[30] It is linked with the MAD in that both directives have a strong focus on disclosure of information to the market: the TD mandates the disclosure of minimum levels of periodic disclosure of information by issuers, while the MAD requires disclosure of 'inside information' to the market and prohibits misuse or unauthorised disclosure of such information prior to its public disclosure.[31] The MAD is relevant not just for listed entities, but also for any entity whose securities are traded on prescribed markets in the UK.[32] The MAD changed the definition of what constitutes market abuse[33] and was implemented in the UK through changes made to part VIII of the Financial Services and Markets Act 2000 (FSMA 2000) and the FSA Handbook.

8.1.4 Corporate finance firms

Making or advising on a public offer is a form of regulated activity under FSMA 2000 and therefore requires authorisation.[34] That process brings the relevant firms (normally investment banks and/or corporate brokers) within the regulatory perimeter and requires them to comply with the FSA Handbook in advising on and managing a public offer. Firms undertaking those activities will often be the 'sponsor' that is required in the case of premium listed firms.[35] The sponsor has specific obligations which it owes to the FSA as the Listing Authority to ensure that the company satisfies the listing criteria and is guided through the listing process.[36]

---

[26] See generally H Jackson and E Pan, 'Regulatory Competition in International Securities Markets: Evidence from Europe in 1999—part 1' (2001) 56 *Business Law* 653.

[27] Directive 2004/109/EC [2004] OJ L390/38.

[28] Directive 2003/6/EC [2003] OJ L96/16.

[29] A related development was that all companies whose securities are admitted to trading on a regulated market in the EU were required to implement International Accounting Standards from 1 January 2005 (see Regulation 1606/2002/EC [2002] OJ L243/1).

[30] This includes the insertion in the FSA Handbook (Disclosure Rules and Transparency Rules, DTR) of the rules relating to disclosure of the acquisition and disposal of major shareholdings following the repeal of ss 198–220 of the Companies Act 1985 with effect from 20 January 2007. See further Chapter 13.1.

[31] See further Chapter 13.4.7.

[32] Markets 'prescribed' for the purposes of the market abuse regime in the UK are not limited to 'regulated markets': for example, AIM is included.

[33] From that contained in pt VIII of FSMA 2000 as originally enacted. See Chapter 13.4.

[34] See Chapter 3.5 regarding regulated activities. Note that an issuer does not require authorisation for a public offer as that activity is not undertaken by way of business.

[35] See the Listing Rules, LR 8.2.1R.

[36] See the Listing Rules, LR 8.3.

The FSA Handbook focuses in particular on the conflict of interest faced by a corporate finance firm in those circumstances. That conflict arises from the duties that are owed at the same time to the issuer and to the investment clients of the firm. One aspect of the conflict is that an issuer wants to maximise the issue price whereas new investors want to buy at the lowest price possible. Another aspect is that corporate finance firms may want to give preference to favoured clients whereas the issuer is likely to be more concerned with attracting long-term investors who can support the strategic objectives of the issuer. A further consideration is the impartiality of investment research produced by a firm advising on an IPO.[37]

In recognition of these conflicts, the FSA Handbook provides guidance to corporate finance firms that:

A firm will wish to note that when carrying on a mandate to manage an offering of securities, the firm's duty for that business is to its corporate finance client (in many cases, the corporate issuer or seller of the relevant securities), but that its responsibilities to provide services to its investment clients are unchanged.[38]

The FSA Handbook goes on to suggest ways in which the conflict of interest can be managed, such as by agreeing with the issuer how the offering will be allocated in the case of oversubscription, how the price will be set and how the firm's proprietary trading unit will participate in the offering.

8.2 The Structure of the UK listing regime

In the past, the UK listing regime comprised a unified set of rules that were referred to as the Listing Rules. They covered the conditions for admission, disclosure in the listing particulars, periodic and ongoing disclosure obligations and continuing obligations. However, the increasing influence of EU regulation and the division of these matters between different directives led to the FSA adopting a structure for the listing regime that corresponds more closely with the EU structure. Thus, the FSA Handbook block entitled 'Listing, Prospectus and Disclosure' is split into three corresponding sections: Listing (LR), which comprises the conditions for listing and continuing obligations of listed companies; Prospectus (PR), comprising the obligation to publish an approved prospectus and its contents; and Disclosure and Transparency (DTR), comprising disclosure and corporate governance requirements for issuers.

---

[37] See Chapter 15.3.4.

[38] SYSC 10.1.13 G. This is in addition to the other conflict of interest provisions of the FSA Handbook (implementing the Markets in Financial Instruments Directive) that apply to all investment firms: see Chapter 15.2.5.

8.2.1 Official listing

While, as mentioned above, the EU regulatory framework has shifted its focus away from 'official listing', it remains important in the UK context for two reasons. First, the designation 'listed' distinguishes securities admitted to 'official listing' from those that are not. Securities that are not admitted to the official list are not 'listed' for this purpose even if they are admitted to trading on a market such as the Alternative Investment Market (AIM). The essential distinction for the investor is that 'official listing' imposes more onerous admission conditions on companies by comparison with 'unlisted' securities. The designation 'listed' also implies (at least in the case of equity shares) that the securities are traded on a regulated market,[39] which is subject to more onerous regulation than markets which do not fall into that category.

The legal framework governing listing and public offers is as follows:

1 Securities which are to be admitted to 'official listing' are governed by part VI of FSMA 2000.[40] This applies also to securities when a public offer is made at the same time as listing (in which case the offer is referred to as an IPO).

2 Public offers of unlisted securities are regulated by the PD. This is relevant when the securities are not to be admitted to 'official listing' (eg when admission is to AIM).

3 Offers of securities falling outside both part VI of FSMA 2000 and the PD are subject to the provisions of section 21 of the Financial Services and Markets Act 2000, which regulates the activity described as 'financial promotion'.[41]

4 Certain matters relating to the allotment of shares and debentures remain within the scope of company law.[42]

5 Special rules, implementing the 'passporting' principle, apply when a company wants to make a simultaneous offer of its securities in two or more Member States of the EU.[43]

Admission to listing is controlled by the FSA. It is the 'competent authority' for the purposes of the EU directives relating to listing and public offers, which require such an authority to be designated in each Member State. When discharging its responsibilities, the FSA must have regard to six regulatory principles, which are similar to the principles that must be observed by the FSA when discharging its general functions under FSMA 2000 as a whole.[44] Listing particulars or a prospectus (when listing is accompanied by

---

[39] This is the case at least for equity shares. Debt instruments and derivatives may be admitted to the Professional Securities Market, which is not a regulated market for EU purposes.

[40] As amended by implementation of the PD.

[41] See Chapter 3.6 regarding financial promotion. In these circumstances, the offer must be approved by a person authorised under FSMA 2000.

[42] See J Birds (ed), *Boyle & Birds' Company Law*, 8th edn (Bristol, Jordans, 2011) ch 7.

[43] See ss 87H and 87I FSMA 2000.

[44] See Chapter 3. Note that the 'general functions' in s 2(4) FSMA 2000 do not apply to the FSA's role as competent authority (s 72(2) and sch 7 FSMA 2000). The Act's regulatory objectives (ss 3–6) therefore do not apply to the FSA as competent authority. This reflects the dominance of EU directives (based primarily on the single market integration objective) in relation to listing and public offers and the obligation of the competent authority to give effect to the EU directives.

a public offer) must be approved by the appropriate regulator (either the FSA or the competent authority in another EEA Member State) and published.

Applications for listing must be made to the UKLA, which is required to make a decision on admission within 6 months.[45] A listing application can only be made by or with the consent of the issuer of the securities concerned.[46] This removes the possibility of a listing application being made by a substantial shareholder who may not be able to satisfy the disclosure obligations imposed by FSMA 2000 and the Listing Rules. An application may be refused if, for a reason relating to the issuer, the competent authority considers that granting it would be detrimental to the interests of investors.[47] If the competent authority decides to refuse an application for listing, the applicant may refer the matter to the Upper Tribunal.[48]

The concept of the official list as a single category has been eroded over time by a number of developments. One is the policy adopted in the UK whereby 'superequivalent' requirements have been imposed over and above the minimum standards set by EU directives. This led to the designation of 'primary listing', requiring compliance with the 'superequivalents', and 'secondary listing', based on the EU directives' minimum standards. Secondary listing was available to all companies incorporated outside the UK, although in practice it was mainly used by non-EU companies. Another factor was the emergence and growth of depositary receipts as a form of foreign listing and the creation of a special listing regime for that type of security, based on the EU directives' minimum standards. All three categories (primary, secondary and depositary receipt) were typically referred to as forms of 'London listing' despite the presence of significant differences in the relevant listing rules.[49] In response to concerns that the reputation and status of a London listing was being threatened by this confusion, the FSA made changes to the structure of the listing regime that took effect in 2010.[50] The new structure is based on two segments, 'premium' and 'standard', which are intended to provide a clearer description of the type of listing of the relevant securities and the obligations associated with listing.[51]

---

[45] FSMA 2000, s 76.

[46] FSMA 2000, s 75(2).

[47] FSMA 2000, s 75(5). It is virtually unknown for this provision to be used as a basis for rejecting an application and it does not form the basis for a 'merit-based' approach to regulating listing and public issues (see n 11 above).

[48] FSMA 2000, s 76(6). Note that the Upper Tribunal replaced the Financial Services and Markets Tribunal in April 2010: see the Transfer of Tribunal Functions Order 2010, SI 2010/22.

[49] The problem was further exacerbated by the tendency to refer to admission to AIM as 'London listing' despite AIM not being part of the Official List. The confusion was compounded by the fact that AIM is run by the London Stock Exchange, which is a recognised investment exchange and operates the main market for listed securities in the UK.

[50] For background see FSA, 'A Review of the Structure of the Listing Regime', Discussion Paper (DP) 08/1 (2008); 'Consultation on Amendment to the Listing Rules and Feedback on DP 08/1,' Consultation Paper (CP) 08/21 (2008); 'Listing Regime Review', CP 09/24 (2009); 'Listing Regime Review: Consultation on Changes to the Listing Categories Consequent to CP09/24', CP 09/28 (2009).

[51] For a graphic illustration of the new regime and the categories of securities associated with each segment see FSA CP 09/28 (2009) 11.

8.2.2 Premium listing

This segment is reserved for equity securities, reflecting the fact that in the past the 'superequivalent' requirements imposed by the FSA were framed by reference to equity securities, while only minimum EU directive standards[52] were applied to debt securities. That basic approach remains in place and the designation 'premium' is intended to convey the more onerous regulatory obligations (and hence investor protection) associated with the segment.

Among the conditions specified for admission to this segment (over and above those mentioned above for any form of official listing) are:

1. The market value of the shares to be listed must be at least £700,000 (though, in practice, an applicant may have difficulty in finding a broker or issuing house to sponsor the issue,[53] and may find the costs involved make an official listing prohibitively expensive unless the value of the securities involved is substantially greater than this).
2. The company must normally have a trading record of at least 3 years and must have unqualified audited accounts for those 3 years.
3. The company must demonstrate that: (i) at least 75% of its business is supported by a historic revenue earning record which covers the period for which accounts are required under condition 2; (ii) it controls the majority of its assets and has done so for at least the period referred to in condition 2; and (iii) it will be carrying on an independent business as its main activity.[54] This is intended to permit investors to make an independent assessment of the company's business prospects (eg where the listing applicant has been demerged from a larger group).
4. The company must be able to state that it is satisfied, after due and careful inquiry, that it has sufficient working capital for at least the next 12 months.[55]
5. The shares must be freely transferable and at least 25% must be in the hands of the public after the flotation.
6. Equity shares must be admitted to trading on a regulated market for listed securities operated by a Recognised Investment Exchange. All other securities must be admitted to trading on a Recognised Investment Exchange's market for listed securities.[56]
7. The shares must be eligible for electronic settlement, which will take place within CREST.

Following admission, a premium listing is distinguished from a standard listing by a range of 'superequivalent' requirements. Important examples are:

---

[52] These are the standards set by the CARD and the TD.

[53] LR 8.2.1R sets out the requirement to have a sponsor in the case of a premium listing of equity securities.

[54] Note that the previous requirement to show independence from a controlling shareholder has been removed.

[55] This is the only forward-looking statement which an applicant is required to make. The requirement can be set aside in certain cases (eg entities whose solvency is regulated).

[56] This permits such securities to be traded on the Professional Securities Market, which is not a 'regulated market' for the purposes of the EU directives.

- the 'continuing obligations' (LR 9), which control the relationship between an issuer and its shareholders;
- the Listing Principles (LR 7), which are designed to help issuers identify their obligations under the Listing Rules;
- the 'significant transactions' rules (LR10), which require disclosure and (in some cases) shareholder approval for major transactions;
- the 'related party' rules (LR 11), which set safeguards for transactions between an issuer and related parties; and
- rules covering repurchases of the issuer's own shares (LR 12).

8.2.3 Standard listing

Prior to the restructuring of the UK listing regime, which took effect in April 2010, this form of listing was applicable to secondary listing of shares by foreign companies and listing of debt securities by any issuer. Prior to 2005, a company seeking a secondary listing in the UK was required to have a listing in its country of incorporation but that restriction was removed in that year, prompted by the need to provide for listing of EU companies in accordance only with the (minimum) requirements of the EU directives. The 2010 restructuring makes a standard listing available to UK incorporated companies on the basis that it will provide a level playing field and greater choice for UK companies. The requirements for admission to a standard listing are less onerous than in the case of a premium listing. Conditions 2, 3, 4 and 7 in 8.2.2 above do not apply in the case of a standard listing, which is based on the minimum requirements set by the EU directives.

8.2.4 Foreign listing: context

Foreign listing refers to a company listing its securities in a country other than the one in which it is incorporated.[57] There are several reasons why foreign listings occur. One is that the country in which a company is incorporated does not have the scale of capital market that is appropriate to the company's requirements. This can arise in a number of different circumstances. First, a limited shareholder base in the country of incorporation may restrict the ability to raise capital. Secondly, there may be limited trading opportunities in the company's shares in the stockmarket of the country of incorporation (eg as a result of poor liquidity). Thirdly, a deliberate choice may be made to incorporate the company in a jurisdiction without a developed capital market in the knowledge that it will seek a foreign listing in the jurisdiction in which the company has most of its business operations.[58] There may also be taxation advantages to be gained through foreign incorporation.

---

[57] In the past this was often referred to in the UK as 'overseas listing'. See generally I MacNeil and A Lau, 'International Corporate Regulation: Listing Rules and Overseas Companies' (2001) 50 *International and Comparative Law Quarterly* 787.

[58] This is a common occurrence in Hong Kong: see S Chan, I MacNeil and A Lau, 'Lawyers' Perceptions of Overseas Incorporated Companies Listed in Hong Kong' 16 (2001) *Managerial Auditing Journal* 290–96.

In principle, two forms of foreign listing can be distinguished: a 'primary' or a 'secondary' foreign listing. A primary foreign listing occurs when a company that has no listing in its country of incorporation obtains a listing in another country.[59] A secondary listing occurs when a company incorporated and listed in its home country obtains a listing in another country.[60] From the regulatory perspective, a company with a primary foreign listing is treated no differently to other listed companies, meaning that it is subject to the full requirements applicable to listing in that country. In the case of a secondary listing, some concessions from the standard requirements for listing may be permitted.[61]

The rationale for a secondary listing differs from a primary listing because in this situation a company will already have a listing and therefore the main issue is whether there are advantages in having a second listing on a different market. Research suggests that, for London, the following factors are of broadly similar significance: the large investor base in the UK, the liquidity of the London stockmarket and the possibility of raising new capital.[62] As the London market has a global role in capital raising and trading shares of foreign companies, it is an attractive listing destination for foreign companies who wish to extend their shareholder base and to ensure the level of liquidity in the trading of their shares that will be required by large institutional investors. Other factors may also be relevant, such as the ability to issue shares to investors within the secondary listing jurisdiction to finance a takeover and the facilitation of share ownership by local employees. The regulatory regime is also a significant factor and may encourage some companies to have their shares admitted to trading on AIM[63] rather than the official list as a result of the less onerous regulatory regime.

The 'bonding' explanation for foreign listings predicts that high standards of regulation in one country will attract listings from countries with lower standards of regulation.[64] This results not from any desire to be more heavily regulated per se, but from the expectation that a company which 'bonds' to a higher regulatory standard (particularly as regards the quantity and quality of information made available to investors) will benefit from a higher share price. The result of regulatory competition according to the 'bonding' hypothesis is that there will be a general movement towards higher regulatory standards in listing rules as a result of competition between jurisdictions.

It is possible for companies seeking a foreign listing to list securities that have been 'repackaged' specifically for that purpose. This occurs frequently in the case of depositary receipts,[65] which are attractive to companies because of the less onerous regulatory obligations applicable to them by comparison with listing the underlying securities. The rationale for the lower regulatory burden is that the relevant securities cannot be sold

---

[59] For UK incorporated companies this is a relatively rare occurrence.

[60] New York, London, Hong Kong and Singapore are the main destinations for companies seeking a foreign listing.

[61] For an assessment of the concessions made (in the past) by the UKLA and Hong Kong listing rules see Chan et al, n 58 above.

[62] See Chan et al, ibid.

[63] See section 8.2.7 below for more detail on AIM.

[64] See I MacNeil, 'Competition and Convergence in Corporate Regulation: The Case of Overseas Listed Companies' (2001), available at SSRN: http://ssrn.com/abstract=278508 (accessed on 20 August 2011).

[65] See Chapter 4.9 for a discussion of the nature of depositary receipts.

freely to the public in the secondary listing jurisdiction and therefore the information asymmetry basis for regulation is not as strong as if that were possible.[66]

In 2007 the FSA initiated a review of the listing regime. The review was prompted by two main concerns. One was that a degree of confusion had emerged as regards the use of the term 'official listing' as a result of the emergence of different segments and markets offered by the FSA and the London Stock Exchange.[67] The other concern was to ensure that the UK remained competitive as a listing destination for foreign companies. The outcome of that review was that changes to the listing regime were implemented with effect from 6 April 2010. The most significant change was that the listing segments were redesignated 'premium' and 'standard',[68] with the former being reserved for equity shares of commercial companies, closed-end investment funds and open-ended investment companies who meet the enhanced requirements applicable to this category. Other categories of securities that had in the past been eligible for a 'primary' listing (eg debt securities and global depositary receipts) are now restricted to the 'standard' category. Moreover, a clear distinction is drawn between the premium category, where issuers are subject to requirements that exceed those contained in relevant EU directives (so-called 'superequivalents' or 'gold plating') and the standard category, where issuers are subject only to the minimum standards set by the EU directives.

8.2.5 Foreign listing: the UK listing regime

Prior to the restructuring of the UK listing regime in 2010, the terminology of 'primary and secondary' foreign listing and the general approach mentioned above were adopted in the UK. Since then, the concept of primary listing has been merged into premium listing (above) and the concept of secondary listing has been merged into standard listing (above).[69] However, the change in terminology has not altered the underlying differences between the two forms of listing as far as intensity of regulation is concerned, since, as explained above, that forms the basis of the distinction between the two segments in the new structure. All issuers of equity securities now have a choice between a premium and a standard listing. In the case of EU issuers, access to a standard listing is easier than for non-EU issuers since the admission and prospectus requirements are common to all EU members and those issuers can use the 'passporting' provisions contained in the PD. For non-EU issuers, a standard listing is likely to be the more obvious choice, and will be the only choice if the relevant securities are debt or depositary receipts.

Changes made to the obligations of premium listed foreign companies as part of the 2010 restructuring are also a relevant factor in considering a premium listing. Prior to

---

[66] Regarding the form and regulation of secondary listing in the US see JC Coffee, 'Competition among Securities Markets: A Path Dependent Perspective', Columbia Law School, The Center for Law and Economic Studies, Working Paper No 192 (2002), available at SSRN: http://ssrn.com/abstract=283822 (accessed on 20 August 2011).

[67] See FSA DP 08/1, above n 50, ch 3 for an overview of those segments and markets.

[68] This superseded the previous division between 'primary' and 'secondary' listing.

[69] The new structure follows the established pattern of applying more onerous admission requirements and continuing obligations to a premium listing by comparison with a standard listing.

the 2010 restructuring, there were some concessions that were granted to primary listed (now premium listed) foreign companies. They related to compliance with the Combined Code of Corporate Governance,[70] shareholders' pre-emption rights and compliance with the Takeover Code. In recognition of differences in their governance structure and shareholders' rights arising from the law of their jurisdiction of incorporation, foreign companies were required only to disclose significant ways in which their governance practices differed from the Combined Code and were not required to give effect to shareholders' pre-emption rights. The Listing Rules were in the past silent as regards compliance with the Takeover Code and that remained the case when the Code was placed on a statutory basis (following implementation of the EC Takeovers Directive), since the UK Takeover Panel generally does not have jurisdiction in relation to companies incorporated outside the UK even if they are admitted to trading on a regulated market in the UK. The FSA chose to change its approach to the Combined Code and pre-emption rights in the 2010 restructuring, with the result that foreign companies are required to 'comply or explain' against the Combined Code and to observe pre-emption rights when they make cash offers.[71] No action was taken in respect of the Takeover Code since the FSA lacks any legal basis to require compliance by companies which do not fall within its scope. However, the FSA has noted the market pressure created by the FTSE UK Series Index, which takes into consideration compliance with all three of these issues for the purposes of inclusion of a company in an index.[72]

8.2.6 Admission to trading on a regulated market

It is a requirement for admission to listing that equity shares[73] must be traded on a regulated market for listed securities but admission to listing does not itself secure that outcome. A second regulatory barrier must be overcome, which is admission to trading on a regulated market.[74] In the past, these two regulatory stages were combined as the London Stock Exchange (LSE) was the 'competent authority' for listing[75] and had an effective monopoly over trading in listed securities. Two developments led to change. The first was the demutualisation of the LSE, resulting in it becoming a company listed on the LSE. The second was the emergence of competitors to the LSE in the form both of recognised investment exchanges and alternative markets.[76] These developments made it inappropriate for the LSE to continue to act as a regulator ('competent authority' for the purposes of the EU directives) and therefore the Treasury exercised its power to

---

[70] As it was then known. It is now referred to as the UK Corporate Governance Code.

[71] See FSA CP 09/24, above n 50, for the FSA's policy statement on these issues.

[72] This may carry direct implications for investment by investors whose mandate is linked explicitly with certain indices. See Chapter 5.6 regarding investment mandates.

[73] All other securities must be admitted to trading on a Recognised Investment Exchange's market for listed securities. This permits those securities to be traded on the Professional Securities Market, which is not a 'regulated market' for the purposes of the EU directives.

[74] See further Chapter 12.3.1 for the meaning of this term.

[75] Under the relevant EU directives.

[76] See further Chapter 12.3.

transfer responsibility to the FSA.[77] The new structure involves a division of regulatory responsibility between the FSA, which is responsible for compliance with the listing rules, and recognised investment exchanges, which are responsible for compliance with their rules relating to trading (eg trade reporting, execution of transactions).[78] In addition to the LSE, a market for listed securities is operated by PLUS Markets Ltd, which is a recognised investment exchange under FSMA 2000.[79]

8.2.7 Admission to trading on other markets

The CARD is concerned only with admission to the Official List. There are currently no EU or UK statutory conditions for admission of securities without an official listing to trading on markets. Conditions for admission refer to requirements relating to the issuer or the securities that are to be admitted and can be considered separately from the obligation to publish an approved prospectus that is contained in the PD. In the absence of regulatory provisions, admission to trading on markets is regulated contractually by individual markets.

The most prominent market example of a market that has chosen not to be a regulated market is AIM, which is operated by the London Stock Exchange. The conditions for admission to AIM are less onerous than the Official List, reflecting the objective that AIM should provide a market for relatively new companies.[80] The main conditions are as follows:[81]

1. The company must be permitted by its national law to offer its securities to the public. In the UK, this means that it must be a public limited company.
2. The securities to be traded on the market must be freely transferable and eligible for electronic transfer (via CREST).
3. The company must appoint and retain a nominated adviser (NOMAD) and a nominated broker.
4. The company must state that it has sufficient working capital to meet its requirements for the 12 months following its date of admission to AIM.
5. The company must accept continuing obligations with regard to such matters as preparation of accounts, disclosure of substantial transactions and shareholder approval for fundamental changes of business.

By comparison with the admission requirements for a primary listing, there is no minimum requirement for shares to be held in public hands, no requirement for a 3 year trading record and no minimum market capitalisation. It follows that it is easier for a company

---

[77] See the Official Listing of Securities (Transfer of Competent Authority) Regulations 2000, SI 2000/968. The Treasury has power to transfer (by order) the functions of the competent authority to another person: FSMA 2000, s 72(3) and sch 8.

[78] See further Chapters 12.3.1 and 13.1.2.

[79] See http://www.plusmarketsgroup.com/(accessed on 16 August 2011).

[80] For more detail see www.londonstockexchange.com (accessed on 16 August 2011).

[81] See the AIM rules for companies at http://www.londonstockexchange.com/companies-and-advisors/aim/documents/aim-rules-for-companies.pdf.

to meet the admission requirements for AIM than it is to satisfy the requirements for admission to the 'official list'.

The NOMAD plays a key role in AIM's regulatory framework in two ways. First, it is the NOMAD and not AIM (nor its operator the London Stock Exchange) that is responsible for determining if a company is eligible to join AIM. Secondly, there is no regulatory approval required for the admission document that an AIM applicant must submit to the exchange prior to admission. Compliance with AIM's requirements for the admission document is ensured by the requirement that the NOMAD must confirm compliance. If a prospectus is required (typically because a non-exempt public offer is being made in conjunction with admission to AIM), it will be vetted by the FSA in the same manner as applies to listed companies.

In the case of debt securities, depositary receipts and convertibles, it is possible for listed securities to be admitted to the Professional Securities Market (PSM), despite the fact that it is not a regulated market.[82] This has the result that the relevant securities are admitted to the official list but there is no requirement to produce a prospectus (so long as the offer is an exempt offer for the purposes of the PD) since that obligation is triggered by admission to a regulated market. It also has the effect that the continuing disclosure obligations derived from the TD do not apply to those securities. In particular, it means that the requirement to prepare financial information according to the International Financial Reporting Standards (IFRS), or an EU-approved equivalent standard, does not apply to the listing particulars or ongoing disclosure linked with the relevant securities. This provides an attractive option for issuers by comparison with the more rigorous disclosure associated with raising equity capital in a standard public offer and is justified from a regulatory perspective by the 'wholesale' nature of the PSM, defined by reference to the type of security eligible to be admitted to the market.

8.3 Disclosure obligations imposed by the UK listing regime

Disclosure obligations represent the core of the rules that comprise the UK listing regime. In recent years their structure and formulation have been heavily influenced by the PD (applicable to the contents of a prospectus) and the TD (applicable to securities admitted to trading on a regulated market).

8.3.1 The rationale for and role of disclosure obligations

The rationale for disclosure obligations is that regulatory intervention in financial markets should focus on ensuring that investors are sufficiently informed to be able to make

---

[82] For a description of the PSM see http://www.londonstockexchange.com/companies-and-advisors/psm/ psmbgoverview.pdf (accessed on 20 August 2011).

rational investment decisions. That approach dates back at least as far as the securities legislation enacted in the US in the wake of the 1929 Wall Street Crash. Mandatory disclosure envisages that issuers will be required to provide sufficient information to investors to enable them to overcome the information asymmetry that might otherwise deter investment. It is an approach that recognises the potential for disclosure to operate as a regulatory technique in its own right or, in the words of Justice Brandeis, that 'Sunlight is said to be the best of disinfectants; electric light the most efficient policeman'.[83]

A later development was the linkage of mandatory disclosure obligations with the efficient market hypothesis (EMH), which predicts the extent to which stockmarkets are 'informationally efficient'.[84] Efficiency in this sense refers to how quickly and fully the prices of securities reflect available information. While the extent to which stockmarkets in the real world correspond to this model remains contentious, it is beyond doubt that EMH has exerted a significant influence on regulation, both in terms of reliance on disclosure as a regulatory technique and in terms of the framing of disclosure obligations. Reservations have been expressed regarding the extent of reliance on disclosure as a regulatory technique,[85] especially in the wake of the 2008/9 financial crisis,[86] but it has largely retained its prime position in the post-crisis regulatory framework.

8.3.2 The requirement for and role of a prospectus and listing particulars

Public offers of securities are often made in conjunction with a listing,[87] but there is no necessary link between the two.[88] Securities can be listed without a public offering (through an introduction to listing) and a public company can make an offer of securities to the public without the shares being listed. Public offers are essentially substantial sales of securities outside regulated markets. Following the decline of official listing as a key concept within the EU regulatory regime, the prospectus has emerged as the key document. The PD requires that an approved prospectus must be published when a public offer is made or when relevant securities are admitted to trading on a regulated market. Thus, even in the case of an 'exempt offer' (below), admission to trading on a regulated market will trigger the requirement for publication of a prospectus. The use of listing

---

[83] L Brandeis, 'Other People's Money' [1913] *Harper's Weekly*, available at http://www.law.louisville.edu/library/collections/brandeis/node/196 (accessed on 16 August 2011).

[84] Se generally K Pilbeam, *Finance and Financial Markets*, 3rd edn (Basingstoke, Palgrave Macmillan, 2010) ch 10. Note that EMH offers three possible models of informational efficiency: weak, semi-strong and strong.

[85] See S Schwarcz, 'Rethinking the Disclosure Paradigm in a World of Complexity' (2004) 1 *University of Illinois Law Review* 1.

[86] See E Avgouleas, 'What Future for Disclosure as a Regulatory Technique? Lessons from Behavioural Decision Theory and the Global Financial Crisis' in I MacNeil and J O'Brien (eds), *The Future of Financial Regulation* (Oxford, Hart Publishing, 2010) ch 12.

[87] In these circumstances, the offer is of securities that are to be listed and the offer is conditional on, inter alia, the securities being admitted to listing.

[88] The link will often arise from the requirement that at least 25% of shares to be listed must be in public hands. For some companies, the simplest way to comply will be by making a public offer in conjunction with listing.

particulars is now confined largely to instances in which securities are admitted to listing without triggering the requirements for publication of a prospectus. In practice, that means primarily the admission of debt securities to the Professional Securities Market.

To determine if publication of a prospectus is required, it is necessary to consider first the meaning of a public offer in the UK. Following the definition in the PD, there will be a public offer if there is a communication to any person in the UK presenting sufficient information on transferable securities[89] and the terms on which they are offered to enable an investor to decide to buy or subscribe for the securities.[90] A rights issue falls within the definition of an offer to the public[91] and so normally requires the publication of a prospectus. So too does a placing through an intermediary.[92]

Certain offers are designated as exempt from the requirement to publish a prospectus.[93]

- Qualified investors. This exemption applies if an offer is made only to persons falling into that category. It includes (FSA) authorised firms and national and local government entities. A qualified investor can act as an agent on behalf of a client in respect of an exempt offer so long as he can make decisions without reference to the client.
- Limited numbers of investors. This exemption applies when the securities are offered to no more than 100 persons, other than qualified investors.
- Minimum consideration. This exemption applies where the minimum payable by any person acquiring securities is 50,000 euros.
- Minimum denomination. This exemption applies when the securities are denominated in amounts of at least 50,000 euros.
- Maximum consideration. There are two overlapping provisions. Offers in which the total consideration is less than 2.5m euros are excluded from the requirement for a prospectus, whereas offers where the total consideration for the securities cannot exceed 100,000 euros are categorised as exempt offers (similarly to the other exemptions mentioned above).[94]
- Takeover offers. Offers made in connection with a takeover are exempt provided that a document is available containing information that is regarded by the FSA as equivalent to a prospectus.[95]
- In addition to the category of exempt offers, there are certain exemptions that apply (only) to the admission of securities to trading on a regulated market.
- 10% exemption. This exemption applies when the shares offered represent, over a period of 12 months, less than 10% of the number of the same class already admitted to trading on the same regulated market.[96]

---

[89] Transferable securities are defined in FSMA 2000, sch 11A. Note that some important categories are excluded (eg government bonds and units in open-ended collective investment funds).
[90] FSMA 2000, s 102B.
[91] FSMA 2000, s 102B(1).
[92] FSMA 2000, s 102B(4).
[93] FSMA 2000, s 86.
[94] The relationship between the two provisions is not entirely clear. See Birds, above n 42, ch 19.21.
[95] PR 1.2.2R(2) and PR 1.2.3R(3). See Chapter 11.3 regarding takeover offers.
[96] PR 1.2.3R(1).

- Shares converted or exchanged. Shares resulting from the conversion or exchange of other transferable securities are exempt provided that shares of the same class are already admitted to trading on the same regulated market.[97]
- Bonus shares and shares issued in lieu of dividends.[98]
- Shares already admitted to trading on another regulated market. This exemption applies when shares have been admitted to trading on another EEA regulated market for at least 18 months.[99]

Provision is made in the PD for issuers to adopt a tripartite form of prospectus. It comprises: a registration document containing information relating to the issuer; a securities note relating to the securities to be offered; and a summary in non-technical language not exceeding 2,500 words. The purpose of this structure is to facilitate rapid access by issuers to the capital market since a registration document, once approved, is valid for 12 months. During this period, an issuer would have to prepare (and have approved) only a securities note and a summary in order to satisfy the requirement to publish a prospectus. Moreover, the possibility introduced by the PD to incorporate information by reference to other documents approved by or filed with the FSA (such as annual or interim reports) offers further scope for expediting the process. While there are examples of the tripartite structure being used,[100] it has been noted that in terms of 'speed to market' it compares unfavourably with the comparable procedure that operates in the US.[101]

8.3.3 Disclosure obligations for prospectuses and listing particulars

As a result of the maximum harmonisation approach adopted by the PD and its implementing Regulation,[102] the content of prospectuses now follows a standardised format. The contents of the prospectus are linked with the nature of the issuer and the securities to be offered, and for this purpose the Prospectus Regulation[103] draws a distinction between wholesale and retail investors, with the former benefiting from a less onerous disclosure regime. In either case, the content of the prospectus is determined by detailed 'schedules' of minimum information[104] attached to the Prospectus Regulation and 'building blocks' that provide additional information for instruments or transactions that have special characteristics (eg a guarantee of some aspect of the issue by a third party). While national regulators such as the FSA cannot set requirements for a prospectus other than those derived from the PD and Prospectus Regulation, there are provisions that

---

[97] PR 1.2.3R(7).

[98] See Chapter 7 as to the meaning of these terms.

[99] PR 1.2.3R(8).

[100] See E Ferran, 'Cross-Border Offers of Securities in the EU: The Standard Life Flotation' (2006), available at SSRN: http://ssrn.com/abstract=955252 (accessed on 20 August 2011).

[101] See J Oakes and I MacNeil, 'Capital Raising: A Transatlantic Perspective' (2009) 4(2) *Capital Markets Law Journal* 155.

[102] The Prospectus Directive Regulation, 2004/809/EC [2004] OJ L149/1.

[103] See the preamble, para 14.

[104] Issuers are free to provide more information since it is only legislators and regulators who are restricted by the policy of maximum harmonisation.

permit the FSA to require the inclusion of additional information deemed necessary for investor protection.[105] It can also authorise omission of information if its disclosure would be detrimental to the public interest or to the issuer (provided that the omission would be unlikely to mislead the public), or if the information is only of minor importance for an informed investment decision.[106]

In addition to setting detailed requirements, the PD also imposes a more wide-ranging disclosure obligation. A prospectus must contain the necessary information to enable investors to make an informed assessment of:

- the assets and liabilities, financial position, profits and losses, and prospects of the issuer of the securities; and
- the rights attaching to the securities.[107]

While the precise formulation of this obligation has changed by comparison with the version that was in place prior to the implementation of the PD, there is as yet no indication that the change has proven to be a significant factor for the purposes of determining what must be disclosed or liability for non-disclosure.

Historical financial information contained in a prospectus should be presented in accordance with the EU-adopted IFRS.[108] Listed companies have been required to report in accordance with these standards since 2005.[109] However, the extension of this principle to non-EEA issuers has proven to be problematic. While provision is made for historic financial information in a prospectus to be presented in accordance with accounting standards that are equivalent to the IFRS,[110] the process for determining equivalence has been complex and politically charged. The outcome has been that the transitional period within which non-EEA issuers must comply has been extended twice (to 2009 and then 2011) pending a more complete resolution of the equivalence issue.

8.3.4 Periodic disclosure obligations

All companies, whether listed or not, are required to publish an annual report and accounts, and to make an annual return to the Registrar of Companies.[111] Listed companies, however, have always been subject to more extensive periodic disclosure obligations. The rationale for that approach has been that the proper functioning of securities markets requires investors to be fully informed about a company's activities and prospects in order that the prices of securities reflect the economic fundamentals. It is only under those conditions

---

[105] FSMA 2000, s 87J.

[106] FSMA 2000, s 87B.

[107] FSMA 2000, s 87A(2), implementing Art 5 of the PD.

[108] See recital 28 and the annexes to the Prospective Directive Regulation (809/24/EC [2004] OJ L149/1). That regulation was a 'level 2' measure within the so-called 'Lamfalussy' legislative structure (see Chapter 2.9).

[109] The requirement to report in accordance with IFRS is contained in EC Regulation 1606/2002 [2002] OJ L243/1. The purpose of IFRS is expressed by recital 2 as follows: 'In order to contribute to a better functioning of the internal market, publicly traded companies must be required to apply a single set of high quality international accounting standards for the preparation of their consolidated international statements.'

[110] Art 35 of the Prospectus Regulation.

[111] Companies Act 2006, ss 423 and 854 respectively. See further Chapter 10.3.

that a securities market can perform its function of allocating capital efficiently to competing uses. Disclosure obligations are now referenced to securities that are admitted to trading on a regulated market (rather than, as in the past, only those admitted to official listing) and appear in the Transparency section of the DTR component of the FSA Handbook, reflecting the influence of the TD. Among the additional obligations imposed on relevant issuers are:

Annual report. The timeframe for production of the annual report is 4 months from the end of the accounting reference period, compared with the 6 month deadline set by the Companies Act.[112] A management report must be compiled[113] and responsibility statements must be given by identified persons in respect of the financial statements and the management report. These statements are in addition to the provisions of the Companies Act 2006, which impose criminal liability on directors who approve accounts that do not comply with the requirements of the Act.[114] The DTR provision goes beyond the Companies Act by requiring the responsibility statement to confirm that the management report includes a fair review of the development and performance of the business and the position of the issuer and the undertakings included in the consolidation taken as a whole, together with a description of the principal risks and uncertainties that they face.[115]

Interim report. An interim report with prescribed contents must be made available within 2 months of the end of the period to which it relates.

Interim management statements. In the case of issuers that do not produce quarterly reports, a statement must be made in the prescribed form during each of the first and second 6 month periods of a company's financial year.

Corporate governance statement. An issuer must include a corporate governance statement in its directors' report setting out details of the code to which the issuer is subject, the extent to which it departs from that code and the reasons for so doing. The corporate governance statement must contain a description of the main features of the issuer's internal control and risk management systems in relation to the financial reporting process.

While in principle financial information that forms part of these disclosures must be presented in accordance with IFRS, non-EEA issuers benefit from transitional provisions permitting the use of their national accounting standards.[116]

---

[112] Companies Act 2006, s 442. For private companies the period allowed is 9 months.

[113] This can overlap with the directors' report required by s 417 of the Companies Act 2006.

[114] Companies Act 2006, s 414. Non-compliance with the Act may result from non-compliance with relevant accounting standards or the broader requirement that accounts represent a 'true and fair view' of the financial position of the company (s 393).

[115] DTR 4.1.12R.

[116] Commission Regulation 1569/2007, expiring in 2011.

8.3.5 Ongoing disclosure obligations

Ongoing disclosure requires particular types of information to be publicised whenever they occur. They are linked both with efficient price formation (by ensuring that markets are up to date with new developments) and also with limiting the potential for insider dealing to take place (since the faster that new developments become public knowledge, the less opportunity there is for insiders to use private information for their own benefit). The relevant rules are now found in the Disclosure segment of the DTR block in the FSA Handbook and largely implement Article 6 of the MAD and its related implementing measures.[117] That article provides that 'Member States shall ensure that issuers of financial instruments inform the public as soon as possible of inside information which directly concerns the said issuers'.[118] Provision is made for an issuer to delay the public disclosure of inside information so as not to prejudice its own legitimate interests, provided that such omission would not be likely to mislead the public and provided that the issuer is able to ensure the confidentiality of that information. Further clarification of the meaning of 'inside information' for the purposes of the disclosure obligation is provided by the MAD Implementing Directive.[119] It provides that issuers are deemed to have complied with the MAD Article 6 disclosure obligation 'where, upon the coming into existence of a set of circumstances or the occurrence of an event, albeit not yet formalised, the issuers have promptly informed the public thereof'.[120] This can be taken to mean that the obligation to disclose 'as soon as possible' does not arise until the inside information has become certain.[121] It should be noted that this qualification of the meaning of 'inside information' is only for the purposes of the disclosure obligation of issuers and does not apply for the purposes of the prohibition on the disclosure of inside information or trading on the basis of inside information. For those purposes, the MAD Implementing Directive makes clear that inside information includes circumstances which may reasonably be expected to come into existence or events that may be reasonably expected to occur.[122]

8.3.5 The mechanics of disclosure

Prior to 2001, information was submitted by listed companies to the Regulatory News Service (RNS), operated by the FSA and funded in part by fees paid to the FSA by

---

[117] Prior to the implementation of the TD, The London Stock Exchange's Listing Rules had required ongoing disclosure of material developments in the business of an issuer or changes in their financial position that were likely to have a significant effect on the share price. For an example of enforcement of that obligation, see the case of Shell plc, in which the FSA imposed a £17m fine in respect of the announcement of misleading proven oil reserves: available at http://www.fsa.gov.uk/Pages/Library/Communication/PR/2004/074.shtml (accessed on 19 November 2011).

[118] See Herbert Smith, 'Regulatory Update' (2010) 5(4) *Law and Financial Markets Review* 314 regarding the FSA penalty imposed on JJB Sports for failing to disclose information to the market.

[119] Commission Directive 2003/124, OJ L339 70.

[120] Art 2(2).

[121] This is the interpretation favoured by JL Hansen and D Moalem, 'The MAD Disclosure Regime and the Twofold Notion of Inside Information: The Available Solution' (2009) 4(3) *Capital Markets Law Journal* 323.

[122] See Art 1(1).

listed companies. The RNS then distributed the information to the market. The FSA was concerned about the monopoly position enjoyed by the RNS in carrying out this function and decided, following consultation, to open that function to competition.[123] In order to provide this service, an organisation must now be approved by the FSA and thereby become a designated Primary Information Provider (PIP).[124]

8.4 Responsibility for inadequate disclosure

Inadequate disclosure refers to a failure to disclose in accordance with the relevant disclosure obligations outlined above. It can arise from non-disclosure, limited disclosure, false disclosure, misrepresentation or failure to disclose within the time limit set by the relevant obligation. In view of the centrality of disclosure for the efficient pricing of securities in the market, it is essential that the law identifies who bears legal liability for inadequate disclosure, the circumstances in which liability arises, the standard of liability that applies and the sanctions that may be imposed. The formulation of all these factors carries important consequences for deterring inadequate disclosure, but there is no common European approach. While the PD[125] and TD[126] require Member States to ensure that legal liability attaches to certain persons, the liability is based on national law since there has been no harmonisation. This represents a considerable limitation on the operation of the single market since enforcement of the (now very substantial) harmonised core of prospectus and disclosure law is dependent on national liability rules and the associated procedures for their enforcement. Nor is it entirely clear how the law relating to prospectus liability is determined. Even if it is likely that such liability arises in tort rather than contract, there remains some uncertainty. A case can be made for each of (i) the location where the securities are held, (ii) the location of the market on which they are traded and (iii) the state of origin (ie the state responsible for approving the prospectus).

The EU model is very different to that in the US, where the Securities and Exchange Commission (SEC) is able to take enforcement action against all SEC-registered companies, irrespective of where they are incorporated or where their securities are traded. Moreover, as discussed below, the approach of the law is not uniform as differing considerations have been to the fore in the formulation of the law in relation to prospectuses, periodic disclosures and ongoing disclosures.

---

[123] See FSA Policy Statement, 'Proposed Changes to the UK Mechanism for Disseminating Regulatory Information by Listed Companies' (November 2001).
[124] See sch 12 to the Listing Rules for details of designated PIPs.
[125] Art 6.
[126] Art 7.

8.4.1 Prospectuses and listing particulars

The disclosure obligations applicable to a prospectus[127] can be enforced in three different ways. First, a person who knowingly or recklessly gives false or misleading information to the FSA commits a criminal offence.[128] Secondly, where there is a contravention of part VI of FSMA 2000 or the prospectus rules, the FSA may impose a financial penalty on the issuer or any other person to whom a relevant provision of the PD applies.[129] The FSA can take similar action against a director of the applicant who is knowingly concerned in the contravention.[130] Thirdly, a person responsible for a prospectus is liable to pay compensation to a person who has acquired securities and suffered loss as a result of[131] any untrue or misleading statement in the particulars or the omission from the prospectus of any matter required to be included by the general duty of disclosure.[132] The following persons are responsible for a prospectus relating to shares:[133]

(a) the issuer;
(b) if the issuer is a body corporate:
    (i) each person who is a director of that body corporate when the prospecus is published; and
    (ii) each person who has authorised himself to be named, and is named, in the prospectus as a director or as having agreed to become a director of that body corporate either immediately or at a future time;
(c) each person who accepts, and is stated in the prospectus as accepting, responsibility for the prospectus;
(d) in relation to an offer:
    (i) the offeror, if this is not the issuer; and
    (ii) if the offeror is a body corporate and is not the issuer, each person who is a director of the body corporate when the prospectus is published;
(e) in relation to a request for the admission to trading of transferable securities:
    (i) the person requesting admission, if this is not the issuer; and
    (ii) if the person requesting admission is a body corporate and is not the issuer, each person who is a director of the body corporate when the prospectus is published; and
(f) each person not falling within any of the previous paragraphs who has authorised the contents of the prospectus.

---

[127] And, where relevant, listing particulars.
[128] FSMA 2000, s 398.
[129] FSMA 2000, s 91.
[130] FSMA 2000, s 91(2).
[131] Note that the requirements to show reliance on the information (that was not disclosed or misrepresented) and inducement (to enter the contract) do not apply to the statutory remedy (as they do to the common law remedy for deceit).
[132] FSMA 2000, s 90. The general duty of disclosure is contained in s 80. Note that the general remedy provided by s 150 FSMA 2000 for breach of statutory duty is not available in the case of breaches of the listing and disclosure rules.
[133] FSA Handbook, PR 5.5.3. Persons responsible for listing particulars are specified in The FSMA 2000 (Official Listing of Securities) Regulations 2001 (SI 2001/2956) Art 6, which corresponds to categories a, b, c and f. In the case of a prospectus, the offeror need not be the issuer (eg the offeror could be an institutional investor selling a large holding).

Neither an issuer nor its directors are liable if the issuer has not made or authorised the offer or the request for admission to trading in connection with which the prospectus has been published. A director is not liable if a prospectus is published without his knowledge or consent and, on becoming aware of its publication, he, as soon as practicable, gives reasonable public notice that it was published without his knowledge or consent. In the case of a prospectus relating to securities other than shares, the relevant provisions exclude directors from liability. The rationale for this exclusion is that investors in debt securities can negotiate for contractual forms of protection (eg covenants) that are not available for shares. In the case of shares, investors rely heavily on disclosure for valuation purposes and so a strong form of liability (extending beyond the issuer) is necessary to ensure that the required information is published.

The statutory remedy in respect of inadequate disclosure is subject to a number of defences.[134] One is the 'reasonable belief' defence, which applies when loss is caused by inadequate disclosure in circumstances in which the relevant person believed (having made reasonable enquiries) that adequate disclosure was made.[135] Another defence is that inadequate disclosure was caused by reliance on the statement of an expert. Nor is liability incurred when inadequate disclosure is remedied by a correction published in an appropriate manner.

The most obvious category of claimant in respect of a breach of the statutory compensation remedy is a person who buys from the company (or its financial adviser, in the case of an offer for sale) in reliance on false information contained in a prospectus. However, the relevant provision[136] extends to market purchasers and also to anyone who contracts to acquire an interest (such as an option) in the securities provided that a causal link between loss and inadequate disclosure in the prospectus can be established. There is no express provision governing the period during which a prospectus can be taken to have been a casual influence in an investor's decision to buy shares, but it can be said as a matter of principle that its influence must decline over time as circumstances change and the issuer makes further disclosures as required by the FSA's Disclosure and Transparency Rules.

The statutory compensation remedy leaves in place other (common law) remedies applicable to false or misleading information in prospectuses.[137] They are rescission (or damages) for misrepresentation, damages for breach of a duty of care or damages for deceit. Prior to the introduction of the statutory compensation remedy, investors had no option but to rely on those remedies, but that is less common nowadays since those remedies are more restrictive than the statutory remedy in their scope and formulation.[138] This is evident, for example, with regard to the position of investors who buy in the secondary

---

[134] They are set out in sch 10 to the Act.

[135] This defence reflects the policy that liability should be based on the civil standard of fraud, which requires a deliberate attempt to mislead. Liability is not imposed as a result of mere negligence.

[136] FSMA 2000, s 90.

[137] See s 90(6) FSMA 2000. Note that the statutory remedy under s 150 FSMA 2000 (see Chapter 6.5) does not apply to breaches of rules made under pt VI of the Act (covering listing, prospectuses and disclosure rules).

[138] For more detail see Birds, above n 42, ch 19.

market. In *Possfund Custodian Trustee Ltd vs Diamond and Others*,[139] the court was required to consider whether a common law duty of care was owed by persons responsible for a prospectus offering shares that were to be quoted and traded on the Unlisted Securities Market.[140] The court decided that it was not possible to conclude that there was no common law duty owed by persons responsible for an unlisted prospectus to investors who bought in the secondary market. This followed consideration of the purpose of a prospectus in its modern context as being a document on which investors in the secondary market intend to rely, rather than the narrow view established in the nineteenth-century cases, which viewed a prospectus as being limited to providing information in respect of a particular allotment of shares.[141] The result is that there remains some uncertainty as to the common law position of buyers in the secondary market.

No reference is made in the statutory compensation remedy to the measure of damages to be awarded to the claimant. Older cases based on the prospectus liability provisions in company law had applied the measure of damages applicable to the tort of deceit.[142] This measure permits the recovery of all losses directly flowing from inadequate disclosure, whereas damages for breach of duty of care are restricted by remoteness rules limiting liability to foreseeable losses. While the absence of case law on the FSMA 2000 version of the statutory remedy means that the law is not entirely clear, it has been suggested that the courts would follow the deceit measure.[143] The implications of that approach are illustrated by the case of *Smith New Court Securities Ltd v Scrimgeour Vickers (Asset Management) Ltd*.[144] In that case, a buyer of shares induced by deceit sustained loss as a result of a fraud within the company, which meant that the shares could be sold for only a fraction of the purchase price. Although the deceit had not caused the fraud within the company, the court held that the loss flowed directly from the deceit since the buyer was effectively 'locked in' as a result of the effect of the fraud on the marketability of the shares. The buyer was therefore awarded the difference between the purchase price and the eventual sale price.

8.4.2 Periodic and ongoing disclosures

Prior to the implementation of the TD, there was no statutory regime for liability in respect of periodic disclosures. It was in principle possible for the FSA to sanction instances of inadequate disclosure that were breaches of the Listing Rules, but that would not provide

---

[139] [1996] 2 All ER 774. The case was for the striking out of the plaintiff's claim on the basis that it disclosed no cause of action. Consideration of the merits was therefore confined to whether there was a cause of action.

[140] The legal background to the case was that s 150 of the Financial Services Act 1986 (FSA 1986) gave a remedy to anyone who bought securities in reliance on a prospectus (whether in a public offer or in the secondary market), whereas (in the opinion of the judge in this case) the relevant provision of FSA 1986 applicable to unlisted securities did not provide a remedy to investors who bought in the secondary market.

[141] See *Peek v Gurney* (1873) LR 6 HL 377.

[142] See eg *Clark v Urquhart* [1930] AC 28, HL.

[143] P Davies, 'Liability for Misstatements to the Market: A Discussion Paper' (HM Treasury, March 2007) para 107.

[144] [1997] AC 254, HL.

compensation to an investor who suffered loss.[145] Moreover, the alternative common law remedies mentioned in 8.4.1 above are even more difficult to establish in the context of periodic disclosures because in those circumstances there is no contractual link between the issuer and the investor comparable to that between an issuer and an investor who buys into an issue of securities for which a prospectus has been published.[146]

As required by the TD, a statutory compensation remedy was introduced in the UK when the Directive was implemented.[147] It applies to securities traded on a securities market[148] situated or operating in the UK or where the UK is the issuer's home state. In its original form, the statutory remedy applied only to annual financial reports[149] (and the preliminary announcements that typically precede them), half-yearly financial reports and interim management statements; the liability regime for periodic disclosures did not extend to ongoing disclosures that are required by the MAD and its implementing measures. In recognition of the anomaly[150] that this created between liability for periodic and ongoing disclosures (and in recognition of the limitations of the liability regime for periodic disclosures), the government commissioned a review of issuer liability by Professor Paul Davies in 2006.[151] This was followed by proposals from the government to extend the statutory regime to cover ongoing disclosures.[152] These proposals were implemented in 2010 by way of regulations amending section 90A of and Schedule 10A to FSMA 2000.[153]

The statutory remedy in respect of periodic and ongoing disclosures (section 90A) follows the approach adopted for prospectuses by adopting the fraud standard of the civil law as the basis of liability. That approach is evident in the references in points 3 and 4 below to the knowledge of a relevant person acting for the issuer: the effect is to exclude liability for mere negligence. However, section 90A liability differs from that applicable to a prospectus (section 90) in several significant ways, as indicated below.

1. Section 90A includes within its scope buyers, holders and sellers of securities, whereas section 90 extends only to those who have 'acquired' securities.

---

[145] It would be possible for the FSA to use its power to require restitution or compensation to be paid by an issuer, but there are no recorded instances of that occurring.

[146] The absence of a contractual link reflects the fact that, while the prospectus represents an offer to investors that forms the basis of a contract to buy shares, an investor buying in the 'after-market' does not contract on the basis of the prospectus.

[147] See s 90A FSMA 2000.

[148] Note that the regime extends beyond regulated markets.

[149] Including the directors' report accompanying the accounts.

[150] For a discussion of the origins and nature of the anomaly see L Burn, 'Only Connect—the Importance of Considering Disclosure Requirements in the Light of Their Legal Consequences' (2007) 2(1) *Capital Markets Law Journal* 41.

[151] See Davies, above n 143; P Davies, 'Review of Issuer Liability: Final Report' (HM Treasury, June 2007).

[152] See HM Treasury, 'Extension of the Statutory Regime for Issuer Liability' (July 2008). Ongoing disclosures for these purposes means information published by the issuer whether voluntarily or as a result of an obligation.

[153] Financial Services and Markets Act 2000 (Liability of Issuers) Regulations, SI 2010/1192 (effective 1 October 2010).

2. Only the issuer can be liable to investors under section 90A.[154]
3. The issuer is liable in respect of an untrue or misleading statement only if a person discharging managerial responsibilities within the issuer knew the statement to be untrue or misleading, or was reckless as to whether it was untrue or misleading.
4. The issuer is liable in respect of the omission of any matter required to be included in published information only if a person discharging managerial responsibilities within the issuer knew the omission to be a dishonest concealment of a material fact.
5. The issuer is liable for dishonest delay in publishing information.
6. Dishonesty (for the purposes of points 3 and 4 above) is conduct which is (i) regarded as dishonest by persons who regularly trade on the securities market in question and (ii) the person was aware (or must be taken to have been aware) that it was so regarded.
7. The requirement of reliance is retained and an additional requirement (by comparison with the common law of deceit) is imposed whereby the reliance must be reasonable by reference to the time and the circumstances.

While section 90A does extend the liability regime in a meaningful way, there remains a considerable burden for an investor to discharge all the requirements that are necessary for a successful claim. In those circumstances, it seems likely that the deterrent effect of FSA and reputational sanctions will continue to be more influential factors in encouraging full disclosure by comparison with legal liability.

---

[154] It was decided to continue to exclude directors and advisers from liability on the basis that they would remain liable to the company for breach of duty and could also be exposed to sanction by the FSA if 'knowingly concerned' in the contravention by the issuer (under s 91(2) FSMA 2000).

Corporate Governance— Overview and Evolution

This chapter deals with corporate governance in listed companies. The term 'corporate governance' is used in different ways, depending on its context. One definition is that it refers to how companies are directed and controlled.[1] That is a very broad definition which is capable of covering a wide range of issues. Another is that it refers to 'the ways in which suppliers of finance to corporations assure themselves of getting a return on their investment'.[2] That is a more restrictive definition in which governance mechanisms are viewed as being a monitoring device for investors. Yet another definition is that corporate governance refers to the various mechanisms associated with company law that shape the way company managers exercise their discretion.[3] That definition focuses attention on corporate governance as a system of rules or guidelines that control the exercise of discretion by company managers, and in particular the board of directors.

The law plays a crucial role in defining the sphere within which discretion can be exercised. Company law, for example, determines the respective roles of shareholders and directors in making decisions within a company and determines the powers available to directors in running a company. However, two characteristics of company law in particular help to explain why the formal legal framework has increasingly come to be regarded as an inadequate means to control the exercise by directors of their wide powers. First, legal remedies, such as challenging decisions or actions taken by directors on the basis that they are beyond their powers or represent an improper use of powers, represent an *ex post* form of control in that they deal with problems after they have occurred. They are also complicated by the legal rules that determine who is able to institute legal action on behalf of a company.[4] Secondly, the power given to shareholders to appoint and

---

[1] This was the definition adopted in the Cadbury Report (Gee & Co Ltd, 'Report of the Committee on the Financial Aspects of Corporate Governance', 1992) para 2.5.

[2] A Shleifer and R Vishny, 'A Survey of Corporate Governance' (1997) 52 *Journal of Finance* 737.

[3] See J Parkinson, 'The Role of "Exit" and "Voice" in Corporate Governance' in S Sheikh and W Rees (eds), *Corporate Governance and Corporate Control* (London, Cavendish, 1995) 75.

[4] See generally J Birds (ed), *Boyle & Birds' Company Law*, 8th edn (Bristol, Jordans, 2011) ch 18.

remove directors[5] represents a 'nuclear option' and does not necessarily create genuine accountability in respect of decisions or conduct on the part of directors which may be objectionable from the shareholders' perspective but which is not a 'sacking offence'. Corporate governance has emerged as a process for establishing and developing control mechanisms and detailed standards within this sphere. The main focus of corporate governance is on strategic direction, high-level decision-making, supervision of management[6] and legitimate expectations for accountability. Corporate governance is relevant for investors because each of these issues is of crucial importance to the long-term relationship between investors and companies and to the valuation of investors' shareholdings.[7]

9.1 Corporate governance and ownership structure

The structure of share ownership is relevant for corporate governance because different ownership patterns create different incentives for investors to become involved in corporate governance. This can be illustrated by comparing two hypothetical countries. Assume that in country A ownership of listed companies is typically widely dispersed, meaning that no single investor has a sufficiently large holding to be able to exercise a strong influence through the exercise of votes. By way of contrast, assume that in country B listed companies typically have a single large shareholder who has sufficient voting power to be able to dominate decision-making. In country A, it is likely that there will be no incentive for a shareholder to become actively involved in corporate governance because that shareholder will have to bear the cost while all other shareholders will share the benefits, if any, that are reflected in the share price.[8] It can therefore be expected that in country A considerable emphasis will be placed on alternatives to active involvement in corporate governance and in particular the development of mechanisms (such as stock exchanges) that provide an exit mechanism for dissatisfied shareholders who are unwilling to become actively involved in corporate governance. This process has been described as shareholders choosing 'exit' (selling) over 'voice' (active involvement in corporate governance) in respect of poorly performing companies.[9] In country B, it is

---

[5] The Companies Act 2006, s 168 provides that a company may by ordinary resolution remove a director before the expiration of his period of office, notwithstanding anything in any agreement between it and him.

[6] Corporate governance differs from 'management' in that the governance structure sits above management, sets the objectives for management and monitors its implementation of those objectives. See B Tricker, *Corporate Governance, Principles, Policies and Practices* (Oxford, Oxford University Press, 2009) ch 2.

[7] See M Maher and T Andersson, 'Corporate Governance: Effects on Firm Performance and Economic Growth' in L Renneboog et al (eds), *Convergence and Diversity of Corporate Governance Regimes and Capital Markets* (Oxford, Oxford University Press, 2000).

[8] This is an example of the classic 'free rider' problem. See generally M Becht, P Bolton and A Röell, 'Corporate Governance and Control', ECGI Finance Working Paper No 02/2002, available at http://www.ecgi.org/wp/search_year.php?year=2002 (accessed on 16 August 2011).

[9] The terminology is derived from A Hirshman, *Exit, Voice and Loyalty, Responses to Decline in Firms, Organizations and States* (Cambridge, MA, Harvard University Press, 1970).

likely that the single large shareholder (aka 'blockholder') will take a more active role in corporate governance for the simple reason that much of the benefit of that action will accrue to that shareholder. Moreover, the emphasis on exercising 'voice' in that country might well be expected to lead to less emphasis on 'exit' and therefore a reduced role for financial markets by comparison with country A.

Institutional investors dominate share ownership in the UK.[10] This remains the case even after the phase of popular capitalism during the 1980s in which small private investors were encouraged to buy shares in the privatisations of several large state-owned organisations. Institutional investment takes several forms.[11] Pension funds account for the largest percentage, followed by insurance companies (primarily life assurance funds) and collective investment schemes. Individual investors' direct holdings are relatively small, although it is of course true that, ultimately, all institutional investment is held on behalf of individual investors. In common with the US, but unlike most other countries, most listed companies in the UK do not have a single dominant shareholder. Shares in UK and US companies are widely dispersed, as even the large institutional shareholders referred to above rarely hold more than 3% of a listed company.[12] Elsewhere, it is common for companies to have a single large shareholder (a concentrated shareholding structure).[13]

Different explanations have been offered as to why there has been such divergence in the historical evolution of the pattern of share ownership.[14] One is that concentrated shareholding is a mechanism that allows for effective monitoring of company management.[15] On this view, the presence of a large shareholder acts as a counterweight to the tendency of boards of directors to have effective control of a company. Another explanation is that widely dispersed shareholding developed in countries in which small shareholders were well protected against self-interested action on the part of boards of directors and majority shareholders.[16]

On this view, the quality of investor protection attracts small shareholders into share ownership because they feel secure about being treated fairly. Another possible explanation is that political considerations have influenced the evolution of the pattern of share

---

[10] See P Myners, 'Institutional Investment in the United Kingdom: A Review' (March 2001) (Myners Report), available at http://archive.treasury.gov.uk/docs/2001/myners_report0602.html (accessed on 16 August 2011) 7 for a table showing the distribution of share ownership in the UK. See also the Office for National Statistics, 'Share Ownership Survey 2008', reporting that individual ownership of UK listed shares fell to 10.2% at the end of 2008. As recently as 1994 that figure was above 20%.

[11] See generally Chapter 5.

[12] This is the threshold at which the FSA Handbook requires disclosure of the identity of a shareholder. See Chapter 13.1.3.

[13] See eg R La Porta, F Lopez-de-Silanes, A Shleifer and R Vishny (hereafter LLSV), 'Corporate Ownership around the World' (1999) 54 *Journal of Finance* 471.

[14] See H Demsetz and K Lehn, 'The Structure of Corporate Ownership: Causes and Consequences' (1985) 93 *Journal of Political Economy* 1155.

[15] See A Shleifer and M Vishny, 'Large Shareholders and Corporate Control' (1986) 94 *Journal of Political Economy* 461; D Leech and J Leahy, 'Ownership Structure, Control Type, Classification and the Performance of Large British Companies' (1991) 101 *Economic Journal* 1418.

[16] See LLSV, 'Legal Determinants of External Finance' (1997) 52 *Journal of Finance* 1131; 'Law and Finance' (1998) 106 *Journal of Political Economy* 1113; 'Investor Protection and Corporate Governance', available at http://papers.ssrn.com/sol3/papers.cfm?abstract_id=183908 (accessed on 16 August 2011).

ownership by discouraging the concentration of industrial power in small groups.[17] This has been an issue in particular in the US, where, historically, there has been a stronger emphasis on competitive markets than in Europe and a corresponding distrust of accumulation of industrial and commercial power.

Company finance is relevant for corporate governance because different forms of finance create differing legal rights and expectations regarding involvement in decision-making within companies. This issue has already been examined in Chapter 7 in terms of the differing position of contributors of equity and loan capital to a company. However, the extent to which the corporate sector as a whole relies on different sources of finance is also relevant for corporate governance. In this respect, a distinction is typically made between 'bank-centred' systems of corporate governance, in which companies rely more heavily on loan capital, and 'market-centred' systems of corporate governance, in which companies typically rely more on equity rather than loan capital. Linked with this is the fact that companies in 'bank-centred' systems tend to have controlling shareholders.[18]

Both systems have advantages and disadvantages, and this is reflected in the fact that many countries can be described as 'hybrid' in that they do not fall squarely into one category or the other. The market-based system lays considerable emphasis on disclosure of financial information so as to allow shareholders to make informed investment decisions, but tends to encourage a short-term focus on performance and exit rather than voice. This system is associated primarily with the US and the UK. The bank-centred system allows for the development of long-term relationships between companies and providers of (loan and equity) capital but tends to suffer from lower standards of disclosure and the appropriation of private benefits by controlling shareholders at the expense of minorities. It is associated primarily with countries such as Germany, Japan and Italy.[19]

9.2 Company law and corporate governance

Shareholders' rights are controlled by company law and are an important determinant of the structure and process of corporate governance.[20] They are particularly important for determining the key relationships between shareholders and others stakeholders (such as creditors and employees), and between shareholders and the board of directors. In

---

[17] See MJ Roe, 'A Political Theory of American Corporate Finance' (1991) 91 *Columbia Law Review* 10. Roe's account cannot be regarded as a generalised explanation of the evolution of all systems of dispersed ownership. With respect to the UK see B Cheffins, 'Law, Economics and the UK's System of Corporate Governance: Lessons from History' (2001) 1 *Journal of Corporate Law Studies* 71.

[18] See LLSV, above n 16.

[19] For an extensive discussion of the relative roles of banks and financial markets in the UK, Germany and Japan see N Dimsdale and M Prevezer, *Capital Markets and Corporate Governance* (Oxford, Clarendon Press, 1994).

[20] For a comparative review of shareholders' rights in different jurisdictions and an analysis of the degree of convergence see M Siems, *Convergence in Shareholder Law* (Cambridge, Cambridge University Press, 2008).

the UK, corporate governance tends to focus most on the latter relationship, and in that context shareholders' rights can be broadly classified into four groups: decision-making rights; appointment and removal rights; shareholding rights; and intervention rights.

As regards the first category, a characteristic of the UK system is the wide range of decisions that are reserved to the shareholders. They include (in the case of a listed company): the power to approve changes to the constitution;[21] decisions to issue shares[22] or disapply pre-emption rights;[23] the approval of certain transactions between directors or their associates and the company;[24] and the approval of 'Class 1' transactions under the listing rules[25]. The overall effect of these decisions is to limit the power of the board, which would otherwise be commensurately broader since the default provision in the model articles grants the board all the powers of the company.[26]

The powers of shareholders with regard to the appointment and removal of directors are also significant in this context. While the formal legal rights are not particularly unusual in an international context, the power to remove[27] is simpler than in many other jurisdictions, since dismissal is possible through an ordinary resolution without having to show good cause.[28] The recent change in the UK Code of Corporate Governance is also significant in this regard since it now provides that all directors of FTSE 350 companies be subject to annual election by shareholders, thereby limiting the need to resort to removal.

Company law is also concerned with the balance between the legal rights of controlling shareholders and minorities. Company law generally permits majority rule to prevail within companies and allows all shareholders to vote on resolutions in accordance with their own interests.[29] However, there are important protections against the abuse of majority rule. One is the requirement that certain resolutions require more than a simple majority. While most decisions can be taken by ordinary resolution, which requires approval only by a majority of shareholders who vote on the issue, some decisions (eg a change in the company's articles of association[30]) can be made only by special resolution, which requires approval by a three-quarters majority of shareholders who vote. This provides some protection to minorities in respect of important decisions that are made by a company, but still leaves open the possibility of exploitation by the majority.

---

[21] Companies Act 2006, s 21. Although most systems of corporate law require such approval, some US states devolve power to directors to make changes to bylaws, thereby altering the distribution of power as between shareholders and the board: see R Kraakman et al, *The Anatomy of Corporate Law, A Comparative and Functional Approach* (Oxford, Oxford University Press, 2004) 138.

[22] Companies Act 2006, s 549.

[23] See further Chapter 7.3.2.

[24] Companies Act 2006 pt 10, ch 3.

[25] See FSA Handbook, LR 10. The 'unanimous consent' rule also empowers shareholders to take decisions, albeit that it is of more relevance for private companies than for public limited companies.

[26] See Art 3 of the Model Articles for Public Companies (Schedule 3) in The Companies (Model Articles) Regulations 2008, SI 2008/3229.

[27] Companies Act 2006, s 168.

[28] For a summary of the position in other major jurisdictions see Kraakman et al, above n 21, 37–38.

[29] See generally P Davies, *Gower and Davies' Principles of Modern Company Law*, 8th edn (London, Sweet & Maxwell, 2008) Chapter 19.

[30] Companies Act 2006, s 21.

Two other forms of control do, however, limit the extent to which such exploitation can occur. The first is the remedy provided to minorities in respect of 'unfairly prejudicial conduct'.[31] It has been viewed as primarily of relevance to shareholders in small (generally private) companies and has not been used to any significant extent by shareholders in listed companies, who often simply prefer to 'exit' by selling in the market rather than engaging in expensive litigation. The remedy permits a minority shareholder or group of shareholders to petition the court for a remedy in circumstances when a company is being run in a manner that is prejudicial to their interests. This might be because the directors are acting without regard to their fiduciary duties or because controlling shareholders are favouring their own interests at the expense of the minority.[32] The most common remedy sought by shareholders in these circumstances is an order requiring the other shareholders to buy the shares of the minority at a price fixed by an independent valuer.

A second legal mechanism that limits exploitation of a minority is the possibility of the minority bringing a 'derivative' action.[33] The most blatant example of such circumstances is where a majority use their voting power to transfer company assets or opportunities to themselves.[34] The law's approach in these circumstances, broadly stated, is to modify the operation of the principle of majority rule so as to allow an oppressed minority to take action to prevent or remedy the relevant act of the majority.[35]

The relevance of these legal principles for corporate governance in the UK is that they create an underlying legal framework in which routine exploitation of minority shareholders by a majority is made difficult. The dispersed nature of share ownership in the UK also limits the potential for exploitation of minorities as it results in the absence of controlling shareholders in most listed companies. In this respect the UK differs from many other countries,[36] where concentrated share ownership leads to the corporate governance agenda being framed much more in terms of controlling the appropriation of private benefits by controlling shareholders rather than controlling the exercise of discretion by directors. It is therefore not surprising to find that virtually no attention has been paid to minority rights in the development of corporate governance codes in the UK. Minority rights are already entrenched in the law and there is therefore no obvious need to remedy any deficiency by adopting additional provisions in corporate governance codes.

[31] See s 993 of the Companies Act 2006.
[32] For a discussion of the techniques through which this may occur see S Johnson, R Laporta, F Lopez-de-Silanes and A Shleifer, 'Tunneling' (2000) 90 *American Economic Review* 22.
[33] See pt 11 of the Companies Act 2006.
[34] See eg *Prudential Assurance Co Ltd v Newman Industries Ltd* (No 2) [1981] Ch 257.
[35] See generally Birds, above n 4, ch 17.
[36] See eg LLSV, above n 13.

9.3 Corporate governance and corporate social responsibility

Corporate governance is nowadays often understood to encompass the concept of corporate social responsibility (CSR). That concept has been defined as a voluntary process by which companies integrate social and environmental concerns in their business operations and in their interaction with stakeholders.[37] It differs from philanthropy in that CSR focuses on how business is done and its impact on society and the environment. Philanthropy, in contrast, focuses on how profits earned from business are distributed rather than how they are earned in the first instance. CSR is linked with the broader understanding of corporate governance, which focuses on the relationships of all stakeholders in a company and not just the narrower focus on the relationship between the board and shareholders. In that sense, corporate social responsibility represents a move away from so-called 'shareholder value' to a broader view of the nature and purpose of companies.

The growth in awareness of CSR and its implementation through company codes of conduct has been driven by several factors.[38] Non-government organisations have played a central role particularly in drawing attention to the labour practices of multinational companies. The 'business case' for CSR has also been influential, with many companies recognising that 'reputational capital' can be built on the basis of practices that implement CSR. Linked with that is market and consumer pressure that may be brought to bear on companies which engage in unethical practices. Finally, increasing public concern over the environmental impact of business has prompted demands for greater accountability on the part of companies regarding the environmental impact of their activities.

These influences have led to the recognition of so-called environmental, social and governance (ESG) issues within the statutory reporting framework, as well as the development of new reporting frameworks that aim to enhance the accountability of companies with respect to CSR issues. In the UK, the business review that must be included in the directors' annual report is required to provide information about:

1. environmental matters (including the impact of the company's business on the environment);
2. the company's employees; and
3. social and community issues.[39]

---

[37] See EC Commission Green Paper, 'Promoting a European framework for Corporate Social Responsibility' COM(2001) 366 final, para 2.20.

[38] See generally D McBarnet, A Voiculescu and T Campbell (eds), *The New Corporate Accountability, Corporate Social Responsibility and the Law* (Cambridge, Cambridge University Press, 2007).

[39] Companies Act 2006, s 417(5), applicable to quoted companies. The obligation to provide the information is qualified by the proviso that the information must be provided 'to the extent necessary for an understanding of the development, performance or position of the company's business'.

Other initiatives have taken that process further forward. In the UK, the Association of British Insurers' (ABI) Guidelines on Responsible Investment Disclosure[40] set out a wide range of ESG disclosures that are recommended for all companies (not just quoted companies, as in the case of the statutory business review). In particular, the ABI guidelines recommend disclosure in the annual report of whether:

1. as part of its regular risk assessment procedures, the board of directors takes account of the significance of ESG matters to the business of the company;
2. the board has identified and assessed the significant ESG risks to the company's short- and long-term value, as well as the opportunities to enhance value that may arise from an appropriate response;
3. the board has received adequate information to make this assessment and that account is taken of ESG matters in the training of directors; and
4. the board has ensured that the company has in place effective systems for managing and mitigating significant risks, which, where relevant, incorporate performance management systems and appropriate remuneration incentives.

At the international level, the Global Reporting Initiative (GRI) has exerted a powerful influence on ESG reporting. It is a voluntary initiative run through an Amsterdam-based foundation. The GRI's objectives are to benchmark corporate performance with respect to laws, codes, performance standards and voluntary initiatives; demonstrate commitment to sustainable development; and compare organisational performance over time. It promotes and develops the standardised approach to sustainable information (broadly understood) through a standard disclosure profile and performance indicators. The GRI framework is focused on stakeholder accountability and therefore its focus is broader than the normal accounting framework; the latter focuses on the entities that are owned by a company, whereas GRI reporting encompasses the entire supply chain with which a company is linked. The majority of the world's largest companies now report in line with the GRI Guidelines.[41]

While the success of CSR in prompting the development of ESG reporting frameworks is clear, what is less obvious is whether CSR has a material impact on the decision-making process within companies. The central problem is that, if implemented in its true spirit, CSR is likely to result in a conflict with the duty of directors to 'promote the success of the company for the benefit of its members as whole'.[42] The ABI guidelines overcome this impasse by referring to ESG issues as 'risks to the long and short-term value of the business' and that it is 'incumbent on institutional investors to consider these risks and opportunities in the context of their overarching objective of enhancing shareholder value'. Thus, while ESG issues are to be integrated into decision-making, it

---

[40] Available at http://www.ivis.co.uk/PDF/7.1_ABI_RID_guidelines.pdf (28 July 2011). Compliance with these guidelines is monitored and made available to investors by the Institutional Voting Information Service (IVIS) run by the ABI.

[41] See KPMG, 'International Survey of Corporate Responsibility Reporting' (2008) 4, available at http://www.kpmg.com/Global/en/IssuesAndInsights/ArticlesPublications/Pages/Sustainability-corporate-responsibility-reporting-2008.aspx.

[42] Companies Act 2006, s 172.

seems clear that they are managed in the way that companies manage other risks that may interfere with its objectives. Viewed in that light, the conflict is clearly resolved by diluting the meaning of CSR for the purposes of board decision-making.

However, there are mechanisms which have been used by CSR activists to promote a more meaningful adoption of CSR into the decision-making process and practices of companies.[43] One technique has been shareholder activism, meaning the use of the legal rights of shareholders (such as tabling a resolution, asking questions at shareholders' meetings or calling a shareholders' meeting) to promote CSR. Another has been the use of private law remedies to seek to enforce commitments made by companies in their (voluntary) codes of conduct.[44] Contractual techniques have also been developed to promote CSR whereby governments or other large buyers require compliance by contractors (and in some cases also their subcontractors) with CSR standards (eg those set by the International Labour Organisation for child labour). Beyond those influences, the capacity of CSR to contribute to compliance with legal standards should not be underestimated, especially in those areas of regulation (such as tax and financial regulation) where companies may devote considerable resources to minimising their costs.[45]

9.4 Theories of corporate governance

There are many different theories and philosophies of corporate governance.[46] Four of the most influential are discussed in turn below.

9.4.1 Principal/agent theory

Corporate governance is concerned with the accountability of directors to shareholders. This relationship has been characterised by economists as a principal/agent relationship in which shareholders (the principal) face the problem of how to monitor the conduct and performance of directors (the agent).[47] The main risk faced by shareholders is that directors will act in a self-interested manner rather than in the best interests of the company, thereby imposing 'agency costs' on the shareholders.[48] However, the risks faced by shareholders must also be balanced by consideration of the most efficient governance structure for

---

[43] See McBarnet et al, above n 38, ch 1.

[44] See *Kasky v Nike, Inc*, 45 P 3d 243 (Cal 2002), discussed in McBarnet et al, ibid.

[45] McBarnet, ibid, ch 1, referring to CSR operating *beyond* law, *through* law and *for* law.

[46] See Tricker, above n 6, ch 9. See also T Clarke (ed), *Theories of Corporate Governance, The Philosophical Foundations of Corporate Governance* (London, Routledge, 2004).

[47] See MC Jensen and WH Meckling, 'Theory of the Firm: Managerial Behaviour, Agency Costs and Ownership Structure' (1976) 3 *Journal of Financial Economics* 305.

[48] The directors are often described in the literature as having a tendency to engage in 'shirking' or securing 'perks' for their own benefit.

companies. In this context, it has been argued that so-called 'director primacy' is the most efficient approach because directors are better placed to make corporate decisions than are shareholders.[49] On this basis, an overly zealous approach to resolution of the principal/agent problem may be self-defeating as corporate performance may suffer if shareholders intervene too much in corporate decision-making.

One possible way to limit agency costs is for only limited powers to be given to directors. However, this poses a problem for anything other than very small companies since most shareholders do not want to be involved in routine decision-making within companies. The approach taken by company law and (for listed companies) the Listing Rules is that, while the board of directors is given broad authority to conduct the company's affairs, shareholder approval is required for a number of important matters. They include changes to the constitution under company law and substantial transactions under the Listing Rules. This division of responsibility goes some way towards resolving the agency problem inherent in delegating responsibility to a board of directors, but it cannot remove the risk that directors will exercise their powers in a self-interested fashion rather than in the best interests of the company.

Concern over the potential for such self-interested action has been evident in two aspects of corporate governance. The first has been to ensure that the board of directors contains individuals who are independent of management. The purpose of such independent (non-executive) directors is to ensure that decisions of the board are based on the interests of the company as a whole and not just the interests of the executive directors who are responsible for running the company. The second has been to ensure that directors are not excessively remunerated at the expense of the shareholders. This poses a difficult problem of balance because incentives (eg in the form of share options) have always been regarded as important in motivating management.

9.4.2 Transaction cost economics

Transaction cost economics provides a perspective on corporate governance that focuses on the costs of carrying out business activities within an organisation by comparison with the alternative of carrying out the same activity through multiple transactions in the market. It is derived from the seminal contribution of Ronald Coase in his 1937 article 'The Nature of the Firm'.[50] Coase explained the emergence of firms (irrespective of their legal structure) by reference to their capacity to reduce the transaction costs that arise from carrying out business entirely through market transactions. According to Coase, a firm is able to replace some market transactions with an authority structure that is capable of replacing market transactions as a means of conducting business. That authority structure is built on the governance structure of the firm and the relationship

---

[49] See eg S Bainbridge, *The New Corporate Governance in Theory and Practice* (Oxford, Oxford University Press, 2008).

[50] R Coase, 'The Nature of the Firm' (1937) 4 *Economica* 386, reproduced in L Putterman and R Kroszner, *The Economic Nature of the Firm,* 2nd edn (Cambridge, Cambridge University Press, 1996) ch 7.

between the firm and its employees.[51] Thus, according to Coase, the nature of the firm and the extent to which it replaces market transactions is dependent on the extent to which the firm, as an institution, is able to economise on transaction costs by comparison with market transactions.

From this perspective, the capacity of corporate governance to limit transaction costs and improve the performance of firms is critical.[52] That capacity is linked with the costs imposed by corporate governance, such as disclosure costs, enforcement costs and operating costs (eg with respect to independent directors and board committees that are typically required by governance codes). While there are considerable costs associated with corporate governance, the general consensus among investors is that good corporate governance does have the capacity to improve operating performance, which should ultimately be reflected in share prices.[53] It has proven more difficult to establish a clear causal link between governance and performance, not least because there are many factors that affect performance.[54]

As far as the structure and approach of corporate governance are concerned, transaction cost economics has been used to promote the principle of shareholder primacy.[55] The argument is that share capital is a 'firm-specific investment', meaning in principle that it is permanent and cannot be removed because of legal restrictions relating to legal capital. In that sense, share capital is 'locked in' to a company even if the identity of the shareholders changes. Moreover, as the manner in which the share capital is managed is at the discretion of the board of directors,[56] shareholders are in a different position to creditors or employees who have the benefit of more complete contractual and regulatory protection. Thus, the argument is made that, in order to attract equity capital, shareholders must be given residual control to allow the company to raise equity capital at reasonable cost. Without that control, the cost of equity capital would rise or, in extreme situations, might not be available at all. While that approach does have some merit, other approaches to corporate governance focus more on the potential benefits (rather than costs) to shareholders that may result from the integration of stakeholder interests into the process of corporate governance.

---

[51] Thus, for example, a firm is able to direct an employee to perform a task, to supervise the process continuously and to make adjustments to the process as necessary, whereas that may not be possible if the task is allocated to a contractor through the market.

[52] See O Williamson, *The Economic Institutions of Capitalism* (The Free Press, 1985) chs 4 and 6.

[53] See R Newell and G Wilson, 'A Premium for Good Governance' (August 2002) 3 *McKinsey Quarterly* 20.

[54] See S Bhagat and B Bolton, 'Corporate Governance and Firm Performance' (2008) 14 *Journal of Corporate Finance* 257, finding that good governance is a predictor of superior operating performance but is not directly linked with share price performance; ABI, 'Governance and Performance in Corporate Britain, Evidence from the IVIS Colour-Coding System', Research Paper 7 (2008), suggesting that compliance with governance requirements in the UK is linked with superior operating and share price performance; see also M Maher and T Anderson, 'Corporate Governance: Effects on Firm Performance and Economic Growth' (OECD, 1999), available at http://www.oecd.org/dataoecd/10/34/2090569.pdf for a review of the literature and consideration of governance systems other than the UK and US.

[55] See further G Kelly and J Parkinson, 'The Conceptual Foundations of the Company' in J Parkinson, A Gamble and G Kelly (eds), *The Political Economy of the Company* (Oxford, Hart Publishing, 2000) ch 6.

[56] The extent to which that is the case is itself a function of the model of corporate governance adopted in any particular system.

9.4.3 Stakeholder theory

The concept of 'stakeholders' in a company has now become widespread. It refers to the notion that there are different groups who all have a stake in the success of a company. Shareholders and employees are always regarded as stakeholders, but customers or suppliers may or may not be regarded as stakeholders depending on their relationship with a company. The nature of a stakeholder's interest in a company differs from a shareholder in two important ways. First, there is no convenient method of measuring a stakeholder's interest analogous to the role performed by a company share. Secondly, unlike shareholders, there are substantial differences in the legal rights of different stakeholders.

Stakeholding is relevant to ownership rights in a company because it influences the residual rights of ordinary shareholders. To the extent that legal rights are allocated to other stakeholders, they limit the ownership rights of ordinary shareholders. Put another way, the characterisation of shareholders as 'owners' of a company is linked with the initial allocation of rights in the company among stakeholders. This allocation can occur in two distinct ways. First, it is possible for internal regulation to allocate rights within a company. For example, employees could be given some form of board representation or, if that is regarded as too radical, directors could simply be required to take account of the interests of employees.[57] Secondly, it is possible for external regulation to control the manner in which a company interacts with stakeholders and others. Examples are health and safety legislation, environmental regulation and statutory minimum wages. In principle, it is possible for stakeholders' interests to be recognised through either route.

The most contentious issue is to determine who should be recognised as stakeholders and how extensive the rights of the respective groups of stakeholders should be. The following groups all have some claim in this respect.

Shareholders

Shareholders are often described as the 'owners' of companies[58] and this reflects the fact that they ultimately control companies through their voting power. Their ownership is, however, residual, in the sense that shareholders exercise control subject to the rights of other stakeholders. The rationale for allocating control rights to shareholders is that it is necessary to compensate for the uncertain nature of the return provided by equity investment and the indefinite duration of their investment in the company. Put another way, shareholders are not guaranteed a financial return and bear the risk of failure because creditors' claims are given priority on insolvency: they therefore require control rights as an incentive to engage in equity investment.[59] Indeed, it is difficult to envisage that equity investment could exist without the allocation to shareholders of residual control rights.

---

[57] Section 172(1)(b) of the Companies Act 2006 requires the latter.
[58] See eg para 6.1 of the Cadbury Report, above n 1.
[59] See Kelly and Parkinson, above n 55.

Even so, it remains the case that the extent of those residual rights is a function of the rights allocated to other stakeholders.

Creditors

The case for creditors to be recognised as stakeholders is based on the significance of their contribution to company financing, through either loans or trade credit. The argument is that they have a substantial interest in the success or failure of companies and the process of corporate governance because they have a substantial investment in them. However, it has not generally been accepted in the UK that creditors' interests should be recognised in decisions made by a board of directors. Two reasons can be suggested for this. First, it is open to creditors to determine contractually the nature of their relationship with a company.[60] Secondly, the nature of the risks faced by creditors differs from that faced by shareholders in that creditors have an agreed return on their investment and their claims are given priority over shareholders in the event of insolvency. The most recent review of company law in the UK has followed this approach, concluding that it is not appropriate to require a board of directors to take account of creditors' interests.[61]

Employees

The claim of employees to be recognised as stakeholders is based on either the simple observation that they are essential to the success of a company or the more complex argument that, like shareholders, they make a firm-specific investment and that, in those circumstances, it is efficient for the corporate sector as a whole to award control rights to employees so as to minimise transaction costs.[62] Inherent in the second argument is the idea that employment contracts are, in essence, incomplete or 'relational' contracts and control rights act as a substitute for more detailed or 'complete' contracts. In some other countries, these arguments have been used to justify representation of employees at board level;[63] in the UK, however, there has been resistance to employee representation at board level (albeit that company law leaves the matter entirely to the shareholders). Even the requirement that directors take account of employees' interests[64] is of little direct relevance because it cannot be enforced directly by employees. Recognition of employees' interests in the UK has largely been developed through external regulation, such as health and safety regulation and employment law.

---

[60] See Chapter 7.5 for a discussion of this issue.

[61] See Company Law Review Steering Group (CLRSG), 'Modern Company Law for a Competitive Economy, Developing the Framework' (March 2000) paras 3.72–3.73. The position changes when a company approaches insolvency as in those circumstances the shareholders' financial interest is worthless and directors must act to preserve the value of creditors' claims: see *Liquidator of West Mercia Safetywear Ltd v Dodd* [1988] BCLC 250 (CA).

[62] See Kelly and Parkinson, above n 55.

[63] See CJ Meier-Schatz, 'Corporate Governance and Legal Rules: A Transnational Look at Concepts and Problems of Internal Management Control' (1988) 13 *Journal of Corporation Law* 431.

[64] Companies Act 2006, s 172(1)(b).

Customers/suppliers

The customers and suppliers of companies are clearly essential to its success, but that observation does not in itself establish a claim to the status of 'stakeholder'. It is possible to apply the 'firm-specific' investment argument (above) to some instances in which companies have a particularly close relationship with specific customers or suppliers, but that would probably be the exception rather than the norm. Reflecting this, customers' interests are largely recognised through external regulation (eg the law relating to sale and product safety) and they are given no status within the internal organisation of companies. Suppliers have traditionally been in the same position,[65] but it is now required that directors take account of all these interests.[66]

Society at large

The idea that society at large can be considered a stakeholder in companies is reflected in the development of the concept of corporate social responsibility. This refers to the idea that companies should be expected (and may indeed have economic incentives) to act in a manner that is socially responsible.[67] This goes beyond observing the minimum requirements set by the law and includes a company's approach to the environment, equal opportunities and remuneration. In essence, it deals with the issue of whether or not a company is viewed in its own right as a responsible citizen. The increasing acceptance of corporate social responsibility as an issue relevant to the monitoring by shareholders of management and to an assessment of a company's prospects is reflected to some extent in the widespread adoption by companies of ethical codes that extend beyond compliance with legal and regulatory obligations.[68]

9.4.4 Stewardship theory

Stewardship theory has its roots in psychology and sociology, and adopts a model of man based on a steward whose behaviour is ordered such that pro-organisational, collectivistic behaviour has a higher utility than individualistic, self-serving behaviour.[69] Contrary to the principal/agent model, stewards believe that their interests are aligned with that of

---

[65] It is possible to argue that suppliers have not been afforded the same degree of protection as customers as they often bear the risks arising from limited liability when a company fails. However, there are legal mechanisms available to suppliers to protect their interests (such as retaining legal title to goods until full payment is made).

[66] Companies Act 2006, s 172(1)(e).

[67] See generally Department of Trade and Industry (DTI), 'Business and Society, Corporate Social Responsibility Report' (2002).

[68] See K Bondy, D Matten and J Moon, 'Multinational Corporation Codes of Conduct: Governance Tools for Corporate Social Responsibilty?' (2008)16(4) *Corporate Governance* 295, 302, finding 'that codes are more often used as tools for governing traditional business issues such as ensuring compliance with laws and regulations, improving the corporation's reputation, and guiding employees in terms of expected workplace behavior'. That study focused on codes in Canada, the UK and Germany.

[69] See generally J Davis, F Schoorman and L Donaldson, 'Towards a Stewardship Theory of Management' (1997) 22(1) *Academy of Management Review* 20.

the company and it owners and therefore the steward's interests and utility motivations are directed to organisational rather than personal objectives. As a result, stewardship theory focuses on governance structures that facilitate and empower rather than those that monitor and control. The extent to which the model may influence the relationship between owners and managers and the governance structure of a company is dependent on the degree or risk that is acceptable to each side and the degree of trust that is present in the relationship. Stewardship theory predicts that the performance of the company will be maximised and costs minimised where both sides voluntarily select a stewardship relationship rather than a principal agent relationship.

While it may be difficult to identify the influence of stewardship theory in the techniques and language that is employed by governance codes (which tend to be heavily influenced by principal/agent theory), its influence is clearly evident in company law in the UK, which generally provides very broad discretion to the board of directors. However, to the extent that the development of codes of corporate governance can be viewed as a means of making the exercise of that discretion more transparent and accountable, there is implicit recognition that the risk preference and trust of investors is quite low with regard to the decisions and actions of the board. Thus, while stewardship theory may be employed successfully in private companies or mutual organisations, where there may be scope for a greater degree of trust as between owners and managers, it has not gained acceptance as a technique for public listed companies at their current stage of evolution.

9.5 Evolution of corporate governance codes

The development of corporate governance codes can be viewed largely as a response to the relatively wide sphere of discretion enjoyed by directors in running companies and the limited obligations placed on institutional shareholders in monitoring and controlling companies. The existence of wide discretion in both spheres carries benefits in terms of flexibility but also creates potential problems. As regards directors' discretion, the main risks are excessive or inappropriate risk taking, manipulation of financial results and excessive remuneration. From the shareholders' perspective, it is less obvious that discretion in exercising voting rights poses risks, but for the corporate sector as a whole it is likely that the absence of any formal or informal requirement to vote will tend over time to weaken shareholder monitoring.

Developments in corporate governance in the UK over the past two decades address both these issues. The specific impetus for change was a number of high-profile corporate failures that highlighted the risks associated with ineffective control of company management.[70] However, the concerns underlying the developments in the 1990s had been

---

[70] See generally B Cheffins, *Company Law, Theory, Structure and Operation* (Oxford, Oxford University Press, 1997) 612–13.

evident for a long time.[71] The Cohen Committee, set up in 1945 to review company law, observed that:[72]

> The illusory nature of the control theoretically exercised by shareholders over directors has been accentuated by the dispersion of capital among an increasing number of small shareholders who pay little attention to their investments, so long as satisfactory dividends are forthcoming, who lack sufficient time, money and experience to make full use of their rights as occasions arise and who are, in many cases, too numerous and too widely dispersed to be able to organise themselves.

Later initiatives also recognised problems but the prevailing support for self-regulatory solutions was an important factor in preventing statutory intervention. For example, the Jenkins Committee, which recommended changes in company law in 1962, warned against excessive regulation of the corporate sector.[73] In 1973 the CBI published a report entitled The Responsibilities of the British Public Company[74] in which it argued that self-regulation and evolution in corporate governance were preferable to statutory intervention. Many of the principles contained in the current UK Code of Corporate Governance can be traced back to the Principles of Corporate Conduct adopted by the CBI at that time. The tendency to favour self-regulation over statutory intervention was continued by the government-sponsored review of company law that preceded the Companies Act 2006 on the basis that it provides for a more competitive and effective system of regulation than statutory regulation.[75]

Another factor supporting self-regulation then and now is the activity of investor bodies such as the Institutional Shareholders Committee (ISC), the Investment Management Association (IMA), the ABI and the National Association of Pension Funds (NAPF).[76] These bodies represent the collective interests of institutional investors in listed companies. While they could no doubt operate effectively whether corporate governance was subject to statutory intervention or not, their existence and power makes self-regulation workable. These bodies are able, through their members' extensive shareholdings, to ensure that companies comply with codes that they have endorsed. Without such organisations, much of the impetus for developing and implementing codes of corporate governance would be missing. Although they act primarily in their own interests, their activities also bring benefits to other investors.

The self-regulatory approach underpinned the development of corporate governance in the UK during the 1990s. None of the codes have a formal legal status. Nor do they form part of the Listing Rules, with the result that non-compliance cannot threaten a company's listed status. Reliance is instead placed on disclosure of the extent to which

---

[71] See generally S Sheikh and S Chatterjee, 'Perspectives on Corporate Governance' in Sheikh and Rees, above n 3, ch 1.

[72] Board of Trade, Report of the Company Law Committee (1945) Cmnd 6659.

[73] Board of Trade, Report of the Company Law Committee (1962) Cmnd 1749, 3 para 11.

[74] CBI, 'The Responsibilities of the British Public Company: Final Report of the Company Affairs Committee' (1973).

[75] See CLRSG, 'Modern Company Law for a Competitive Economy: Final Report' (1998) paras 1.28 and 3.5.

[76] See Chapter 5.7 for more detail regarding these organisations.

a listed company has complied with the relevant code. This opens up the possibility of institutional investors applying pressure on companies who do not comply. On the assumption that the codes have introduced measures that improve governance, it is also likely that disclosure of non-compliance will have a negative influence on a company's share price as the market will assume that such a company operates a suboptimal governance structure.

The Financial Reporting Council (FRC), the London Stock Exchange and the accountancy profession established a Committee on the Financial Aspects of Corporate Governance in May 1991. Its first report (the Cadbury Report in 1992) represents the most significant landmark in the development of a code of corporate governance in the UK. It produced a Code of Best Practice that dealt with the structure and role of the board of directors, the role of non-executive directors, directors' remuneration, and reporting and controls. This was followed in 1995 by a second report from the Greenbury Committee, whose remit was to set out best practice in determining and accounting for directors' remuneration. The final report of the Committee (the Hampel Report in 1998) considered the implementation of the Cadbury and Greenbury Reports and was given the fresh task of examining the roles of directors, shareholders and auditors in corporate governance. Following the final report, the committee produced the Combined Code, which consolidated the recommendations of all three reports. A revised version of the Combined Code was published in 2003 and incorporated the 'Turnbull Guidance on Internal Control',[77] the 'Smith Guidance'[78] (on audit committees) and the 'Higgs Suggestions for Good Practice'.[79] Following the FRC's review of the Code and its subsequent revision in 2010, it became known as the UK Corporate Governance Code. The change in title was linked with changes in the UK listing regime, which resulted in foreign companies with a premium listing being required to report against the Code.[80] The new title was intended to communicate more clearly the Code's status as the UK's recognised corporate governance standard.

The UK Code is appended to but does not form part of the Listing Rules. A company with a premium listing is, however, required to state in its annual report and accounts:

1. how they applied the main principles of the UK Code (the 'appliance statement'); and
2. whether they have complied with the guidance in the Code, and to give reasons for any areas of non-compliance (the 'compliance' statement).[81]

The rationale for this approach is explained in the following terms:

> The 'comply or explain' approach is the trademark of corporate governance in the UK. It has been in operation since the Code's beginnings and is the foundation of the Code's flexibility.

---

[77] Turnbull Committee, 'Internal Control: Guidance for Directors on the Combined Code' (Institute of Chartered Accountants in England and Wales, September 1999).

[78] R Smith, 'Audit Committees: Combined Code Guidance' (January 2003).

[79] D Higgs, 'Review of the Role and Effectiveness of Non-executive Directors' (Janaury 2003).

[80] See further Chapters 8.2.2 and 8.2.5.

[81] LR 9.8.6R(6). In referring to a company's approach to the Code, a distinction should be drawn between 'conformance' and 'compliance'. A company may conform to the Code by explaining why it does not comply with guidance.

It is strongly supported by both companies and shareholders and has been widely admired and imitated internationally.[82]

Some observations can be made about this approach.[83] First, if flexibility is desired because there is no clear link between corporate governance standards and company performance, it can be questioned whether there is any point in having any standards. In other words, if it is not clear that the objective (improved performance) can be achieved by the means proposed (corporate governance standards), the nature of the proposed standards makes little difference. Secondly, if the preoccupation with flexibility is instead simply to allow companies to adapt rules to suit their own particular circumstances, so as to avoid a 'one size fits all' approach, it is not clear that that this can only be achieved outside a formal legal framework. For example, the process by which a company can 'tailor' its articles of association from default rules set by company law provides a clear analogy that could be applied to the Code. However, it must be recognised that the speed with which the Code can be and has been updated does offer a significant advantage by comparison with the long delays associated with reform of company law. Moreover, the FRC's 2009 review of the Code confirmed that there was a strong preference among investors for retaining the current self-regulatory approach and little enthusiasm for the FRC or Financial Services Authority (FSA) to take on a more formal role in enforcement.[84]

In the majority of cases, companies have chosen to comply with the Code rather than to explain deviations. Moreover, in those cases where there has been non-compliance, the explanations offered by the relevant companies have often been poor—and in some cases no explanation has been offered at all.[85] Empirical studies of compliance have concluded that the 'comply or explain' process is linked with performance in several ways. One is that companies with a record of non-compliance tend to outperform compliant companies. That may be understood by reference to the willingness of investors to tolerate non-compliance in the case of companies where the management have a good record and to intervene only when performance deteriorates.[86] Another is that returns of non-compliers differ significantly according to the quality of explanations. That can be explained on the basis that poor (or non-existent) explanations may be an indicator of poor governance, and also that the market pays little attention to the quality of explanations and places greater emphasis on compliance.[87] The FRC explained the tendency to focus on compliance in its 2009 review of the Code on the basis that there was a view

---

[82] 'Comply or explain' preamble to the Combined Code (2010 version), para 1.

[83] See generally C Riley, 'The Juridification of Corporate Governance' in J de Lacy (ed), *The Reform of UK Company Law* (London, Cavendish, 2002).

[84] The FRC's role in enforcement derives from its remit over the content of companies' annual report and accounts. The FSA's role derives from its function as the UK Listing Authority. Neither body has been active in enforcing the disclosure requirements under the Code: see I MacNeil, 'The Evolution of Regulatory Enforcement Action in the UK Capital Markets: A Case of "Less is More"?' (2007) 2(4) *Capital Markets Law Journal* 345.

[85] S Arcot and V Bruno, 'In Letter But Not in Spirit: An Analysis of Corporate Governance in the UK' (May 2006), available at SSRN: http://ssrn.com/abstract=819784 (accessed on 16 August 2011).

[86] I MacNeil and X Li, 'Comply or Explain: Market Discipline and Non-compliance with the Combined Code' (2006) 14(5) *Corporate Governance: An International Review* 486.

[87] S Arcot, V Bruno and A Grimaud, 'Corporate Governance in the UK: Is the Comply or-Explain Approach Working?' (2010) 30(2) *International Review of Law and Economics* 193.

among many participants that explaining rather than complying means that something is necessarily wrong.[88] However, since a box-ticking approach to compliance with the Code effectively removes the flexibility provided by the 'comply or explain' approach, the FRC encouraged companies to consider carefully whether non-compliance was beneficial and, if so, to provide a clear explanation to shareholders of why it has reached that view.

The approach adopted in the UK has attracted considerable international support, extending beyond common law jurisdictions with which the UK shares a similar approach to corporate law.[89] The EU's first move was the adoption of a recommendation inviting Member States to take steps to introduce provisions concerning the role of non-executive directors in listed companies, either on a 'comply or explain' basis or through legislation.[90] Subsequently, the EU adopted a requirement that companies whose securities are admitted to trading on a regulated market is required make a corporate governance statement in its annual report containing at least the following information:

(a) a reference to:
 (i) the corporate governance code to which the company is subject, and/or
 (ii) the corporate governance code which the company may have voluntarily decided to apply,
 and/or
 (iii) all relevant information about the corporate governance practices applied beyond the requirements under national law.
 Where points (i) and (ii) apply, the company shall also indicate where the relevant texts are publicly available; where point (iii) applies, the company shall make its corporate governance practices publicly available;
(b) to the extent to which a company, in accordance with national law, departs from a corporate governance code referred to under points (a)(i) or (ii), an explanation by the company as to which parts of the corporate governance code it departs from and the reasons for doing so. Where the company has decided not to apply any provisions of a corporate governance code referred to under points (a)(i) or (ii), it shall explain its reasons for doing so;
(c) a description of the main features of the company's internal control and risk management systems in relation to the financial reporting process;[91]

The implementation of this requirement in EU Member States is linked with the status and content of the Code in each country and therefore there is no harmonisation beyond the high level adoption of the 'comply or explain' principle in the 2006 Accounting Directive.[92] That in itself distinguishes the EU as separate from the US which has not adopted the 'comply or explain' approach to corporate governance but has instead stuck with its long-standing statutory approach.[93]

---

[88] FRC, '2009 Review of the Combined Code: Final Report' (December 2009).

[89] Australia, Hong Kong and Singapore all have 'comply or explain' codes of corporate governance.

[90] Commission Recommendation 2005/162/EC [2005] OJ L52/51. Recommendations are not binding in Member States.

[91] Art 1(7) of Directive 2006/46/EC [2006] OJ L224/1.

[92] See F Wymeersch, 'The Enforcement of Corporate Governance Codes' (2006) 6(1) *Journal of Corporate Law Studies* 113.

[93] The Dodd-Frank Act of 2010 is the latest stage in the evolution of the US approach. The earlier Sarbanes-Oxley Act of 2002 attracted considerable criticism for the costs it imposed on non-US companies that were SEC-registered as a result of having securities listed in the US.

9.6 Shareholder engagement

While codes perform an important function in terms of setting appropriate board structures and decision-making processes, effective corporate governance demands ongoing engagement by shareholders in the form of monitoring and the exercise of voting rights. In the absence of such engagement, directors will not be properly held to account for their decisions and matters that are reserved for shareholder decision-making may fall under the influence of the board or a small group of shareholders. In those circumstances, the danger is that the company will not be run in the interests of the general body of shareholders and other stakeholders (to the extent that their interests must be considered).

The adoption of the Stewardship Code by the FRC in July 2010 represents an important step in the facilitation of engagement.[94] The preface to the Code sets out its objectives clearly: 'The Stewardship Code aims to enhance the quality of engagement between institutional investors and companies and to help improve long-term returns to shareholders and the efficient exercise of governance responsibilities.'

Both in origin and development, the Code has been an industry-sponsored initiative.[95] The original statement on 'The Responsibilities of Institutional Shareholders in the UK' was published by the ISC in 1991. Following the recommendations of the Myners Report in 2001 on incorporating shareholders activism into fund management mandates, the ISC developed best practice guidance for the investment industry by way of its 2002 Statement of Principles on the responsibilities of institutional shareholders and their agents in respect of investee companies. The statement was reviewed and reissued in 2004 and 2007, and was published in the form of a Code in November 2009. Like its predecessor, the Code applies to institutional investors on a 'comply or explain' basis. In reporting terms, this entails providing a statement on the institution's website that contains:

- a description of how the principles of the Code have been applied and
- disclosure of the specific information listed under Principles 1, 5, 6 and 7; or
- an explanation if these elements of the Code have not been complied with.

As with the Combined Code, that approach is intended to permit flexibility, so that institutional investors subject to the Code can in appropriate circumstances choose not to comply and explain why.

9.6.1 Voting

The law relating to the manner in which shareholders are able to exercise their votes is fundamental to the framework of corporate governance. This is so because voting rights

---

[94] The Code is reproduced on the FRC website at http://www.frc.org.uk/corporate/investorgovernance.cfm (2010).

[95] See generally I MacNeil, 'Activism and Collaboration Among Shareholders in UK Listed Companies' (2010) 5(4) *Capital Markets Law Journal* 419. The text below draws on this article.

are central to the 'property' that is owned by a shareholder. Those property rights are derived primarily from the contract that is represented by the company constitution and that contract is widely recognised as being incomplete because it cannot anticipate all future events that will give rise to issues regarding shareholders' rights. A governance structure, in which voting rights play a central part, creates the possibility for investment to be attracted into a company despite the incomplete nature of the rights granted to investors by the company constitution. It follows that the manner in which the law controls the exercise of voting rights is fundamental to the relationship between shareholders and a company, as well as to the relationship among shareholders.

The default rule under company law is that each share in a company carries one vote.[96] This rule can be varied by the articles of association to create non-voting shares or to provide enhanced voting rights to certain shares. In the case of listed companies, resistance on the part of institutional investors to non-voting or weighted voting shares has resulted in the default rule becoming the norm. Listed companies that in the past did not adopt the principle of one vote per share have now largely been forced to fall in line.

The person entitled to vote is the registered owner of a share and company law prohibits the interest of any other person being recorded in a company's register of shareholders.[97] While this rules out an indirect investor (eg a person holding through a nominee) being recorded as the legal owner, it does not preclude arrangements that allow indirect investors to exercise voting rights. Such arrangements can be created through a contract between an indirect investor and an intermediary (who is the registered holder) supported by changes to a company's constitution (so as to recognise the vote of the indirect investor).[98] Entitlement to vote carries with it no obligation to vote. Some shareholders are passive in the sense that they generally do not vote on resolutions and this is generally attributed to the fact that most regard themselves as having a shareholding too small to exert influence over resolutions.[99] The result may be that it is possible for a relatively small shareholding to give effective control over a company. However, the Stewardship Code now requires fund managers to have a policy on voting and, particularly with regard to contentious issues such as remuneration, there has been a marked increase in voting in recent years.[100]

At one time, it appeared that the common law might have developed a rule requiring shareholders to vote by reference to interests other than their own. That possibility arose from a line of case law relating to the exercise of powers by a company. In one case, it

---

[96] Companies Act 2006, s 284. It was not always so: see C Dunlavy in Hopt et al (eds), *Comparative Corporate Governance, The State of the Art and Emerging Research* (Oxford, Oxford University Press, 1998); see also HG Manne, 'Some Theoretical Aspects of Share Voting' (1964) 64 *Columbia Law Review* 1427.

[97] Companies Act 2006, s 126. The prohibition does not apply to companies registered in Scotland.

[98] See R Nolan, 'Indirect Investors: A Greater Say in the Company' (2003) 3 *Journal of Corporate Law Studies* 73, citing the example of BP's enfranchisement of holders of depositary receipts (explained in Chapter 4.9) issued in connection with its takeover of Amoco and ARCO. The Companies Act 2006, pt 9 permits a company to recognise the rights of persons other than the registered shareholder; however, only the registered shareholder has the right to sell.

[99] But see below Chapter 9.4.2 for evidence of recent changes in behaviour.

[100] See the ABI/IVIS Review 2009 at http://www.abi.org.uk/Media/Releases/2010/04/IVIS_Review_2009_.aspx (accessed on 16 August 2011); see also KM Sheehan, 'Is the Outrage Constraint an Effective Constraint on Executive Remuneration? Evidence from the UK and Preliminary Results from Australia' (2007), available at http://ssrn.com/abstract=974965 (accessed on 16 August 2011).

was held that the general principle applicable to all instances of the exercise of powers by a company is that the power must be exercised 'bona fide for the benefit of the company as a whole'.[101] That principle has proven difficult to apply to resolutions adopted by a company, in the main because it qualifies the general principle that shareholders, including controlling shareholders, are entitled to vote according to their own interests provided that such action is not illegal or fraudulent, or oppressive towards those who oppose it.[102] The clear implication of a requirement to vote bona fide for the benefit of the company as a whole is that a much wider duty would be imposed on shareholders than simply to avoid oppression of a minority.

Later cases attempted to clarify the meaning of such a duty. On one occasion[103] the court took the view that the determination of whether a resolution was bona fide in the interests of the company was for the shareholders and not the court to decide, subject to the right of the court to intervene if it could not reasonably be regarded as being in the interests of the company. On another,[104] 'bona fide' was taken to mean simply the honest opinion of the particular shareholder casting his vote, and 'the company as whole' was taken to be a reference to the interests of an individual hypothetical member. The implication was that a particular shareholder was required, before casting his vote, to consider the position of such a hypothetical shareholder, assuming such a person could be identified. A later case[105] illustrated the difficulty of applying such a test: in that case there were only two shareholders in the company, and the interests of a hypothetical shareholder were equated with those of the minority shareholder despite the ostensible application of the approach adopted in *Greenhalgh*. The decision in *Clemens* is of particular interest in that the majority shareholder was prevented from authorising a new issue of shares because the result of the new issue would be to reduce the shareholding of the minority shareholder to below 25%, resulting in the minority shareholder being unable to block a special resolution.

The net result is that, in the absence of special circumstances such as those that applied in *Clemens* (which could not arise in the case of a listed company), shareholders are entitled to vote simply by reference to their own interests. Such control as does exist over voting has developed through two routes. The first is the legal restrictions on the manner in which shareholders can vote. While the general rule is that shareholders are entitled to vote according to their own interest, they cannot use their votes to ratify[106] breaches of directors' duty in respect of acts that are illegal or fraudulent.[107] Nor can shareholders who are connected with a director who is in breach of duty

---

[101] *Allen v Gold Reefs of West Africa Ltd* [1900] 1 Ch 656, 671 per Lindley MR.

[102] *Northwest Transportation Co v Beatty* (1887) 12 AC 589, 593.

[103] *Shuttleworth v Cox Brothers* [1927] 2 KB 9.

[104] *Greenhalgh v Arderne Cinemas* [1950] 2 All ER 1120.

[105] *Clemens v Clemens Bros Ltd* [1976] 2 All ER 268. See also V Joffe, 'Majority Rule Undermined?' (1977) 40 *Modern Law Review* 71.

[106] Ratification enables a principal to 'cure' an act of an agent that exceeds the authority of the agent or is in breach of duty.

[107] See *Franbar Holdings Ltd V Patel and others* [2008] EWHC 1534.

vote on a resolution to ratify the breach.[108] The second type of control over voting is self-regulation on the part of institutional investors.[109] These restrictions are intended to enhance the ownership rights of institutional investors by taking a uniform line on the authorisation of certain action (eg share issues) and cannot be viewed as restrictions in the same way as the common law rules, which are focused on the prevention of oppression of minority shareholders.

It can be concluded, therefore, that the law gives shareholders a relatively free hand in exercising their votes. This creates an environment that is, at least at the level of the individual shareholder, conducive to the adoption of an activist stance in respect of corporate governance. The law does not require an activist stance, but it does facilitate it. However, as discussed in 9.1 above, there are other factors that work in the opposite direction.

9.6.2 Activism and collaboration

The term 'shareholder activism' is used here to refer to the extent to which shareholders become involved in active monitoring and supervision of companies in which they are invested. Shareholders generally have two options when there is a liquid market in the relevant securities. The first is that they can engage in monitoring and supervising the company with a view to ensuring that it is operating efficiently and according to their wishes.[110] The second is that they do not engage in monitoring and supervision, but instead simply sell the securities of companies with which they are dissatisfied. The first option has been characterised as the exercise of 'voice' and the second as 'exit'.[111] The extent to which the exit option is available is dependent on the liquidity of the capital market and the degree to which shareholdings are concentrated. If shareholdings are typically concentrated (as indicated by the presence of controlling shareholders), it will be more difficult to exercise the exit option and therefore there may be no alternative but to exercise the voice option. On the other hand, the conditions under which the exit option is generally available (widely dispersed share ownership) are such that the exercise of voice in a meaningful manner by a single investor is usually not possible. Exit and voice are therefore not alternatives in all circumstances. The legal framework in the UK surrounding the exercise of voting rights by shareholders supports the 'voice versus exit' analysis. As noted above, shareholders are under no duty to vote and when they do they are entitled to vote as they wish. Moreover, the UK, unlike some other countries,[112] does

---

[108] Companies Act 2006, s 239. This section also prevents the relevant director voting on the resolution if he is a shareholder.

[109] See eg the voting restrictions adopted by the Pre-Emption Group in respect of the disapplication of pre-emption rights, discussed in Chapter 7.3.2.

[110] For a discussion of how investors do this, see S Gillan and L Starks, 'Corporate Governance, Corporate Ownership and the Role of Institutional Investors: A Global Perspective' Working Paper 2003-01 (John Weinberg Centre for Corporate Governance, University of Delaware, 2003), available at SSRN: http://ssrn.com/abstract=439500 (accessed on 16 August 2011).

[111] See n 9 above regarding the origin of this terminology.

[112] See B Black and J Coffee, 'Hail Britannia? Institutional Investor Behaviour under Limited Regulation' (1997) 92 *Michigan Law Review* 1.

not generally restrict the ability of shareholders to collaborate over voting on resolutions, thereby making it possible, at least in principle, for some form of collective voice to be exercised.

Shareholders have largely been passive investors in the UK.[113] The Hampel Committee Report commented:[114] 'Typically institutions used not to take much interest in corporate governance . . . Institutions tended not to vote their shares regularly, and to intervene directly with company managements only in circumstances of crisis.'

In 2001, Paul Myners[115] wrote to the then Chancellor Gordon Brown setting out the conclusions of his review into institutional investment in the UK. He commented that: 'the review is clear that fund managers remain unnecessarily reluctant to take an activist stance in relation to corporate underperformance, even where this would be in their clients' financial interests'.[116] While this conclusion was influential in prompting a number of changes in the legal and regulatory framework, and in the practices of institutional investors, the issue came to the fore once again in the wake of the global financial crisis. Sir David Walker observed in his 2009 review of corporate governance in UK banks and other financial institutions that: 'With hindsight it seems clear that the board and director shortcomings discussed in the previous chapter would have been tackled rather more effectively had there been more vigorous scrutiny and persistence by major investors acting as owners.'[117]

A number of explanations can be offered for this. One is that there is little incentive for an individual shareholder to engage in costly monitoring of listed companies. Any benefits to the share price resulting from that monitoring have to be shared with other investors, whereas the costs have to be borne by the individual shareholder (the classic 'free rider' problem). While such monitoring might be an attractive proposition for a controlling shareholder, who can retain much of the value derived from monitoring, the relatively widely dispersed nature of share ownership in the UK makes that scenario unlikely. The obvious solution might be collective action. However, while institutional investors do engage in collective action in relation to matters which affect their collective interest, monitoring individual companies raises issues of competitive advantage as between institutional investors. Institutional investors are competitors and are unlikely to collaborate in monitoring companies on a routine basis[118] because monitoring is an integral part of investment management. Another explanation is that the nature of retail investment products creates a complex link between the ultimate investor and the investee

---

[113] See eg A Peacock and G Bannock, *Corporate Takeovers and the Public Interest* (Aberdeen, Aberdeen University Press, 1991) 32, who refer to a 1991 NAPF survey showing that nearly a quarter of pension funds had a policy of never using their shareholders' voting rights, while only 20% had a policy of voting at all times.

[114] Para 5.2. ABI, 'Statement of Voting Policy and Corporate Governance Good Practice' (1998) 32 indicated some change: 'ABI members have made an active voting policy a priority and this is reflected in their creditable voting record in recent years.' By 2008, all members of the Investment Management Association had policy statements on engagement and most made them public: see IMA, 'Survey of Fund Managers' Engagement with Companies' (2008).

[115] Now Lord Myners.

[116] Myners Report, above n 10.

[117] 'A Review of Corporate Governance in UK banks and Other Financial Industry Entities' (July 2009) 60, available at http://www.hm-treasury.gov.uk/walker_review_information.htm (accessed on 16 August 2011).

[118] For examples of collaboration on specific issues see Black and Coffee, above n 112.

company, and thereby discourages activism on the part of those persons and organisations that together link the company and the ultimate investor.[119]

The system under which a substantial proportion of institutional funds are managed in the UK is another explanation for shareholder passivity.[120] Pension funds in particular tend to be managed under relatively short-term contracts, with the result that there may be little incentive to incur monitoring costs that do not yield an immediate benefit.[121] Potential conflicts of interest may also contribute to passivity. They are likely to arise when there are business links between investors and companies (eg between a bank shareholder and a company that is a customer of the bank) that could be threatened if an active stance were to be adopted. It is also possible that widespread use of nominees and custodians, which results in an 'ownership' chain being interposed between an investor and an issuer, results in either confusion over exactly who is entitled to exercise voting rights or administrative difficulty in passing voting rights down the 'ownership' chain.[122]

The Stewardship Code aims to enhance the quality of engagement between institutional investors and companies not only because of its potential to improve corporate performance but also as way of ensuring that institutional investors discharge their fiduciary duties to the clients whose funds they manage. The following principles are of particular significance in this regard:

- Principle 3: Institutional investors should monitor their investee companies.
- Principle 4: Institutional investors should establish clear guidelines on when and how they will escalate their activities as a method of protecting and enhancing shareholder value.
- Principle 5: Institutional investors should be willing to act collectively with other investors where appropriate.

Both observation and measurement of shareholder activism is complicated by the fact that much of it takes place behind closed doors and that in many instances a public initiative is the outcome of a failed private dialogue between a company and shareholders.[123] Public initiatives may be informal in that they may do no more than publicly contest the management's view of a particular issue. That represents an important and potentially powerful form of intervention at key points in a company's development, such as at the time of a strategic acquisition.[124] However, public intervention with a longer-term objective or a broader focus, such as a change in strategy, is likely to take the form of a

---

[119] See J Gray, 'Personal Finance and Corporate Governance: The Missing Link: Product Regulation and Policy Conflicts' (2004) 4 *Journal of Corporate Law Studies* 187.

[120] See generally Chapter 5.6.

[121] J Coffee, 'Liquidity versus Control: The Institutional Investor as Corporate Monitor' (1991) 91 *Columbia Law Review* 1277, 1325 makes the same point in respect of the US.

[122] Although it is the registered owner of shares who is entitled to vote, it is possible for voting rights to be passed down an 'ownership' chain through contractual provisions in custody agreements.

[123] See IMA, above n 114, 19; se also J McCahery, Z Sautner and L Starks, 'Behind the Scenes: The Corporate Governance Preferences of Institutional Investors' ECGI Finance Working Paper No 235/2009, available at SSRN: http://ssrn.com/abstract=1571046 (accessed on 16 August 2011).

[124] The proposed acquisition by Prudential of AIA provided several examples of public intervention by shareholders: see eg 'Investors Sharpen Knives for Pru Chiefs', *Financial Times*, 21 June 2010.

shareholder-sponsored resolution. As already noted, such resolutions are binding in the UK. While they are rare in the case of large listed companies, empirical studies agree that poorly performing companies are most likely to be the target of such resolutions.[125] Moreover, it is not surprising that the relative ease with which directors can be removed in the UK results in resolutions with that objective being the most common form of public intervention.

As envisaged by the guidance to Principles 4 and 5 of the Stewardship Code, collaboration represents an escalation of unilateral activism. In a system of dispersed shareholding such as the UK, collaboration among shareholders can create a coalition that is able to exercise influence over the incumbent board. As a technique for resolving the agency problem in corporate governance and exercising effective discipline over management, it offers a functional equivalent to blockholding, which has emerged as the more common solution to that problem worldwide.[126] The degree of influence that can be exerted by a coalition is linked with the intervention options that are open to shareholders at critical levels of ownership (such as calling a general meeting at the 5% ownership level[127]), since the threat posed by a coalition that has sufficient votes to trigger those measures will often be sufficient to secure the cooperation of the incumbent board. Reflecting past practice,[128] the Stewardship Code envisages that 'collaborative engagement may be most appropriate at times of significant corporate or wider economic stress, or when the risks posed threaten the ability of the company to continue'.[129] Collaboration is clearly viewed as appropriate only in a sub-set of circumstances in which intervention is appropriate since Principle 4 leaves (individual) institutional investors to formulate their own policy on intervention, including the circumstances in which it is appropriate. The preference for individual over collective intervention is clearly evident in the ladder for escalation provided in the guidance to Principle 4, in which joint intervention is the fourth step after three stages of individual dialogue with the company. That preference for individual over joint action also reflects a long-standing tradition of equality of treatment for shareholders and strong minority rights, both of which can be viewed as antidotes to the threat of excessive influence being wielded by blockholders and the risk of value-decreasing behaviour associated with that influence.[130] There is ultimately a trade-off that has to be made between the potential benefits that may arise from blockholder influence as a disciplinary mechanism and the risks that may arise from undue influence and value-

---

[125] As regards the UK see B Buchanan, J Netter and T Yang, 'Proxy Rules and Proxy Practices: An Empirical Study of US and UK Shareholder Proposals' (2009), available at SSRN: http://ssrn.com/abstract=1474062 (accessed on 16 August 2011); as regards the US see S Gillan and L Starks, 'The Evolution of Shareholder Activism in the United States' (2007) 19(1) *Journal of Applied Corporate Finance* 55.

[126] See Becht et al, above n 8.

[127] Under s 303 of the Companies Act 2006.

[128] See eg the interview-based study of British institutional investment in Black and Coffee, above n 112, 31: 'What types of issues trigger the formation of a coalition? Most interviewees responded that it usually took a financial crisis, including a sharp decline in share price . . .'.

[129] Stewardship Code, Principle 5, Guidance.

[130] Such value decreasing behaviour can be in the form of expropriation of private benefits or collusion with management at the expense of minority shareholders: see Becht et al, above n 8, 5.2.

decreasing behaviour: and while most systems of corporate governance prioritise the former (as evidenced by a legal and institutional framework that supports blockholding), the UK has placed relatively greater emphasis on the latter in its legal and institutional framework.[131]

---

[131] The same conclusion tends to be made in respect of the US, but care should be taken in characterising the US system as one of dispersed ownership: see A Pichhadze, 'The Nature of Corporate Ownership in the USA: The Trend Towards the Market Oriented Blockholder Model' (2010) 5(1) *Capital Markets Law Journal* 63–88.

Corporate Governance— Board Structure and Operation

This chapter focuses in more detail on three issues that have been the main focus of the UK Corporate Governance Code. The first is the structure and operation of the board of directors. In the UK, this issue has been approached largely through a 'shareholder primacy' model of corporate governance, in which the balance of power between the shareholders and the board is tilted in favour of the shareholders.[1] The second issue is the remuneration of directors, which has been a contentious and problematic issue ever since the Cadbury Committee first initiated the development of the system of corporate governance in the form of a Code.[2] The financial crisis focused further attention on that issue, particularly for Financial Services Authority (FSA)-authorised firms, and while there has been a regulatory response it remains to be seen what its effect will be. The chapter concludes with an examination of the legal and regulatory framework for audit. The reliability of audit reports and links between companies and their auditors have been an underlying concern in corporate governance for some time. The more recent trend has been for regulatory intervention to focus on risk management and internal controls, thereby shifting the focus of the board and the auditor's attention from *ex post* reporting to *ex ante* assessment and control of risk within a broad framework that is set by shareholders.

---

[1] For the merits of the alternative model of 'director primacy' see S Bainbridge, *The New Corporate Governance in Theory and Practice* (Oxford, Oxford University Press, 2008).

[2] For a general overview see The Work Foundation, 'Life at the Top, Is Managing Time the Route to Smarter Working?', available at http://www.theworkfoundation.com/assets/docs/publications/164_Life_at_the_Top.pdf (22 August 2011).

10.1 The board of directors

Companies have two decision-making organs: the general meeting of shareholders and the board of directors. The general meeting of shareholders is the senior body in the sense that it ultimately controls appointment to and removal from the board of directors. That relationship is reinforced by the requirement that the board must 'promote the success of the company for the benefit of its members as a whole'.[3] The powers of the board are determined largely by a company's constitution as there are relatively few matters that are required by company law to be reserved for decision-making by the shareholders in general meeting.[4] It is therefore largely for each company to determine the extent to which powers are delegated to the board of directors. The articles of association set out the powers of the board and, unless changed by the company (through a special resolution adopted by the general meeting of shareholders), the default provisions contained in the model articles for public companies will take effect.[5] Broad powers offer the benefit of flexibility and facilitate an entrepreneurial approach to running the business, but they also pose the risk that directors may abuse their powers, for example by acting in a self-interested manner.

10.1.1 Board decision-making

While the UK favours a 'shareholder primacy' model of corporate governance, it operates within a framework in which the board of directors is typically given very broad powers. That approach recognises the operational expertise of the board and the practical difficulties (at least in public listed companies) of shareholders becoming involved on a routine basis in operational decision-making. The model articles for public companies provide that, 'subject to the articles,[6] the directors are responsible for the management of the company's business, for which purposes they may exercise all the powers of the company'.[7]

The model articles for public companies provide a reserve power to the shareholders who may by special resolution direct the directors to take, or refrain from taking, specified action.[8] In the case of listed companies, however, it is rare for the general meeting

---

[3] Companies Act 2006, s 172. The board must have regard to the interests of other stakeholders, but it is the interests of shareholders which are predominant.

[4] See Chapter 9.2 for decisions reserved to shareholders. The Companies Act does, however, allocate some mandatory tasks to the board, eg the duty to prepare accounts, considered below.

[5] The model articles are contained in The Companies (Model Articles) Regulations 2008 SI 2008/3229. The articles of companies formed before these regulations took effect (on 1 October 2009) continue to govern those companies.

[6] This proviso recognises that other provisions of the articles of a company may limit or qualify the powers of the board. For example, there may be limits relating to raising loans on behalf of the company.

[7] Article 3 of the Model Articles for PLCs, above n 5.

[8] Article 4 of the Model Articles for PLCs, ibid. No such resolution invalidates anything which the directors have done before the passing of the resolution.

to be given that power by the articles. The rationale is that shareholders invest in listed companies because they offer separation of the functions of ownership and operational control, and therefore it is inappropriate for such companies to have mechanisms that run contrary to that principle.[9] However, this only exacerbates the nature of the principal/agent problem in listed companies and gives rise to particular problems when, as is generally the case, directors are permitted to set their own remuneration. In that context, the concerns of principal/agent theory regarding the likelihood of directors over-rewarding themselves are particularly evident.

The model articles for public companies permit the board to delegate any of its powers to any person or any committee. This enables a chief executive to be empowered to make and implement decisions without reference to the board. It also enables issues to be delegated to committees who are better placed to make a decision than the full board. The UK Corporate Governance Code provides that decisions in respect of three key issues must be delegated to a board committee: nomination of individuals who will be proposed for approval by the shareholders as a director; appointment and removal of auditors; and setting the remuneration of executive directors. The rationale for this requirement is to introduce some degree of independence to these decisions, primarily through the role of independent directors on the relevant committees. In the case of banks and financial institutions, there is also a recommendation in the *Walker Review*[10] that there be a risk committee of the board separate from the audit committee with responsibility for oversight and advice to the board on the current risk exposures of the entity and future risk strategy.

Board decisions are normally taken by simple majority voting.[11] A decision of the board duly adopted in accordance with company law and the company's constitution binds the company since the board is authorised to act on behalf of the company. The same principle applies to matters that are properly delegated by the board to an individual (such as a CEO or an executive director) or a committee. In that sense, the board can be said to act in a collective manner since the company will be bound to decisions adopted by the board even when there is dissent within the board. The UK Code of Corporate Governance emphasises that dimension of the operation of a board in its first principle: 'Every company should be headed by an effective board which is collectively responsible for the long-term success of the company.'

However, that perspective of the board as a collective decision-making entity must be qualified in two important ways. First, from the perspective of legal duties and liability, each director stands in principle on his or her own.[12] It may be that more than one director may be implicated in a breach of duty, but that is a matter that must be shown in each case: it cannot be presumed to be so. Secondly, in the case of FSA-authorised

---

[9] The position will differ in many private companies where there will often be an expectation that shareholders should be directly involved in running the business.

[10] D Walker, 'A Review of Corporate Governance in UK Banks and Other Financial Industry Entities' (July 2009) (Walker Review), available at http://www.hm-treasury.gov.uk/walker_review_information.htm (17 August 2011).

[11] See Articles 13 and 14 of the Model Articles for PLCs.

[12] That approach is implicit in the language of the Companies Act 2006, which refers to duties owed by a director rather than duties owed by the board.

firms, the regulatory system does not explicitly recognise collective responsibility: regulatory obligations fall either on an individual or on the regulated entity.[13] Thus, collective responsibility in the sense that is used in the Code should be understood to refer more to expectations about the commitment and range of skills and experience that directors bring to the board rather than a description of responsibility in the legal or regulatory sense.

10.1.2 Board structure

In the UK, the law relating to the structure of boards of directors is sparse.[14] A minimum number of directors is specified,[15] but the law does not mandate the structure of the board of directors of a company or by whom they should be appointed. Nor does the law prescribe whether a board of directors should consist of a single or two tiers,[16] whether any of the directors should be independent of management or whether any particular tasks should be undertaken by committees of the board.

There are, however, sound reasons why, at least in the context of listed companies, board structure would evolve in a manner whereby shareholders would be able to monitor and control the decisions of directors.[17] The decision-making process in listed companies can be characterised as having four stages: initiation, ratification, implementation and monitoring. Initiation and implementation are usually termed management, whereas ratification and monitoring are usually termed 'decision control', and are the central focus of corporate governance. In listed companies, agency problems will usually be minimised if there is some separation of these two functions. If there is no separation, shareholders face the risk that directors will act in a self-interested manner. It is likely that, even without formal legal intervention, shareholders would establish board structures that minimised this risk. One way of doing this is to appoint to the board independent directors[18] who have no operational involvement in the company. The UK Corporate Governance Code adopts this approach by requiring that the board include an appropriate combination of executive and independent directors and to establish board committees dominated by those directors to take the lead in making key decisions. The main principle of the Code dealing with the composition of the board provides that: 'The board and its committees should have the appropriate balance of skills, experience, independence and knowledge

---

[13] See I MacNeil, 'The Evolution of Regulatory Enforcement in the UK Capital Markets: A Case of "Less is More"?' (2007) 2(4) *Capital Markets Law Journal* 345, 357.

[14] See CA Riley, The Juridification of Corporate Governance' in J de Lacy (ed), *The Reform of UK Company Law* (London, Cavendish Publishing, 2002) 179–201.

[15] The Companies Act 2006, s 154 requires two directors for a public company and one for a private company.

[16] A two-tier board normally comprises a management board and a supervisory board. For a comparative analysis of this issue as between Germany and the UK (following the introduction of the Combined Code) see P Davies, 'Board Structure in the UK and Germany: Convergence or Continuing Divergence?', available at http://ssrn.com/abstract=262959 (2 August 2011).

[17] See E Fama and M Jensen, 'Separation of Ownership and Control' (1983) 26 *Journal of Law and Economics* 301.

[18] In the UK, such directors are referred to as 'non-executive' directors (NEDs), thereby distinguishing them from executive directors who have responsibility for managing the company's business.

of the company to enable them to discharge their respective duties and responsibilities effectively.'[19]

It remains to be seen whether the considerable effort devoted to board structure will yield benefits in terms of financial performance. Initial indications based on empirical research were not encouraging. One study based on data drawn from the period 1994–96 concluded that there was at best a weak link between the internal governance structures established by the Cadbury Code[20] and performance.[21] The authors suggested three possible conclusions: first, it simply may not be possible to protect shareholders' interests by mandating board structure; secondly, the study may reflect inappropriate non-executive appointments; and thirdly, it may not be appropriate to mandate a 'one size fits all' rule applicable to board structure. Another study examined the relationship between board structure and performance in newly listed companies in the period 1990–94.[22] It concluded that there was no evidence of any link between adherence to governance guidelines and enhanced performance in newly listed companies during that period. However, a later study did conclude that compliance with the Cadbury recommendations had a positive impact in limiting the manipulation of accounting information and disciplining senior management.[23] Nevertheless, it remains difficult to establish clear links between board structure and performance, not least since many factors other than board structure contribute to performance and using share prices as a measure of performance is problematic since investors may discount the benefits of good governance with the result that future share price performance is no better or worse than for companies with mediocre or poor governance.[24]

---

[19] Section B: Effectiveness, Main Principle B1. This principle was amended in the 2010 version of the Code to include references to skills and experience following concern that an overemphasis on independence had limited the pool of potential NEDs for some companies: see Financial Reporting Council (FRC), '2009 Review of the Combined Code: Final Report' (December 2009) 16.

[20] This was the first version of the UK Code of Corporate Governance (see further Chapter 9.3).

[21] See C Weir, D Laing and P McKnight, 'An Empirical Analysis of the Impact of Corporate Governance Mechanisms on the Performance of UK Firms', available at SSRN: http://ssrn.com/abstract=286440 (accessed on 17 August 2011).

[22] See R Buckland, 'UK IPO Board Structures and Post-Issue Performance' Aberdeen Papers in Accountancy, Finance & Management Working Paper 01-05, available at SSRN: http://ssrn.com/abstract=276049 (accessed on 22 August 2011).

[23] See EB Dedman, 'The Cadbury Code Recommendations on Corporate Governance—A Review of Compliance and Performance Impacts' (2002) 4 *International Journal of Management Reviews* 335.

[24] This may explain why, in a study of compliance with the Combined Code over the period 1998–2004, it was found that returns on a portfolio of compliers did not significantly exceed that of non-compliers: see s Arcot, V Bruno and A Grimaud, 'Corporate Governance in the UK: is the Comply or-Explain Approach Working?' (2010) 30(2) *International Review of Law and Economics* 193. That outcome can be rationalised on the basis that the expected benefits of good corporate governance are discounted by investors. However, operational performance measured by reference to accounting data may yield different results: see See s Bhagat and B Bolton, 'Corporate governance and firm performance' (2008) 14 *Journal of Corporate Finance* 257, finding that good governance is a predictor of superior operating performance but is not directly linked with share price performance.

10.1.3 The role of independent non-executive directors

In principle, independent directors can serve two different purposes. In countries such as the UK, where listed companies generally do not have a controlling shareholder, they can protect against the possibility of directors engaging in self-interested conduct. This can take a variety of forms, since directors are likely to value not just financial rewards but also status and power over increased resources.[25] Company law already provides some protection through the fiduciary duties of directors and the statutory provisions requiring disclosure of a personal interest in transactions.[26] Independent directors provide a different type of control over self-interested action in that they should have sufficient business experience and involvement in a company's affairs to be able to 'smell trouble' and exert their influence to prevent it.[27] In countries where controlling shareholders are frequently found in listed companies, the presence of independent directors on the board can serve the different purpose of protecting minority shareholders from the expropriation of private benefits by the controlling shareholder at the expense of other shareholders. This can occur, for example, by awarding contracts to other businesses controlled by that shareholder or selling assets to associates at an undervalue.

The UK Corporate Governance Code is based on the belief that appropriate board structures and decision-making processes will have a beneficial effect on corporate governance and ultimately on corporate performance. To this end, it requires that non-executive directors (NEDs) should comprise not less than half of the board.[28] The NEDs should be independent of management and free from any business or other relationships that could materially interfere with the exercise of their independent judgement.[29] NEDs are not involved in operational aspects of the business in the way that executive directors are, so should be able to take a more detached and independent view of the company's performance and prospects. The Code also defines a particular role for NEDs by reference to the operation of several board subcommittees that carry out key functions. A nomination committee should be appointed, comprising a majority of NEDs, to make recommendations to the board on all new board appointments.[30] A remuneration committee, comprising only non-executive directors, should be established with authority delegated to it by the board to set remuneration for all executive directors and the chairman.[31] Finally, an audit committee comprising only non-executive directors should be established to keep under review the scope and results of the audit and the conduct of the auditors.[32] In the case of banks and financial institutions, the role of the chief risk officer

---

[25] The extent to which such conduct causes a welfare loss to shareholders is sometimes termed the residual loss.

[26] See generally J Birds (ed), *Boyle & Birds' Company Law*, 8th edn (Bristol, Jordans, 2011) ch 16.

[27] See generally R Gilson and R Kraakman, 'Reinventing the Outside Director: An Agenda for Institutional Investors' (1991) 43 *Stanford Law Review* 863.

[28] Section B Supporting Principles and Code provision B.1.2.

[29] Code provision B.2.1.

[30] Code provision B.2.1. Once appointed, a director's appointment must be confirmed by an ordinary resolution of shareholders. Moreover, directors of FTSE 350 companies are subject to annual election by shareholders (Code provision B.7.1).

[31] Code provision D.2.1.

[32] Code provision C.3.1.

(CRO) complements the broader role of NEDs. The Walker Review recommends that such firms should be served by a CRO who should participate in the risk management and oversight process at the highest level on an enterprise-wide basis and have a status of total independence from individual business units.[33]

10.2 Directors' remuneration

Concern over the scale of the remuneration of directors of listed companies has grown considerably in recent years. In the 1980s it was largely prompted by the 'fat cat' allegations that surrounded the large rises in remuneration awarded to directors in the newly privatised utilities. In recent years, concern has focused on the mismatch between remuneration and performance, the perception being that in some cases directors have been rewarded excessively for either failure or mediocre performance.[34] The financial sector has been the subject of special attention in the wake of the financial crisis and, as discussed below, specific measures have been adopted in that field.

10.2.1 The company law framework

There is relatively little substantive control exerted by company law over the remuneration of directors. The Companies Act 2006 does not control either the decision-making process or the level of remuneration of directors, leaving the matter to be settled by the company's articles of association. Moreover, there are only very limited grounds on which the courts are willing to review remuneration awarded to directors.[35] In those cases in which the courts have struck down remuneration awarded to directors, the underlying reason has not been that the awards were excessive. For example, in *Re Halt Garage (1964) Ltd*[36] the remuneration was struck down as being a disguised return of capital and therefore contrary to the legal doctrine of maintenance of capital.[37] In *Guinness v Saunders*,[38], the award was struck down because a committee of the board lacked the power under the

---

[33] See recommendation 24 of the review, above n 10.

[34] See Department of Trade and Industry (DTI), '"Rewards for Failure" Directors' Remuneration—Contracts, Performance & Severance' (June 2003); House of Commons Trade and Industry Committee, 'Rewards for Failure', Sixteenth Report of Session 2002–03 (HC 914).

[35] See R Day, 'Challenging Directors' Bonuses: The Application of Directors' Duties to Service Contracts' (2009) 30(12) *Company Lawyer* 374, 376, concluding that 'the service contracts of directors which contain incentives to short-term risk without a balance of equally valuable long-term objectives, and which encourage the pursuit of one or more agendas at the expense of a holistic agenda, are contrary to the fiduciary duties of directors'. That approach has not found favour with the courts.

[36] [1982] 3 All ER 1016.

[37] See Chapter 7.4.

[38] [1990] 2 AC 663 (HL).

company's articles to pay remuneration to one of its own members since that power was reserved to the full board.

The model articles for public companies provide that directors are entitled to such remuneration as the directors determine and that the remuneration may take any form.[39] The decision is therefore in the hands of the board, subject to the requirements of the UK Code of Corporate Governance, as to how decisions on remuneration should be made (in the case of listed companies). Moreover, the board is free to structure remuneration as it wishes, again subject to the requirements of the Code (and institutional investor guidelines[40]). Recent years have seen a substantial increase in the use of performance related pay, often in the form of the award of shares or share options in the company. In relation to performance-related pay, company law retains its policy of non-interference and such controls as have emerged have been in the form of the Code, the listing rules made by the UKLA or guidelines adopted by institutional investors.

Instead of substantive control, the emphasis in company law is on disclosure of directors' remuneration, the rationale being that disclosure will inform shareholders and encourage them to exercise effective control over remuneration.[41] Members are, however, entitled to inspect directors' service contracts.[42] If a director's service contract runs for more than two years and can only be terminated by the company in specified circumstances,[43] shareholders must approve the contract.[44] Additional disclosure requirements apply in the case of premium listed companies.[45]

The requirement for disclosure of remuneration policy (previously contained in the Combined Code[46]) has now become statutory and shareholders have been given a more substantial role in voting on remuneration policy.[47] The rationale for this approach is that, while there had been adequate disclosure of directors' remuneration packages (as a result of the requirements of the Listing Rules), there was inadequate compliance with the Greenbury recommendations on the disclosure of remuneration policy.[48] Directors of quoted companies are now required to prepare a remuneration report containing specified

---

[39] Article 23 of the Model Articles for public companies.

[40] Discussed below.

[41] That approach is also reflected in the EC Commission Recommendations regarding remuneration of directors in listed companies: see eg Commission Recommendation C(2009) 3177, (SEC) 2009 580.

[42] Companies Act 2006, ss 228 and 229.

[43] No guaranteed term can prevent termination of a service contract for good cause, such as material breach or gross misconduct. Nor is it possible to limit the power of a company to dismiss a director at any time without good cause under s 168. However, dismissal without good cause will give rise to liability to compensate the director for dismissal.

[44] Companies Act 2006, s 188. The period was reduced from 5 to 2 years by the 2006 Act. This is the only statutory provision that provides for remuneration to be approved by shareholders.

[45] See FSA Handbook LR 9.8.8R, requiring disclosure of the company's policy on remuneration and details of each director's remuneration.

[46] See s 1.B.3 of and sch B to the April 2002 version of the Code.

[47] Companies Act 2006, s 420. The requirement was first introduced in 2002—see n 49 below for the current requirements.

[48] See DTI, 'Directors' Remuneration', Consultative Document URN 01/1400 (December 2001); L Roach, 'The Directors' Remuneration Report Regulations 2002 and the Disclosure of Executive Remuneration' (2004) 25 *Company Lawyer* 141.

information.[49] This information is more extensive than would otherwise be required by company law or the Listing Rules.[50] Moreover, a listed company must consider at its annual general meeting a resolution approving the remuneration report and the existing directors must ensure that the resolution is put to the vote at that meeting. The vote has been described as 'advisory', meaning that it cannot change contractual agreements relating to remuneration that have already been concluded. A vote does, however, provide a mechanism for shareholders to signal dissatisfaction and require a change in practice. That option has increasingly been taken up by shareholders abstaining or voting against remuneration resolutions as a way of indicating dissatisfaction with excessive pay and inappropriate incentive packages.[51]

10.2.2 The Corporate Governance Code provisions

The UK Corporate Governance Code introduced some potentially significant changes in the practice of setting directors' remuneration. First, following the earlier recommendation of the Cadbury Committee,[52] it requires companies to establish a remuneration committee comprised of independent non-executive directors with delegated responsibility for setting the remuneration of executive directors and the chairman.[53] The board itself or, where required by the articles of association, the shareholders should determine the remuneration of the non-executive directors within the limits set by the articles.[54] These procedures are intended to limit the conflicts of interest that inevitably arise if executive directors are responsible for setting their own remuneration.[55] Secondly, the Code sets companies an objective of limiting or reducing directors' service contracts to a period of 1 year or less.[56] This has important implications for payments made to directors in cases of early termination. A company has the right to remove (by ordinary resolution) a director before expiration of his period in office and notwithstanding anything in its

---

[49] Companies Act 2006, s 420. The specified information is contained in Regulation 11 of and sch 8 to the Large and Medium-sized Companies and Groups (Accounts and Reports) Regulations, SI 2008/410; and Regulation 9 of and sch 3 to the Small Companies and Groups (Accounts and Directors' Report) Regulations SI 2008/409.

[50] The DTI Consultative Document, above n 48, highlights three differences: the remuneration report has a clearer focus on forward looking disclosure of remuneration policy; there is a requirement for information on performance linkage by comparison with a company's peer group; and there is disclosure of the role of the board and remuneration committee in respect of their consideration of directors' remuneration.

[51] See theABI/IVIS Review at http://www.abi.org.uk/Media/Releases/2010/04/IVIS_Review_2009_.aspx; see also KM Sheehan, 'Is the Outrage Constraint an Effective Constraint on Executive Remuneration? Evidence from the UK and Preliminary Results from Australia' (2007), available at http://ssrn.com/abstract=974965. Sheehan concludes that 'outrage' among shareholders prompted changes to contract terms; performance criteria for long-term incentive plans; and 're-tests' for such plans.

[52] See (Cadbury) Code of Best Practice, para 3.3.

[53] Code provision D.2.2.

[54] Code provision D.2.3.

[55] The possibility of non-executive directors being involved in setting their own remuneration poses less risk of conflict of interest because their expectations are generally much lower, reflecting the part-time nature of their role.

[56] Code provision D.1.5. The Cadbury Code of Best Practice had recommended that directors' service contracts should not exceed 3 years without shareholders' approval (para 3.1).

articles or in any agreement between it and him.[57] Early termination can result in two types of payment being made to a director. One is compensation for loss of office as a director; the other is damages for breach (through early termination) of a service contract. Company law requires that the former type of payment must be disclosed to and approved by the shareholders.[58] Damages for breach of a service contract are specifically excluded from this statutory provision.[59] The result is that, according to company law, substantial payments can be made to directors following early termination in respect of damages for remuneration that would have been paid in the unexpired period of their service contracts; and such payments do not require disclosure or approval. Restriction of service contracts to a maximum period of 1 year in accordance with the Code would limit the potential for such payments to be made. Companies may also consider the advantages of providing explicitly in directors' service contracts for such compensation except in the case of removal by misconduct (in which case it is the director who is in breach of contract and the company has no liability in damages).[60] Linked with this is the recommendation made by the Code that companies should avoid rewarding poor performance when making early termination payments and should take a robust line on a departing director's duty to mitigate loss.[61]

The Code requires all new long-term incentive schemes (as defined in the Listing Rules[62]) to be approved by shareholders.[63] They include bonuses linked to service and/ or performance over periods longer than one financial year. The language adopted in the revised 2010 version of the Code reflects investor and public concern that in many cases remuneration of directors in listed companies has risen too rapidly and has not been matched by a commensurate improvement in performance. Thus, main principle D.1 of the remuneration section of the Code recognises the need to pay sufficiently to attract and retain directors of the quality required to run the company but warns against the risk of paying too much. The supporting principles refer to the need for the performance-related elements of executive directors' remuneration to be stretching and designed to promote the long-term success of the company.[64]

---

[57] Companies Act 2006, s 168.

[58] Companies Act 2006, s 217.

[59] Companies Act 2006, s 220.

[60] See s 1, para B.1.9 of the Combined Code (April 2002 version). That option is rarely pursued as a result of the difficulty of proving a breach of contract and the adverse publicity that it may attract.

[61] Section 1, para B.1.10. The duty to mitigate loss following breach is a general principle of contract law.

[62] See the definitions section of the Listing Rules.

[63] Code provision D.2.4. The Listing Rules do, however, exempt from that requirement long-term incentive schemes in which all employees participate or an arrangement where the only participant is a director of the listed company and the arrangement is established specifically to facilitate, in unusual circumstances, the recruitment or retention of the relevant individual (see LR 9.4.2R). The Listing Rules also permit share options to be granted without shareholder approval subject to conditions as to the exercise price: see LR 9.4.4R.

[64] See also Schedule A to the Code, The Design of Performance-related Remuneration for Executive Directors.

10.2.3 Institutional investor guidelines

Also relevant in this context are the guidelines on executive remuneration adopted by the ABI/NAPF.[65] These guidelines are concerned with the structure of remuneration, the conditions attaching to share incentive schemes, and disclosure to and approval by shareholders of various aspects of remuneration. They recognise a role for both fixed and variable pay and for both long- and short-term incentives. Variable pay should generally take the form of bonuses linked to performance targets that are disclosed in the remuneration report.[66] Pension entitlement and other benefits accruing during a year should also be disclosed. Share incentive schemes are subject to detailed rules. Underlying these rules is a recognition that they involve either the commitment of shareholders' funds (to buy shares for distribution to scheme members) or dilution in shareholders' equity (when options are granted to buy shares at a discount to the market price in the future). A limit of 10% of issued ordinary share capital applies to the capital of a company that can be used for all share incentive schemes over a 10 year period.[67] Vesting[68] of options should normally be subject to performance conditions that extend over 3 years or more.[69] It is recognised that any retesting of performance conditions for all share-based incentive schemes is unnecessary and unjustified. Finally, all new share-based incentive schemes and material changes to existing schemes should be subject to approval by shareholders.

10.2.4 Remuneration in FSA-authorised firms

The Walker Review[70] drew attention to the risks posed to financial stability by excessive and inappropriate remuneration. Its engagement with remuneration in financial institutions represented an extension of concern over excessive and inappropriate remuneration that has been at the centre of the corporate governance debate for the last 20 years.[71] Walker stopped short of recommending any kind of cap on remuneration,[72] opting instead for enhancement of disclosure[73] and expansion of the role of the remuneration committee 'to

---

[65] See 'Executive Remuneration—ABI Guidelines on Policies and Practices' (December 2009), available at http://www.ivis.co.uk/ExecutiveRemuneration.aspx.

[66] See n 49 above and accompanying text.

[67] ABI Guidelines, above n 65, para 8.1.

[68] Vesting refers to the acquisition of a right to exercise the option. The grant of an option does not in itself lead to its exercise as the conditions for its exercise may not be met.

[69] ABI Guidelines, above n 65, para 5.5.

[70] Above n 10.

[71] For an overview of recent developments in the EU and at the international level, see G Ferrarini and M C Ungureanu, 'Executive Pay at Ailing Banks and Beyond: A European Perspective' (2010) 5(2) *Capital Markets Law Journal* 197.

[72] Although that did not in itself preclude the government from using its power as controlling shareholder in bailed-out banks such as RBS and Lloyds/HBOS to implement some form of cap.

[73] The Financial Services Act 2010, s 4 implements Walker's recommendation by authorising the Treasury to make regulations requiring (enhanced) disclosure of remuneration paid to executives of FSA-authorised firms. The Treasury published draft regulations in March 2010, but they were not passed into law following the change of government in May 2010.

cover all aspects of remuneration policy on a firm-wide basis with particular emphasis on the risk dimension'.[74]

While the FSA's mandate does not directly encompass governance issues, there are inevitable overlaps between governance and regulation, especially in the context of the control of risk.[75] The FSA viewed excessive and inappropriate remuneration as a 'contributory factor rather than a dominant factor behind the financial crisis', but nevertheless took the view that regulatory intervention in remuneration was justified as a means of promoting effective risk management and facilitating effective governance by shareholders. Its intervention took the form of changes to the Senior Management Arrangements, Systems and Controls (SYSC) component of the FSA Handbook requiring compliance with a new Remuneration Code that is also inserted into that component. The Code comprises a mixture of rules, guidance and evidential provisions,[76] with the core obligation being that: 'A firm must establish, implement and maintain remuneration policies, procedures and practices that are consistent with and promote effective risk management.'[77]

The use of guidance and evidential provisions limits the extent to which the Code is mandatory and aims to avoid a 'one size fits all' approach to remuneration. However, amendment of the Code with effect from January 2011 has had the effect of making its provisions more prescriptive. The changes reflect broader powers given to the FSA to regulate pay in authorised firms by the Financial Services Act 2010.[78] In its revised form the Code applies to a wider set of firms and has a wider geographical reach through its application to the global operations of UK groups and UK subsidiaries of third country groups. It is also more prescriptive as regards structure of remuneration, deferral of variable remuneration and the percentage of variable remuneration that must be taken in shares.[79]

10.3 Accounts, audit and internal controls

The significance of accounting and audit to the development of corporate governance standards in the UK is made evident by three factors. First, doubts over the reliability of audit reports given in respect of the accounts of failed companies were significant in prompting demands for the introduction of corporate governance standards.[80] Secondly,

---

[74] Walker Review, above n 10, Recommendation 29.

[75] For a general discussion, see I MacNeil, 'Risk Control Strategies: An Assessment in the Context of the Credit Crisis' in I MacNeil and J O'Brien (eds), *The Future of Financial Regulation* (Oxford, Hart Publishing, 2010) ch 9.

[76] See Chapter 3.6.2 for an explanation of the structure and content of the FSA Handbook of Rules and Guidance.

[77] FSA Handbook, SYSC 19A.2.1R.

[78] FSA 2010, s 6.

[79] See generally FSA, 'Revising the Remuneration Code', Consultation Paper 10/19 (July 2010).

[80] See the preface to the Cadbury Report (see Chapter 9.3).

the accountancy profession itself recognised this concern and the associated need to bolster the standing of the profession by participating directly in the process of creating standards. The Cadbury Committee was established by the Financial Reporting Council (FRC), the London Stock Exchange and the accountancy profession, and its remit was essentially to focus on financial reporting and audit.[81] Thirdly, responsibility for review and associated development of the UK Code of Corporate Governance and the Stewardship Code lies with the FRC, which is the body charged with overall responsibility for financial reporting and regulation of the accounting and auditing professions in the UK.

10.3.1 Accountability and audit

The UK Corporate Governance Code adopts standards that are built around an existing legal framework that distinguishes the roles of directors and auditors in relation to financial statements. According to company law, directors are responsible for preparing the annual report and accounts of a company.[82] The overriding obligation is to prepare accounts that provide a 'true and fair view' of the financial position of the company.[83] That obligation is closely linked with the broader fiduciary duties owed by directors to the company, since a central principle of the law relating to fiduciaries is that they are required to account to their principal in regard to their stewardship of assets and their conduct of the business of the principal. The concept of accounting, in the technical sense in which it is now most often used, is derived from the obligation of a fiduciary 'to give an account' to the principal.

Directors are also required to prepare a directors' report, which must contain prescribed information relating to the directors and the company's business.[84] The more recent requirement to prepare a 'business review'[85] introduces two features into accountability that are not normally present in the statutory accounts.[86] The first is that the business review contains a forward-looking aspect covering 'the main trends and factors likely to affect the future development, performance and position of the company's business'. The second is that the business review promotes accountability to stakeholders other than the shareholders: thus, it requires the company to provide information about environmental matters, the company's employees and social and community issues. The extent of that information is to some extent controlled by the company itself since the requirement is to provide information to the extent necessary for an understanding of the development, performance or position of the company's business. While this form of disclosure

---

[81] Hence the reference to the 'financial aspects of corporate governance' in the designation of the Cadbury Committee. See Appendix 1 of the Cadbury Report for a statement of the Committee's remit.

[82] See Companies Act 2006, s 394. These accounts are sometimes referred to as the 'statutory accounts'.

[83] Companies Act 2006, s 393(1).

[84] Companies Act 2006, s 416.

[85] Companies Act 2006, s 417. The antecedent of the 'business review' was the 'operating and financial review', which was more onerous and was quickly withdrawn: for background see D Arsalidou, 'The Withdrawal of the Operating and Financial Review in the Companies Bill 2006: Progression or Regression?' (2007) 28(5) *Company Lawyer* 131.

[86] The comments below on the business review are based on the provisions of s 417 applicable to quoted companies.

can potentially provide valuable information for stakeholders other than shareholders to take action to protect their interests, it will also often be of interest to shareholders and potential investors, who increasingly take an interest in issues linked with corporate social responsibility.[87]

The UK Corporate Governance Code reinforces the accountability of directors by adopting the principle that 'The board should present a balanced and understandable assessment of the company's position and prospects'.[88] It goes on to say that this responsibility extends to interim and other price-sensitive public reports and reports to regulators, as well as to information required to be presented by statutory requirements. In response to criticism of the limited usefulness of financial reports in informing readers as to how the business model generates profits for the company and what the future risks are judged to be, the Code now requires directors to include in their annual report an explanation of the business model and the strategy for delivering the objectives of the company.

The role of auditors under company law is to state whether the annual accounts have been properly prepared, whether they are consistent with the company's accounting records and whether they provide a 'true and fair' view of the company's financial position.[89] In respect of the directors' report, the auditor must state in his report on the company's annual accounts whether in his opinion the information given in the directors' report for the financial year for which the accounts are prepared is consistent with those accounts.[90] The role of the auditor is therefore one of verification that the directors have properly carried out their obligation to prepare accounts that present a 'true and fair' view. The auditor's report must be either qualified or unqualified, and must include a reference to any matters to which the auditor wishes to draw attention by way of emphasis without qualifying the report.

The Code requires companies to appoint an audit committee of at least three non-executive directors, all of whom should be independent.[91] The duties of the audit committee should include keeping under review the scope and results of the audit, its cost effectiveness, and the independence and objectivity of the auditors. Where the auditors also supply a substantial volume of non-audit services to the company, the committee should keep the nature and extent of such services under review, seeking to balance the maintenance of objectivity and value for money. The risk posed by non-audit services is that the objectivity of the audit opinion may be compromised by the payment of fees in connection with non-audit work, with the result that shareholders can no longer rely on the verification provided by the auditors of the accounts that are prepared under the direction of the directors. To that end, the Code requires that the annual report should explain to shareholders how, if the auditor provides non-audit services, auditor objectivity and independence is safeguarded.

---

[87] See further Chapter 9.3 regarding CSR.
[88] Section C: Accountability, Main Principle.
[89] Companies Act 2006, s 495.
[90] Companies Act 2006, s 496.
[91] Code provision C.3.1. The FRC Guidance on Audit Committees (formerly known as the 'Smith Guidance') suggests ways in which this principle can be implemented.

In the event of the removal or resignation of the auditors, various statutory protections and procedures are triggered. The underlying rationale of these provisions is that removal or resignation of the auditors is a potential 'red flag' as to the existence of problems within a company that ought to be revealed to shareholders. First, the auditor can be removed only by (ordinary) resolution of the shareholders in general meeting.[92] Secondly, special notice[93] of such a resolution must be given and (if passed by the shareholders' meeting) the resolution publicised (through notification to the registrar of companies) within 14 days; this is unusual, since normally only special resolutions of a company require registration. An auditor may resign by depositing a notice to that effect at the company's registered office, but the notice is not effective unless it is accompanied by the required statement in connection with the circumstances connected with his ceasing to hold office.[94] The company is required to send the statement to shareholders and the auditor is required to send it to the Registrar of Companies, thereby making it available to the general public.[95] Both the company and the auditor are required to notify the appropriate audit authority that the auditor has ceased to hold office and to provide a statement of the circumstances.[96] In the case of quoted companies, members have the power to require the company to publish on its website a statement setting out any matter relating to the audit of the company's accounts or the circumstances connected with an auditor of the company ceasing to hold office that the members wish to raise at the next accounts meeting of the company.[97]

The Markets in Financial Instruments Directive (MiFID) contains important provisions relating to 'whistleblowing' by auditors with respect to investment firms. It provides that auditors are required to report to the competent authority (in the UK, the FSA) any fact or decision which is liable to:

1. constitute a material breach of the laws, regulations or administrative provisions which lay down the conditions governing authorisation or which specifically govern pursuit of the activities of investment firms;
2. affect the continuing functioning of the investment firm; or
3. lead to the refusal to certify the accounts or to the expression of reservations.[98]

Auditors making a disclosure to the authorities under this provision are protected from liability that might otherwise be incurred through disclosure of information relating to an audit client.[99]

---

[92] Companies Act 2006, s 510.

[93] Special notice is a procedure defined by s 312 of the Companies Act 2006. It requires 28 days notice of the resolution to be given to the company and 14 days to the members (in each case before the meeting at which it is proposed). A general meeting of shareholders requires only 14 days notice under s 307.

[94] Companies Act 2006, ss 516 and 519. In the case of an unquoted company, no statement need be made if the auditor considers that there are no circumstances that need to be brought to the attention of members or creditors of the company.

[95] Companies Act 2006, ss 520 and 521.

[96] Companies Act 2006, ss 522 and 523.

[97] Companies Act 2006, s 527. Members exercising this right must number at least 100 or represent 5% of the voting rights in the company.

[98] Art 55 MiFID.

[99] Ibid.

10.3.2 Risk Management and Internal controls

Underlying the approach of the UK Corporate Governance Code to risk management and internal controls is the view that the board is responsible for setting the risk appetite of the company, establishing a system of internal control and reviewing its effectiveness. That approach is reflected in the main principle (C) of the Code dealing with the matter: 'The board is responsible for determining the nature and extent of the significant risks it is willing to take in achieving its strategic objectives. The board should maintain sound risk management and internal control systems.'

The Code does not attempt to determine or even provide guidance on the nature or extent of the risks that a company should undertake. It focuses instead on the effective control of risk, and the disclosure of the nature and extent of that risk and of the main features of the internal control and risk management systems to investors.[100] Thus, effective disclosure is essential to permit the shares of a company to be priced relative to the business risk that is faced by the company and to enable long-term investors to engage with the company on that issue. The Turnbull guidance[101] provides companies with guidance on how to implement the provisions of the Code. While it emphasises the responsibility of the board for establishing, reviewing and updating internal controls and risk management, it also recognises that 'such a system is designed to manage rather than eliminate the risk of failure to achieve business objectives, and can only provide reasonable and not absolute assurance against material misstatement or loss'. The experience in the financial sector during the financial crisis that began in 2007 certainly supports that viewpoint. A major cause of the crisis was the failure of the boards of banks and financial institutions to understand the risks to which they were exposed. Shareholders were particularly exposed to that failure since they, rather than creditors (such as bondholders and depositors), bore the brunt of the losses that were suffered by the banks. Thus, as the residual risk-bearers in companies, shareholders rely very heavily on the ability of companies to identify and manage risk.

In the case of FSA authorised firms, there are additional provisions relating to systems and controls in the FSA Handbook, specifically the Principles for Business and the Senior Management, Arrangements, Systems and Controls (SYSC).[102] Principle 3 of the Principles for Business provides that: 'A firm must take reasonable care to organise and control its affairs responsibly and effectively, with adequate risk management systems.'

---

[100] The disclosure requirement in the Code is supplemented by a provision in the listing regime: FSA rule DTR 7.2.5 R requires companies to describe the main features of the internal control and risk management systems in relation to the financial reporting process. Moreover, under s 497A Companies Act 2006 the auditor of a company subject to that DTR rule must state in its report on the company's annual accounts whether in its opinion the information is consistent with those accounts.

[101] FRC, 'Internal Control: Revised Guidance for Directors on the Combined Code' (October 2005), available at www.frc.org.uk.

[102] These rules implement the provisions of MiFID and the MiFID Implementing Directive relating to organisational requirements, compliance and risk management.

The SYSC provides that, where the Code is relevant to a firm,[103] due credit will be given for compliance with the Code when assessing compliance with the FSA Handbook.[104] While there is much common ground between the FSA Handbook and the Code, the former does not follow the emphasis of the latter on the collective responsibility of the board. Indeed, the SYSC requires that:

> A firm must take reasonable care to maintain a clear and appropriate apportionment of significant responsibilities among its directors and senior managers in such a way that:
> (1) it is clear who has which of those responsibilities; and
> (2) the business and affairs of the firm can be adequately monitored and controlled by the directors, relevant senior managers and governing body of the firm.[105]

From the FSA's perspective, the responsibilities associated with internal controls and risk management can therefore be attached to individuals as well as to the firm. This process of attribution of responsibility to individuals is supported by the FSA's 'approved person' regime under which FSA approval is required for individuals who perform 'controlled functions'.[106] Individuals with senior management responsibilities covered by SYSC also fall within the 'approved persons' regime and are therefore subject to the sanctions available to the FSA under that regime. The primary sanction is withdrawal of 'approved person' status, which provides credible deterrence by threatening individuals with removal of the 'approved' designation, thereby limiting the roles they can undertake within an authorised firm.

---

[103] It will be relevant when the firm has a primary listing in the UK. Not all FSA-authorised firms have a primary listing, hence only the SYSC may be applicable.

[104] SYSC 3.1.3 G.

[105] SYSC 2.1.1 R.

[106] See generally Chapter 3.9.4.

Corporate Governance—
Takeovers

This chapter deals with the regulatory regime for takeovers. The UK was a pioneer in developing a regulatory regime for takeovers. In its original form, that regime was self-regulatory. The rules, in the form of the Takeover Code, were made and administered by the Takeover Panel, relying primarily on market discipline to sanction those companies and advisory firms who did not comply. Over time, the Takeover Code became linked with the system of financial regulation through provisions that recognised the Code and imposed sanctions on those companies within the remit of the Code and Financial Services Authority (FSA)-authorised firms who did not comply with the Code. Following the implementation of the EU Takeovers Directive, the regulatory regime in the UK was placed on a statutory footing. However, despite the change in formal legal status, there has been relatively little change in the working of the regulatory system in the UK. There are two main reasons: one is that the UK system exerted a strong influence on the regulatory techniques adopted by the Takeovers Directive and therefore implementation of the Directive in the UK did not require significant changes to the rules (as it did in some other Member States); the other is that the Takeover Panel continued to act as the competent authority for takeovers following implementation of the Directive, with the result that the smooth operation of the system was not interrupted.

11.1 Takeovers: definition

The term 'takeover' is often used in different ways to describe different types of transaction. The EU Takeovers Directive provides the following definition:

'Takeover bid' or 'bid' shall mean a public offer (other than by the offeree company itself) made to the holders of the securities of a company to acquire all or some of those securities, whether mandatory or voluntary, which follows or has as its objective the acquisition of control of the offeree company in accordance with national law.[1]

That definition focuses on a change of control in the relevant company[2] through the acquisition of securities. A change of control is the result of the transfer of voting rights attached to the relevant securities (normally shares). Although not explicitly stated, there are other important principles that underlie that definition. First, the legal entity in which control is to alter remains the same. It may subsequently change but, if that is the case, it is not the direct consequence of the takeover.[3] Secondly, since the legal structure and assets of a company are not altered by a takeover (as defined), it follows that the rights of creditors are not altered or prejudiced by a takeover. Thus, there is no need to seek the consent of creditors to a takeover (as defined) or to provide them with any form of protection from the possibility of takeover.[4]

Mergers, in the sense that the term is used in the relevant European directives[5] governing their form and process, refer to transactions in which the undertaking, property and liabilities of public companies are transferred to other public companies or to companies formed specifically for the purpose of the merger. This differs from a takeover in that control over the transferring company remains in the hands of the existing shareholders but its business has been merged with that of another company, effectively leaving it as a 'shell company' holding the consideration paid for the sale of the business. While the term 'merger' is often applied in a loose sense to takeovers in which the intention is to present the bidder and target as being of equal standing, it is preferable to regard the two techniques as separate legal concepts because both the process[6] and the outcome differ between the two. Mergers in the true sense are relatively rare, not least because they give rise to the need to secure the consent of creditors for the transfer of liabilities to the new entity.[7]

Takeovers and mergers have other important dimensions linked to competition law and policy. For example, they may lead to a reference by the Office of Fair Trading to

---

[1] Art 2(1)(a) of Directive 2004/25/EC [2004] OJ L142/12.

[2] Companies fall within the scope of the Directive when the relevant securities (which are the subject of the takeover bid) are admitted to trading on a regulated market. See Chapter 13 as to the meaning of a regulated market.

[3] For example, following a change of control through takeover a company's assets and business may be integrated with that of the bidder and the company subsequently wound up.

[4] That is not to say that creditors are not free to protect themselves through contract terms, which they often do (eg by providing that a contract will end if control of the company changes).

[5] Directive 2011/35/EU [2011] OJ L110/1 concerning mergers of public limited liability companies (codifying and superseding Directive 78/855/EEC [1978] OJ L295, 36) and Directive 92/891 [1982] OJ L378/47 concerning the division of public limited liability companies, both implemented in the UK by pt 27 of the Companies Act 2006.

[6] The process for a merger is a scheme of arrangement, discussed below. A takeover can be in the form of a contractual offer (see below) or a scheme of arrangement.

[7] While rights can be transferred by a creditor to a third party without the consent of the debtor, liabilities cannot be transferred without the consent of the creditor. The logic is that the identity of the creditor does not matter to the debtor (who simply has to pay), whereas the identity of the debtor does matter to the creditor (because it affects the ability to pay).

the Competition Commission under the Enterprise Act 2002[8] or to an examination by the European Commission of offers with a Community dimension under the EC Merger Control Regulation.[9] The purpose of the investigations which follow such references is to establish if the proposed mergers are likely to have anti-competitive effects.[10] If they do, they will either be blocked or have conditions attached to them so as to remove the anti-competitive effects. There are also taxation implications for the offeror and the shareholders of the offeree,[11] and there are employment law consequences under the Transfer of Undertakings (Protection of Employment) Regulations 2006.[12] The Listing Rules require offerors which are listed companies to notify a Regulated Information Service[13] of takeover offers that fall within certain financial thresholds (the 'class tests') and to secure shareholder approval for offers that represent 'class 1' transactions.[14]

11.2 The rationale for takeovers

11.2.1 Economic considerations

There a several economic arguments that are typically made to support takeovers. One is rationalisation. It may well be that there are scale economies that can be achieved through a combination of the activities of the relevant companies or possibly technical improvements that may be possible through close collaboration. Another argument is that a takeover would lead to greater efficiency as a result of either vertical or horizontal integration. The former implies that different stages of the manufacturing or service process are linked together, whereas the latter implies that different stages of market access are linked together (eg wholesale and retail). Another argument is that a takeover may be a mechanism to expand market share more quickly than would be possible through organic growth; this argument is particularly to the fore in the case of cross-border takeovers, since it is often more difficult to expand into foreign markets in which a company lacks experience.

While these arguments focus primarily on the benefits of a takeover for the bidder's shareholders, they are not irrelevant to a target company's shareholders. Where a takeover is in the form of a 'share for share' offer, the prospects for the combined entity is a fundamental matter for those shareholders to consider in deciding whether to accept a takeover

---

[8] See M Furse, *The Law of Merger Control in the EC and the UK* (Oxford, Hart Publishing, 2007).

[9] Regulation 139/2004/EC [2004] OJ L24/1.

[10] See Furse, above n 8, ch 5. The UK and EC systems adopt different approaches to the determination of whether mergers are likely to have anti-competitive effects.

[11] See The Rt Hon The Lord Millett, A Alcock, M Todd QC (eds), *Gore-Browne on Companies*, 45th edn (Bristol, Jordans, looseleaf) pt X1, ch 48.

[12] See O Hyams, *Employment Aspects of Business Reorganisations* (Oxford, Oxford University Press, 2006).

[13] This will result in the information being made public.

[14] See FSA Handbook, LR 10: Significant Transactions.

bid. However, where the bid is financed by cash alone, the prospects of the combined entity are of little relevance to target shareholders. In that situation they are concerned primarily with the price and the extent to which the price reflects the prospects of the target as a separate entity (ie the alternative to accepting the bid). The adequacy of the price will be judged also by reference to the 'bid premium' that the bidder is prepared to pay. The rationale for such a premium is that a bidder ought to pay a price higher than the prevailing market price to acquire control, since control has a value resulting from the ability to appoint and dismiss board members and to set strategy.

11.2.2 Takeovers as a governance technique: the market for corporate control

Takeovers can be viewed as a governance technique in the sense that they open up the possibility of a change of control in companies. The consequence of a change of control is likely to be that the new controller will take steps to change the composition of the board with the objective of improving financial performance. Thus, it is possible to view takeovers as performing a disciplinary function since directors will be aware that underperformance may lead to the company being taken over and their being replaced.[15] Of course, since it is quite likely that steps will have been taken by shareholders to improve performance before a takeover bid emerges, the success (or otherwise) of those measures is closely linked both to the emergence of a bidder and the likelihood of a bid succeeding. A takeover bid is a governance technique of last resort since shareholders will be unlikely to accept if they believe that performance can be improved should the target remain independent.

The operation of a market for corporate control, through the mechanism of takeovers, is linked with the pattern of share ownership[16] and the operation of public markets for shares. It is notable that the market for corporate control developed first and remains most active in the US and the UK, which are both characterised by relatively widely dispersed share ownership and highly developed capital markets. Dispersed share ownership facilitates takeovers because there is unlikely to be a controlling shareholder and it is easier for a bidder to build up a stake prior to launching a bid.[17] Moreover, dispersed share ownership tends to discourage shareholder engagement as a solution to underperformance and therefore makes it more likely that a takeover bid will be seen as the best solution. By way of contrast, concentrated share ownership tends to discourage the emergence of a market for corporate control since there is likely to be less liquidity and 'blockholders' will be more inclined to engage with companies to solve underperformance. Of course, to the extent that there is some convergence over time between dispersed and concentrated systems of shareholding (for example, as a result of the policy of the Takeovers Directive

---

[15] See generally H Manne, 'Mergers and the Market for Corporate Control' (1965) 73 *Journal of Political Economy* 110.
[16] See generally Chapter 9.1.
[17] See further Chapter 9.1.

of encouraging takeovers), it is likely that the differences between systems will become less over time.

11.3 The legal and financial structure of a takeover bid

The regulatory framework for takeovers does not prescribe the legal or financial structure of a takeover bid. It is therefore a matter primarily for the bidder to decide and the choice will be influenced primarily by the capacity of the relevant structure to contribute to a successful bid. In the case of the legal structure, there is a choice available between a contractual offer and a scheme of arrangement. In the case of the financial structure, the main issue is how the bidder will finance the bid, and that will depend to a large extent on the existing financial position of the bidder and its ability to raise equity or debt to finance the bid.

11.3.1 Contractual offer

A contractual offer, as the term implies, is an offer made by the bidder to the shareholders in the target company to acquire sufficient shares to give the bidder control over the target. In principle, any form of payment may be offered for the relevant shares. As with any offer, the offeree is free to reject the bid. In this type of takeover bid, neither the target company nor its board of directors has any direct role in accepting or rejecting the offer. Thus, there is no compulsion or pressure that can be exerted over shareholders who choose not to accept the offer. From the bidder's perspective, this form of takeover bid has the disadvantage that it may leave the bidder with a controlling shareholding that falls short of the 75% threshold that is required to control the company's constitution.[18] In those circumstances, a bidder would have to accept the presence of minority shareholders who were able to exert significant influence within the company through their ability to block special resolutions. There are two options open to a bidder who wants to avoid that outcome. One is to make it a condition of the offer that the bidder secures a high threshold of acceptances (eg 90%), thus ensuring full control once the potential to trigger the 'squeeze out' procedure[19] is taken into account. The other is to revise the bid price during the course of the bid so as to increase the level of acceptances to a level (above 75%) at which the power of minority shareholders is insignificant.[20]

---

[18] That is the threshold required to pass a resolution to change the company's constitution under s 21 of the Companies Act 2006.

[19] See Chapter 11.7.

[20] In the case of a revised offer, all shareholders in the target company are entitled to accept the revised offer even if they have already accepted the original offer: Takeover Code rule 32.3.

11.3.2 Scheme of arrangement

A scheme of arrangement is a compromise or arrangement agreed between a company[21] and its members and/or creditors. There is in principle no limit to the type of compromise or arrangement that can be covered; it can, for example, be used for debt rescheduling or to give effect to a takeover bid. A scheme differs from a contractual offer (above) in that it represents a binding agreement between a company and the members or creditors whose rights are affected by the proposal. In the case of a contractual offer, the rights of creditors of the target are not affected since the debtor (the target company) remains unchanged as a legal entity even though its shareholders may change.[22] Under a scheme, members who do not agree to its terms are bound if it is approved by the requisite majority. In that sense, there is compulsion exerted over the minority by the (requisite) majority of members. From the bidder's perspective, this offers the advantage that, once the scheme is approved by the members, it will acquire 100% of the shares that are the subject of the scheme. A scheme therefore avoids the uncertainty associated with a contractual offer as to the extent of control that may be secured by the bidder over the target. For that reason (and others), the scheme has increased in popularity in recent years as the legal structure for takeover bids that are supported by the board of a target company ('recommended bids').[23] However, a scheme is less likely to be used in the case of bids that are not supported by the board of a target company ('hostile bids') since a scheme is a proposal made by a company to its shareholders and it is the board that is empowered to act on behalf of the target company in making that proposal.[24] If the board refuses to act, the bidder is unlikely to be able to proceed and may well have to fall back on the alternative of a contractual offer.

There are three main requirements for a takeover that is structured as a scheme.[25] First, it must be approved by a meeting of the members and/or creditors of the (target) company at a special meeting convened at the direction of the court.[26] Consent is required only if the scheme affects the rights of members and/or creditors. In cases where the rights of different classes of shares are affected, the consent of the relevant class of shareholders is required. The notice summoning the meeting must be accompanied by a statement explaining the effect of the scheme and any material interests

---

[21] A company can adopt a scheme under pt 26 of the Companies Act 2006 if it is capable of being wound up under the Insolvency Act 1986. This means that foreign companies (which are not incorporated in the UK) may fall within the scope of pt 26: see *Re La Seda de Barcelona SA* [2010] EWHC 1364 (Ch) and *Re Lehman Brothers International (Europe) (In Administration)* [2009] EWCA Civ 1161.

[22] A takeover offer does not affect the legal capital or assets of the target and therefore the position of creditors is not in principle prejudiced by a takeover offer.

[23] See the Takeover Panel Annual Report 2007–2008, reporting that schemes regulated by the panel rose to represent 41% of takeovers in that year compared with 10% in 2001–02.

[24] See Chapter 10.1.1 regarding the powers of the board.

[25] These requirements are set out in pt 26 of the Companies Act 2006.

[26] There is no requirement for meetings or approvals on the part of the transferee company (the bidder), although such meetings and approvals may be triggered by other relevant requirements. In the case of merger schemes proposed by a public company see ss 907, 922 and 938 CA 2006. A meeting may also be necessary if the scheme involves the issue of shares by the bidder other than on a pre-emptive basis (see Chapter 7.3.2) or, in the case of a listed company, the scheme falls within the 'class rules' contained in the Listing Rules, above n 14.

of directors in the scheme. Secondly, the scheme must be approved by the requisite majority of members, which is a majority in number representing 75% in value of the members or class voting.[27] Thirdly, following approval by the members, the scheme must be approved by the court.[28]

In exercising its discretion to approve a scheme, the court will have regard to whether the proposal is such that an intelligent and honest man, a member of the class concerned and acting in respect of his interest, might reasonably approve.[29] While members of a particular class may in principle vote as they wish, it has been held that an allegation that a voting shareholder has a collateral interest, if made out, could result in the court disenfranchising the relevant member.[30] Issues may arise on the hearing of the petition regarding the valuation of creditors' interests and, linked to that, the duty of the company (and its directors) to take account of the interests of creditors. The scheme in *Re Bluebrook Ltd, IMO (UK) Ltd and Spirecove Ltd*[31] represented a restructuring of a carwash business run by the last two companies, who were indirect subsidiaries of the first. The overall effect was to transfer all the assets of the group into a new group and to give the senior lenders the bulk of the equity in that new group. No assets were to be left in the group to pay the mezzanine lenders, who were thereby shut out. The justification advanced for this approach was that the value of the group was such that the mezzanine lenders and other creditors had no economic interest in the group because the value of its assets was significantly less than the senior debt. The mezzanine lenders argued that they were unfairly prejudiced by the scheme and did not accept that the value of the group was less than the senior debt. On the valuation issue, the court held, after reviewing the evidence, that there was not sufficient support for the mezzanine lenders' argument. On the issue of breach of duty owed to (all) creditors, the court recognised that a company must pay proper regard to the interests of creditors, but recognised in this case that the mezzanine lenders were negotiating effectively for themselves and that in any event they did not have an economic interest to which the directors could have regard.

Once approved by the court, a copy of the scheme must be filed with the Registrar of Companies,[32] at which point it takes effect.

11.3.3 Forms of payment to target shareholders

Any type of takeover requires the bidder to pay the target shareholders a price that will be sufficient to persuade them to sell. The market expectation is that a bidder will pay a premium over the prevailing market price in order to secure control over

---

[27] This represents a dual test for approval of the resolution, unlike a special resolution of a company which simply requires 75% of those voting for approval. The same principle applies to creditors, based on the value of their claims.

[28] The High Court in England or the Court of Session in Scotland (s 1156 Companies Act 2006).

[29] *Re Alabama, New Orleans, etc Railway Co* [1891] 1 Ch 213 (CA). See also J Payne, 'Schemes of Arrangement, Takeovers and Minority Shareholder Protection' (2011) 11 *Journal of Corporate Law Studies* 67.

[30] *Re Linton Park plc* [2005] All ER (D) 174.

[31] [2009] EWHC 2114 (Ch).

[32] Filing with the registrar means that the scheme is open to inspection by the public.

a company. In the case of cash offers, the bidder will need to have cash available from either internal or external sources. Internal resources are primarily retained profits (reserves), while external resources can include the proceeds of loans or share issues made with the intention of having funds available for takeovers. External resources can also be provided by the underwriting of a cash alternative to a share-for-share offer. This involves an underwriter agreeing to provide cash payments to shareholders in the target as an alternative to shares in the bidder. In some cases, such as when a bid is mandatory under the Takeover Code,[33] the bidder must offer cash or a cash alternative to a share-for-share offer. Such arrangements are popular with investors, as they may not want to take shares in the bidder, and can therefore improve the likelihood of a bid succeeding. For the bidder, however, an underwritten cash alternative adds to the cost of a share-for-share offer.

Alternatively, the bidder may offer its own shares in exchange for shares in the target.[34] Since there is no limit to the number of shares that can be issued by a company, the bidder is free to issue any number of shares as payment to the target shareholders.[35] Whether shares in the bidder will be accepted by the target shareholders is another matter. The decision of the target shareholders on this issue turns on their view as to the respective value of the shares in each company and the quality of the board and management of each company. The following example illustrates the issues (assuming that each company is listed in the UK).

Company A wants to bid for company B.

Company B has 200 million shares in issue and the current market price is £1, giving a market capitalisation of £200m.

Company A believes that B's shareholders would accept an offer of 120p. The consideration for the takeover would therefore be £240m. Company A has 100 million shares in issue and they currently trade at £5, giving a market capitalisation of £500m.

At this point the bid will require an issue of 48 million shares in A (ie an issue valued at £240m).

When the bid is announced, A's shares fall to £4.50.

At this point the bid will require an issue of 53.3 million shares in A to maintain its value at £240m.

A significant factor for A will be the effect of the proposed acquisition on its earnings and dividend-paying capability. The scenario described above would be consistent with a market expectation that the proposed takeover would have a negative impact on the earnings and dividends of A. The increased cost of capital associated with the increased number of shares required to fund the takeover may have the effect of causing the

---

[33] See rule 12 of the Code.

[34] This form of bid is generally referred to as a 'share for share' offer or a 'paper' offer since it is financed by the bidder's own shares.

[35] The company law rules relating to adequate and proper payment for shares are disapplied in this case by s 594 Companies Act 2006, the rationale presumably being that the market correctly values the target shares which form the consideration for the new issue by the bidder.

takeover to be abandoned. Equally, a positive market reaction to the proposed takeover would reduce its cost by lowering the number of shares that A would be required to issue to fund the bid. In that sense, market expectations, which relate essentially to the future prospects of the combined entity, largely determine both the cost of a share-for-share takeover and its outcome.

11.4 Regulation of takeovers[36]

11.4.1 Policy issues

Regulation of takeovers is a relatively recent development. Its origins are linked with the growth of takeovers in the UK in the 1950s and 1960s, and in particular the emergence of hostile takeovers.[37] This led to the creation, on a self-regulatory basis, of the Takeover Panel and the adoption of the Takeover Code in 1968. The main concern underlying this self-regulatory initiative was to ensure that takeovers were conducted in an orderly manner and in particular that shareholders in target companies were treated equally. The Code is not directly concerned with broader policy issues of whether takeovers are socially beneficial or whether they have anti-competitive effects.[38]

However, it is not possible for a regulatory regime governing takeovers to ignore entirely the issue of whether takeovers are socially beneficial, since a basic question for the design of the regime is the extent to which it should facilitate takeovers. An unstated principle underlying both the Takeovers Directive and the Takeover Code is that takeovers perform a useful function and should therefore be facilitated. That objective is particularly evident in the Takeovers Directive, since one of its effects is to remove barriers to takeovers that had in the past been erected in various Member States.

A policy of facilitation of takeovers can be justified in principle on the basis that takeovers may have the effect of making the corporate sector more efficient. By opening up the possibility of more successful companies taking over the less successful, it is possible to envisage a Darwinian process of evolution in which enterprises that adapt best to their economic environment survive while those less capable of adapting to that environment are eliminated. However, that theoretical analysis is not always evident in practice. In particular, empirical evidence points to two weaknesses in the theory. First, it is not clear that takeovers target the weakest companies as measured by their operating

---

[36] The material in this section is drawn in part from I MacNeil, 'Takeovers and Mergers' in J Birds (ed), *Boyle & Birds' Company Law*, 8th edn (Bristol, Jordans, 2011) ch 20.

[37] For a general overview of the historical development see J Armour and D Skeel, 'Who Writes the Rules for Hostile Takeovers, and Why?—The Peculiar Divergence of US and UK Takeover Regulation', available at http://ssrn.com/abstract=928928 (accessed on 16 August 2011).

[38] Competition aspects of takeovers are dealt with under a separate regulatory regime established under the EU Merger Control Regulation, above n 9, and the Competition Act 1998.

performance.[39] Secondly, although target shareholders benefit from the payment by the bidder of a bid premium, bidder shareholders often suffer from lower returns from the combined enterprise following conclusion of a bid.[40] Both weaknesses in the theory may be linked to some extent with the principal/agent problem in corporate governance since 'empire-building' bids pursued by directors may serve their own interests but not those of the shareholders whom they serve.

11.4.2 Governance issues

Takeover bids raise a number of governance issues within the bidder and target companies.[41] For the bidder, the first issue is who can approve the making of a takeover bid. While the model articles for public companies establish a default position in which the board can authorise any transaction,[42] there are two potential limitations. First, in the case of a share-for-share offer, the board will require authority to issue the relevant shares.[43] Although directors are often authorised to make relatively small share issues to new investors, most share issues made to fund takeovers are likely to fall outside that authorisation and will therefore require approval by shareholders.[44] Secondly, in the case of listed bidders, the Listing Rules require that shareholders approve Class 1 transactions.[45] The rationale for that approval requirement is that a Class 1 transaction fundamentally alters the business of the company.

From the target company's perspective, the most basic issue is who has responsibility for accepting the takeover bid. As noted above, the manner in which shareholders accept a bid and the extent to which dissenting shareholders may become bound to accept a bid varies between a contractual offer and a scheme of arrangement. However, that perspective ignores the potential intervention of the board in the takeover process. Both the Takeovers Directive and the Takeover Code adopt a principle of board neutrality according to which the board should not influence the outcome of the takeover. This does not imply that the board can do nothing; indeed, both the Takeovers Directive and the Takeover Code require the board to act, for example by ensuring that independent

---

[39] See J Franks and C Mayer, 'Hostile Takeovers and the Correction of Managerial Failure' (1996) 40 *Journal of Financial Economics* 163, finding little evidence of poor performance prior to bids in UK takeovers in the 1980s; and M Maher and T Anderson, 'Corporate Governance: Effects on Firm Performance and Economic Growth', available at http://www.oecd.org/dataoecd/10/34/2090569.pdf (accessed on 16 August 2011) IV.3.

[40] See M Martynova, S Oosting and L Renneboog, 'The Long-Term Operating Performance of European Mergers and Acquisitions', ECGI Finance Working Paper No 137/2006/TILEC Discussion Paper No 2006-030 (November 2006), available at SSRN: http://ssrn.com/abstract=944407.

[41] The discussion here focuses on bidders and targets that are structured as companies under the Companies Act 2006. In the case of a bidder, it may well be that it is a different type of legal entity, such as a Limited Partnership, Limited Liability Partnership or a company formed outside the UK. Note that the scope of the Takeover Code is defined by reference to the target and not the bidder.

[42] See Chapter 10.1.1 regarding the powers of the board.

[43] Companies Act 2006, ss 550 and 551. The authority may be contained in the Arts or given by special resolution.

[44] See Chapter 7.3.1 regarding the general principles governing the issue of new shares.

[45] A Class 1 transaction is one in which ratios relating to assets, profits, turnover and consideration to market capitalisation and gross capital exceed 25%: see FSA Handbook, LR 10: Significant Transactions.

advice is given to shareholders as to the merits of the bid. But the principle does limit the defensive and frustrating measures that can be adopted by a board that opposes a bid.

11.4.3 The Takeovers Directive

The long gestation period of the Takeovers Directive and its approach to several key issues reflect basic differences among Member States in regard to takeovers. At the time that the Directive was first proposed (1989), there was an active takeover market only in the UK. Other Member States were generally either suspicious of takeovers or simply hostile to them. That approach reflected two principal concerns. One was that facilitation of takeovers through the medium of a directive would create a market for control across Europe which would threaten the independence of companies based in countries without a tradition of takeovers or without a well-developed capital market. The other was that takeovers concentrated too much power in the hands of shareholders in a way that was not compatible with those models of corporate governance that placed greater emphasis on stakeholders other than shareholders.

The outcome was a directive which permits opt-outs in relation to several key provisions and therefore failed to establish a harmonised system of takeover regulation within the EU. While the Directive bears a close resemblance in some respects to the Takeover Code in the UK (for example, the General Principles of the Code are reproduced verbatim in Article 3 of the Directive), the opt-outs mean that the application of the General Principles can vary widely between Member States (and in some cases between companies in the same Member State). The opt-outs arise in respect of defensive measures and the so-called 'breakthrough' provision of the Directive, both of which are discussed in more detail below. The main purpose of the relevant provisions is to remove impediments to takeovers, but the opt-outs have the effect of limiting the extent to which that will occur.

Prior to the adoption of the Takeovers Directive, there were no provisions in UK company law that dealt with impediments to takeovers. The Takeover Code did contain some provisions which limited the ability of the board of an offeree company to take frustrating action during the course of a bid, but there was no attempt made to control impediments to takeovers in the form of the capital structure of a company. Such impediments, which can arise, for example, from special voting rights attached to particular classes of shares or other provisions in a company's constitution, have the capacity to limit the possibility of takeovers in the sense that control may be entrenched in the hands of a controlling shareholder or a group of shareholders. This was not historically a matter of great concern in the UK for several reasons. First, company law in the UK historically emphasised the freedom of shareholders to structure the constitution as they wished, relatively free from regulatory control. Secondly, the dispersed system of shareholding which became established in the UK in the middle of the twentieth century meant that that there was relatively little concern over the possibility of control of listed companies becoming entrenched in the hands of a controlling shareholder. And finally, resistance on the part of institutional investors to differential voting structures or restrictions on share transfer[46] meant that listed companies with different classes of shares carrying different voting rights were not a feature of the UK capital market. The position differed in continental Europe, which did not have the same historical tradition as the UK. Nor did many Member States have much experience in developing and administering a takeovers regime. In order for the Takeovers Directive to facilitate takeovers in continental Europe it was therefore necessary for the Directive to address directly the issues of entrenchment of control through capital structure as well as the freedom enjoyed by boards of directors in some other Member States to take frustrating action after a bid was announced. Article 11 of the Directive (the 'breakthrough' provision) addresses the first issue and Article 9 the second. However, the political sensitivity of facilitating takeovers (and thereby opening up the possibility of greater foreign control over enterprises) resulted in a compromise whereby the two provisions were made subject to an opt-out regime. This regime permits Member States not to require compliance with Article 9(2) and (3) (the prohibition on an offeree board adopting frustrating measures after a bid is announced) and Article 11. The UK has not taken advantage of the possibility of opting out of Article 9, mainly because the prohibition on frustrating action has been such a fundamental part of the Takeover Code for so long.[47] However, the UK has taken advantage of the opt-out in respect of Article 11, with the result that the Takeover Code does not require compliance with this provision. Instead, companies are able to decide for themselves whether to give effect to the provision.[48] The process by which this decision is made is controlled by part 28 of the Companies Act 2006.[49]

11.5 The Takeover Panel

The Companies Act 2006 places the Takeover Panel on a statutory footing,[50] whereas in the past it had operated on a self-regulatory basis. The Act assumes the existence of the Panel and does not alter its legal status as an unincorporated association, although it does make clear that it can sue and be sued in its own name.[51] The Act does not interfere with the existing structure or mode of operation of the Panel. Authority is given for the continuation of existing practice by the express power to delegate functions of the Panel either to a committee or to an officer or member of the Panel.[52] This permits the

---

[46] See the UK Listing Authority's Listing Rules, LR 2.2.4R, requiring shares admitted to the 'official list' to be freely transferable.

[47] See rule 21 for the current version. The position is made clear by s 943(1) CA 2006, requiring the Panel to adopt rules which give effect to Art 9. No such requirement is imposed in respect of Art 11.

[48] As required by Art 12(2) of the Directive when a Member State has opted out of Art 11.

[49] See further Birds, above n 36, ch 20.4.

[50] Companies Act 2006, s 942.

[51] Companies Act 2006, s 960. Unincorporated associations cannot normally sue and be sued in their own name.

[52] Companies Act 2006, s 942(3).

day-to-day business of the Panel to continue to be handled by the Panel Executive—consisting of the Director-General, the Deputy Director-General(s), the Secretary and their staff reporting directly to the Chairman.[53] The day-to-day business of the Panel Executive consists chiefly of monitoring all takeover and merger transactions to ensure as far as possible that the proposals and the manner of their execution conform to the spirit and to the detailed provisions of the Code, on the basis that such rulings are subject to reference to the full Panel. The Director-General or his deputies are available at all times to give rulings on points of interpretation of the Code. Such rulings now have binding effect under the Companies Act 2006.[54] They aim to give these rulings as promptly as is necessary to ensure the free functioning of the takeover and merger business.[55] Companies and their advisers are encouraged to consult the Panel Executive on points requiring clarification either by telephone or by meetings at short notice. Practice statements are published by the Panel Executive indicating how it normally interprets the Code in particular circumstances.

The move to a statutory framework for the Panel and Code raised concern[56] that tactical litigation might emerge as a threat to the rapid decision-making that had been a hallmark of the operation of the Panel during its time as a self-regulatory body. Several provisions of the Companies Act 2006, in combination, have the effect of largely excluding this possibility. The first is that contraventions of the Takeover Code do not make any transaction void or unenforceable.[57] This removes the uncertainty and potential costs that would arise if takeover transactions could be challenged on that basis. The second is that contraventions of the Takeover Code do not give rise to a right of action for breach of statutory duty.[58] Such an action, were it available, could have an equally disruptive effect as parties could argue that contraventions had resulted in a takeover bid either being thwarted or succeeding as a result of the contravention. Finally, the Panel and its members, staff and officers are exempt from liability in connection with the discharge or purported discharge of the Panel's functions.[59] This removes the possibility of tactical litigation being targeted at the Panel itself as a means of disrupting its decision-making processes.

The Companies Act 2006 enables the Panel to impose sanctions for breaches of the Code or failure to comply with a direction. This represents a significant change from the position under the self-regulatory regime, which relied on the reputational benefits of voluntary compliance with the Code. The Panel is required to publish a policy statement in respect of sanctions that were not available under the Takeover Code prior to the

---

[53] The staff of the Panel comprises mainly secondees from City of London firms associated with takeovers.

[54] Companies Act 2006, s 945(2).

[55] As noted below, the Code applies to mergers whereas the Takeovers Directive does not.

[56] See Department of Trade and Industry, 'Company Law Implementation of the European Directive on Takeover Bids, A Consultative Document' (January 2005) para 2.39.

[57] Companies Act 2006, s 956(2).

[58] Companies Act 2006, s 956(1). This follows the pattern established in respect of most regulatory rules created under the Financial Services and Markets Act 2000 (FSMA 2000) as a result of s 150(2) FSMA 2000 and Art 3 of the FSMA 2000 (Right of Action) Regulations 2001, SI 2001/2256.

[59] Companies Act 2006, s 961.

implementation of the 2006 Act.[60] This requirement applies most obviously to financial penalties, should they be included in the Code at some future date.[61] The Act also sets out factors that the Panel must have regard to when imposing sanctions. They include the seriousness of the breach or failure in question, the extent to which the breach was deliberate or reckless, and whether the person subject to the penalty is an individual. The Panel is able to revise a policy statement at any time, but that freedom should be understood to be subject to the legitimate expectations of those who relied on the version in force when a breach occurred. Also relevant in this context is the FSA rule prohibiting authorised persons from acting for an offeror who is not complying or is not likely to comply with the Takeover Code.[62] So too is the possibility of enforcement action by the FSA based on breach of the FSA's Principles for Business.[63]

The Companies Act 2006 also enables the Panel to adopt rules providing for the payment of compensation in respect of breaches of its rules.[64] Provision has now been made in the Code for compensation to be payable in respect of breaches of a limited number of rules.[65] Another innovation is the possibility of court enforcement of the Code on the application of the Panel.[66] This is possible when the court is satisfied that there has been or is likely to be a contravention of a rule-based requirement or a disclosure requirement. Reflecting its new statutory power to impose sanctions, the Panel is now also equipped with investigative powers. The Panel is able to require the production of documents and the provision of information that is reasonably required in connection with the exercise of its powers.[67]

Closely linked with the sanctions available to the Panel are the new criminal offences[68] of failing to comply with the requirements of the Takeovers Directive (as implemented by the Takeover Code) in respect of offer documents[69] or response documents.[70] When an offer document does not comply with the relevant rules an offence is committed by the person making the bid (the offeror) and any director, officer or member of that body who caused the document to be published. The offence is not one of strict liability as there is a requirement to show intent but there is no materiality requirement, meaning that even minor non-compliance may result in the attachment of criminal liability. A person will be guilty if he knew that the offer document did not comply or was reckless as to whether

---

[60] The sanctions that were available in the past were: private and public censures; suspending or withdrawing an exemption; reporting conduct to a regulator such as the FSA; and publishing a statement indicating that a person is likely not to comply with the Code, thereby triggering regulatory and professional rules that prevented firms acting on behalf of that person (eg MAR 4.3.1R below).

[61] The absence to date of financial penalties in the Code distinguishes the Panel from the FSA, which routinely imposes financial penalties.

[62] See FSA Handbook, MAR 4.3.1R.

[63] This option is available in the case of firms that are authorised under FSMA 2000.

[64] Companies Act 2006, s 954. The rule is widely framed, permitting the Panel to order compensation to be paid to any person if it is just and reasonable. There are no recorded instances of the exercise of this power.

[65] See s 10(c) of the Introduction to the Code.

[66] See CA 2006, s 955.

[67] CA 2006, s 947(1)–(3).

[68] See CA 2006, s 953.

[69] See Rule 24 of the Code.

[70] See Rule 25 of the Code. These offences apply only to the (narrow) definition of takeovers in the Directive and not to the wider meaning adopted in pt 28 of the Companies Act 2006.

it complied and failed to take all reasonable steps to secure that the offer document did comply. The position differs in respect of a response document in that responsibility lies not with the offeree company but only with its directors and officers, who will be guilty subject to the same conditions applicable to their liability in respect of an offer document (above).

11.6 The Takeover Code

Unlike the Takeovers Directive, the Code does not define its scope by reference to a definition of a 'takeover'. The Code states in its introduction that it is concerned with regulating takeovers and mergers, however effected, including statutory mergers and schemes of arrangement. It makes clear also that it applies to other transactions which result in a change of control in companies falling within the Code.

The scope of the Code by reference to companies has become more complex since the introduction of the Takeovers Directive. The scope is defined by reference to companies in receipt of an offer (target companies), and there are two main categories that fall within the scope of the Code:

- Public companies with their registered office in the UK or with securities admitted to trading on a regulated market in the UK.
- Private companies in some limited circumstances in which their shares have been traded on public markets in the previous 10 years.

As required by the Takeovers Directive, the Code also provides for shared jurisdiction in circumstances in which a company has links with more than one Member State through the location of its registered office and the location in which its securities are traded on a regulated market.

The Takeover Code adopted a 'principles-based' approach to the regulation of takeovers long before that term came into general use in other regulatory domains. The overall approach of the Code is made clear in the introduction, which provides that:

> The Code is based upon a number of General Principles, which are essentially statements of standards of commercial behaviour. They are expressed in broad general terms and the Code does not define the precise extent of, or the limitations on, their application. They are applied in accordance with their spirit in order to achieve their underlying purpose. In addition to the General Principles, the Code contains a series of rules. Although most of the rules are expressed in less general terms than the General Principles, they are not framed in technical language and, like the General Principles, are to be interpreted to achieve their underlying purpose. Therefore, their spirit must be observed as well as their letter.[71]

The General Principles of the Code are as follows:

---

[71] Introduction to the Takeover Code, para 2(b).

1. All holders of the securities of an offeree company of the same class must be afforded equivalent treatment; moreover, if a person acquires control of a company, the other holders of securities must be protected.

2. The holders of the securities of an offeree company must have sufficient time and information to enable them to reach a properly informed decision on the bid; where it advises the holders of securities, the board of the offeree company must give its views on the effects of implementation of the bid on employment, conditions of employment and the locations of the company's places of business.

3. The board of an offeree company must act in the interests of the company as a whole and must not deny the holders of securities the opportunity to decide on the merits of the bid.

4. False markets must not be created in the securities of the offeree company, of the offeror company or of any other company concerned by the bid in such a way that the rise or fall of the prices of the securities becomes artificial and the normal functioning of the markets is distorted.

5. An offeror must announce a bid only after ensuring that he/she can fulfil in full any cash consideration, if such is offered, and after taking all reasonable measures to secure the implementation of any other type of consideration.

6. An offeree company must not be hindered in the conduct of its affairs for longer than is reasonable by a bid for its securities.

The detailed rules of the Code provide for the application of these principles to the takeover process. Several of the most important rules are referred to in the sections that follow below. No significant changes to the Code were necessary to implement the Takeovers Directive. However, part 28 of the Companies Act does put the Code on a statutory basis, and provides formal powers to the Takeover Panel in relation to making rules and enforcing the Code.

11.6.1 The terms of the offer

As a general rule, the terms of a takeover bid are not controlled by the Takeover Code or the Takeovers Directive. The terms are a commercial matter for the bidder to set and for the shareholders in the target company to accept or reject as they see fit. However, there are some important exceptions to this principle. An important condition which is imposed by the Takeover Code is that it must be a condition of a voluntary offer that the bidder secures more than 50% of the relevant (voting) shares. The purpose of the rule is to ensure that a takeover will only be implemented if control has passed to the bidder. For this purpose, control is viewed as the ability to pass an ordinary resolution (requiring 50% of the votes cast) rather than the higher threshold (75% of votes cast) required for a special resolution. If the 50% threshold is not met, effective control has not passed to the bidder and therefore the basic objective of the takeover has not been achieved. In those circumstances, the underlying logic of the choice available to target shareholders—either to exit or to accept a change in control of the company—is no longer relevant: thus, the appropriate solution is for the bid to lapse.

In the case of takeovers which fall within the scope of the merger control regimes[72] in the UK or EU, it must be a condition of the bid that it will lapse if it is referred to the Competition Commission in the UK or the EU Commission initiates action under the Merger Regulation[73] before the closing date for the offer or the date (whichever is later) when it is declared unconditional.[74] The rationale for this rule is that the outcome of a merger reference may be that the merger cannot proceed or that it can only proceed subject to certain conditions. Thus, until the outcome is known, it would be pointless to proceed with a bid which might subsequently have to be unravelled to comply with the outcome of the relevant merger investigation. Once the outcome is known, it is possible for a new bid to be made, although both the outcome of the merger investigation and changes in market conditions may mean that a new bid will only be possible on different terms.

11.6.2 Equality of treatment of target shareholders

The first general principle of the Takeover Code (above) refers to the requirement of equal treatment of shareholders, reflecting the long-standing principle of company law that all shareholders of the same class are to be treated equally.[75] The first general principle also refers to the need to protect shareholders once a person acquires control of a company. The two issues are linked in the sense that de facto control of a company may be acquired from a select group of shareholders, who may be paid a bid premium as part of the process. In those circumstances, the remaining shareholders are faced with the prospect of a change in control of the company without having the opportunity to exit the company in the same manner as those from whom the bidder has acquired control.

The Takeovers Directive and the Takeover Code attempt to deal with this issue through the requirement that a bidder who acquires de facto control is required to make an offer (a 'mandatory offer') to the remaining shareholders. In the Takeover Code, the rule is triggered when a person acquires shares carrying 30% or more of the voting rights of a company.[76] The mandatory offer must be made to the holders of all equity shares, whether voting or non-voting, and to the holders of all transferable securities carrying voting rights. As to the terms of the offer, it must not be conditional on the offeror acquiring shares carrying more than 50% of the voting rights; and it must be in cash or

---

[72] Note that these regimes define 'mergers' so as to include takeovers within the meaning adopted by the Takeovers Directive and the Takeover Code.

[73] Above n 9.

[74] Rule 12 of the Takeover Code. The rule applies to takeovers structured as a scheme of arrangement if the relevant merger reference or action by the EU Commission occurs before the shareholders' meeting that votes on the scheme.

[75] The Takeover Code applies the principle more broadly than company law, for example by requiring that non-voting equity shareholders and the holders of non-equity voting securities (eg preference shares) be included in a 'mandatory offer'.

[76] Rule 12 of the Takeover Code. For the purposes of this rule, shares acquired by (other) persons 'acting in concert' with that person are included in the calculation. See Takeover Panel Practice Statement 26 regarding shareholder collaboration and concert parties. The effect of the statement is to restrict the circumstances in which shareholder collaboration will trigger a requirement to make a mandatory bid.

be accompanied by a cash alternative at not less than the highest price paid by the offeror or any person acting in concert with it for any interest in shares of that class during the 12 months prior to the announcement of that offer. The effect of the rule is to create a shareholding threshold at 29.99% beyond which a shareholder cannot increase its stake without making a general offer to all shareholders on the terms required by the Code. The underlying premise is that a shareholder who reaches a 30% shareholding has secured de facto control of the company and that following this acquisition of control the remaining shareholders should be offered the opportunity to exit the company on equivalent terms to those shareholders who have already sold.

The principle of equality is also evident in several other rules in the Takeover Code. Rule 14 is relevant where the target has more than one class of equity share capital and requires that a comparable offer is made to each class, whether it carries voting rights or not. Rule 16 prohibits any attempt by the bidder to enter into special deals with selected target shareholders by offering them favourable conditions that are not available to all shareholders.[77] Rule 20 deals with equality of information, providing that information about parties to an offer must be made equally available to all offeree company shareholders as nearly as possible at the same time and in the same manner. Finally, rule 32 deals with circumstances in which an offer is revised during the period that it is open for acceptance: in those circumstances, all shareholders who have already accepted the offer are entitled to the revised terms.

11.6.3 Defensive measures

The Takeover Code adopts the principle that the board of a target company should remain neutral during the course of a takeover and should adopt defensive measures only with the consent of shareholders.[78] The underlying principle is that it is the shareholders and not the board who should decide on the merits of the bid.[79] To give effect to the principle, the Code requires that the board refrain from taking action, such as the issue of shares, sale of assets of a material amount or entering into contracts other than in the ordinary course of business. While the Takeovers Directive permits Member States to opt out of the Article 9 provisions on defensive measures, the UK has chosen not to do that on the basis that the prohibition on defensive measures has been such a fundamental part of the Takeover Code for so long.[80] Moreover, it remains open to question whether the regulatory emphasis on limiting defensive measures has been a necessary or proportionate

---

[77] This does not prevent a bidder taking binding undertakings from shareholders in advance of a bid to accept an offer at a certain minimum price. This provides some reassurance to the bidder that the bid will be successful. In those circumstances, all shareholders are treated equally since they will all receive the same bid price (including any revision).

[78] Rule 21. The Code refers to 'frustrating' action, but the underlying concept is the same as the 'defensive' measures referred to in the Takeovers Directive.

[79] In that respect, the UK approach differs from that in the US, which permits the board in some circumstances to adopt defensive measures: see P Davies and K Hopt, 'Control Transactions' in R Kraakman et al (eds), *The Anatomy of Corporate Law* (Oxford, Oxford University Press, 2004) ch 7.

[80] The position is made clear by s 943(1) of the CA 2006, requiring the Panel to adopt rules which give effect to Art 9.

response to the risks faced by target shareholders, as in many instances the capacity to adopt defensive measures will be limited by principles of corporate law.[81]

11.6.4 The role and duties of the target board

Underlying General Principle 2 of the Takeover Code is the belief that takeovers can only operate effectively as a corporate governance mechanism if shareholders have sufficient time and information to enable them to reach a properly informed decision on the bid. Thus, the Code requires the board of the offeree company to obtain competent independent advice on any offer and the substance of such advice to be made known to its shareholders.[82] The target board is not required to advise the shareholders as to whether or not they should accept the offer (or how to vote in the case of a takeover structured as a scheme of arrangement), but it is required to make known to shareholders its opinion on the offer. That opinion must include:

1. the effects of implementation of the offer on all the company's interests, including, specifically, employment; and
2. the offeror's strategic plans for the offeree company and their likely repercussions on employment and the locations of the offeree company's places of business.[83]

Since the recommendation of the board of the target company to its shareholders that a bid should be accepted is likely to carry some weight and improve the prospects of the bid being successful, the bidder will normally be keen to secure the recommendation of the target board. To this end, it may enter into an agreement with the target board to that effect. Whether, in those circumstances, the agreement represents a binding contract obliging the target board to recommend the bid is a matter of contractual interpretation.[84] Moreover, even if it does bind the board, it cannot have the effect of preventing the board from subsequently recommending a later bid that offers better terms. The rationale for this approach is that the board is required to act in the best interests of the company for the benefit of its members as a whole.[85] Thus, an agreement to recommend a bid must be understood to incorporate that obligation and it cannot be overridden.[86] That principle is particularly significant for the purposes of enabling competing bids to be brought forward, since it provides a basis for the board of the target to take account of a new bid when advising shareholders. While recommending a bid opens up the target board to possible legal liability in respect of the advice given, they will only be liable if the advice

---

[81] See D Kershaw, C Gerner-Beurle and M Solinas, 'Is the Board Neutrality Rule Trivial? Amnesia about Corporate Law in European Takeover Regulation', LSE Law, Society and Economy Working Papers 3/2011, available at www.lse.ac.uk/collections/law/wps/wps.htm.

[82] Rule 3. The relevant advice is normally provided by an investment bank. However, the adviser must not be part of the same corporate group as the target company, nor can it be an existing or recent adviser.

[83] Takeover Code, rule 25.1.

[84] See eg *Dawson International plc v Coats Patons plc* 1988 SLT 854, where the agreement was interpreted as not giving rise to a contractual obligation.

[85] Companies Act 2006, s 172. See also general principle 3 of the Takeover Code.

[86] *Dawson International*, above n 84.

is given negligently.[87] Thus, it is unlikely that liability will arise if advice is given after careful consideration of the merits of the bid and the advice of the independent adviser appointed in respect of the bid.

11.6.5 Review of the Takeover Code

In early 2010, the Panel announced a review of certain aspects of the Code.[88] The review was prompted by concerns, which were crystallised by the takeover of Cadbury plc by Kraft Foods Inc, regarding the extent to which the operation of the Code favoured bidders over target companies. In particular, the concern focused on the extent to which the Code facilitated hostile bids and the role of short-term investors in deciding the outcome of a bid. Three of the possible reforms that were discussed would have had far-reaching consequences. They were:

1. Raising the acceptance condition threshold above '50% plus one'. This would have altered the long-standing principle that a takeover offer need be conditional only on the offeror securing control of the target.[89]
2. Disenfranchising shares acquired during the offer period. This was viewed in some quarters as a means to limit the role of short-term investors in deciding the outcome of a bid.
3. Requiring bidder shareholders to approve takeover offers. This would have been a new requirement as the Code has traditionally focused on protecting shareholders in target companies.

In its response to the consultation, the Panel rejected the three proposals outlined above. However, it did propose significant measures, including:[90]

1. A prohibition on (i) undertakings given to an offeror by an offeree company board to take any action to implement a transaction to which the Code applies, or to refrain from taking any action which might facilitate a competing transaction to which the Code applies; and (ii) inducement fee agreements.[91]
2. Disclosure of fees paid to advisers.
3. Clarification of the matters that a target board can take into account in giving their opinion and recommendation on the offer.

---

[87] Ibid.

[88] See Takeover Panel PCP 2010/2, Consultation Paper Issued by the Code Committee of the Panel (June 2010).

[89] See Rule 10 of the Code.

[90] See generally Takeover Panel 2010/22, Review of Certain Aspects of the Regulation of Takeover Bids (October 2010).

[91] This refers to so-called 'break fees' paid by a target to a bidder in the event that a bid does not proceed to completion. Such fees are currently permitted subject to a maximum of 1% of the offer consideration (see rule 21.2 of the Code). So-called 'success fees' paid to advisers are not covered by that proposal—the Panel concluded that such fees should not be prohibited.

Further developments on these issues are awaited and are likely to be linked with the government's review of so-called 'short-termism' in capital markets.[92]

11.7 'Breakthrough' provisions

The breakthrough provision in Article 11 of the Takeovers Directive is intended to facilitate takeovers by ensuring that in a bid situation there will be equivalence between the economic interest in a company acquired by a bidder and the voting power of the bidder. It provides a mechanism whereby a bidder can overcome a capital structure that entrenches voting power in the hands of certain shareholders through techniques such as non-voting shares or enhanced voting shares. The Takeovers Directive makes it optional for Member States to enforce this provision and the UK has taken advantage of the opt-out, with the result that the Takeover Code does not give effect to the provision.[93] While that approach may appear anomalous in view of the UK's long-standing policy of facilitating takeovers, it was justified on the basis that entrenchment of control is not an issue in UK listed companies[94] and therefore the rule addressed a problem that did not exist in the UK system of corporate governance. Moreover, the requirement of the Directive that any Member State opting out of Article 11 must allow companies to decide for themselves whether to give effect to the breakthrough rule (in their articles of association) means that the application of the rule has effectively been delegated to shareholders. That approach is in keeping with the long-standing tradition in the UK of providing flexibility to companies in determining their legal structure.

Another aspect of the 'breakthrough' rule, and one which makes its application very complex in cross-border bids, is the 'reciprocity' option contained in Article 12 of the Directive. This permits a Member State to specify that Article 11 can only be relied on by a bidder against a target company where the bidder is also subject to Article 11 (ie there is reciprocity between the target and the bidder). The UK rejected the possibility of adopting this provision on the basis that it would represent a form of protectionism that was not compatible with the policy of an open takeovers regime and also that it would add another layer of complexity to the regime. In the case of Member States who do rely on the reciprocity opt-out, the effect is to protect their companies from takeovers, since a bidder will only be able to rely on the 'breakthrough' provision if the bidder itself is bound by the breakthrough rule.

---

[92] See Department for Business Innovations & Skills, 'A Long-Term Focus for Corporate Britain: a Call for Evidence', available at http://www.bis.gov.uk/Consultations/a-long-term-focus-for-corporate-britain?cat=closed awaitingresponse (7 July 2011).

[93] Unlike the position in relation to Art 9 of the Directive, the Companies Act 2006 does not require the Takeover Panel to give effect to Art 11.

[94] See generally Chapter 9.1.

The substance of the breakthrough rule is set out in Article 11 of the Directive. Article 11(2) provides that any restrictions on the transfer of securities provided for in the articles of association of the offeree company shall not apply vis-à-vis the offeror during the time allowed for acceptance of the bid laid down in Article 7(1). A similar provision in Article 11(3) applies to any restrictions on the transfer of securities provided for in contractual agreements between the offeree company and holders of its securities, or in contractual agreements[95] between holders of the offeree company's securities entered into after the adoption of the Directive. The objective of these provisions is to facilitate the transfer of control as a result of a bid by disregarding the relevant restrictions.

Article 11(3) contains several provisions which have the same effect in relation to restrictions on voting rights. First, restrictions on voting rights provided for in the articles of association of the offeree company shall not have effect at the general meeting of shareholders which decides on any defensive measures in accordance with Article 9. Secondly, restrictions on voting rights provided for in contractual agreements between the offeree company and holders of its securities, or in contractual agreements[96] between holders of the offeree company's securities entered into after the adoption of the Directive, do not have effect at the general meeting of shareholders which decides on any defensive measures in accordance with Article 9. Thirdly, multiple-vote securities shall carry only one vote each at the general meeting of shareholders which decides on any defensive measures in accordance with Article 9.

Article 11(4) provides the crucial breakthrough mechanism that permits a bidder to secure effective control of a target. It provides that, where, following a bid, the offeror holds 75% or more of the capital carrying voting rights, no restrictions on the transfer of securities or on voting rights referred to in paragraphs 2 and 3 nor any extraordinary rights of shareholders concerning the appointment or removal of board members provided for in the articles of association of the offeree company shall apply. Furthermore, multiple-vote securities shall carry only one vote each at the first[97] general meeting of shareholders following closure of the bid, called by the offeror in order to amend the articles of association or to remove or appoint board members.[98] The effect of this provision is to enable an offeror who has acquired 75% of voting capital (though not necessarily 75% of the votes) to control the key issues of changes to the constitution and changes to the board of directors. From a bidder's perspective, these two issues are the 'crown jewels' of the target company in the sense that they represent effective control.

A special resolution must be adopted for a company to opt in to Article 11. The result is that the company's constitution is aligned with the Directive as special resolutions form part of a company's constitution. In that sense, the breakthrough provision in the Directive will apply not just as a regulatory rule but as part of the company constitution, which

---

[95] Eg a pre-emption provision in a shareholders' agreement that requires the parties to offer shares to each other before offering them to outsiders. Without the breakthrough provision, such an agreement could limit the holder's ability to accept a takeover offer.

[96] Eg in a shareholders' agreement.

[97] The express reference to the first general meeting indicates that the bidder has only one chance to 'breakthrough' the relevant restrictions as they will be reactivated at any subsequent meeting.

[98] A bidder who reaches the 75% threshold has the right to call a general meeting: see CA 2006, s 969.

can be enforced by shareholders (including a bidder who has acquired shares). Notification of an opt-in decision must be given to the Panel and to the designated supervisory authority of any EEA state other than the UK in which the company has voting shares admitted to trading on a regulated market within 15 days of the resolution being passed. This is in addition to the recording of the resolution at Companies House as required by the Companies Act.[99]

It is possible for a company to reverse the effect of an 'opt-in' resolution by subsequently adopting an 'opt-out' resolution. The UK implementation of this requirement goes beyond the Takeovers Directive by stipulating, in the interests of legal certainty, the time at which the 'opt-out' resolution becomes effective. This may not be earlier than the first anniversary of the date on which a copy of the opting-in resolution was forwarded to the registrar. The effect is to delay the legal effect of an 'opt-out' resolution, thereby limiting its relevance as a potential response to a takeover bid.

Article 11(5) provides that, where rights are removed as a result of the operation of the breakthrough provision or the adoption of an 'opt-in' resolution, 'equitable compensation' shall be paid to the holders of those rights as determined by member states. This does not apply in the case of Article 11(3) and (4), where the restrictions on voting rights are compensated for by specific pecuniary advantages. Thus, it would seem that the application of the breakthrough provision to preference shares (in circumstances in which they have voting rights) would not attract compensation. Article 11 does not apply where Member States hold securities in the offeree company that confer special rights on the Member States which are compatible with the Treaty, or to special rights provided for in national law which are compatible with the Treaty, or to cooperatives.

The UK implementation of the Directive contains no express provisions providing for the payment of compensation in the case of an 'opt-in' resolution. The justification for this approach was that such a resolution is subject to the normal legal and bargaining framework under which changes may be made to the constitution, which allows for the possibility of compensation to be paid. While that approach certainly follows the tradition in the UK, there must remain some doubt whether there has been adequate implementation of the Directive.

11.8 'Squeeze-out' and 'sell-out' rights

The rationale underlying the provisions of the Takeovers Directive and the Companies Act 2006 relating to so-called 'squeeze-out' and 'sell-out' rights is that, when a bidder has secured a 90% shareholding in the target company, the governance structure changes such that the minority is no longer able to exercise any significant influence within the company. The solution that has been adopted is to enable the bidder to require the

---

[99] CA 2006, ss 29–30.

dissenting shareholders[100] to sell and to enable such shareholders to require the bidder to acquire their shares. In the case of the bidder acquiring shares, the rationale is that a minority of 10% or less may simply be a troublemaker that lacks any real power other than to disrupt the business and governance of the company. In the second case, the rationale is that the dissenting shareholders should be given the opportunity to reconsider their rejection of the bid once it becomes clear, after the bid has closed, that their fate is to be a powerless minority. The relevant provisions apply only to a takeover in the form of a contractual offer since in the case of a scheme of arrangement there can be no dissenting shareholders once the scheme is approved by the requisite majority.

As far as compulsory acquisition ('squeeze-out') is concerned, the buyer must reach the 90% shareholding by virtue of acceptances of the offer; thus, shares already held are excluded. Moreover, where the shares are voting shares, not less than 90% of the voting rights must be acquired by virtue of acceptances of the offer.[101] There is a 3 month 'deadline' from the last day on which the offer can be accepted during which notices starting the process of compulsory acquisition can be given.[102] Reflecting the fact that the Takeover Code allows the offeror to extend the period for acceptance,[103] an overall time limit of 6 months starting from the date of the offer applies in the case of takeover bids not subject to the Takeovers Directive (eg bids for companies that are not admitted to trading on a regulated market). The terms (including price) on which the shares must be acquired are those of the relevant takeover offer.

Dissenting shareholders may apply to the court, which may do two things. It may order that the offeror shall not be entitled and bound to acquire the shares. The court may also be asked to adjust the terms of the acquisition, and this power in its new form makes clear that the court is able to set such terms as it thinks fit.[104] However, under a new provision,[105] the court cannot require consideration of a higher value than that specified in the offer unless the holder shows that the offer value would be unfair, nor can it require consideration of a lower value than the offer. Moreover, the problems faced by courts in assessing the true merits of a takeover bid will still apply. These include judicial reliance on the 90% level of acceptance as indicating that sound commercial judgement must be behind the decision of such a large majority. There is also the difficulty for dissenting shareholders in matching the means, access to expert advice and internal corporate information that the offeror will have at its command.

In the case of the 'sell-out' rights of dissenting shareholders,[106] the 90% threshold is calculated differently since it includes shares already held by the bidder. The result is that the threshold for the operation of 'sell-out' rights is likely to be reached before that which

---

[100] The dissenting shareholders are those who did not accept the offer from the bidder.

[101] The addition of this second limb to the threshold resulted from the implementation of Art 15(2) of the Takeovers Directive. In the case of listed companies, the second limb is unlikely to represent a significant hurdle as differential voting rights are now rare.

[102] Companies Act 2006, s 980(2).

[103] See Rule 31.

[104] Companies Act 2006, s 986(1)(b). The corresponding provision in s 430C(1)(b) CA 1985 had simply referred to the power of the court to specify different terms of acquisition from those of the offer.

[105] Companies Act 2006, s 986(4).

[106] Meaning those shareholders who did not accept the takeover offer before it closed.

triggers the operation of the offeror's 'squeeze-out' rights. Once a dissenting shareholder has exercised his rights, the offeror is entitled and bound to acquire the dissenter's shares 'on the terms of the offer or on such terms as may be agreed'.[107] Where the takeover offer gave a choice of consideration to those who accepted its terms, this choice is preserved for dissenting shareholders who exercise their rights to be bought out.[108] If the parties cannot agree on the terms of the offer, then either side may apply to the court. The terms may then be 'such as the court thinks fit'.[109] Unlike the equivalent jurisdiction where the offeror compulsorily acquires shares, it may be noted that the court here has no power to prevent the shareholder having his shares bought. It can only change the terms. It would appear that there has been very little need for this form of relief but, together with the right to be bought, it forms a useful protection when minority shareholders are 'locked into' a company under the overwhelming control of the offeror.

---

[107] Companies Act 2006, s 985(2).

[108] Companies Act 2006, s 985(3). Similar provision is made as in the case of an offeror compulsorily acquiring shares where the consideration is not in cash and the offeror is no longer able to provide it, etc. See s 985(5).

[109] Companies Act 2006, s 986(3).

Part 4

Markets and Participants

Trading Markets— Overview

Trading markets have been at the centre of much of the discussion that has already been presented in this book. Their significance has increased over the past 20 years as most asset classes have seen a material increase in the level of trading activity.[1] The purpose of this chapter is to examine in more detail the operation and regulation of such markets. It begins by considering the different types of organisational structure to which the term 'market' is applied and the impact that technological innovation is having on regulatory developments. The EU regulatory framework established by the Markets in Financial Instruments Directive (MiFID) and its implementation in the UK are then examined. Next, consideration is given to the role and regulation of clearing and settlement—the 'post-trade' or 'operations' side of the investment business. The chapter ends with an outline of the law governing the insolvency of participants in trading markets.

12.1 Trading markets: nature and typology

The main function of trading markets is to provide a forum for the trading of securities.[2] The operation of trading markets is dependent on the transferability of securities, and this is reflected in the requirement of the UK Listing Authority (UKLA, a division of the

---

[1] See FSA, 'The Prudential Regime for Trading Activities', Consultation Paper (CP) 10/4 (2010) ch 4, for a review of the evolution of trading markets. See also R Michie, *The Global Securities Market; A History* (Oxford, Oxford University Press, 2008).

[2] See R Lee, *What is an Exchange?* (Oxford, Oxford University Press, 2000) ch 1. Lee defines a market's structure to include the full set of rules governing data dissemination, order routing and order execution. A broader definition is given by S Valdez, *An Introduction to Global Financial Markets*, 5th edn (Basingstoke, Palgrave Macmillan, 2007) 161: 'It [a stock exchange] provides the regulation of company listings, a price formation mechanism, the supervision of trading, authorisation of members, settlement of transactions and publication of trade data and prices.'

Financial Services Authority (FSA)) Listing Rules that listed securities must be freely transferable.[3] By way of contrast, in private and unlisted public companies, the articles of association may and often do restrict transfer of shares. This reflects the absence, in most cases, of an organised market for shares in such companies, along with the fact that small companies often operate on a basis similar to a partnership and therefore wish to restrict share-ownership to persons with whom the existing shareholders feel comfortable in running the business.

There is no legal or regulatory requirement for transfer of securities to take place through an organised or regulated market.[4] The attraction of markets, especially regulated markets, is that they provide liquidity and ensure some degree of investor protection. Liquidity refers to the ease with which investors can buy or sell securities.[5] Investors value liquidity because it enables securities to be converted into cash: all things being equal, investors will therefore pay more for a liquid security than an illiquid one. Protection of investors who trade in investment markets is an important issue because it creates confidence in the operation of markets and therefore encourages the process of investment. Investor protection encompasses issues such as transparency and market integrity, which are discussed in greater detail in Chapter 13.

Trading markets also have a role in raising new capital for companies, but, in comparison with other sources of corporate finance, that function is quite limited. In other words, there is relatively little 'new' capital raised by companies through initial public offers (IPOs) or through subsequent share issues.[6] The more common pattern is for an IPO to serve as a mechanism through which existing shareholders can sell their shares to the public. In this sense, the market provides liquidity to those shareholders and serves a vital function in encouraging their initial investment in the knowledge that success will bring with it the opportunity to sell out via an IPO.

A basic distinction can be drawn between organised and unorganised or 'over-the-counter' (OTC) markets.[7] An organised market operates under a set of standard rules relating to admission to trading, the process of trading and the settlement of transactions. It may have a central location or may simply link the various participants together electronically. 'Over-the-counter' markets operate on an ad hoc basis, with no market infrastructure. The 'market' is simply a collection of individual transactions relating to similar securities. There may be established market customs and practices, but there is no organised market. The Eurobond, derivatives and money markets operate as OTC markets. Their operations are characterised by the use of standard form documentation[8] and reliance on trade customs, which, if sufficiently well established, are considered to

---

[3] See LR 2.2.4R (1).

[4] See Chapter 4 for more details on the transfer of shares and debentures

[5] See generally M O'Hara, *Market Microstructure Theory* (Oxford, Blackwell, 1995).

[6] See the sources cited in Chapter 7, n 1. See also R La Porta et al, 'Legal Determinants of External Financing' (1997) 52 *Journal of Finance* 1131.

[7] See D Marcus and L Tshikali, 'Some Misconceptions about OTC Markets' (2010) 4(3) *Law and Financial Markets Review* 263.

[8] For example, the forms devised by the International Swaps and Derivatives Association (ISDA; see www2. isda.org (accessed on 19 November 2011)) are the standard terms for derivatives transactions.

be implied contract terms.[9] Markets can also be distinguished by reference to the securities traded on the market. The market for debt instruments with a maturity of less than a year is referred to as the money market, while the market for debt instruments with more than a year to maturity is referred to as the debt capital market. The market in ordinary shares is referred to as the equity capital market. A distinction is made in the case of both the equity and debt capital markets between the primary market, in which securities are offered to the public for the first time, and the secondary market, in which trading of those securities subsequently takes place.

Another distinction is between regulated and unregulated markets. MiFID uses the term 'regulated market' to mean a market that is regulated by the competent authority of its home Member State. In the UK, the equivalent term is a recognised investment exchange (RIE). The essential feature of a regulated market is that it operates subject to rules set by MiFID and the national system of regulation (such as the Financial Services and Markets Act 2000 (FSMA 2000) in the UK) relating to financial stability and investor protection. There is no requirement for an exchange operator to secure recognition as a 'regulated market', but there are several incentives that encourage operators towards that outcome. First, 'regulated market' status carries with it the assurance that the exchange operates under a formal system of regulation that is intended to promote fair and efficient markets. This is likely to appeal to companies because they will be keen to attract investors and ensure that there is a liquid market in their securities. Secondly, there are incentives within the regulatory system that encourage (and sometimes require) investment intermediaries (eg brokers) to use regulated markets.[10] Thirdly, there are tax advantages for intermediaries registered with an RIE (or a 'multilateral trading facility', or MTF) in the UK, in the form of exemption from Stamp Duty.[11]

It is possible for markets to operate without being regulated in this manner and, when they do so, they are generally referred to as alternative investment exchanges or electronic communication networks.[12] Such markets are unregulated in the sense that they are not regulated as markets but their operators, who are normally broker-dealers, are regulated in respect of the activity of dealing in investments (as a principal) and arranging deals in investments (as an agent). The essential difference is that alternative markets are regulated in a different way to recognised markets. To date, recognised exchanges have generally been subject to more onerous obligations than alternative markets and hence have incurred higher regulatory costs.[13]

Markets can also be distinguished on the basis of their dealing systems. Order-driven systems are those in which buyers and sellers are directly matched together, usually

---

[9] See generally E Peel, *Treitel, The Law of Contract*, 12th edn (London, Sweet & Maxwell, 2007) 236–37.

[10] For example, capital adequacy requirements are lower for transactions undertaken on regulated markets.

[11] Exemptions from stamp duty on trades in UK equities (at the rate of 0.5% on the value of purchases) are only available to RIE- or MTF-registered intermediaries and only in respect of 'onexchange' transactions.

[12] An additional category is a 'service company' which is not authorised as a broker-dealer but is subject to a special 'light-touch' regulatory regime, reflecting the limited range of activity in which it is authorised to engage and its lack of direct contact with private investors. Such companies are mainly technology companies who provide order-routing and post-trade processing (settlement) to market participants.

[13] See eg FSA Discussion Paper, 'The FSA's Approach to Regulation of the Market Infrastructure' (January 2000) 39–44.

via a computer system. The precise manner in which matching occurs can vary (eg by reference to price considerations or the time at which an instruction is input), but the essential point is that there is no third party involvement in the pricing process (although third parties such as brokers may be responsible for inputting investors' instructions). For that reason, order-driven systems are best suited to markets in which investors are willing to participate directly (rather than through intermediaries). Quote-driven systems are based around buy/sell quotes made on a continuous basis by market-makers, who trade as principals and provide liquidity to the market.[14] Historically, the London Stock Exchange (LSE) was a quote-driven market, but a substantial volume of trade is now conducted through the order-matching system SETS (Stock Exchange Trading System), which combines order-book functionality with a quote-driven facility for participation by market-makers (as well as the anonymity and protection provided by clearing and central counterparty facilities).[15]

Distinctions can also be drawn by reference to the investors in different markets. The term 'wholesale market' refers to the market in which institutional investors purchase securities, while the term 'retail market' refers to the purchase of securities (directly or indirectly through investment funds) by private individuals. The retail market is characterised by the presence of 'packaged' products. These are financial products such as investment funds or investment-linked life assurance that offer indirect investment in securities.[16]

12.2 Market regulation: overview

From the economic perspective, a major concern is that markets should operate efficiently. This can be understood in different ways. Allocative efficiency refers to the manner in which the capital market allocates capital to competing uses. It should operate so as to allocate capital to the projects with the highest present value (broadly speaking, those that will generate the highest return on capital); if it does not, it will not be operating efficiently. Informational efficiency refers to the ability of the market to price securities accurately by reference to available information.[17] Operational efficiency refers to the extent to which markets are able to minimise the transaction costs (eg brokerage and administrative costs) associated with dealing in securities.

These underlying economic principles are linked to the historical development of market regulation. Disclosure obligations were first introduced when the Joint Stock

---

[14] See Chapter 14.1.2.
[15] See section 12.5 regarding clearing and central counterparties.
[16] See Chapter 4 on investments and Chapter 6 on the retail investment market.
[17] The efficient market hypothesis (in its strong form) holds that the market is efficient in pricing securities on the basis of all known information. If true, it would render pointless any attempt to discover information (eg through fundamental analysis) that is not already discounted in the price of a security. See generally K Pilbeam *Finance and Financial Markets*, 3rd edn (Basingstoke, Palgrave Macmillan, 2010) ch 10.

Companies Act 1844 required information to be disclosed to the Registrar of Companies prior to incorporation. In the modern context, disclosure (at different levels) is mandated by the Companies Act 2006 for all companies and by the Disclosure and Transparency rules (DTR) for listed companies.[18] The objective is to promote allocative and informational efficiency by providing the information necessary for investors to choose between competing uses for their capital. They also promote informational efficiency by allowing the market to price securities at the time of an initial listing/offer and on an ongoing basis.

Market transparency obligations require the reporting and publication within defined time limits of transactions that take place on a market. They promote informational efficiency in that they allow investors to make pricing decisions by reference to the prices at which other investors are trading. More controversial are regulatory rules (such as prohibitions against insider dealing) which promote market integrity. While they may be seen to limit informational efficiency by preventing prices moving to their true level, they can be justified on two grounds.[19] First, they address an information asymmetry problem (as between 'insiders' and 'outsiders') that has the potential to damage confidence in the operation of capital markets and thereby limit their potential role in the financial system. Secondly, they reduce the cost of capital for companies because the presence of insider dealing is likely to raise transaction costs for investors. These issues are discussed in more detail in Chapter 13.

12.3 The EU market regulation framework

The structure of trading markets reflects many different influences, but it is nevertheless clear that regulation has exerted a critical influence in recent times. In the European context, MiFID[20] has been particularly important. It has pursued the twin objectives of creating a single capital market within the EU and promoting competing between execution venues as a means to reduce transaction costs for investors.[21] It has also introduced harmonised rules across the EU covering transparency obligations and conduct of business regulation. The EU market regulation framework adopts a progressive system of regulation, with regulated markets representing the most intense form of regulation and the highest standards of investor protection. Below that level, the regulatory regime recognises that

---

[18] Disclosure obligations for listed companies are dealt with in more detail in Chapter 8.

[19] Plus the more general reason that insider dealing is simply not fair because it represents a wealth transfer to insiders. See H McVea, 'What's Wrong with Insider Dealing?' (1995) *Legal Studies* 390.

[20] Directive 2004/39/EC [2004] OJ L145/1.

[21] There may also have been unintended consequences. The London Stock Exchange has argued that excessive focus on competition between trading venues drew attention away from decreasing competition between broker-dealers, leading to a significant impact in overall costs for investors (eg FTSE 100 spreads widened considerably between 2007 and 2008). It also drew attention to the conflicts of interest inherent in investment firms running their own trading venues either independently or in collaboration with each other. See the LSE response to CESR 08-872, 'Call for Evidence on the Impact of MiFID on Secondary Market Functioning' (November 2008).

investors (particularly professional investors in the wholesale markets) may be prepared to sacrifice standards of investor protection in return for lower transaction costs and access to a broader range of financial instruments.

12.3.1 Regulated markets

As noted elsewhere in this book, the concept of a regulated market is central to the delimitation of the scope of the MiFID regime as well as the listing regime.

MiFID provides the following definition:

> 'Regulated market' means a multilateral system operated and/or managed by a market operator, which brings together or facilitates the bringing together of multiple third party buying and selling interests in financial instruments– in the system and in accordance with its non-discretionary rules—in a way that results in a contract, in respect of the financial instruments admitted to trading under its rules and/or systems, and which is authorised and functions regularly and in accordance with the provisions of Title III;[22]

This definition focuses attention on the market operator and the obligations imposed by MiFID in connection with the operation of the market. The market operator requires authorisation[23] and must 'be of sufficiently good repute and sufficiently experienced as to ensure the sound and prudent management and operation of the regulated market'.[24] Organisational requirements are imposed on the market regarding matters such as risk management, technical operations, fair and orderly procedures for execution of orders, and adequate financial resources. Discretion is left to Member States in setting admission standards for issuers whose financial instruments are admitted to trading on a regulated market,[25] with the result that there is scope for competition between regulated markets in attracting issuers. MiFID also extends its 'passporting' principle to regulated markets in two significant ways. First, it requires that authorised investment firms must have the right of membership or access to a regulated market in a host state through a branch or through remote access or membership, without having to be established in the host state. Secondly, it requires that the rules of a regulated market must provide for direct or remote participation in trading by investment firms and credit institutions.[26]

---

[22] Art 4(1)(14) MiFID. This definition has the effect of excluding clearing and settlement from its scope. As noted below, these activities are generally excluded from the scope of the MiFID regime other than in regard to access rights for investment firms.

[23] This requirement distinguishes regulated markets from MTFs and systematic internalisers, which are authorised as investment firms rather than market operators.

[24] Art 37 MiFID.

[25] Although it should be noted that admission to the 'official list' remains subject to the minimum standards set by the CARD: see Chapter 8.1.3.

[26] Art 42(5) and recital 47 MiFID.

12.3.2 Multilateral trading facilities

While regulated markets and OTC markets have coexisted in one form or another since securities were first traded, alternative trading systems (ATS) are a relatively new development.[27] They have emerged over the past 20 years mainly as a result of new technology, which has encouraged securities firms to compete with regulated markets by cutting transaction costs for investors.[28] Their focus in on the wholesale market, and retail investors are generally excluded because of the additional counterparty risk that they pose.

ATS raise a number of regulatory issues.[29] First, as they operate without the full rigour of the recognition or transparency requirements applicable to regulated markets, there is a 'level playing field' issue in respect of the regulation of organisations that perform similar functions. As ATS derive at least some of their competitive advantage from a lower burden of regulation, the regulated exchanges have some grounds for arguing that they face unfair competition. Moreover, although ATS have in the main aimed to attract professional investors (who are assumed to be well informed as to market practices), there remains scope for confusion over the terms on which they transact business, particularly if the ATS is within a securities firm operating as a broker-dealer. In these circumstances there may be confusion regarding when the firm is acting as principal or agent for a customer when a transaction is being executed through an 'in-house' MTF. There may also be confusion over regulatory obligations such as 'best execution'.[30]

Secondly, there has been concern over the impact which ATS have on transparency and liquidity.[31] In a securities market in which virtually all securities transactions take place in a single regulated market (the model that applied in most of Europe until the 1990s), transparency is ensured through transaction reporting and publication rules such as those contained in MiFID. In such a market, the absence of alternative dealing venues for investors ensures that liquidity in the regulated market will be maximised as all dealing is centralised in that market. The position is different when, as occurred in the late 1990s, the market structure changes to one in which regulated markets are competing with alternative systems. Transparency for the market as a whole will decline if ATS are not subject to transparency obligations, as there will be a part of the market in which transactions are not visible. Liquidity may also decline if the market for particular securities fragments into segments traded on regulated markets and others on ATS. It is thus possible to envisage a scenario in which ATS deliver benefits in the form of lower

---

[27] See generally S Prigge, 'Recent Developments in the Market for Markets for Financial Instruments', available at http://ssrn.com/abstract=258593 (accessed on 19 November 2011).

[28] See S Claessens, T Glaessner and D Klingebiel, 'Electronic Finance: Reshaping Financial Landscapes around the World' Financial Sector Discussion Paper No 4 (World Bank, September 2000), available at www.worldbank.org (accessed on 19 November 2011).

[29] See generally FSA Discussion Paper, above n 13.

[30] See Chapter 6.3.

[31] See FSA, 'Alternative Trading Systems', CP 153 (October 2002); H Allen, J Hawkins and S Sato, 'Electronic Trading and its Implications for Financial Systems', Bank for International Settlement Papers No 7 (2001), available at www.bis.org (accessed on 19 November 2011).

transaction costs for investors but exert a negative influence on the securities market as a whole by lowering its transparency and reducing liquidity.

The response of regulators has been to bring ATS within the scope of the regulatory system without subjecting them to the full rigour of the regulation applicable to regulated markets. The process was begun through the adoption in 2002 by The Committee of European Securities Regulators (CESR[32]) of seven standards applicable to ATS that were intended to give effect to this objective. Those principles were given effect in the UK through changes to the FSA rulebook.[33] Following the implementation of the MiFID regime, the regulatory status and obligations of ATS are now set out in that directive and its implementing measures. Within that regime, the term 'multilateral trading facility' has now largely replaced the older terminology of 'alternative trading systems'.[34] MiFID defines an MTF as follows:

> 'Multilateral trading facility (MTF)' means a multilateral system, operated by an investment firm or a market operator, which brings together multiple third party buying and selling interests in financial instruments—in the system and in accordance with non discretionary rules –in a way that results in a contract in accordance with the provisions of Title II;[35]

While this definition focuses regulatory attention on those systems that replicate the 'functionality' of regulated markets by creating facilities for trading between buyers and sellers, it also distinguishes it from a regulated market. Significantly, MTFs are treated as investment firms and are therefore subject to the MiFID rules applicable to investment firms rather than those applicable to regulated markets.[36] While the transparency regime applicable to trading on MTFs is broadly similar to that applicable to regulated markets[37], a lower intensity of regulation is apparent in several other aspects of the regulatory regime. There are no 'admission to trading' requirements set by MiFID for MTFs, the underlying premise being that MTFs provide a trading service for sophisticated investors rather than a public market in the true sense. Similarly, the requirements relating to disclosure by issuers and operating conditions are less demanding than the comparable obligations that are imposed on regulated markets.[38]

---

[32] Replaced by ESMA as from 1 January 2011.

[33] See FSA CP 153, above n 31; FSA, 'Alternative Trading Systems Instrument 2003', FSA 2003/45 (2003).

[34] The majority of MTFs offering trading in shares admitted to regulated markets (24) were launched after the entry into force of MiFID in November 2007, although some were already established by that time (eg AIM, Chi-X and others offering trading in bonds).

[35] Art 4(1)(15) MiFID.

[36] An operator of a regulated market remains free to operate an MTF, as the London Stock Exchange does in the case of AIM. This freedom facilitates segmentation of markets to appeal to different types of investors and promotes competition.

[37] MTFs are regulated very similarly to regulated markets as regards transparency, although the latter argue that they are subject to more stringent and costly requirements (eg regulated markets verify that issuers comply with disclosure obligations).

[38] See Art 14 MiFID for the requirements applicable to an MTF.

12.3.3 Systematic internalisers

This concept was first introduced into the EU regulatory regime by MiFID and its objective is to bring within the pre-trade transparency regime the process of order execution through 'internalisation' of orders within an investment firm. That practice, which had in particular been common in the UK, was possible in cases where a firm was able to match client buy and sell orders internally without executing the transaction through an organised market. From a regulatory perspective, this practice raised concerns regarding transparency (as such transactions were not subject to reporting requirements) and the risk that liquidity and price formation across the entire market would suffer. MiFID provides the following definition: '"Systematic internaliser" means an investment firm which, on an organised, frequent and systematic basis, deals on own account by executing client orders outside a regulated market or an MTF.'[39]

According to this approach, a distinction is drawn between firms that internalise client orders on an ad hoc basis and those that undertake this function on a systematic basis. In the latter case, they fall within the regulatory definition and become subject to transparency requirements that are not otherwise applicable. The underlying rationale is that in those circumstances an investment firm is acting in a manner similar to an MTF or regulated market so far as execution of transactions is concerned. Those transparency requirements are in addition to the other regulatory requirements that are imposed on investment firms.

12.3.4 Dark pools

In Europe, the operation (by regulated markets, MTFs or investment firms authorised under MiFID) of 'dark pools'[40] is made possible by waivers granted by national regulators from the pre-trade transparency obligations[41] imposed by MiFID. Dark pools are less of a market force in Europe than in the US and lag some way behind European MTFs, which are subject to pre-trade transparency, but the position may well change as MTFs expand their dark pool activity.[42]

---

[39] Art 4(1)(7) MiFID.

[40] This is a market term and not one adopted in regulatory rules either in the US or Europe.

[41] Note that 'dark pool' trades remain subject to post-trade publication in the normal way unless eligible for deferred publication. See Chapter 13 regarding transparency obligations.

[42] In the US, dark pools are alternative trading systems that, in contrast to electronic communication networks (ECNs), do not provide their best-priced orders for inclusion in the consolidated quotation data. There are 32 dark pools in the US that actively trade 'national market system' stocks and they account for around 8% of the trading volume in such stocks, although some sources suggest a share of trading volume up to twice as high.

12.3.5 Assessment

Commenting on its effect, the CESR noted some significant changes that have resulted from the implementation of MiFID.[43] First, established exchanges have seen their positions challenged as MTFs[44] have won some of their business as well as attracting trade from the MTF space.[45]

Secondly, competition between regulated markets remains quite low as each focuses on trading in shares admitted to their own market rather than pan-European trading of shares listed on other EU markets (although some MTFs operated by regulated markets do this).

Exchanges that operate as regulated markets have generally been less sanguine than CESR about the effects of MiFID. The Federation of European Stock Exchanges (FESE) has been quite critical, arguing that MiFID has resulted in price discovery suffering and investors' orders being executed increasingly in venues that are owned by the sell side, with execution venues operated by neutral operators being restrained by restrictive rules.[46] FESE pointed the finger at broker crossing networks that should be classified as MTFs (or Systematic Internalisers) but are able to act OTC because they do not declare themselves part of those regimes. It also suggested that MTFs operated by investment firms were more lightly regulated than those operated by regulated markets. Moreover, FESE also argued that there was no evidence of MiFID having lowered overall trading costs (ie direct and indirect costs, including spreads and market impact costs).[47] Another concern raised by FESE (based on a study of the implementation policies of different firms and also of conflict of interest problems arising from ownership links between broker-dealers and execution venues) was the very different ways in which the MiFID 'best execution' obligation is implemented in different Member States.

These observations illustrate the inherent difficulty in balancing the policy objectives of (i) consolidation in trading interest, with the aim of improving liquidity and price discovery, and (ii) competition between trading venues, with the aim of lowering transaction costs. Finding the right balance is difficult, particularly as technology, market developments and trading strategies mean that the contours of the market are always changing and quite often in subtle ways that may not always be visible to or carry significant meaning for regulators. Similar concerns are evident in the US, where the Securities and Exchange Commission (SEC) published a concept release on equity market structure

---

[43] See CESR, 'Impact of MifID on Equity Secondary Markets', CESR/09-355 (June 2009).

[44] MTFs are functionally equivalent to a regulated market but operate under a less onerous regulatory regime. Their relationship as competitors with regulated markets is similar to that between registered markets and ECNs in the US, albeit that the regulatory obligations differ in each system.

[45] The extent to which this has occurred is made evident by the data collected by FESE (the Federation of European Stock Exchanges). It shows that the leading MTF (Chi-X) is now the third largest trading venue in Europe for equities after the London Stock Exchange and NYSE/Euronext: see FESE, 'European Equity Market Report 2011', available at http://www.fese.be/en/?inc=art&id=8.

[46] See FESE response to CESR 08-872.

[47] That contention does not correspond with other research findings. See Oxera, 'Monitoring Prices, Costs and Volumes of Trading and Post-trading Services' (July 2009), available at www.oxera.com, finding that since 2006, the costs per transaction charged by trading platforms has decreased by 33%. The extent to which those savings have been passed on to investors is not, however, clear.

focusing in particular on three areas of concern: market performance and quality; high-frequency trading; and undisplayed liquidity (including so-called dark pools).

As regards market performance and quality, the SEC has questioned whether the current market structure adequately meets the needs of long-term investors. Underlying that question is the recent rise in the volume of short-term trading by professional investors and changes in technical systems and practices that have facilitated the surge in such short-term trading activity. The SEC's main concern is not to restrict short-term trading per se but to identify whether market structure and practices have moved too far to accommodate short-term traders to the cost of long-term investors. Linked with that issue is the increasing prevalence of high-frequency trading, which has now risen to represent 60–70% of equity trading volume in the US and 30–50% in the EU.[48] The SEC has identified systemic risks to the integrity of the equity market arising from the enormous message traffic of automated trading systems, and to the stability of market prices and the solvency of proprietary traders arising from connected trading strategies that amplify fluctuations in market prices. More widespread financial distress might also be transmitted through banks that lend to finance the trading activity of broker-dealers. While the SEC has already taken action to address concerns over market access,[49] broader measures may well follow the concept release.

While some institutional investors in Europe have welcomed dark pools as a way to lessen the market impact of trading in large sizes, regulated markets have been much less enthusiastic, pointing to the risks to price discovery posed by fragmentation and the conflicts of interest posed by dark pools affiliated to broker-dealers. Similar concerns over price discovery have been raised by the SEC in its concept release. In particular, the SEC is concerned that the significant percentage of the orders of long-term investors that are executed either in dark pools or at OTC markets raises fundamental questions about the structure and role of public markets, which are increasingly a venue for the execution of high-frequency trading. A related factor is the degree to which different types of investor can access dark pools: while public markets generally operate on the principle of open access, dark pools generally do not.

These issues are complex, and are unlikely to be amenable to rapid or long-lasting solutions. Recent years have shown that markets change rapidly and regulators have only limited capacity to steer the direction of change. It is clear, however, that the role of public markets has changed dramatically and that, in response, the pace of regulatory change is likely to accelerate in the near future.

---

[48] Source: FSA, 'Financial Risk Outlook 2010', 51.
[49] See SEC Market Access Release at http://www.sec.gov/news/press/2010/2010-7.htm.

12.4 The UK market regulation framework

Market regulation in the UK is based on two sources. The first is part 18 of FSMA 2000, relating to RIEs, which in the main continues the regime that applied under the Financial Services and Act 1986 (FSA 1986). A more recent addition is the provisions contained in the FSA Handbook which give effect to MiFID. As discussed above, MiFID creates a regulatory regime for multilateral trading facilities and systematic internalisers. That regime was implemented in the UK through changes made to the MAR component of the FSA Handbook.

12.4.1 Recognised investment exchanges

Reflecting the historic role of exchanges as regulators rather than regulated entities, an RIE is exempt from FSMA 2000. To be recognised, an exchange must comply with the requirements set by the Act and regulations made by the Treasury under the Act.[50]

These regulations require an exchange applying for 'recognised' status to satisfy, inter alia, the following conditions:

1. The exchange must have adequate financial resources.
2. The exchange must be a fit and proper person to perform the functions of a recognised investment exchange.
3. The exchange must ensure that business conducted by means of its facilities is conducted in an orderly manner and affords proper protection to investors.
4. The exchange must comply with the requirements of the MiFID regime relating to pre- and post-trade publication of information.
5. The exchange must have effective arrangements for monitoring and enforcing compliance with its rules.
6. The exchange must have default rules which, in the event of a member of the exchange being or appearing to be unable to meet his obligations in respect of one or more market contracts, enable action to be taken in respect of unsettled market contracts to which he is a party.
7. The exchange's rules must make provision for payment to be required (subject to netting) from a defaulter in respect of unsettled market contracts.

Once recognised, an exchange operates without the controls imposed on authorised persons, but the FSA can nevertheless veto rule changes and issue directions to an exchange. The description of RIEs as 'exempt' is somewhat misleading in that the recognition process brings them clearly within the scope of FSMA 2000 system of regulation and the FSA's residual powers ensure that it exercises considerable influence over the manner in which

---

[50] The FSMA 2000 (Recognition Requirements for Investment Exchanges and Clearing Houses) Regulations 2001, SI 2001/995.

they operate. The FSA has power to impose notification requirements;[51] give directions requiring compliance with legal and regulatory obligations;[52] revoke a recognition order;[53] and deal with complaints relating to recognised status.[54] Moreover, for certain purposes (see eg the reduction of financial crime objective in section 6 FSMA 2000), RIEs are treated as regulated persons. The scope of their exemption is limited as it relates to activities carried on as part of the business of an exchange or in connection with the provision of clearing services. There is no exempt person status in respect of other activities undertaken by RIEs.[55]

In the past, there was a link between RIE status and regulatory responsibility for listing and public offers in the sense that the LSE was designated as the 'competent authority' by the relevant EU directives.[56] However, following the change in status of the LSE when it became a company listed on the exchange, its function as 'competent authority' for listing and public offers was transferred to the FSA. The rationale was that it was not appropriate for regulatory functions to be undertaken by a commercial organisation that ran (on a 'for profit' basis) the market it regulated. The UKLA now makes and monitors compliance with the listing and public offers rules. RIEs do, however, retain a role in that they are responsible for 'admission to trading' (which is now a separate regulatory process from admission to the official list) and are also responsible for setting and enforcing trading rules.

The RIE regime does not directly regulate participants who trade on the relevant exchange as its focus is on the exchange itself as a regulated entity. Participants include broker-dealers, banks and institutional investors, who are already regulated by the FSA in respect of their investment activities, as well as private investors. In respect of trading on exchanges by these participants, the FSA Handbook focuses on capital adequacy (solvency), the standards to be observed in trading and the manner in which client assets and money are safeguarded. Three broad categories of market participant can be distinguished for this purpose.[57] The first is professional investors who trade as principals for their own account (eg market-makers). The main concern of the regulatory system is that such traders have adequate capital to meet their obligations. The second category is professional investors who act on behalf of others (eg fund managers or stockbrokers). The main focus of the regulatory system in this area is to safeguard the interests of the clients of the professional investor through rules relating to client assets and conflicts of interest. The third category is private investors, and in this area the regulatory system

---

[51] FSMA 2000, s 293.

[52] FSMA 2000, s 296.

[53] FSMA 2000, s 297.

[54] FSMA 2000, s 299. Note, however, that the FSA cannot use its general rule-making power in connection with RIEs, nor do senior managers of RIEs fall within the APER regime discussed in Chapter 3.9.4.

[55] Any application for permission in respect of such other activities is treated as an application relating only to that other activity.

[56] See Chapter 2.5.2.

[57] This categorisation is adopted to illustrate the broad objectives of FSA regulation of market participants. The more technical regulatory categorisation and the relevant rules applicable to each category are dealt with in Chapter 15.

adopts a protective stance in recognition of the limited knowledge and expertise of most private investors.

Nor does the RIE regulatory regime directly control the manner in which dealing in securities is organised, although the system will be scrutinised by the FSA for compliance with recognition requirement 3 (above) prior to the making of a recognition order. In principle, therefore, there is no regulatory preference at the recognition stage in favour of order-driven or quote-driven systems. The general movement towards order-driven markets is largely a function of advances in technology, lower costs and the greater scope for anonymity on the part of buyers and sellers offered by such systems.

Recognised investment exchanges (and clearing houses) enjoy a favoured position in relation to competition law. They are exempt from the prohibitions contained in chapter 1 (anti-competitive agreements) and chapter 2 (abuse of a dominant market position) of the Competition Act 1998.[58] The rationale for the exemption is the separate system of competition scrutiny established by FSMA 2000[59] in respect of recognised bodies. This approach avoids the possibility of routine challenge to the validity of market contracts on the basis that the rules of the exchange under which the contract is made are anti-competitive. The following are exempt from the chapter 1 prohibition:

1. the constitution of a recognised body;
2. the constitution of an applicant for recognition;
3. the regulatory provisions of a recognised body;[60]
4. a decision of a regulatory body in respect of its regulatory provisions or practices;
5. the practices of a recognised body; and
6. an agreement the parties to which include an RIE or RCH (recognised clearing house) or persons subject to its rules to the extent that the agreement is required or encouraged by the recognised body's regulatory provisions or practices.

Despite their exemption, RIEs are nevertheless subject to a separate system of competition scrutiny established by FSMA 2000. This involves submission of their rulebook (at the time of recognition) and subsequent rule changes to the Office of Fair Trading, and potentially also to the Competition Commission. The Treasury is empowered to order an RIE to rectify any anti-competitive conduct or rules.

RIEs (as well as their officers and staff) have immunity from liability in damages. The liability in damages can be based on any cause of action (such as negligence, breach of statutory duty, defamation or breach of confidence). The immunity is in respect of anything done or omitted in the discharge of the recognised body's regulatory functions[61] unless it is shown that the act or omission was in bad faith. There is no immunity in respect of acts or omissions which are unlawful as a result of section 6(1) of the Human Rights Act 1998 (a public authority acting in contravention of a Convention right). There

---

[58] There is no exemption from the equivalent provisions of EC competition law contained in Arts 101 and 102 of the TFEU Treaty.

[59] Sections 302–11.

[60] See s 302(1) FSMA 2000 for the meaning of regulatory provisions.

[61] Regulatory functions, as defined in s 3 FSMA 2000, cover obligations arising from recognition requirements made by the Treasury under s 286 FSMA 2000.

was no comparable immunity provided to RIEs under FSA 1986. The formulation of the immunity in this section is similar, but not identical, to that provided to the FSA.[62] The section leaves open the possibility of judicial review and court orders other than damages being sought against an RIE.

12.4.2 Multilateral trading facilities and systematic internalisers

The MiFID regime for MTFs and systematic internalisers is implemented in the MAR component of the FSA Handbook. The implementation adopts a 'copy out' approach, with the result that no additional obligations are imposed by the FSA Handbook.[63] The MiFID requirements for publication by investment firms of information relating to trades in shares admitted to trading on regulated markets undertaken outside a regulated market or MTF are similarly implemented through the MAR component of the FSA Handbook.

12.5 Clearing

The term 'clearing' is used in different senses with respect to banking and stock exchanges respectively. In banking, clearing is used in a narrow sense to refer to the calculation of payment obligations: 'In its narrow sense, "clearing system" is a mechanism for the calcuation of mutual positions within a group of participants ("counterparties") with a view to facilitate the settlement of their mutual obligations on a net basis.'[64] In this context, the main function of clearing is to reduce (through netting[65]) the number of payments that have to be made by participants to each other. Without netting, each payment would be treated separately (gross payments), resulting in many individual payments between banks. Netting can operate on either a bilateral or multilateral basis. In the former case, netting operates separately between each pair of counterparties in the system. In the latter case, netting operates so as to result in each participant having to make only one payment into the system in respect of all transactions for which payment is due at a particular point

---

[62] By s 1 and sch 1, para 19 FSMA 2000.

[63] Irrespective of the potential benefits of 'gold-plating', the nature of the MTF regime and the operation of 'passporting rights' would in any case make it difficult to apply additional requirements to MTFs at the national level.

[64] B Geva, 'The Clearing House Arrangement' (1991) 19 *Canadian Business Law Review* 138, quoted in R Cranston, *Principles of Banking Law*, 2nd edn (Oxford, Oxford University Press, 2002) 279.

[65] Netting is a contractual form of set-off, which is a legal remedy available to a debtor enabling debts owed by the creditor to be deducted from the creditor's claim. See J Benjamin, *Financial Law* (Oxford, Oxford University Press, 2007) ch 12. In Scotland, set-off is referred to as compensation: see generally W McBryde, *Contract*, 3rd edn (Edinburgh, Thomson W Green, 2007) 740.

in time.[66] In both cases, the effect of netting is to enhance liquidity in the market as a result of the lower net payments that are required on an ongoing basis.

'Clearing' in the context of stock exchanges encompasses the narrow banking definition above but also refers to the process by which a clearing house becomes a counterparty to transactions undertaken on the exchange and thereby guarantees performance of the contract. This function is referred to as that of a central counterparty (CCP). The legal mechanism by which a CCP takes over a contract entered into by a member is novation.[67] It has two significant effects: first, it eliminates direct contractual relations between members; and secondly, it subjects all contracts to the terms set by the CCP.[68] From a market perspective, this has the effect of shifting counterparty risk from individual members and concentrating it in the CCP. This function of clearing houses evolved first in commodities markets in the nineteenth century, was later adopted in relation to transactions on exchanges trading futures and options, and has now been extended to some forms of trading on stock exchanges and also to some OTC transactions.[69] The rationale for clearing houses assuming the role of counterparty (in return for a fee) is that it reduces the credit risk associated with the default of a counterparty.[70] This has been a particular concern in derivatives markets, where the prices of the relevant contracts are subject to greater volatility than is the case in the securities market generally. Clearing houses undertake their counterparty function only in relation to members, who are required to meet ongoing financial requirements, which serve the function of limiting the exposure of the clearing house to potential defaults.[71]

Another important development has been the creation of a central counterparty system for trading on SETS, the London Stock Exchange's electronic order book. LCH.Clearnet acts as counterparty to such transactions, thereby allowing anonymous trading on SETS without any risk being posed to participants resulting from the fact that they do not know the identity of the other side to the transaction. In this sense, a central counterparty is a guarantor who has been described as the seller's buyer and the buyer's seller.[72] Virtually all order-driven markets operate some form of CCP system as it is vital to provide some

---

[66] See Cranston, above n 64, 287 for more detail. He observes that bilateral netting reduces payments in a system with n participants to $n(n-1)/2$, while multilateral netting reduces payments to n.

[67] See Chapter 4.4.3 for an explanation of novation.

[68] See further J Huang, *The Law and Regulation of Central Counterparties* (Oxford, Hart Publishing, 2010) ch 4. Huang also observes (at 176) that the operation of CCPs supports anonymous trading in securities that are cleared through the CCP (so long as the trading process is anonymous) and thereby enhances liquidity.

[69] See R Kroszner, 'Can the Financial Markets Privately Regulate Risk? The Development of Derivatives Clearing Houses and Recent Over-the-Counter Innovations', available at http://ssrn.com/abstract=170350 (accessed on 19 November 2011).

[70] As noted by Huang, above n 68, 52, CCPs effectively distribute counterparty risk across their members (who ultimately bear the cost of any default by a member). This characteristic of CCP operation has been an important influence in the adoption by the EU Commission of a proposed regulation that would require some OTC derivatives transactions to be made subject to mandatory clearing through a CCP: see 'Proposal for a Regulation on OTC Derivatives, Central Counterparties and Trade Repositories' (COM)2010 484.

[71] This function can be characterised as risk management across the entire membership of a CCP: Huang, ibid, 53.

[72] Although analogous to a guarantee, the legal mechanism under which the CCP operates is novation (see Chapter 4.4.3). A trade between buyer and seller is subject to novation at the point of execution, being replaced by two new contracts, between buyer and LCH as seller and seller and LCH as buyer respectively. These transactions are then passed on to CREST for settlement.

security to transactions in which buy/sell instructions are matched electronically without revealing the identity of the parties. The operation of this CCP system at a relatively low cost is made possible by limiting its availability to clearing members of LCH.Clearnet and integrating it into the CREST settlement system.

The FSMA 2000 makes provision for clearing houses to become recognised and 'exempt' in the same manner as investment exchanges.[73] The recognition requirements are very similar to those applicable to investment exchanges.[74] Of particular significance in the context of financial stability is the requirement that the clearing house must have default rules which, in the event of a member of the clearing house being or appearing to be unable to meet his obligations in respect of one or more market contracts, enable action to be taken to close out his position in relation to all unsettled market contracts to which he is a party.[75] The rules must provide: (i) for all rights and liabilities of the defaulter under or in respect of unsettled market contracts to be discharged, and for there to be paid by or to the defaulter such sum of money (if any) as may be determined in accordance with the rules; and (ii) for the sums so payable by or to the defaulter in respect of different contracts to be aggregated or set off so as to produce a net sum.[76] The 'market contract' regime discussed below in the context of insolvency (12.7) applies to clearing houses in the same way as it does to settlement facilities, and provides further support for the role of clearing houses and CCPs in managing counterparty risk and promoting financial stability.

12.6 Settlement

The term 'settlement' is also used differently in banking and investment contexts. In banking, settlement is the transfer of value to discharge a payment obligation.[77] In the investment context, settlement can also bear this meaning (eg in respect of exchange-traded derivatives which are settled by a monetary transfer) but it also refers to the performance of the mutual obligations of buyer and seller under a contract for the transfer of legal title to securities. The buyer's obligation is to pay the price and the seller's is to deliver a valid legal title to the buyer (irrespective of the form in which legal title is

---

[73] The regulatory regime is in principle the same whether or not a clearing house undertakes the function of CCP.

[74] See FSMA 2000 (Recognition Requirements for Investment Exchanges and Clearing Houses) Regulations 2001, SI 2001/995, sch 1, pt III. The main difference is the absence of requirements relating to proper market conduct and disclosure by issuers in the case of clearing houses.

[75] SI 2001/995 sch 1, pt IV, para 24.

[76] Ibid, para 25.

[77] Cranston, above n 64, 278.

recorded). Settlement follows on from clearing, but is logically distinct from it even if the two services are provided by the same organisation.[78]

12.6.1 The settlement process

The timing of settlement in securities markets is determined by the design of the system, which can take two forms.[79] Rolling settlement involves settlement on a given number of days after the trade date $(t + x)$. In 1989, the G30[80] recommended that final settlement of cash transactions[81] should occur on $t + 3$, that is, 3 days after the settlement date. This is the system currently in use on the LSE. Account settlement involves all transactions within a set period being settled on a fixed day after the end of the period. Such a system was operated in the past by the LSE, with all transactions during a 2 week period being settled on the following Monday. In principle, it is also possible to operate 'real time' settlement, in which transfer of legal title and payment occur simultaneously with the making of a contract, but that poses technical and logistical problems which are difficult to resolve, at least in the context of the equity market.

12.6.2 Regulatory issues and response

Settlement plays a key role in the operation of trading markets. Routine failures in the settlement system pose a number of risks. First, they create credit and liquidity risk for the party whose counterparty defaults on a transaction (eg A does not pay B the agreed price for securities on the agreed date and B is therefore forced to borrow to meet its commitments to C). Secondly, settlement defaults on a sufficiently large scale have the potential to create systemic risk across the whole financial system. Thirdly, settlement problems may result in investors withdrawing from particular types of investment or from particular countries in which settlement problems cause a significant rise in transaction costs.

These issues have been addressed in several different ways by both regulators and market participants. The International Organisation of Securities Commissioners has stressed the importance of the principle of 'delivery versus payment' (DvP) as a method of minimising the risks associated with settlement. The essence of the principle of DvP is

---

[78] In so-called 'vertical silos', trading, clearing and settlement are provided by the same organisation, and that raises issues of access and anti-competitive behaviour that may not be easy to resolve.

[79] See generally the International Organisation of Securities Commissioners Consultative Report, 'Recommendations for Securities Settlement Systems' (2001), available at www.iosco.org (accessed on 19 November 2011). The report notes that the longer the period from trade execution to settlement, the greater is the risk that (i) one of the parties may become insolvent or default on the trade and (ii) prices of securities will depart from contract prices, creating the potential for non-defaulting parties to incur a loss in replicating the unsettled contract.

[80] The Group of Thirty is an international non-profit body that researches and advises on choices available to market practitioners and policymakers: see www.group30.org (18 August 2011).

[81] If settlement occurs immediately or shortly after a trade (eg 3 days as occurs in the UK equity market), a market is described as a cash market: if it is in the future, it is a forward or futures market.

that, if delivery of legal title to securities occurs simultaneously with payment, the credit and liquidity risks associated with settlement are minimised.[82] The CREST/Euroclear settlement system, which settles most transactions in the UK, operates a form of DvP.

The regulatory response within the EU has been very limited. Neither clearing nor settlement is an investment service within the scope of MiFID, and neither is in general subject to the MiFID regulatory regime.[83] One reason for that omission has been the sheer complexity of the system in Europe, where settlement is spread across multiple entities and jurisdictions which operate under different technical, legal and taxation regimes governing ownership and transfer of securities.[84] While the 2003 Giovannini Report[85] examined these barriers to integration and liberalisation in some detail and proposed measures for their resolution, the approach adopted within MiFID focuses on the relatively narrow issue of access rights to settlement systems.[86] Member States must ensure that investment firms from other Member States have the right of access to settlement systems in their territory for the purposes of finalising or arranging the finalisation of transactions in securities. Regulated markets are required to offer all their members and participants the right to designate the system for the settlement of transactions in financial instruments undertaken on the regulated market. However, that requirement is subject to the necessary technical requirements being in place to support the choice made by members or participants, and has led one commentator to conclude that 'It is as if the passengers could take all trains, but the different railway systems remain unconnected'.[87]

The capital adequacy rules derived from the Capital Requirements Directive[88] also promote the honouring of settlement obligations by requiring securities firms to allocate capital against transactions that have not settled by the due date. This is achieved by requiring firms to include in their calculation of financial resources[89] an allowance ('counterparty risk requirement') for transactions on which a counterparty has defaulted by not settling on the due date.[90] In effect, this results in a financial penalty being applied in respect of unsettled transactions in the sense that the allocation of capital (financial

---

[82] See *Delivery versus Payment in Securities Settlement Systems* (Basle, Bank for International Settlements, 1992), available at www.bis.org (accessed on 18 August 2011).

[83] Note, however, that custody is an investment service falling within MiFID (and a regulated activity under FSMA 2000) and will therefore be subject to authorisation and supervision if carried out in conjunction with settlement.

[84] The position in Europe can be contrasted with the US, which has a much more integrated settlement system as a result of the adoption of uniform legal provisions for ownership and transfer of securities (Uniform Commercial Code, Art 8) and the economies of scale and SEC backing enjoyed by the Depository Trust & Clearing Corporation, through which the bulk of clearing and settlement is undertaken.

[85] Giovannini Group, 'Cross-border Clearing and Settlement Arrangements in the European Union' (First Report, 2001; Second Report, 2003).

[86] See generally K Löber, 'The Developing EU Legal Framework for Clearing and Settlement of Financial Instruments', European Central Bank, Legal Working Paper Series No 1 (February 2006) 27–29.

[87] E Wymeersch, 'Securities Clearing and Settlement: Regulatory Developments in Europe' in G Ferrarini and E Wymeersch (ed), *Investor Protection in Europe: Corporate Law Making, MiFID and Beyond* (Oxford, Oxford University Press, 2006) 465, 477.

[88] See Chapter 2.9.2.

[89] Firms are required to calculate their financial resources (regulatory capital) on a daily basis for the purposes of regulatory reporting and on an intra-day basis to verify their capability to enter into transactions.

[90] See Annex II to the CRD (Directive 2006/49/EC). The provision is in respect of the difference between the agreed settlement price and the market price multiplied by a factor that increases over time. It reflects the

resources) to cover settlement risk means that it cannot be used to support the firm's business (eg by using that capital to trade in securities). Moreover, as the 'counterparty risk requirement' increases the longer a trade remains unsettled (ie as the period of default increases), there is a strong incentive for firms to ensure that settlement occurs as quickly as possible.

12.6.3 Settlement in the UK

In the UK, as elsewhere, settlement nowadays typically takes place in dematerialised form.[91] Dematerialisation differs in principle from 'immobilisation'. In the latter case, ownership of an entire issue of securities is in the hands of a central securities depositary (CSD), and ownership is recorded and transferred through entries in accounts held by intermediaries with the CSD. Immobilisation can be used for registered securities that are issued in certificated form or for bearer securities as the system replaces the circulation of paper documents with account entries (at the CSD). Under that system, it is the CSD which is the legal owner of the securities and the interest of investors is indirect. In a dematerialised system, paper certificates are eliminated and ownership is recorded and transferred by the operator of the settlement system. Ownership of the securities in a dematerialised system can be direct, with the result that members are recognised by issuers as the legal owner (as opposed to a CSD in an immobilised system).[92]

Secondary legislation introduced in 1995 resulted in the establishment of the CREST transfer system and the replacement of most share certificates by electronic records. CREST is now operated by Euroclear UK & Ireland, part of the Euroclear Group, which operates securities settlement systems in several European countries. CREST came into operation in April 1997, replacing Talisman, the former settlement system operated by the LSE. Euroclear is an approved operator under the relevant Regulations[93] and also a recognised clearing house[94] under FSMA 2000.

The CREST system provides settlement facilities for shares and other financial instruments, in particular UK government bonds, money market instruments, covered warrants, UK and Irish unit trusts, and open-ended investment company and exchange traded funds, as well as a wide range of international securities, including Eurobonds.[95] Ownership and transfer are 'dematerialised' in the sense that CREST operates on an 'uncertificated' basis,

---

risk that a firm may have to buy securities in the market to meet delivery obligations to clients as a result of the default of a counterparty.

[91] See Chapter 4 regarding transfers of securities in certificated and dematerialised form.

[92] See generally J Benjamin, *Interests in Securities* (Oxford, Oxford University Press, 2000) chs 1 and 9; M Yates and G Montagu, *The Law of Global Custody*, 3rd edn (Haywards Heath, Tottel, 2009) ch 9.

[93] The Uncertificated Securities Regulation 2001 (SI 2001/3755). See Chapter 4.4.3.

[94] Clearing houses undertake two functions. First, they operate systems that enable settlement of mutual obligations on a net basis. Secondly, they act as counterparties in transactions, thereby reducing the credit risk that is associated with transactions, especially when the identity of the other party is not known (eg in order-driven markets such as the LSE's SETS).

[95] Settlement of foreign securities is achieved through links with foreign settlement systems. Foreign securities cannot be admitted to CREST as the Uncertificated Securities Regulations (see Chapter 4.4.3) are effective only in the UK.

with legal title being constituted by entries in the operator register (although it remains possible for an issuer to have certificated shares). While issuers of securities maintain an issuer register that is a mirror image of the (CREST) operator register, it is the latter that is definitive for the purposes of ownership. In order to reduce risk for market participants and credit providers, the system operates on the basis of an advanced form of DvP in which there is simultaneous and irrevocable transfer of cash and securities for all sterling- and euro-denominated transactions.

CREST operates a 'direct' form of settlement in which CREST members own securities directly.[96] Securities are transferred within CREST by the operation of an account system that parallels the register maintained by the issuer. The accounts CREST maintains for members show the same information as the issuer's register. A transfer is made by debiting the CREST account of the seller and crediting the account of the buyer (or, in the case of buyers who are not CREST members, the member of CREST acting for the buyer). This form of direct transfer of ownership within CREST differs from certificated transfer in that a buyer of certificated securities becomes the legal owner only on entry in the issuer register (and not on delivery of the certificate to the buyer).

12.7 Insolvency

The insolvency of a market participant who trades on an investment exchange gives rise, in principle, to two main problems. The first is that the relevant person is likely to default on settlement obligations.[97] RIEs and RCHs are required to have rules to deal with this contingency. In the case of the LSE, the rules provide for a member firm to be declared a defaulter if it is unable to fulfil its obligations in respect of one or more market contracts, or appears to be or is likely to become so unable.[98] The significance of that process is that responsibility for the calculation of amounts due to and from the defaulter is transferred to the exchange.[99]

The second problem is whether the general principles of insolvency law should be applied to such contracts and, if so, how.[100] A particular concern is that, if market participants are exposed to the risk that a payment due to them from a counterparty may become the subject of competition among the general creditors of that counterparty fol-

---

[96] However, investors who are not CREST members hold their securities indirectly through such members.

[97] In the case of major firms (eg Lehman Bros in 2008), default may carry systemic consequences for other firms and threaten financial stability.

[98] See the Rules of the London Stock Exchange, default procedures, section D100, available at http://www.londonstockexchange.com/traders-and-brokers/rules-regulations/rules-lse-2011.pdf. A defaulter ceases to be a member but is bound by the default rules.

[99] The exchange is entitled to fix 'hammer' prices in respect of unsettled contracts with a defaulter, which may deviate from the contract price. The practice has given rise to the description of a defaulter as having been 'hammered'.

[100] On the general principles of insolvency law see R Goode, *Corporate Insolvency Law*, 2nd edn (London, Sweet & Maxwell, 1997).

lowing insolvency, the credit risk associated with market transactions will be increased and the market will operate less efficiently than if they are protected from that risk.[101] This concern is reflected in the legal provisions governing 'market contracts'.

Part VII of the Companies Act 1989 established a special regime modifying the general law of insolvency for 'market contracts'.[102] That regime is based on several principles.

1. The procedures of a recognised exchange or clearing house take precedence over insolvency proceedings. To this end, it is made clear that none of the following shall be regarded as to any extent invalid at law on the grounds of inconsistency with insolvency law:
   (a) a market contract;
   (b) the default rules of an RIE or RCH;[103] and
   (c) the rules of an RIE or RCH as to the settlement of market contracts not dealt with under its default rules.[104]

2. A person with control over the assets or documents of a defaulter is required to give an RIE or RCH such assistance as it may reasonably require for its default proceedings. This applies notwithstanding any duty of that person under the enactments relating to insolvency.[105]

3. On completion of default proceedings, an RIE or RCH is required to report to the FSA on its proceedings, stating in respect of each creditor or debtor the sum certified by them to be payable to or from the defaulter or, as the case may be, the fact that no sum is payable.[106]

4. The sum so certified can be claimed on the bankruptcy/insolvency of the defaulter.[107]

5. The law relating to transactions at an undervalue, unfair preferences and transactions defrauding creditors is disapplied in respect of market contracts entered into by an RIE or RCH under its default rules and a disposition of property in pursuance of such a market contract.[108] This allows an RIE or RCH to act under its default rules free from the threat that transactions made under those rules may be challenged by a defaulter's general creditors.

---

[101] This will be so as the market is likely to reflect the credit risk of market participants in setting prices as well as the underlying fundamentals of a security.

[102] Market contracts are defined by s 155 of the Companies Act 1989. The definition requires the contract to be between a member of the recognised exchange (or clearing house) and a third party, and to be subject to the rules of the exchange. The definition does not apply to contracts made on an ATS (as it is not a recognised exchange).

[103] An RIE is subject to the same requirements as a clearing house with regard to default rules and the netting of amounts due from or to defaulters: see section 12.5.

[104] Companies Act 1989, s 159.

[105] Companies Act 1989, s 160.

[106] Companies Act 1989, s 162.

[107] Companies Act 1989, s 159.

[108] Companies Act 1989, s 162. See Goode, above n 100 regarding transactions at an undervalue, unfair preferences and transactions defrauding creditors.

The general approach established by the Companies Act 1989 is developed further by the EU Directive on Settlement Finality in Payment and Securities Settlement Systems.[109] The purpose of the Directive is to reduce the risks associated with participation in payment and securities settlement systems by minimising the disruption caused by insolvency proceedings brought against a participant in such a system. It pursues this objective by requiring that the rules of a designated settlement system will prevail over the provisions of national insolvency laws. The scope of the Directive is defined by reference to participants in designated[110] payment and settlement systems. This differs from the provisions of part VII of the Companies Act 1989, which apply to 'market contracts' (see above). There is, however, substantial overlap between these two sets of legal rules as the insolvency of a participant in a designated settlement system will normally have implications for 'market contracts' entered into by that participant.[111]

The Directive carries important consequences for transfer orders and netting.[112] As regards transfer orders, the Directive provides that they become final and irrevocable once they enter the relevant system. This has the effect that transfer orders are protected from the insolvency of a market participant so long as they are entered into the system before the opening of insolvency proceedings.[113] The Directive also protects the netting[114] of payments from challenge under national insolvency law so long as the relevant transfer orders are entered into the system before the opening of insolvency proceedings. There are also important provisions relating to the enforceability of financial collateral in the event of the insolvency of a market participant. Their effect is that rights to collateral security provided to a market participant in connection with a system are insulated from the insolvency of a counterparty. All these provisions carry important implications for financial stability because they provide certainty as to the status of market transactions following the insolvency of a participant.[115]

The special regime applicable to financial collateral arrangements is also relevant in the context of insolvency of market participants.[116] The regime applies to arrangements under which cash or financial instruments are transferred outright or by way of a security interest as collateral in a capital market transaction. The purpose of such arrangements is to provide an additional right to a counterparty in the event of default. The special regime facilitates the creation of such arrangements by dispensing with some of the formalities

---

[109] Directive 98/26/EC [1998] OJ L166/45, implemented in the UK by the Financial Markets and Insolvency (Settlement Finality) Regulations 1999 (SI 1999/2979). See generally L Sealy, 'The Settlement Finality Directive—Points in Issue' [2000] *Company Financial and Insolvency Law Review* 221.

[110] Designation in the UK is by the FSA or Bank of England.

[111] Art 13 of the Settlement Finality Regulations expressly states that the Regulations do not disapply pt VII of the Companies Act 1989.

[112] Note, however, that the Directive applies only to settlement and not clearing.

[113] Art 3(1).

[114] For the meaning of this term see n 65 above and accompanying text. The Directive applies both to bilateral and multilateral netting.

[115] That does not imply that the insolvency of a major participant cannot give rise to difficulty or contagion: the fallout from the collapse of Lehman Bros provides an example of the difficulties that can arise in determining who owns securities and has rights to collateral following insolvency.

[116] The regime is derived from the EC Directive on Financial Collateral Arrangements 2002/47 [2002] OJ L168/43 (as amended), implemented in the UK by The Financial Collateral Arrangements (No 2) Regulations 2003 SI 2003/3226 (as amended).

normally associated with the creation of such arrangements.[117] It also facilitates their enforcement by disapplying the operation of various provisions of insolvency law that would otherwise limit or prevent the enforcement of financial collateral arrangements.[118]

---

[117] See eg Arts 4 and 5 of the 2002 Directive, dispensing with the requirement for charges (security interests) granted by a company to be registered with the Registrar of Companies.
[118] See Art 10.

Trading Markets—Transparency and Integrity

This chapter examines transparency and integrity in trading markets. The policy objectives underlying the relevant rules are succinctly encapsulated by the recitals to the relevant EU directives. Recital 44 of the Markets in Financial Instruments Directive (MiFID)[1] provides that:

> With the two-fold aim of protecting investors and ensuring the smooth operation of securities markets, it is necessary to ensure that transparency of transactions is achieved and that the rules laid down for that purpose apply to investment firms when they operate on the markets.

Integrity in the context of trading markets refers to the extent to which market participants and investors are treated fairly, in particular by reference to the availability of public information relating to securities. Recital 2 to the EU Market Abuse Directive (MAD)[2] articulates that concern as follows:

> An integrated and efficient financial market requires market integrity. The smooth functioning of securities markets and public confidence in markets are prerequisites for economic growth and wealth. Market abuse harms the integrity of financial markets and public confidence in securities and derivatives.

Recital 12 to the MAD goes on to say that:

> Market abuse consists of insider dealing and market manipulation. The objective of legislation against insider dealing is the same as that of legislation against market manipulation: to ensure the integrity of Community financial markets and to enhance investor confidence in those markets. It is therefore advisable to adopt combined rules to combat both insider dealing and market manipulation.

[1] Directive 2004/39/EC [2004] OJ L145/1. See generally Chapter 2.9.1.
[2] Directive 2003/6/EC [2003] OJ L96/16.

These issues, as well as their implementation into the legal and regulatory framework in the UK, are considered in this chapter.

13.1 Market regulation: transparency

Transparency refers to the extent to which regulators and investors are able to observe activity in markets. It is an important regulatory issue because transparency influences the efficiency of markets. Economic theory holds that, for markets to operate efficiently, investors must be fully informed when making investment decisions.[3] Disclosure obligations imposed on listed companies[4] attempt to ensure that this is the case with regard to information concerning the business of an issuer of securities, but the activity of other investors is also relevant in rendering investors fully informed. This can arise in three ways. First, information regarding the price and size of transactions informs investors about the likely terms on which they will be able to trade. Secondly, information regarding the identity of substantial holders of a particular security provides information to investors regarding potential changes of control. Thirdly, acquisitions and disposals by directors and senior managers of an issuer provides investors with a valuable perspective on the valuation of securities as those individuals have access to better information within the company. Each aspect is dealt with by a different part of the regulatory system.

Recent changes in market structure outlined in Chapter 12 have given rise to concerns that overall transparency within securities markets has declined as trading volume has migrated away from public regulated markets to other markets and trading venues. In this context, transparency can be taken to refer to two different concepts. One is the degree to which transactions are visible to regulators: transparency in this sense assists in the supervision of firms (eg as regards risk control and market abuse) and the monitoring of aggregate market trends. The other is the degree to which the market is transparent to participants on an *ex ante* (as regards the terms for future trades) and *ex post* (as regards the terms of completed trades) basis. Transparency in this sense contributes to market efficiency by informing investors of the prices (and other trade terms) that are available across the market and the terms on which recent transactions have been undertaken. It also informs investors as to the liquidity in relevant instruments and provides a basis for discharging regulatory obligations owed to clients such as 'best execution'.

Since transparency underpins the operation of markets and regulatory surveillance in such a central manner, it is hardly surprising that the onset of the volatility that followed the financial crisis in 2008 heightened concerns over transparency that were already emerging from changes to market structure. These concerns were particularly to the fore in Europe, which does not have any equivalent of the 'national market system' that oper-

---

[3] See PD Spencer, *The Structure and Regulation of Financial Markets* (Oxford, Oxford University Press, 2000) 1–3 for a discussion of the conditions under which financial markets can be expected to operate efficiently.

[4] See generally Chapter 8.

ates in the US. Although, as discussed below, there is some degree of harmonisation of transparency rules within the EU, the system leaves considerable discretion to Member States, particularly in the context of non-equity instruments that are traded outside regulated markets.

13.1.1 Transaction reporting (to regulators)

The harmonised EU regime for the reporting of transactions to regulators applies to any financial instrument admitted to trading on a regulated market.[5] Investment firms are required to report details of transactions to the competent authority as quickly as possible and no later than the close of the following working day. The regime is formulated on a 'minimum standards' basis, permitting Member States to adopt 'superequivalent' requirements,[6] as has been the case in the UK. While the scope of the regime is limited to financial instruments admitted to trading on a regulated market, any trading of such instruments in other locations is subject to the reporting requirements. Thus, regulators have access to information about trading in such instruments by authorised firms operating in 'over-the-counter' (OTC) markets, 'multilateral trading facilities' and 'dark pools'. However, it seems clear that there is still some way to go in developing the EU regime to a point where regulators' market intelligence matches the rigour and complexity of the regulatory obligations that are imposed by MiFID on investment firms. Two issues in particular have proven to be problematic.[7] One is the difficulty encountered in reaching a consistent definition of the meaning of 'execution of a transaction' (which triggers the reporting obligation) across different Member States. The other is the identification of the capacity in which transactions are undertaken (as principal or on behalf of a client) for the purposes of determining whether regulatory obligations owed to clients (eg 'best execution') have been discharged. In the meantime, much depends on the capacity and capability of national regulators to cooperate so as to capture trading information from multiple trading locations.[8]

13.1.2 Trade reporting (to market participants)

The EU trade-reporting regime requires regulated markets and multilateral trading facility (MTFs) to provide both pre- and post-trade transparency for shares (only) admitted to trading on a regulated market. Pre-trade information encompasses current bid and offer prices and the depth of trading interest at those prices.[9] This information must be made

---

[5] Art 25 MiFID.

[6] See Chapter 3 for an explanation of this term.

[7] See CESR, 'Technical Advice to the European Commission in the context of MiFID Review—Transaction Reporting' CESR/10-292 (April 2010).

[8] Note Art 25(3) MiFID, requiring the competent authority to which information is reported to ensure that the competent authority of the most relevant market in terms of liquidity for those financial instruments also receives this information.

[9] Level 2 and 3 rules apply this requirement in greater detail to different market models.

available to the public on reasonable commercial terms and on a continuous basis during normal trading hours.[10] While pre-trade obligations are also imposed on systematic internalisers, the rules are much more complex than for regulated markets and MTFs, reflecting difficulties in negotiating a compromise[11] between the proponents of broad and narrow regimes.[12] Moreover, transactions that take place outside regulated markets, MTFs or through systematic internalisers are not subject to pre-trade disclosure requirements. Included in that category are transactions that fall within waivers granted by the national authorities as permitted by MiFID.[13]

The post-trade transparency regime for regulated markets and MTFs requires publication of the price, volume and time of the transactions executed in respect of shares admitted to trading on regulated markets. Details of all such transactions must be made available on a reasonable commercial basis and as close to real time as possible.[14] However, the scope of the post-trade regime extends beyond regulated markets because all investment firms[15] are subject to the obligation to publicise information relating to transactions (in shares admitted to trading on a regulated market) outside a regulated market or MTF.

Trade-reporting for asset classes other than shares was left to the Member States to determine and few have taken any action, with the result that transparency in non-equity instruments was generally poor at the time of the onset of the financial crisis. While in the early stages of the crisis the Committee of European Securities Regulators (CESR)[16] remained of the view that no changes were necessary to enhance transparency in non-equity instruments, the focus of the Financial Stability Forum on the issue prompted a reappraisal.[17] Subsequently, having examined the operation of the TRACE system in the US operated by FINRA in respect of OTC transactions as well as recent market-based initiatives in Europe, CESR concluded that 'there would be value for market participants in receiving access to greater post-trade information'.[18] In particular, CESR was of the view that greater transparency had the capacity to bolster market confidence (by reducing information asymmetry) and enhance liquidity in normal times, not just in crisis situations. Further developments on this front are awaited.[19]

---

[10] Art 44 MiFID.

[11] That compromise reflects the inherent tension between publication as a mechanism to improve price formation and threats to liquidity that may result from dealers having to publicise trading information that may compromise their capacity to take large risk positions in securities subject to the regime.

[12] See Arts 22 and 27 MiFID.

[13] See Arts 44(2) and 29(2) MiFID. These waivers are central to the operation of so-called 'dark pools'. See Chapter 12.3.4.

[14] Arts 45(1) and 30(1) MiFID.

[15] While this obligation applies to systematic internalisers, it also applies to investment firms undertaking any other 'off-exchange' transactions in shares that are admitted to trading on a regulated market.

[16] CESR was the level-three committee in the 'Lamfalussy' structure, which was replaced by the European Securities and Markets Authority (ESMA) as from 1 January 2011. See further Chapter 2.9.4.

[17] See Financial Stability Forum, 'Report of the Financial Stability Forum on Enhancing Market and Institutional Resilience' (April 2008).

[18] CESR, 'Transparency of Corporate Bond, Structured Finance Product and Credit Derivative Markets', CP 08-1014 (2008) para 106.

[19] For a discussion of the different considerations applicable to debt markets by comparison with equity markets and the difficult balance that needs to established between transparency and liquidity, see Centre for

In the secondary equity market, investors have noted that MiFID's reform of market structure has resulted in greater fragmentation of trading among competing venues and decreases in overall transparency and market data quality.[20] In particular, MiFID does not require or incentivise the consolidation of post-trade market data in the way that used to occur in the past, when the main market in each EU country published data and monitored its quality. Moreover, that outcome differentiates Europe from the US, where consolidation of market data has been required since 1975 and is available to the market at reasonable cost. This situation has led the ABI[21] in the UK to argue in favour of a mandated 'consolidated tape' in Europe in the interests of transparency, lower trading costs and the enhancement of the 'best execution' obligation owed to clients.[22] Another concern has been that the MiFID waivers for pre-trade transparency that permit the operation of 'dark pools' in the EU are overused and inconsistently applied by national regulators. CESR has responded by indicating that it favours moving to a more 'rules-based' approach from the 'principles-based' regime now in place.[23] CESR has also recommended the extension of the transparency regime for equities to equity-like instruments admitted to trading on a regulated market, such as depositary receipts and exchange-traded funds.[24]

13.1.3 Disclosure of substantial shareholdings

The UK has a long-standing system of ownership disclosure in respect of voting shares, based on the principle that the ownership profile of a company is a significant factor in equity investment and that relevant information should be in the public domain so as to enable investors to make informed decisions. The rules in the UK applied historically to all public companies (not just listed companies) and the regime took effect when an equity stake reached 3% of the shares in issue. When a similar regime was adopted in EU law[25] it adopted a 5% threshold, but the UK implemented the EU regime on a superequivalent basis so as to preserve the original 3% threshold. The UK implementation transferred the ownership disclosure regime from the Companies Act to the Financial Services Authority (FSA) Handbook and narrowed its scope to companies whose shares are admitted to trading on prescribed markets.[26]

The relevant provisions require that an interest of 3% or more in the voting share capital of an issuer with shares admitted to trading on a regulated market must be disclosed

---

Economic Policy Research, 'European Government Bond Markets: Transparency, Liquidity and Efficiency' (May 2006).

[20] See CESR, 'Impact of MiFID on Equity Secondary Markets', CESR/09-355 (June 2009) para 153.

[21] The Association of British Insurers, an influential investor organisation in the UK.

[22] ABI, 'Response to CESR's Call for Evidence on the Impact of MiFID on Secondary Market Functioning', CESR/08-872 (2008).

[23] CESR, 'Technical Advice to the European Commission in the Context of MiFID Review—Equity Markets', CESR/10-394 (April 2010).

[24] Ibid.

[25] See Art 13 of the Transparency Obligations Directive, 2004/109/EC [2004] OJ L390/38.

[26] See FSMA 2000, s 89A(1), 3(a) and the Disclosure and Transparency (DTR) component of the FSA Handbook.

to the issuer.[27] Subsequent changes from that level that exceed a 1% threshold must also be disclosed. Shareholdings held on behalf of investors by some investment managers, custodians and market-makers are excluded from the disclosure obligation, the rationale being that they are unlikely to influence the exercise of voting control over a company. While the disclosure obligation is imposed on a shareholder whose shareholding triggers the relevant threshold, it is also possible for a company itself to take the initiative. This is made possible by the preservation in the Companies Act 2006 of the right of any public company to serve a notice requiring information about interests in its shares on any person that it has reasonable cause to believe is interested in its shares or has been so interested in the previous 3 years.[28] That process allows a company to discover the true identity of the holder of shares that are held by nominees or in trust. An issuer must, following receipt of a notification of a substantial shareholding, disclose to the public as soon as possible, and in any event not later than the end of the trading day following receipt of the notification, all the information contained in the notification.[29]

However, it soon became clear that derivative positions, which were not covered by either the UK or EC regime, were being used to circumvent the ownership disclosure rules. The result was that substantial shareholdings and the associated voting control could be acquired covertly without disclosure to the market. In 2007 the FSA drew attention to several problems that arose from this practice: inefficient price formation resulting from 'hidden voting' that would not be reflected in market pricing; distortion to the market for corporate control; diminished market confidence as investors would not be well informed as to the exercise of influence within companies; and information asymmetry as between investors, only some of whom are likely to know about derivative positions.[30] In response, the FSA introduced a comprehensive regime that requires disclosure of financial instruments that have a similar economic effect to instruments that provide an entitlement to acquire shares with voting rights attached.[31] Such instruments must be aggregated with shares and relevant financial instruments to determine whether disclosure is required. The UK rules took effect on 1 June 2009. CESR has proposed the introduction of an EU-wide disclosure regime for economic equivalent financial instruments that are currently excluded from the Transparency Directive.[32]

---

[27] DTR 5.1.2R. While this obligation is framed by reference to regulated markets, exchange-regulated markets (such as AIM) are also covered by the regime.

[28] See Companies Act 2006, pt 22 esp s 793 (replacing s 212 of the Companies Act 1985).

[29] DTR 5.8.12R.

[30] See FSA, 'Disclosure of Contracts for Difference', Consultation Paper (CP) 07/20 (November 2007).

[31] See FSA Handbook, DTR 5.3.1R and see guidance at 5.3.3.G.

[32] See CESR, 'CESR Proposal to Extend Major Shareholding Notifications to Instruments of Similar Economic Effect to Holding Shares and Entitlements to Acquire Shares', CESR/09-1215b (January 2010). CESR proposed a broad definition as per the UK model since the creation of new instruments has the capacity to result in avoidance. CESR also notes that rules were introduced in France on 1 November 2009. Outside the EU, Hong Kong, Switzerland and Australia have taken action. In the US, a broader disclosure regime was in place prior to the financial crisis, requiring disclosure of beneficial interests above 5% held directly or indirectly, with some special exemptions for institutional investors who hold in the ordinary course of business.

13.1.4 Disclosure of transactions by persons discharging managerial responsibilities

Finally, there are disclosure requirements relating to transactions by persons discharging managerial responsibilities (PDMR) in the shares of an issuer which are admitted to trading on a prescribed market.[33] A PDMR is required to notify the company of the occurrence of all transactions conducted on their own account in the shares of the issuer, or derivatives or any other financial instruments relating to those shares, within four business days of the day on which the transaction occurred.[34] The issuer is then required to pass that information to a Regulatory Information Service Provider for the purposes of disclosure to the market. The rationale for such a disclosure requirement is twofold. First, it reinforces the prohibitions on insider dealing by recording changes in the interests of PDMRs in the share capital of the company. PDMRs are generally first in line to gain access to inside information and it is therefore important to protect against abuse of that position through insider dealing. Secondly, transactions entered into by PDMRs provide an important signal to investors as regards the directors' and senior managers' evaluation of the company's prospects.

13.2 Market integrity: overview

Insider dealing did not attract formal regulatory attention in the UK until legislation was introduced in 1980.[35] By that time, there was already a long history of regulating insider dealing in the US. Statutory regulation was introduced in the US by the Securities Exchange Act 1934, but even before then the common law in some states had already begun to control insider dealing. Why should there have been such a difference in approach in two countries which shared a common legal heritage and led the world in the development of financial (and particularly equity) markets in the nineteenth and twentieth centuries? Two explanations can be offered. First, the tendency in the UK to permit self-regulation in financial markets meant that insider dealing was regarded as a matter of internal market discipline rather than a matter of public interest. Hence, insider dealing was not viewed as being in the same category as other forms of 'white collar' crime. A second explanation, linked to some extent with the first, is that the state courts in the US adopted an interventionist stance in respect of insider dealing. This was achieved by extending fiduciary duties to dealings between company directors and

---

[33] Following implementation of the MAD, these rules moved from the Companies Act to the DTR component of the FSA Handbook.

[34] DTR 3.1.2R, implementing Art 6(4) of the MAD and Art 6(1) of the MAD Implementing Directive 2004/72/EC.

[35] The relevant provisions were contained in the Companies Act 1980. See further B Rider et al, *Market Abuse and Insider Dealing*, 2nd edn (Edinburgh, Tottel Publishing, 2009) ch 3.

shareholders so that directors with inside information were required either to disclose the relevant information or refrain from dealing.[36] The emphasis in company law in the UK on directors' duties being owed to the company alone largely ruled out the possibility of the common law regulating insider dealing in this way.[37]

In the EU, the rationale for the prohibition has been that insider dealing has a negative effect on market integrity, resulting in a loss of confidence in the market and therefore an unwillingness to use the market to transform savings into investments.[38] The negative effect on market integrity results from the information asymmetry caused by the presence of 'insiders' in a market. The result of 'insiders' being routinely present in a market is that 'outsiders' are likely to adjust their price expectations to reflect the likelihood of dealing with better-informed buyers or sellers. The aggregate effect of this across the market as a whole is likely to be that transaction costs will increase (eg market-makers will widen spreads) and therefore the cost of capital for companies will rise.[39] This will be the case even if investors are confident that full information is provided when a company first makes a public offer, as trading in the secondary market will reflect the presence of 'insiders' and new share issues will have to be priced consistently with valuations in the secondary market. Another consideration is that large controlling shareholders might be tempted to make profits from insider dealing (as they are likely to have access to inside information) rather than engage in monitoring, which would benefit all shareholders equally. There may also be a depressing effect on valuations as investors lose confidence in the likelihood of being treated fairly in a market in which insiders are routinely trading.

13.3 The criminal law on insider dealing

In the UK, the criminal law prohibition of insider dealing is contained in part V of the Criminal Justice Act 1993 (CJA 1993).[40] It establishes three separate offences:[41]

[36] See generally S Bainbridge, 'The Law and Economics of Insider Trading: A Comprehensive Primer', available at hhttp://papers.ssrn.com/abstract=261277 (accessed on 20 November 2011).

[37] See *Percival v Wright* [1902] 2 Ch 421, a case in which directors of a company bought shares from shareholders without disclosing that the company was in takeover negotiations. It was held that, as the directors did not owe a fiduciary duty to the shareholders, disclosure was not required. Company law in the UK does not rule out the possibility of directors owing fiduciary duties to shareholders in specific circumstances, but there is no instance of this principle being applied to insider dealing in the way that occurred in the US.

[38] This is evident in the preambles to both the 1989 Directive on Insider Dealing (89/592 [1989] OJ L334/30) and the 2003 Market Abuse Directive (2003/6 [2003] OJ L96/16). The 1989 Directive was implemented in the UK by pt V of the Criminal Justice Act 1993. It was superseded by the 2003 Directive in October 2004.

[39] See U Battychara and H Daouk, 'The World Price of Insider Trading' (2002) 57 *Journal of Finance* 75. On one measure, the authors conclude that enforcement of insider dealing laws reduces the cost of equity by around 6% per year. See also I MacNeil, *Editorial*, 'Insider Trading and $64m Questions' (2011) 5(4) *Law and Financial Markets Review*.

[40] These provisions implemented the 1989 EC directive on insider dealing (now repealed and replaced by the Market Abuse Directive).

[41] Section 52.

- dealing;
- encouraging another person to deal; and
- disclosing information.

In each instance, the person must have information as an insider. This will be the case only if the information is inside information and the person has it, and knows he has it, from an inside source. Inside information is defined as information which:[42]

(a) relates to particular securities or to a particular issuer of securities or to particular issuers of securities and not to securities generally or to issuers of securities generally;
(b) is specific or precise;
(c) has not been made public; and
(d) if it were made public would be likely to have a significant effect on the price of any securities.

A person has information as an insider if and only if:[43]

(a) it is, and he knows that it is, inside information; and
(b) he has it, and he knows that he has it, from an inside source.[44]

A person has information from an inside source if and only if:

(a) he has it through—
  i. being a director, employee or shareholder of an issuer of securities; or
  ii. having access to the information by virtue of his employment, office or profession; or
(b) the direct or indirect source of his information is a person within paragraph (a).

The reference to the accused 'knowing' that information is inside information and 'knowing' that he has it from an inside source effectively imposes a requirement of *mens rea* (intent).[45] This requirement distinguishes the criminal offence of insider dealing from the market abuse regime, where the principle does not apply because the proceedings are civil (administrative) rather than criminal in nature.[46]

For any of the offences to be established, the relevant securities must be price-affected securities, meaning that publication of the relevant inside information would be likely to have a significant effect on the price of the securities.[47] This is not to say that the inside information must relate to the securities relevant to the offence. It is possible for the offence to be committed by dealing in other securities if they are price-affected (eg

---

[42] Section 56.
[43] Section 57.
[44] This is sometimes referred to as 'tipee liability' as it arises most frequently in situations in which an insider provides a 'share tip' to another person. In that situation, the insider has committed the disclosure offence and the other person will commit the dealing offence if he trades on the basis of the tip.
[45] *Mens rea* (intent to commit a crime) must be shown by the prosecution in the case of common law crimes. In the case of statutory offences, it is possible for this requirement to be set aside and such offences are referred to as imposing 'strict liability' as it is only necessary to show that the accused performed the relevant act.
[46] But see below section 13.4.9 regarding the characterisation of regulatory proceedings under the market abuse regime.
[47] Information falling within this category is subject to the obligation imposed by the Listing Rules to publicise the information to the market. See Chapter 8.3.5.

dealing in the shares of a competitor whose shares are likely to rise or fall when the inside information becomes public).

It is also necessary to establish that the dealing occurred on a regulated market or that the person dealing relies on a professional intermediary[48] or is himself acting as a professional intermediary. The Act contains a number of defences, some of which are general in their scope, others which apply to specific situations. The exemption given to market-makers allowing them to continue trading even when in possession of inside information is of particular significance:[49] it recognises that, since market liquidity relies on the continuous provision of dealer quotes, the ability to provide those quotes should not be constrained by concerns over insider trading. Were market-makers required to comply with the law on insider dealing, considerable disruption would be caused in quote-driven markets (not least since inside information may be acquired inadvertently).[50]

Prosecutions for insider dealing are undertaken by the FSA in England[51] and the Lord Advocate in Scotland. Few prosecutions have been pursued. The main problem is that the prosecutor is required to produce evidence that shows beyond reasonable doubt that the offence has been committed. The presence of any reasonable doubt will result in acquittal of the accused. There are problems in collecting the necessary evidence to sustain a prosecution as in many cases 'insiders' will go to considerable trouble to cover their tracks (eg dealing through nominees and offshore companies). Even when evidence can be collected, it may be difficult to corroborate.[52]

However, in the wake of the financial crisis, the FSA policy of 'credible deterrence' led to a new focus on criminal prosecution of insiders. There were six successful prosecutions between 2009 and 2011, several of which implicated professionals working in the financial markets.[53] The most severe sentence imposed was 40 months' imprisonment, and in each case a confiscation order was imposed to recover the profits earned from insider dealing.[54]

Market manipulation is, in certain circumstances, a criminal offence under the Financial Services and Markets Act 2000 (FSMA 2000).[55] Manipulation is not defined in the Act,[56] but is generally understood to refer to devices such as transactions in which there is no change of ownership (giving a false impression of liquidity in the relevant security) or price positioning (such as heavy buying of a security to influence the level of an index

---

[48] Eg when a deal involves either a broker (acting as agent for the accused) or a dealer (trading on her own account) operating outside the regulated markets.

[49] Section 53 and sch 1, para 1.

[50] A similar approach is adopted under the market abuse regime: see section 13.4.6 re the 'safe harbour' for executing client orders.

[51] FSMA 2000, s 402. The FSA must comply with any conditions or restrictions imposed by the Treasury. See FSA Handbook, ENF 15 for FSA policy on prosecuting offences (especially ENF 15.5.1G).

[52] See eg *Mackie v HMA* 1994 SCCR 277.

[53] See Herbert Smith, 'Financial Regulatory Developments' (2011) 5(4) *Law and Financial Markets Review* 314.

[54] The maximum sentence under s 61 of the Criminal Justice Act 1993 is 7 years. There is no limit to fines which may be imposed (on indictment).

[55] See s 397(3) for a definition of the offence and subss 4 and 5 for defences.

[56] Section 397 does not refer explicitly to 'market manipulation' but to 'any course of conduct which creates a false or misleading impression as to the market in or the price or value of any relevant investments'.

at a particular time). It may also take the form of a false announcement made on behalf of an issuer with a view to supporting the share price.[57]

13.4 The market abuse regime

13.4.1 Evolution of the UK regime

The perceived failure of the criminal law to deal effectively with cases of insider dealing and market manipulation led to calls for powers to be given to the FSA to impose regulatory sanctions for such behaviour. The FSA (and the regulatory bodies which preceded it) already had such powers under the Financial Services Act 1986 (FSA 1986) regulatory framework[58] as such behaviour was prohibited either by core rule 28 or by the Statements of Principle made under the Financial Services Act 1986. It was therefore possible for regulators to take disciplinary action under those provisions.[59]

However, there were three main problems associated with this system of regulatory sanctions. First, action against insider dealing based on core rule 28 was limited to behaviour falling within the (criminal law) definition of insider dealing in CJA 1993. This was seen as unduly restrictive by comparison with the type of behaviour that could be regarded broadly as 'market abuse'. Secondly, disciplinary action was limited to authorised firms and their employees as the relevant rules (above) did not apply to the public at large (they applied only to authorised firms and their employees). Thirdly, reliance on the high-level principles as a basis for disciplinary action against behaviour considered to be 'market abuse' would, even if it were legally possible,[60] leave the FSA open to the criticism that is was failing to specify in sufficient detail conduct which it regarded as contrary to high-level principles.

The market abuse regime was introduced to resolve these problems. It comprises part 8 of FSMA 2000 and the Code of Market Conduct (MAR) that the FSA is obliged to make under section 119 of the Act. The purpose of the Code is to define more clearly the types of behaviour that constitute market abuse. Behaviour will not be considered to be market abuse if it falls within a 'safe harbour' designated by the Code. A safe harbour is a conclusive description of behaviour that is not market abuse, made under section 119(2) FSMA 2000.

---

[57] See further B Rider et al, *Market Abuse and Insider Dealing*, 2nd edn (Edinburgh, Tottel Publishing, 2009) ch 5.14.

[58] See I MacNeil and K Wotherspoon, *Business Investigations* (Bristol, Jordans, 1998) paras 4.4 and 4.58.

[59] See eg *R (Fleurose) v SFA* [2001] EWHC Admin 1085, a case in which the SFA (Securities and Futures Authority, a self-regulatory organisation under FSA 1986 and the FSA's predecessor as regulator of broker/dealers) took disciplinary action against a trader on the basis of FSA Statements of Principle 1 and 3.

[60] *R (Fleurose) v SFA*, ibid, lent support to the view that it was possible.

While not formally designated as safe harbours, two forms of FSA guidance are significant for determining the scope of the market abuse regime. The first is that behaviour conforming to the rules on 'Chinese walls' does not in itself constitute market abuse.[61] The second is that behaviour conforming to the rules in the Disclosure and Transparency component of the FSA Handbook relating to the timing, dissemination or availability, content and standard of care applicable to a disclosure, announcement, communication or release of information does not in itself amount to market abuse.

The definition of behaviour that constitutes market abuse is more open ended because it comprises provisions which do not have the conclusive character of the 'safe harbour' provisions above. Those provisions are evidential provisions and guidance. Evidential provisions are in effect presumptions that can be rebutted.[62] It follows that, while such provisions may point to the likelihood of certain behaviour being considered market abuse, it is in principle possible to convince the FSA that the behaviour is not in fact market abuse. Guidance consists of information and advice given by the FSA with respect to the Act and rules made under it.[63] There is no obligation to follow guidance and failure to follow it does not automatically mean that a person has engaged in market abuse.

13.4.2 The EU Market Abuse Directive

MAD,[64] taken together with the implementing measures[65] adopted under the so-called 'Lamfalussy' process, required changes to be made to FSMA 2000, the Code of Market Conduct, the Price Stabilising Rules, the UK Listing Rules and the Conduct of Business Sourcebook (COBS). MAD encompasses but also extends beyond the criminal law the concepts of insider dealing and market manipulation discussed above. It is a 'minimum standards' directive, meaning that it requires Member States to adopt its provisions but leaves them free to set additional requirements. MAD provides some discretion to Member States as to the nature of the measures (criminal, regulatory or civil) that give effect to the provisions of the Directive. It does require, however, that administrative (ie regulatory) sanctions can be taken against persons responsible for non-compliance (Article 14).

---

[61] MAR 1.10.2 G and SYSC 10.2.2R. See Chapter 15.2.5 regarding the nature and function of Chinese walls.

[62] See s 149 FSMA 2000 for a definition of evidential provisions. They are designated 'E' in the Code.

[63] It is indicated by the letter 'G' in the Code.

[64] Directive 2003/6/EC [2003] OJ L96/16. See generally M Avgouleas, *The Mechanics and Regulation of Market Abuse* (Oxford, Oxford University Press, 2005).

[65] Commission Directive 2003/124/EC implementing Council Directive 2003/6/EC as regards the definition and public disclosure of inside information and definition of market manipulation [2003] OJ L339/70; Commission Directive 2003/125/EC implementing Council Directive 2003/6/EC as regards the fair presentation of investment recommendations and the disclosure of conflicts of interest [2003] OJ L339/73; Commission Regulation EC/2273/2003 implementing Council Directive 2003/6/EC as regards exemptions for buy-back programmes and stabilisation of financial instruments [2003] OJ L336/33; Commission Directive 2004/72 implementing Directive 2003/6/EC as regards accepted market practices, the definition of inside information in relation to derivatives on commodities, the drawing up of lists of insiders, the notification of managers' transactions and the notification of suspicious transactions [2004] OJ L162/70.

In its consultation on the implementation of MAD,[66] the Treasury canvassed views on whether the UK should retain the scope of its existing market abuse regime where it was wider than the Directive. The outcome was a compromise under which the UK retained provisions in FSMA 2000 that prohibit a wider range of behaviour than MAD, but those provisions were made subject to a 3 year 'sunset' clause, meaning that they would automatically lapse on 30 June 2008 unless new legislation were adopted to allow them to remain in force. Such legislation was adopted,[67] extending the 3 year period until 31 December 2009, and subsequently further extended to 31 December 2011.[68] That (extended) period is referred to below as the 'transitional period' and the retained provisions that are not required by MAD are referred to as superequivalents.

13.4.3 The scope of the regime

The Market Abuse Regulations[69] extended the scope of the market abuse regime by reference to the markets and instruments covered. The old regime applied only to markets based in the UK, although the coverage of markets was wider than required by MAD as it included markets run by UK recognised investment exchanges that are not EEA-regulated markets (eg the London Stock Exchange's Alternative Investment Market (AIM) as from October 2004). The new regime applies to the following prescribed markets:

1. all markets which are established under the rules of a UK recognised investment exchange;
2. the market known as OFEX; and
3. all other markets which are regulated markets.[70]

The Market Abuse Regulations also extended the scope of qualifying investments (above) so as to include:

- transferable securities;[71]
- units in collective investment undertakings;
- money-market instruments;
- financial-futures contracts, including equivalent cash-settled instruments;
- forward interest-rate agreements;

---

[66] See HM Treasury/FSA Consultation Paper, 'UK Implementation of the EU Market Abuse Directive' (June 2004).

[67] In the form of the Financial Services and Markets Act 2000 (Market Abuse) Regulations 2008, SI 2008/1439.

[68] The Financial Services and Markets Act 2000 (Market Abuse) Regulations 2009 SI 2009/3128. The future of the 'sunset' clause is linked with implementation of the EU Commission's review of the market abuse regime: see the proposals for a new EU regulation and directive at http://ec.europa.eu/internal_market/securities/abuse/index_en.htm (accessed on 20 November 2011).

[69] The Financial Services and Markets Act 2000 (Market Abuse) Regulations 2005, SI 2005/381.

[70] Art 4 of the Financial Services and Markets Act 2000 (Prescribed Markets and Qualifying Investments) Order 2001, SI 2001/996 (as amended by the Market Abuse Regulations). 'Regulated market' has the meaning given in Art 4.1.14 MiFID. Note that the scope of the superequivalent provisions in s 118(4) and (8) is narrower: they apply only to prescribed markets in the UK.

[71] As defined in MiFID: see Art 69 and Annex 1, s C.

- interest-rate, currency and equity swaps;
- options to acquire or dispose of any instrument falling into these categories, including equivalent cash-settled instruments (this category includes in particular options on currency and on interest rates);
- derivatives on commodities; and
- any other instrument admitted to trading on a regulated market in a Member State or for which a request for admission to trading on such a market has been made.[72]

The result is that orders executed from the UK in relation to any such instrument that is admitted to trading on a prescribed market (including EEA-regulated markets) fall within the market abuse regime even if the market on which the trade is executed is not a prescribed market.[73] However, the scope of the superequivalent sections remains limited as they apply only to behaviour in respect of investments admitted to trading on prescribed markets operating in the UK.[74]

13.4.4 The definition of market abuse

The Market Abuse Regulations substantially amended FSMA 2000, section 118. Instead of the three forms of market abuse previously contained in that provision, there are now seven. The elements of the definition relating to behaviour, inside information and *mens rea* (intent) are worthy of particular note.

Behaviour

- Behaviour constituting market abuse can take the form of any kind of conduct (including an act or omission) of one or more persons (including legal persons[75]), and must occur in the UK.
- MAD did not adopt the 'regular user' test, which had been employed as a core element of the definition of market abuse in the original formulation of FSMA 2000, section 118. This feature was regarded by the Treasury as making necessary the recasting of FSMA 2000, section 118 as it might mean that behaviour prohibited by the Directive would be exculpated in the UK.[76] However, the regular user test was retained in the superequivalent subsections (4) and (8), which retain the original definition of market abuse during the transitional period.
- The disclosure form of market abuse referred to in subsection (3) makes an exception in respect of disclosure that is made in the proper course of employment, profession

---

[72] See Art 5 of SI 2001/996 (as amended).

[73] See the FSMT decision in *Jabre v FSA*, case 36 (for text see http://www.tribunals.gov.uk/Finance/Decisions/Financial.htm). In that case, it was held that the market abuse regime covered short sales executed from London in the Tokyo market of shares that were traded on the London market (SEAQ International).

[74] See Regulation 4 of SI 2001/996 as amended by Regulation 10 of the Market Abuse Regulations.

[75] That distinguishes the market abuse regime from the criminal offence of insider dealing, which can be committed only by individuals.

[76] See para 3.14 of the Treasury Consultation, above n 66.

or duties.[77] That latter provision was the subject of a preliminary ruling by the European Court of Justice in November 2005,[78] which indicates that the exception is to be interpreted strictly and that the sensitivity of the inside information is to be taken into account in determining if particular circumstances fall within the exception.

- Behaviour conforming to 'accepted market practices' will, in limited circumstances, mean that it falls outside the definition of market abuse. Those circumstances are where the accepted market practice is followed for the purposes of effecting transactions or orders to trade which—

  (a) give, or are likely to give, a false or misleading impression as to the supply of, or demand for, or as to the price of, one or more qualifying investments; or

  (b) secure the price of one or more such investments at an abnormal or artificial level.[79]

The factors relevant to the FSA's determination of whether a practice is an accepted market practice are set out in the FSA Handbook.[80]

Inside information

The definition of inside information for the purposes of the market abuse regime differs from that which applies in the context of the criminal offence of insider dealing. In general terms, information is inside information for the purposes of the market abuse regime if it:

1. is not generally available;
2. relates, directly or indirectly, to one or more issuers of the qualifying investments or to one or more of the qualifying investments; and
3. would, if generally available, be likely to have a significant effect on the price of the qualifying investments or on the price of related investments.[81]

In relation to a person charged with the execution of orders concerning any qualifying investments or related investments, inside information includes information conveyed by a client and related to the client's pending orders which:

1. is of a precise nature;
2. is not generally available;

---

[77] This provision implements Art 3(a) MAD, which in turn follows Art 3(a) of the (now repealed) Insider Dealing Directive.

[78] European Court of Justice, judgment of 22 November 2005 in Case C-384/02 (Grongaard and Another), reference for a preliminary ruling under Art 234 regarding Art 3 of the Insider Dealing Directive 89/592/EEC.

[79] FSMA 2000, s 118(5).

[80] MAR 1, Annex 2: Accepted Market Practices. See also Case C-445/09 *IMC Securities BV v Stichting Autoriteit Financiële Markten* [2011] EUECJ regarding the manipulation of market prices through the placing of simultaneous buy and sell limit orders, which was held by the European Court of Justice to constitute market abuse for the purposes of MAD.

[81] Information would be likely to have a significant effect on price if and only if it is information of a kind which a reasonable investor would be likely to use as part of the basis of his investment decisions.

3. relates, directly or indirectly, to one or more issuers of qualifying investments or to one or more qualifying investments; and
4. would, if generally available, be likely to have a significant effect on the price of those qualifying investments or the price of related investments.

Information is precise if it:

1. indicates circumstances that exist or may reasonably be expected to come into existence, or an event that has occurred or may reasonably be expected to occur; and
2. is specific enough to enable a conclusion to be drawn as to the possible effect of those circumstances or that event on the price of qualifying investments or related investments.[82]

In *David Massey v The Financial Services Authority*,[83] the Tribunal considered the requirements in section 118C that the information be 'precise' and that it would, if generally available, be likely to have a significant effect on the price of the qualifying investments or on the price of related investments. It concluded that information could be precise where it was possible that it would have an effect on the price and the effect would likely be negative. There was no requirement for certainty in regard to this issue. Moreover, whether or not the information would have a significant effect on the price, it was nevertheless information of a kind which a reasonable investor would be likely to use as part of the basis of his investment decisions falling within FSMA 2000, section 118C(6) and therefore inside information.

Mens rea *(intent)*

There is no express requirement of *mens rea*, or 'intent', in establishing market abuse. However, there are three ways in which intent may be relevant. First, if market abuse is regarded as a statutory criminal offence, at least for the purposes of the European Convention on Human Rights (ECHR), a requirement of 'mens rea' could be implied.[84] Support for the view that it is a criminal offence is provided by the judgment of the European Court of Justice in the *Spector* case.[85] Secondly, insiders who fall within FSMA 2000, section 118B(e) must know that the information is inside information and therefore may avoid liability if they do not have such knowledge (actual or constructive). Thirdly, intent (or, more specifically, its absence) may be relevant for the purposes of the imposition of a penalty under FSMA 2000, section 123. However, in that context, the interpretation of the Code of Market Conduct by the Financial Services and Markets Tribunal in *Winterflood et al v FSA*[86] indicates that, in the case of behaviour that creates

---

[82] FSMA 2000, s 118C.

[83] Upper Tribunal (Tax and Chancery Chamber) [2011] UKUT 49 (TCC).

[84] *Sweet v Parsley* [1970] AC 132.

[85] Case C-45/08 *Spector Photo Group NV v Commissie Voor Het Bank-Financie-En Assurantiewezen (CBFA)* [2010] CMLR 30.

[86] *Winterflood Securities Ltd, Stepehn Sotiriou & Jason Robins v FSA*, Financial Services and Markets Tribunal case 66; for text see http://www.tribunals.gov.uk/finance/Documents/decisions/FinancialServicesMarketsTribunal/066_WinterfloodSecuritiesLimitedStephenSotiriouJasonRobins.pdf.

a false or misleading impression or positions prices at an artificial level, defences based on provisions of the Code that are referenced to intent will be interpreted narrowly.

The decision of the European Court of Justice in *Spector* carries important implications for the relevance of intent. The decision focuses on the reference in Article 2(1) of MAD to 'using' inside information. According to that decision, the fact that a primary insider who held inside information traded on the market in financial instruments to which that information related implied that he 'used that information' within the meaning of Article 2(1) of MAD, but without prejudice to the rights of the defence and, in particular, the right to be able to rebut that presumption. While the FSA regards FSMA 2000 section 118(2)[87] as consistent with the decision in *Spector*, it did delete an inconsistent provision in its Handbook[88] that suggested that the Authority would require evidence of a person's intention as a separate element. The effect of that change will be to simplify and facilitate market abuse cases that are pursued by the Authority.

13.4.5 Safe harbours

Safe harbours are intended to provide certainty to market participants with regard to behaviour that does not constitute market abuse. The implementation of MAD resulted in changes to the safe harbours. Several of the safe harbours are of particular importance in the context of this book:[89]

- Behaviour in conformity with relevant provisions of the Takeover Code does not constitute market abuse.
- Dealing in financial instruments by market-makers for their own account will not in itself constitute market abuse.
- The dutiful carrying out of, or arranging for the dutiful carrying out of, an order on behalf of another (including as portfolio manager) will not in itself amount to market abuse (insider dealing) by the person carrying out that order.
- Disclosure of inside information required by statutory or regulatory obligations does not in itself constitute market abuse.
- Behaviour conforming with the EU buy-back and stabilisation regulation[90] does not in itself constitute market abuse.

13.4.6 Mandatory disclosure of inside information by issuers

As noted in the recitals to MAD: 'Prompt and fair disclosure of information to the public enhances market integrity, whereas selective disclosure by issuers can lead to a loss

---

[87] FSMA 2000, s 118(2) provides as follows: '(2) The first type of behaviour [that is market abuse] is where an insider deals, or attempts to deal, in a qualifying investment or related investment on the basis of inside information relating to the investment in question.'

[88] MAR 1.3.4E.

[89] See MAR generally. The designation 'C' is reserved for 'safe harbours' under the market abuse regime.

[90] Above n 65.

of investor confidence in the integrity of financial markets.'[91] In pursuit of that policy, Article 6(1) of MAD requires that: 'Member States shall ensure that issuers of financial instruments inform the public as soon as possible of inside information which directly concerns the said issuers.'[92]

The link between prompt disclosure of inside information and market integrity is reinforced by Principle 4 of the Listing Principles (for premium listed companies[93]), which requires that: 'A listed company must communicate information to holders and potential holders of its listed equity shares in such a way as to avoid the creation or continuation of a false market in such listed equity shares.' MAD also prohibits selective disclosure of inside information by requiring that any disclosure to a third party that is not protected by a duty of confidentiality[94] must also be made public.[95] It is possible for an issuer to delay disclosure so as not to prejudice its own legitimate interests[96] provided that such omission would not be likely to mislead the public and provided that the issuer is able to ensure the confidentiality of the information. That represents a difficult judgement for an issuer and one that carries the risk of failing to make a timely disclosure.[97]

13.4.7 Compliance and supervision

As noted in Chapter 3, authorised firms bear primary responsibility for establishing and maintaining compliance systems and controls that are appropriate to the nature, scale and complexity of their business.[98] Those systems and controls must encompass compliance with the market abuse regime, and there are some specific requirements that are of particular relevance to this. The first is the conduct of business rules relating to personal account dealing by the staff of investment firms. A firm must establish and maintain arrangements which ensure that a relevant person with access to confidential information is not able to enter into a personal transaction[99] that is prohibited by MAD.[100]

The second is the system of suspicious transaction reporting. A firm which arranges or executes a transaction with or for a client in a qualifying investment admitted to trading on a prescribed market and which has reasonable grounds to suspect that the transaction might constitute market abuse must notify the FSA without delay.[101] If an investment firm or a credit institution is obliged to make a notification to the FSA under this section, it must transmit to the FSA the following information: a description of the transaction,

---

[91] MAD, recital 24.

[92] That requirement is implemented in the UK through the FSA Handbook, DTR 2.2.1R.

[93] For the meaning of that term, see Chapter 8.2.2.

[94] Disclosures to auditors or professional advisers are protected by a duty of confidentiality. Disclosures made to investors or financial analysts are not.

[95] MAD, Art 6(2), implemented by DTR 2.5.1(3) R.

[96] Such as the completion of a major transaction that is being negotiated.

[97] See Chapter 8.3.5 for further discussion of the disclosure obligation and Chapter 8.4 for liability in the case of failure to make a timely disclosure.

[98] See also SYSC 6.1.1R.

[99] This includes transactions on behalf of close family and associates.

[100] COBS 11.7.1R.

[101] SUP 15.10.2R.

including the type of order (such as limit order, market order or other characteristics of the order), the type of trading market and the reasons for suspicion that the transaction might constitute market abuse. In addition the following information must be provided to the FSA as soon as it becomes available: (i) the means for identification of the persons on behalf of whom the transaction has been carried out, and of other persons involved in the relevant transaction; (ii) the capacity in which the firm operates (such as for own account or on behalf of third parties); and (iii) any other information which may have significance in reviewing the suspicious transaction.[102]

A firm itself (in addition to its staff) may be implicated in market abuse and become the subject of FSA proceedings.[103] In this context, the FSA has made clear that the conduct of an employee can be attributed to an employer for the purposes of establishing market abuse without the need to show any additional conduct or failing (eg in respect of systems or trading procedures) on the part of the firm.[104] While the conduct of the firm will be relevant if it relies on the 'reasonable precautions' defence,[105] that defence will not succeed where precautions that have been implemented in other firms (eg procedures relating to dealing after an individual has become 'wall-crossed') have not been adopted.[106]

13.4.8 Enforcement

The FSA can take enforcement action when a person has engaged in market abuse or has required or encouraged another person to engage in such behaviour. The normal warning and decision notice procedure associated with FSA disciplinary action must be followed in these circumstances.[107] Where the response to a warning notice indicates that the relevant person believed on reasonable grounds that his behaviour was not market abuse (or requiring or encouraging market abuse) or that he took all reasonable precautions and exercised all due diligence to avoid such behaviour, the FSA may not impose a penalty.[108] This comes close to but does not expressly create a requirement for intent in respect of behaviour constituting market abuse.

Disciplinary proceedings for market abuse are civil in character.[109] While this was the intention of the government at the time of the introduction of FSMA 2000, doubts were expressed at the Committee stage of the FSMA Bill as to whether the market abuse regime was sufficiently different from the criminal law of insider dealing to be considered civil in character for the purposes of the ECHR.[110] The significance of the categorisation

---

[102] SUP 15.10.6R.

[103] Firms may be monitored by regulated markets which are required by Art 43 MiFID to monitor compliance with the market abuse regime.

[104] FSA Final Notice of 1 August 2006 (Philippe Jabre and GLG Partners LP).

[105] In FSMA 2000, s 123(2)(b).

[106] See FSA Final Notice, above n 104.

[107] See s 126 FSMA 2000.

[108] FSMA 2000, s 123(2).

[109] *R (Fleurose) v SFA*, above n 59.

[110] See Annex C to the First Report of the Joint Parliamentary Committee on the Financial Services and Markets Bill (HC 328-I).

of the market abuse regime as civil or criminal lies in the safeguards which are available to the defence in criminal cases. While the ECHR requires a fair hearing in all cases before courts and tribunals, a number of safeguards apply specifically to criminal cases. Moreover, the determination of whether an 'offence' is criminal or civil is ultimately determined under the ECHR, not under national law. In recognition of the potential for legal challenges to the market abuse regime based on its criminal character, FSMA 2000 provides two important protections to the 'defence'. First, legal assistance is available to a person who appeals an FSA decision on market abuse to the relevant Tribunal.[111] Secondly, compelled evidence is not admissible in market abuse cases.[112] Such evidence arises when there is an obligation on a person to answer questions posed by an FSA investigator.[113] The availability of these two safeguards does raise some doubt as to whether the market abuse regime can properly be considered civil in character. It also reduces the likelihood that the issue will be tested, as it has considerably narrowed the grounds on which it could be argued that the safeguards associated with a criminal trial have not been provided.

In principle, the FSA has discretion as to the penalties it imposes for market abuse.[114] It is, however, required to issue a statement of policy with respect to the imposition of penalties and the amount of penalties. The policy must take account of:[115]

1. whether the relevant behaviour had an adverse effect on the market in question and, if so, how serious that effect was;
2. the extent to which that behaviour was deliberate or reckless; and
3. whether the person on whom the penalty is to be imposed is an individual.

The FSA's policy statement on penalties in market abuse cases is published at DEPP 6.3 in the FSA Handbook.

It is also possible for enforcement action to be taken against an authorised firm in respect of market abuse as, unlike the criminal offence of insider dealing, the market abuse regime applies to firms as well as individuals. Enforcement action against a firm may relate to failures in respect of its systems and controls in circumstances where the firm failed to take effective measures to prevent market abuse.[116]

The onset of the financial crisis in 2008 heightened long-standing concerns on both sides of the Atlantic that insider trading and market manipulation were rife despite regulatory rhetoric about a commitment to clean markets. This accusation was particularly relevant in the UK, where the tradition of 'light touch regulation' left the regulator open to the charge of not taking sufficiently seriously its role in protecting markets and investors

---

[111] FSMA 2000, s 134 provides for the creation of such a scheme. The Financial Services and Markets Tribunal was replaced by the Upper Tribunal (Tax and Chancery Chamber) in April 2010: see the Transfer of Tribunal Functions Order 2010, SI 2010/22.

[112] Section 174(2).

[113] Sections 171 and 172 require persons under investigation to answer questions.

[114] Section 123. The penalty of £17m imposed on Shell Transport and Trading Company plc—see www.fsa.gov.uk/Pages/Library/Communication/PR/2004/074.html (accessed on 20 November 2011)—is the largest penalty to date.

[115] Section 124(2).

[116] See FSA Decision Notice to Philippe Jabre and GLG Partners (28 February 2006).

from such practices. Prompted by such charges, it is evident that both the Securities and Exchange Commission (SEC) and the FSA have stepped up their enforcement activity in this area since the onset of the crisis, with both agencies launching a series of high-profile investigations that have targeted complex networks said to be operating among professional investors.[117] In the UK context at least, that approach represents new ground since in the past market abuse investigations have focused on simpler cases that have not implicated powerful players in the investor community.

13.4.9 Liability in civil law

Section 150 FSMA 2000 provides that a contravention by an authorised person of a rule[118] is actionable at the suit of a private person[119] who suffers loss as a result of the contravention, subject to the defences and other incidents applying to actions for breach of statutory duty.[120] It also provides that rules may prescribe circumstances in which this remedy is available to a non-private person.[121] The relevant rules provide that the remedy is available to institutional investors in respect of contraventions of rules that relate to dealing on the basis of unpublished price-sensitive information. There are, however, no recorded instances of the remedy having been pursued in those circumstances.

It has been held that shareholders who suffered loss as a result of market abuse represented by failure to disclose information to the market have no remedy against the company under FSMA 2000.[122] That surely cannot be right since section 150 FSMA 2000 provides a general remedy to private persons (for breach of statutory duty) in respect of contraventions of rules. While there are some exclusions (above), there is no general exclusion in respect of market abuse (see MAR 2.2.9 for a partial exclusion relating to buy-backs and stabilisation). Thus, it would seem wrong to conclude (as the Court did in the *Cable and Wireless* case[123]) (i) that the powers given by this section (and section 383) to the FSA to punish market abuse indicate that there was no intention on the part of Parliament to provide a remedy and (ii) that there is an 'absence of an express cause of action'.

---

[117] See the Herbert Smith briefing, above n 53. For SEC action, in particular the high-profile case against hedge fund Galleon, see http://www.sec.gov/spotlight/insidertrading.shtml.

[118] Listing rules, financial resources rules and short-selling rules are not rules for the purposes of this section: see s 150(4). Principles set out in the PRIN section of the FSA Handbook are also excluded: s 150(4) and PRIN 3.3.4R.

[119] Private person is defined by Art 3 of the FSMA 2000 (Rights of Action) Regulations 2001, SI 2001/2256. See *Titan Steel Wheels Ltd v The Royal Bank of Scotland Plc* [2010] EWHC 211 (Comm) for an unsuccessful attempt by a commercial company to bring itself within the definition of a private person (with the aim of pursuing a claim for losses on structured products which speculated on currency movements).

[120] This includes contributory negligence as a partial defence. See *Spreadex Ltd v Sanjit Sekhon* [2008] EWHC 1136 (Ch), where a customer was found to be 85% responsible for losses sustained on spread bets.

[121] The FSMA 2000 (Rights of Action) Regulations 2001, SI 2001/2256, Art 6.

[122] *Hall v Cable and Wireless Plc; Martin v Cable and Wireless Plc; Parry v Cable and Wireless Plc Queen's Bench Division (Commercial Court)* 21 July 2009 [2009] EWHC 1793 (Comm).

[123] Ibid.

13.5 Market regulation—short-selling

Short-selling is a technique whereby market participants attempt to profit from a fall in the price of a security. In essence, it involves the sale of a security (for future settlement) that one does not own in the expectation that it will subsequently be possible to buy the security in the market to satisfy the delivery obligation. A distinction can be drawn between naked short-selling and covered short-selling. In the former case, the short-seller relies entirely on liquidity in the market to buy the security to meet the delivery obligation. In the latter case, the short-seller 'borrows' the security from an institutional investor, sells it and then buys it back so as to return it to the investor.[124] Naked short-selling raises systemic risk concerns since there may be widespread failure to settle transactions should liquidity in the relevant securities suddenly dry up. Covered short-selling does not pose the same risk but does raise issues linked to the market abuse regime.

When the uncertainty associated with the financial crisis prompted increased market volatility in 2008, the capacity for short-selling to destabilise the shares of financial institutions who were engaged in capital raising, as well as the broader market, became apparent. It was clear in particular that, in some instances, short-selling was accompanied by the creation of false and misleading market rumours. In the UK, the FSA responded by introducing, on an emergency basis, a prohibition on short-selling of financial sector stocks and a disclosure obligation in respect of short positions.[125] The policy reason given by the FSA for the prohibition was that, while short-selling was 'a legitimate technique in normal market conditions',[126] it can be used to support abusive practices and may contribute to disorderly markets when 'herding' leads to prices overshooting in response to the signal that a share is overvalued.[127] Introduction of the disclosure obligation was justified on the basis that information about the aggregate short position in a single stock could help the market judge the extent to which short-selling is driving the price of that stock and in throwing light on the individual funds/participants who are engaged in short-selling.

The legal nature of the prohibition and disclosure obligation[128] was that either the creation of a short position or failure to disclose an existing position would constitute market abuse. While the prohibition was not renewed when it expired,[129] the disclosure obligation

---

[124] The arrangement with the institutional investor is referred to as 'stock-lending' and a fee is payable to the investor linked to the duration of the arrangement. Since securities are fungible, the short-seller need only return securities of the same class to the investor.

[125] The measures took effect on 18 September 2008: see FSA, 'Temporary Short Selling Measures', CP 09/1 (2009).

[126] That view reflects the potential for short-sellers to contribute to efficient price formation by exerting downward pressure on prices which they believe will fall in the future.

[127] FSA CP 09/1, above n 125, 4.

[128] The disclosure obligation is triggered when a net short position (representing an economic interest in the issued share capital of an issuer) exceeds or falls below 0.25, 0.35, 0.45 and 0.55%, and each 0.1% threshold thereafter. Disclosure in this context means public disclosure, not just disclosure to the regulator.

[129] On 16 January 2009.

was extended until June 2009 and then indefinitely.[130] The Financial Services Act 2010 gives the FSA broader powers to make rules on short-selling, including restrictions based on financial stability grounds.[131] At the EU level, a model for a pan-European short-selling disclosure regime has been proposed by CESR.[132] Also relevant in this context is the change in regulatory style that is now evident in the UK in the wake of the financial crisis and in particular the greater willingness on the part of the FSA to take enforcement action over alleged infringements of the market abuse regime.[133]

---

[130] See FSA, 'Extension of the Short Selling Disclosure Obligation', CP 09/15 (June 2009).

[131] See s 8 of the Act (inserting s 131B into FSMA 2000, with effect from 8 June 2010). Such rules do not fall within the FSMA 2000, s 150 remedy for breach of statutory duty. However, there is no express exclusion of the existing short-selling rules which were made under other provisions of FSMA 2000 (ss 119, 121, 149, 156 and 157(1)). It follows that the s 150 remedy is available in respect of breaches of those rules. See also Chapter 3.9.6.

[132] See CESR, 'Model for a Pan-European Short selling Disclosure Regime', CESR/10-088 (2010). It differs from the UK disclosure model in that it has a lower (0.2%) threshold for disclosure of short positions in shares to regulators and a higher threshold (0.5%) for public disclosure. See also the EU Commission proposal for a Regulation on Short Selling and certain aspects of Credit Default Swaps (COM(2010) 482 final), which follows the CESR model.

[133] See J Symington, 'The FSA and Enforcing the Market Abuse Regime' (FSA, November 2008) referring to credible deterrence and the role of criminal prosecutions.

14

Market Participants—Role and General Legal Principles

The term 'market participants' is used here to refer to persons who are involved in a professional capacity in the transaction of investment business. It excludes investors on the basis that their primary concern is with the ownership of investments. The term 'market participant' therefore applies to persons or organisations with a professional involvement in the process of investment. It covers stockbrokers, market-makers, custodians, central securities depositaries (CSDs), merchant banks, investment banks, commercial banks and credit rating agencies.[1] Persons involved in the transaction of investment business primarily in the 'retail market' (such as independent financial advisers and appointed representatives) are dealt with in Chapter 6.

Market participants differ from 'investors' in that, although they do sometimes act as investors in their own right,[2] they act more frequently in the role of agents for investors (eg a stockbroker) or as parties to a contract with investors (eg a market-maker). The nature of their business and the incentives under which they operate therefore differ from those of investors. Market participants are generally more concerned with valuation and trading of securities and transaction costs than with exercising ownership rights. This is because their role is primarily to facilitate the acquisition and transfer of ownership of investments by investors.

---

[1] Custodians and CSDs are categorised for this purpose as market participants rather than investors because, although they are often the registered owners of shares (and therefore the legal owners), they are not the beneficial owners of shares.

[2] Market-makers and other proprietary traders become owners of the securities they trade on their own account, but they generally hold these securities for very short periods. The purpose of their ownership is to provide liquidity to the market (and by doing so make trading profits) rather than to exercise ownership rights.

14.1 The role of market participants

Market participants are involved in the process of investment and undertake several different functions. Maturity transformation is undertaken primarily by commercial banks, though in some cases by investment funds. In the banking context, the transformation results from the taking of short-term deposits and using them to provide long-term loans such as mortgages. This process gives rise to liquidity risk in terms of the capacity of the bank to repay deposits as well as the inherent credit risk that arises from lending money. Execution services are provided by brokers and market-makers, and give rise mainly to counterparty risk. Advisory services are provided by brokers and investment banks (often within the same financial conglomerate), and relate to a wide range of matters, such as investment recommendations made to fund managers and corporate finance advice given to issuers of securities and companies considering major transactions such as a takeover.

14.1.1 Stockbrokers

Stockbrokers act as agents for investors in the purchase of securities.[3] Prior to the 'Big Bang' in 1986, the London Stock Exchange was organised on the basis of 'single capacity'. This meant that the function of market-makers (or 'jobbers' as they were then known) was separated from that of brokers.[4] Investors were not permitted to transact business directly with market-makers,[5] so had to use a broker. When a 'dual capacity' system was introduced in 1986, permitting the functions of broker and market-maker to be performed by the same organisation,[6] institutional investors were able to deal directly (on a principal-to-principal basis) with market-makers.[7]

Stockbrokers also perform the function of acting as sponsor (or corporate stockbroker) for listed companies. The Listing Rules require that each listed company appoint a sponsor whose role is to liaise between the UKLA and listed companies and to advise the companies on compliance.[8]

---

[3] In that capacity they undertake the regulated activities of dealing in investments as an agent and arranging deals in investments. If they offer discretionary portfolio management to clients they also require permission to manage investments. See Chapter 3.5.

[4] Historically, the London Stock Exchange did not always require single capacity. See R Michie, *The London Stock Exchange, A History* (Oxford, Oxford University Press, 1999) 113–15.

[5] Historically, this prohibition did not prevent market-makers having direct contact with investors in overseas markets; see Michie, ibid.

[6] Commonly referred to as a 'broker-dealer', following the practice in the US, which already permitted dual capacity firms.

[7] For an account of the Big Bang see J Littlewood, *The Stockmarket, Fifty Years of Capitalism at Work* (London, Pitman, 1998) ch 27.

[8] FSA Handbook, LR 8.2.1R requires primary listed companies to have a sponsor. See further Chapter 8.2.2.

14.1.2 Market-makers

Market-makers trade as principals in securities on exchanges where they are members.[9] They are required to register with the relevant exchange the securities in which they trade and then become subject to an obligation to make a continuous two-way (buy/sell) market in those securities.[10] It is this requirement that provides liquidity to the market. The quote must be made in the minimum number of shares applicable to that security (normal market size). The 'spread' between the bid and offer prices is the profit made by the market-maker and is determined by competition in the market.

As members of an exchange, market-makers are subject to the rules of the exchange and may also be subject to regulatory rules made under the Financial Services and Markets Act 2000 (FSMA 2000), depending on the type of person they deal with. Institutional investors dealing on a principal-to-principal basis with market-makers will typically be classified as professional clients unless they choose to be treated as eligible counterparties.

14.1.3 Custodians

Custodians safeguard and administer assets on behalf of others.[11] A substantial proportion of securities are now held through custodians, the main attractions being:

1. security of paper documents of title from loss or theft;
2. specialist services, such as record-keeping, valuation and performance measurement;
3. savings in transaction costs resulting from the custodian's investment in specialist systems and the possibility of some transfers of securities being effected simply by changes in the records of the custodian; and
4. the simplification of legal and regulatory issues by holding securities through a custodian established in the country of the issuer.

A distinction can be drawn between intermediary and non-intermediary custody.[12] The former refers to the deposit with a custodian of a share certificate or certificate of negotiable securities indorsed to the investor. In this situation, there remains a direct link between the issuer of the security and the investor because the investor remains the legal owner of the security.[13] Non-intermediary custody refers to a situation in which a custodian becomes the legal owner of the relevant securities (eg the registered owner of

---

[9] They require authorisation to engage in the regulated activity of dealing in investments as principal (see Chapter 3.5).

[10] See 'Market-Makers Rules' in London Stock Exchange, 'Rules of the London Stock Exchange', available at http://www.londonstockexchange.com/traders-and-brokers/rules-regulations/rules-lse-2011.pdf (accessed on 12 August 2011) 55.

[11] They require authorisation to engage in this activity: see Chapter 3.5.

[12] See generally M Yates and G Montagu, *The Law of Global Custody*, 3rd edn (Haywards Heath, Tottel, 2009).

[13] This form of custody was traditionally termed 'bailment'.

company shares). In this situation, the direct ownership link between the issuer and the ultimate investor is broken.

This is not to say that the investor in non-intermediary custody becomes irrelevant. Three mechanisms ensure that the investor continues to have a significant link with the investment. First, the custody contract between investor and custodian will often specify the manner in which the custodian is to hold the investment on behalf of the investor. Such rights are, however, personal in nature and do not give the investor an ownership link with the investment.[14] Secondly, it will often be clear from the circumstances in which custody is created that a custodian holds investments on trust for the investor, with the result that the investor has a beneficial interest in the rights held by the custodian.[15] This will be the case even if it is not possible for the existence of the beneficial interest of the investor to be formally recorded.[16] Thirdly, the relevant rules in the Financial Services Authority (FSA) Handbook (COBS and CASS) protect the investor by creating a number of safeguards in the creation and performance of custody.

Non-intermediary custody can be either single- or multi-tier. The former, as the name suggests, involves a single custodian holding legal title to investments in which the investor has a beneficial interest. Multi-tier custody (or 'sub-custody') involves more than one custodian holding investments on behalf of an investor. Such arrangements are common in respect of overseas investments, with local custodians often being used by a global custodian (or 'lead custodian') to simplify investment in a particular country, region or category of security. As immobilisation of securities is often encountered in overseas investment, it will also often be the case that the local custodian holds through a central securities depositary that is the legal owner of the securities.

Two critical issues arise in non-intermediary custody: first, what is the nature of the investor's interest in the investment, and secondly, what rights does the investor have against the custodian(s)? Many different contractual permutations are possible, but several general points can be made:

1. The investor will usually have a contractual relationship with only one custodian (the 'lead custodian').
2. It will often be possible to infer the creation of a trust at each level of custody, with each party's respective interest being passed down to the investor.[17]
3. Each investor shares common ownership of the pool of a particular security held by the custodian. When an investor deposits securities with the custodian, he has a claim to have returned an equal amount of the same securities, but not the same securities that were deposited. In other words, the pool held by the custodian for investors in

---

[14] See N Papasyrou, 'Immobilisation of Securities—Part Two: Personal Rights of Indirect Holders' (1996) 11 *Journal of International Banking Law* 459.

[15] See Yates and Monatgu, above n 12, chs 1 and 3.

[16] Section 126 of the Companies Act 2006 prevents any beneficial interest from being recorded in the shareholders' register of a company registered in England.

[17] See J Benjamin, *Interests in Securities* (Oxford, Oxford University Press, 2000).

a particular security comprises fungibles and the investor has no right to require the return of the deposited securities in specie.[18]

4. Because there are separate trusts at each level, only the lead custodian owes a fiduciary duty to the investor.
5. It is possible for the fiduciary duty owed by a custodian to be modified by contract.[19]
6. The existence of a trust in principle precludes the custody assets being claimed by creditors of the custodian should the custodian become insolvent, although problems may arise if the investments are held in a pooled fund that does not have segregated client-specific holdings.

While some of these issues remain subject to some doubt in the UK,[20] other jurisdictions have adopted measures to clarify matters. This is particularly true of the nature of the investor's interest in a pool of securities held by a custodian for investors. In the US, a revised version of Article 8 of the Uniform Commercial Code[21] makes clear that investors have (real) property rights in securities held on their behalf by custodians, not merely personal claims.[22] Belgium and Luxembourg have adopted similar measures, primarily to support the operations of major custodians with headquarters in those countries who hold in custody a large proportion of internationally traded securities.[23]

14.1.4 Central securities depositories

CSDs are a key component of systems of immobilised securities.[24] They hold legal title to immobilised securities and record transfers between the underlying investors. Such transfers have no effect on the legal ownership of immobilised securities, which remain with the depository, but give the ultimate investor an ownership right in relation to the deposited securities.[25] Depositories differ from custodians as legal title to immobilised

---

[18] See R Goode, 'The Nature and Transfer of Rights in Dematerialised and Immobilised Securities' in F Oditah (ed), *The Future for the Global Securities Market: Legal and Regulatory Aspects* (Oxford, Oxford University Press, 1996) ch 7.

[19] *Kelly v Cooper* [1993] AC 205. Exclusions of liability in standard form documentation are subject to a reasonableness test under s 3 (England) and s 17 (Scotland) of the Unfair Contract Terms Act 1977. Benjamin, above n 17, 45 notes that it is customary for custodians to accept liability for ordinary negligence.

[20] See Financial Markets Law Committee, 'Property Interests in Investment Securities' (2004), available at www.fmlc.org (accessed on 20 November 2011), for background and proposals to clarify the legal regime in the UK.

[21] The UCC is a uniform law intended for separate enactment by each state of the US. The revised Art 8 has been enacted in almost all the states of the USA: see SL Schwarcz, 'Intermediary Risk in a Global Economy' (2001) 50 *Duke Law Journal* 1541.

[22] Regarding the distinction between real and personal rights see Chapter 1.2. Art 8 UCC makes clear that an account entry represents a proprietary right that can be vindicated by an investor if a custodian becomes insolvent.

[23] On the legal and technical arrangements for holding securities in the EU see generally the First Giovannini Report, 'Cross Border Clearing and Settlement Arrangements in the European Union' (2001), available at http://ec.europa.eu/internal_market/financial-markets/docs/clearing/first_giovannini_report_en.pdf (accessed on 12 August 2011).

[24] See Chapter 1.2 for an explanation of the principle of immobilisation.

[25] In English law, this takes the form of beneficial ownership. See Goode, above n 18, 125. In other legal systems an account entry may give an investor legal ownership of the relevant securities,

securities always remains with the relevant depository, whereas it may be transferred between custodians.

CSDs are found in countries in which issuers of securities in immobilised form are resident. In the US, a large proportion of securities are issued in this form and are held by the Depositary Trust & Clearing Corporation. In the UK, Euroclear (which has absorbed the CREST settlement system) provides depositary services, but the CREST system operates on the basis of dematerialisation rather than immobilisation.[26]

14.1.5 Merchant and investment banks

The terms 'merchant' and 'investment' bank are sometimes used interchangeably nowadays but their derivation reflects different regulatory and corporate finance traditions in the UK and USA. Merchant banks in the UK were historically merchants who diversified into banking principally through the provision of finance.[27] The Accepting Houses Committee developed from this background as a body representing their interests as acceptors[28] of Bills of Exchange, which were commonly used as a means of payment in international trade. The merchant banks were also historically involved in taking deposits and making short-term loans, principally in connection with international trade. Corporate finance became an important part of the business of merchant banks that were members of the Issuing Houses Association.

Investment banks in the US were so named so as to distinguish them from commercial banks during the period when there was a prohibition on combining banking and securities business. That prohibition was introduced by the Glass-Steagall Act 1934 in the wake of the Wall Street Crash of 1929 as a result of concern over the involvement of commercial banks in the speculative stockmarket boom of the late 1920s.

Two developments led to the distinction between merchant and investment banks on the one hand and commercial banks on the other becoming blurred. First, the relaxation of ownership restrictions in the London Stock Exchange, combined with the 'Big Bang' in 1986, meant that it was possible for financial conglomerates to be formed in the UK comprising merchant and commercial banking, broker-dealing in securities and fund management. Conglomerates also emerged in the US. While the Glass-Steagall Act of 1934 prohibited the combination of banking and securities business, its effect was mitigated by exceptions and liberal court decisions.[29] The partial repeal[30] of the Act in

---

[26] See Chapter 12.6.3. CREST does not operate on the basis of immobilisation as CREST members have direct legal ownership of securities within the CREST system and are shown as the registered holder in the issuer's records. In the case of shares, this means that the CREST member is a member (shareholder) in the company.

[27] See generally C Clay and B Wheble, *Modern Merchant Banking* (Cambridge, Woodhead-Faulkner, 1976).

[28] See s 54 of the Bills of Exchange Act 1882 for more detail on the position of an acceptor of a bill of exchange.

[29] See R Cranston, *Principles of Banking Law*, 2nd edn (Oxford, Oxford University Press, 2002) 99.

[30] As a result of the Gramm-Leach-Bliley Act of 1999 (also referred to as the Financial Services Act of 1999). See generally KA Summe, 'The repeal of Glass-Steagall and the Modernisation of the US Financial System' (2000) 21 *Company Lawyer* 189.

1999 further assisted the emergence of conglomerates. Whether one now refers to such conglomerates as merchant or investment banks makes little difference in most cases.

A major concern resulting from the combination of a number of different functions in a single organisation is the possibility that the interests of different clients may differ and the organisation may find itself unable to serve all those interests simultaneously. That issue is addressed by fiduciary duties under the common law (below) and by FSA regulatory rules (Chapter 15).

The involvement of investment banks in securities markets takes a number of different forms. First, they often act as financial advisers to companies whose shares are being listed.[31] The Listing Rules require that an applicant for a premium listing must have a sponsor, who needs to be authorised under FSMA 2000 to undertake that function.[32] In this capacity, they organise the writing of the prospectus and assume responsibility (and therefore also legal liability) for some of the contents of the prospectus.[33] They often also act as underwriter of the share issue made by such a company at the time of listing.[34] Secondly, investment banks often acts as stockbrokers and market-makers.[35] They assumed this role when the Stock Exchange relaxed the ownership restrictions for member firms in the early 1980s and many of the previously independent stockbroking and jobbing firms were bought by banks.

More recently, 'prime brokerage' has become a major part of the activity of many investment banks. This is a market term and has no precise meaning for legal or regulatory purposes. However, the nature of the activities typically undertaken by a prime broker brings them within the regulatory perimeter of FSMA 2000. Prime brokers aim to provide a range of services to hedge funds so as to enable the fund managers to focus on the core activity of investment strategy and selection. The core services offered by prime brokers include: the provision of credit lines to enable funds to leverage their positions or meet short-term obligations, stock-lending,[36] custody,[37] and clearing and settlement.[38]

While 'prime brokerage' itself is not a regulated activity, the core services are within the regulatory perimeter, with the result that supervision is undertaken by the FSA and the overall regulatory capital position of the investment bank must take account of those activities.

---

[31] This is a regulated activity under FSMA 2000: see Chapter 8.1.4.

[32] See n 8 above. The nominated adviser (NOMAD) required for admission to AIM requires similar authorisation.

[33] Principally any profit-forecast included in the prospectus. See further Chapter 8.4.

[34] Underwriting is a regulated activity under FSMA 2000: see Chapter 3.5.

[35] These are regulated activities under FSMA 2000: see Chapter 3.5.

[36] See Chapter 13.5 for the meaning of this term.

[37] See *Re Lehman Brothers International (Europe) (In Administration)*, also known as *Lomas v Rab Market Cycles (Master) Fund Ltd* [2009] EWHC 2545 (Ch), holding that the proper construction of a prime brokerage agreement was that the counterparty to the agreement retained a beneficial interest in the securities held by the broker as custodian and in cash derived from those securities. As a result, the counterparty was a secured creditor for both cash and securities in the broker's administration.

[38] See further Chapter 12.5 and 12.6. Prime brokers may act as intermediaries for hedge funds in clearing and settlement systems.

14.1.6 Commercial banks

Commercial banks are those whose business is primarily lending money raised from deposits or from other banks.[39] Commercial banking business is regulated mainly through the system of prudential supervision, which focuses on the solvency of financial institutions. Historically, the Bank of England was responsible for the authorisation and supervision of banking business, but this role was transferred to the FSA in 1998.[40]

Increasingly, however, commercial banks also have an involvement in the investment markets, through stockbroking, fund management, or life assurance and pensions subsidiaries. When they carry on such business they are subject to the relevant regulatory regime, in addition to the system of prudential supervision that applies to banking. In particular, the regulatory provisions relating to material interests and conflicts of interest are applicable when the bank acts in different capacities for different clients or acts as a principal in a transaction with a client. A common pattern in recent years has been for banks to act as a sales outlet for a life assurance and pensions company with which they have an ownership link, an arrangement commonly referred to as 'bancassurance'.[41]

14.1.7 Credit-rating agencies

Credit-rating agencies are private-sector organisations that assess the likelihood of timely payment on debt securities.[42] They have been described as 'the universally feared gatekeepers for the issuance and trading of debt securities'.[43] Investors in domestic and international debt securities[44] markets increasingly rely on the credit rating attached to an issue of such securities. It avoids the need for investors to engage in their own assessment of creditworthiness. Rating agencies use similar, though not identical, ratings. Standard & Poor's ratings for long-term debt securities can be referred to as an example. Their highest rating is AAA, followed by AA, A, BBB and below. Marginal modifications within these ratings are indicated by the attachment of + and – designations. The higher the rating, the lower the risk of default associated with the particular issue.[45] Ratings below BBB– are deemed 'non-investment grade' (or 'junk bonds'), indicating considerable risk associated with full and timely payment on the securities. This categorisation can have considerable

---

[39] Banks lend to each other in the 'inter-bank' money market, also referred to as the wholesale money market.

[40] Under proposals brought forward by the government in 2010, responsibility for banking supervision will return to the Bank of England, within which a new Prudential Regulation Authority will be established: see Chapter 3.1.

[41] See Chapter 6.1.

[42] The best-known credit rating agencies are Standard & Poor's, Moody's Investors Service Inc and Fitch Investors Service Inc, all based in the US, but with worldwide operations. See K Pilbeam, *Finance and Financial Markets*, 3rd edn (Basingstoke, Palgrave Macmillan, 2010) ch 6.18 for a more detailed description of the rating systems used by Moody's and Standard & Poor's.

[43] S Schwarcz, 'Private Ordering of Public Markets: The Rating Agency Paradox' [2002] *University of Illinois Law Review* 1, 2.

[44] Including sovereign debt. As illustrated by the Eurozone crisis, changes to credit ratings attached to sovereign debt may carry serious consequences for interest rates and currencies. See D Zandstra, 'The European Sovereign Debt Crisis and Its Evolving Resolution' (2011) 6(3) *Capital Markets Law Journal* 285.

[45] A rating relates to a particular issue of debt securities and not the creditworthiness of the issuer.

implications for the type of investor who is able to purchase such securities and may increase the interest rate payable by a borrower.[46]

Credit ratings are generally solicited by and paid for by issuers of debt securities. This undoubtedly creates a potential conflict of interest in that there may be a temptation to overstate the capacity of the issuer to meet its obligations. In reality, the concern of the agencies with their reputation has often resulted in this potential conflict of interest being subordinated to the need to maintain their reputation in the market.[47] The freedom afforded to rating agencies to issue unsolicited ratings has been challenged as abusive in the US (on the basis that they effectively force unwilling issuers to pay for a rating), but has been upheld on the basis of the US constitutional provisions relating to freedom of speech and the press.[48] The liability of rating agencies for negligence is a matter that appears to be untested in the UK courts. In the US, the courts have held that, in order for liability to be attached to a rating agency, it must be shown that they acted recklessly and not simply negligently.[49]

Outside the US,[50] credit rating agencies were not regulated prior to the crisis.[51] However, they formed a material part of the regulatory structure since, as the FSA commented, 'the regulatory framework places significant reliance on external ratings as part of the calculation of capital requirements under the Capital Requirements Directive'.[52] In that sense, a significant aspect of capital adequacy regulation was contracted out to private organisations whose initial allocation of credit ratings and subsequent changes (especially downgrades) would carry serious implications for the entire global financial system, especially as leverage increased over time.

Prior to the financial crisis, investors relied to an inappropriate extent on credit ratings in making investment decisions, especially in the case of structured finance products such as CDOs,[53] where credit ratings in many cases became a substitute for fundamental analysis and due diligence by investors.[54] Over-reliance on credit ratings was also evident

[46] For example, insurance companies and investment funds may be restricted to investment in 'investment-grade' debt securities.

[47] See Schwarcz, above n 43, 13, citing research on the long-term default rates of debt securities with different credit ratings. However, the recent record of the rating agencies is less impressive: see FSA, 'The Turner Review, A Regulatory Response to the Global Banking Crisis' (March 2009) 76, available at http://www.fsa.gov.uk/Pages/Library/Corporate/turner/index.shtml, regarding the role of overstated credit ratings in the financial crisis.

[48] See Schwarcz, above n 43, 17.

[49] See the cases cited by Schwarcz, ibid, fn 78.

[50] See T Möllers, 'Regulating Credit Rating Agencies: The New US and EU Law—Important Steps or Much Ado about Nothing?' (2009) 4 *Capital Markets Law Journal* 477, for a comparison of the US and EU approaches.

[51] While Art 81 of the Capital Requirements Directive (2006/48 [2006] OJ L177/1) required that credit ratings used in connection with the risk weighting of assets (for the purposes of the calculation of regulatory capital) be issued by a rating agency that was recognised as 'eligible' by at least a single Member State, this process did not amount to licensing or supervision in a form comparable to that imposed on banks, insurers and investment firms under the EU regulatory regime.

[52] FSA, 'A Regulatory Response to the Global Banking Crisis', Discussion Paper 09/2 (March 2009) para 1.57, available at http://www.fsa.gov.uk/pubs/discussion/dp09_02.pdf.

[53] Collateralised debt obligations. These instruments are a technique for repackaging underlying debt obligations for onward sale to investors in the form of asset-backed bonds.

[54] FSA Regulatory Response, above n 52, para 1.54.

in the operation of the financial guarantee insurance market, where ratings of both the insurers and the underlying credit risk covered by guarantees were the main drivers of the market.[55] While these considerations alone raised serious concerns about the central role that credit ratings occupied, they were given further weight by the conflicts of interest that are faced by the credit rating agencies. These conflicts arise from the business model operated by the agencies under which they charge issuers for ratings and are often (particularly in the case of innovative products in structured finance) employed to provide consulting services in respect of the products that they will rate.[56] The risk in such cases, even where there are internal processes for managing conflicts, is that the agency provides a favourable rating to an issuer to secure fees.[57] For the system as a whole, this has the effect both of overpricing the relevant products at the outset and of creating the potential for systemic instability as a wave of selling by investors follows subsequent downgrades.[58]

The relatively rapid adoption by the EC authorities of a regulation[59] on credit rating agencies in 2009 reflected the causal impact of credit ratings in the financial crisis,[60] the relatively undeveloped state of EC regulation and the rather weak 'comply or explain' framework adopted by the International Organisation of Securities Commissioners (IOSCO) Code of Conduct,[61] which relies on voluntary compliance. The new EU framework is based on registration and supervision, undertaken primarily by the national authority in the country where registration is sought[62] but with a role for the European Securities and Markets Authority,[63] to which the application is to be made in the first instance, and for a college of supervisors drawn from the competent authorities of Member States in which the activities of the credit rating agency is likely to have a significant impact. Among the requirements for registration are important provisions relating to conflicts of interest and disclosure of credit-rating methodology.

The new regulatory regime is also viewed by the EU authorities as a means to tackle the lack of qualitative competition in the market for credit ratings since regulatory approval (combined with increasing convergence between the US and EC regimes) has the capacity to overcome the entry barrier for new entrants posed by their lack of

---

[55] See the Joint Forum (comprising the Basel Committee, the International Organisation of Securities Commissioners and the International Association of Insurance Supervisors), 'Differentiated Nature of Financial Regulation' (January 2010) 78, available at http://www.bis.org/publ/joint24.pdf.

[56] See F Partnoy, 'How and Why Credit Rating Agencies Are Not Like Other Gatekeepers', available at http://ssrn.com/abstract=900257.

[57] Ibid, 70.

[58] Some institutional investors may be forced to sell by their investment mandate following downgrades, contributing to a downward spiral.

[59] Regulation (EC) 1060/2009 [2009] OJ L302/1, implemented in the UK by the Credit Rating Agencies Regulations 2010, SI 2010/906 with effect from 7 June 2010.

[60] See Recital 10 of the Regulation.

[61] See IOSCO, 'Code of Conduct Fundamentals for Credit Rating Agencies', available at http://www.iosco.org/library/pubdocs/pdf/IOSCOPD173.pdf.

[62] The primacy of national regulators is reflected in the fact that the registration decision (Art 14(4)) and enforcement measures (Art 23) are reserved to the competent national authority, albeit subject to consultation obligations.

[63] This replaced the Committee of European Securities Regulators with effect from 1 January 2011: see further Chapter 2.9.4.

market reputation. However, even the Regulation itself recognises the initial and provisional nature of the regulatory regime that it creates: there remain important issues to be clarified and developed, especially as regards the boundary between consulting and credit rating activities, the capacity of individual Member States to supervise credit rating agencies, and the appropriateness of the existing rating recommendations and symbols for structured finance products.[64]

14.2 Private law claims

While market participants are subject to regulatory rules that carry important implications for the manner in which they conduct business with customers, private law remains of considerable significance, not least because the intensity of regulation with regard to transactions in the wholesale market is less intense than in the retail market. While, in principle, a distinction can be drawn between private law claims and the enforcement of regulatory rules, there may well be overlap between the two categories. The overlap may arise in three ways. First, it is possible for regulatory obligations to shape the content of contractual duties.[65] Secondly, breach of a regulatory duty may also represent a tort/delict, thereby giving rise to a private law claim. Thirdly, there may be a direct claim for loss resulting from breach of the regulatory rule.[66]

The most common forms of common law claims relating to financial transactions are considered below.

14.2.1 Choice of jurisdiction and governing law

So far as transactions with an international (including EU) dimension are concerned, the possibility of bringing a private law claim before the UK courts[67] is linked to the issue of whether the UK courts have jurisdiction over the matter. In the case of persons (including legal persons) domiciled[68] in Member States of the EU, jurisdiction is determined by the

---

[64] See Möllers, above n 50, 499–500.

[65] This can result from incorporation by reference of regulatory duties or the process of interpretation and construction of contracts by the courts.

[66] See Chapter 3.9.6.

[67] A distinction should be drawn for this purpose between the three legal systems in the UK: England & Wales, Scotland and Northern Ireland. While all three are bound by the EU jurisdiction regulation, cases falling outside the regulation are governed by the common law applicable to each jurisdiction.

[68] As applied to the UK, the domicile of a company is the location of the registered office or the place of incorporation. For other Member States, the domicile of a company is determined by the location of its 'statutory seat': see Art 60 of the regulation (below n 69). In the case of individuals, domicile is determined by the internal law of the Member State seised of the matter.

EU Jurisdiction Regulation.[69] This established a general principle that such persons may (subject to the provisions of the Regulation) be sued in the courts of the Member State of their domicile. However, the Regulation recognises the principle of party autonomy in connection with jurisdiction and provides (subject to some exceptions) that the parties can determine which Member State's courts are to have jurisdiction over matters covered by their agreement.[70] That principle was applied in the case of *Maple Leaf Macro Volatility Master Fund v Rouvroy and Trylinski*.[71] The issues may be more complicated where there are a series of linked transactions with different jurisdiction provisions.[72] Where there is no agreement as to jurisdiction, persons domiciled in a Member State may be sued in matters relating to contract in the courts for the place of performance of the obligation in question.[73] In the case of tort/delict claims jurisdiction, the default rule is that the courts of the place where the harmful event occurred has jurisdiction.[74]

The determination of the governing law for a contract is a separate matter from the determination of jurisdiction. The governing law determines which system of law is to apply for the purposes of determining matters of substantive law related to a contract such as its validity, interpretation, performance and breach. The governing law applies irrespective of which court has jurisdiction over the matter. The governing law is determined by the EU Rome I Regulation,[75] which superseded the Rome Convention of 1980 on the Law

[69] Council Regulation 44/2001/EC [2001] OJ L12/1. The regulation superseded the Brussels Convention of 1968. Its status as a regulation means that it is directly applicable in Member States without need for implementation into national law.

[70] Art 23 of the regulation. An express jurisdiction clause is not required. It is sufficient that the natural interpretation of a contractual provision suggests that a choice has been made: *7E Communications Ltd v Vertex Antennentechnik GmbH* [2007] 1 WLR 2175.

[71] [2009] EWHC 257 (Comm). The court also had jurisdiction under Art 23 by virtue of the English jurisdiction clause in the funding agreement. The defendants did not enter the funding agreement as consumers and Art 15 did not apply. In the case of the claims in deceit, the court had jurisdiction under Art 5 because the harmful event occurred in England as that was where the plaintiff suffered its damage when it committed itself to accepting the deal and sending its subscription form.

[72] In *UBS v HSH Nordank AG* [2009] EWCA Civ 585, an action was brought in England by HSH for a negative declaration relating to jurisdiction over a range of claims made by HSH alleging mis-selling and mis-management in connection with the sale of collateralised debt obligations (CDOs). The case was complicated by the presence of different jurisdiction and governing law provisions at different levels of the transaction, thus leaving the court with two main issues to settle: first, the allocation of the dispute to the relevant level of the transaction: and secondly, the resolution of conflict between overlapping jurisdiction clauses. In approaching these issues, the court stressed that 'the essential task is to construe the jurisdiction agreement in the light of the transaction as a whole' and 'Where there are numerous jurisdiction agreements which may overlap, the parties must be presumed to be acting commercially, and not to intend that similar claims should be the subject of inconsistent jurisdiction clauses'. In this instance, the court decided that the New York jurisdiction clause contained in the agreements that represented the commercial centre of the transaction applied to all disputes arising from the transaction and thereby made the negative declaration in favour of HSH (which had simultaneously initiated proceedings in New York).

[73] That may raise difficult questions in the case of financial contracts, and it is for that reason that many contain express jurisdiction clauses. The regulation provides that the place of performance of the obligation is 'in the case of the provision of services, the place in a Member State where, under the contract, the services were provided or should have been provided' (Art 5(1)(b)).

[74] Art 5(3), giving effect to the principle of *lex locus delicti*.

[75] EC Regulation 593/2008 [2008] OJ L177/6. In the case of non-contractual claims, the governing law is determined by the Rome II Regulation EC/864/2007 [2007] OJ L199/40, which permits a choice of law in limited circumstances and otherwise sets the governing law by reference to the principle of *lex locus delicti*.

Applicable to Contractual Obligations. Rome I provides a complete system[76] of conflict of law rules for EU Member States and required changes to be made to the law in the UK.[77] Rome I recognises the principle of party autonomy and permits the parties to choose the applicable law.[78] Such a choice can be made expressly or by implication, and can relate to the whole or part of the contract. Where no choice of law is made by the parties, the contract is governed by the law of the country with which it is most closely connected.[79] The principle of 'characteristic performance'[80] is adopted by Rome I as a proxy for the closest connection, but even that principle does not necessarily resolve the uncertainty that may exists with regard to international financial contracts that may be connected with many countries by reference to currencies, stock exchanges, standard contract terms and location of traders. For that reason, an express choice of law is favoured in standard financial market documentation as a means of providing certainty as to governing law. In some contexts that certainty may be essential for proper pricing of a contract (eg where the substantive law of different systems which might be the governing law in the absence of choice differs in relation to the rights of the contracting parties).

14.2.2 Contract

Contracts are based on the consent of each party, freely given. When consent is not freely given, the law responds by providing, in effect, that the innocent party is released from the obligations contained in the contract. There are two main circumstances in which this can occur.

The first is where one party breaches a condition precedent to the contract.[81] The essence of such a condition is that it has to be satisfied before a contract comes into existence.[82] For example, it might be made a condition precedent to a contract that a

---

[76] The universal application is made clear by Art 1(1): 'This Regulation shall apply, in situations involving a conflict of laws, to contractual obligations in civil and commercial matters.' Thus, there is no limitation of scope by reference to matters such as domicile (as in the case of jurisdiction).

[77] See the Law Applicable to Contractual Obligations (England and Wales and Northern Ireland) Regulations 2009 (SI 2009/3064). Regulation 2 disapplies in relation to England and Wales and Northern Ireland the Contracts (Applicable Law) Act 1990 as regards contracts concluded on or after 17 December 2009. Regulation 2(a) of the Law Applicable to Contractual Obligations (Scotland) Regulations 2009/410 (Scottish SI) does the same for Scotland. These contracts are now dealt with under Rome I. The 1990 Act gave effect to the 1980 Rome Convention in the UK. After the commencement of Rome I, that Convention will only apply to contracts concluded before the commencement of Rome I.

[78] Art 3 of the Rome I Regulation.

[79] Art 4(1) of the Rome I Regulation. So far as the UK is concerned, the reference to country means the three legal systems in the UK, with the result that Rome I generally applies to conflicts of law within the UK: see regulation 5 of the Law Applicable to Contractual Obligations (England and Wales and Northern Ireland) Regulations 2009 (SI 2009/3064).

[80] Art 4(2) of the Rome I Regulation.

[81] In Scots law, this is referred to as a contract subject to a suspensive condition. See W McBryde, *Contract*, 3rd edn (Edinburgh, Thomas W Green, 2007) para 5-35.

[82] See *Bettini v Gye* (1876) 1 QB 183 and *Murdoch & Co Ltd v Greig* (1889) 16 R 396 for analysis of the law in England and Scotland respectively.

borrower or an issuer of shares has no outstanding litigation being pursued against it.[83] If the condition is not satisfied, there can be no contract because the consent of each party is predicated on the satisfaction of the condition. Breach of a condition precedent therefore may result in there being no contract and no obligations on either side.

The second is where a seller of a financial product makes a misrepresentation that induces a customer to enter into a contract. A distinction is drawn between misrepresentations that are made fraudulently (intentionally), negligently and innocently. In each case, the innocent party is entitled to rescind the contract.[84] Rescission involves the innocent party giving notice to the other party that he regards the contract as terminated. The legal nature of rescission is that the contract is voidable, meaning that it remains valid until set aside by the process of rescission. For this to occur, each party must be able to restore to the other benefits that have been obtained under the contract (*restitutio in integrum*). For example, in the case of a sale of shares induced by misrepresentation, the buyer would be required to transfer the shares to the seller in return for repayment of the purchase price.

A misrepresentation has no effect unless it is material and induces the other party to enter the contract.[85] That issue was considered in *Bankers Trust International plc vs PT Dharmala Sakti Sejahtera*,[86] a case involving an interest rate swap. The court concluded, on the basis of the facts, that a case for rescission had not been established. In explaining the circumstances in which a misrepresentation might be made, Mance J said:

> A description or commendation which may obviously be irrelevant or may even serve as a warning to one recipient, because of its generality, superficiality or laudatory nature, or because of the recipient's own knowledge and experience, may constitute a material representation if made to another less informed or sophisticated receiver.[87]

The relevance of the recipient's actual and apparent expertise in the assessment of whether a misrepresentation was made was explained as follows:

> Whether there was any and if so what particular representation must thus depend on an objective assessment of the likely effect of the proposal or presentation on the recipient. In making such an assessment, it is necessary to consider the recipient's characteristics and knowledge as they appeared, or ought to have appeared, to the maker of the proposal or presentation. A recipient holding himself out as able to understand and evaluate complicated proposals would be expected to be able to do so, whatever his actual abilities.[88]

This case suggests that the courts are likely to take a more robust view of transactions between commercial organisations dealing with each other as principals than they would

---

[83] See eg s 2(a)(iii) of the ISDA Master Agreement, which makes it a condition precedent to a party's payment and delivery obligations that an actual or potential event of default is not then current with respect to the other party.

[84] As regards English law, see E Peel *Treitel, The Law of Contract*, 12th edn (London, Sweet & Maxwell, 2007) 401–03; as regards Scots law, see McBryde, above n 81, paras 15-66–15-73.

[85] See eg *Raiffeisen Zentralbank Osterreich AG v Royal Bank of Scotland* [2010] EWHC 1392 (Comm).

[86] [1996] CLC 518. For a discussion of this case see T Little, 'Suitability the Courts and the Code' (1996) *European Financial Services Law Review* 119; S Greene, 'Suitability and the Emperor's New Clothes' (1996) *European Financial Services Law Review* 53.

[87] At 530.

[88] Ibid.

do if one party were a private investor. A similar approach is evident in respect of the issue of whether a duty of care is owed by one party to the other in the context of principal-to-principal transactions between commercial organisations.[89]

Claims based on breach of contract are also possible, but do not feature significantly in the reported cases. This may be explained to some extent by the use of mechanisms that protect against the effect of breach of contract. They include the taking of security to cover loans or, in the case of exchange-traded derivatives, the practice of requiring 'margin' to be paid by reference to value of the relevant instrument. Another factor is the effect of netting,[90] which permits relevant debts due by A to B to be offset against the relevant claims of A against B. All these mechanisms help to mitigate the effect of a breach of contract on the financial position of the innocent counterparty and limit the need to resort to litigation to recover losses.

14.2.3 Tort/delict[91]

Claims arising in tort in respect of financial transactions are most likely to be for damages in respect of misrepresentation. It is possible, when the innocent party has suffered loss, for damages to be recovered in respect of fraudulent and negligent misrepresentations. Such a claim can be pursued either as an alternative to or in addition to a claim for rescission of a contract as a result of misrepresentation.[92] In the case of an innocent misrepresentation, no damages are available in Scotland,[93] but in England damages may be awarded in lieu of rescission.[94]

The general conditions applicable to a claim in damages for negligent misrepresentation were established in the case of *Hedley Byrne & Co Ltd v Heller.*[95] The plaintiff in that case suffered a loss as a result of extending credit to a firm in reliance on a banker's reference given by the defendant. While the decision in the case was that the defendant bank was not liable as the reference was given 'without responsibility', the House of Lords clarified the circumstances in which liability would arise. The central issue was the definition of circumstances in which a duty of care can arise as between two parties. The House of Lords held that a duty of care arises when there is a 'special relationship' between two parties. It has been said in a number of cases that three conditions must be met for this to occur. First, it must be reasonably foreseeable by the representor that the representee will rely on the relevant statement. Secondly, there must be a sufficiently close relationship between the parties ('proximity'). Thirdly, it must be reasonable in all

---

[89] See section 14.2.3.

[90] See further Chapter 12.5.

[91] The Scots law counterpart of tort is delict.

[92] *Newbigging v Adam* (1886) 34 Ch 582, 592, *Archer v Brown* [1985] QB 401, 415. See also Companies Act 2006, s 655, which reverses the common law rule (established in *Houldsworth v City of Glasgow Bank* (1880) 5 App Cas 317) that a person induced by fraud to subscribe for a company's shares could not claim damages unless he rescinded (and thereby ceased to be a shareholder).

[93] *Manners v Whitehead* (1898) 1 Fraser (Court of Session Reports) 171.

[94] Misrepresentation Act 1967, s 2(2).

[95] [1964] AC 465.

the circumstances for the law to impose such a duty. Moreover, even if a duty of care is shown to exist, the plaintiff must show a causal link between the breach of duty[96] and the loss that he has suffered.

Several cases have applied these principles in the context of dealings in the financial markets. The most far reaching in terms of its analysis of the existence and scope of a duty of care as between a market participant and its customers is *Bankers Trust International plc vs PT Dharmala Sakti Sejahtera*.[97] That case arose from the sale by Bankers Trust International (BTI) of several, ultimately loss-making, interest-rate swaps to the defendant (DSS). Among the defences put forward by DSS to BTI's claim for payment were that (i) misrepresentations made by BTI during the sale of the derivatives gave DSS the option of rescission and (ii) BTI was in breach of a duty of care owed to DSS to ensure that the derivatives were suitable and safe products for DSS. The circumstances of the case were that both BTI, a leading player in the derivatives market, and DSS, a substantial commercial organisation with general financial expertise but no special expertise in derivatives, were acting as principals in the transactions, which were exempt from the Financial Services Act 1986 but subject to the London Code of Conduct.[98]

As regards DSS's second claim (that BTI owed a duty of care to ensure that derivatives were suitable and safe), the court found in respect of the first transaction that DSS did not ask, and were not entitled to expect, BTI to act as their advisers generally. In respect of the second transaction, the issue of causality came to the fore in that it was accepted that BTI owed a duty of care not to make inaccurate statements and to make a balanced presentation of the risks arising from the transaction. However, DSS failed to show that a full and fair presentation would have led to a different result (such as withdrawal from the transaction or negotiation of different terms). There was therefore a failure to show a causal link between BTI's representations and the loss suffered by DSS. It was, moreover, stated that courts should not be too ready to read duties of an advisory nature into the type of (informed principal-to-principal) relationship that existed between BTI and DSS.

While that case may have created some uncertainty as to when the courts would find that a duty of care was owed by one party to another in the absence of an agreement to provide advice, two subsequent cases suggest that the courts will uphold an 'arm's length' agreement where it is supported by the documentation and surrounding circumstances. In *Peekay Intermark Ltd v ANZ Banking Group Ltd*[99] it was established that an employee of the defendant had misrepresented the nature of an investment product. However, the bank sought to, and was held to be entitled to, rely on a provision in the agreement that the customer had taken independent advice on the suitability of the product and did not rely on the defendant's advice. Subsequently, in *JP Morgan Chase v Springwell Navigation Corporation*[100] the court was asked to rule that losses resulting from the purchase

---

[96] The fact that a customer has suffered loss as a result of advice does not in itself prove that there has been a breach of duty: see eg *Stafford v Conti Commodity Services Ltd* [1981] 1 All ER 691, holding that the principle of *res ipsa loquitur* could not be applied to deduce negligence from losses sustained in the commodities market by a customer who followed the erroneous advice of a broker.

[97] [1996] CLC 518.

[98] The London Code of Conduct for Principals and Firms in the Wholesale Markets (Bank of England, 1995).

[99] [2005] EWHC 830 (Comm).

[100] [2008] EWHC 1186 (Comm); upheld on appeal [2011] EWHC 1785.

of complex debt instruments by the investment vehicle of a wealthy Greek ship-owning family were recoverable from the defendant on the basis that it owed a duty of care to advise appropriately on the investments. There was no written agreement between the bank and the customer according to which the bank was to provide advice and on the facts the court held that there was no duty of care owed to the customer.[101]

14.2.4 Fiduciary duty

Fiduciary duty arises independently of contract as a result of a relationship of trust between two parties.[102] A fiduciary relationship does not arise automatically between market participants and their customers.[103] It does, however, arise in circumstances in which a market participant acts as agent or trustee for a customer or as its partner.[104] It can also arise on an ad hoc basis, and it is this possibility that opens up the potential for a customer of a financial firm to argue that a fiduciary relationship exists in a particular instance that does not fall within the established cases. The attraction for the customer of establishing the existence of a fiduciary duty is essentially that the firm is bound to a higher standard than would the case in an 'arm's length' transaction. The core obligation of a fiduciary has been defined in the following terms: 'The distinguishing obligation of a fiduciary is the obligation of loyalty. The principle is entitled to the single-minded loyalty of his fiduciary.'[105]

It has, however, proven quite difficult to establish that fiduciary duties exist on an ad hoc basis in the case of financial transactions.[106] Arguments along these lines were rejected in *JP Morgan Chase v Springwell Navigation Corporation* (above) and in *Titan Steel Wheels v Royal Bank of Scotland*.[107] In both cases, reliance was placed on provisions in the relevant contracts providing that no advice or recommendation was offered to the customer and that, if required, the customer was to take independent advice. However, were a customer to succeed in establishing the existence of an ad hoc fiduciary duty, it seems likely that a court would take account of relevant regulatory rules in determining the content of that duty.[108]

---

[101] This approach was subsequently followed in *Standard Chartered Bank v Ceylon Petroleum Corp* [2011] EWHC 1785.

[102] It may be that there is a contract between them but even if there is, the contract is unlikely to spell out in detail the conduct expected from the fiduciary. A contract can, however, limit fiduciary duty—see *Kelly v Cooper* [1993] AC 205 and Law Commission, 'Fiduciary Duties and Regulatory Rules', Report No 236 (1995).

[103] For example, banks are not automatically in a fiduciary relationship with their customers. However, they may become fiduciaries in specific circumstances such as: becoming a financial adviser or advising a customer on a particular transaction. See Cranston, above n 29, 187–91.

[104] The reference here is to a partner in the law of partnership and not any broader usage of that term.

[105] Millet J in *Bristol & West Building Society v Mothew* [1998] Ch 1, 18.

[106] The same point could be made more broadly with regard to commercial transactions generally: see eg *Re Goldcorp Exchange Ltd* [1995] 1 AC 74, where the Privy Council declined to find a fiduciary relationship where a company sold gold to customers and stored it on their behalf.

[107] [2010] EWHC 211.

[108] See Law Commission Report No 236, above n 102. See also the discussion of *Gorham v BT* [2001] 1 WLR 2129 at Chapter 6.5.1.

Fiduciary duty also encompasses an obligation of confidentiality. Issues related to confidentiality are particularly likely to arise in a conglomerate because, even if there is functional segregation within the firm, knowledge possessed in one part of a single corporate entity or partnership is treated in law as known in all parts of that entity.[109] Even where the conglomerate is not a single entity (eg because it has a group structure), common directorships may result in attribution of knowledge between group companies because the knowledge of a director (as agent) is attributed to the company (the principal). This approach to attribution of knowledge can lead to a number of problems. For example, an investment bank dealing as principal for its own account in company A may have been given information by company B relating to A during the course of providing corporate finance advice to B. If B passed the information to the bank in the context of a fiduciary relationship, the bank is prohibited from using the information for its own purposes.[110] A conflict of interest would also exist in this situation when an analyst working for the bank advises a client on company A. While the analyst is obliged, in principle, to use all the information that the law attributes to the bank in framing the recommendation, the duty of confidentiality owed to B creates a conflict of interest.

In applying the common law of fiduciary duty, the courts have generally taken a strict approach. Thus, in *Boardmann v Phipps*,[111] for example, a fiduciary (a solicitor to a trust) was required to account for profits to trustees despite the fact that the trust benefited from the action taken by the fiduciary in acquiring and liquidating a company in which the trust held a shareholding that it was not able to increase. The House of Lords held that the fiduciary was required to account to the trustees for the profits on the basis that they were earned as a result of the relationship with the trust (albeit that a substantial sum was awarded to the solicitor as compensation for work undertaken in relation to the trust's shareholding). This approach can be contrasted with the narrower approach adopted by the FSA regulatory rules to conflicts of interest[112] and suggests that the common law remedy is likely to remain more attractive than an action based on breach of the regulatory rules.

14.2.5 Claims in restitution/unjustified enrichment

Claims in restitution (unjustified enrichment in Scotland) arise when property or benefits are transferred other than under a contract and the person holding the property has no legal basis for doing so. There are two main circumstances in which market participants are likely to face claims for restitution of property. The first is where property has been transferred under a contract that is void because of a lack of contractual capacity of one of the parties. This formed the basis of one of the claims arising in the local authority swaps cases. In *Westdeutsche Landesbank Girozentrale v Islington LBC*[113] a derivatives contract

---

[109] *Harrods Ltd v Lemon* [1931] 2 KB 157.
[110] The basic principle is derived from *Boardmann v Phipps* [1967] 2 AC 46.
[111] Ibid.
[112] See Chapter 15.2.5.
[113] [1996] AC 669.

was held to be void as a result of the lack of contractual capacity of the local authority to enter into a derivatives contract. The House of Lords held that the local authority could recover money paid under the contract.

Haugesund Kommune, Narvik Kommune v Depfa ACS Bank[114] concerned swap agreements entered into by two Norwegian municipal authorities. The swaps effectively provided a capital sum to each *kommune* in return for payment over a number of years of sums that were to be funded by the revenue provided to the *kommunes* from their interest in local power stations (although that revenue was neither assigned nor charged in security, it simply provided a relatively secure revenue stream). With the capital sum, each *kommune* (eventually) became the holder of a CDO, which fell sharply in value. The *kommunes* eventually stopped the repayments and challenged the legal validity of the swaps on the basis that they lacked legal capacity to enter such agreements. Although it was accepted that public authorities under Norwegian law have similar capacity to a natural person unless it is limited, the *kommunes* were prohibited by the Local Government Act from entering into loans (with some limited exceptions). Thus the essential question was whether the swaps were loans. The court held that they were in essence and that the *kommunes* lacked the capacity to enter into the agreement. On that basis, they could not be enforced, but that left the matter of the large capital advances made by Depfa to the *kommunes*. On that issue, the court held that Depfa (having taken Norwegian advice on the issue of capacity and having been wrongly advised) had entered into the swaps under a mistake of law (as opposed to taking a conscious risk that the swaps might be invalid) and was therefore entitled to recover the payments that had been made to the *kommunes*. Nor were the *kommunes* able to argue that a change of position meant that they were not obliged to make restitution. That defence did not apply to circumstances such as these, where the risks associated with investing the capital sums were well known in advance.

A second instance in which a claim in restitution may be made is where profits have been made by a fiduciary in contravention of fiduciary duty. Those profits are held on trust for the benefit of the fiduciary and may be the subject of a claim in restitution.[115]

14.2.6 Statutory invalidity

Financial contracts often include exclusion clauses with the aim of clarifying that the seller does not provide advice to or accept responsibility for any losses suffered by the customer as a result of the buying a financial instrument.[116] The question then arises if these exclusion clauses are subject to the Unfair Contract Terms Act (UCTA) 1977 or the Unfair Terms in Consumer Contracts Regulations 1999, and, if so, whether they satisfy

---

[114] [2009] EWHC 2227 (Comm).

[115] *Boardmann v Phipps*, above n 110.

[116] For example in *Titan Steel Wheels Ltd v The Royal Bank of Scotland Plc* [2010] EWHC 211 (Comm) the contract provided that 'except to the extent that the same resulted from its gross negligence, wilful default or fraud, the Bank was not liable for any loss of opportunity, loss resulting from any act or omission made under or in relation to or in connection with the banking terms or the services provided thereunder, any decline in the value of the investments purchased or held by the bank on Titan's behalf, or any errors of act or judgment howsoever'.

the requirements of the relevant provisions for the terms to be valid. Also relevant in this context is section 3 of the Misrepresentation Act 1967.[117] The most obvious starting point is the 1977 Act, since its provisions relating to exclusion clauses relating to negligence are framed so as to cover, in principle, terms in contracts between commercial parties.[118] A broad interpretation of those provisions could lead to the conclusion that they apply not only to exclusion clauses in the classic sense[119] but also to contract terms which define the basis on which services will be rendered (the implication being that those terms may adjust the manner in which the principles of negligence would otherwise apply to the relationship between the parties). However, in the context of contracts between parties in the wholesale financial market, the courts have been reluctant to apply the unfair contract terms legislation so as to limit the contractual freedom of the parties. That policy was succinctly expressed in *JP Morgan Chase v Springwell Navigation Corporation*[120] in the following terms:

> Thus terms which simply define the basis upon which services will be rendered and confirm the basis upon which parties are transacting business are not subject to section 2 of UCTA 1977. Otherwise, every contract which contains contractual terms defining the extent of each party's obligations would have to satisfy the requirements of reasonableness . . . The reluctance of the courts to interfere in contracts concluded between commercial parties in relation to substantial transactions reflects the strong business need for commercial certainty . . .[121]

That policy was subsequently followed in *Titan Steel Wheels Ltd v The Royal Bank of Scotland Plc*.[122] Moreover, further reassurance regarding the courts' respect for party autonomy in the case of commercial agreements between sophisticated counterparties was provided by the finding in both cases that the relevant contract terms would have passed the reasonableness test had it been applicable. In *Titan Steel Wheels Ltd v The Royal Bank of Scotland Plc* the court justified that conclusion in the following terms:

> 1. There was complete equality of bargaining power. Titan was a substantial entity that was a customer of the Bank. It was open to Titan to choose any bank and indeed it did take its custom elsewhere.
> 2. The terms were not simply standard for the Bank but, it would appear, to many banks including the Irish banks from which Titan bought products.
> 3. There was no difficulty in Titan seeking (as the terms expected) advice from another quarter if desired.[123]

---

[117] This provision subjects contract terms which attempt to exclude or restrict liability for misrepresentation (or the available remedies) to a test of reasonableness. It applies to England only.

[118] See, in respect of England, s 2; and in respect of Scotland, s 16.

[119] See the example in n 116 above.

[120] [2010] EWCA Civ 1221.

[121] Mrs J Gloster at 602, 604. In that case the relationship between bank and customer extended over a long period of time, but at no time was the customer (Springwell) classified as a private customer. Reference was made to the earlier decision of the Court of Appeal in *IFE v Goldman Sachs* [2006] EWCA Civ 811, where a similar approach was adopted in the context of the application of s 3 of the Misrepresentation Act 1967 to the terms of a syndicated loan agreement.

[122] [2010] EWHC 211 (Comm).

[123] Steel J at para 105.

Further reassurance was provided in that case by the finding that, even had UCTA 1977 been applicable to the contract, the relevant terms were reasonable by reference to the nature of the parties and the circumstances in which the contracts were concluded.

Further support for the 'arm's length' model of contracting in the wholesale markets is provided by subsequent cases. In *CRSM Spa v Barclays Bank Ltd*,[124] the court followed the approach in *Springwell*[125] and *Peekay*,[126] holding that the plaintiff was estopped from making a misrepresentation claim by a contract term providing that it had understood and accepted the risks of entering the transaction. In *Camarata Property Inc v Credit Suisse Securities (Europe) Ltd*,[127] it was alleged that the plaintiff investor had suffered loss on an investment note issued by a Lehman Bros entity as a result of the negligence or gross negligence of the defendant bank under an investment advisory service agreement. The effect of the relevant terms and conditions was that the defendant was liable only if its employee was guilty of gross negligence in the advice that was given. The court held that the employee was not in the circumstances guilty of negligence for failing to assess the counterparty risk of dealing with a Lehman Bros entity and therefore the defendant was not liable. Moreover, the 'exclusion' relating to gross negligence was held to satisfy the reasonableness test in section 11 of the Unfair Contract Terms Act 1977.

The Unfair Terms in Consumer Contracts Regulations 1999 are of less direct relevance to the wholesale market because they are limited in scope to consumer contracts. However, the definition of consumer in the Regulations[128] leaves open the possibility that transactions which are conducted in the manner typically adopted in the wholesale market may fall within the their scope. Those circumstances arose in the case of *Maple Leaf Macro Volatility Master Fund v Rouvroy and Trylinski*.[129] The case concerned a dispute that arose from a funding arrangement entered into between a hedge fund (Maple Leaf) and the defendants with the objective of securing control of Belvedere, a French company in which they were respectively CEO and deputy CEO as well as substantial shareholders. The transaction involved the creation by the defendants of a special purpose vehicle (SPV) that was to hold collateral against the funding advanced by Maple Leaf, primarily in the form of warrants in Belvedere. The dispute arose as a result of the defendants failing to set up the SPV and Maple Leaf being left with warrants in Belvedere which plummeted in value. To the extent that the 1999 Regulations could be applied to the funding arrangement (and they could not apply to the price/remuneration aspects), the court followed *Bryen & Langley v Boston*,[130] holding that so long as the relevant terms were not imposed on the 'consumer' in contravention of the requirements of good faith there could be no issue of unfairness. The court found no indication of breach of the requirement of good faith (fair dealing) in this case.

---

[124] [2011] EWHC 484 (Comm).

[125] Above n 120.

[126] Above n 99.

[127] [2011] EWHC 479.

[128] The definition is provided by Art 3(1) as follows: 'consumer' means any natural person who, in contracts covered by these Regulations, is acting for purposes which are outside his trade, business or profession.

[129] [2009] EWHC 257 (Comm).

[130] [2005] EWCA 973.

Market Participants— Regulatory Structure and Rules

This chapter focuses on the regulatory framework applicable to participants in the wholesale financial markets. It follows the approach adopted in Chapter 14 whereby market participants are regarded as persons involved in a professional capacity in the transaction or execution of investment business. It begins by examining the system of customer classification adopted by Markets in Financial Instruments Directive (MiFID) and implemented in the Financial Services and Markets Act 2000 (FSMA 2000) regulatory regime in the UK. The classification represents a technique for tailoring the application of regulatory rules (in particular conduct of business rules) to the different needs of the retail and wholesale markets. The chapter then goes on to consider the prudential regulation of financial resources (or regulatory capital) rules applicable to investment firms, which are also largely based on the requirements set by the EU regime. The system of customer classification is not applied in this sphere as regulatory capital protects against the aggregate risks of insolvency faced by all customers and counterparties of an investment firm.

15.1 Customer classification

A distinction between investors and market participants is relevant for the regulatory system because the traditional role of the regulatory system has been to provide investor protection. This means, among other things, protecting investors from the information asymmetry problems that they face in entering into investment transactions with market participants. However, there are many transactions in financial markets between professionals, in respect of which the information asymmetry rationale for regulation does not apply because both parties are sophisticated and can make informed decisions. In Chapter 14, these transactions were referred to as 'arm's length' transactions between parties in the 'wholesale' financial market. The objective of the regulatory system is to identify those transactions and supply an appropriate degree of investor protection, bearing in mind the ability of the parties to take care of their own interests.

The FSMA 2000 system of regulation undertakes this task by using customer classification to allocate regulatory rules to transactions according to the parties to the transaction and the context within which it occurs. That policy is based on a number of statutory provisions:

1. that regulation should be proportionate to the benefits it provides;[1]
2. that the Financial Services Authority (FSA) should take into account the differing degrees of experience and expertise of investors;[2] and
3. that the FSA may make rules that make different provisions for different cases and may, in particular, make different provisions in respect of different descriptions of authorised person, activity or investment.[3]

Client classification operates by reference to transactions, with the result that, in respect of different transactions, a client to which an authorised firm provides services can fall within different classifications. It is the responsibility of a firm to categorise its clients.[4] The relevant categories are set out below.[5]

Eligible counterparty

An eligible counterparty is a client that is either a per se eligible counterparty or an elective eligible counterparty. Each of the following is a per se eligible counterparty (including an entity that is not from an EEA state that is equivalent to any of the following):[6]

1. an investment firm;
2. a credit institution;
3. an insurance company;
4. a collective investment scheme authorised under the Undertakings for Collective Investment in Transferable Securities Directive or its management company;
5. a pension fund or its management company;

---

[1] FSMA 2000, s 2(3)(c).

[2] FSMA 2000, s 5(2)(b).

[3] FSMA 2000, s 156.

[4] See FSA Handbook, COBS 3.3. Failure to categorise correctly may in itself be a breach of regulatory rules, but mere procedural requirements may be overlooked if the firm has in fact followed the requirements applicable to a transaction with the relevant category of customer: see *Spreadex Ltd v Sanjit Sekhon* [2008] EWHC 1136 (Ch). See also *Wilson v MF Global UK Ltd* [2011] EWHC 138, holding that the test for determining whether a client was properly categorised as an 'intermediate client' (under the pre-MIFID system) was whether reasonable care had been taken to determine that the client had sufficient experience and understanding to be classified as an intermediate customer (*Spreadex Ltd v Sanjit Sekhon* applied).

[5] They are derived from MiFID regime, which is implemented by the conduct of business (COBS) component of the FSA Handbook.

[6] Unless and to the extent that it is given a different categorisation.

6. another financial institution authorised or regulated under EU legislation or the national law of an EEA state;

7. an undertaking exempted from the application of MiFID under either Article 2(1)(k) (certain own account dealers in commodities or commodity derivatives) or Article 2(1)(l) (locals) of that directive;

8. a national government or its corresponding office, including a public body that deals with the public debt;

9. a central bank; and

10. a supranational organisation.[7]

A firm is entitled to treat a client as an eligible counterparty if the client requests that status but only in respect of transactions for which the client would otherwise be treated as a professional client.

Professional client

This category follows the same pattern as above in distinguishing between a per se and an elective professional client. The per se category includes all the categories shown above for a per se eligible counterparty except central banks and supranational organisations.[8] It also includes large undertakings, partnerships and trusts which meet certain financial thresholds.[9]

A firm may treat a client as an elective professional client if it complies with points (1) and (3) and, where applicable, point (2) below:

(1) the firm undertakes an adequate assessment of the expertise, experience and knowledge of the client that gives reasonable assurance, in light of the nature of the transactions or services envisaged, that the client is capable of making his own investment decisions and understanding the risks involved (the 'qualitative test');[10]

(2) in relation to MiFID or equivalent third country business[11] in the course of that assessment, at least two of the following criteria are satisfied:

   (a) the client has carried out transactions, in significant size, on the relevant market at an average frequency of 10 per quarter over the previous four quarters;

   (b) the size of the client's financial instrument portfolio, defined as including cash deposits and financial instruments, exceeds EUR 500,000;

   (c) the client works or has worked in the financial sector for at least one year in a professional position, which requires knowledge of the transactions or services envisaged;

(the 'quantitative test'); and

(3) the following procedure is followed:

---

[7] COBS 3.6.2R. For the purposes of this rule a financial institution includes institutions in the banking, securities and insurance sectors.

[8] It follows that those two categories must always be eligible counterparties.

[9] See COBS 3.5.2R.

[10] If the client is an entity, the qualitative test should be performed in relation to the person authorised to carry out transactions on its behalf.

[11] This refers to business falling within the scope of MiFID regime or, in the case of non-EEA firms, business that would fall within that regime if the establishment from which the business is carried on in the UK was a firm subject to MiFID regime.

> (a) the client must state in writing to the firm that it wishes to be treated as a professional client either generally or in respect of a particular service or transaction or type of transaction or product;
> (b) the firm must give the client a clear written warning of the protections and investor compensation rights the client may lose; and
> (c) the client must state in writing, in a separate document from the contract, that it is aware of the consequences of losing such protections.[12]

While the FSA rules do not generally distinguish between per se and elective professional clients for the purposes of the application of rules, the FSA Handbook guidance that 'An elective professional client should not be presumed to possess market knowledge and experience comparable to a per se professional client'[13] carries implications for the application of the suitability and appropriateness rules as both are linked to the knowledge and experience of the client. That issue is considered in more detail below.

Retail client

This category covers clients who are not eligible counterparties or professional clients.[14] It includes private individuals who are not authorised under FSMA 2000, as well as enterprises that fall below the financial thresholds applicable to per se professional clients.

A firm must allow a professional client or an eligible counterparty to request recategorisation as a client that benefits from a higher degree of protection.[15] It is the responsibility of a professional client or eligible counterparty to ask for a higher level of protection when it deems it is unable to properly assess or manage the risks involved. A firm may, either on its own initiative or at the request of the client concerned: (i) treat as a professional client or a retail client a client that might otherwise be categorised as a per se eligible counterparty; or (ii) treat as a retail client a client that might otherwise be categorised as a per se professional client; and if it does so, the client will be recategorised accordingly.

In the case of a firm (F1) that provides services to another firm (F2) which acts as agent for another client (C) (eg a market-maker dealing with a stockbroker acting as an agent for a client), the FSA Handbook adopts the general rule that it is F2, not C, who is the client of F1. However, this is subject to alteration so that C can be treated as the client of F1, with the result that F1 will owe regulatory duties to C.[16] The FSA Handbook also deals with circumstances in which F1 can rely on information provided by F2 relating to C. It provides that:

> (a) F1 may rely upon:
>   (a) any information about C transmitted to it by F2; and
>   (b) any recommendations in respect of the service or transaction that have been provided to C by F2.

---

[12] COBS 3.5.3R.
[13] COBS 3.5.7G.
[14] COBS 3.4.1R.
[15] See generally COBS 3.7.
[16] COBS 2.4.3R. Note the any reallocation of regulatory duties does not affect the common law duties of an agent owed by F2 to C. Regulatory and common law duties are not coextensive.

(b) F2 will remain responsible for:
   (a) the completeness and accuracy of any information about C transmitted by it to F1; and
   (b) the appropriateness for C of any advice or recommendations provided to C.

(c) F1 will remain responsible for concluding the services or transaction based on any such information or recommendations in accordance with the applicable requirements under the regulatory system.

Many transactions conducted between market participants are likely to fall within the eligible counterparty regime. From the regulatory perspective, this has the effect of disapplying a substantial part of the FSA conduct of business rules other than generally applicable regulatory rules, which are considered next.

15.2 Generally applicable regulatory rules

Only a relatively small part of the FSA Handbook is generally applicable to transactions falling within the scope of regulated activity. This results from the policy that regulatory controls should be tailored to the needs of the relevant parties to a transaction and that in the case of transactions between sophisticated parties (eligible counterparties and professional clients) the need for regulatory intervention is much less than in cases where services are provided to retail clients.

The following are generally applicable rules:

15.2.1 The Principles for Businesses (PRIN)[17]

The PRIN are a general statement of the fundamental obligations of firms under the FSMA 2000 regulatory system.

The Principles

1. Integrity. A firm must conduct its business with integrity.
2. Skill, care and diligence. A firm must conduct its business with due skill, care and diligence.
3. Management and control. A firm must take reasonable care to organise and control its affairs responsibly and effectively, with adequate risk management systems.
4. Financial prudence. A firm must maintain adequate financial resources.
5. Market conduct. A firm must observe proper standards of market conduct.
6. Customers' interests. A firm must pay due regard to the interests of its customers and treat them fairly.

[17] See the FSA Handbook at www.fsa.gov.uk (accessed on 20 November 2011).

7. Communications with clients. A firm must pay due regard to the information needs of its clients, and communicate information to them in a way which is clear, fair and not misleading.
8. Conflicts of interest. A firm must manage conflicts of interest fairly, both between itself and its customers and between a customer and another client.
9. Customers: relationships of trust. A firm must take reasonable care to ensure the suitability of its advice and discretionary decisions for any customer who is entitled to rely upon its judgment.
10. Clients' assets. A firm must arrange adequate protection for clients' assets when it is responsible for them.
11. Relations with regulators. A firm must deal with its regulators in an open and cooperative way, and must disclose to the FSA appropriately anything relating to the firm of which the FSA would reasonably expect notice.

The role of the Principles in the FSMA 2000 regulatory system is discussed in chapter 3.7.3 and the implications of breach are considered below.[18]

15.2.2 Statements of Principle and Code of Practice for Approved Persons (APER)

The APER regime under FSMA 2000 focuses on the competence and integrity of individuals who carry out 'controlled functions'.[19] It is linked with and expands on Principles 1 and 2 of the Principles for Businesses (above).

Statements of Principle issued under section 64 of the Act

Principle 1   An approved person must act with integrity in carrying out his controlled function.
Principle 2   An approved person must act with due skill, care and diligence in carrying out his controlled function.
Principle 3   An approved person must observe proper standards of market conduct in carrying out his controlled function.
Principle 4   An approved person must deal with the FSA and with other regulators in an open and cooperative way and must disclose appropriately any information of which the FSA would reasonably expect notice.
Principle 5   An approved person performing a significant influence function must take reasonable steps to ensure that the business of the firm for which he is responsible in his controlled function is organised so that it can be controlled effectively.

---

[18] See section 15.3.5.
[19] See Chapter 3.9.4 for more detailed discussion of the role of the APER regime in the UK regulatory system.

Principle 6   An approved person performing a significant influence function must exercise due skill, care and diligence in managing the business of the firm for which he is responsible in his controlled function.

Principle 7   An approved person performing a significant influence function must take reasonable steps to ensure that the business of the firm for which he is responsible in his controlled function complies with the relevant requirements and standards of the regulatory system.

15.2.3 The Code of Market Conduct[20]

The statutory provisions relating to market abuse and the Code of Market Conduct apply to all persons trading relevant securities on markets in the UK. They are discussed in Chapter 13.

15.2.4 Client assets and client money

Market participants often assume responsibility for the safekeeping of clients' investments or money under various types of contractual arrangement. Some arrangements involve the firm itself undertaking the safekeeping, others provide for this task to be delegated to a professional custodian. Principle 10 (Clients' assets) of the FSA's Principles for Businesses requires a firm to arrange adequate protection for clients' assets when it is responsible for them. The relevant Client Assets (CASS) apply in general to custody services and the holding of client money for any category of client. Their objectives are:

1. To protect clients by restricting the commingling of client and firm assets. This is achieved through rules relating to the segregation of firm and client assets, registration and recording of ownership.
2. To minimise the risk of client assets being used by a firm without the client's agreement or contrary to the client's wishes.[21] This is achieved mainly through a requirement that the terms on which safe custody is provided are notified to the client and a general prohibition against firms using clients' assets for their own account.[22]
3. To prevent the client's assets being treated as the firm's assets in the event of insolvency. This is mainly achieved through the agreements that must be made between firms and custodians who hold the assets of the firm's clients. Those agreements must detail the manner in which assets are held, following the principle of segregation of firm and client assets.

The collapse of Lehman Bros in 2008 exposed flaws in the existing client assets regime. In response, the FSA made some changes with a view to strengthening the regime and

---

[20] The Code is part of the Market Conduct (MAR) section of the FSA Handbook, which is itself part of the Business Standards block.

[21] Eg the risk that a firm might use client assets for stock-lending.

[22] FSA Handbook, CASS 2.3.2R.

reducing risk.[23] They require enhanced oversight of client assets and money. A firm must allocate to a director or senior manager exercising a significant influence function[24] responsibility for:

1. oversight of the firm's operational compliance with CASS; and
2. reporting to the firm's governing body in respect of that oversight.

They also require greater disclosure from prime brokers as to the status and extent of assets held on behalf of clients.[25] Prime brokers[26] must make available to each of its clients to whom it provides prime brokerage services a statement:

1. showing the value at the close of each business day of required items[27]; and
2. detailing any other matters which that firm considers are necessary to ensure that a client has up-to-date and accurate information about the amount of client money and the value of safe custody assets held by that firm for it.

Custody of investments

Custody is a 'regulated activity' for the purposes of FSMA 2000 if the relevant assets include 'investments' or 'contractually based investments'.[28] A firm must establish adequate organisational arrangements to minimise the risk of loss or diminution of clients' safe custody assets, or the rights in connection with those safe custody assets, as a result of the misuse of the safe custody assets, fraud, poor administration, inadequate record-keeping or negligence. A firm is permitted to register legal title to client investments in its own name or that of a professional custodian acting on its behalf. In that situation, the legal title is held by the registered owner on trust for the client.[29]

Some modifications are made to the scope of the conduct of business rules governing custody in particular cases. A trustee firm or depositary acting as custodian for a trust or collective investment scheme is required to comply with only a limited number of the

---

[23] See FSA, 'Enhancing the Client Assets Sourcebook'. Consultation Paper (CP) 10/9 (2010).

[24] The significant influence function is a 'controlled function' for the purposes of APER and therefore brings the relevant person within the scope of the APER regime: see further Chapter 3.9.4.

[25] This addresses so-called 're-hypothecation' risk, which is the risk that client assets may be used by the prime broker (under a 'right of use' in the prime brokerage contract) as collateral in transactions which it enters as principal, with the result that the assets may become subject to proprietary claims by the counterparty of the prime broker.

[26] See Chapter 14.1.5 for an explanation of this term.

[27] See CASS 9.2.1R. The items include: (i) the total value of safe custody assets and the total amount of client money held by that prime brokerage firm for a client; (ii) total collateral held by the firm in respect of secured transactions entered into under a prime brokerage agreement, including where the firm has exercised a right of use in respect of that client's safe custody assets; (iii) the location of all of a client's safe custody assets, including assets held with a sub-custodian; and (iv) a list of all the institutions at which the firm holds or may hold client money, including money held in client bank accounts and client transaction accounts.

[28] See Art 40 of the Regulated Activities Order (RAO, SI 2001/544) and Chapter 14.3.3.

[29] There may be several layers of trust interposed between the client and the legal owner. This might arise where, for example, a retail client holds a share through a nominee company operated by a stockbroker which holds all its client investments through a custodian. In that situation, the rights of the beneficial owner can be exercised only at each level of the ownership chain. See further J Benjamin, *Interests in Securities* (Oxford, Oxford University Press, 2000) ch 2.

rules, reflecting the extensive regulation of this activity under the relevant regulations[30] as well as common law duties. A firm that merely arranges safeguarding and administration of assets is subject to a limited set of rules, including a requirement that it undertake a proper risk assessment of the custodian.

Client money

There are special rules applicable to the holding of client money.[31] The effect of the statutory provision and relevant rules is that a statutory trust is created in respect of clients' money, which has the effect of 'ring-fencing' the money in the event of the firm's insolvency.[32] The trust arises immediately on receipt of the money by the firm and is not conditional on the money being allocated to a segregated account.[33] In the event of a deficiency in client funds, a 'pooling' system operates so that the deficiency is shared among clients, with payments being made pro rata according to entitlement.[34] The pooling operates by reference to all client money and not just that held in segregated accounts. Moreover, entitlement to share in the pool is based on a client's contractual entitlement to have money segregated and not simply to his having a proprietary interest in the pool (as a result of segregation having occurred). However, a simple debt due to a client is not 'client money' for these purposes as there is no property which is sufficiently identified for the purposes of the creation of a trust.[35]

15.2.5 Conflicts of interest

The implementation of the MiFID regime in the UK has resulted in a recasting of the conduct of business rules, which apply when a service is provided by a firm irrespective of the categorisation of the client.[36] The first requirement is that firms identify conflicts of interest between the firm and a client of the firm or between one client of the firm and

---

[30] See Chapter 4.10.

[31] These rules are made under s 139 FSMA 2000 and are contained in CASS 7. As was the case with the relevant provision of the Financial Services Act 1986 (s 55(5)), FSMA 2000, s 139(3) states that, as regards Scotland, the reference to money being held on trust is to be read as a reference to its being held as agent for the person on whose behalf it is held. In the past, this served the purpose of avoiding the complications, real or imagined, associated with the Blank Bonds and Trusts Act 1696. Following the repeal of that Act by the Requirements of Writing (Sc) Act 1995, it is not clear why it is necessary for s 139 to apply in a different way to Scotland.

[32] See FSA, 'Protecting Client Money on the Failure of an Authorised Firm', CP 38 (January 2000) Annex B for more detail and the history of client money rules.

[33] *Re Lehman Bros International (Europe) (In Administration)* [2010] EWCA Civ 917. But note that an honest mistake in failing to treat money as client money (such as paying it into the firm's own account) will not lead to the creation of a trust: *Re Global Trader Europe Ltd (In Liquidation)* [2009] EWHC 602 (Ch).

[34] The creation of a pooling system expressly disapplies the rule in Clayton's case (*Devaynes v Noble* (1816) 1 Mer 572, 35 ER 767), which adopts a 'first in–first out' approach to credit and debit transactions in a (banking) current account. See R Cranston, *Principles of Banking Law*, 2nd edn (Oxford, Oxford University Press, 2002) 160–63 for more detail.

[35] *Re Lehman Bros*, above n 33.

[36] See generally FSA Handbook, SYSC 10.1.

another client. In considering whether a conflict of interest arises a firm is required to consider as a minimum whether the firm:

1. is likely to make a financial gain, or avoid a financial loss, at the expense of the client;
2. has an interest in the outcome of a service provided to the client or of a transaction carried out on behalf of the client, which is distinct from the client's interest in that outcome;
3. has a financial or other incentive to favour the interest of another client or group of clients over the interests of the client;
4. carries on the same business as the client; or
5. receives or will receive from a person other than the client an inducement in relation to a service provided to the client, in the form of monies, goods or services, other than the standard commission or fee for that service.[37]

However, the circumstances that should be treated as giving rise to a conflict of interest are narrower than is the case under fiduciary duty in the common law. The FSA Handbook guidance provides that:

> It is not enough that the firm may gain a benefit if there is not also a possible disadvantage to a client, or that one client to whom the firm owes a duty may make a gain or avoid a loss without there being a concomitant possible loss to another such client.[38]

The common law, by way of contrast, does not limit the existence of a conflict of interest in this manner. It is the existence of a conflict of interest and the action of the principal in that situation that matters, not whether loss has been caused to the client.[39] It follows that compliance with the regulatory regime relating to conflicts of interest does not necessarily protect a firm from common law claims in respect of profits made or losses avoided by a firm in circumstances in which no disadvantage has been caused to the client.[40]

Firms are required to establish, implement and maintain a conflicts of interest policy which identifies, by reference to the specific services and activities carried on by the firm, the circumstances which constitute or may give rise to conflicts of interest. The policy must specify procedures to be followed and measures to be adopted to manage such conflicts. In particular, the policy must focus on the independence of relevant persons carrying out different functions so as to:

- control the exchange of information that may harm a client's interests;
- separate the provision of services to clients from activities undertaken by the firm as principal;
- remove remuneration incentives that may create a conflict of interest;
- remove inappropriate influence over the way in services and activities are carried out; and

---

[37] SYSC 10.1.4R.

[38] SYSC 10.1.5G.

[39] See *Boardmann v Phipps* [1967] 2 AC 46; *Industrial Development Consultants v Cooley* [1972] 1 WLR 443. The FSA Handbook cites recital 24 of the MiFID Implementing Directive as the basis of its approach, but that does not disapply the broader common law approach to conflicts of interest.

[40] See Chapter 14.2.4.

- prevent simultaneous or sequential involvement in activities where such involvement may impair the proper management of conflicts of interest.[41]

Implementation of the policy focuses on managing conflicts of interest. A firm must maintain and operate effective organisational and administrative arrangements with a view to taking all reasonable steps to prevent conflicts of interest from constituting or giving rise to a material risk of damage to the interests of its clients.[42] If those arrangements are not sufficient to ensure, with reasonable confidence, that risks of damage to the interests of a client will be prevented, the firm must clearly disclose the general nature of the conflict before undertaking business for the client so as to allow the client to make an informed decision with respect to the service.

The FSA Handbook recognises the role of so-called 'Chinese walls' in managing conflicts of interest. A Chinese wall is an arrangement[43] that requires information held by a person in the course of carrying on one part of its business to be withheld from, or not to be used for, persons with or for whom it acts in the course of carrying on another part of its business. In that sense, Chinese walls are like information firewalls that separate a conglomerate into different regulatory components. FSMA 2000 enables the FSA to make 'control of information' rules, which are in effect rules recognising Chinese walls.[44] The only rule made by the FSA under this power is a rule providing that, where a firm establishes and maintains a Chinese wall, it may withhold information or not use the information held and limit the transfer of information between departments.[45] The result of this rule is that:

1. acting in conformity with this rule provides a defence against a prosecution (under section 397 FSMA 2000) for making misleading statements or practices or engaging in a course of conduct creating a false or misleading impression;
2. behaviour conforming with this rule does not amount to market abuse; and
3. acting in conformity with this rule is a defence to an action for damages under section 150 FSMA 2000, where that action is based on a breach of a relevant requirement to disclose or use information.[46]

A related rule deals with attribution of knowledge. It provides that when any of the Conduct of Business (COBS) or CASS rules apply to a firm that acts with knowledge, the firm will not be taken to act with knowledge for the purposes of that rule if none of the relevant individuals involved on behalf of the firm acts with that knowledge as a result of the operation of a Chinese wall.[47] This means that, when a Chinese wall is in operation, individuals on the 'other side of the wall' will not be regarded as being in possession

---

[41] SYSC 10.1.11R.

[42] Contrast the strict rule under the common law according to which transactions in which an agent has a conflict of interest can be avoided by the principal without any reference to the issue of whether the terms are fair to the principal or not: see *Aberdeen Railway v Blaikie Bros* (1854) 1 Macq 461, 471–72.

[43] These arrangements can take a variety of different forms, such as physical segregation of staff and relevant client information or secure digital document rooms with restricted access.

[44] FSMA 2000, s 147.

[45] SYSC 10.2.2R.

[46] SYSC 10.2.3G. See also Chapter 13.4.6 regarding 'safe harbours' under the market abuse regime.

[47] COBS 10.2.4R.

of knowledge denied to them as a result of the effective operation of the Chinese wall. This has the effect of disapplying, within the limited scope of the rule, the common law rules on the attribution of knowledge which generally attribute information known by an agent to the principal.[48]

15.3 Conduct of business regulation: rules of limited application

Following the approach of the MiFID regime, the FSA Handbook frames conduct of business rules so as to be generally applicable to any client, irrespective of their categorisation. It then makes various exceptions and modifications to the general rules so as to tailor their application to the different client categories. The most extensive exceptions are made in the case of eligible counterparties.[49] The exceptions and modifications made in the case of professional clients are less extensive, but nevertheless carry significant implications for the manner in which a firm transacts business with those clients.

15.3.1 Suitability

In principle, the suitability requirement applies in the same way to all clients.[50] However, there are two ways in which its application to eligible counterparties and professional clients differs from its application to retail clients. The first is linked to the scope of the rule. It applies only to personal recommendations and decisions to trade (under a discretionary investment management agreement) for a client. It therefore excludes 'arm's length' transactions in which each party acts as a principal. As was observed in Chapter 14, this type of transaction is common in the wholesale financial market. The second modification is derived directly from the MiFID regime and relates to the assessment of suitability in the case of professional clients. If a firm makes a personal recommendation or manages investments for a professional client[51] in the course of MiFID or equivalent third country business, it is entitled to assume that, in relation to the products, transactions and services for which the professional client is so classified, the client has the necessary level of experience and knowledge for the purposes of the

---

[48] *Lloyds Bank v EB Savory & Co* [1933] AC 201, per Lord Wright at 235. See further G Mc Cormack, 'Conflicts of Interest and the Investment Management Function' (1999) 20 *Company Lawyer* 2–13; Law Commission, 'Fiduciary Duties and Regulatory Rules', Report No 236 (1995).

[49] See COBS 1, Annex 1: Application.

[50] See Chapter 6.3.4 for the content of the rule.

[51] The same reasoning applies to an eligible counterparty as it is only possible to be treated as such if a client is already a professional client.

basic suitability rule.[52] However, that does not exhaust the content of the suitability rule, which also encompasses consideration of the client's investment objectives and capacity to bear risk. In this regard, the modification of the suitability rule is more narrowly framed, as it is only in respect of per se professional clients that a firm is entitled to assume that the client is able financially to bear any related investment risks consistent with his investment objectives.[53]

15.3.2 Appropriateness

As outlined in Chapter 6.3.4, the appropriateness rule applies to non-advised services and applies only in circumstances in which the suitability rule is not applicable. It does not apply to eligible counterparty business. In the case of a professional client, a firm is entitled to assume that such a client has the necessary experience and knowledge in order to understand the risks involved in relation to those particular investment services or transactions, or types of transaction or product, for which the client is classified as a professional client.[54] This is a broader modification than in the case of suitability (above) as the effect is to remove all obligations owed by a firm regarding appropriateness in respect of non-advised services. It thereby facilitates 'arm's length' transactions between investment firms and professional clients.

15.3.3 Dealing and managing

The rules in this section apply when a firm is conducting designated investment business[55] with or for a customer. Taken together, they are intended to protect customers from a range of possible abuses that can occur when authorised firms manage funds or deal on behalf of their customers.

Best execution

As stated by the FSA, 'In most major jurisdictions in the world, regulation of best execution is acknowledged as having two main purposes: providing consumer protection and contributing to market efficiency'.[56] Except in some limited circumstances, a firm

[52] The basic rule is expressed in COBS 9.2.2 R (1)(c) as follows: (1) A firm must take reasonable steps to ensure that a personal recommendation, or a decision to trade, is suitable for its client. (2) When making the personal recommendation or managing his investments, the firm must obtain the necessary information regarding the client's: (a) knowledge and experience in the investment field relevant to the specific type of designated investment or service; (b) financial situation; and (c) investment objectives; so as to enable the firm to make the recommendation, or take the decision, which is suitable for him.

[53] COBS 9.2.8R. Quite what this means in terms of a firm making its own assessment of suitability for an elective professional client is not clear. It would seem to imply that in the case of a hedge fund (which is not a per se professional client) that a firm providing services (eg a prime broker) is required to undertake its own assessment of the objectives and risk-bearing capacity of the fund.

[54] COBS 10.2.1R.

[55] See Chapter 6.3

[56] FSA, 'Best Execution', CP 154 (2002) 7.

must provide best execution when it executes a customer order.[57] A firm must establish internal arrangements to give effect to this obligation. It must also prepare an order execution policy, provide it to clients and secure their consent to it. The obligation applies when agency or contractual duties are owed to a client.[58] It also applies in cases where a firm deals as principal with a client as a means of executing the client's order. While best execution applies in principle to orders in respect of all financial instruments, FSA guidance recognises that its operation must take into account the different ways in which markets for different financial instruments operate.

To provide best execution, a firm must take all reasonable steps to obtain, when executing orders, the best possible result for its clients taking into account the execution factors, which are price, costs, speed, likelihood of execution and settlement, size, nature and any other consideration relevant to the execution of an order. If the client provides specific execution instructions, the firm discharges its best execution obligation by following those instructions.

A firm need not have access to all competing exchanges and trading platforms but, if it does, they are encompassed by the best-execution principle. The firm is required to pass on to the customer the price at which it deals for the customer. It is possible for a firm to 'internalise' an order, meaning that the firm is both the execution venue for the transaction and the contractual counterparty to the customer. This occurs in broker/dealer firms when matching client orders are 'crossed' within the firm rather than being executed individually through a market-maker or order-matching system. When this occurs, the requirement for 'best execution' remains relevant and the firm must carry out the transaction by reference to the outcome (price and other considerations) available through execution on alternative venues.

The FSA has, however, stressed that the obligation of best execution is more than the achievement of best price.[59] It requires attention to the overall costs of trading, both implicit and explicit, which are ultimately borne by the customer. A decision on how to execute an order will therefore require a firm to consider the order type, size, settlement arrangements and timing along with any other conditions set by the customer.

Client order handling

Several matters are encompassed by this heading.[60] They have in common the potential for clients' interests to be prejudiced as a result of the manner in which a firm handles client orders.

The first relates to customer order priority. Order priority may affect the interests of customers because a firm's own account orders (or other customer orders) may move the price of a security against a customer. A firm must implement procedures and arrangements which provide for the prompt, fair and expeditious execution of client orders,

---

[57] See generally COBS 11.2.

[58] That formulation is unusual as few regulatory rules are based expressly on the existence of underlying private law obligations.

[59] See FSA CP 154, above n 56.

[60] See generally COBS 11.3.

relative to other orders or the trading interests of the firm. These procedures or arrangements must allow for the execution of otherwise comparable orders in accordance with the time of their reception by the firm. A firm must not misuse information relating to pending client orders, and shall take all reasonable steps to prevent the misuse of such information by any of its relevant persons. For the purposes of this rule any use by a firm of information relating to a pending client order to deal on own account in the financial instruments to which the client order relates, or in related financial instruments, should be considered a misuse of that information.

The rules relating to aggregation and allocation of orders deal with circumstances in which client (and possibly firm) orders are aggregated so as to take advantage of better terms in the market for large orders. In those circumstances the aggregated order will not always be executed in a single tranche and therefore there is some risk of client disadvantage in the allocation of the transaction to individual client accounts. The rules seek to mitigate this risk by requiring firms to have an order allocation policy that must be followed and by requiring that allocation of client orders that are combined with firm orders must be allocated in a way that is not detrimental to the client.

15.3.4 Investment research

Following the bursting of the 'dotcom' bubble in the year 2000, regulators around the world became particularly concerned over the impartiality of investment research produced and distributed by regulated firms such as investment banks. In the US, the Securities and Exchange Commission (SEC) took legal action against 10 of the nation's top investment firms and secured a $1.4 billion dollar settlement.[61] In the UK, the FSA began a process of consultation with a view to ensuring that research held out to clients as impartial or objective is produced according to appropriately high standards for conflict management.[62] Following that consultation, the FSA took the following action:[63]

1. It amended the Conduct of Business Sourcebook to provide guidance on the management of conflicts of interest in particular situations arising in the context of corporate finance business.[64] The most obvious conflict in this area arises when a firm owes duties both to a client for whom it is carrying out a public offer of securities and to investment clients who may be interested in buying those securities.

---

[61] See www.sec.gov/litigation/litreleases/lr18438.htm (accessed on 18 August 2011). In its complaints, the allegations of which the defendants neither admit nor deny, the Securities and Exchange Commission alleged that, from approximately mid-1999 through mid-2001 or later, all of the firms engaged in acts and practices that created or maintained inappropriate influence by investment banking over research analysts, thereby imposing conflicts of interest on research analysts that the firms failed to manage in an adequate or appropriate manner. The complaints also alleged supervisory deficiencies at every firm.

[62] See FSA, 'Investment Research—Conflicts and Other Issues', Discussion Paper 15 (2002); 'Conflicts of Interest: Investment Research and Issues of Securities', CP 171 (2003); 'Conflicts of Interest: Investment Research and Issues of Securities', CP 205 (2003).

[63] For general background see FSA, 'Conflicts of Interest in Investment Research', Policy Statement 04/6 (March 2004).

[64] See the Conflicts of Interest (Corporate Finance and Investment Analysts) Instrument 2003 (FSA 2003/70, attached to CP 205, above n 62).

2. It amended the COBS rules relevant to investment firms dealing ahead of investment research (so-called 'front-running').[65] The dealing ahead rules are aimed at ensuring that a firm does not use knowledge of the content, and timing of publication, of a research report to inform its proprietary dealing and thereby to prefer its own interests above those of its clients. The old rules contained a number of exemptions which were closed.[66]

3. It amended the COBS rules so as to require investment firms to establish and implement a policy, appropriate to the firm, for managing effectively the conflicts of interest that might affect the impartiality of investment research that is held out as being impartial.[67]

Further changes in the regulatory rules were necessary to implement the MiFID regime. Investment research is now defined for regulatory purposes as:

> research or other information recommending or suggesting an investment strategy, explicitly or implicitly, concerning one or several financial instruments or the issuers of financial instruments, including any opinion as to the present or future value or price of such instruments, intended for distribution channels or for the public, and in relation to which the following conditions are met:
> (a) it is labelled or described as investment research or in similar terms, or is otherwise presented as an objective or independent explanation of the matters contained in the recommendation;
> (b) if the recommendation in question were to be made by an investment firm to a client, it would not constitute the provision of a personal recommendation.[68]

Condition (b) effectively disapplies the suitability obligation (above) since that applies only to recommendations that are personal to the recipient. Investment research provides a generic form of recommendation that is not personal to the recipient. The regulatory rules apply to a firm which produces, or arranges for the production of, investment research that is intended or likely to be subsequently disseminated to clients of the firm or to the public, under its own responsibility or that of a member of its group. The appropriateness rule (above) does not apply because investment research is an 'ancillary service' under the MiFID regime and not a core service within the scope of the rule.

The main focus of the regulatory rules relating to research is on conflicts of interest between financial analysts and clients.[69] MiFID requires that firms introduce organisational and administrative arrangements such that conflicts of interest that may arise in the provision of investment services are identified, managed and/or disclosed. These rules focus not only on the relationship between financial analysts and their clients but also on the relationship between analysts and issuers. Analysts must not promise favourable research coverage to issuers and issuers are not permitted to review draft research before its dissemination if it includes a recommendation or target price. FSA Guidance sug-

---

[65] See COBS 12.2.5R, implementing Art 25(2)(a) of the MiFID Implementing Directive. The exceptions to this rule include a market-maker undertaking the transaction in good faith in the normal course of market-making.

[66] See FSA 2003/70, above n 64, for an account of the old rules.

[67] See the Conflicts of Interest (Investment Research) Instrument 2004 (FSA 2004/24, attached to FSA Policy Statement 04/06, above n 63).

[68] FSA Handbook Glossary, implementing Art 24(1) of the MiFID Implementing Directive.

[69] See generally COBS 12.2.

gests that analysts should not become involved in activities other than the preparation of investment research where such involvement is inconsistent with the maintenance of the financial analyst's objectivity. It suggests that the following should ordinarily be considered as inconsistent with the maintenance of a financial analyst's objectivity:

1. participating in investment banking activities such as corporate finance business and underwriting;
2. participating in 'pitches' for new business or 'road shows' for new issues of financial instruments; or
3. being otherwise involved in the preparation of issuer marketing.[70]

15.3.5 Liability for breaches of regulatory rules

As noted in Chapter 6.5, FSMA 2000 provides a remedy to clients of a firm who suffer loss as a result of a breach of the Act or associated regulatory rules.[71] That remedy is generally limited to a 'private person', which excludes legal entities that suffer loss in the course of carrying on business of any kind. Thus, professional clients will normally be excluded from that category even if they are recategorised as a retail client for the purposes of a particular transaction.

Breach of the Principles for Businesses may lead to enforcement action by the FSA, but does not affect the validity of a transaction or give rise to a claim in damages under section 150 FSMA 2000.[72]

15.4 Financial resources

In the case of investment firms, the focus of the prudential rules on capital adequacy differs from banks. Investment firms are mainly exposed to market risk, whereas banks are primarily exposed to credit risk.[73] Moreover, the nature of the market risk faced by investment firms varies considerably. Those taking risks as a principal are directly exposed to market volatility and may pose systemic threats as a result of their inability to settle transactions with counterparties.[74] By way of contrast, those investment firms (including fund managers) who act as agents do not pose the same degree of systemic risk

---

[70] COBS 12.2.9G.

[71] FSMA 2000, s 150.

[72] See PRIN 3.4.4R.

[73] Universal banks or investment banks may be exposed to both types of risk. However, in those cases a distinction is drawn between the two types of risk for the purposes of calculating regulatory capital.

[74] The collapse of Lehman Bros, which was an investment firm (regulated by the SEC) rather than a bank, provides the clearest example of the risk posed by investment firms. Potential causes of failure include: a general decline in the firm's markets affecting income levels; adverse movements in positions in securities held by the firm; default by a customer or counterparty; adverse currency or interest rate movements.

since changes in the market values of securities are borne by clients rather than the firm itself. In those cases, the regulatory concern focuses more on ensuring that the asset base is sufficiently liquid to meet claims as they fall due and that operational risk[75] is mitigated through appropriate organisational and risk-management techniques.

15.4.1 The CAD regime

The Capital Adequacy Directive (CAD)[76] establishes common financial resources rules for investment firms operating in the EU. The scope of the Directive is defined by reference to the definition of an investment firm in MiFID, with the result that investment firms falling within MiFID are subject to the CAD.[77] In recognition of their very limited threat to financial stability (and therefore the disproportionate cost that would be imposed by CAD's capital requirements), limited exemptions from the CAD regime are provided to firms undertaking restricted activity. The exemptions apply only to investment firms ('exempt CAD firms'[78]) that are only authorised to provide the service of investment advice and/or receive and transmit orders from investors without holding money or securities belonging to their clients and which for that reason may not at any time place themselves in debt with those clients.[79]

CAD requires firms that fall within its scope to satisfy both initial and ongoing capital requirements. Both sets of requirements are calibrated by reference to the nature and scale of activities that are undertaken by investment firms, the objective being to reflect the degree of risk posed by a firm in its capital requirement. Banks are subject to the same requirements as investment firms with respect to their investment business, and the capital that is counted against investment activity cannot in principle be counted against banking activities.[80]

CAD is implemented in the UK through the GENPRU and BIPRU components of the FSA Handbook.[81] Following the approach of CAD, a distinction is first drawn between exempt CAD firms and CAD investment firms. The latter category is then divided into subcategories based on the initial capital requirements set by CAD (below): BIPRU

---

[75] This is the risk of loss resulting from inadequate or failed internal processes, people and systems or from external events (including legal risk): see Art 4(22) of the 2006 Banking Directive, 2006/48/EC [2006] OJ L177/1.

[76] Directive 2006/49/EC [2006] OJ L177/201. The directive is framed as a 'minimum standards'directive, leaving it open to Member States to engage in 'gold-plating' (see further Chapter 2.9).

[77] See Art 3(1)(b) CAD, referencing Art 4(1)(1) MiFID. The effect of that reference is that restricted-activity investment firms that are exempt from MiFID as result of the Art 3 exemption do not fall within the CAD regime. See further Chapter 6.1.2.

[78] This follows the terminology adopted by the FSA in its Handbook implementation of CAD.

[79] Art 3(1)(b)(iii) CAD.

[80] If 'double-counting' were permitted, the objectives of capital regulation would be circumvented and integrated banks would have an unfair competitive advantage over investment firms.

[81] GENPRU is the General Prudential Sourcebook, which applies to banks, insurers, building societies and BIPRU investment firms. BIPRU is the Prudential Sourcebook for Banks, Building Societies and Investment Firms. In the case of firms to which CAD does not apply (including exempt CAD firms), the IPRU (INV) component of the FSA Handbook applies.

50k, BUPRU 125k and BIPRU 730k firms, respectively.[82] A further distinction is drawn between a limited licence firm[83], a limited activity firm[84] and a full scope BIPRU firm. While the last category is subject to the full range of rules derived from CAD, the prior two categories benefit from the exemptions provided by CAD in respect of the requirement to hold capital against operational risk.[85] The CAD regime follows the model of the Basel Accord by imposing minimum capital requirements (Pillar 1) and then permitting the competent authorities to set additional requirements based on the specific risk profile and risk-management systems of a particular firm (Pillar 2, Supervisory Review).[86]

15.4.2 Initial capital requirements

The initial capital requirements relate to the minimum level of share capital and reserves that are required for an investment firm to become authorised. CAD sets an initial level of capital of 125,000 euros where the investment firm does not deal in financial instruments for its own account or underwrite issues of financial instruments on a firm commitment basis but holds clients' money and/or securities and offers one or more of the following services: reception and transmission of investors' orders for financial instruments, execution of investors' orders and management of individual portfolios.[87] Member States may reduce the amount referred to 50,000 euros where a firm is not authorised to hold clients' money or securities, to deal for its own account,[88] or to underwrite issues on a firm commitment basis. So-called exempt CAD firms are not entirely exempt from initial capital requirements, though they are subject to a much lighter regime. They must

1. provide initial capital of 50,000 euros;
2. have professional indemnity insurance or some other comparable guarantee against liability arising from professional negligence in the required form;[89] or
3. have a combination of initial capital and professional indemnity insurance in a form resulting in a level of coverage equivalent to that referred to in point 1 or 2.

All other firms are subject to an initial capital requirement of 730,000 euros.

---

[82] See generally BIPRU 1.1.

[83] This type of firm is not authorised to deal on its own account and underwrite and/or place financial instruments on a firm commitment basis: see Art 20(2) CAD.

[84] This is a BIPRU 730k firm that deals on its own account only for the purpose of fulfilling or executing a client order or gaining entrance to a clearing or settlement system or a recognised exchange when acting in an agency capacity or executing a client order: see Art 20(3) CAD.

[85] See generally FSA Handbook, PERG 13: Guidance on the Scope of MiFID and the Recast CAD. See also Chapter 3.8 (Risk Control under FSMA 2000).

[86] Pillar 3 of the Basel framework (market discipline) is not directly applicable to investment firms as it requires disclosure of the management of credit risk in order to strengthen market monitoring.

[87] Art 5(1) CAD.

[88] Dealing on own account includes proprietary trading and market-making: see FSA Handbook, PERG 13.3.

[89] It must cover the whole territory of the EU, representing at least 1,000,000 euros applying to each claim and an aggregate 1,500,000 euros per year for all claims. The ability to use insurance recognises that it can provide similar *ex post* protection to investors as is provided by regulatory capital *ex ante*.

15.4.3 Ongoing capital requirements

The ongoing capital requirements of the CAD reflect the changes made by the Basel II Accord to the capital requirements for banks. Basel II was designed to introduce more risk-sensitive capital requirements (both for credit and market risk), and to that end it permitted the use of internal models to measure risk. Its impact on investment firms was felt principally with regard to the treatment of the trading book and operational risk. As regards the trading book, a more flexible approach was adopted by CAD, which provides that:

The trading book of an institution shall consist of all positions in financial instruments and commodities held either with trading intent or in order to hedge other elements of the trading book and which are either free of any restrictive covenants on their tradability or able to be hedged.[90]

Moreover, CAD provides that trading intent shall be evidenced on the basis of the strategies, policies and procedures set up by the institution to manage the position or portfolio. Thus, some discretion was provided to firms as to whether financial instruments are allocated to the trading book or the banking book, and in hindsight it seems clear that this provided an incentive to shift risk from the banking book to the trading book so as to reduce regulatory capital requirements.[91]

The basic obligation imposed by CAD is that firms must have 'own funds'[92] that are always equal to or greater than their capital requirement set by CAD.[93] The capital requirement is the sum of:

- the capital requirements for position risk, settlement and counterparty risk and large exposure risk in respect of the trading book;
- the foreign exchange and commodity risk in respect of all business risks;
- credit risk; and
- operational risk.[94]

Calculation of the financial resources requirement is a complex process. The objective is to increase the financial resources that are held by a firm as each of the categories of risk increases. Position risk is the risk arising from the net position of an investment firm across the securities in which it trades on its own account. Calculation of the position risk requirement involves separate calculation of the specific and general risk associated

---

[90] Art 11(1) CAD.

[91] See the FSA, 'The Turner Review, A Regulatory Response to the Global Banking Crisis' (March 2009), available at http://www.fsa.gov.uk/Pages/Library/Corporate/turner/index.shtml (Turner Review), 58.

[92] Own funds for this purpose follows the definition adopted for banks in Art 57 of Directive 2006/48/EC. It includes share capital and reserves. It also includes fixed-term preference shares and subordinated loan capital if binding agreements exist under which, in the event of the bankruptcy or liquidation of the institution, they rank after the claims of all other creditors and are not to be repaid until all other debts outstanding at the time have been settled.

[93] That high-level requirement is reflected in Principle 4 of the FSA's Principles for Business, which requires firms to maintain adequate financial resources.

[94] The operational risk requirements are derived from the 2006 Banking Directive whereas CAD provides for the calculation of the other risk requirements.

with each type of financial instrument.[95] Firms may adopt internal models (such as value at risk[96]) to calculate this risk[97] so long as the model meets the requirements of the CAD and is approved by the competent authority. Counterparty risk reflects the risk posed by the default of a firm's counterparties (eg failure to settle a transaction by the due date). The collapse of Lehman Bros provides a clear example of the systemic implications of that risk, with many firms around the world having a substantial exposure to its default.[98] The capital charge for settlement risk penalises firms by requiring additional financial resources to be available when a firm has unsettled transactions. Foreign exchange risk is the risk that arises when a firm's trading book or, more generally, its balance sheet, income and expenses are denominated other than in the currency of its books of account. In those circumstances, adverse exchange rate movements pose a potential risk and therefore financial resources are required to cover that risk.

The inclusion of operational risk as a discrete element within the capital require-ment follows the approach of the Basel II Accord, which gave greater prominence to that category of risk. The approach for investment firms follows that which has been applied to banks.[99] In its most basic form, it imposes a capital charge of 15% of annual net income (excluding capital gains and irregular items). A more sophisticated approach distinguishes between different lines of business within a firm, applying different charges to each line (the standardised approach). Finally, it is possible for a firm to calculate its own exposure to operational risk (the Advanced Measurement Approach). However, in recognition of the considerable cost[100] imposed by the operational risk requirement and the limited systemic risk posed by many investment firms, there are important exemptions provided by CAD.[101] The first relates to firms that are not authorised to deal on their own account, offer portfolio management services or investment advice. Those firms ('limited licence' firms in the FSA Handbook) are exempt from the CAD requirement to hold capital against operational risk. The second exempt group are investment firms that deal on their own account only for the purpose of fulfilling or executing a client order or for the purpose of gaining entrance to a clearing and settlement system or a recognised exchange when acting in an agency capacity or executing a client order (a 'limited activity firm' in the FSA Handbook). Both these types of firm are instead subject to a 'fixed overhead requirement',[102] which had been used in the past as a proxy for the (mainly liquidity) risk faced by investment firms. The requirement is one-quarter of the previous year's overheads, subject to adjustment by the competent authority in the event of a material change in a firm's business since the preceding year.

---

[95] See Chapter 1.1 for an explanation of general and specific risk.

[96] Value at risk (often abbreviated to VAR) is a statistical technique for modelling the probable loss that may be suffered by a bank or investment firm as a result of market movements under different scenarios, by refer-ence to past experience. See the Turner Review, above n 91, 22 for a critique of its role in the financial crisis.

[97] As well as foreign exchange and commodity risk.

[98] See M Singh and J Aitken, 'Counterparty Risk, Impact of Collateral Flows, and Role for Global Counter-parties', IMF Working Paper 09/173 (2009).

[99] See Arts 103 and 104 and Annex X of the 2006 Banking Directive.

[100] See PWC, 'Study on the Financial and MacroEconomic Consequences of the Draft Proposed New Capital Requirements for Banks and Investment Firms in the EU' (2004).

[101] See Art 20 CAD.

[102] See Art 21 CAD.

Index